8TH EDITION

BUSINESS
CYCLES
AND
FORECASTING

Lloyd M. Valentine
Professor of Economics Emeritus
University of Cincinnati

Dennis F. Ellis
Professor of Business Economics
The University of Michigan - Flint

Library of Congress Cataloging-in-Publication Data
Valentine, Lloyd M.
    Business cycles and forecasting/Lloyd M. Valentine, Dennis F. Ellis. - 8th ed.
      p.   cm.
    Includes bibliographical references.
    ISBN 0-538-80575-7
    1. Business cycles.   2. Business forecasting.   I. Ellis, Dennis F.   II. Title.
    HB3730.V29   1991
    338.5'4--dc20   90-33876
                                      CIP

1 2 3 4 5 6 7 8 9 D 8 7 6 5 4 3 2 1 0
Printed in the United States of America

COLLEGE DIVISION South-Western Publishing Co.

HG65HA   CINCINNATI   DALLAS   LIVERMORE

PREFACE

This is the eighth edition of *Business Cycles and Forecasting*. Every edition required revision to reflect significant changes in the economy and in the advances made in the field of economics. The current edition has been completely reworked to that end. Throughout the revision our overriding goal has been to do our best to present the ideas in as understandable a manner as possible. It is a textbook designed for learning.

The eighth edition also introduces a new author, Dennis F. Ellis. Dr. Ellis is Professor of Business Economics at The University of Michigan - Flint and did extensive reviewing work on the seventh edition of this text. He is also active in economic forecasting and consulting work.

Business Cycles and Forecasting is used in a variety of courses and in a variety of ways. Some users think of it as a text on business conditions analysis; others use it as an intermediate macroeconomics text; for still others it is their forecasting text. It is intended for both economics and business majors at the intermediate level and for the required course in economics for MBA students.

The organization of the book reflects the authors' conviction that to be able to intelligently analyze and forecast economic conditions (or simply to make sense out of what is going on in the economy), a theoretical foundation is an absolute necessity. In addition, some feel for historical experience contributes to the acquisition of the perspective so necessary for worthwhile analysis and forecasting. To this end the first four chapters of Part 1 present a survey of some of the important historical features of the fluctuations or cycles in the aggregate economy. Chapter 5 deals with cycles in specific industries including building and various agricultural crops, as well as a discussion of the Kondratieff cycle.

Part 2 is a short course in intermediate macroeconomic theory or national income analysis. Chapter 6 is a careful and rigorous discussion of the fundamental building blocks of aggregate economic analysis. Chapter 7 summarizes the most important elements of the classical macroeconomic model, while Chapters 8 through 12 develop the core of the contemporary basic macroeconomic model.

Part 3 summarizes the major schools of business cycle theory as developed by their leading advocates. This was once virtually the entire content of courses in business cycles and was, prior to Keynes, the main outlet for thinking about aggregate economics. At that time speculation about economic relationships predominated over rigorous theoretical and empirical study. Even today, these early theories provide valuable insight into the processes of economic activity.

Part 4 is devoted to forecasting on the aggregate level, the industry level, and the level of the individual firm. The use of econometrics has become more prevalent in forecasting, and Part 4 has been revised to reflect this. Chapter 15 now includes a discussion of nonlinear trends, as well as modelling of regional economics. Chapter 16 presents the leading, coincident, and lagging indicator system of projecting turning points. This chapter also introduces the reader to the workings of a simple "full blown" econometric model. The forecasting uses of such models is presented along with the potential for "what if" kinds of simulations. Techniques for forecasting durable goods are found in Chapter 17. This chapter also introduces the reader to the stock adjustment model. Chapter 18 presents an introduction to forecasting models used in the investment category of GNP. Statistical techniques of forecasting are continued in Chapter 19 with a discussion of a building block approach to projecting prices of individual commodities. Sales forecasting is the topic of Chapter 20, and here the traditional methods of classical decomposition, and relations of sales with GNP are presented.

The purpose of Part 4 is not to make econometricians out of students but rather to expose them to the use of economic theory in statistical forecasting. The emphasis remains on the economics, with a healthy respect for the pitfalls of forecasting. On the other hand, since no action can be taken, whether in business or government policy, without some explicit or implicit forecast, the goal should be to make the best forecast possible with the techniques and information available.

Part 5 considers the issues of public policy to promote economic stabilization and growth, with the emphasis on monetary and fiscal policies. The faith of the public, and of economists themselves, in the ability to manage the economy by governmental action goes through cycles of its own. The stance that is taken in these chapters is that economic policy can have a very positive effect, but with all of the uncertainties involved, we should try to be aware of the possible undesirable consequences, and we should not expect more than can be delivered.

The authors have done their best to avoid polemics in presenting both the theory and the policy discussions. Instead our aim has been to offer a balanced treatment, believing that there is something to be gained from an open-minded study of diverse points of view. The factors responsible for producing changes in the levels of economic activity and national income are not completely understood in all of their ramifications, but most of the basic determinants are clear. The business cycle is no longer a totally unsolved riddle, and there exists a large measure of understanding of the factors that promote economic growth. As knowledge of the causal factors steadily increases, economic forecasting will become more accurate.

As must be the case for any textbook authors, our debts are great to the many individuals who have influenced our thinking. They include our own teachers, our colleagues, our students, the many professors and students who have used earlier editions of this book and have been kind enough to offer helpful suggestions for its improvement. Our developmental editors at South-Western Publishing, who also qualify as friends, deserve special mention for their professionalism in minimizing the errors of the authors. For this we particularly wish to thank Marvin Good and Alice Denny for their work over several editions of the book.

While it is impossible to thank everyone who has contributed to the eighth edition of *Business Cycles and Forecasting*, the following persons deserve special acknowledgment: David Fand from Wayne State University; Peeth Kartha and Clark Chastain, both from The University of Michigan - Flint; and Xiao Ming Shen, a graduate student at the University of Cincinnati. We also express our appreciation to our colleagues who reviewed the manuscript as it was in process:

Thomas Kopp, Siena College
Hassan Pirasteh, Southern Oregon State College
Ajmer Singh, Western Oregon State College
Ron Straight, Howard University
Stan Wisniewski, Howard University

Lloyd M. Valentine
University of Cincinnati
Dennis F. Ellis
The University of Michigan - Flint

CONTENTS

INTRODUCTION TO BUSINESS FLUCTUATIONS

Fluctuations in economic activity are a part of life. At times, they are of all-consuming interest and concern to people in their capacities as business decision makers, family breadwinners, budgeters, and wealth managers. Changes are continually taking place in prices, in wages, in the level of employment, and in other economic factors; these changes affect the fortunes of all of us, not only in our country but in the world. The early pioneers on the frontiers of civilization could largely ignore economic changes since they built their own homes from native timber, raised their own food, and made their own clothes. However, in an economy of interdependence in which almost everyone works for a living and uses the money received to buy goods and services, the state of economic activity is of primary concern to all.

The benefits of a free-enterprise system have been evident to other societies. There is now a greater movement towards the use of capitalistic approaches throughout the world. Economic systems that once relied on a great deal of economic planning are currently experimenting with the use of the price mechanism. Eventually these economies also will experience the ups and downs of business cycles.

PART 1

This introductory part attempts to set the stage for the later parts that deal with the analysis of the causal factors in economic fluctuations, the forecasting of future economic activities, and policies designed to mitigate the more severe and costly sorts of fluctuations. The first five chapters look at the historical record to encourage a perspective for current viewing of the economy. The patterns of business cycles and their regularities are given considerable study. Chapters 1 through 4 of this part deal with general cycles, that is, cycles in the overall or aggregate economy, while Chapter 5 treats a number of specific cycles, that is, cycles in particular segments of business activity. This discussion provides a review of the background needed to understand what is happening in the economy during cyclical fluctuations. These features of the American economy will be used in the explanation of why the cycle develops as it does. If the economy were changed materially, the cycle would be changed or perhaps even eliminated in the form in which it has occurred.

NATURE OF ECONOMIC FLUCTUATIONS AND FORECASTING

The volume of economic activity in America has been increasing since early colonial days. This has been true not only because population and the number of workers have increased but also because our productivity has increased as methods have been developed to turn out more and more goods with a given amount of labor. This growth of economic activity has not taken place, however, at a steady rate. It was very rapid during World War II and the early postwar years and much slower in the 1930s and the late 1970s. Nor has growth taken place without interruption. There have been several periods of minor decreases in economic activity even in the prosperous years since the end of World War II. From time to time there have been much more serious and protracted interruptions in the forward push of economic progress. This happened from 1929 to 1933 and also in several earlier periods in our history.

NATURE AND SIGNIFICANCE OF ECONOMIC FLUCTUATIONS

Severe fluctuations in production, employment, prices, and other phases of economic activity are of primary importance as economic, social, and political factors. They affect not only the economy and society at large but also the living styles and standards of individuals of all ages and in all walks of life.

Economic problems and their impact on the people exist at all times and in all societies. The economics profession dedicates itself continuously to work on the solutions. Economic fluctuations exacerbate these problems, and to the degree that these fluctuations can be made milder, the problems and suffering can be lessened.

The first observation to make is that business fluctuations happen over time. In other words, the study must be dynamic rather than static.

If economic activity could change instantaneously, the statistics of business activity would look different than they do. But, in fact, most activity takes time: time for decisions to be made, time to arrange financing, time to order materials and hire or lay off workers, time to change production rates, and so on. Recognizing time lags of different lengths for different economic processes plays an important role in the understanding of business conditions analysis.

Market economies such as that of the United States, as opposed to planned economies, have certain characteristics that make them subject to change in their own peculiar fashion. Some of these are desirable, such as the growth arising from technological improvements in products or in production processes. Others are not at all desirable because they can result in periods of unemployment or inflation. In general, planned economies, as we have been able to observe them, are more cumbersome in their ability to change and adapt to new developments. In market economies, the rule is: Change, or suffer the consequences.

Depression Periods in Economic Activity

It is difficult to comprehend the full effect on the lives of individuals of periods of severe depression in economic activity. Those who are unable to find employment in a period of depression are forced to curtail consumption of goods and services to such an extent that real deprivation often exists. The psychological impact on their lives is more difficult to measure, but is certainly great. The effect on the attitudes of young people who are just entering the labor force and cannot find employment can be highly detrimental to the social framework of the nation. This is especially true of young people who are members of minority groups since these groups often are hit hardest by unemployment. Older workers who lose their jobs during the decline in business activity on the downswing of the cycle may find it almost impossible to find gainful employment on a regular basis even after the depression ends.

Depression periods have also often been periods of declines in the general level of prices, that is, of deflation. In a period of deflation, debtors find their loans and the interest payments on them more difficult to repay since it takes more purchasing power to do so than it did at the time the loan was made. This creates problems for business people and farmers who mortgaged their property in a period of high prices and must pay off mortgages and meet interest payments in a period of falling prices. The same is true for individuals buying a house on which they have a substantial mortgage. Not only does it take additional real income to repay the loan and interest on it, but problems arise if an individual is forced to move. More dollars may be owed than the house will bring on the market and, as a result, there will still be some debt remaining after the sale, so nothing would remain for a payment on a new home.

Even when the price level does not decline absolutely during recession periods, often there is a period of failing rates of increase in the price level, which creates serious problems in many fields of activity. For example, during the inflation of the 1970s, farmers saw land values rising rapidly. In the anticipation of prices continuing to rise at a similar pace in the future, many farmers expanded their landholdings by going into debt. When, during the early 1980s, prices did not rise as fast as expected, servicing the debt became very difficult and foreclosures resulted. The disinflation of the 1980s created difficulties for all those who had made contracts to deliver goods or services at prices based on the expectation of higher rates of inflation than actually occurred.

Business fluctuations also create problems for society at large. From the economic standpoint, there is the loss of goods that might have been produced during the period of less than full employment. This will amount to billions of dollars even in relatively minor downturns and is staggering in major depressions. There is also a loss of capital equipment that deteriorates faster than it is replaced. As a result, it is more difficult to achieve high levels of production in the ensuing prosperity period, and the nation is permanently poorer than it would have been if capital had been replaced and expanded at more normal levels.

Business failures increase rapidly during periods of depressed business activity, especially in major depressions. This involves losses not only for the owners, but generally also for creditors. Such losses to creditors have been substantial even in minor downturns. Business failures also have an adverse effect on the employees of the concerns that fail and on the communities in which they are located.

Depressions also create social problems that become especially severe during protracted periods of large-scale unemployment. The crime rate increases, especially among the younger people who have not been firmly established in their jobs and homes or who are just entering the labor force and find it impossible to get jobs. Marriages are postponed, and birth rates drop, which intensifies the depression since demand for housing and consumer goods related to homemaking and rearing a family is further reduced.

The political repercussions of business fluctuations are also of great importance. When large numbers of people are unemployed, they are easily swayed by demagogues who promise them food and shelter in exchange for some freedoms. At least part of the rise of communism, and especially fascism, can be traced to such situations in periods of greatly depressed business activity. In democratic nations, there is tremendous pressure on the government during times of subnormal business activity to do something about unemployment and other problems associated with depressed economic conditions. The result is that the trend toward government regulation and public ownership of business is greatly accelerated.

Boom Periods in Economic Activity

Severe problems also occur when demands are made on the economy that are beyond its ability to supply. Increasing output in itself creates no macroeconomic problems, but the effect of demand in excess of the ability to supply leads to an increase in the general level of prices. Prices do not change uniformly but do so at different rates in different sectors of the economy, which creates problems. It leads to inequities among individuals and groups and also to a less than optimum allocation of resources.

Inflation creates serious problems for the individual. Debts may become easier to pay off, but problems in planning insurance, investment, and retirement programs increase. The face value of life insurance policies remains unchanged, but the proceeds buy less. The same is true of many pension programs that guarantee a fixed dollar amount. Personal investment also becomes a problem since bonds and savings and loan shares lose purchasing power as prices go up, and the average individual does not have the necessary analytical or financial ability to invest in common stocks in such a way as to keep up with inflation.

Many groups in society suffer a loss in real income during inflationary periods and try to use political pressure to stop it. The pay of government workers, teachers, employees in regulated industries, and others lags behind the rise in prices, and this makes it difficult to recruit and hold good workers. The teaching profession is likely to be hard hit since, when income fails to keep up with prices, fewer students, especially the good ones, plan to become teachers and thus a shortage exists for several years.

In the United States, the desire to avoid the undesirable consequences of economic fluctuations led to the enactment of the Full Employment Act of 1946, which stated that it was the policy of the federal government to plan its activities affecting the economy so as to promote full employment. The government is also under continuing pressure to use its powers and influences to control inflation as well as deflation. This was formalized by Congress in 1978 in the Humphrey-Hawkins Act, which specified targets for both unemployment and inflation. Government programs in agriculture have been directed toward stabilizing agricultural income and in housing toward stabilizing overall economic activity.

TYPES OF VARIATIONS IN ECONOMIC ACTIVITY

Economists recognize different types of variations in economic activity. These are the trend, business cycles, seasonal fluctuations, and irregular or random fluctuations.

Trend

Although economic activity does not proceed smoothly and is interrupted by periods of decline followed by increased activity, there is an underlying long-run tendency for economic activity to increase or decrease that is referred to as the trend. *Trend* is the persistent underlying movement that takes place in economic activity in general or in a sector of the economy over a period of years. It is the basic growth or decline that would exist if there were no periods of boom or depression or less pronounced variations in economic activity.

The trend in total economic activity is a linear one; that is, activity has grown at a more or less constant rate over a period of years. This trend in the United States has been upward due to many factors. The development of a new continent was a major factor until around 1900. The rapid increase in population, the increasing stock of capital goods, technological progress, the increased education and skills of the labor force, increased managerial skills, and the discovery of new sources of raw materials have also been significant.

The trend of total economic activity is the combined result of the trends of individual industries and businesses. A successful new industry usually grows rapidly in its early stages. Growth then levels off to a more gradual rate. In time, the industry becomes integrated with the economy, and its growth is largely governed by the growth in the

general economy. The trend of growth of such a new industry is a cur-
vilinear one; that is, it resembles an elongated S. As the demand for
goods and services changes, some industries may pass their peak and
decline. This may be a gradual downward movement, as in the case of
coal furnaces, or a rapid decline, as in the case of a product that has
become obsolete, such as wagon wheels.

Business Cycles

Changes in the level of economic activity caused by the trend are
overshadowed by continually recurring variations in total economic
activity. Several years of expansion in total economic activity are followed by a period of slower growth or of contraction in such activity.
These fluctuations occur in total economic activity, not just in a particular industry or sector of the economy. Such expansions and contractions in the level of activity occur at about the same time in most
sectors of the economy. This sequence of fluctuations is a recurring
one, but it is not periodic; that is, such variations do not occur at regular time intervals and do not last for the same periods of time. The
amplitude of movement from the low point of activity to the high point
of activity is not the same. These fluctuations have become known as
business cycles. Any connotation of a high degree of regularity, however, that the term "cycles" may give is not warranted by serious study
of the data on total economic activity, production, employment, prices,
or any other major economic series. On the other hand, the recurrence
of ups and downs in business is more regular than would be expected
if it were a random process.

Seasonal Fluctuations

Seasonal fluctuations are changes in economic activity during the
course of a year that occur in a more or less regular pattern from year
to year. Such changes are related to the changing seasons of the year,
to holidays, or to the calendar. The canning or freezing of fruit, for example, must take place during that season of the year when the fresh
fruit is available. Other seasonal patterns are related to customs in our
society, such as sales arising out of Christmas gift purchases and the
Easter parade. The changing date of Easter leads to a changing seasonal
pattern in those sectors of economic activity that are affected. Other
seasonal variations occur because of the unequal number of days in
the month in our calendar and the unequal distribution of holidays

that are generally observed. Most industries or products are subject to their own particular seasonal influences; some coming from the demand side and some from the supply side.

Irregular or Random Fluctuations

Economic activity in various sectors of the economy, and to some degree in the total economy, is also affected from time to time by such exogenous factors as a widespread drought, a major flood, or a political disturbance. It also may be affected by a major strike. Some minor variations in economic activity are due to more or less unpredictable factors, such as unusual absenteeism resulting from a flu epidemic. Others may be due to purely random factors, such as a technological breakthrough in production or a sudden change in fashions or fads. These various factors are known as *irregular* or *random fluctuations*.

PRICE LEVEL CHANGES

The changes in economic activity involved in the trend, the business cycle, seasonal factors, and irregular or random fluctuations affect the general level of prices. For example, there is some tendency for prices to rise during the upswing of a business cycle as the demand for goods and services grows faster than the ability of the economy to provide goods and services; there is also some tendency for prices to decline during the downswing of the cycle. Changes in the price level from time to time may also be primarily related to changes in the money supply or the money standard, rather than to real changes in the level of economic activity. For example, during the Vietnam War, the money supply was greatly increased by the methods used to finance the war, and prices rose until the supplies of money and goods were in balance. At other times (although not in recent years), the basic movement of prices has been downward. This was true in the 1870s and 1880s because economic activity was expanding and the money supply was more or less fixed. By the same token, the rapid price increases in the 1978–1981 period were brought to a halt by restricting the growth in the money supply.

FORECASTING AND ECONOMIC FLUCTUATIONS

When making decisions about the future course of a business, management must take into consideration all of the factors that are likely to have some effect, both external and internal. Business fluctuations are among the major external factors that affect a business and are therefore of prime importance in making management decisions.

The Relationship of Economic Changes to Business Management

The primary function of management in a business is to determine the objectives of the business in both the long and the short runs. Management must then make plans to carry out these objectives, organize human and material resources to put the plans into action, implement the plans, and control the activities of the business to be sure that all is going according to the plan. Economic analysis and forecasting are involved in all of these steps in management, but primarily in determining objectives and in developing long- and short-range plans to carry out these objectives.

In determining its objectives, each business must decide on the commodities it plans to produce and sell, the price range of its products or services, the geographic region in which it plans to sell, the potential market for the products, the share of the market it can realistically hope to get, the prospective return on capital, and the like. Such objectives can only be realistic and well-balanced if management has analyzed trends in the economy and has forecast the demand for its products over time, the prices at which it will sell, the cost of the factors of production, and so on. Thus, an analysis of trends and current developments in the economy and a forecast of such trends and current developments are basic to establishing sound business objectives and in developing long-range and short-range plans to carry out such objectives.

The Need for Forecasting in Business

Some business people and economists still feel that forecasting is impossible in their businesses or, at best, is so indefinite as to be hazardous as a basis for business decisions. The statement is frequently made that forecasting may have succeeded well for others but "our business is different." The fact remains, however, that in any business in which raw materials must be purchased before orders are received or in which substantial capital equipment is used, some form of forecasting is being done, even if unwittingly.

If a business plans to continue operating at present levels, the forecast implicitly made is that present levels of business are predicted for the future. For most businesses this is not true for any period of time since they are continually affected by changing business conditions. Another frequent basis for business decisions is that past trends will continue. If, for example, business has been increasing at a rate of about 5 percent a year, that rate of increase is expected to continue for the next year or several years. This can be a hazardous assumption because growth does not continue at the same rate indefinitely in a dynamic economy.

In many concerns in which the top officials feel that forecasting cannot be done, someone is actually doing the forecasting. For example, a manufacturer of appliances used in home construction felt that the level of business could not be forecast successfully. The manufacturer believed that current orders were the only real guide to follow in planning production. Since orders usually were received several weeks ahead of the requested delivery date and since the appliances could be assembled in several days, this looked like a reasonable procedure. Some of the raw materials, however, had to be ordered as much as five months in advance to allow for delivery and fabrication. Since no one would venture a forecast, not even the purchasing agent, the clerk who did the ordering had to decide when to order materials. The clerk tried to follow production but, of course, got behind on an upswing owing to the time required to obtain materials. As pressure increased for raw materials when business increased, the clerk ordered faster. As business turned down, the firm received large stocks when they were no longer needed.

In effect, what was happening was that the order clerk was forecasting. The clerk knew little about the prospects of the business and acted in response to pressure from superiors to either obtain materials in a hurry or reduce excess stocks. The manufacturer finally called in outside consultants for advice on reorganizing the purchasing department and was surprised when told that top management was to blame because no forecast existed.

Nature of Forecasting

Business has no alternative to some type of forecasting, since aimless drifting is unthinkable in a well-managed organization. The basic question really concerns the approach that is to be used in forecasting. It can be done in a mechanical way as, for example, predicting a 5 percent increase in sales, since this has been the average experience over the last few years. Or it can be done by relying on one of several series that have generally led to changes in business activity in the past, such as changes in stock prices. On a somewhat more sophisticated level, it can be done by studying the economic and business situation and then intuitively deciding what will happen.

The scientific approach in this field is the same as in any field. It involves a knowledge and understanding of what has happened in the past, what is currently happening in the economy, and why it is happening. Only when phenomena are understood is it possible to predict with any degree of accuracy what will happen and, in the light of such predictions, take the proper action.

Our knowledge of the causal factors at work in business fluctuations is not comprehensive enough to make it possible to forecast with complete accuracy. But it is advanced enough to make possible more reliable indicators of future events than can be done with unscientific approaches. The forecasts that can be made more than justify the time and money spent on them. As knowledge increases in this field, better and better results will be forthcoming.

Forecasting can be qualitative or quantitative, ranging from hunches derived from unspecified sources, to econometric models with hundreds of equations. Qualitative forecasting may be in the form of judgmental models or may be developed through questionnaire surveys. Quantitative approaches include naïve models, such as trend extrapolation or data-smoothing formulas, but also extend to extremely complex interdependent systems of equations. Techniques may include simple and multiple regression analysis and, ultimately, the whole range of statistical analysis.

Forecasting may also involve the indicators approach developed by the National Bureau of Economic Research. The basic goal of indicators analysis is to determine the likely timing of upturns and downturns of economic activity. Forecasting can also be categorized by time: short run, intermediate, and long run. Short-run forecasts range up to two years, intermediate forecasts range between two and five years, and long-run ones are as long as or longer than five years.

Benefits from a Forecasting Program

The only certainty about any specific forecast is that it will be wrong, at least to some degree or in some particular area. It has been said that, "He who lives by the crystal ball must be prepared to eat glass." With the present knowledge of business fluctuations, it is impossible to gauge all variables exactly. As a rule, however, it should be possible in most businesses to forecast total sales for a quarter of a year ahead within a range of 5 percent above or below the actual figure and for a year ahead within a range of 10 percent. Such results are usually accurate enough to be of real aid in managing a business, even if sales and production forecasts of individual products are off somewhat more. Such forecasting is a valuable managerial tool for business planning.

Ultimately, of course, it is the bottom line that matters most. A better forecast should permit a business unit to make a greater profit, and increase the owners' equity, more than a poorer forecast would. Thus, forecasting both demand side and supply side are important, as is the timing of changes on either side. Economic units whose goal is neither profit nor wealth maximization nevertheless have need of a forecast to maximize whatever it is they wish to maximize.

While accuracy of forecasting is the major criterion, there are other objectives of a good forecast. These other desirable features include usefulness and timeliness. A forecast prepared for management should take into account that its readers are not likely to have much technical forecasting expertise. Thus, the presentation should be straightforward and clear and not rely on technical jargon. It should state exactly the assumptions used in making the forecast in order to allow the user to evaluate them. It should also discuss the probable range of accuracy. Whoever prepares the presentation of the forecast should keep the purposes of the forecast in mind so that it becomes a useful document.

Timeliness is also important. A forecast made for a particular purpose must be available in time for the decision to be made when it is needed. It does no good to have a perfectly accurate forecast if that forecast reaches the decision makers after the decision has to be made.

Another important aspect to remember is the cost of the forecasting process relative to the benefits expected to be derived from it. If the costs exceed the benefits, the activity is obviously uneconomical.

Consideration of Every Contingency. Every contingency? Certainly not! The world is far too complex for that. However, when a forecast is prepared, consideration of the events or developments that might render the forecast inaccurate should be included. A forecasting program should help a business to meet almost any eventuality. A good forecast considers all factors that might influence a business, including remote possibilities. If management studies the forecasts carefully, it will at least not be caught unaware when the unexpected happens. It is impracticable to prepare in advance for every contingency, but knowing what can happen and spotting unusual situations early will go a long way toward preventing serious difficulties.

Study of Past Record. Forecasting forces a decision-making unit to study its past record carefully. This must be done to determine past trends and the most likely pattern in the future. A study of the past is also necessary to determine if any regular seasonal pattern exists. Furthermore, an analysis of past cyclical movements should be made in developing data for future forecasting. The determination of the trend, cycle, and seasonal pattern requires the recognition of all sporadic or unusual factors. An analysis of these compared with a study of the past policies of the business will often reveal both good and bad courses taken by management. Such study can provide the basis for avoiding the same mistakes in the future and for continuing the policies that have proved successful.

Study of Outside Factors. Another important benefit of forecasting is that it forces management to look at all the outside factors affecting the business. In this way, executives are kept informed of the governmental and social environment in which they make decisions. Favorable trends may be discerned and developed, or action may be taken to combat unfavorable aspects of a situation before they develop too far. Such awareness of the social and governmental milieu in which business operates is important for the preservation of free private enterprise in a democratic system.

Limitations and Problems of a Forecasting Program

Several problems are likely to be encountered in a forecasting program. One problem is that top management may expect a greater degree of accuracy from a forecast than is possible with the present knowledge of business and economic factors. Many top executives, especially in smaller concerns, feel that a forecast made once a year should be accurate enough to use as a basis for planning a year ahead with no future review or change. Such accuracy is seldom possible, however, since the numerous factors affecting business are constantly changing. Forecasting must be a continuous process.

Another problem is obtaining cooperation among various groups that participate in developing and using the forecast. When sales are bad, sales departments, at times, are inclined to be overly pessimistic. Other departments may argue for levels of production that are too high, in order to make per unit costs look more favorable. This emphasizes the need for an independent forecasting group rather than one under the direction of the sales or production planning department.

Small businesses have a special problem in the forecasting area. Their forecasting problems may not keep one trained person occupied, and they cannot afford to pay for the required background and experience. They are also at a disadvantage in finding a good forecaster, since the number of persons qualified in this area is small. A possible solution is to have forecasting services set up locally, serving clients in a manner similar to law offices or tax consulting services.

The Need for Forecasting in Government

The many activities of the federal government and its widespread obligations in the economic sphere cannot be carried on without an analysis of current economic activity and forecasts of future economic activity. This has to be done to carry out governmental responsibilities under the Full Employment Act, and the Council of Economic Advisers has been established for this purpose. The level of economic activity must also be forecast to develop the annual budget of the federal government. To estimate receipts of the federal government, which come to a large degree from personal and corporate income taxes, it is necessary to forecast personal income and corporate profits. This, of course, cannot be done without forecasting the level of total economic activity and the level of prices.

The Department of Agriculture must forecast the prospective supply of farm products, the level of farm prices in general, and the supply and prices of particular commodities to plan its crop control and price support programs. The Board of Governors of the Federal Reserve System must forecast the demand for money and credit and the basic supply and demand factors at work in the economy to develop and carry out its monetary policies.

The various housing agencies must forecast supply and demand in developing their programs. In fact, every agency that deals with economic matters must analyze the factors at work in the economy and forecast future economic conditions. State and local governments, too, are finding that forecasting is an absolute necessity. Forecasting has become one of the important activities of government, and the skill and accuracy with which it is done are major factors in the success or failure of governmental programs.

MAJOR CHARACTERISTICS OF THE ECONOMY

We now wish to review some of the general characteristics of the economic environment that are relevant to an understanding of the causes of instability. The economies of the world differ in greater or lesser degree with respect to these characteristics, and any economy that is not stagnant will find them changing; at times subtly, and at other times, in a dramatic fashion. Such changes can be very important in the analysis of economic fluctuations. Accordingly, one needs some understanding of the institutions and historical forces at work in the economy being studied.

Consumer Freedom of Choice

Consumer sovereignty is a fundamental principle of democratic capitalism. By and large, freedom of the individual to make economic choices is characteristic of the economy of the United States. Consumers are free to spend their income as they see fit. Choices are made among various types of goods and services, and the timing of the purchases is left to the consumer. If the individual elects not to spend on commodities in the immediate period, a further decision must be made as to the form in which the increased wealth will be held: money, bonds, insurance, equity securities, and so on, or the reduction of debt. While this kind of freedom is priceless, it is also one of the factors that gives the economic system some of its unstable characteristics.

When consumers, businesses, peoples of other countries, and governments are free to determine their purchases, total spending can sometimes be inadequate to employ all the resources that are available for use, or sometimes total spending is more than the value of the goods that can be produced. Consumers are vital in determining the rate of economic growth of the system since capital expansion, which is the essence of growth, is limited by the amount of saving.

Classical economists admitted to some temporary difficulties as consumer preferences shifted from certain goods to other goods, but believed that flexible prices and mobility of the factors of production would eliminate them. It was inconceivable, however, to Ricardo and later classicists that less total spending by consumers could result in any excess of labor or other resources. Their way of phrasing this proposition was that a general glut was impossible. The reasoning was that the interest rate would fall, causing investors to increase their demand for resources and leading households to revise their spending plans upward so that total resources would be employed but with a lower percentage of them devoted to present or consumption goods. This line of analysis, known as Say's law, has played such an important role in the development of the understanding of how economic systems work that we shall come back to it again and again. In particular, Chapter 7 is devoted to an exposition of the classical model of the aggregate economy.

Profit Motive

In the U.S. economic system, most production is done for the market. Most business firms cannot wait until the orders come in to produce precisely the amount needed. Instead, they try to estimate what the demand will be when the goods are ready for the market, and what the costs will be when they are actually incurred in the production process. The possibility of error is great. Both revenue and cost forecasts can be wrong so that undesired inventory accumulation or attrition, or conversely, serious price changes, may easily arise. Unexpected outcomes provoke responses by the business community that cause further changes in the important variables of the economy. The problems arise because production takes time. If output could be created instantaneously, no inventories would be maintained, and no possibility of error in expectations would exist.

Sometimes government officials and other observers admonish business people to make decisions "for the good of the nation" rather than on the basis of the self-interest principle or profit motive. During depressions, business is asked to expand; and when inflation appears to be the problem, restraint is in order. In general, if there is a conflict between the larger good and self-interest, business decision makers are well advised to ignore and, in fact, do ignore such admonitions. By relying on the profit motive, we get into difficulties, but it is not clear that any alternative criterion would be superior or as good.

Business decisions concerning prices, production, investment, and so on may be made upon the basis of careful, rational appraisals of all factors in the business situation. But, they may also be influenced by psychological factors: waves of optimism or pessimism; the desire to follow in the footsteps of competitors; or fear of the future outlook because of international uncertainties, governmental policies, and the like.

The bases on which decisions are made have changed somewhat as the economy has developed so that the role of business decisions in the cycle is not necessarily the same today as it was a generation ago. More and more firms are taking a longer-range point of view, realizing that it is better to maximize long-run profits or stockholders' equity than short-run profits. This often means that, in the short run, prices are set at a lower level than the market will bear in order to maximize long-run profits. This tends to narrow the range of price fluctuations over the cycle in those fields where such a policy is followed and thus to change the characteristics of the cycle to this extent.

In many cases, modern management decides inventory policies, working capital policies, and the timing and amount of investment in new plants and equipment on the basis of careful studies of the long-range demand for its product. As such actions reach sizable proportions, it eliminates excessive accumulation of inventory and the building of unnecessary plants and equipment and thus, by reducing activity somewhat during the boom, changes some of the characteristics of the cycle.

The Industrial Structure

Elements of great importance in the analysis of business fluctuations are the degree of price flexibility and output responsiveness to changing conditions. According to the traditional theory of the firm, both purely competitive firms and unfettered monopolies respond immediately to changes in supply or demand by altering price or output. Only casual observation is needed, however, to see that the prices of some goods and services seem to remain quite stable even though cost conditions and demand change markedly.

Competitive prices become rigid when governments impose controls over them, such as under agricultural price supports; when government is the sole or major buyer; or in other cases, such as milk, where it is deemed in the public interest. Monopoly prices are rigid when set by government or when they must be approved by a governmental agency, which, of course, describes public utilities. Monopolies might also maintain constant prices to avoid more direct and pervasive involvement by government. Most firms in the real world are somewhere between the poles of pure competition and pure monopoly, and here our micro theory is less helpful.

There are a number of explanations for the price stability that is fairly characteristic of oligopolistic markets. One is that collusion, tacit or overt, exists; in this situation, any change in price or other policy could precipitate a falling-out among the members. This is a way the firms can live together without damaging price wars or extreme price fluctuations. Another explanation involves the kinked demand curve established if each firm believes that if it raises its price, other firms in the industry will not raise their prices, and if the firm lowers its price, the others will follow suit. Under these circumstances variations in cost will not change price or output unless the cost changes are extreme. In some activities, the cost of changing prices is considerable and, consequently, will not be done unless circumstances have definitely changed and are expected to be relatively permanent. Sometimes, price stability has as its source the organizational structure of the firm, and internal political considerations may lead to the no-change decision. If the firms are large, as they frequently are in the oligopoly case, fear of government involvement in one way or another may induce the firms to leave well enough alone; that is, to keep prices where they are.

In general, where prices are relatively inflexible, the response to changes in demand or cost conditions is a more pronounced change in output than where prices are flexible. In unrestricted agricultural markets, for example, price varies considerably as demand changes, and output variations are less pronounced. In contrast, automobile sales and output vary directly as demand varies, and price changes are more moderate. This relationship between price and output variability in particular industries, and the differences in this respect among industries, has a great deal to do with the character of business fluctuations, so we shall come back to this question later.

Much has been written and discussed in recent years of the evolution of the structure of industry in the United States from capital-intensive, so-called "smokestack," industries to generally more labor-intensive, service industries. While the importance of this change has been sometimes exaggerated, it has obvious implications for business conditions analysis. For example, manufacturing output and employment normally fluctuate more severely during business cycles than is the case of service firms.

The Structure of the Labor Market

Another important factor in shaping the cycle in the present-day United States is the position of labor unions. When workers were largely unorganized, wages were cut rapidly in a period of declining business to bring costs into line with declining prices. This is what one would expect to happen under any perfectly competitive system in which workers compete with each other for the available jobs. With the advent of powerful labor unions, however, the wage is fixed by collective bargaining between union negotiators and representatives of management. The wage rate is usually set for a specified period, though in some contracts it is tied to a cost-of-living index. When wage rates are fixed through union contracts or by minimum-wage laws, a reduction in the demand for a product will result in a greater reduction of employment in that industry than would otherwise occur.

In the United States, the labor force that is unionized is estimated to be 17 percent. Thus, while the vast majority of workers' wages are not directly determined through the collective bargaining process, they are surely affected by it. Furthermore, when unions go on strike, many nonunion workers and industries are also forced to stop or slow down their activities.

In business cycle analysis, it is important to distinguish between real wages and money wages. Constant money wages during a period of rising consumer goods prices result in falling real wages. Real wages rise if the consumer price index falls at a faster rate than money wages; if money wages and prices rise or fall at the same rate, real wages remain constant. We raise a question to be taken up later: Are business decisions, and the decisions of workers, based on the real wage or on the money wage?

The Financial System

According to national income determination theory, saving that is not matched by concurrent, voluntary investment expenditures brings about a reduction in aggregate economic activity. Financial institutions have evolved over the years to aid in the process of accepting funds from those who are willing to give up their ability to command goods currently (savers), and to make the funds (and therefore the ability to command resources) available to investors. In this sense, financial institutions are intermediaries between savers and investors. They also act as intermediaries between savers and dissavers and, to some extent, between disinvestors and investors. To serve this important function, they must tailor their liabilities to the manifold needs and personalities of savers; on the other hand, the nature of the credit granted must be such as to fit the needs of those who wish to use the funds. As economic conditions change, financial institutions and financial instruments must also change to avoid serious problems. As a general rule, the financial community is very adept at meeting the changing needs of their customers, and, if not inhibited by legal restrictions, technological advances are adopted quickly.

In the highly developed economies, savers have a wide spectrum of assets from which to choose for the composition of their wealth. They can elect to hold real assets such as houses, land, gold, furniture, and artwork. They can own businesses directly, or indirectly through share ownership of corporations. A large part of the wealth of individuals is in the form of bonds, which are the liabilities (or debts) of financial and nonfinancial business units.

Large sums of wealth are held in the form of deposits or other liabilities of institutions such as commercial banks, savings banks, savings and loan associations, credit unions, and money market funds. Holders find attractive the safety and liquidity of these assets, as well as the assets' ability to yield some return. Each of these depository institutions attempts to tailor its services and accounts to service the needs of a category of savers in order to attract depositors. Product differentiation is an especially important aspect of financial institutions.

Savers also hold large amounts of government bonds, especially federal, but also municipals issued by state and local governmental units. Savings bonds issued by the U.S. government are bonds whose prices do not vary as market rates of interest vary. Some savers prefer bonds for that reason. Others, who are willing to accept more risk, and who generally are more wealthy, can hold marketable government securities whose prices rise when interest rates fall, and fall when interest rates rise. Governments, as well as private units, attempt to make the conditions attached to their liabilities attractive to different classes of buyers.

A very familiar class of financial institution or financial intermediary is the life insurance company. Life insurance, as it is generally sold in the United States, represents a combination of protection and investment. As a way of holding wealth, life insurance policies are a very attractive way for many people to accumulate assets. Pension funds also serve this purpose and have grown impressively in recent decades.

The financial institutions we have discussed, as well as the many more we have not mentioned, specialize in providing particular kinds of assets for savers and wealth holders whose needs and desires differ. The features of long-term versus short-term; risky versus safe; liquid versus illiquid; large potential versus smaller, more certain return provide sufficient variety to meet the requirements of most of the population.

The other side of the behavior of financial institutions focuses on their assets, which, in some ways, are dictated by the nature of their liabilities. Depository institutions, in order to keep their liabilities liquid and safe, must choose assets that in their totality must also be liquid and safe. Hence, they hold considerable amounts of cash and government securities. In order to earn the income needed to provide the services and return a yield to depositors, depository institutions make loans to business and consumers, but stress the security of the loans.

Though any financial institution must be concerned about the safety of the loans it makes or the securities it buys and holds, some can accept somewhat more risks than others. The risk can be minimized by developing expertise by specializing in the financing of certain kinds of loans, such as real estate mortgages, or loans for certain industries or activities.

Investment depends on these intermediary institutions that accumulate the funds of individuals, businesses, and governments who do not immediately need them and deploy them to others who wish to use resources in excess of those currently available. An important part of business conditions analysis is the study of the relative strengths of the flows of savings by households and investment demands by the business sector. When these two flows are significantly different, important changes take place in the economy. We will delve into this subject in considerable depth in later chapters.

THE ROLE OF THE FEDERAL GOVERNMENT IN THE ECONOMY

Given the complexity of the federal government's role in the economy, we can only summarize the topic here. The consensus of what the proper role of government is has changed considerably over the history of our nation. It always has been, and no doubt always will be, the subject of widespread debate; however, the range of disagreement is narrowed by the understanding of how the economic system operates. But whether or not we agree with the actions taken by government, we must know what those actions are and take account of them in our analysis.

When our country was first established, the basic attitude was "that government is best which governs least." Interferences with the functioning of the economy arose primarily from war financing or from governmental changes in banking rules and regulations (for example, prior to the crash of 1837, the "wildcat" banking period of the Jackson administration). As time passed, the federal government assumed an increasingly larger role in the economic system. Beginning with the passage of the Interstate Commerce Act in 1887, which regulated railroad rates, governmental regulation has spread to many sectors of the economy. The federal government continues to engage in business on a large scale in such projects as the production of electrical energy and atomic energy.

The role of the federal government in pricing agricultural products also has decided effects on the course of the business cycle. Before the advent of the New Deal, agricultural production was left almost entirely to the decisions of individual farmers, although some attempts were made to stimulate production during World War I and to take surpluses off the market during the Hoover administration. Since 1933, however, various aspects of agricultural production and pricing have been controlled by the federal government.

In past cycles, agricultural prices and food prices in general usually dropped rapidly and gave the cycles some of their characteristics. With governmental control of some agricultural prices, this characteristic of the cycle has changed, and past price-quantity interrelations have been altered.

While there recently has been some movement away from direct agricultural controls, the federal government has turned its policy attention to the areas of environmental controls, health and safety regulations, and the broad class of activities referred to as "consumerism." Many of these activities have serious effects on the operations of business enterprise and, in some cases, have had significant impact on the overall performance of the economy.

We could continue to enumerate the points at which the federal government impinges upon the operations of the different segments of the economy. This type of governmental policy might be termed *structural economic policy*, since it alters the relationships among the basic units of the system. Increasingly, the viewpoint has been growing that the federal government should not restrict its influence to structural policy, but should be responsible for the assurance that the level of total economic activity behaves in a desirable manner. We might refer to this type of policy as *aggregative economic policy*. In this connection, the role of the federal government includes full employment policy, anti-inflationary policy, economic growth policy, and a balance-of-payments policy. The tools used are monetary and fiscal policy. Chapter 22 is devoted to the study of these aggregative tools.

QUESTIONS

1. How do business fluctuations affect individuals? Society at large? Governments?
2. What is the trend of economic activity?

3. Describe the business cycle. Comment on the use of the word "cycle" in describing this type of economic fluctuation.
4. Describe the seasonal variations in business activity.
5. Give several examples of irregular fluctuations that may affect the level of economic activity.
6. Explain how economic analysis and forecasting are related to determining business objectives.
7. Describe the role of forecasting in business planning.
8. What is the nature of forecasting as it is used in business planning?
9. Discuss the advantages and limitations of forecasting in business.
10. Discuss the role of forecasting in governmental activities.
11. How would the susceptibility to business fluctuations differ in an economy such as ours where consumer freedom of choice exists as contrasted to a controlled economy where the state decides what commodities the people will get?
12. The level of employment and unemployment can be affected by structural economic policy and by aggregative economic policy. Under what conditions would you expect each of these policies to be most effective?

READINGS

Adams, F. Gerard. *The Business Forecasting Revolution.* New York: Oxford University Press, 1986. Chapters 1 and 2.

Ascher, William. *Forecasting, An Appraisal for Policy-Makers and Planners.* Baltimore: The Johns Hopkins University Press, 1978. Chapters 1, 2, and 4.

Bails, Dale G., and Larry C. Peppers. *Business Fluctuations, Forecasting Techniques and Applications.* Englewood Cliffs, NJ: Prentice Hall, 1982. Part I.

Butler, William F., et al. *Methods and Techniques of Business Forecasting.* Englewood Cliffs, NJ: Prentice-Hall, Inc., 1974.

Economic Report of the President. Washington, D.C.: United States Government Printing Office, annually.

Frumkin, Norman. *Tracking America's Economy.* Armonk, NY: M. E. Sharpe, Inc., 1987.

Granger, C. W. *Forecasting in Business and Economics.* Boston: Academic Press, 1989.

Heath, Daniel (ed). *America in Perspective: Major Trends in the United States through the 1990s.* Boston: Houghton Mifflin Company, 1986.

Makridakis, S., and S. Wheelwright. *Forecasting Methods for Management,* 5th ed. New York: John Wiley & Sons, 1989.

THE HISTORICAL RECORD
OF BUSINESS CYCLES
IN THE UNITED STATES

The story of American economic development is one of dramatic growth in total output as a new continent was being populated and developed. It is also a story of increased output per capita and the development of many new goods and services to meet the needs and wants of consumers. This growth has not been continuous because it has been interrupted by many periods of decline in economic activity. Most of these have been short and mild, but several have been severe and protracted.

Economic activity from the end of the Revolutionary War to the present can be divided into several periods in which the factors at work were somewhat different from what they were in the period taken as a whole. The period from the end of the Revolutionary War in 1783 to the beginning of the Civil War in 1861 was one of rapid development on an extensive scale. The population of the country grew rapidly and pushed westward past the eastern mountain ranges to the Mississippi River and beyond.

The Civil War marked a distinct political and economic turning point in our history. The time between the outbreak of the Civil War and the beginning of World War I was a period of rapid growth in which manufacturing replaced agriculture as the dominant American industry. The end of the period has been set at 1914 because World War I had a pronounced influence on the American economy, especially in its relationships to the rest of the world, and also because the passage of the Federal Reserve Act in 1913 materially changed the nature of banking and credit in the American economic system.

The next period begins with the outbreak of World War I in Europe in 1914 and runs to 1950. Following World War I, several new industries developed very rapidly—specifically, the automobile and its attendant industries, electrical utilities, and a host of electrical appliance manufacturers. The exuberant period of the late 1920s culminated in the "crash of 1929," and the worst economic depression the country had ever seen followed. The economy was in the process of struggling to reach full recovery when World War II brought on all the demand for its output the economy was capable of producing.

The fourth period begins in 1950 and continues to 1970. The postwar baby boom had profound effects on the economic system throughout the 1950s and 1960s. The housing and education industries were especially affected. The early 1950s was the time of the Korean War, and the late 1960s had the Vietnam conflict. The decade of the 1950s saw three short business cycles followed by a period of sustained expansion throughout most of the 1960s.

The fifth period starts in 1970 and continues to the present. The Vietnam War ended in 1973; the economy continued its expansion but was plagued by persistent inflationary pressures. A severe recession occurred from 1973 to 1975. The remainder of the decade included economic improvement until the short cycle of 1980 and the long slump of 1981–1982 followed by a strong recovery.

A SURVEY OF THE PERIOD FROM 1861 TO 1914

The period from 1861 to 1914 was one of continued rapid growth in population and in total economic activity. It was a period in which manufacturing and trade increased rapidly and surpassed agriculture in their contributions to the total production of goods and services in the economy.

The rate of increase in population after 1860 was slower than it had been before that period. The westward movement of the population was so rapid that by 1900 the frontier had all but disappeared. As a result, unemployment in the cities during depression periods became a more serious problem, because previously, as long as free land had existed, many of the unemployed had moved west to begin life anew.

In 1859, agriculture accounted for 30 percent of the total realized private production income; by 1914, it had declined to 20 percent. Manufacturing became more important, increasing from 12 percent of the total to 21.5 percent, and trade increased from 12 percent to 20 percent.[1]

---

1. Robert F. Martin, *National Income in the United States, 1799–1938* (New York: National Industrial Conference Board, 1939), p. 60.

Changes in agriculture that affected the whole economy took place during this period. In 1860, agriculture was based on the use of "cheap land," which could always be deserted for new land. By 1900, the frontier was gone and a period of intensive development of available land was begun. The development of machinery to harvest cereal crops, such as the combined harvester and thresher, made it possible to produce more food at a lower cost. It meant, however, that farming was becoming a business that required a high degree of managerial skill and sizable amounts of capital. Lowered costs and increased production also meant lower prices for farm products.

A major development in the field of transportation was the rapid growth of the railroad network. In 1860, there were 30,000 miles of railroad in the United States; by 1916, the railroad network had increased to 260,000 miles.

The volume of foreign trade increased significantly from 1860 to 1914, and its composition also changed. In 1860, agricultural products accounted for 80 percent of total exports, and finished manufactures accounted for about 10 percent; by 1914, agricultural products constituted 40 percent of total exports and finished manufactures 30 percent.[2]

During the Civil War, Congress passed the National Banking Act, which authorized the establishment of banks with a national charter. These banks were permitted to issue bank notes, using government bonds as collateral. A tax was placed on state bank notes, which drove them out of circulation and left national bank notes as the most important form of money, except for small change. Since the debt of the federal government was not increasing, the volume of national bank notes was restricted by the amount of available government bonds for collateral. This led to a shortage of currency, especially in the fall of the year when crops were being marketed, and created problems in several depression periods.

During this period, the level of national income showed a decided rise. Measured in terms of constant dollars based on the 1926 cost of living, the increase was 508 percent. Also measured in 1926 dollars, the 1859 per capita income was $296, and the per capita income of 1914 was $565, an increase of 91 percent.[3]

---

2. Ernest L. Bogart and Donald L. Kemmerer, *Economic History of the American People* (New York: Longmans, Green & Co., Inc., 1943), p. 369.

3. Martin, *National Income*, p. 6.

Depression of 1873

The major depression that began in 1873 was due in part to unsound commitments by the financial institutions and also in part to the operation of the money and banking system of that period. The banks had not engaged in any large-scale credit expansion before 1873, nor were their reserves unusually low. Under the National Banking Act, national banks were required to keep a set percentage of reserves against deposits and could keep part of them in other banks. Between 70 and 80 percent of these deposits were concentrated in seven large New York banks. There was normally a demand for funds late in the fall to meet the needs of the crop-moving period. As a result of this demand, these seven banks had a sizable deficiency in the required 25 percent reserve of legal tender notes and specie against their deposits by mid-September of 1873. They were forced to call in some of their loans to meet reserve requirements. This happened at the same time that several brokerage houses failed and banks called in loans in this field. A financial panic and runs on the banks followed, and they were forced to suspend specie payments. Despite the financial panic and the suspension of specie payment, most of the national banks were sound since only a few of them failed during this period.

The depression that followed this panic was long and severe. Business declined until the middle of 1879. This is the longest period of contraction in any cycle in American history. Business failures were not as spectacular during the downturn as they were during the initial panic, but they increased slowly year by year. Unemployment also increased and became a serious problem, especially in the industrial centers in the eastern part of the country. Prices declined steadily until they were at much lower levels than in 1873, and this led to distress in agricultural communities.

The basic cause of the 1873 depression was the over-expansion of the preceding period, especially in railroads. The years from 1868 to 1872 witnessed extraordinarily rapid growth, especially in the upper Mississippi valley, and the real cause for the decline was the completion of most of the railroad network that could be operated profitably at this time. The eastern part of the country had fairly adequate railroad coverage. There was still room for development, especially west of the Mississippi River; but railroads in this area found it difficult to operate profitably without being tied in with the eastern network of railroads. The lack of bridges across the Mississippi River made this impracticable. It was not until several years later that such bridges were successfully built and business increased sufficiently to resume profitable railroad development in the western part of the country.

A SURVEY OF THE PERIOD FROM 1914 TO 1950

The period from 1914 to 1950 was marked by wide variations in economic activity. The early years were boom years owing to the demands for goods arising out of World War I. The decade of the 1920s was a period of boom and speculation, and that of the 1930s one of worldwide depression. This was followed by a new boom period during World War II and continued prosperity during most of the 1940s.

The rate of increase in population slowed from the previous periods, especially in the years before World War II. Between 1910 and 1920, population increased 15 percent and between 1920 and 1930, 16 percent, but in the decade of the 1930s, only 7 percent. In the 1940s, population increased 15 percent.

The trends in manufacturing continued in the same pattern as in the previous period. The rate of manufacturing output increased rapidly when measured either in absolute output or on a per capita basis. The trend toward large business establishments with increased efficiency based on scientific management and industrial research also continued.

Mechanization in agriculture also progressed at a faster rate. The most significant development in the early part of this period was that of the gasoline tractor. Power machinery was developed for harvesting and threshing. The mechanization reduced the amount of labor needed to produce farm products and freed labor for jobs in industry.

A revolution in transportation took place in the early part of this period with the development of the automobile. The auto was a luxury in 1914, but by 1929, over 5.6 million had been sold as a result of assembly-line production, which cut costs drastically. The airplane was also developed as a major form of transportation in the late 1920s and continued to increase in importance throughout the remainder of the period.

The foreign trade of the United States increased rapidly, and its composition changed materially. In 1914, exports of goods and services were somewhat above $2 billion, and they increased to $10.5 billion in 1945. The composition of exports also changed during this period. In 1914, agricultural products were more significant than manufactured goods, but during the 1940s, agricultural products were only about 20 percent of all merchandise exported.[4]

The difficulties with the currency system led to the establishment of the Federal Reserve System in 1913. Provision was made for an elastic currency that would increase with the demands of industry and commerce. The total resources of the banking system increased significantly during this period, but the number of banks decreased markedly.

One of the outstanding developments was the growth in consumer credit, especially in installment financing of the sale of durable consumer goods. It grew rapidly after the end of World War I as a method of financing the growing sales of automobiles and consumer durables.

National income and personal income increased significantly. In dollars of constant purchasing power, using 1972 as 100, per capita personal income went up from an estimated $1,883 in 1929 to $2,392 in 1950.[5] Gross national product increased from $38.6 billion in 1914 to $284.6 billion in 1950.

Prelude to the Great Depression

The economic and political changes arising out of World War I affected the U.S. economy during the war period and, to some extent, during much of the 1920s and 1930s. The level of economic activity in the United States increased materially when World War I broke out in Europe in 1914. The United States supplied military equipment to some of the European countries engaged in the war. The level of activity grew even more when the United States entered the war in 1917. The increased demand for goods and the inflationary methods used to finance the war led to rapid increases in prices.

At the end of the war in November 1918, a severe slump in business activity was expected; and after the armistice there was some decline in the volume of business. But by the summer of 1919, the U.S. economy was again in a boom period, and prices rapidly rose. The European demand for peacetime goods increased greatly at the end of the war, and the favorable U.S. merchandise balance of trade for 1919 was more than $4 billion. The federal government also continued to operate

---

4. Bogart and Kemmerer, *Economic History*, p. 803; and *Survey of Current Business* (July 1973), p. 51.
   5. U.S. Department of Commerce, *The National Income and Product Accounts of the United States, 1929–76* (Washington, D.C.: United States Government Printing Office, 1981), Table 2–1.

at a deficit until the late summer of 1919. Another reason for the business boom was that the Federal Reserve System did not restrain the supply of money and credit until the beginning of 1920, since the banks were committed to take up a large part of the Victory Loan during April and May of 1919.

By late 1919, the monetary situation was completely reversed. In the third quarter of 1919, the federal government balanced its budget and had a surplus from the fourth quarter of 1919 through 1920. Foreign trade fell in early 1920 when European currencies were no longer pegged to the dollar at prewar rates. When the Federal Reserve System was free from its commitments to government financing, it raised discount rates to discourage borrowing.

There was a serious break in prices in August 1920, and a drastic drop in December of the same year that carried the wholesale price index down almost 100 points.[6] The break in commodity prices was followed by a depression in 1920 as business readjusted to lower price levels. The slump in business activity was rather severe, but it did not last very long.

The basic cause of the 1920 depression was the unbalanced situation created by inflation during the war. The rise in the price level was caused primarily by the inflationary methods used to finance the war. This inflationary finance continued into the postwar period until the government balanced its budget. Added to this factor were the unusual demands for goods from Europe caused by wartime shortages and improperly adjusted currency exchange rates. When these inflationary stimulants were removed, the price level dropped rapidly. During the period of rapid price declines, business was on a day-to-day basis. As soon as it was apparent that prices were stabilized, business picked up. There were no serious maladjustments to correct other than those caused by price imbalance, which resulted in a short depression.

The depression of 1920 ended in 1922 and was followed by a period of record prosperity. Development was especially marked in the construction and automobile fields, and a boom of unprecedented proportions occurred in the stock market. During these years, the general price level was experiencing some minor fluctuations, but on the whole it remained remarkably stable, except that prices of common stocks climbed. The rapid rise in stock prices was in part based upon

---

6. Warren M. Persons, *Forecasting Business Cycles* (New York: John Wiley & Sons, Inc., 1931), pp. 143–147.

a similarly rapid increase in the amount of credit used in the stock market. According to Federal Reserve figures, from 1927 to October 1929, loans to brokers more than doubled.[7]

This credit structure for stock purchases was especially vulnerable because stocks were purchased with small margins of the purchaser's funds, often only 10 percent. As a result, the market was very vulnerable in a downturn, since if prices dropped about 10 percent, the banks would ask for an additional margin to protect themselves; however, the investors frequently did not have such a margin. The banks, therefore, sold the stocks, thus adding greatly to the supply and driving stock prices down even further.

The Great Depression

The first generally recognized sign of real difficulty in the business situation began with several breaks in security prices in October 1929. On October 29th, the most severe break occurred, and in early November, Standard and Poor's index of common stock prices declined from 213 to 160.[8] The collapse in the stock market was a spectacular turning point in one phase of the total economic situation, but in retrospect, it appears that the upper turning point in business was reached about the middle of the year. In some countries this worldwide depression had begun earlier. The depression, however, was not severe in any nation until after the decline began in the United States in the third quarter of 1929.[9]

Business continued to decline through 1932 when the level of production was just over 50 percent of prosperity levels. General employment decreased about 25 percent by 1932, and factory employment by one third. The slump was especially severe in the construction industry, which had been one of the mainstays of the boom through 1928. This decline in all phases of business activity led to a rapid decrease in wholesale and consumer prices.

World trade also declined rapidly, and international investment was drastically curtailed during this period. The ability of debtor countries to meet their international obligations was seriously impaired by

---

7. *Banking and Monetary Statistics* (Washington, D.C.: Board of Governors of the Federal Reserve System, 1943).

8. Ibid., pp. 480–481.

9. *The Recovery Problem in the United States* (Washington, D.C.: The Brookings Institution, 1936), pp. 27–28.

the deepening depression in the individual countries and by the contraction in world trade. In addition, political factors were superimposed on the already weakened debt structures, and this situation led to a financial and monetary collapse. Elections held in Germany in October 1930 showed that the Nazi party was steadily increasing in strength.

Fifteen countries followed the lead of Great Britain in abandoning the gold standard. Because of uncertainties in international financial relationships, foreign trade declined at a rapid rate, and this helped deepen the depression in the United States. Not only did it add to general uncertainty, but it also led to a quick decline in the prices of agricultural products and raw materials.

Government Action. During the period from 1929 through 1932, the Hoover administration took various steps to stem the economic tide. Early in 1932, the Reconstruction Finance Corporation (RFC) was established to lend money to railroads, insurance companies, banks, building and loan associations, various agricultural credit agencies, and business corporations that were in financial difficulties. The federal government made additional capital available to the Federal Land Bank System to increase long-term credit to agriculture. The Federal Home Loan Bank System was set up with an initial capital of $125 million to discount first mortgages on residential real estate and thus provide additional credit in the housing field.[10] Despite the financial assistance rendered to the banking system by the RFC, many banks failed. During the early hours of March 4, 1933, the day on which President Franklin D. Roosevelt was inaugurated, the New York banks were closed. Banks in other parts of the country followed their lead, and the new President took office with every bank closed. On March 9, Roosevelt called Congress into emergency session, and on that day, Congress passed a hurriedly drawn emergency banking act that provided for additional funds for distressed banks as well as for the reopening of banks that were basically in a sound condition. Roosevelt's firm action dispelled a great deal of fear and uncertainty; money flowed back into the banks, and some confidence in the banking system returned.

The emergency banking legislation also gave the President authority over gold during the continuance of the crisis. All gold was ordered turned in to the Federal Reserve System, and the Treasury began to

---

10. Horace Taylor, *Contemporary Economic Problems and Trends* (New York: Harcourt, Brace & Co., 1938), p. 57.

raise the price of gold by buying at increasing prices all gold that was presented to it. The government embarked on a policy aimed at raising prices to pre-depression levels. The first Agricultural Adjustment Act, which was passed shortly after the banking legislation, provided for the restriction of agricultural production in exchange for payments to farmers. The National Recovery Act was likewise passed in the early days of the New Deal. This act gave business groups the right to draw up codes of fair competition to set minimum prices on their products or services, provided they set maximum hours of work and minimum wages for labor. Large sums of money were appropriated for direct relief and for public works projects. An extensive Social Security program of unemployment insurance and old-age and other benefits was instituted.

Causal Factors. The immediate causes of the 1929 depression appear to be the stock market collapse and the uncertainty of the international situation and its effect on financial markets. The basic causes went much deeper than these more spectacular events.

One of the causes of the 1929 depression was the unbalanced situation in world agriculture. The treaty of peace at the end of World War I called for the breakup of the Austro-Hungarian Empire and the setting up of autonomous countries in central Europe based upon the political principle of the self-determination of peoples. Each new nation tried to become as self-sufficient as possible, especially in food supplies. This movement, in addition to increases in agricultural production in the war-ravaged areas of Europe, led to large-scale increases in food production.

Problems were also created because several factors that had led to increased consumer spending during the twenties all but disappeared after 1929. The flow and pattern of consumer purchasing power were changed temporarily by the substantial profits that were being made in the security markets. Undoubtedly, a large part of these realized profits went back again into the purchase of securities, but also some were spent on consumer goods. Thus, a portion of the money arising out of the bank credit used to finance the purchase of the stock was used for consumption expenditures. This additional source of funds for consumption expenditures was only available while stock prices increased and made capital gains possible.

The amount and pattern of consumer spending were also greatly affected by the rapid increase in installment credit. The amount of outstanding consumer credit doubled between 1923 and 1929, and a substantial portion of this credit was used for the purchase of durable goods.[11] The volume of consumer credit dropped significantly in 1930 as automobile sales fell and general economic activity decreased.

Another cause of the depression was the overbuilding of houses in the 1920s. The residential construction industry had reached its high point in 1928 and was declining in 1929. Apparently, the basic reason for a decline in construction was an exhaustion of the effective demand for new housing.

Another cause of the depression is to be found in developments in the automobile field and in the changes in the economy produced by the automobile. From 1922 to 1929, the number of automobiles manufactured increased rapidly as the automobile became a part of the American way of life. By 1929, the automobile industry had passed its point of rapid growth and had become integrated with the rest of the economy; its growth was in response to increases in population and in real income. During the period of rapid growth, large amounts of capital were invested in plants to produce automobiles and in their materials, such as steel sheets, plate glass, upholstery, and rubber. Rapid development took place in related fields, such as gasoline refining. Much capital was invested in highway construction and in the development of business establishments along the highways.

Rural shopping habits were changed as motor cars made it possible to go to larger towns for goods. New facilities were built to meet these changed habits. In short, the automobile and related developments led to large-scale capital investment in the period of rapid development prior to 1929. The rapid increase in the level of nonresidential construction came to a halt because the rapid expansion in the automobile and related industries had slowed down as the demand for these new goods reached a saturation point at current income levels. The changes required in the pattern of production to adjust to this new situation were major factors in the protracted period of depression in the 1930s.

Monetary policies must share some of the blame for the economic unbalance that led to the depression. This is particularly true since credit helped materially to finance the boom in real estate and in the security markets. Stock market speculation continued unabated in 1929, but the Federal Reserve took no vigorous action to halt it. This was due to a controversy between the Board and the twelve Federal Reserve Banks on the proper policy to follow. The Federal Reserve

---

11. Rolf Nugent, *Consumer Credit and Economic Stability* (New York: Russell Sage Foundation, 1939), p. 124.

Banks urged the use of quantitative measures, such as a higher discount rate and open-market operations, but the Federal Reserve Board urged direct pressure on banks making security loans. The major action taken in 1929 was the adoption of a policy that banks that were large-scale lenders to the stock market could not get credit from their Federal Reserve Bank. The policies adopted by the Federal Reserve were not restrictive enough to halt stock speculation but were too restrictive to help promote a vigorous business expansion.

There is also a serious question about the effectiveness of monetary policy after the decline in the stock market and in business activity had begun. The Federal Reserve added somewhat to bank reserves during the stock market collapse in late 1929 but did not pursue a vigorous policy of monetary ease during most of 1930 and 1931. Federal Reserve authorities felt that a larger money supply would not help stimulate the economy because most banks had excess reserves during this period, and banks could not force the use of their funds. One vigorous critic of monetary policy during this period, Professor Milton Friedman, feels that reserves were in excess only in a narrow legal sense, because banks had found that the Federal Reserve would not lend them funds as a "lender of last resort" when they really needed them.[12] The debate over Federal Reserve policy in the great depression is not resolved, but it is clear that it failed to act vigorously enough in the early stages of the downturn to prevent a financial crisis.

Fiscal policy must also share some of the blame for the deteriorating financial situation. The federal government ran modest deficits in the depression years, but total government spending by all levels of government declined. The policy of the Hoover administration and during the first years of the Roosevelt administration was to balance the budget, if at all possible. In fact, tax rates were increased sharply in 1932 in an attempt to balance the budget, contributing to the deepening depression.

Recovery. Under the impetus of the government programs mentioned previously, industrial production increased after 1933 and continued upward to 1937. By early summer 1937, business had reached the peak of a new cycle, although during this recovery period its growth rate was not as dramatic as that of the 1920s. Employment was about the same as in 1929; but since the labor force had also grown, in 1937, approximately eight million people were out of work.

---

12. Milton Friedman and Anna Jacobson Schwartz, *A Monetary History of the United States, 1867–1960* (Princeton, NJ: Princeton University Press, 1963), p. 348.

The 1937 Recession and Recovery

Recovery had not yet carried the economy back to full employment levels when another recession occurred in 1937. The decline in business activity, which began in the latter half of 1937 and continued into the first half of 1938, was rapid. Industrial production dropped by over 25 percent in a short time, but it did not reach the low levels of 1932 or 1933. The greatest decline during this depression occurred in the production of durable goods.

During the recovery period after 1933, governmental deficits added to the income stream. In 1936, the deficit of the federal government was unusually large owing to the cashing of bonus certificates for veterans of World War I. However, in 1937, receipts of all governmental units exceeded expenditures by $685 million.

In addition to the decrease in the deficit of the federal government, funds in the hands of consumers were further reduced when Social Security tax collections increased by over $1 million in 1937 from the 1936 level, and no provision was made for paying out any funds until a later period. The net result of the operations of the federal government was a decrease in borrowing from $3.8 billion in the calendar year 1936 to about $300 million in 1937.[13] This rapid shift in government finances was a major factor leading to the downturn in 1937.

Another factor that influenced the business situation at this time was the June 1936 Revenue Act, which contained an undistributed profits tax. This tax caused the payment of a larger sum in dividends on 1936 corporate income than would otherwise have been the case, and this added to consumer income in the latter part of 1936 and the early part of 1937. Its long-range effect on business expansion, however, was repressive in that many businesses were afraid of the implications of such a tax. Prices of agricultural commodities increased in 1936 because of the severe drought. There was a decline in speculative activity in world commodity markets in April 1937, and the prices of raw materials declined after that time and with them the speculative demand for goods.

The federal government reacted to the decline in business in 1937 by stepping up its public works program, which was financed by again running a deficit. More orders for airplanes and armaments were placed in this country by European countries as the international situation deteriorated, and these orders helped increase the level of busi-

---

13. *National Income Supplement to Survey of Current Business* (July 1947), pp. 21–23.

ness activity. Almost all phases of economic activity in the United States increased rapidly in late 1939 after World War II began in Europe. The United States became the "Arsenal of Democracy."

The World War II Period

When the United States entered the war in December 1941, over five million of her people were still unemployed. Within a short time, however, demand became so large that it was impossible for the economy to produce enough war goods without reduction of production in industries serving civilian needs and wants.

The increased demand for goods for military operations, as well as increased purchasing power in the hands of a much larger labor force as the unemployed were absorbed into the armed forces or in war production, led to price control and rationing in an attempt to prevent inflation. The Office of Price Administration was set up, and it rationed items such as tires, automobiles, typewriters, gasoline, bicycles, fuel oil, shoes, processed foods, and meats and fats. It also established maximum prices on various commodities and set ceilings on rent.

Because of war expenditures, the total federal budget increased rapidly. In fiscal year 1941, the federal government spent $12.8 billion, of which approximately half was directly war-related. Total expenditures increased to $100.4 billion in fiscal year 1945, of which 90 percent was for war expenditures.[14]

Although part of the cost of the war was raised through increased taxation, a substantial part was raised by government borrowing. The United States Treasury sold almost $157 billion of securities. The Federal Reserve System facilitated the financing of the war by supplying reserves to the banking system through the purchase of over $20 billion of government securities.[15]

The Reconversion Period

The reconversion period was viewed with misgivings by many who felt that the economy would return to prewar depression levels. As the economy shifted back to peacetime production at the end of 1945 and in 1946, the controls were lifted one by one. Control over prices was modified shortly after the end of the war and was allowed to lapse on

---

14. *Tax and Expenditure Policy for 1950, A Statement on National Policy by the Research and Policy Committee for Economic Development* (New York: 1950), p. 38.
15. *Federal Reserve Bulletin* (January 1950), p. 61.

June 30, 1947, except for rent control in housing shortage areas. Prices rose rapidly when controls were lifted.

In 1946, both production and employment decreased. Most of the difference in production, however, was accounted for by the elimination of overtime work. In 1947, production and employment again increased; the year was one of virtually full employment of labor and resources, and a strong seller's market continued. Prices continued upward during 1947 as supply and demand were seeking a new balance. During the second quarter of the year, there was some tendency for domestic business to level off.

Demand by foreign countries increased generally and reversed the easing tendencies that were beginning to appear in some lines of business. As the world agricultural situation became worse because of poor crops in 1947, the foreign demand for farm products created new pressure on prices. Foreign countries drew on their dollar resources so rapidly that they soon were all but exhausted. This led Secretary of State George C. Marshall to suggest a foreign aid program; Congress passed the European Recovery Program the following year. This program kept foreign demand at a high level, but not at the level of the second quarter of 1947.

Factors Leading to Inflation. Several factors accounted for the postwar increases in prices after the period of wartime price control. There was a large demand for consumer durable goods since the output of these goods had been drastically curtailed during the war. Wartime savings, larger than usual because of patriotic appeals and the shortage of goods, were available for postwar purchases. The changed situation from a partially employed economy in the prewar period to a fully employed economy in the postwar period also made price increases likely. The most important reason for inflation in the postwar period was the method of wartime finance. As already pointed out, the government resorted to borrowing on a large scale, and the banks of the country bought government bonds from private investors in large quantities. With a greatly increased money supply and the increased demand for goods, it was inevitable that prices should rise.

The 1949 Readjustment. During 1948, the economy continued to operate at close to capacity levels. Wartime income tax rates were cut in the spring of 1948, and the extra income left in the hands of consumers had an expansionary effect on the economy. In 1948, the price level increased more slowly than it had in 1947, and the rate of increase in consumption expenditures also began to level off. Business people did not adjust immediately to this change in the rate of increase in business activity and thus found themselves with excessive inventories. As a result, industrial production declined about 8 percent.

One reason that business did not decline further was that personal consumption expenditures held up and even increased slightly toward the end of 1949. This was due in part to the payment of unemployment compensation to most of the workers who were out of work and also to the effects of lower federal income taxes under the 1947 Revenue Act. Perhaps most important was the willingness of consumers to keep expenditures up, even in the face of some falling off in business.

It became evident in the second half of 1949 that inventory liquidation had gone too far. Buying for stock was resumed in more normal proportions, and early in 1950, business picked up. A new boom began later in the year as the Korean War and large-scale rearmament led to an intensified demand for goods.

A SURVEY OF THE PERIOD FROM 1950 TO 1970

The social, political, and economic consequences of World War II continued to have important bearing on the economy of the 1950s and 1960s. The low birth rates of the 1930s and the war years of the 1940s were replaced by the exceptionally high birth rates of the late 1940s, which continued throughout the 1950s. These demographic facts had and continue to have important implications. Education and housing enjoyed boom conditions throughout the two decades. The process of shifting production from manufacturing and agriculture toward the service industries continued apace in this period. Population movements toward the South and West, and relatively away from the older areas of the country, were taking place. The percentage of the population classified as rural fell from 43.5 percent in 1950 to 30.1 percent in 1970.

The period was influenced by political unrest around the world beginning with the Korean conflict in the early fifties and the long Vietnam engagement of the late sixties and early seventies. These had important influences on the federal budget and Federal Reserve actions that affected the inflation rate.

The entire period was one of a satisfactory rate of economic growth, and the business cycles that did occur were relatively mild. It was sometimes said that the business cycle was obsolete. Chronic unemployment seemed to be becoming a problem, partly because of the labor force growing at a more rapid rate than total demand, and partly because of the gradual decrease in the demand for unskilled labor. Government welfare programs of various kinds gave some people an alternative to employment, and downward wage rigidity seemed to be increasing.

The Korean War Period

The Korean War started on a small scale as a United Nations (UN) police action, but it developed into a major conflict lasting several years. This war had a significant effect on our economy because the bulk of the UN forces and most of the war material supplied were American.

The demand for goods arising out of the Korean War led to renewed inflationary pressures. Government deficits were not the cause of price rises in the last half of 1950, since the Treasury had an excess of cash income over cash outgo of almost a billion dollars in the last half of the year. The explanation lies in private spending. Consumers, fearing the shortages of World War II, spent large sums on various types of durable and semi-durable goods. Business also spent heavily for inventories and capital investment.

Under these conditions, Federal Reserve Bank credit increased materially. The Board of Governors of the Federal Reserve System wanted to act to restrict expansion, but could not do so as long as it felt obligated to support the bond market by buying all government securities at par or better. The Treasury wanted to follow a pattern of low interest rates as it did in World War II, and this, of course, required price-support operations, since interest rates would have gone up in a free market as the demand for funds increased.

An agreement between the Treasury and the Federal Reserve System was announced in March 1951. This accord was designed to check credit expansion without the use of direct controls. Government bonds were no longer bought in the market by the Federal Reserve to maintain a set pattern of interest rates. The Federal Reserve was not to stay out of the market completely but continued to buy and sell some securities so as to maintain an orderly market. As the private demand for funds increased because of a boom in residential building and in the capital markets, interest rates rose, and the price of long-term securities somewhat dropped.

The 1953 Recession and Recovery

Business continued upward in the first half of 1953. By summer, the rate of increase in business activity had slowed down, and there was some fear that a recession might occur. The Federal Reserve System eased credit to prevent a downturn or to make any downturn that might occur less serious. A downturn began in the third quarter of 1953 and continued through the second quarter of 1954. The 1953–1954 downturn was largely a readjustment to a lower level of defense expenditures made possible by the end of the Korean War.

The lower expenditures led to some decrease in business investment expenditures and to liquidation of inventories in late 1953 and 1954. Consumers also reduced expenditures on durable goods somewhat, especially on automobiles, because many had purchased late-model cars in the postwar period.

The recession did not result in a protracted depression for several reasons. Personal income held up well because many sectors of the economy were not affected, and personal taxes were cut by over $3 billion. Unemployment compensation also helped cushion the decline in income of those unemployed.

Economic activity increased rapidly in 1955, and personal consumption expenditures increased, especially on durable goods. Inflationary pressures began to develop during this prosperity period. To prevent serious inflation, the Federal Reserve System followed a highly restrictive monetary policy. Reserve requirements were raised, and the discount rate was raised several times.

The 1957–1958 Recession and Recovery

In late summer 1957, the economy experienced the beginning of the third postwar recession. In some ways, this recession was the most severe of the three readjustments, although the period of decline was the shortest. By August 1958, unemployment had increased to 7.7 percent of the civilian labor force. Gross national product declined 2.5 percent, but disposable personal income changed little.

A number of causal factors were at work in the 1957–1958 recession. One was the slowing down of capital expenditures because plant and equipment had been expanded faster than the increase in demand for goods and services. Another was the shift in consumer expenditures. Less money was spent on durable goods and more on nondurables and services, which resulted in a decline in production and liquidation of inventories.

Business reached the low point of the recession in April 1958, and then started upward. The boost came in part from the ending of inventory liquidation as consumer expenditures increased on nondurable goods. There was also an increase in residential construction as interest rates eased and mortgage funds were made more easily available under programs of the Federal Housing Administration and the Veterans Administration. Increased federal, as well as state and local, government expenditures also helped increase business activity.

The first half of 1959 was a year of strong economic recovery that showed some signs of turning into a boom. The economy suffered a severe setback, however, when the longest steel strike on record began shortly after midyear. When the steel strike ended in November, there was a new surge in economic activity. Inventories were rebuilt rapidly through the first quarter of 1960, and production and gross national product reached new highs by midyear.

The 1960–1961 Recession

The fourth postwar recession began in the second half of 1960. Industrial production dropped during the second half of the year and into early 1961. Gross national product eased somewhat during the last quarter of 1960 and fell somewhat further in the first quarter of 1961. Unemployment, however, posed more of a problem than in earlier postwar recessions. One reason for the increased unemployment was the increasing size of the labor force resulting from an increasing birth rate after 1939. Another was the accelerated pace of automation resulting from new technological advances and rising labor costs.

The 1960–1961 recession was due to several factors. Inventories that had been depleted by the steel strike were rebuilt rapidly in the first quarter of 1960. This buildup led to an increase in production that could not be sustained when inventory building ceased. Residential construction also slowed down since the huge backlog of deferred demand had been met and mortgage money for residential financing was more difficult to obtain and more costly than it had been during the 1957–1958 downturn and early recovery period. Consumer buying also weakened somewhat after midyear, especially the purchase of durable goods. Consumers had a good stock of automobiles and other durables so demand was no longer pressing.

The Prosperity Period of the 1960s

The prosperity period that followed the mild recession of 1960–1961 was the longest in our history. There was some retardation in the rate of advance in economic activity in late 1962, which was more pronounced in industrial production than in gross national product. There was some intensification of economic activity in 1965 and especially in 1966 as American participation in the Vietnam War greatly increased. Policies that were designed to slow inflation led to a slowdown in the forward movement of the economy in the first quarter of 1967, but the economy moved forward again in the second quarter and continued to advance until late 1969.

Several characteristics of the early years of this prosperity period before it was affected by the Vietnam War are somewhat unusual. Wholesale prices remained almost completely stable from 1961 through 1964 and then started to move upward slowly in 1965 as demand accelerated. Labor cost per unit of output remained relatively stable throughout the period from 1961 through 1966. This was due to wage increases that, to a large extent, were held within average increases in productivity and to major expenditures by industry on more efficient plant and equipment.

The money supply also was increased gradually during most of this period. In the early part of 1962, there was a reduction in the money supply, but the supply was increased sharply in the second half of the year as the rate of advance in economic activity slowed. The federal government had a cash deficit that did not vary significantly in amount during the first four years of this period. One major reason for the unusual length of this prosperity period was that many things that led to cyclical unbalance did not occur until 1965 and 1966.

This does not mean that the prosperity period was without problems. The unemployment rate did not fall below 5 percent of the labor force until late 1964, and unemployment was especially severe among teenagers. The Vietnam War led to additional demands for military personnel, goods, and services, but even under the impetus of war demands, the unemployment rate did not drop much below 4 percent. Many of those who were still unemployed were for all practical purposes unemployable in a highly mechanized economy without an upgrading of their labor skills.

The problem of a deficit in the balance of payments also persisted during this period of prosperity. Campaigns to increase exports had some measure of success, and foreign investment was reduced by a Voluntary Foreign Credit Restraint Program. The measures taken were not sufficient, however, to solve the problem of the balance of payments.

In 1966, a new problem arose when interest rates climbed to the highest levels since the early twenties. The demand for funds from all sectors of the economy was high and increasing, especially the demand for bank loans from business. To prevent serious inflation arising out of the demands of the Vietnam War, in December 1965, the Federal Reserve raised the discount rate and acted generally to restrict the supply of money and credit. The result was a slowdown in residential construction during the summer of 1966. The stock market also reacted to higher interest rates and reduced profit prospects; by mid-1966, the average price of industrial common stock had dropped by some 20 percent from the high points reached in 1965.

There were signs in late 1966 that the economy was slowing down. The Federal Reserve acted to stimulate the economy by increasing the money supply at the end of the year and into the first half of 1967. There was a very sharp recovery in economic activity in the second half of 1967 that continued until late 1969. Inflation continued at an accelerated rate during this period primarily because of a high level of private spending and inflationary policies followed by the federal government in the 1967 slowdown in economic activity. The federal budget for fiscal 1969 showed a slight surplus, and by mid-1969, the Federal Reserve was following a policy of severe credit restraint. Interest rates rose to higher levels than in 1966 and, in some cases, were the highest since Civil War days.

The 1969 Recession

The economy experienced another recession in late 1969 that lasted during most of 1970. This recession was among the mildest in our history. Gross national product (GNP) in current dollars continued to expand and declined only very slightly in constant dollars. Industrial production dropped by 6.6 percent from its high point and employment by 1.6 percent. The general price level continued to increase at a high rate during this recession period. The GNP implicit price deflator rose at an annual rate in excess of 5 percent.[16]

This recession was not mild, however, in the financial markets. The prices of common stocks declined somewhat more than in the earlier postwar recessions, but not as much as in the depression of 1937 or 1929–1933. Before the recession, the prices of long-term debt securities were falling as interest rates rose to unusually high levels and continued to do so during the first half of the recession period. A dramatic event was the failure of the Penn-Central Railroad to meet its obligations, which resulted in its filing for bankruptcy.

---

16. Solomon Fabricant, *Recent Economic Changes and the Agenda of Business-Cycle Research* (New York: National Bureau of Economic Research, Inc., 1971), p. 27.

This recession was not caused by inventory liquidation or a decline in business capital investment. Business continued to add to inventories throughout the recession, and 1970 was a record year for capital outlays. The major cause was the restrictive monetary policy followed by the Federal Reserve in the second half of 1969 and into early 1970 in an effort to slow down the rate of inflation. Consumers also increased their level of saving to near a twenty-year high because of uncertainties related to inflation and the continuation of the Vietnam War.

A SURVEY OF THE PERIOD FROM 1970 TO THE PRESENT

Real GNP declined seriously in the 1973–1975 recession and recovered at a steady rate to the end of the decade. A minor cycle occurred within the year 1980, and by late 1981, another decline in activity had begun. Throughout the 1970s, inflation was a constant problem as the rate of growth in the money stock and the rate of growth in prices were both about 6 percent in the first half of the decade and 8 percent in the second half.[17] Interest rates were very high during this period, reflecting in large part the public's perception of continuing future inflation. This made it particularly hard on home buyers and on durable goods manufacturers and users.

Concern was being shown for the observed decline in labor productivity. Whereas in the post-World War II years before 1970, the trend growth of productivity had been about 2.5 percent annually, in the 1970s, it fell to just over 0.5 percent. Since nominal wages were increasing faster than productivity, the real cost of labor was increasing, putting more pressure on unemployment and prices. Hope for improvement in labor productivity was not very great, since such improvement depends upon increase in the capital stock, which in turn depends upon personal saving, and personal saving had been low during the period.

A shock to the economy occurred when the Organization of Petroleum Exporting Countries (OPEC) raised substantially the price of oil in 1978–1980. Crude oil had been priced at about $15 per barrel in 1978 and rose to $36 in 1980. The increase was a great shock because the U.S. domestic petroleum industry had been controlled and regulated to keep energy prices artificially low. The natural consequences

---

17. James E. Glassman and Ronald A. Sage, "The Recent Inflation Experience," *Federal Reserve Bulletin* (May 1981), pp. 389–397.

were profligate use of the resource, a decline in domestic production, and very large imports of lower cost foreign crude oil. Ultimately, most of the domestic controls were taken off, and petroleum prices stabilized as consumers and producers reacted to the higher prices.

The 1973–1975 Recession

The recession that began late in 1973 was the most severe of the recessions in the post-World War II period, and it was also the longest. It began in November 1973, and lasted through March 1975, a period of sixteen months. Real GNP in terms of 1972 prices declined 6.6 percent, well over twice the decline in the recession of 1957–1958, which was the most severe of the earlier recessions in the postwar period. Industrial production dropped almost 15 percent, a somewhat larger decline than in the most severe recession before that in the postwar period. The other postwar recessions varied in length between eight and eleven months.

Construction also declined significantly. Total construction contracts in early 1975 were 25 percent below the average level in 1973. Housing starts fell 63 percent from 1973 to 1974. Inventories also created problems in the 1973–1975 recession. Inventories generally lag GNP, but the lag was unusual in this recession. Inventories increased in each quarter of 1974. In the first two quarters, inventories rose in the materials and supplies fields as producers attempted to build stocks that had been in short supply. In the last two quarters, inventories rose because sales declined and stocks had become excessive in relationship to sales. This was especially true in the last quarter of 1974. There was a massive liquidation of inventories in the first two quarters of 1975, and the liquidation continued at a slower pace during the remainder of the year.

Employment dropped from a record 79.9 million in October 1974, to 76.6 million in February 1975, and three-fourths of the reduction was in manufacturing. In the spring of 1975, the unemployment rate rose to a postwar high of 9.2 percent.[18]

The GNP deflator rose almost 10 percent in 1974 compared with less than 6 percent in 1973. The price level increased in each recession period after the end of the Korean War, but earlier increases were at a much slower rate than in 1974. Consumer prices also increased rapidly, going up at an 11 percent rate.[19]

---

18. *Federal Reserve Bulletin* (February 1976), p. A52.
19. Ibid., pp. A53–A55.

Interest rates rose to unprecedented levels. On July 3, 1974, major banks raised their prime rates to a record 12 percent. The high interest rates and poor business conditions led to a major decline in stock prices. Early in December, the Dow industrials closed at 578, the lowest level since October 1962, and well below the high at 892 for the year in mid-March.[20]

The 1973–1975 recession, like all severe recessions in modern times, was worldwide so far as industrial nations are concerned. The acceleration of output in the first half of 1973 in France, West Germany, Italy, the United Kingdom, Japan, and Canada was at an exceptionally high rate. This was followed by an equally sharp deceleration of output in all countries and a general recession.[21] In some cases, as in the United States, the recession was the most severe in recent years.

The 1973 1975 recession also differed from earlier postwar recessions in that it consisted of two distinct phases. The first phase was a response to constraints on aggregate supply; the second stage, which began in early fall 1974, also reflected a reduction in demand for goods and services.

Total spending for goods and services rose substantially during the first three quarters of the recession with only a minor halt after the peak of the cycle. Money expansion continued to be rapid during the first two quarters of the recession, whereas this period is usually characterized by slow monetary growth. The chief cause of the downturn during this period came from the supply side. The ability of the nation to produce was reduced by increased energy costs, unfavorable weather leading to crop reductions and higher prices, the cost of environmental and safety programs, the effect of dollar devaluations, and the unbalancing effects on production of price controls. The result was a decline in the quantity of goods available for consumption while prices went up. After the first phase of the recession, the second phase was also affected by the more typical lack of demand at prevailing prices and institutional arrangements. Total spending declined sharply in the last quarter of 1974 and the first quarter of 1975.

Causes of the 1973–1975 Recession. Like all severe recessions, the recession of 1973–1975 had its immediate and its longer-run causal factors. The major immediate causal factor was inflation in the United States, which was part of a worldwide inflation in major industrial countries. This was due in part to relatively easy monetary and fiscal

---

20. *Business Conditions*, Federal Reserve Bank of Chicago (January 1975), pp. 16–17.
21. "Inflation and Stagnation in Major Foreign Industrial Countries," *Federal Reserve Bulletin* (October 1974): pp. 683–698.

policies in the years preceding 1973. This was true not only in the United States, but in all major industrial countries. There were also several additional inflationary factors involved. In 1973, farm prices rose rapidly due to poor crops in many parts of the world. Oil prices also increased dramatically as a result of the actions of OPEC countries. There was an increase in raw material prices generally as a worldwide boom ran up against a relatively fixed supply. Inflation had an effect not only on interest rates and stock prices, but also on consumers. Increased prices for oil products and food left consumers with less money for other products. Higher wage rates that were to help, at least in part, offset inflation provided no greater real wages, and, under our system of progressive income taxes, a larger percentage of real income went to the federal government.

Inventory buildup was excessive, and this also helped cause recession. Goods were so scarce during the boom that many businesses failed to see signs that the boom was ending, and they thus continued to build stocks. When stocks had to be liquidated, demand was further reduced, and this led to more severe recession.

The more basic causes of the recession of 1973–1975 go back to some of the developments in the preceding period.[22] In a real sense, 1973 marked the end of a period that began in 1958 or as late as 1961, just as 1933 marked the end of a period that began in 1921. Total employment rose in every year from 1961 through 1973, as did disposable personal income and personal consumption expenditures, both on a per capita basis and in real terms.

The period from 1961 through 1964 was one of sustained expansion in which unemployment fell to 5 percent of the labor force and productivity grew rapidly. About 1965, speculative excesses developed in several fields. One such excess was in corporate mergers and acquisitions, especially in the era of conglomerates. The effect of such action on projected profits per share diverted management from its more basic tasks of increasing technology and profit prospects. Many conglomerates were a disappointment with respect to earnings, and the prices of their stocks dropped dramatically.

Other stocks also were involved in a speculative market for common stocks. The volume of trading on the New York Stock Exchange doubled between 1966 and 1971. In the two-year period of 1967–1968,

---

22. This section relies heavily on a paper presented by Arthur F. Burns, Chairman, Board of Governors of the Federal Reserve System, at a meeting of the Society of American Business Writers and published in the *Federal Reserve Bulletin* (May 1975), pp. 273–279.

the average price per share on the New York Stock Exchange went up 40 percent, while earnings went up less than 2 percent. Needless to say, the stock market could not and did not sustain such a record of growth, but dropped to lower levels. Such stock speculation was aided by mutual funds of the "performance" type. A similar stock market boom took place in all major industrial countries.

A speculative wave also hit the real estate markets. Real estate investment trusts (REITs) supplied high risk construction loans for condominiums, recreational developments, shopping centers, and the like. The result was overbuilding; by 1972, the vacancy rate for office buildings reached 13 percent, and many projects were in serious financial trouble.

The inventory boom began in 1973 as several other speculative excesses were diminishing. There were signs in early 1973 that there was a reduction in consumer spending, but these signs were missed as business rushed to get "scarce" goods before the price rose even higher.

Fiscal policy was not used to stop speculative excesses but became more expansive. Taxes were cut in 1964, 1965, 1969, and 1971, and spending was increased for social programs and the war in Vietnam. Corporations allowed their equity positions to deteriorate and liquidity to decrease. Large banks relied more heavily on volatile short-term funds to finance their loan customers, and some state and local governments followed unsafe financial practices. Some resorted to excessive short-term borrowing, while others issued so-called "moral obligation" bonds, which some investors wrongly regarded as equal in credit rating to "full faith and credit" obligations. These excesses could only lead to problems that needed correction, and this helped intensify the 1973–1975 recession.

Recovery from the 1973–1975 Recession. To stimulate recovery, monetary policy became much more expansive in early 1975. Fiscal policy became stimulative late in 1974 and expansionary in 1975 because of an increase in expenditures and a sizable tax cut, especially for lower income groups. Interest rates declined from the high levels of 1973 and 1974 and thereby made expansion easier to finance. Inflation also slowed from the high rates of 1973 and 1974.

Recovery from the 1973–1975 recession began in the fourth quarter of 1975. Consumers led the way to recovery with increased expenditures on nondurable goods. As excess inventories were worked off in field after field, production was again called for to meet current demand. The U.S. trade surplus hit a record level in 1975 as imports were reduced and exports expanded.

The Period of the 1980s

Economic activity continued to expand throughout the remainder of the 1970s and peaked in the first quarter of 1980. During this expansion period, persistent inflation was experienced with the consumer price index increasing at a rate of 5 percent at the beginning of 1977 and ranging upward to over 14 percent in 1980, after which it began to subside somewhat. The most dramatic price increases took place in energy costs and in home ownership. The home-ownership index increased both because of increases in home prices and because of the marked increase in mortgage interest rates.[23] High and volatile market interest rates also characterized the period. For example, in 1977, the bank prime rate was just over 6 percent and in December 1980, rose to 21.5 percent.

The Brief 1980 Recession. During the first half of 1980, the U.S. economy was subjected to some strain. The National Bureau of Economic Research designated the turning points of the brief cycle of 1980. The peak was determined to be in January and the trough in July. Beginning late 1979, the growth of the money stock slowed substantially and then declined sharply for three months in early 1980. In late 1979, the price of oil was raised substantially. The cost of crude oil rose from $12.93 per barrel in December 1978 to $27.85 per barrel in May 1980. The impact of the rise in energy prices was not distributed evenly across all sectors of the economy, but most of the impact was felt in those industries and products which were heavy users of energy, such as automobiles. The sharp increase in the price of energy, relative to other prices, was the primary cause of the drop in the growth rate of real output from 4.8 percent in 1978, to 1 percent in 1979 and continuing at between 1 to 2 percent in early 1980.[24]

Early in 1980, the credit markets were thrown into turmoil with the introduction of a major selective credit restraint program. Because of the uncertainty caused by this restraint program, demand for short-term credit surged in 1980. In the first two months of 1980, business loans at commerical banks increased at a 24 percent annual rate. Part of this increase in credit demand was the result of the credit control program. The borrowing that would have taken place later in the year was concentrated earlier, because potential borrowers were uncertain if credit would be available later on.

With the Federal Reserve trying to restrain credit, the resulting de-

23. "The Recent Inflation Experience," *Federal Reserve Bulletin* (May 1981), pp. 389–397.

24. Albert E. Burger, "What Happened to The Economy in The First Half of 1980," *Review*, Federal Reserve Bank of St. Louis (August/September 1980), pp. 9–15.

mand had the effect of pushing interest rates up sharply. As market interest rates climbed above ceiling rates and rates set by state usury laws, financial institutions found it difficult to hold and acquire funds, and thus had difficulty in performing their traditional functions. Housing was one sector that suffered from these developments.

In the second quarter of 1980, there was a reversal of money supply growth—from slow growth to faster growth. This reversal in money growth did help correct the recessionary impact of the earlier slow money supply growth. In the last half of 1980, the economy did turn upward. However, the problems of high inflation and high interest rates continued to persist.

The 1981–1982 Recession. The recovery was a brief and halting one. The downswing that followed was sharp and lasted for approximately sixteen months. The National Bureau of Economic Research designated the peak as July 1981 and the trough as November 1982. This recession was associated with a concerted effort on the part of the Federal Reserve System to combat the inflation that had characterized the period of the 1970s. The consumer price index, which had increased at annual rates of 13.5 percent in 1980 and 10.3 percent in 1981, fell to 6.2 percent in 1982 and 3.2 percent in 1983. This period of disinflation, however, brought about a steep downturn which was accompanied by increased unemployment.

From the start of the recession in July 1981 through the first quarter of 1982, real output declined by 5.7 percent. The unemployment rate, which had been 7.6 percent in 1981, increased to 9.7 percent and 9.6 percent, respectively, in 1982 and 1983. The peak unemployment rate of 10.8 was reached in December 1982.

The manufacturing sector was especially hard hit. Over the first nine months of the recession, industrial production declined by 13.6 percent. At the start of the recession, manufacturing capacity utilization was 79.9 percent, and at the bottom of the recession, it had fallen to 67.6 percent. Manufacturing employment declined by over 2 million jobs during the early stages of the recession. The drop in manufacturing output and employment placed economic pressure on the regional economies of the northeast and the upper-midwest.

The rate of increase in labor costs decelerated considerably. Part of the slowing was due to early negotiation of expiring contracts and the renegotiation of contracts in a number of major industries. Many of the new contracts involved wage and fringe benefit concessions. The reductions in labor costs did relieve production cost pressure and enhanced the competitive position of firms in these industries.

Personal consumption expenditures (adjusted for inflation) fell sharply early in the recession. The weakness in consumer spending was concentrated in the durable goods sector, especially autos. In the fourth quarter of 1981, total auto sales (domestic plus foreign) fell to an annual rate of 7.4 million units. This was the lowest sales figure in more than a decade. The industry responded with rebates and other sales promotions, which did increase auto demand and sales. But, as has generally occurred, when major rebates and promotions ended, auto purchases declined sharply.

The effects of the recession were reflected in federal government expenditures and receipts. The federal deficit was $61.2 billion in 1980, $63.8 billion in 1981, but grew to $145.9 billion in the recession year of 1982.

As the recession developed in late 1981, short-term interest rates moved down. But long-term interest rates remained high during most of the recessionary period. This reflected doubts by the credit markets that the progress made on reducing inflation would be sustained over the long run. This skepticism was related to the fact that, during the 1960s and 1970s, episodes of reduced inflation had been short-lived. Periods of deep downturns in business activity, for example, 1973–75, had been followed by reacceleration of even faster price increases, for example, 1979–80. High long-term rates were also fostered by the prospect of huge deficits in the federal budget, even as the economy started to recover. Fears of big deficits led to expectations of future credit market pressures and also sustained the feeling of inflationary expectations.

In international markets, the value of the dollar appreciated on most world markets. The appreciation of the dollar was associated with the declining inflation rate in the United States and to the rise in dollar interest rates. Because of a strengthening dollar, as well as slowing economic growth abroad, real exports of goods and services declined in 1981. The value of imports, which grew steadily through most of 1981, declined sharply in 1982. At that stage in the recession, the weakness in aggregate demand did show up in smaller imports.

The Mid-to-Late 1980s. The recovery that started in November 1982 was a strong one and generally followed the typical pattern of past expansions. In fact, the expansion continued on through 1988 and proved stronger than during comparable cyclical periods since World War II—the only exception might be the period during the Korean War buildup. The expansion that started in 1982 represents the longest peacetime expansion on record. Real GNP grew faster and levels of economic slack declined faster than in the average expansion.

This economic expansion was consumer led. Strength in consumer spending provided the major impetus for the expansion continuing for several years. Personal income, in nominal terms, rose rapidly, and with falling inflation, most of that nominal gain was translated directly into sizable increases in real purchasing power. Consumer spending for new cars and housing was particularly strong. Consumer spending for autos, in real terms, grew by 50 percent above the recession levels of 1981–82. Lower interest rates, innovations in housing finance, and stable housing prices provided underlying support for increases in housing demand.[25]

With the rise in consumer spending, economic conditions in the business sector also improved. Output, sales, profits, productivity, and investment spending did grow during the economic upturn. Widespread investment and adoption of computer-based technologies was recognized by business as necessary in order to remain competitive with foreign producers.[26]

During this time period, fiscal policy was very stimulative. The federal budget deficit grew from $61.3 billion to $205.6 billion in 1986. The major reasons for growth in the federal deficit relate to continued growth in government and a sizable cut in income tax rates. The rapid growth in government debt was of concern to the Congress and the Administration, and they did provide some progress in reducing government spending. One piece of legislation, the Gramm-Rudman-Hollings Bill, required reductions in government spending so as to reach a balanced budget in five years.

The value of the U.S. dollar relative to foreign currencies grew rapidly from the trough of the recession, from 1980 to 1985. Also, during this period, consumer demand was very strong. This, combined with a strong value of the dollar, was reflected in a rapid rise in merchandise imports, which accounted for 15 percent of real domestic expenditures on goods and services. The increase in imports was widespread, occurring in both the consumer and capital goods sectors as well as in industrial supplies. The imports did help in bringing down inflation in the early 1980s, but the impact was uneven across the country. The farm belt and the industrial north were hard hit. The end result of the high value of the dollar and strong consumer demand was a long period of deficits in the merchandise trade balance.

---

25. "Monetary Policy Report to Congress," *Federal Reserve Bulletin* (August 1984), pp. 612–613.
26. Ibid., p. 614.

Beginning in 1986, the value of the dollar started to depreciate against most foreign currencies. The underlying reasons for the downward movement in the exchange value of the dollar was the slow progress of the United States in reducing its trade imbalance and the narrowing of interest rate differentials between the United States and major foreign economies. From mid-1986, the U.S. trade picture started to turn around. However, the progress has been slow.

The inflation figures changed dramatically with the onset of the recession in early 1980. During 1979, 1980, and 1981, consumer prices rose by 11.3 percent, 13.5 percent, and 10.3 percent, respectively. From 1983 through 1987, inflation hovered between 2 and 4 percent. During the period of the eighties, energy prices remained quite volatile, but in general, the trend was downward. Falling energy prices were a contributing factor for the significant slowing in the measure of aggregate inflation.

The downturn in the early 1980s had a significant impact on employment and unemployment. Total employment declined by 1 percent during the 1981–82 recession, and the unemployment rate reached a peak of 10.6 percent. With the recovery beginning in late 1982, the unemployment rate showed a steady decline. The recession in early 1980 impacted the country in uneven regional patterns. The industrial belt of the northeast and the central midwest were especially hard hit. For example, in some of the industrial centers, the unemployment rate approached 25 percent.

The economic recovery that started in November 1982, as described above, is not without conditions that cause analysts' concern. Federal deficits are at record levels with little prospect for much improvement. The dollar was extremely strong in the early 1980s, but declined starting in 1986. The negative trade balance is improving very slowly and this has increased support in favor of protectionist legislation. Monetary policy was criticized for being erratic and generating uncertainty in the money and capital markets. The Federal Reserve was also criticized for not expanding the money supply fast enough, but its Board of Governors remained committed to an anti-inflation stance.

SUMMARY

In this chapter, we have attempted to give a very general description of the history of the U.S. economy. We have emphasized the business cycle features of that experience, in the sequence in which they happened, without much explanation of why things happened as they did. Also, implicitly, we have used some economic theory to focus on the particular variables and relationships without spelling out that theory. It remains for the later chapters of the book to bring this confusing mass of detail into some kind of order. That is one of the most important functions of business cycle theory: to determine which relationships and which variables are helpful in explaining why the economy behaves as it does.

QUESTIONS

1. In the early years of its history the United States was an agricultural society and economy. Over the years, agriculture became more mechanized and the whole economy became more industrialized. How do you think the good and bad times of the earlier period differed from the business cycles of the later periods?
2. Describe the immediate and basic causal factors at work in the 1873 depression.
3. Why was the depression that began in 1929 a long and severe one?
4. Why did business turn down in 1937 before full employment was achieved?
5. Outline the steps that were taken to adjust the economy to the demands of World War II.
6. How would economic conditions probably have differed in 1946 and 1947 if almost all of the cost of the war had been raised by taxation?
7. What led to the 1949 readjustment?
8. (a) Describe the nature of the 1953–1954 downturn. (b) Discuss the factors that led to this downturn.
9. How does the 1973–1975 recession compare with earlier post-World War II recessions?
10. Outline the basic causes of the 1973–1975 recession.
11. What led to economic recovery in 1975?
12. The paragraph that precedes the summary of this chapter mentions a number of concerns expressed by economists and others during 1987 and 1988. By the time you are reading this book, you might know whether they turned out to be resolved or whether they continue to be problems, Discuss these issues.

READINGS

Bartlett, Bruce R. *Reaganomics Supply Side Economics in Action*. Westport, CT: Arlington House Publishers, 1981.

Blicksilver, Jack. *Views on U.S. Economic and Business History*. Atlanta: Georgia State University, 1984.

Bowsher, Norman N. "1974—A Year of Inflation, Production Cutbacks, and Oil-Induced Payments Deficits." *Review*, Federal Reserve Bank of St. Louis (December 1974), pp. 2–10.

———. "Two Stages to the Current Recession." *Review*, Federal Reserve Bank of St. Louis (June 1975), pp. 2–8.

Burger, Albert E. "What Happened to The Economy in The First Half of 1980." *Review*, Federal Reserve Bank of St. Louis (August/September 1980), pp. 9–15.

Cole, A. H. "Statistical Background of the Crisis of 1857." *Review of Economic Statistics* (November 1930), pp. 170–180.

"Consumer Income, Spending, and Saving. 1960–1970." *Economic Review*, Federal Reserve Bank of Cleveland (June 1971), pp. 10–18.

Craf, John R. *A Survey of the American Economy, 1940–1946*. New York: North River Press, Inc., 1947.

Denison, Edward F. *Trends in American Economic Growth, 1929–1982*. Washington, D.C.: The Brookings Institution, 1985.

Economic Report of the President. Washington, D.C.: United States Government Printing Office, 1947 to date.

Federal Reserve Bulletin. Current issues.

Feldstein, Martin. *The American Economy in Transition*. Chicago: University of Chicago Press, 1980.

Gordon, Robert J. (ed.). *The American Business Cycle: Continuity and Change*. NEBR Studies in Business Cycles, Vol. 25. Chicago: University of Chicago Press, 1986.

Kuznets, Simon. *Modern Economic Growth: Rate, Structure, and Spread*. New Haven: Yale University Press, 1966.

Mirowski, Philip. *The Birth of The Business Cycle*. New York: Garland Publishers, 1985.

North, Douglas C., and Terry L. Anderson. *Growth and Welfare in the American Past*, 3d ed. Englewood Cliffs, NJ: Prentice-Hall, Inc., 1983.

Olson, Mancur. *The Rise and Decline of Nations: Economic Growth, Stagflation and Social Rigidities*. New Haven, CT: Yale University Press, 1982.

Sorkin, Alan L. *Monetary and Fiscal Policy and Business Cycles in the Modern Era*. Lexington, MA: Lexington Books, 1988. Chapter 4.

Stein, Herbert. *Presidential Economics: The Making of Economic Policy from Roosevelt to Reagan and Beyond*. New York: Simon and Schuster, 1984.

Stigler, George J. *Trends in Output and Employment*. New York: National Bureau of Economic Research, Inc., 1947.

U.S. Department of Commerce. "The Business Situation." *Survey of Current Business*, monthly.

Wood, Christopher. *Boom and Bust*. New York: Atheneum Press, 1989.

3

PATTERNS IN BUSINESS FLUCTUATIONS

In order to make sense of the confusing mass of historical data generated by economic activity, it is helpful to categorize the various forms of fluctuations and to develop techniques of analyzing them. This chapter is basically designed to do this, although much of the rest of the book will extend the discussion in a number of directions.

The generally agreed-upon classes of business fluctuations are trend, cycles, and seasonal and random variations. Each of these results from a different class of causality factors, and discovering and understanding the nature of these causes is the aim of business conditions analysis. The data involved may be either general or specific. *General data* deal with global aggregates such as Gross National Product (GNP), national employment or unemployment rates, or total investment. *Specific data* are less aggregated or global, such as poultry production in Missouri or total imports of color television sets.

MEASUREMENT OF SEASONAL VARIATIONS

Seasonal variations are the results of changes from one season of the year to the next that may be due to changes in the weather, in customs related to the seasons of the year or to holidays, or to the unequal number of days in the months in our calendar. A *seasonal variation* exists in any economic series when there is a regular pattern of variation in the series over a specific period of time, usually a year, but sometimes less than a year. This may be a regularly recurring pattern from year to year, or it may be a changing pattern in which changes regularly occur as, for example, an increased proportion year by year of December sales of a commodity for Christmas-giving.

There are several reasons for calculating a measure of seasonal variation. The best form for data for measuring and forecasting cyclical changes is that in which an adjustment has been made to eliminate the effects of seasonal variations. This adjustment eliminates the effect of a regular factor and puts the major stress on the variable factors at work.

A measure of seasonal variation also is needed in developing a sales forecast for an industry and, especially, for an individual business. The basic forecast is made without regard to the seasonal variation. A measure of seasonal variation is then used to put the data in the annual forecast of sales on a month-by-month basis throughout the year.

Before calculating a measure of seasonal variation, the analyst should be sure that regular variations of this type exist. The factors causing the variations should be studied to make certain which factors cause an observed variation. At times, random factors may produce variations for a period that appear to be regular. If a measure of seasonal variation is thus calculated, it not only is useless for analysis and prediction, but also adds a source of error that may make such analysis and prediction impossible.

The most widely used measure of the seasonal variation is found by the ratio-to-moving-average method. A 12-month moving average is calculated from monthly data of sales or production for a period of several years. Since such a moving average always includes each of the twelve months of the year, it averages out the seasonal fluctuations in the data. This means that the moving average contains the trend, the cycle, and any irregular factors that may have affected the data. By dividing the original monthly data by the 12-month moving average, which includes everything but the seasonal factor, it is possible to obtain a measure of the seasonal variation.

The basis for this procedure may be shown in equation form, using the following symbols: T for the trend, S for the seasonal factor, C for the cyclical factor, and I for the irregular factors.

The original data may then be expressed in terms of the above symbols as $T \times S \times C \times I$. The 12-month moving average averages out the seasonal factor and, therefore, contains the trend and cyclical and irregular factors. It may be expressed as $T \times C \times I$.

Dividing the original data containing trend, seasonal, cyclical, and irregular factors by the 12-month moving average containing the trend, cyclical, and irregular factors gives a measure of the seasonal factor as shown below.

$$\frac{\text{data}}{\text{moving average}} = \frac{T \times S \times C \times I}{T \times C \times I} = S$$

Table 3-1

Monthly Sales of the Super Ice Cream Company, 1984–1988
(Thousands of Dollars)

	1984	1985	1986	1987	1988
January	40	50	52	55	58
February	47	60	62	65	68
March	64	77	79	83	86
April	81	96	99	102	106
May	122	137	140	144	149
June	143	158	163	165	170
July	154	167	174	175	180
August	149	159	165	166	171
September	102	108	114	116	120
October	71	75	78	81	85
November	58	61	62	64	67
December	49	54	56	58	61

Source: Hypothetical data.

The hypothetical example of the calculation of the seasonal index of the sales of the Super Ice Cream Company illustrates the method. For simplicity, a period of 5 years has been used, but in actual practice it is best to use a period of 10 or 12 years. Monthly sales from 1984–1988 are shown in Table 3-1.

The first step is to find a 12-month moving average of the sales data. To do this, it is necessary to find a 12-month moving total and then to divide it by 12 to get the moving average. These calculations are shown in Table 3-2 on page 62.

The original data are divided by the 12-month moving average, and the result is expressed as a percentage to determine the year-by-year seasonal factors. For example, the sales figure of $52,000 for January 1986 is divided by the 12-month moving average for that month of 101.58 to get a seasonal factor of 51.2 percent. The results of these calculations are shown in Table 3-3 on page 63.

Since unusual factors may affect the seasonal pattern in any one year, the seasonal factors for several years are averaged to obtain a typical figure for each month. If necessary, these typical seasonal factors are then adjusted proportionately up or down to total 1,200 percent, or an average of 100 percent a month. After all, the seasonal index for

Table 3-2

Calculation of a 12-Month Moving Average of the Monthly Sales of the Super Ice Cream Company, 1984–1988

	12-Month Moving Total Centered at the 7th Month[1]					12-Month Moving Average Centered at the 7th Month				
	1984	1985	1986	1987	1988	1984	1985	1986	1987	1988
January		1161	1219	1263	1297		96.75	101.58	105.25	108.08
February		1174	1226	1264	1302		97.83	102.17	105.33	108.50
March		1184	1232	1265	1307		98.67	102.67	105.42	108.92
April		1190	1238	1267	1311		99.17	103.17	105.58	109.25
May		1194	1241	1270	1315		99.50	103.42	105.83	109.58
June		1197	1242	1272	1318		99.75	103.50	106.00	109.83
July	1080	1202	1244	1274	1321	90.00	100.17	103.67	106.17	110.08
August	1090	1204	1247	1277		90.83	100.33	103.92	106.42	
September	1103	1206	1250	1280		91.92	100.50	104.17	106.67	
October	1116	1208	1254	1283		93.00	100.67	104.50	106.92	
November	1131	1211	1257	1287		94.25	100.92	104.75	107.25	
December	1146	1214	1261	1292		95.50	101.17	105.08	107.67	

Source: Table 3-1.

[1] Actually the average for the set of data from January through December 1984 is the average for the middle of the year, that is, between June and July. For greater refinement, the July figure can be calculated by taking this figure and the figure between July and August found by averaging the data from February 1984 through January 1985, and averaging these two figures.

Table 3-3

Original Monthly Sales Data of the Super Ice Cream Company
for 1984–1988 Divided by the 12-Month Moving Average
in Percentage Form

	1984	1985	1986	1987	1988
January		51.7	51.2	52.3	53.7
February		61.3	60.7	61.7	62.7
March		78.0	76.9	78.7	79.0
April		96.8	96.0	96.6	97.0
May		137.7	135.4	136.1	136.0
June		158.4	157.5	155.7	154.8
July	171.1	166.7	167.0	164.8	163.5
August	164.0	158.5	158.8	156.0	
September	111.0	107.5	109.4	108.7	
October	76.3	74.5	74.6	75.8	
November	61.5	60.4	59.2	59.7	
December	51.3	53.4	53.3	53.9	

Source: Tables 3-1 and 3-2.

annual data is 1 or 100 percent. These steps are shown in Table 3-4 on page 64.

When a longer period of years is used, it is often desirable to find some average other than the arithmetic mean to arrive at a typical seasonal pattern. This may be done by placing the items in an array, that is, arranging them from low to high and then taking the middle item or median, or by taking an average of the middle three or five items. It is also possible to use a modified arithmetic mean, that is, to eliminate any unusually low or high items and then take an arithmetic average of the rest.

If the seasonal variation in any field changes, it is necessary to alter the procedure used in finding typical seasonal factors. Instead of calculating an average January figure, for example, the proper procedure is to plot the January crude seasonal figures for the period being studied and then to draw a trend line showing the change that is taking place. It is usually best to draw this trend line freehand, especially if it is being done by someone who has a thorough knowledge of the changes taking place. The trend may also be fitted by means of a formula either for a straight line or for a curve. The use of such formulas is considered more fully in the next section of this chapter on the mea-

Table 3-4

Calculation of the Refined Seasonal Factors from the
Crude Seasonals of the Super Ice Cream Company

	Jan.	Feb.	Mar.	Apr.	May	June	July	Aug.	Sept.	Oct.	Nov.	Dec.
1984							171.6	164.0	111.0	76.3	61.5	51.3
1985	51.7	61.3	78.0	96.8	137.7	158.4	166.7	158.5	107.5	74.5	60.4	53.4
1986	51.2	60.7	76.9	96.0	135.4	157.5	167.9	158.8	109.4	74.6	59.2	53.3
1987	52.3	61.7	78.7	96.6	136.1	155.7	164.8	156.0	108.7	75.8	59.7	53.9
1988	53.7	62.7	79.0	97.0	136.0	154.8	163.5					
Average seasonal	52.2	61.6	78.2	96.6	136.3	156.6	166.8	159.3	109.2	75.3	60.2	53.0
Seasonal index	52.0	61.3	77.9	96.2	135.7	155.9	166.1	158.6	108.7	75.0	59.9	52.8

Source: Table 3-3.

Table 3-5

Typical Seasonal Factors for the Super Ice Cream Company Expressed as a Percentage of the Year's Business

January	4.3	May	11.3	September	9.1
February	5.1	June	13.0	October	6.2
March	6.5	July	13.8	November	5.0
April	8.0	August	13.2	December	4.8

Source: Tables 3-1 and 3-4.

surement of the secular trend. The same thing is done for each of the 12 months. The current seasonal factors are then found by projecting the trend line for each of the 12 months one year ahead and then adjusting these figures on a proportionate basis to add to 1,200.

A seasonal index such as that calculated from the sales of the Super Ice Cream Company shows the percentage of each month's sales in relation to average monthly sales as 100. For example, January sales are 52.0 percent of the average, July sales 166.1 percent, and so on. It is helpful at times to express the seasonal factor for each month as the average percentage of the business for the year done in that month. January sales in this case are $\frac{52.2}{1,200}$ of the year's business, or 4.3 percent. Figures for each month as a typical percentage of the year's business are shown in Table 3-5.[1]

MEASUREMENT OF THE SECULAR TREND

After the seasonal variation has been calculated and then eliminated from a series of data, it is possible to calculate the long-term or secular trend. This trend is the persistent underlying movement that has taken place in a series of data over a period of time long enough to cover several business cycles. It is the basic growth or decline that would exist if there were no cycle.

In the absence of the cycle, the growth of any economic series, such as the production of a new product like microwave ovens, would prob-

---

1. A more sophisticated approach to the determination of seasonal adjustments than that described here is used by the Bureau of the Census. It adjusts for the number of working days in months and for extreme values in the data. It is described in U.S. Department of Commerce, "The X-II Variant of the Census Method II Seasonal Adjustment Program," Technical Paper No. 15, 1967 revision (Washington, D.C.: United States Government Printing Office, 1967).

ably approximate a curve like an elongated S. Any new industry will probably grow slowly at first, experience a period of rapid growth while it is becoming integrated into the economy, and then grow more slowly in the relationship to increases in total economic activity.

The long-term trend in total economic activity in the United States has been gradually rising at an approximately constant rate. This is partly true because of increases in population that are continuing, albeit at a reduced rate. Increases in productivity and in the proportion of the population in the labor force have, in all probability, more than offset the decreasing rate of population growth. The quantity of capital in use has been increasing, and from all available evidence it appears that its effectiveness has also increased. American industry has likewise developed methods of economizing on materials and labor by improving design, by using by-products, by developing more ways to efficiently plan work, and by introducing labor-saving techniques. In some fields, natural resources of the highest quality are being depleted, but this factor, leading to a slowdown in the rate of growth, has been more than offset by the development of substitute materials and synthetic products. The system of distribution is also becoming more efficient through the introduction of self-service facilities and the development of larger, more economical units. The net result of all of these factors has been a more or less constant rate of increase in total economic activity.

There are several reasons for calculating a measure of the trend of an economic series. It can be used to project the most likely level of that series over a long period as, for example, ten or twenty years in the future. Such a projection is valid only if the factors that led to its growth in the past continue. It is possible to calculate a measure of the trend from any series showing a significant change in magnitude over a period of time, even when year-by-year changes are largely random; but projections made from such measures are useless. A measure of the trend is also useful as a means of analyzing the changes resulting from the business cycle in the past. In forecasting for a calendar quarter or a year ahead, the cycle may easily overshadow the trend so that a measure of the trend is of limited usefulness in short-run forecasting.

Since most economic series are in the stage in which they are growing in relationship to changes in population and national income, their current growth can be effectively measured by a straight-line trend, even though an S-shaped curve would be needed to describe their total growth. The straight line that most closely approximates the growth in the total economy or in an industry that is growing in relation to increases in population and national income is the line of least squares. It is a line from which the sum of the squared vertical deviations is at a minimum. This line was not developed as a logical explanation of the growth in these series, but was adapted from the physical sciences because it produces a good fit.

The following example shows the calculation of this line for the sales of the Super Ice Cream Company from 1984 through 1988. This is much too short a period for calculating a trend, which should cover several cycles, but it is now used to illustrate the method of getting the least-squares line. The formula for any straight line is $Y=a+bx$, in which Y is the trend value for each year expressed in terms of the original data. The symbol a is the average of the original data and establishes the height of the trend line in the middle year of the series. The slope of the line is determined by the value of b, which measures the annual deviation from the average value of the trend at the midpoint of the series. The following example shows its calculation.

Sales of Ice Cream for Each Year
(Thousands of Dollars)

1984	$1,080
1985	1,202
1986	1,244
1987	1,274
1988	1,321

Year	Production Y	Years from Midpoint x	xY	x^2
1	1,080	-2	-2,160	4
2	1,202	-1	-1,202	1
3	1,244	0	0	0
4	1,274	1	1,274	1
5	1,321	2	2,642	4
	6,121	0	554	10

The value of a is found by dividing the sum of the original data (Y) by the number of years, or N; thus,

$$a = \frac{\Sigma Y}{N} = \frac{6,121}{5} = 1,224.2$$

The value of b is found from the following formula:

$$b = \frac{\Sigma xY}{\Sigma x^2}$$

In this case, it is $\frac{554}{10}$, or 55.4. The straight-line formula is then $Y = 1{,}224.2 + 55.4x$. The values of Y (in thousands of dollars) for each year are found by adding or subtracting 55.4 for each year from the midyear, as shown below.

1984	1,113.4	(1,224.2 minus 2 × 55.4)
1985	1,168.8	(1,224.2 minus 1 × 55.4)
1986	1,224.2	(average value)
1987	1,279.6	(1,224.2 plus 1 × 55.4)
1988	1,335.0	(1,224.2 plus 2 × 55.4)

To express the trend in monthly values, it is necessary to divide the value of a and the value of b each by 12. Thus in the example, the trend equation for monthly sales of ice cream is $Y_m = 102.02 + 4.62x$ with the origin at July 1, 1986. The monthly trend value should be placed in the middle of the month. Since July 1 is the origin for the annual data, the origin for the monthly data would have to be two weeks later, that is, 1/24 of a year. Thus to shift the origin to July 15, 1986, use the equation: $Y_m = 102.02 + (4.62)(1/24) = 102.02 + 0.19 = 102.21$.

The b value of 4.62 means that the monthly sales will increase by 4.62 per year, which is the same as saying that monthly sales will increase 1/12th of 4.62, or 0.385 production units per month. We calculated above that the trend value of sales for July 1986 is 102.21, so the trend value of sales for August 1986 is $Y_{Aug.} = 102.21 + 0.385 = 102.6$.

Start at the origin date trend value of sales of 102.21, and simply add 0.385 units per month for all succeeding months, and subtract 0.385 per month for all earlier months. For 1986, the calculations of trend values for monthly sales are shown here:

January	99.90	= February value − 0.385
February	100.29	= March value − 0.385
March	100.67	= April value − 0.385
April	101.02	= May value − 0.385
May	101.44	= June value − 0.385
June	101.83	= Origin − 0.385
July	102.21	= Origin

August	102.60	= Origin + 0.385
September	102.99	= August value + 0.385
October	103.37	= September value + 0.385
November	103.76	= October value + 0.385
December	104.14	= November value + 0.385
	1,224.22	

Notice that the summation of the monthly trend values is equal to the annual trend value for 1986 calculated previously.

In the above example, the number of years for which sales data were available was an odd number of years, 1984 through 1988. For an even number of years, the deviations (years) from the midpoint of the data are somewhat different. For example, suppose there are six years of data for ice cream sales, using sales of Super Ice Cream Company from 1983 through 1988. The data represent annual sales as of July 1 of each year.

	Years	Production Y	Years from Midpoint X
1	1983	1,000	−5
2	1984	1,080	−3
3	1985	1,202	−1
	midpoint		0
4	1986	1,244	+1
5	1987	1,274	+3
6	1988	1,321	+5
		7,121	

The middle of the data is between 1985 and 1986, or January 1 of 1986. The data for 1985 are one deviation below the midpoint and are noted −1. Sales in 1986 are one deviation above the midpoint and are noted +1. Note that the midpoint is January 1, and +1 represents July 1 of 1986—a period of six months from the midpoint. So, to go to July 1 of 1987 we need to traverse twelve months, or two six-month deviations from the midpoint. Thus, 1987 is +3 deviations from the midpoint. The rest of the calculations remain the same—same formulas for a and b.

At times, it may be desirable to express the long-term trend by means of a curved line rather than a straight line. This should be done, however, only if the analyst is convinced that such a curve actually represents the basic growth of the economic series at hand. Formulas are available for many types of curves, such as the second degree parabola, the compound interest curve, and several different forms of S-shaped curves.[2]

In many cases, it is probably better to draw a trend line freehand rather than to use a formula that may not accurately express the rate of growth.

THE CONCEPT OF THE BUSINESS CYCLE

One of many definitions of the word *cycle* is a "series that repeats itself." In mathematics, a sine wave or cycle is a series that repeats itself perfectly. Nothing of the sort should be expected in economic series. The word *fluctuation* might better describe the behavior of economic variables. Still, some series are more systematic than would be implied by the more general term *fluctuation*.

The business cycle is the movement of some aggregate measure of economic activity upward and downward over time. The periodicity is not precise; that is, the length of time of the upward and downward movements will vary. Similarly, the amount of the movement upward and downward will differ over time. Yet it is true that business expansions do not continue forever; an upper turning point always occurs. And a contraction of economic activity always reverses itself.

In the analysis of business cycles, various authors have had different conceptions of how best to study the phenomenon. The two views we will consider here are those of Joseph A. Schumpeter and the National Bureau of Economic Research.

Schumpeter's Three-Cycle Schema

Schumpeter drew on the work of other business cycles theorists to conclude that there were three distinct cycle lengths. He named them after the person who did the most definitive work on each.

First, he accepted the existence of a positive trend in overall economic activity in the developed economies. The Kondratieff cycles—

---

2. For a discussion of the methods of deriving such curves, the reader is referred to a comprehensive text in statistics such as Charles T. Clark and Eleanor W. Jordan, *Introduction to Business and Economic Statistics* (7th ed. Cincinnati: South-Western Publishing Company, 1985); and Werner Z. Hirsch, *Introduction to Modern Statistics* (New York: The Macmillan Company, 1959). The latter book also discusses a method of testing the significance of a measure of the trend that differentiates a measure based on random data from one based on a true trend. Such tests are also described for measures of seasonal and cyclical variations.

Figure 3-1   Idealized Schumpeter Three-Cycle Schema

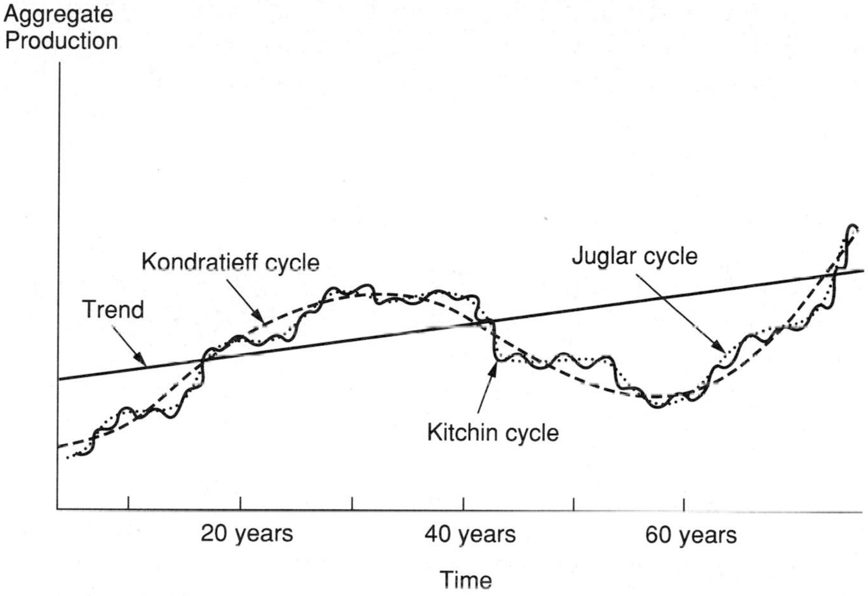

long waves averaging fifty-four years—oscillate around this trend. Juglar cycles—of nine to ten years' duration—in turn, oscillate around the Kondratieff waves. Kitchin cycles—of about forty months' duration—are superimposed on the Juglar cycles. We could further impose the seasonal and random variations to complete the picture. The Schumpeter picture, then, would have a trend and a Kondratieff cycle lasting fifty to sixty years; for each Kondratieff wave, there would be six Juglar cycles; and for each Juglar cycle, we would find three Kitchin cycles.

An approximation to what Schumpeter had in mind is shown in Figure 3-1. Except for the seasonal and irregular variations in the series, what would be seen in the plotting of actual data would be only the shortest cycles, that is, the Kitchin cycles. In other words, if you could erase the trend, the Kondratieff, and the Juglars, you would have the "real world"—again, except for the seasonal and irregular variations.

While the approach by the National Bureau of Economic Research (NBER), which is to be considered next, has become the favored one by virtue of the preeminence of the NBER in cycle research, it is the case that many economists still prefer to study business cycles categorized, as Schumpeter did, by various time lengths. Those who follow

Schumpeter's approach find value in explaining the different length cycles with somewhat different theories or stress different phenomena. For example, it would be difficult to argue that a nine-year, or fifty-year, cycle could be explained by inventory adjustments, which is the most accepted explanation of the forty-month average cycle.

The NBER Approach

One of the most complete and most frequently used definitions of the business cycle has been developed by the NBER. It rejects the Schumpeterian notion of different families of business cycles. Over the time period of a cycle, there is only one cycle. The working concept used by the NBER in its research is:

Business cycles are a type of fluctuation found in the aggregate economic activity of nations that organize their work mainly in business enterprises: a cycle consists of expansions occurring at about the same time in many economic activities, followed by similarly general recessions, contractions, and revivals, which merge into the expansion phase of the next cycle; this sequence of changes is recurrent but not periodic; in duration, business cycles vary from more than one year to ten or twelve years; they are not divisible into shorter cycles of similar character with amplitudes approximating their own.[3]

Several important factors are included in this definition:

1. The business cycle refers to fluctuations in aggregate economic activity rather than in a particular industry or sector of the economy.
2. It is a phenomenon of an economy that has developed sufficiently to organize its activity in business units.
3. Expansions and contractions occur at about the same time in many phases of economic activity.
4. This sequence is recurrent but not periodic; that is, one cycle follows another in a continuous process but the cycles are not of equal length.
5. These cycles cannot be further subdivided into shorter cycles that have similar characteristics or the same amplitude of fluctuation from the low point of activity to the high point, and from the high point to the next low point.

---

3. Wesley C. Mitchell, *What Happens During Business Cycles* (New York: National Bureau of Economic Research, Inc., 1951), p. 6.

A measure of the cycle is valuable for historical analysis of past cyclical movements. It cannot be used for mechanical projection into the future since cycles do not develop in a perfectly regular pattern. Some of the factors in the cycle do develop in somewhat similar ways, and there is some consistency in cycle patterns. This makes a measure of past cycles of some value as an aid in analyzing the present situation. Such elements of similarity in the cyclical pattern will be described in Chapter 4.

Several methods have been developed for measuring the business cycle. The most widely used is the residual method, in which the cycle is found by eliminating the other factors in the data. The NBER has developed a method of directly determining the cycle. It has become significant since more and more of the data from the intensive business cycle research of the NBER are being published in this form. These two methods will be considered in this section.

Residual Method

The residual method of calculating the cycle is based on the elimination of the trend and seasonal factors. The first step is to find a *normal factor* by multiplying the trend by the seasonal variation (i.e., TS). The original data are then divided by the normal factor to obtain the cyclical and irregular factors (i.e., $\frac{TSCI}{TS}$). For example, the trend value of sales of the Super Ice Cream Company for 1984 was $1,113,400.[4] Since the trend of sales was increasing at a rate of $55,400 a year, or $4,617 a month, the trend figure at an annual rate for January 1984 is $1,088,006 ($1,113,400 minus $5\frac{1}{2} \times \$4,617$); for February 1984, it is $1,092,624, and so on. The seasonal pattern shows that business in January is normally 4.3 percent of the business for the year. In this case, normal sales in January are 4.3 percent of $1,088,006, or $46,784; normal sales in February are 5.1 percent of $1,092,624, or $55,724; and so on.

Deviations from such normal sales based on the trend and the seasonal are due to cyclical and irregular factors. In the above examples, actual sales for January 1984 were $40,000, so they were $6,784 below normal due to cyclical and irregular factors.

---

4. The trend value for 1984 is 1,113.4 expressed in thousands of dollars, or $1,113,400.

Table 3-6

Calculation of the Cyclical and Irregular Factors in the Sales of
the Super Ice Cream Company for Each Month of 1984
(Thousands of Dollars)

	Trend (Monthly Figures at an Annual Rate)	Normal (Trend and Seasonal)	Actual Sales	Cyclical and Irregular Factors	
				Deviations from Normal	Percentage of Normal
January	1,088.1	46.8	40	−6.8	85.5
February	1,092.7	55.7	47	−8.7	84.4
March	1,097.3	71.3	64	−7.3	89.8
April	1,101.9	88.2	81	−7.2	91.8
May	1,106.5	125.0	122	−3.0	97.6
June	1,111.1	144.4	143	−1.4	99.0
July	1,115.7	154.0	154	0.0	100.0
August	1,120.3	147.9	149	+1.1	100.7
September	1,124.9	102.4	102	−0.4	99.6
October	1,129.5	70.0	71	+1.0	101.4
November	1,134.1	56.7	58	+1.3	102.3
December	1,138.8	54.7	49	−5.7	89.6

Actual figures may also be expressed as a percentage of normal sales (i.e., $\frac{TSCI}{TS} \times 100$). Sales of $40,000 in January 1984, for example, were 85.5 percent of normal sales of $46,784. Deviations resulting from cyclical and irregular factors for each month of 1984 are shown in Table 3-6. Thus, it appears from our hypothetical data for 1984 that the ice cream industry was in an expansion phase of the business cycle, reaching its peak in November of the same year.

The irregular factors cannot be eliminated from the data but can be smoothed out by means of one or a series of moving averages. The most frequent procedure is to use a three-month moving average, since most irregular factors affect a series for only a few months.

This residual method leaves a cyclical pattern that is correct only if the trend and seasonal have been correctly measured. It shows the cycle divorced from the trend and may thus give a somewhat false impression, since the trend that has occurred during the period of the cycle may be an integral part of the fluctuations that are taking place.

Figure 3-2   Simplified Cycle Pattern

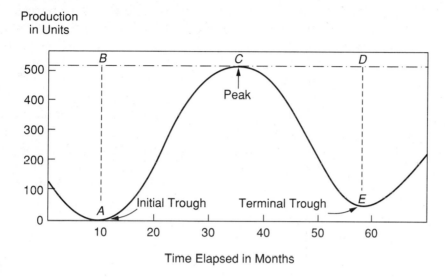

The NBER Method

The NBER has developed a method for isolating and analyzing cyclical and irregular fluctuations directly, rather than by first calculating a normal figure and expressing these factors as deviations from the norm.

Since business fluctuations are continuous, it is necessary to agree on a consistent method of isolating individual cycles. A cycle could be considered as the interval from one peak of business activity to the next, from one trough or low point to the next, or perhaps in other ways. The NBER measures the cycle from trough to trough. Thus, a cycle begins at the initial trough at point A in the simplified pattern in Figure 3-2, develops to the peak at point C, and ends at the terminal trough at point E.

The *duration* of the cycle is measured from A to E, in Figure 3-2, about 48 months. The duration of the expansion is measured from B to C, about 25 months; and the duration of the contraction is measured from C to D, about 23 months. The *amplitude* of the expansion is measured from A to B, about 520 production units; and the amplitude of the contraction from D to E is about 470 units.

It is also necessary to establish the dates of the initial trough and terminal trough to isolate a cycle and, for some purposes, to establish the peak. This may be done for a series by noting the low point in the cycle, the high point, and the following low point. These points should, of course, correspond in a general way to the time period of the cycle in total economic activity. Since there is no comprehensive series available that covers all economic activity, it is necessary to determine the dates of the cycle in total activity in a different way. The NBER has analyzed many areas of economic activity and, on the basis of such study, has determined when aggregate economic activity reached cyclical highs and lows. The NBER has developed reference dates showing the time of the initial trough, the peak, and the terminal trough of cycles in aggregate economic activity.[5] The cycle based on such reference dates measured from the initial trough through the peak to the terminal trough is called the *reference cycle*. For example, July 1980 is the initial trough of the reference cycle in the early 1980s; July 1981 is the peak; and November 1982 is the terminal trough.

To analyze the data for any series on economic activity, the first step is to eliminate the variations caused by seasonal factors. The seasonally adjusted data are then studied to find the specific cycles in the data by looking for troughs and peaks, which correspond in a general way to the reference dates for troughs and peaks. The specific cycles also are measured from the initial trough through the peak to the terminal trough in those series that fluctuate in a similar manner to total economic activity. In those series that move in an inverse fashion from general economic activity, as, for example, commercial failures, the cycle is measured from the initial peak through the trough to the terminal peak.

Plotting Data for Cyclical Comparisons

A visual presentation of cycle patterns may be obtained by plotting cycle relatives. This may be done for the reference cycle by plotting cycle relatives for each of the nine stages of the cycle from the initial trough through the peak to the terminal trough. Several cycles may be plotted on the same chart for cyclical comparisons. Comparison may not be easy when cycles are of varying lengths.

The most important times for cyclical comparison are often those around reference cycle troughs and peaks. As a cycle develops, it is not possible to divide the cycle into stages since this can only be done when the cycle is complete. It is possible, however, to present cyclical

---

5. The process by which the dating of business cycles is decided has been told in an interesting and informative way in Geoffrey H. Moore, *Business Cycles, Inflation, and Forecasting*, 2d ed. (Cambridge, MA: Ballinger Publishing Co., 1983), Chapters 1 and 2.

Figure 3-3 Cyclical Comparison Charts: Coincident Series

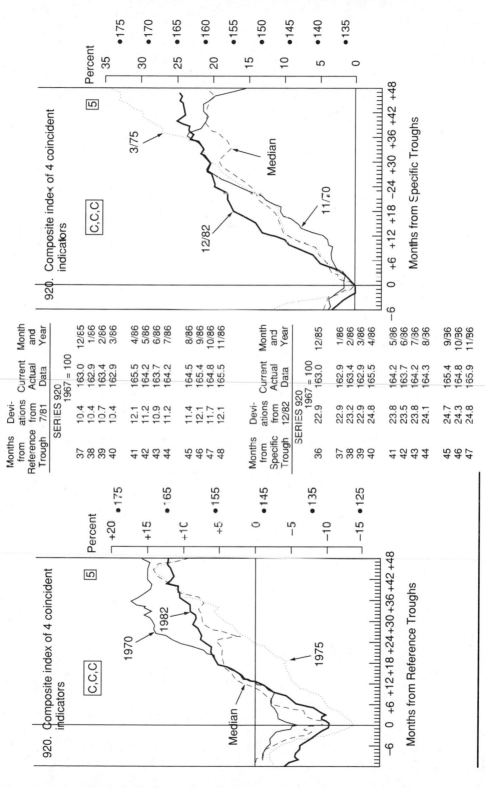

920. Composite index of 4 coincident indicators

Months from Reference Trough	Deviations from 7/81	Current Actual Data	Month and Year
		SERIES 920 1967 = 100	
37	10.4	163.0	12/85
38	10.4	162.9	1/86
39	10.7	163.4	2/86
40	10.4	162.9	3/86
41	12.1	165.5	4/86
42	11.2	164.2	5/86
43	10.9	163.7	6/86
44	11.2	164.2	7/86
45	11.4	164.5	8/86
46	12.1	165.4	9/86
47	11.7	164.8	10/86
48	12.1	165.5	11/86

Months from Specific Trough	Deviations from 12/82	Current Actual Data	Month and Year
		SERIES 920 1967 = 100	
36	22.9	163.0	12/85
37	22.9	162.9	1/86
38	23.2	163.4	2/86
39	22.9	162.9	3/86
40	24.8	165.5	4/86
41	23.8	164.2	5/86
42	23.5	163.7	6/86
43	23.8	164.2	7/86
44	24.1	164.3	8/86
45	24.7	165.4	9/86
46	24.3	164.8	10/86
47	24.8	165.9	11/86

Source: *Business Conditions Digest* (December 1986), p. 109.

Figure 3-4   How to Read Cyclical Comparison Charts

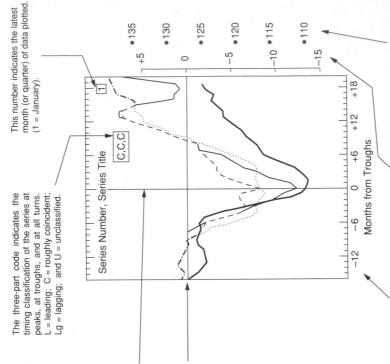

This number indicates the latest month (or quarter) of data plotted. (1 = January).

The three-part code indicates the timing classification of the series at peaks, at troughs, and at all turns. L = leading; C = roughly coincident; Lg = lagging; and U = unclassified.

Series Number, Series Title

C,C,C

This scale measures time in months before (−) and after (+) reference trough dates (left panel) and specific trough dates (right panel).

This scale shows deviations (percent or actual differences) from reference peak levels (left panel) and specific trough levels (right panel).

This scale shows actual series units and applies only to the current business cycle (heavy solid line).

Months from Troughs

These charts show graphically, for selected indicators, the path of the current business cycle. To set the current movements in historical perspective, cyclical paths over generally similar histori-cal periods also are shown. The selected periods are superimposed to compare the current business cycle with corresponding historical patterns and to facilitate critical assessment of the amplitude, duration, and severity of the indicators' current movements.

1. For most indicators, two cyclical comparison charts are shown. In the left panel, compari-sons are based on reference peak levels and reference trough dates; in the right panel, compari-sons are based on both the levels and the dates of the specific troughs in each indicator. (See the charts on the following pages.)

2. The vertical line represents trough dates; reference trough dates in the left panel and specific trough dates in the right panel. The current cycle and the corresponding historical periods are positioned so that their reference trough dates (left panel) and specific trough dates (right panel) are on this vertical line.

3. The horizontal line represents the level of data at reference cycle peaks (left panel) and specific cycle troughs (right panel). The current cycle and the corresponding historical periods are positioned so that their reference peak levels (left panel) and specific trough levels (right panel) are on this horizontal line.

4. For most series, deviations (percent or actual differences) from the reference peak and specific trough levels are computed and plotted. For series measured in percent units (e.g., the unemploy-ment rate), these units (actual data) are plotted rather than deviations. The deviations (if plotted) and actual data for the current cycle are shown in the tables accompanying the charts.

5. For series that move counter to movements in general business activity (e.g., the unem-ployment rate), an inverted scale is used; i.e., declines in data are plotted as upward movements, and increases in data are plotted as downward movements.

6. Several curves are shown in each chart. The heavy solid line (———) describes the current cycle. The broken line (- - -) represents the median pattern of the seven post-World War II cycles. The other lines represent selected business cycles. In the left panel, each line is labeled according to the year of the reference trough; in the right panel, each line is labeled according to the date of the specific trough.

7. These charts use the business cycle (reference) peak and trough dates designated by the National Bureau of Economic Research, Inc.

Peaks: Nov. 1948 (IVQ 1948), July 1953 (IIQ 1953), Aug. 1957 (IIIQ 1957), Apr. 1960 (IIQ 1960), Dec. 1969 (IVQ 1969), Nov. 1973 (IVQ 1973), Jan. 1980 (IQ 1980), July 1981 (IIIQ 1981).

Troughs: Oct. 1949 (IVQ 1949), May 1954 (IIQ 1954), Apr. 1958 (IIQ 1958), Feb. 1961 (IQ 1961), Nov. 1970 (IVQ 1970), Mar. 1975 (IVQ 1975), July 1980 (IIIQ 1980), Nov. 1982 (IVQ 1982).

Source: *Business Conditions Digest* (July 1988), p. 105.

data using a somewhat different technique. Data on such series as GNP, industrial production, or unemployment may be shown as they develop in the period immediately preceding or following a reference trough or peak. Data on a quarterly or monthly basis are expressed as percentage deviations from the level of the series at the reference peak or trough. Series presented in percentage form, such as unemployment data, are plotted directly. Figure 3-3 shows a chart for a composite index of coincident series around the trough of the current recession.

Figure 3-4 shows one page from a recent issue of *Business Conditions Digest* (BCD) for study by the reader and presents the BCD explanation of how to read cyclical comparison charts. Note that the panel on the left compares the variables with the reference cycles, while the panel on the right compares the variables with the specific cycles.

QUESTIONS

1. Describe the ratio-to-moving-average method of calculating the seasonal index.
2. How is a changing seasonal calculated?
3. Describe the method of calculating a trend line by the least-squares method.
4. Describe the residual method of isolating the cycle.
5. What can be done to remove the effect of irregular factors?
6. How does the NBER use the term "reference cycle"? "Specific cycle"?
7. How are reference cycle relatives calculated? Specific cycle relatives?
8. How can the amplitude of the cycle be determined from specific cycle relatives?
9. How do the residual method and the NBER method differ in handling the trend?
10. Describe cyclical comparison charts. How may they be used in studying cycles as they develop?
11. Contrast the NBER approach to the study of business cycles with that of Professor Joseph A. Schumpeter.

READINGS

Burns, Arthur F., and Wesley C. Mitchell. *Measuring Business Cycles.* New York: National Bureau of Economic Research, Inc., 1946.

Clark, Charles T., and Eleanor W. Jordan. *Introduction to Business and Economic Statistics*, 7th ed. Cincinnati: South-Western Publishing Co., 1985. Part 4.

Kuznets, Simon. *Seasonal Variations in Industry and Trade*. New York: National Bureau of Economic Research, Inc., 1933.

Lehman, Michael B. *The Dow Jones-Irwin Guide to Using The Wall Street Journal*, 2d ed. Homewood, IL: Dow Jones-Irwin, 1987. Chapters 1–3, 8–10.

Moore, Geoffrey H. *Business Cycles, Inflation, and Forecasting*, 2d ed. Cambridge, MA: Ballinger Publishing Co., 1983.

Nelson, Charles R. *The Investors Guide to Economic Indicators*. New York: John Wiley & Sons, 1987. Chapters 6 and 9.

Newbold, Paul, and Theodore Bos. *Introductory Business Forecasting*. Cincinnati: South-Western Publishing Co., 1990.

Sietz, Neil. *Business Forecasting: Concepts and Microcomputer Applications*. Reston, VA: Reston Publishing Company, Inc., 1984. Chapters 1 and 5.

Sommers, Albert T. *The U.S. Economy Demystified*. Lexington, MA: Lexington Books, 1985.

CHAPTER 4

BEHAVIOR OF THE CYCLE

We will begin the study of the statistical record of the behavior of the cycle with an analysis of the most common length of the cycle, its expansion and contraction phases, and the extent of the deviations from these patterns. We will focus next on the international conformity of business cycles, especially in the major industrial countries. The extent to which the cycle has affected all phases of American business will then be discussed, followed by a study of the timing of various phases of economic activity in relationship to the turning points in the reference cycle. We will give special attention to the important series that lead and lag in the cyclical process. We will describe and analyze the varying amplitudes of different economic series in past cycles, the nature of the cycle in inventories, and the factors that cause that cycle. In conclusion, we will discuss some aspects of the general cycle pattern as it develops during expansion and contraction.

LENGTH OF THE CYCLE

In forecasting changes in the level of economic activity, it is helpful to know what pattern, if any, has existed in the length of the cycle and in the expansion and contraction phases of the cycle.

Length of the Cycle in Years

Using the NBER's definition and measuring the length of the cycle from trough to trough, American business cycles from 1854 to the present have varied in length between 2 and 10 years. The average length of the cycle has been 4 years and the most common length 3 years. Three-fourths of the cycles have been between 3 and 5 years in length. Table 4-1 shows the length of American business cycles from 1854 to 1983.

Table 4-1

Length of American Business Cycles, 1854–1990*

Length in Years	Number of Cycles	
1	0	
2	2	
3	10	
4	9	
5	4	
6	2	
7	1	(June 1938 – October 1945)
8	1	(December 1870 – March 1879)
9	0	
10	1	(February 1961 – November 1970)

Sources: Adapted from Arthur Burns and Wesley Mitchell, *Measuring Business Cycles* (New York: National Bureau of Economic Research, Inc., 1946).

*The cycle whose trough occurred in November 1982 had not yet reached a designated peak by early 1990.

Length of the Cycle in Months

For cycles between 1854 and 1983 for which the NBER has established monthly reference dates, the full cycle varied from 28 months to 117 months, with an average of 51 months. The expansion periods varied from 10 months to 106 months, with an average of 33 months; and the contraction periods from 6 months to 65 months, with an average of 18 months. Thus, it can be seen that there is neither a uniform length of the cycle nor uniform periods of expansion or contraction.

There is no uniform relationship between the length of the expansion phase in an individual cycle and the length of the contraction phase in that cycle. In some cases, the expansion period is much longer than the contraction period, as was the case in the cycle that reached its peak in May 1937. In others, the two periods are of about equal length; and in still others, the contraction phase is decidedly longer than the expansion period, as was the case in the cycle that reached its trough in March 1879.

In the post-World War II period, expansions have been considerably longer than the average, and contractions have been considerably shorter than the average. The seven postwar contractions have been 11, 10, 8, 10, 11, 16, 6, and considerably shorter than 16 months long.

Since 1920, 10 of the 14 contractions have lasted 14 months or less. The contraction in the post-World War I depression, however, lasted 18 months and in the depression that began in 1929, 43 months.

The duration of expansion and contraction periods, and of the full cycle for reference cycles from December 1854 through November 1982 is presented in Table 4-2.

CONFORMITY IN BUSINESS CYCLE PATTERNS

Business cycles pervade all areas of economic activity and affect all countries that have economies organized in a free enterprise-pecuniary basis. The most highly industrialized countries show the most pronounced cyclical patterns. Major cycles have occurred at about the same time in industrialized countries such as England, France, Germany, Japan, and the United States. Minor cycles have not occurred at the same time, nor has each country had the same number of cycles. The United States has had more cycles than England, France, the Netherlands, Sweden, and Germany. The amplitude of both contractions and expansion phases of the cycle is significantly more pronounced in the U.S. economy than in the other major economies. Furthermore, some countries may be in a recovery or in a prosperity stage while others are still in a recession stage.

This lack of conformity in international cycle patterns has continued in more recent years. The 1960–1961 recession in the United States was not generally experienced in other countries, though there was some decline in economic activity in Canada and Japan. In 1970, industrial production showed little or no growth in Canada, Japan, and most European countries. The 1973 recession affected all major industrial nations organized on a free enterprise basis. The 1980 recession in the United States was shared by a number of its trading partners, particularly England, but others such as Japan, Switzerland, and Italy continued to enjoy economic expansion. The 1982 recession was fairly widespread among the industrialized nations, and these countries did feel the impact of a recession. The recovery from the trough of the recession was initially uneven among the industrialized countries, but, over time, all the industrialized countries experienced recovery.

The cycle in the United States is also by no means an all-pervasive phenomenon that carries every economic activity with it. A sample of economic time series, such as those published in government publications, shows that some series are reaching their peaks at many dif-

Table 4-2

Duration of Business Cycle Expansions and Contractions in
the United States, 1854–1990

Business Cycle			Duration (in Months) of—		
Trough	Peak	Trough	Expansion	Contraction	Full Cycle
Dec. 1854	June 1857	Dec. 1858	30	18	48
Dec. 1858	Oct. 1860	June 1861	22	8	30
June 1861	Apr. 1865	Dec. 1867	46	32	78
Dec. 1867	June 1869	Dec. 1870	18	18	36
Dec. 1870	Oct. 1873	Mar. 1879	34	65	99
Mar. 1879	Mar. 1882	May 1885	36	38	74
May 1885	Mar. 1887	Apr. 1888	22	13	35
Apr. 1888	July 1890	May 1891	27	10	37
May 1891	Jan. 1893	June 1894	20	17	37
June 1894	Dec. 1895	June 1897	18	18	36
June 1897	June 1899	Dec. 1900	24	18	42
Dec. 1900	Sept. 1902	Aug. 1904	21	23	44
Aug. 1904	May 1907	June 1908	33	13	46
June 1908	Jan. 1910	Jan. 1912	19	24	43
Jan. 1912	Jan. 1913	Dec. 1914	12	23	35
Dec. 1914	Aug. 1918	Mar. 1919	44	7	51
Mar. 1919	Jan. 1920	July 1921	10	18	28
July 1921	May 1923	July 1924	22	14	36
July 1924	Oct. 1926	Nov. 1927	27	13	40
Nov. 1927	Aug. 1929	Mar. 1933	21	43	64
Mar. 1933	May 1937	June 1938	50	13	63
June 1938	Feb. 1945	Oct. 1945	80	8	88
Oct. 1945	Nov. 1948	Oct. 1949	37	11	48
Oct. 1949	July 1953	May 1954	45	10	55
May 1954	Aug. 1957	Apr. 1958	39	8	47
Apr. 1958	Apr. 1960	Feb. 1961	24	10	34
Feb. 1961	Nov. 1969	Nov. 1970	106	11	117
Nov. 1970	Nov. 1973	Mar. 1975	36	16	52
Mar. 1975	Jan. 1980	July 1980	58	6	64
July 1980	July 1981	Nov. 1982	12	16	28
Average, all cycles:					
30 cycles, 1854–1982			33	18	51
14 cycles, 1919–1982			41	14	55
8 cycles, 1945–1982			45	11	56

Source: *Business Cycle Developments* (February 1976) and *Business Conditions Digest* (April 1985).

ferent times during the cycle.[1] Many series do not move in complete conformity with the general business cycle but are undergoing expansion and contraction at different times. During a prosperity period, many, but by no means all, of the series are expanding; and during a recession not all series are contracting.

CYCLICAL TIMING OF ECONOMIC SERIES

Most types of economic activity expand and contract in phase with overall economic activity. Some series are inverted; that is, they are moving in opposition to the direction of business in general.

Inverted timing occurs to a large extent because of the form in which economic data are reported. If the employment series being studied is the number of people at work, it will move with the business cycle, showing positive timing. If, instead, the employment situation is viewed from the number of people unemployed, the series will show inverted timing. Since in most cases the form in which economic data are expressed is not arbitrary but is designed for ease of use and compilation, the NBER has kept all of the time series it has studied in their original form. This explains the inverted position of such series as commercial failures and idle freight cars, in addition to unemployment.

Even though most economic series expand and contract with general business, they do not move in perfect unison with the cycle in overall activity. Many of them typically have leads and lags at reference cycle peaks and troughs. Such leads and lags can be measured from the reference cycle turning point dates as developed by the NBER. These are the dates presented as the troughs and peaks of cycles since 1854 in Table 4-2 on page 84.

Table 4-3 presents some of the most important series that typically lead at reference cycle peaks and troughs, those that move at about the same time as the reference cycle, and those that typically lag.

The series shown here are those chosen in an extensive study by the Department of Commerce in 1975 and updated in 1989. Over the years, the particular series included in the so-called "short list" may vary simply because some statistical series may be somewhat more consistent in their behavior than others, but the economic processes involved are quite faithful. For example, the construction of a new series on investment spending may be a superior indicator to other such

---

1. *Survey of Current Business*, current issues.

Table 4-3

Timing at Peaks and Troughs of Important Economic Series

Leading Index Components

Average weekly hours of production or nonsupervisory workers, manufacturing
Average weekly initial claims for unemployment insurance, state programs
Manufacturers' new orders in 1982 dollars, consumer goods and materials
   industries
Vendor performance, percent of companies receiving slower deliveries
Contracts and orders for plant and equipment, 1982 dollars
New building permits, private housing units (index: 1967 = 100)
Change in manufacturers' unfilled orders in 1982 dollars, durable goods industries,
   smoothed
Change in sensitive materials prices
Stock prices, 500 common stocks (index: 1941–1943 = 100)
Money supply, M2, 1982 dollars
Index of consumer expectations

Coincident Index Components

Employees on nonagricultural payrolls
Personal income less transfer payments, 1982 dollars
Industrial production, total (index: 1977 = 100)
Manufacturing and trade sales, 1982 dollars

Lagging Index Components

Average duration of unemployment
Ratio, manufacturing and trade inventories to sales, 1982 dollars
Change in index of labor cost per unit of output, manufacturing, smoothed
Average prime rate charged by banks
Commercial and industrial loans outstanding, 1982 dollars
Ratio, consumer installment credit outstanding to personal income
Change in consumer price index for services, smoothed

Source: *Business Conditions Digest.*

series measuring investment. Prior to 1988, the leading index contained a twelfth component, an index on net business formation. Since then, the leading index has consisted of only eleven components.

Coincident Economic Indicators

As is to be expected, indexes that reflect aggregate economic activity correspond fairly closely with reference cycle dates.

General Economic Activity. The most highly aggregated series measuring national income or production move in close conformity to the business cycle dating determined by the NBER. Gross national product for the period for which the figures are available moved closely in harmony with reference cycle dates.[2] The Federal Reserve Board Index of Industrial Production in the post-World War II period generally had a short lead at reference peaks and reached its trough at about the same time as reference troughs.

Employment and Hours of Work. Indexes of employment correspond to cyclical peaks and troughs fairly closely. Employment in non-agricultural establishments is practically coincidental with the reference cycle turns at the trough, but at times has had a short lead at the peaks owing to the lead in construction and in industrial durable goods. The measure of unemployment used by the Bureau of Labor Statistics has, in the post-World War II period, generally had a short lead at reference peaks and a lag at reference troughs. The tendency for indexes of employment to be roughly coincidental at peaks and troughs is also shown in series on employment in the durable goods field and in such industries as cement, clay, glass, iron and steel, and machinery. The Bureau of Labor Statistics index of average hours worked per week, however, shows a fairly long lead at reference peaks and a short lead at reference troughs. In other words, one of the first reactions of business to a change in economic conditions is a change in the average hours worked per week rather than in the number of workers employed.

Leading Economic Indicators

Economic activities that are based on longer-term decisions often lead or begin to change in advance of the reference cycle dates.

Construction. Indexes for the construction industry almost always lead reference cycle peaks and troughs. There is also a tendency for related series, such as the production of southern pine lumber, oak flooring, and plumbing fixtures, to move in about the same fashion.

Since contracts lead construction, a lead would be expected in this series, even if construction moved in complete conformity with the cycle. The lead of construction itself at many upper turning points is due to several factors that are inherent in the nature of the cyclical pro-

2. The data on leads and lags in this section are taken from Geoffrey H. Moore (ed.), *Statistical Indicators of Cyclical Revivals and Recessions* (New York: National Bureau of Economic Research, Inc., 1950), and Geoffrey H. Moore, *Business Cycle Indicators*, vol. I (New York: National Bureau of Economic Research, Inc., 1961), and are brought up to date from data in *Business Conditions Digest*.

cess. The accelerator can cause construction to turn down when the rate of increase in demand begins to slow. Innovations lead to building early in the cycle, but this slows down when plant and equipment have been built to produce the new product. The slowdown in construction before the economy turns down may also be due to overbuilding in some fields, which has often been one of the factors producing unbalance. The lead at the lower turning point is due to some of the factors at work in the economy that produce an upturn, such as an innovation, a need for more capacity in some fields as population expands, the lowering of interest rates that makes some projects profitable, and the building of plants to cut production costs.

Industrial Materials and Industrial Durable Goods. The index of sensitive materials prices has shown a tendency to lead at reference peaks and troughs. Inflationary pressures have been so strong since the 1969–1970 downturn that leads have been obscured by the strong pressures for price rises. The tendency to lead cyclical peaks and troughs is probably due in part to changes in demand arising from industries whose activity shows a cyclical lead.

Contracts and orders for plant and equipment lead at both peaks and troughs. The reasons for such leads are similar to those for new building permits. The decision to build a new factory or office building or to buy heavy equipment, just as to build a new house, requires a good deal of time before such activity can take place. Thus the contracts and permits must precede the hiring of workers and the manufacture of the materials required, which is the essence of the business cycle.

Profits. Since profits are a residual after all expenses have been met, they fluctuate much more widely than sales. They begin to decline in some industries before business has reached a peak and to increase before business has reached a trough. In the post-World War II period, the magnitude of changes in profits in such industries was large enough to give profits in total a lead at reference peaks and a short lead at troughs in some cycles, especially the earlier ones in this period.

While no exact series on profit is included in the short list of economic indicators, the effect of profits is felt in the series on stock prices, net business formation, and, indeed, implicitly in all of the series. After all, rising profits constitute a most important signal to proceed in an expansionary way. They provide a signal to stock traders to become bullish; when profits begin to decline, traders become bearish.

New Incorporations and Business Failures. Business failures have a lead at reference peaks and at reference troughs. When the upturn begins, costs lag and profits increase. As costs catch up and as an increasing volume of goods is available from new plants constructed in the upturn, it is more difficult to operate profitably. Some weak concerns fail at this stage, and the number of failures increases as prosperity develops. In the recession period, there is also a lead because most weak concerns have failed after the full effects of lower business levels have had their impact. The concerns still in business are by and large the stronger ones that have weathered the storm. No exact series on business start-ups and failures is included in the short list. However, prior to 1988, a series on net business formation was included.

Consumer Expectations. The Index of Consumer Expectations, a component of the University of Michigan Index of Consumer Sentiment, tracks rising or falling consumer optimism. The index is compiled monthly by the Survey Research Center at the University of Michigan. The survey assesses the human factors in economic affairs. When consumers make spending or saving decisions, consumers are considering expected changes in future income, employment, prices, and interest rates. These shifts in consumer attitudes tend to precede economic activity. The index measures a significant force in the economy and, for many years, has consistently led economic peaks and troughs.

Lagging Economic Indicators

Economic activities that are the result of decisions needing very clear knowledge of the state of the economy often lag or change after the reference cycle dates. However, in recent years, this lag has been greatly shortened as a result of expectations of continued inflation.

Consumer Income and Spending. In the pre-World War II period, there was some tendency for consumer income and spending to lag somewhat in the cyclical process. This lag has disappeared in the post-war period partly because of governmental programs to maintain purchasing power as well as the mild nature of postwar recessions. Personal income has, in recent years, moved in relative harmony with turning points in the cycle, and the same is true of retail sales. In recent cycles, inflationary pressures have been so strong that no cyclical pattern is evident in such data in current dollars.

The ratio of consumer installment credit to personal income, expressed as a percent, lags somewhat. This reflects the heavy use of installment credit for current consumer purchases, regardless of possible near-term changes in income. Also, inflation in the consumer services sector responds after the change in business activity.

Interest Rates. Interest rates have a tendency to lag in the cyclical process. A Federal Reserve Board quarterly index of bank rates on short-term business loans shows a lag at reference peaks and at reference troughs. This same tendency for interest rates to lag is also shown in bond yields. This is, in part, due to the contractual nature of interest payments. Loan contracts are usually signed for a minimum of ninety days, and in many cases, run for years. The lag is also due to the "sticky" nature of interest rates in many situations.

During the inflationary years of the 1970s, this pattern was broken as anticipation of inflation and the uncertainty of the rate of inflation brought about greater volatility in interest rates than had been experienced before. A large part of the recent volatility has been attributed to Federal Reserve policy. This policy has been volatile. At times, the Federal Reserve has focused on controlling the growth of the money stock; at other times, it wished to stabilize interest rates; and at other times, the focus was the price level.

CYCLICAL AMPLITUDE

This section will consider the amplitude over the cycle of various phases of economic activity. First, some observations will be made on the general pattern of cyclical amplitude, and then the pattern in gross national product and in industrial production will be described.

General Pattern

Various phases of economic activity have different amplitudes during the cycle. In the prewar cycles for which data are available in NBER studies, some general patterns are evident. Prices had a lower average amplitude than production in manufacturing inasmuch as producers adjusted to changed demand primarily by reducing output. The amplitude in employment was substantially less than that in production, because many workers had their hours cut rather than be laid off. Payrolls fluctuated somewhat more than production owing to changes in the work week and to overtime pay in prosperity. Profits had a much larger amplitude than production or payrolls. This is to be expected, since it is a residual after all expenses are paid, and fixed costs represent a large part of total business costs.

The relationships have generally held true in the postwar period. Prices have had such an upward bias that they have declined little or not at all in recession periods. An example of such postwar relation-

Table 4-4

Percentage Changes in the Upswing and Downturn
during Reference Cycles in Selected Economic Indicators
in Two Post-World War II Recessions

	Percentage Increase from Initial Trough to Peak		Percentage Decrease from Peak to Terminal Trough	
	1954–1958 Cycle	1970–1975 Cycle	1954–1958 Cycle	1970–1975 Cycle
1. GNP—current dollars	23.9	36.0	1.9	+6.7
2. GNP—1982 dollars	13.2	16.0	2.5	6.6
3. Production—FRB Index	22.1	25.3	12.6	14.9
4. Nondurable goods	20.6	19.8	3.8	13.4
5. Durable goods	21.9	32.5	19.7	16.7
6. Total nonagricultural employment	8.4	9.6	4.0	0.28
7. Nonagricultural employment excluding government	9.5	9.6	7.1	1.6
8. Wholesale prices	6.8	27.8	+0.7	+20.1
9. Profits after tax	29.4	100.9	21.2	15.2
10. Disposable personal income—1982 dollars	15.1	15.6	0.7	4.0
11. Consumer expenditures on durable goods—1982 dollars	15.3	39.8	6.9	10.2

Source: Based on data in the *Survey of Current Business.*

ships may be seen from Table 4-4, which shows changes in major economic variables in the 1954–1958 and the 1970–1975 cycles. Changes in the other postwar cycles show the same general pattern, but the amplitude was smaller, especially in the contraction phase.

Several other significant relationships exist. The amplitude of production of durable goods is much greater than that of nondurable goods. This is consistent with the theories that will be presented later in this book, in particular the acceleration principle and the overinvestment explanations of business cycles. Consumer durables show a more pronounced variation than durable manufacturing in total. This was not generally true in the pre-World War II period. This is probably due to several factors. More consumers have significant amounts of dis-

Table 4-5

Postwar Cyclical Fluctuations in Constant-Dollar GNP

	Timing and Duration			Amplitude and Severity	
	Peak Quarter	Trough Quarter	No. of Quarters of Decline	Percentage Decline	Percentage Decline per Quarter at Annual Rate
Recessions					
1948–49:	1948: IV	1949: II	2	−1.4	−2.9
1953–54:	1953: II	1954: II	4	−3.3	−3.3
1957–58:	1957: III	1958: I	2	−3.3	−6.5
1960–61:	1960: I	1960: IV	3	−1.2	−1.6
1969–70:	1969: III	1970: IV	5	−1.1	−0.9
1973–75:	1973: IV	1975: I	5	−6.6	−5.3
1980:	1980: I	1980: III	2	−2.5	−5.0
1981–82:	1981: III	1982: IV	6	−3.0	−2.0

	Timing and Duration			Amplitude and Strength	
	Trough Quarter	Peak Quarter	No. of Quarters of Expansion	Percentage Increase	Percentage Increase per Quarter at Annual Rate
Recoveries					
1949–53:	1949: II	1953: II	16	28.1	6.4
1954–57:	1954: II	1957: III	13	13.2	3.9
1958–60:	1958: I	1960: I	8	11.7	5.7
1961–69:	1960: IV	1969: III	35	48.0	4.7
1970–73:	1970: IV	1973: IV	12	15.8	5.0
1980–81:	1980: III	1981: III	4	4.2	4.2

Source: *Survey of Current Business* (January 1976), Part I, p. 27, (July 1989), p. 22, (July 1986), p. 26.

cretionary income and so can buy durables in prosperity periods. They seem to have been motivated more by the changing economic outlook than by prospects for long-run changes in income. Business has done more investing than it did during the pre-World War II period on a long-run basis, instead of a short-run profit basis, and has thus reduced the amplitude in the producer durable field. This has been true because of a desire to cut costs by introducing more modern machinery and equipment.

One of the significant factors is the very small change in personal income in the downturn—much smaller than prewar. This is due to a series of factors, such as unemployment compensation, compensatory fiscal policy, agricultural price-support programs, more stable dividend policies, and the like.

Gross National Product

Inflation has been so pronounced in the most recent cycles that comparisons of changes in GNP in recessions and recoveries are best made using constant-dollar GNP figures. In the period since 1949, the percentage increase in constant-dollar GNP in recovery periods has varied between 11.7 percent and 48.0 percent. However, much of this variation is due to the varying lengths of the recovery periods. When comparison is made on the basis of the percentage increase per quarter figured at an annual rate, the difference is narrowed considerably. In recessions, the percentage decline per quarter has varied between 0.9 percent in 1969–1970 to 6.5 percent in 1957–1958. Data for each cycle are presented in Table 4-5.

Industrial Production

The changes in industrial production are more pronounced than changes in GNP in real terms, especially in the downturn. In the post-World War II cycles, the decline in industrial production has been less severe than it was on the average in the prewar period, and the expansion has been somewhat less vigorous than in minor cycles in the same period. The monthly increases in industrial production during expansion periods were not much different from those in contraction periods, but expansion periods were much longer than contraction periods.

FLUCTUATIONS IN INVENTORIES

Changes in inventories play a major role in changes in total economic activity. This has continued to be true in the post-World War II period, even though inventories have been maintained at a lower level in relation to sales than in the prewar period. This influence was more pronounced in downturns than in expansion periods.[3] During the first

---

3. Moses Abramovitz, *The Role of Inventories in Business Cycles* (New York: National Bureau of Economic Research, Inc., 1948), and *Manufacturers' Inventories in the Study of Economic Growth*, thirty-ninth annual report (New York: National Bureau of Economic Research, Inc., 1959), pp. 43–44.

postwar recession, the change in the rate of inventory purchases was somewhat larger than the decline in GNP. In the second recession, inventory adjustment was equal to about 85 percent of the change in GNP and in the third recession, to about 60 percent. In the fourth postwar recession in 1960–1961, the change in inventory investment was more than seven times as great as the decline in GNP. In the 1969–1970 recession, inventories continued to increase, but the annual rate of accumulation was cut from $11.9 billion in the third quarter of 1969 to $2.6 billion in the fourth quarter of 1970.[4] In the 1973–1975 recession, inflationary pressures were so strong that GNP increased by $80.9 billion from the fourth quarter of 1973 to the first quarter of 1975. Inventory liquidation was significant, however, since inventories being built up at a $27.7 billion annual rate in the peak quarter were reduced to a $19.0 billion annual rate in the quarter of the terminal trough. In the 1981–1982 recession, inventories exhibited the same pattern as in the 1973–1975 recession, and the buildup following the 1982 trough was exceptionally vigorous.

The significance of the role of inventories in the cycle is to be expected because of the causal factors at work. The accelerator principle suggests a more than proportionate change in the rate of inventory accumulation on the upswing and in the rate of liquidation in the downturn. Speculative activity also leads to inventory accumulation in a recovery period and to liquidation in a recession.

A detailed study of several series on manufacturers' inventories was made for the NBER by Moses Abramovitz, who found that fluctuations in the volume of inventories conformed well with those of the reference cycle. There was, however, somewhat of a lag in inventory movements behind those of general business. Inventory series in terms of current prices showed a lag approximating three to six months, while deflated series showed a longer lag that was between six and eleven months.[5] An interesting fact is that the series on investment in inventories, that is, changes in the stock of inventory, are all leading series, while the series on the level of inventory continue to be lagging series.[6]

To understand the reasons for the fluctuations in inventories during the course of the cycle, it is necessary to analyze the factors involved in holding inventories. The most common reasons cited for

---

4. Based on data in the *Survey of Current Business*.
5. Abramovitz, *Role of Inventories*, pp. 87, 97.
6. See "Cyclical Indicators by Economic Process," *Business Conditions Digest*, any issue.

holding inventories are to gain the savings that result from buying materials and supplies in larger quantities, to achieve the cost savings that result from smoothing production over a period of time, and to provide a buffer stock against unforeseen contingencies. These benefits from holding inventories are offset in part by the costs incurred in carrying inventories. The level of inventories that a business will normally desire to hold will depend, therefore, on a balance between the costs of holding inventories and the benefits from doing so.

In determining the optimum level of inventories, the costs associated with holding different levels of inventories are first calculated on the basis that the various costs will remain constant over short periods of time and vary only with different levels of inventories. The major costs involved are interest, insurance, taxes, spoilage, obsolescence, storage, and possible price changes. A change in any of these costs will change the costs of holding different levels of inventories and, therefore, also the optimum level of inventories based upon an analysis of costs and benefits.

Two of the major costs of holding inventories—interest charges and price changes, and expectations of such changes—have significant cyclical fluctuation. An increase in the rate of interest will increase the cost of holding inventories and so lead to a reduction in optimum levels, and a reduction will do just the reverse. An expected rise in prices will lead to reduction in the cost of holding inventories and so lead to an increase in optimum inventory levels. An expected decline will have the opposite effect. Since reductions in costs of holding inventories owing to expected price rises are generally greater in the early stages of expansion in business activity than increases in costs resulting from higher interest rates, the net effect from the cost side is to lead to an increase in inventories as expansion gets under way. The opposite is generally true of business contractions, especially in the early stages.

Changes in some of the factors that lead to cost savings from holding inventories also have a cyclical pattern. Consideration will be given in turn to savings from buying in larger quantities, savings from smoothing production, and benefits from holding buffer stocks. In most industries, cost savings are usually realized by buying goods in larger quantities. These savings include quantity discounts both in the purchase price and in transportation costs and also savings from placing and processing fewer orders.

To consider the effect of these factors independently of other factors, let us assume that savings result only from buying in larger quantities and that conditions in the industries supplying the goods have not changed. Under these conditions, a change in the rate of sales would not ordinarily lead to a change in the level of inventories, since savings have been calculated on the basis of savings associated with quantity discounts and less frequent ordering. As the rate of sales increased, a firm would ordinarily consider one of two alternatives: either order more frequently or order in larger quantities. The effect on the level of inventories in either case would be minimal. The increases in the rate of sales associated with an upswing in business activity do not, therefore, lead to a significant increase in inventory owing to cost savings arising from purchasing in larger quantities.

Inventories are also held to achieve even production. Savings result from producing goods at a more or less constant rate rather than adjusting to seasonal shifts in demand. When production is geared to sales, added costs are incurred to hire and lay off workers, to pay overtime or add extra shifts in periods of peak demand, and to pay for raw materials that are likely to be in short supply in periods of peak demand and therefore are more costly. If attempts are made to spread sales more evenly and thus smooth production levels, there are added selling costs. The optimum policy balances the costs of holding inventory against the savings from maintaining smooth production. If production is almost completely smoothed, and average inventory holdings are large enough to meet seasonal needs, an increase in sales will have some effect on average inventories, but it will ordinarily not be as great as a percentage of peak stocks. This is not true, however, if production is only partially smoothed.

When sales go up cyclically in an industry, costs associated with peak periods of production will go up more than normally because of greater delays in getting raw materials, more overtime and shift work, and the like. In this situation, there is a significant saving to be realized from adding to stocks early in an upswing in business. When few firms in an industry maintain smooth production fully, there are significant savings to be gained by an individual firm from increasing stocks early in an expansion period. This is another factor in explaining increases in inventory investment early in the upswing of a cycle.

A third major reason for holding inventories is to provide a buffer stock to serve as a safety factor, if there is a delay in delivery of raw materials or parts, and to be prepared for an unexpected surge in sales. This is true because there are significant costs associated with being out of materials or parts and having to slow production. There are also costs associated with lost sales. The relevant cost factor is the actual cost of being out of stock, multiplied by the probability that this will occur. Cyclical factors will affect the amount of inventory to be held as a buffer. An increase in the rate of sales will increase the probability of running out of finished goods and so lead to an increase in inventories. However, in industries in which stocks are relatively large in relation to sales, the effect will not be large, since the chances are good that production can be increased to meet the added demand before the inventory is depleted.

If sales go up when the supply of raw materials or other goods needed in production is, or is expected to be, tight, the chances of running out of stock are greatly increased, and this leads to an attempt to increase inventories early in an expansion. Again, the effect is greater in an industry in which stocks are relatively low in relation to production than when they are high.

In summary, the result of optimal inventory policy will be an increase in stocks in an upswing in business that is proportionately greater than the increase in sales and a similar reduction in a downturn. These effects will be greatest when significant price rises are expected and when conditions are such that raw materials and parts are expected to be tight. This is generally the situation in the early stages of an upturn.

THE GENERAL CYCLE PATTERN

Each cycle in economic activity is, in many ways, a unique phenomenon, but there are elements that are similar from cycle to cycle. Information on developments during a cycle is available from studies by the NBER and also from data in *Survey of Current Business,* a monthly publication of the U.S. Department of Commerce. Some groups of items have been analyzed over a period of time during segments of the cycle and are helpful in developing information on the general cycle pattern. One such study for the pre-World War II period contains data on thirty-four comprehensive series analyzed by the NBER. They are not inclusive enough to cover all important sectors of economic activity, but enough data are available to present a preliminary picture of the typical cycle.[7]

Data on the complete group of comprehensive series are not available for post-World War II cycles. Information is available, however, on the behavior of a representative group of eleven comprehensive series

7. Wesley C. Mitchell, *What Happens During Business Cycles: A Progress Report* (New York: National Bureau of Economic Research, Inc., 1951).

for the postwar period from 1945 to 1958 covering three complete cycles.[8] Data are also available for the period from 1948 to the present on many comprehensive series in *Business Conditions Digest*.

Some data on costs, prices, and profits in post-World War II business cycles are available in a study by Thor Hultgren that covers cycles in fifteen manufacturing industries and in railroads, public utilities, construction, trade, and telephone companies.[9] Most of the data are for the cycles in the 1947–1961 period. Some data are also available on the cyclical behavior of interest rates in the period from 1945 to 1961 in a study by Reuben A. Kessel.[10] This study analyzes the cyclical behavior of short-term and long-term interest rates including commercial paper rates, the yields on Treasury bills, and Moody's Aaa corporate bonds.

The Expansion Phase of the Cycle

This record of the general cycle pattern will begin at the initial trough of the cycle, and the rest of the cycle is divided into fairly general subperiods. Its purpose is to highlight the rough consistencies or common features in the behavior of certain variables over the cycle.

Expansion Out of the Trough. The outstanding characteristic of this segment of the cycle is the widespread improvement in economic activity. In the pre-World War II period, all comprehensive series showed an increase in business, since all series were rising except business failures, which were falling as expected. Even though all of the comprehensive series were moving with the cycle, there was a variation in the rates of change. Prices of all commodities were going up only 0.5 points per month in the early stages of expansion. Production was increasing 2.0 points per month, construction 3.7 points, shares sold on the New York Stock Exchange 6.6 points, and corporate net profit 11.8 points.

In the post-World War II period, all of the eleven comprehensive series were rising out of the trough, except the number of business failures. The most rapid rate of increase in industrial production occurred in this subperiod just as it did prewar. This was also true of construc-

---

8. From an unpublished research project at Washington University by Robert L. Virgil, Jr., *Comparative Patterns of Behavior by Economic Time Series During Prewar and Postwar American Business Cycles.*

9. Thor Hultgren, *Cost, Prices, and Profits: Their Cyclical Relations* (New York: National Bureau of Economic Research, Inc., 1965).

10. Reuben A. Kessel, *The Cyclical Behavior of the Term Structure of Interest Rates* (New York: National Bureau of Economic Research, Inc., 1965).

tion contracts awarded and of employment in manufacturing industries in the early postwar cycles, but there was little increase in employment in the early months of the cycle that began at the end of 1970.

In the fifteen manufacturing industries in the Hultgren study,
prices were rising in 41 percent of the observations—the smallest percentage for any of the subperiods of expansion—while costs per unit
of output were rising in only 22 percent of the observations, which is
also the smallest for any of the subperiods of expansion. In the beginning of expansions, profit margins as a percentage of sales were rising
in 83 percent of the observations and total profits in 89 percent.

Long- and short-term interest rates were generally rising in the
early stages of expansion, except in the 1961–1969 cycle when bond
rates were about stable. The rates of increase in commercial paper rates
and in Moody's Aaa corporate bond yields were the slowest for any
subperiod in the expansion period.

Expansion of Business Continues. In the prewar period, all of the
series with a regular cycle pattern moved with the cyclical tide, except
the par value of bond sales and the number of shares of stock sold on
the New York Stock Exchange, which began to fall after rising rapidly
in the initial turnaround. The other series with regular cyclical patterns moved more slowly than they did in the beginning of the upturn.

The pattern in the postwar period was similar in some ways to the
prewar period. Only eight of the eleven series expanded in this stage;
the value of construction contracts began falling, and sales of common
stock and of bonds continued to fall. The number of business failures
also moved against the cyclical tide by increasing in the early postwar
cycles, but in the 1958–1961 and 1961–1969 cycles, the number decreased as it had prewar. The rate of growth clearly slowed from that
of the initial turnaround as it had prewar.

The Hultgren study of manufacturing industries shows that prices
rose in 63 percent of the observations compared with 41 percent in the
initial stage. Costs per unit of output rose in 39 percent of the observations compared with 22 percent in the initial stage. Profit margins
were still rising in 75 percent of all observations.

Yields on Treasury bills and commercial paper rates were rising at
the most rapid rate of any stage of expansion. Yields on Moody's Aaa
corporate bonds were rising more rapidly than in the initial stage.

Much Later in the Expansion. Most of the series again rose at a
faster rate as the pace of expansion quickened. In the prewar period,
twenty-eight of the thirty-two comprehensive series having a regular
cyclical pattern rose and four fell. The two series on business failures

are expected to fall as business increases and thus were moving with the tide. Moving against the tide were the value of bond sales at par and bond prices. Most of the other series were increasing faster than they had earlier. Those increasing faster included industrial production, fuel and electricity production, the series on transportation, all of the series on trade having a regular cyclical pattern, factory payrolls, income payments, the number of incorporations, shares sold on the New York Stock Exchange, and net profits of business enterprises. Liabilities in business failures also showed improvement by falling faster.

In the postwar period, all of the eleven comprehensive series were rising in this part of the expansion, except the number of shares of stock traded on the New York Stock Exchange.

In the manufacturing industry study, prices were rising in 74 percent of the observations, and unit costs were rising in 67 percent of the observations, up materially from 39 percent in earlier stages. As a result, profit margins were rising in only 59 percent of the observations compared with 75 percent in earlier stages, but because of increased volume, total profits were still rising in 70 percent of all observations.

Yields on Treasury bills were still rising but at a somewhat slower rate than earlier, and commercial paper rates were rising at a significantly slower rate than in the preceding subperiod, except for 1961–1969 when they were rising rapidly. Yields on Moody's Aaa corporate bonds continued upward.

Nearing the Peak. Business continued to rise as the expansion neared its peak, but fewer series participated in the rise.

In the prewar period, twenty-four series were still moving with the tide, but eight were already moving against it, as follows:

- Liabilities of failures (moving against the tide by increasing)
- Bond sales
- Bond prices
- Number of shares of stock sold on the New York Stock Exchange
- Prices of common stock
- Bank clearings in New York City
- Snyder's index of deposit activity
- Value of corporate security issues

Thus, most of the series on financial transactions were falling in this last subperiod of expansion.

In the postwar period, eight of the eleven series were still expanding near the peak—all, except the value of construction contracts awarded, common stock sales, and bond sales. Industrial production and employment continued upward at about the same rate as earlier or at a somewhat slower rate. Thus, the more rapid increase in production and employment in the prewar cycles of the last stage of expansion compared with earlier did not occur in postwar cycles.

Prices in manufacturing industries were rising in 80 percent of the observations and unit costs in 74 percent, the highest figures for any subperiod of expansion. Profit margins were rising in only 46 percent of all observations, the lowest figure for any subperiod of expansion. Because of increased volume, total profits were still increasing in 70 percent of all observations.

Yields on Treasury bills went up very slowly at the slowest rate in any subperiod of expansion, except in 1961–1969 when they rose rapidly. Commercial paper rates went up at a much slower rate, and the yields of Moody's Aaa corporate bonds went up at a somewhat slower rate.

The Contraction Phase of the Cycle

The contraction phase of the cycle will be described in a similar manner to the expansion phase. In each subperiod, the prewar pattern will be considered first, then the postwar pattern.

Early Stage of Downturn. As business passes the peak, all of the regular series decline in line with the tide of contraction. In the prewar period, the series that had begun to fall before the peak of the cycle all fell faster except bond prices, which were decreasing at a somewhat slower rate. The rate of decrease in commodity prices was small, as was that in income payments. Rapid rates of decrease occurred in the value of construction contracts, the value of new security issues, and the number of shares of stock sold on the New York Stock Exchange. The most rapid change for the worse occurred in corporate profits, and liabilities in business failures were also going up very rapidly.

The postwar cycles did not show the same degree of downturn in the initial turnaround as did prewar cycles. In the prewar cycles, all eleven series included in the postwar study moved with the tide; all decreased except business failures, which went up as business turned down. Postwar increases, in addition to failures, were apparent in the value of construction contracts awarded, except in the 1969–1970 downturn, in the number of shares of common stock sold, in the par value of bond sales, and in bank clearings in New York City. Employment in manufacturing had its slowest rate of decrease just as it did prewar, and it even rose somewhat in the 1969–1970 downturn and the early stages of the 1973–1975 downturn.

In manufacturing industries, prices were still rising in 85 percent of all observations, the highest percentage for any of the subperiods of the cycle; and unit costs were up in 85 percent of all observations, a higher percentage than in any subperiod of expansion. Profit margins were rising in only 28 percent of all observations, and because of decreasing volume, total profits were up in only 19 percent of the observations.

Yields on Treasury bills dropped at the sharpest rate in any of the subperiods of contraction, and commercial paper rates also started to drop significantly. Yields on Moody's Aaa corporate bonds started to decline slowly, except in the 1969–1970 downturn when they continued to rise.

Business Decline Continues. There was no retardation in the rate of decline in this period of contraction as there was in the second subperiod of expansion. In the prewar period, the most rapid rates of decline took place in this subperiod in most sectors of the economy. The only sector of the economy moving counter to the tide was the bond market.

The rate of decline was faster in this subperiod for most, but not all, sectors of the economy. The value of construction contracts fell somewhat more slowly, the value of corporate security issues fell much more slowly, and liabilities in business failures increased at a much slower rate.

After the initial turnaround, the downturn was not as pervasive in postwar cycles as it was prewar when only the par value of bond sales was moving counter to the tide. Stock and bond sales and bank clearings were still going up. Business failures moved with the tide by increasing in number.

The most rapid rate of decline in this subperiod occurred in industrial production, in employment, in manufacturing, and in the AT&T Index, just as it did prewar. Construction contracts awarded also went down most rapidly in this subperiod in the early postwar cycles, whereas prewar the most rapid rate of decline was in the very early stages of contraction.

In manufacturing industries, prices were still rising in 78 percent of all observations and unit costs in 90 percent. Profit margins were rising in only 26 percent of all observations and total profits in the same percentage of observations.

Yields on Treasury bills continued downward at a slower rate than in the initial downturn, while commercial paper rates and yields on Moody's Aaa corporate bonds continued downward at about the same rate as in the initial turnaround stage, except for bonds in the 1969–1970 downturn when they were rising faster.

Much Later in the Downturn. The depression worsened, but at a slower rate. In the prewar period, most series still fell and the number of business failures increased. The liabilities in failures, however, were starting to decline. Most series, however, fell at about the same rate as in the early period or at a slower rate.

For the postwar data, only five of the series were contracting, whereas all but bond sales and business failures went down prewar. Also expanding postwar were stock sales, construction contracts awarded, except in the 1960–1961 contraction, and the two series on bank debits.

Prices in manufacturing industries were rising in only 45 percent of all observations, down from 78 percent in the preceding subperiod; unit costs were rising in 65 percent of all observations compared with 90 percent in the preceding subperiod. Profit margins and total profits were rising in only 26 percent of all observations, the same percentages as in the preceding subperiod. Yields on Treasury bills dropped somewhat faster than earlier, while commercial paper rates and yields on Moody's Aaa corporate bonds dropped at about the same rate.

Nearing the Trough. The decline in economic activity was no longer as pervasive as it was in the previous subperiod. In the prewar period, fourteen series with regular cyclical patterns were already rising. This group included the series on the number of failures, which was still increasing but at a slower rate than earlier.

Other series that were increasing and were still moving with the cycle were those related to financial investment activity, which involves preparation for investments soon to be made. The increases show that the financial situation had become favorable and that plans were under way for a renewal of expansion.

Prewar, many series already moved upward, and the same was true postwar. All were expanding except industrial production, manufacturing employment, and the AT&T Index. Industrial production and the AT&T Index declined at the slowest rate during this last subperiod, just as they did prewar. In the 1969–1970 downturn, production declined rapidly as the contraction approached the trough. Manufacturing employment declined at a more rapid rate now, but slower than in the initial stages of the downturn in the early postwar cycles; however, it declined slowly in 1960–1961 and more slowly in 1969–1970, just as was the case prewar.

Prices in manufacturing industries were rising in only 35 percent of the observations, the lowest rate in any segment of the cycle, and unit costs in 45 percent of the observations, the lowest rate in any segment of contraction. Profit margins were rising in only 19 percent of all observations and total profits in only 11 percent, the lowest percentages in any segment of the cycle.

Yields on Treasury bills continued downward, but at a very slow rate, except in 1969–1970 when they were dropping rapidly. Commercial paper rates continued downward at about the same rate as in previous segments of contraction except for 1969–1970, but yields on Moody's Aaa corporate bonds were nearly stabilized.

QUESTIONS

1. What has been the average length of the cycle? The most common length?
2. How do the lengths of the periods of expansion and contraction compare?
3. Describe the international pattern of business cycles.
4. Discuss the extent to which various phases of economic activity in the United States move with the cyclical tide.
5. Study the list in Table 4-3 of series that typically lead, move with the cycle, and lag. Account for the timing of (a) common stock prices, (b) average weekly hours of production or nonsupervisory workers, manufacturing, (c) labor cost per unit of output, manufacturing, and (d) industrial production.
6. Describe and account for the general pattern of amplitude in various phases of economic activity.
7. Describe the fluctuations in GNP in cycles in the post-World War II period.
8. Describe the fluctuations in industrial production during postwar cycles.
9. How important are fluctuations in inventories over the cycle?
10. Discuss the factors that affect the level of inventories and the effect that cyclical factors have on them.
11. Describe what happens in each of the subperiods of the cycle during expansion. Contrast the prewar and postwar record.
12. Summarize what you feel are the most significant aspects of the behavior of cycles.

READINGS

Abramovitz, Moses. *The Role of Inventories in Business Cycles*. New York: National Bureau of Economic Research, Inc., 1948.

Hultgren, Thor. *Cost, Prices, and Profits: Their Cyclical Relations*. New York: National Bureau of Economic Research, Inc., 1965.

"Inflation and Stagnation in Major Foreign Industrial Countries." *Federal Reserve Bulletin* (October 1974), pp. 683–698.

Kessel, Reuben A. *The Cyclical Behavior of the Term Structure of Interest Rates*. New York: National Bureau of Economic Research, Inc., 1965.

Mitchell, Wesley C. *What Happens During Business Cycles: A Progress Report*. New York: National Bureau of Economic Research, Inc., 1951. Part II.

———. *Business Cycles: The Problem and Its Setting*. New York: Arno Press, 1975.

Moore, Geoffrey. *Business Cycles, Inflation and Forecasting*, 2d ed. Cambridge, MA: Ballinger Publishing Co., 1983.

Sorkin, Alan L. *Monetary and Fiscal Policy and Business Cycles in the Modern Era*. Lexington, MA: Lexington Books, 1988. Chapter 2.

Tatom, John A. "Why Has Manufacturing Employment Declined?" *Review*, Federal Reserve Bank of St. Louis (December 1986), pp. 15–25.

Volcker, Paul A. *The Rediscovery of the Business Cycle*. New York: Free Press, 1978.

Zarnowitz, Victor. "Recent Work on Business Cycles in Historical Perspective: A Review of Theories and Evidence." *Journal of Economic Literature* (June 1985).

5

OTHER FLUCTUATIONS IN ECONOMIC ACTIVITY

Business cycles are usually the most important fluctuations to analyze for the purpose of making forecasts. In some fields, however, seasonal fluctuations lead to wider swings in business activity than those resulting from the cycle, but they are more regular in their pattern and thus easier to predict. Several other types of fluctuations must be understood if a forecasting program is to be successfully carried out. These fluctuations will be analyzed in this chapter.

We will first consider the cycles in building activity. We treat these separately from the business cycle, since the movements do not coincide, and at times, some special factors affect the volume of building. Specific cycles in agricultural production will be studied next, which is followed by a discussion of the seasonal variations that occur in different sectors of the economy. We will then consider the nature of long-run developments in economic activity and the possibility of long waves in such development.

This chapter concludes with a fairly extended discussion of current work being done by economists on the Kondratieff cycle.

CYCLES IN BUILDING ACTIVITY

The construction field is subject to regular cyclical movements that have not always coincided with fluctuations in general business and often have been more severe. The cycle in building activity plays an important part in economic fluctuations, since the building industry is of major importance. In 1988, for example, out of a total employment of 105.5 million in nonagricultural establishments, 15.5 million were employed in contract construction. This by no means indicates the total economic influence of the construction industry since many people are employed in the development of timber, the mining of metals, the manufacture of various building materials, and the furnishing of services related to the construction field. Expenditures on new construction in 1987 amounted to $399 billion out of total expenditures (GNP) of about $4,527 billion.[1]

Characteristics of the Building Industry

Some of the characteristics of the building industry are important in explaining fluctuations in the volume of building activity. It must be first recognized that the building industry is a combination of different types of concerns, some of which build small homes, skyscrapers, other specialized industrial plants, and so on. The industry is also made up of an unusually large number of small firms and of a much smaller number of large contractors engaged in developing large projects or specialized buildings. There also are local differences in the industry in the way of union organization; in the types of buildings permitted under building codes; in the availability of building materials such as stone, sand, and gravel; and in the seasons in which operations are possible.

One of the most important characteristics of the building industry is that it produces a product of unusual durability. Most buildings, especially of the residential type, last for forty or more years. In fact, obsolescence is often more important than actual physical depreciation. The immobility of buildings is of economic importance, since, as population shifts, new buildings must be constructed to take care of the people who change locations. Another important factor is the variation in different buildings, which is especially pronounced in industrial units. Buildings are not directly interchangeable, so that, as the pattern of production and income shifts, there is a demand for some types of buildings that are currently not in existence and a slackening of demand for some types that already exist.

The Building Cycle

A number of attempts have been made to identify a cycle in construction activity, both residential and commercial. Simon Kuznets did early work on many economic activities in the United States and found evidence to indicate a cycle of between 16 and 22 years' duration in the building construction industry. Such length cycles are now referred to as *Kuznets cycles*. In his study, Kuznets developed the con-

---

1. *Federal Reserve Bulletin* (May 1988), A45, A49, and A51.

cept of growth cycles, using rates of growth rather than the absolute data. In those terms, he and others found clear evidence of building cycles before World War I and relatively weak evidence thereafter. Van Duijn has done some recent investigation on investment in structures (residential and nonresidential) in the United States. Using three-year moving averages and expressing the data as percentage deviations from a log-linear trend, he finds peaks in 1955 and 1972 and troughs in 1958 and 1975.

The explanation for Kuznets building cycles typically has run in terms of demographics, particularly migration. Kuznets cycle expansions have generally coincided with emigration waves from Europe. Interestingly, van Duijn points out that the building cycle in Great Britain was just the inverse of the U.S. cycle, and peaks in the United States took place at about the same time as troughs in Great Britain.[2]

If immigration patterns are indeed the true cause of building cycles, we are permitted to be skeptical about their continuance in a 16- to 22-year cycle in modern times, since there would appear to be no particular reason for immigration to run in such cycles.

Causal Factors.   The causes of the differences in the building cycle from the general business cycle, especially the greater length and severity of the major building cycles, are inherent in the nature of the building industry. One of the major reasons for these long and severe fluctuations is the durability of buildings. The basic demand in the economy is for a certain stock of buildings, the vast majority of which are currently in existence, since buildings last from 20 to 50 or more years. For example, let us suppose that a community with 10,000 people has 2,500 dwellings. Suppose further that, on the average, one new house is constructed for each increase of four persons in the population. As population increases, the need for housing in succeeding years varies, as shown in Table 5-1.

The demand for houses in this example increases along with the increases in population, one house being required on the average for each four persons. As population increases by 1.6 percent in the second year, the demand for houses also increases by 1.6 percent, from 2,500 to 2,540 houses. The 160 additional people create a demand for 40 new houses in the second year. The housing construction industry, which had been active only in the replacement business, has now moved from producing zero new houses to 40. In the third year, pop-

---

2. J. J. van Duijn, *The Long Wave in Economic Life* (London: George Allen and Unwin, 1983), pp. 16–17.

Table 5-1

Effect on Housing Demand of Changes in Population

Year	Population	Increase in Population	Percentage Increase in Population	Number of Houses Required	Number of Additional Houses Required	Percentage Differences in Additional Houses Needed
1	10,000	—	—	2,500	—	—
2	10,160	160	1.6%	2,540	40	—
3	10,240	80	0.8%	2,560	20	−50%
4	10,300	60	0.6%	2,575	15	−25%
5	10,420	120	1.2%	2,605	30	+100%

Source: Hypothetical data.

ulation continues to increase, but at a slower rate. The demand for houses increases at the same rate as the increase in population. The demand for new houses, however, is only half of what it was in the previous year; 20 in the third year compared with 40 in the second year. In the fifth year, population and housing demand increase by 1.2 percent, but the demand for new houses doubles the amount in the fourth year. Thus, while population increases by a small amount each year but not by the same amount each year, the demand for new houses shows wide fluctuations. This is an application of the accelerator principle, the theoretical discussion of which is presented in Chapter 9.

Fluctuations in the demand for new buildings are not as extreme as the above example indicates, since a certain amount of building is required for the replacement of existing structures. If buildings on the average lasted 50 years in this community, there would be a demand for about 50 houses a year for replacement. The 15 to 40 new houses a year needed to accommodate increases in population, however, are between 30 and 80 percent of the demand for replacement. In actual practice, houses would not be replaced at a steady rate, and as a result, fluctuations in building activity would be further magnified.

Thus, it can be seen that minor shifts in population growth can lead to large shifts in the rate of demand for new housing. Cycles may easily develop even while population continues to increase but at different rates. In most areas, population does not grow at a smooth rate, and there have been fluctuations in the rate of population growth in many sections of the United States as large as or larger than those used in the above example. Local factors influence rates of population growth, and shifts of population take place as some neighborhoods in a city decline. In addition, changes in income lead to a demand for different types of housing, which increases the demand for new buildings.

Availability of Financing.   Another factor of importance in determining the demand for buildings, and hence the character of the building cycle, is the availability of new financing. Most building is done on borrowed capital. It seems clear from various studies that changes in interest rates will not explain major cycles in building activity. Even when interest rates move in the same direction as building, the changes are not big enough to assign any important causal significance to them. Interest as a cost is overshadowed by such important factors as amortization, taxes, and insurance. The availability of credit, however, rather than the cost, is a major factor in the level of activity in the housing field. During periods of recession in economic activity in which the aggregate demand for credit has eased, funds are freed for investment in mortgages. Savings institutions have a larger inflow of funds partly because of the declining rates of return on Treasury bills and issues of federal agencies. Thus, savings institutions have more money to invest in construction and mortgage loans. Mortgage rates are eased somewhat, and terms of loans are made more attractive. These changes help stimulate a housing boom. As business in general picks up, the reverse process takes place, and a shortage of funds develops for housing. Credit stringency was an important factor leading to the decline in home building in 1956–1957, 1960, 1966, 1969–1970, 1973, and 1980–1981; credit availability was a major factor leading to an upturn in 1958, 1961, 1967, 1971, and 1983. The 1973–1975 recession was severe enough that home building continued to decline even after credit again became available to more than meet needs.

Other Factors.   The level of activity in housing is affected in part by the level of activity in other areas of construction. During recessionary periods in general economic activity, some workers and equipment, made idle because of declining industrial and commercial building, move into the housing field, thus making a housing boom possible. As business activity picks up, the reverse process takes place. Thus, the short cycle in housing is partially out of phase with the general cycle in economic activity and generally reaches a peak early in the recovery period.

Building costs apparently are also one of the factors that should affect the demand for building and thus the building cycle, but studies indicate that no direct relationship is evident. Costs usually move independently of changes in building activity, and such relationship as does exist indicates that building activity causes changes in building costs rather than vice versa. The relationship between the income to be obtained from a building and the cost of the building, however, is an important factor when determining the level of construction.

AGRICULTURAL CYCLES

Fluctuations in agriculture are directly related to cycles in general business, since the purchasing power of farmers forms an important part of the pattern of expenditure for consumer goods. The income of nonfarm consumers also has a substantial effect upon the demand for and prices of agricultural products. However, some cycles in this field have a pattern different from that of the business cycle.

Two-Year Cycles in Agriculture

There is a tendency toward a two-year cycle in the price and production of many crop products. If extremely favorable weather makes it apparent that there will be an unusually large crop of some commodity, such as soybeans, the price will drop to a relatively low level. This price will prevail during most of the crop season and will be the one in existence when new sowings are made. As a result of the low price, some farmers may not feel that it is profitable to raise soybeans and will cut the acreage for this crop. As a consequence, the price in the next crop year, barring other factors of major importance, will tend to be higher. Because this higher price will prevail when another crop is sown, the tendency is to sow a larger acreage, which will lead to a larger crop and lower prices, in turn followed by a smaller crop and higher prices. Thus, there is a tendency toward two-year zigzag cycles.

The cycles result from the way in which supply and prices interact. Supply reacts to the price of a commodity only after a lag, because the production period of most agricultural commodities is more or less fixed. Thus, an exogenous factor, such as the weather and the reaction of producers to prices and profit prospects, leads to cycles in production. The theory that describes such production-price cycles is called the *cobweb theorem*.

The Cobweb Theorem

The business cycle is a phenomenon that occurs over a span of time. Most economic activity, such as production and consumption, usually cannot take place instantaneously. A development may inspire a change in some action, but usually only with a time lag.

Perhaps the clearest example of the way time lags are responsible for fluctuating economic behavior is to be seen in the cobweb theorem. It is demonstrated here on a micro level of analysis, although it also has applications in macroeconomic theory.

In the usual price theory, quantities supplied and demanded of a particular commodity are said to be determined by the current price of that commodity and certain other factors. The analysis is termed "static," because it is essentially timeless. Implicitly, all activity takes place instantaneously. In dynamic analysis, the fact that an activity takes time is considered, and the results are sometimes considerably different from that flowing from static theory.

In the case of the cobweb theorem, it is assumed that the quantity demanded of a good depends upon the price existing at the time the decision to purchase is made. The notation is $Q_{D_t} = f(P_t)$. (In words: quantity demanded in time period t is a function of price in period t.) This isn't always the best assumption, but for many—perhaps most—commodities, it is accurate. It is on the supply side where the most obvious time lag would seem to exist—the production lag. In the cobweb theorem, the assumption is made that the decision of the producers to sell different amounts of the good depends on the price of that good at some critical time in advance of the time of sale. A farmer, for example, must decide early in the spring how many acres of land will be devoted to the production of a certain crop that will be harvested in the fall. The amount of fertilizer and water and other care to be applied must also be determined. In any event, these decisions that determine the quantity that will be produced must be made in some time period before the sale can take place. In other words, $Q_{s_t} = f(P_{t-1})$. (Quantity supplied in period t is a function of the price of the product in period $t-1$.)

Figure 5-1 has been drawn with the supply function slightly steeper than the demand function (ignoring the signs). We can suppose that the example is potatoes, and because of a severe drought last year, the current price (P_0) is above the equilibrium price (P_E). Potato farmers and potential potato growers, observing this relatively attractive price, decide to produce relatively large quantities of potatoes $Q_{s(1)}$. When

Figure 5-1   The Cobweb Theorem

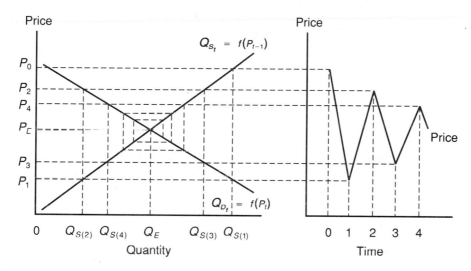

this size crop comes on the market, however, buyers of potatoes will be willing to purchase the entire crop only if the price falls considerably, namely to P_1. P_1, being a price at which little or no profit can be expected, will induce farmers to plan on smaller crops next spring. Many will shift to more promising crops. Thus, the output in time period 2 will be expected to be just $Qs_{(2)}$, a very small output, which, when it is grown and harvested, will bring the higher price (P_2). That higher price will induce a larger output ($Qs_{(3)}$) in the next time period, which, in turn, can be sold only at the lower price, (P_3), and so on. A cycle is in operation, represented on the conventional time diagram on the right side of Figure 5-1. If we were to plot the output figures, they would be inverse to the price figures; that is, when price is high, output is low, and vice versa.

The cyclical process shown in Figure 5-1 is a convergent cycle, so-called because the variables converge toward equilibrium. If the reader will experiment a bit with different shapes of the demand and supply schedules, it will be discovered that if the demand curve is steeper than the supply curve, the result will be an explosive cycle, that is, one in which price and quantity move farther away from equilibrium each time period. If the two curves are drawn with the same slope, the cycle will be one of constant amplitude. When both functions are relatively steep, price will fluctuate widely, and the output cycle will be within a more narrow range; whereas if both curves are relatively flat, the greatest fluctuation will be in output, and the price variation will be mild.

In most industries, considerable qualifications to this simple framework would be necessary to make a realistic picture; but in spite of these, the general theory goes a long way toward explaining many of the cycles that do exist in particular products. One of those qualifications is the ability to store the commodity, but the higher the cost of storage, the closer does the cobweb theorem approach reality. Closely connected with storability is the existence of speculation in the market for the commodity. The extreme swings in price would probably be evened out where a well-developed futures market exists. Perhaps the most important qualification to the theory is the questioning of the hypothesis that the decision to produce is based blindly on present price instead of the more realistic (but impossible to discover) expected future price. Where government sets a minimum or maximum price or where noncompetitive conditions hold, further qualifications are necessary.

Hog and Cattle Cycles

In those fields in which the cycle of production is longer, this same tendency will lead to a longer cycle. One of the best examples is in the hog market, although cattle and other animal markets show the same general pattern. The production and slaughter of hogs has a tendency to move in a series of cycles that are three to four years in length and have been longer. These cycles did not exist during the World War II period, but have since redeveloped. These cycles were due in a significant degree to variations in corn production and the relative price of corn and hogs before the period of government price support and storage programs that helped to stabilize corn prices. In recent years, these cycles have been due primarily to the reaction of hog producers to prices received for hogs. However, they have been longer than the two-year agricultural cycles because of the time required to produce hogs for market. The number of hogs slaughtered in any year is determined by the number of sows that were bred in the preceding year. The spring pig crop, which is marketed from September to March, was born six to nine months previously from sows bred ten to thirteen months previously. The same time relationships hold for the fall pig crop, which is marketed from April to August.

This cycle can be explained as follows. Assume that in the first period under consideration hog slaughter is low, causing relatively high hog prices, and that the pig crop is about normal in size. Slaughter will tend to increase and prices to decrease to more normal levels in the second period as the normal pig crops come to market. The attractiveness of hog prices in period one, however, leads to an above-normal pig crop in period two. In the third period, this larger pig crop will produce a larger than normal rate of slaughter, and prices will drop. The pig crop has, however, declined because of the normal prices in period two. As a result, slaughter and prices will return to normal levels in period four. However, the pig crop will be below normal because of the relatively low prices for hogs in period three, and forces are set in motion to start the cycle over again. These relationships may be summarized as follows:

Period	Slaughter	Prices	Pig Crop
1	Below normal	High	Normal
2	Normal	Normal	Above normal
3	Above normal	Low	Normal
4	Normal	Normal	Below normal
5	Below normal	High	Normal

Hog cycles are somewhat more complicated than the above example, because hog production is governed to some degree by the relative price of corn and other feeds. The production of hogs and the production of corn are interrelated, since most of the corn crop is fed to hogs and corn makes up about two-thirds of the feed used in pork production. Before government price support programs helped stabilize the price of corn, changes in the corn crop had a significant effect on hog production, and to a large degree, the cycle was a corn-hog cycle. This relationship became significant in 1973 and again in 1988–1989, when the price of corn and other feed grains soared because of poor weather in the United States during the 1972 and 1988 fall harvests. Also, poor crops abroad led to the unprecedented demands for feed grains for export.

The corn-hog ratio is the hundredweight price of live hogs divided by the price of corn per bushel. One interpretation is that this ratio is the number of bushels of corn it costs the farmer to produce 100 pounds of pork. For example, if the hundredweight price for hogs is $45, and the price of corn is $3 per bushel, the corn-hog ratio is 15. Suppose that, on the average, it takes twelve bushels of corn to bring a pig up to 100 pounds. This means that for $36 worth of corn ($3 × 12) pork that can be sold for $45 can be produced, a gross gain of $9. (Notice that if the price of corn is $3, either the farmer can buy the corn for that price or, if the farmer grows the corn, it could be sold for $3; either way, the cost is the same.) Thus, the higher the corn-hog ratio, the more profitable it is to keep hogs on the farm putting on weight for longer periods. But the law of diminishing returns works here as well: the larger (or older) the hog gets, the more corn it takes to put on additional weight, so at some point, it is no longer profitable to keep feeding, and the hog is sent to market.

The process works in the following way. An unusually large corn crop, which results from large plantings or unusually good growing conditions, depresses the price of corn. This low price of corn makes it cheaper to raise pigs and thus has a tendency to lead to larger pig crops. The most significant price is not the absolute price of corn, but the relative prices of corn and hogs, or the ratio of the price of hogs to the price of corn. When corn is cheap relative to the price of hogs, the pig crop is increased; and when corn is high, the pig crop is decreased. This leads to cycles, similar to those described above, that are based on the price of hogs without regard to the relative price of corn and hogs. The situation is, however, somewhat more complex and less regular since weather conditions could change the expected yields from a given acreage of corn that was planted on the basis of past price relationships.

The cycle also is accentuated by variations in the length of time that hogs are kept on the farm instead of being sent to market. When the corn-hog ratio is such that it is more profitable to feed hogs and sell them than to sell corn, hogs are kept on the farm and fed longer than normally, and supplies of pork become even smaller than expected on the basis of the pig crop, and prices rise further. When the point is reached at which feeding is no longer profitable, slaughter increases and prices are reduced to more normal levels. At present, there is still some tendency for this to happen, but it has been reduced materially by more stable corn prices and by relatively stable prices of feed supplements. The hog cycle may be further complicated and increased somewhat in length by the number of sows that are available, which is, in part at least, determined by earlier price situations and price expectations.

Since the production period in raising cattle is considerably longer than that in raising hogs, the cattle cycles are of longer duration, having ranged from nine to sixteen years since 1900. They are also less regular, since the longer the time involved, the greater the possibility of outside factors affecting the cycles. Recent cycles have been shorter than earlier ones probably because of better market information. The number of cattle on farms reached a peak of 132 million in 1975. The number declined to 111 million by 1979 and thereafter rose slowly to 115 million in 1983, declining to 102 million in 1987.

Coffee Cycle

One of the longest of the agricultural cycles occurs in the coffee market, because it takes seven years from the time a coffee tree is planted until it yields coffee beans. Therefore a cycle of fifteen or more years occurs in this field. The cycle is no longer as clearly visible as it was some years ago because of the interference of the Brazilian and other governments in the coffee market. However, the cycle has continued to affect coffee production and prices up to the present time.

SEASONAL VARIATIONS

Seasonal fluctuations in the volume of business are important in many fields. We shall see why and look at a few examples next.

Causes of Seasonal Fluctuations

Various factors are responsible for these fluctuations in economic activity that take place during the course of the year. Some segments of the economy are affected by the yearly cycle in weather. Other segments are affected by the customs of society, especially those related to holidays. A third factor that causes data to have seasonal fluctuations is our present calendar.

Climate. Climatic conditions influence the periods of growth and the time of maturity of crops and, also to a lesser extent, of livestock, and thus economic activity related to agriculture undergoes pronounced seasonal fluctuations. The weather also determines the period of ice-free navigation on various bodies of water and thus influences economic activity. For example, during part of the winter, iron ore cannot be transported on the Great Lakes. In some parts of the country, the weather influences operations in the lumber industry and in some types of open-pit mining. In many places, climatic conditions necessitate different types of clothing during various seasons of the year, and the manufacture and sale of clothing show the influence of these variations. In addition, the weather determines which sports are carried on at different times and so leads to a seasonal variation in the sale of sporting goods.

Customs. Human institutions and customs also materially affect the volume of business during the course of the year. Holidays materially affect retail activity, and these influences extend into the manufacturing field. There is a demand for various types of merchandise for Christmas gifts, for new clothing at Easter, for fireworks on the Fourth of July, and so on.

The Calendar. The construction of our calendar gives monthly economic data the appearance of seasonal variations greater than the actual fluctuations in business. The months of the year vary from twenty-eight to thirty-one days. February, for example, is usually almost 10 percent shorter than January, and April is about 3 percent shorter than March. In addition, February has several holidays that make the comparison of the volume of business in February with that in January or March less valid as an indication of the true course of economic activity. The number of Saturdays or Sundays in a month also causes variations, and the changing date of Easter affects sales differently in different years.

Seasonal Patterns in Production

For purposes of analysis, industries with definite seasonal influences may be divided into four basic groups.

The first group consists of those industries in which the supply of raw materials is subject to large seasonal variations, while the demand for the finished product is fairly constant. Most food products are included in this classification.

The second group includes those industries in which the supply of raw materials and the demand for finished products are both subject to large seasonal fluctuations. Examples of this type of industry are the natural fibers, such as cotton and wool, in which there are definite seasonal fluctuations in the demand for the finished products as well as in their production.

The third category embraces industries that make use of raw materials with a fairly constant supply but have a final product that is subject to fairly large seasonal variation in demand. The automobile industry and industries related to it, such as the petroleum industry, are characterized by this type of fluctuation.

The fourth group includes primarily the construction industries, in which there is no necessary seasonal fluctuation in the manufacture of raw materials or in the demand for the final product.

The seasonal movements in some of the component activities of each of these four groups will be presented in general outline, and some comments will also be made on seasonal variations in phases of economic activity other than production.

The supply of most food products is subject to seasonal fluctuations, while the demand is not, but the seasonal fluctuations work out differently in such fields as wheat and flour, dairy products, and fruits and vegetables.

Group 1—Wheat and Flour. The harvesting of wheat is subject to pronounced seasonal fluctuations, since it usually occurs between early June in the southern part of the wheat belt in Texas to late July in the northern wheat belt. Flour milling shows a peak in activity in October but not nearly to the same extent as that for the harvesting of wheat in the summer. There is some peak in flour consumption during the winter months, which is in turn much smaller than that in flour milling.

Stocks of wheat are held at various places—on the farms, in elevators, and at flour mills. The stocks of flour, on the other hand, are usually carried by wholesalers and large bakers.

Group 1—Dairy Products. Seasonal fluctuations in dairy products differ somewhat from those in wheat, because the industry is dealing with a perishable commodity. Since more milk is produced in summer than in winter and since the demand for it shows little seasonal variation, the surplus of summer milk is converted into evaporated milk, butter, and cheese, which are then stored until needed. The summer peak in the production of durable dairy products has a tendency to lower their price and thus produces a seasonal price fluctuation.

Group 1—Fruits and Vegetables. The demand for raw fruits and vegetables would probably remain fairly stable throughout the year in the absence of a seasonal cycle in production. However, their consumption is much heavier in summer, when the supply is large, than it is during other times of the year. The development of the frozen-food industry has tended to smooth out the seasonal fluctuation in consumption, but this industry also has a pronounced seasonal fluctuation, since the freezing of food can be done only at the height of the season for each crop. This is also true of other forms of food processing, such as canning and drying; however, a large part of the seasonal adjustment in this field is made by consumers who adjust their purchases to fluctuations in production.

Group 2—Cotton. In some ways, the seasonal pattern in the movements of raw cotton and cotton textiles is similar to that in the field of wheat and flour milling. The consumption of raw cotton by textile mills does not have any major seasonal fluctuation, even though the harvesting of cotton is concentrated in four months. As in the case of flour, the seasonal peak in mill activity occurs several months after the peak in the harvesting of the crop. This is the case because the farmer carries large and seasonally variable stocks of raw cotton. Cotton differs from wheat, however, since there is also a pronounced variation in manufacturing based upon the seasonal demand for cotton goods. This seasonal variation increases in amplitude the closer one gets to the final consumer. In other words, the retailer has a larger seasonal fluctuation than the wholesaler, and the wholesaler a larger seasonal variation than the manufacturers in the various stages of production.

Group 3—Automobile Field. There is some seasonal variation in the demand for automobiles. This variation is based partly on the demand during the summer for cars for vacation travel and partly on the dates new models are introduced. Increased summer demand is normally more pronounced in low-priced cars than in higher-priced cars. Seasonal variation is smaller for trucks than passenger cars.

Seasonal variations in automobile purchases lead to seasonal variations in the manufacture of automobiles, because the industry, as a rule, does not stock many cars. These variations are carried over somewhat into automobile-parts production, spark plugs and tires for example, and to a lesser degree for the manufacture of upholstery materials and sheet steel. Seasonal variation also affects the gasoline field, but this variation is more in the amount of stock rather than in production, since the technical characteristics of the industry make it difficult to vary production in response to demand.

Group 4—Construction. In the construction field, rain and low temperatures impede activity and thus lead to fluctuations in building activity. Many seasonal problems have been overcome in the construction of major buildings, such as industrial plants and office and apartment buildings, but in the construction of smaller buildings and in the laying of roads and highways, some activity is still impossible in severe weather. Most contractors carry no stock of raw materials, and consequently, there are extreme fluctuations in the demand for materials as building speeds up in the summer months.

The peaks for all materials do not come at the same time, since some are needed early in the process of construction and others somewhat later. Dealers stock some materials, but a large part of the task of meeting fluctuations in demand falls upon manufacturers, especially in the case of heavy equipment. Production of most construction materials proceeds at a much more even rate than the shipment of these materials; the production of some types of brick and lumber is, however, subject to changes in the weather.

LONG WAVES IN ECONOMIC ACTIVITY

A theory of long waves in economic activity was developed by N. D. Kondratieff while he was director of the Conjuncture Institute of Moscow. He studied various series, such as indexes of wholesale prices in England, France, and the United States; bond prices in France and England; and series on wages, foreign trade, and the output of coal, pig iron, and lead.[3] After smoothing out all cycles with a duration of nine years or less from the late 1780s to 1920, he found two complete long waves and the beginning of a third. The first wave began in the late 1780s, rose until 1810–1817, and then declined until 1844–1851. The second wave began at this time, rose until 1870–1875, and then declined until around 1890–1896. The third wave began at this time with an expansion that continued to the period from 1914 to 1920 and then began to decline.

Until quite recently, economists have been skeptical about the existence of such long waves. The earlier dismissal of the Kondratieff cycle was based on the observation that only data expressed in money terms seemed to correspond in a general way to Kondratieff's long waves, whereas no such relationships were found in physical production series. However, the behavior of the economy in the 1970s and early 1980s has encouraged reconsideration of the issue through theoretical and empirical studies. Several studies have been conducted by the System Dynamics Group at MIT.

J. J. van Duijn, a Dutch economist, has recently produced an impressive scholarly work on Kondratieff cycles.[4] He stresses that in order to determine whether or not the cycle is an empirical reality, it is

---

3. Kondratieff's best known article has been translated and his results summarized in "The Long Waves in Economic Life," *Review of Economic Statistics* (November 1935). A more recent translation was done by Guy Daniels, *The Long Wave Cycle* (New York: Richardson and Snyder, 1984).

4. J. J. van Duijn, *The Long Wave in Economic Life* (London: George Allen and Unwin, 1983). Much of the work in this section leans heavily on this study.

Table 5-2

Chronology of Kondratieff Waves

	1st Kondratieff		2nd Kondratieff		3rd Kondratieff		4th Kondratieff	
	Lower	Upper	Lower	Upper	Lower	Upper	Lower	Upper
Kondratieff (1926)	ca. 1790	1810/17	1844/51	1870/75	1890/96	1914/20		
Van Duijn	—	—	1845	1872	1892	1929	1948	1973

Source: Van Duijn, *Long Wave*, p. 63.

first necessary to adjust for the underlying trend. For this purpose, his choice is the S-shaped growth curve suggested by Rostow.[5] Then the cycle is traced as changing rates of growth so that a contraction is not necessarily a decrease in the level of activity, but could be simply a decrease in the rate of growth. He also believes that industrial production series should be on a per capita basis in order to neutralize the effects of population growth.

Van Duijn concludes that the Kondratieff cycle does exist in real production as well as in price-related series. Each of the countries he studied exhibits its own peculiarities due to its own particular growth history. However, when the data of the several countries are combined to form a world industrial production series, he finds a clear long-wave chronology, as seen in Table 5-2. Except for the upper turning point of the third Kondratieff cycle, van Duijn's chronology is very close to that of Kondratieff. Note also that van Duijn dismisses the first Kondratieff cycle as one that cannot be confirmed.

Causes of Kondratieff Waves

If a long-wave cycle is determined to exist by empirical study, what are the explanations of it? Many causes have been alleged, and it may very well be that all of them have played a part in the cyclical process at different historical times.

Many early economists stressed the discoveries of gold as the major causal events initiating the upswing of Kondratieff cycles. It is true that a fairly good correlation between major gold finds and the long waves

---

5. W. W. Rostow, *The Stages of Economic Growth*, 2d ed. (Cambridge: Cambridge University Press, 1971).

can be observed. Furthermore, there is a certain amount of logic to the relationships involved. If gold serves as money during a depression period when prices of goods and services are low, it makes sense to prospect for and increase production of gold, since the value of gold would be relatively high. At that time, wages and other costs of production would be relatively low, making gold production more profitable. But as the supply of money increases, prices of other commodities increase as well, reducing the profitability of the gold industry and thus reducing the output of gold. The decrease in the rate of increase in the supply of money results in recession.

Since gold no longer holds such a pivotal role in the economy, this explanation can hardly be used for contemporary cycles. Money and monetary policy could be advanced as an explanation, but then it would be necessary to explain why money should have such a long cycle, which would be very difficult to do.

Before World War II, wars were frequently cited as the causal factor in the Kondratieff waves. The preparation for and the conduct of war require large expenditures by government and result in expanded aggregate demand and production. Following wars, there were depressions as economies readjusted to peacetime conditions. World War II did not conform to this pattern, as the postwar experiences of the United States and Europe were very different.

An extremely long cobweb cycle for agricultural raw materials has been postulated as the explanation of the Kondratieff cycle. The essential feature of this view is that there are rigidities in the ability of agricultural suppliers to increase or decrease production. During the upswing of the cycle, agricultural prices will rise as demand increases, but supply cannot increase commensurately. It takes a long time for the industry to increase its capital stock. First, it must be determined that the increased demand is permanent, land must then be acquired and adapted to production, the needed machinery must be produced, and so on. Overproduction of these raw materials will happen when the rate of increase in demand slows down; prices will fall, and a downswing of the cycle will ensue. It also takes a long time to eliminate the excess capital.

The causation theories that continue to get support are those dealing with investment in fixed capital and those stressing innovations. Investment in infrastructure, including such industries as steel, shipbuilding, highways and bridges, and transportation, is seen as especially critical to the explanation of long waves. These usually require very large financial commitments and long time spans to complete production. Partly because of these features, decision makers will wait a long time before determining that demand in the industry will be sufficiently long-lasting to warrant increasing capacity. It tends to be the case that investments in heavy industry take place worldwide at about the same time, and worldwide overcapacity results. Since the capital is highly durable, it takes many years for the excess capacity to be eliminated, but when it is, prices rise and investment is again encouraged in many countries. Overinvestment takes place, which means that excess capacity again leads to depressed conditions in the industry.

Simulation Model of the Long Wave

J. W. Forrester and the MIT System Dynamics Group have constructed a dynamic simulation model of the economic long wave. It is basically a multiplier-accelerator model (which will be treated in Chapter 9) stressing investment in the infrastructure industries. The major contribution of this model to the theory of long waves is the elucidation of the long lags involved in the production process. These are physical lags, structural lags, and decision-making lags. The model "relates capital investment; employment, wages, and workforce participation; inflation and interest rates; aggregate demand; monetary and fiscal policy; innovation and productivity; and even political values."[6] Self-ordering plays an important role in the explanation, where the capital goods producers, in order to satisfy the needs of capital users, must first produce the capital to be used in the production of the capital to be used in the later stages of production. Professor van Duijn refers to this as the bootstrap structure.

An example of a simulation from this model is seen in Figure 5-2. The model generates these cycles without the use of shocks to the system, such as gold discoveries, wars, or innovations. It is propelled by constant growth rates in population, technological progress, per capita government activity, and a small amount of random noise.[7]

Innovations and the Long Wave

Empirically, the close association between major innovations and Kondratieff cycles has been well enough documented that most analysts include innovations as a major explanation. Joseph Schumpeter

6. John D. Sterman, "An Integrated Theory of the Economic Long Wave," *Futures* (April 1985): pp. 104–105.
7. Ibid., p. 112. Professor Sterman has developed "STRATEGEM 2: A Microcomputer Simulation Game of the Kondratiev Cycle," which is available from the System Dynamics Group at MIT.

Figure 5-2 _____ Simulated Real GNP, 1800–1984

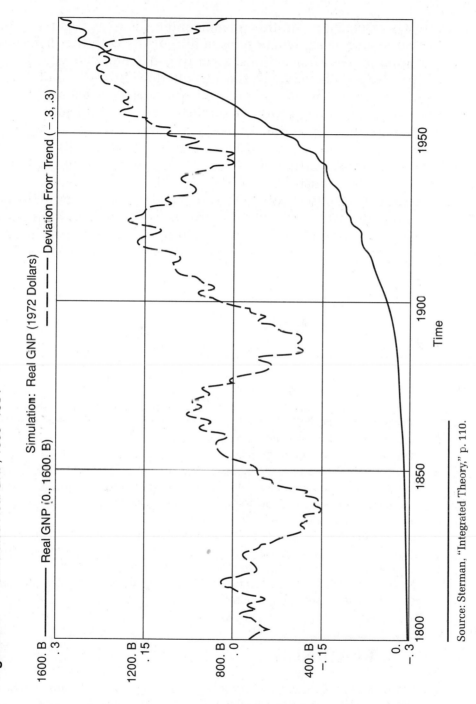

Source: Sterman, "Integrated Theory," p. 110.

is always associated with this phenomenon, since his was the definitive work, and he explains cycles of all lengths with the invention-innovation process. Innovations, according to Schumpeter, can be put into five classes, which require the introduction into the economic system of (1) new products, capital goods, or consumer goods, (2) new methods of producing goods or services, (3) new markets for commodities, (4) the exploitation of newly discovered sources of raw materials, and (5) new means of organizing business activity. The first Kondratieff wave, starting in the late 1780s or early 1790s, was associated with the industrial revolution and the development of steam power, iron, and cotton textiles. The second wave, beginning in the late 1840s, was during the growth of railroads, and the third Kondratieff cycle, starting around the turn of the 20th century, involved the automobile and electricity. The Schumpeterian system is covered in some detail in Chapter 14.

QUESTIONS

1. What is the nature of the building cycle?
2. How are building cycles related to business cycles?
3. Account for the length and severity of the building cycle.
4. Why is the short cycle in housing usually out of phase with the cycle in overall economic activity?
5. Draw three charts depicting the cobweb cycle as (a) convergent, (b) explosive, and (c) of constant amplitude.
6. Describe the hog and cattle cycles. What accounts for them? How has the situation changed since the introduction of agricultural programs to stabilize feed prices and to provide better market information?
7. Why is the coffee cycle one of the longest on record?
8. Briefly describe the factors that lead to seasonal fluctuations in business.
9. Identify the four basic types of seasonal variations in production industries.
10. Briefly analyze the Kondratieff theory of long waves.
11. How is the economy affected by having various cycles in different phases of their cycle as well as the business cycle?

READINGS

Abramovitz, Moses. *Evidences of Long Swings in Aggregate Construction Since the Civil War*. New York: National Bureau of Economic Research, Inc., 1964.

Burns, Arthur F. "Long Cycles in Residential Construction," *Economic Essays in Honor of Wesley Clair Mitchell*. New York: Columbia University Press, 1935.

Forrester, J. W. *Business Structure, Economic Cycles, and National Policy*. Cambridge, MA: MIT System Dynamics Group, D-2245-2, 1975.

Freeman, Christopher, ed. *Long Waves in the World Economy*. Wakefield, NH: Longwood Publishing Group, 1984.

Frumkin, Norman. *Tracking America's Economy*. Armonk, New York: M. E. Sharpe, Inc., 1987.

Goldstein, Joshua S. *Long Waves, Prosperity and War in the Modern Age*. New Haven, CT: Yale University Press, 1988.

Kondratieff, N. D. "The Long Waves in Economic Life." *Review of Economic Statistics* (November 1935).

———. *The Long Wave Cycle*. Translated by Guy Daniels. New York: Richardson and Snyder, 1984.

Long, Clarence D., Jr. *Building Cycles and the Theory of Investment*. Princeton, NJ: Princeton University Press, 1940.

MacAuley, Patrick H. "Economic Trends in the Construction Industry, 1965–80." *Construction Review*, U.S. Dept. of Commerce (May–June 1981), pp. 7–10.

Moore, Geoffrey H. *Business Cycles, Inflation and Forecasting*, 2d ed. Cambridge, MA: Ballinger, 1983.

Solomon, Solomos. *Phases of Economic Growth, 1850–1973: Kondratieff Waves and Kuznets Swings*. Cambridge: Cambridge University Press, 1987.

Sommers, Albert T. *The U.S. Economy Demystified*. Lexington, MA: Lexington Books, D. C. Health and Company, 1985.

Sterman, John D. "An Integrated Theory of the Economic Long Wave." *Futures* (April 1985), pp. 104–131.

———. "A Behavioral Model of the Economic Long Wave." *Journal of Economic Behavior and Organization* (1986), pp. 17–53.

U.S. Bureau of the Census. *Seasonal Analysis of Economic Time Series*. Washington, D.C.: United States Government Printing Office, 1978.

Valentine, Lloyd M. "Kondratieff Cycle," in Douglas Greenwald, ed. *Encyclopedia of Economics*. New York: McGraw-Hill Book Co., 1982, pp. 579–581.

van Duijn, J. J. *The Long Wave in Economic Life*. London: George Allen and Unwin, 1983.

NATIONAL INCOME ANALYSIS

Part 1 of this book examined the historical record of business cycles and other changes in economic activity. Periods of prosperity and depressions that have occurred in the United States were studied without a great deal of discussion of the causal factors at work.

In Part 2, we will focus directly on attempts to explain the way an economy operates and the crucial interrelations that exist that bring about the observed behavior of the system. Chapter 6 introduces the main aggregate economic concepts. These concepts, as they have been used in economic theory, are defined, and the statistical measurements of these concepts and their published sources are given. Considerable consideration is given to how accurately the statistical counterparts approximate the theoretical variables.

Chapter 7 is an overview of the neoclassical school's version of aggregative economic analysis. This is the theory that began to attract so much popular attention and debate in the late 1970s and the 1980s as "supply side economics" and "monetarism." The emphasis in the current research and literature in macroeconomics on "the new classical" and rational expectations theory are extensions of the classical model. Chapter 7 also serves as a necessary background for much of the discussion of business cycle theory in Part 3, since this was the standard framework for most of the authors mentioned therein.

PART 2

Chapters 8 through 12 develop the Keynesian and Neo-Keynesian system of thought that has dominated aggregative economic thought and policy since the 1930s. Chapter 8 reviews the basic Keynesian national income determination model, including operation of the multiplier. The model is presented verbally, graphically, and in the arithmetic of period analysis. Chapter 9 considers the nonconsumption elements of the market for goods and services, primarily investment, but also government expenditures and net foreign demands for the national output. The equilibrium situation of the aggregate market for goods and services is summarized in the *I-S* curve.

Chapter 10 covers the monetary aspects of the economy: the theory of money supply behavior, the demand for money, and the equilibrium situation in the money market summarized by the *L-M* curve. In Chapter 11, the goods market and the money market are then integrated, and the level and the importance of inflation and deflation are considered.

Chapter 12 deals with a number of important topics in national income analysis, such as taxation, alternative theories of consumption, the stagnation thesis, and economic growth theories.

AGGREGATE ECONOMIC CONCEPTS AND MEASUREMENTS

In this chapter we will discuss the meanings of the most important terms and concepts used in aggregative economics, the interrelationships among them, and the statistical approximations that have been developed to measure them. The most fundamental of these terms that are subject to misunderstanding are wealth, income, production, consumption, saving, investment, capital, and profit.

It is worth considerable effort to understand the meaning of these terms, since a great deal of confusion and disagreement are the result of different understandings of what a particular term involves. It would be very easy to give a half dozen different concepts embodied in such words as "capital," "consumption," "saving," "profit," and many other words that belong in the popular domain and are used by economists. Since each of these concepts represents a significant feature of economic behavior, they need to be incorporated in our analysis. We should use qualifying adjectives or explain which notion we have in mind, and we often do, but frequently, we simply hope that the concept intended is clear from its context.

One of the serious stumbling blocks in the understanding of economic relationships is the confusion between flow variables and stock variables. In popular discourse this distinction is often glossed over, but in the study of economics it should not be. For instance, the word "investment" to an economist is strictly a flow, and the associated stock is called "wealth" or "capital." A frequently used analogy is that of water in a bathtub. There is a flow into the tub from a faucet, and an outflow through a drain. When the inflow is greater than the outflow, the stock of water in the tub is increased; when the outflow exceeds the inflow, the stock decreases; and when the inflows and outflows are equal, the stock remains the same. A *flow variable* can be measured only over a period of time, while a *stock variable* can be measured only at a point in time. Similarly, saving is an act that can be performed only over a period of time. The associated stock that results from saving is popularly called "savings." A better practice would be to refer to the accumulated stock simply as "assets" or "wealth."

In national income analysis, as in most of economics, there is usually a difference between the definition of a term designed to permit its measurement and the definition designed for purely analytical purposes. For example, the idea of consumption has been the "using up" of goods and services, or the destruction of utility or value. Since this notion is measurable only in the aggregate, we usually find it expedient to define consumption as purchases by households for current use. Sometimes, the two definitions are very close, but under other conditions, they diverge so much that if a person's analysis is based upon the one idea and the empirical evidence is based upon the other idea, that person may be seriously misled. The definition of consumption as the destruction of value implies that it would be desirable to minimize consumption. However, there is the other side of consumption, which is the receipt of utility by the consumers. The goal of the economy, of course, is to maximize the utility of its people.

Another source of difficulty is that economics deals with transactions, and every transaction has two sides—the buyer's and the seller's. Sometimes, our terms put the emphasis on the one side, and it is forgotten that forces are also operative on the other. For this reason, newspapers frequently report a wave of selling on the stock exchange and ignore the "wave" of buying that is necessarily taking place simultaneously.

A long debate over the equality of saving and investment culminated in the warning of the necessity of distinguishing between planned or intended magnitudes on the one hand and actual or measured magnitudes on the other. It is always necessary to be clear in discussion and analysis whether one is referring to planned magnitudes, which are usually of most interest but difficult, if not impossible, to measure, and actual magnitudes, which are usually of somewhat less interest, but are measurable.

CONCEPTS OF PRODUCTION, INCOME, CONSUMPTION, SAVING, AND INVESTMENT

In this section, we will look first at the most fundamental meaning of these terms. *Production* is the creation of value. Thus, any activity that results in someone being willing to pay more for a good or service than the value of the materials used has produced something. Defined in this way, production is the same thing as income, since all the value created must be allocated or distributed to someone. Under capitalistic principles, the rule is that the income will be distributed to the factors of production responsible for the production. In a complex process, this is difficult to achieve, but we have a large body of thought, called income distribution theory, that attempts to explain this allocative process. It is customary to use the income categories of wages, rent, interest, and profit, even though a rigorous theoretical division of them is not possible. From the viewpoint of the business sector, wages, rent, and interest are elements of cost, and profit is a pure residual between total revenues from the sale of goods and services and contractual costs. From the factor-owner side, wages are the payment for human services, and rent, interest, and profit are derived from the provision of the services of property.

In the aggregate, *income* is the amount of goods and services that could be consumed during a period of time, leaving the stock of wealth of the society at the end of the period the same as it was at the beginning.[1] It thus follows that income is equal to consumption plus capital accumulation, where *consumption* is defined as the destruction of value, and *investment*, or capital accumulation, is the act of adding to the stock of capital or wealth. *Saving* is the process of not consuming as much as was produced during the time period.

If we let Y stand for national income, which we have said is equal to aggregate production, and let C stand for consumption, or destruction of value, the difference between them is what was produced and not destroyed. The result of destroying less than the amount produced is an increase in the stock of physical goods. This is what we defined to be investment, which we label I. But, by definition, this is also saving, S, since it is the amount by which income exceeds consumption. Therefore, $Y \equiv C + I$ and $Y \equiv C + S$, or $I \equiv Y - C$, $S \equiv Y - C$, and $I \equiv S$.

We should keep in mind that these fundamental notions are what we are really interested in, since questions of economic welfare, growth possibilities, and so on must be evaluated in these real terms. However, there are some analytical and statistical reasons for using approximations to these concepts. Consumption, for example, cannot be accurately measured, so we use, as a close estimate, expenditures on consumer goods and services. The difficulty here is defining *consumer goods and services*, and we do this by including all goods and services

---

1. This notion of income is discussed in J. R. Hicks, *Value and Capital*, 2d ed. (London: Oxford University Press, 1946), Chapter 24.

purchased by households that are normally destroyed during the period in which we are interested. Likewise, we cannot discern which part of the expenditures of government add to the society's wealth and which part is currently consumed for present utility. In this case, we devote our attention simply to government expenditures *in toto*. Expenditures by business units on capital account becomes our measure of investment.

Production

In the study of the business firm, we are used to thinking of production as simply the output to be sold. But in the aggregate economy, we are interested in the output of all the firms. There would be a great deal of multiple counting if the sales of all firms were simply added up, since the output of any single firm will necessarily include the value of the output of other firms that were used as intermediate goods. It can also occur that the goods and services sold in the current period were produced in an earlier period and therefore should not be counted as part of current production.

Production is defined as the creation of value (or utility) during a specified time period. The *value added* of a particular producing unit is the value of its sales minus the purchases from other firms, minus any decrease in inventory or capital depreciation during the period of measurement. Notice that our definition of production makes no reference to the physical processes. Much production does involve a physical conversion in which the final product may have little resemblance to the raw materials, as is the case in manufacturing and agriculture. But production takes place even when no physical or tangible commodity is involved. For example, by increasing the demand for the product and hence its price or value measure, advertising can create value or utility, as can storing crops, holding art works, playing music, or transporting goods.

The sum of all of the values added in all of the producing units of the economy equals the net output or production of that economy. That same total can be found by ignoring all of the intermediate production steps and counting only the "final" product values. By *final goods* we mean those that will be neither resold nor embodied in other goods or services. This is required to avoid double counting.

The measurement of the amount of final goods and services produced and bought can be taken from the sides of either the sellers or the buyers. The buyers are classified into sectors called households, governments, business, and the rest of the world; that is, buyers located in other economies. The expenditures by these four sectors are called, respectively, consumption, government expenditures, investment, and net foreign exports.

Income

We stated earlier that production and income are equal, since income is defined as the earnings of the factors of production for their contribution to the current production. An individual may think of his or her income as simply the inflow of funds, but it must be remembered that our concern here is with the income of the aggregate of all individuals. *Thus, the receipt of any funds that are not associated with production in the current time period will not be counted as income.* For example, a person who receives a gift, gambling winnings, an inheritance, a welfare benefit, stock market gains, proceeds from a robbery, and so on, may think of those funds as income, but in each case, the income of someone else is reduced by the same amount so that no net income is involved. These are all examples of "transfer payments." Conversely, an individual may not consider living in an owner-occupied home, food taken from the garden or farm, the use of a refrigerator or automobile, or the value of a do-it-yourself project, as income; but they are. Since these services are not money receipts, they are called "income in kind." Notice that in these and in all other cases, income and production are simultaneous occurrences.

NATIONAL INCOME ACCOUNTING VERSUS BUSINESS ACCOUNTING

A system of accounting is necessary to understand fully the nature and extent of changes that take place in aggregative economic activity. Such a system was developed by the National Bureau of Economic Research (NBER) and is now under the National Income Division of the U.S. Department of Commerce, Bureau of Economic Analysis (BEA). Data on national income and related items are published regularly in the *Survey of Current Business* and are available for 1929 to the present.

The principles on which national income accounting is based are similar to those used in accounting for an individual business. At present, the data that are available regularly on a national basis are income and production data, since no detailed balance sheet for the total econ-

Table 6-1

Income Statement of the ABC Corporation for 1991

Sales		$35,000,000
Less cost of goods sold*		15,000,000
Gross profit		$20,000,000
Wages and salaries	$9,000,000	
Social Security taxes	500,000	
Taxes, other than Income	1,000,000	
Depreciation	1,000,000	
Interest	500,000	
		12,000,000
Net income before taxes		$ 8,000,000
Income taxes		2,400,000
Net income after taxes		$ 5,600,000
Dividends paid		2,000,000
Added to retained earnings		$3,600,000

*Purchases from other firms.

omy is regularly prepared. Furthermore, since information on many phases of economic activity is not available in income statement form, national income figures are developed by estimating some of the items used.

The form in which national income data are presented is different, however, from that used in reporting business income. The usual income statement of a firm begins with a statement of gross sales from which expenses of various types are subtracted to arrive at the net profit or loss. Such a statement is illustrated in Table 6-1. This form of the income statement can be revised somewhat to show the identity between current receipts from sales on one side and the allocations of these receipts on the other. An income statement so revised is shown in Table 6-2.

Production—that is, value added—in this firm is its sales ($35 million) minus its purchases from other firms ($15 million) minus depreciation ($1 million), which equals $19 million. The earnings or income of the individuals supplying factor services to the firm is also $19 million, which includes wages and salaries, $9 million; Social Security taxes, $500 thousand; taxes, other than income, $1 million; interest, $500 thousand; corporate profit taxes, $2.4 million; dividends, $2 mil-

Table 6-2

Income Statement of the ABC Corporation for 1991

Allocations of Sales Receipts		Receipts from Sales	
Goods and materials		Sales to Co. A	$ 5,000,000
purchased from other firms	$15,000,000	Sales to Co. B	10,000,000
Wages and salaries	9,000,000	Sales to Co. C	15,000,000
Social Security taxes	500,000	Sales to other	
Taxes, other than income	1,000,000	companies	5,000,000
Depreciation	1,000,000		
Interest	500,000		
Corporate profit taxes	2,400,000		
Dividends	2,000,000		
Undistributed profits	3,600,000		
	$35,000,000		$35,000,000

lion; and undistributed profits, $3.6 million. The tax amounts and the undistributed profits are included because these amounts have been earned, even though they have not been received by the factor owners.

An income-expenditures-production statement can be visualized for the economic system by aggregating the information found in the statements of all the producing units. Table 6-3 is such a (simplified) consolidated statement. Notice that sales of intermediate goods and

Table 6-3

Consolidated Income–Expenditures–Production Statement

Uses	Sources
Wages	Sales to households = Consumption
Rent	Sales to governments = Government
Interest	expenditures
Profit (includes capital consumption	(Net) Sales to the rest of the
allowance)	world = Exports minus imports
	Sales to business units on capital
	account plus increase in
	inventory = Investment (including
	replacement expenditures)

INCOME = EXPENDITURES

Table 6-4

Sources of GNP, 1989
(In Billions of Dollars)

Personal consumption expenditures	**3,470.0**
Durable goods	473.6
Nondurable goods	1,122.6
Services	1,874.1
Gross private domestic investment	**777.1**
Fixed investment	747.7
Nonresidential	512.5
Structures	145.1
Producers' durable equipment	367.4
Residential	235.2
Change in business inventories	29.4
Net exports of goods and services	**−50.9**
Exports	624.4
Imports	675.2
Government purchases of goods and services	**1,036.7**
Federal	404.1
National defense	302.8
Nondefense	101.3
State and local	632.5
GROSS NATIONAL PRODUCT	$5,233.2

Source: *Economic Report of the President, 1990.* Data are preliminary.

services among firms have been canceled from both sides of this statement except for that portion that is added to the stock of capital or
inventory.

The right half of the statement measures the total production in the
economy during a period of time by measuring final sales. The Department of Commerce publishes its estimates of these magnitudes in
the form shown in Table 6-4. The total is called the *gross national product* or GNP.

Sources of GNP—Definitions

Since forecasts of aggregative economic activity are frequently
made by estimating gross national product from the sales or sources
side of the statement, it is desirable to define each of these terms more
precisely.

Personal consumption expenditures, as the term is used in national income accounting, consist of the purchases of goods and services at market value by individuals and nonprofit institutions and the value of food, clothing, housing, and financial services received as income in kind. Although they do not include the purchase of dwelling units, which are classified as capital goods, they do include an estimate of the imputed rental value of owner-occupied houses.

Gross private domestic investment includes capital goods that are newly produced by private business and nonprofit institutions; all private new dwellings, including those acquired by owner occupants; commissions arising in the sale and purchase of new and existing fixed assets (mainly real estate); and the value of the change in the volume of inventories held by business.

Net exports of goods and services are the net differences between exports and imports of goods and services that have taken place in international transactions, excluding transfers under military grants. They measure the excess of exports of goods and services over imports of goods and services, net transfer payments from the U.S. government to foreigners, and net personal transfer payments to foreigners.

Government purchases of goods and services consist of the net purchases of goods and services by governmental bodies, except the acquisition of land and the current outlays of government enterprises.[2] Thus, this item comprises general governmental expenditures for the compensation of employees, purchases from business (net of sales by government of consumption goods and materials), net government purchases from abroad, and the gross investment of government enterprises. It excludes transfer payments, government interest, and subsidies to business, loans, and other financial transfers. These items are excluded because they do not represent payments to the factors of production for current production. Government interest payments are put into this category because much of the government debt has arisen out of war expenditures that are not, in the usual meaning of the word, productive. Private interest payments are included in the selling price of goods because they are one of the costs involved, representing a payment to capital used in production, and, therefore, they are included in the total of government purchases of goods and services.

---

2. The purchase of land is excluded, since it is a national resource on which productive resources were not expended. The current outlays of government enterprises are excluded, since these do not involve purchases of goods but payments to the factors of production to produce goods and services sold to the private sector. The value of these goods and services is included at the time of sale.

Charges against GNP—Definitions

The left half of Table 6-3 represents charges against GNP in that these payments to factor owners constitute the charges or costs of producing the goods sold on the right-hand side. These charges, from the point of view of the people of the economy, are their incomes. The Department of Commerce reports these estimates in the form shown in Table 6-5.

Most of the factor payments making up the national income categories are self-evident, but additional comments on some of them may be in order. As the term is used in national income accounting, *supplements to wages and salaries* include such items as employer contributions for social insurance, contributions to private pension and welfare funds, compensation for injuries, doctors' fees, pay for the military reserve, and a few other minor items.

Proprietor's income in unincorporated businesses is shown as one sum, since it is not ordinarily broken down on the books of such enterprises into wages of management, rent, interest, and profit. An inventory valuation adjustment is made in arriving at the income figure for this sector of the business community. Such an adjustment is necessary, because, under most accounting systems, profits are taken inclusive of inventory profits or losses due to price changes, whereas only the value of the change in the physical quantity of inventories is considered in national income accounting.

The *rental income of persons* consists of the monetary earnings from the rental of real property, the imputed net rentals to owner occupants of nonfarm dwellings, and the royalties received from patents, copyrights, and rights to natural resources.

Corporate profits are measured without a deduction for depletion charges and exclusive of capital gains and losses, neither of which is related to the production of goods and services. Intercorporate profits are eliminated, and the net receipts of dividends and profits from branch offices abroad are added. An inventory valuation adjustment is also made for corporations. It includes the profits of stock life insurance companies and mutual financial institutions.

Net interest includes all interest accruing to the nation's residents, except interest payments from the government and interest paid by consumers. Such payments are not included in the concept of national income, because they do not add to the value of goods and services, since most government debt has arisen out of military expenditures, and consumer expenditures are not considered productive. An item of imputed interest is added, which consists of the value of financial

Table 6-5

Uses of GNP, 1989
(In Billions of Dollars)

Compensation of employees	3,145.4
Wages and salaries	2,632.0
Supplements to wages and salaries	513.4
Proprietors' income with inventory valuation and capital consumption adjustments	352.2
Rental income of persons with capital consumption adjustment	8.0
Corporate profits with inventory valuation and capital consumption adjustments	298.2
Profits before tax	287.3
Profits tax liability	129.0
Profits after tax	158.2
Dividends	122.1
Undistributed profits	36.2
Inventory valuation adjustment	− 18.5
Capital consumption adjustment	29.4
Net interest	461.1
NATIONAL INCOME	4,265.0
Business transfer payments	31.8
Indirect business tax and nontax liability	416.7
Less: Subsidies less current surplus of government enterprises	9.1
Statistical discrepancy	− 23.4
CHARGES AGAINST NET NATIONAL PRODUCT	4,681.0
Capital consumption allowances with capital consumption adjustment	552.2
CHARGES AGAINST GROSS NATIONAL PRODUCT	5,233.2

Source: *Economic Report of the President, 1990.* Data are preliminary.

services received by individuals from banks and other financial institutions that render financial services free of charge rather than pay interest on balances on deposit and make specific charges for services rendered. Also included is imputed interest on reserves held for individuals by life insurance companies and similar financial intermediaries.

As stated above, aggregate production is identically equal to aggregate income. In Table 6-5, however, it is seen that what the Department of Commerce calls Gross National Product is significantly greater than what it calls National Income (by some $968.2 billion). An explanation is called for. First, GNP is a larger concept than our definition of aggregate production, because it includes all production of plant and equipment without subtracting the amount of plant and equipment destroyed in the production process during the year. To the extent that capital is destroyed in producing goods and services, the value of the capital has been transferred, so to speak, to the produced goods. That amount of value was not produced during the year in question. For example, if a farmer harvests 1,000 bushels of corn after having planted ten bushels of corn, the production of corn during the year would be 990 bushels. Likewise, if 100 lathes are worn out in producing widgets this year, and 100 new lathes are produced during the year, total production should be just the value of the widgets. There has been no addition to the stock of capital.

Net national product (NNP) is GNP minus *capital consumption allowances*. Net national product comes closer to our notion of aggregate production, but has the shortcoming of depending on a very crude approximation of depreciation or capital consumption. The figure for capital consumption allowances is not necessarily very close to the true amount of capital consumption. So while NNP is a better welfare concept, GNP is more accurately measurable. Another reason for the greater popularity of the GNP figure is the belief that it may be more closely related to employment demand than is NNP, though it is not necessarily so.

NATIONAL INCOME

GNP and NNP are estimates of aggregate production or income valued at *market prices* of goods and services. The accounting term *national income* is an estimate of the aggregate output or income valued at *factor prices*. This income concept focuses on income *earned* in producing current output, as opposed to income received, be it disposable or any other criteria.

Again referring to Table 6-5, it can be seen that there is a quantitative difference between net national product and national income. The clue to this difference is that NNP (and GNP) is measured at output prices and national income is measured in input (or factor) prices.

Since the data are gathered from different sources and from a different perspective, one would expect a *statistical discrepancy*—and there always is. However, the substantive reasons for the difference between NNP and national income are accounted for by the existence of *business transfer payments, indirect business taxes and nontax liabilities,* and *subsidies less current surplus of government enterprises.*

Business Transfer Payments

Receipts from business firms to individuals for which the recipient has made no contribution to current production are called *business transfer payments.* Examples of these are pensions to retired employees, scholarships, robberies, bad debts, and gifts. The value of these payments is covered by the revenues of the firms, so they are included in the price of the product and therefore are also included in the calculation of NNP. However, they are not a part of national income since the owners of the factors of production were not compensated to the extent of the transfer payment.

Indirect Business Taxes and Nontax Liabilities

Those taxes or fees paid to governments that are assumed to affect the price of the product are *indirect business taxes.* Included in this category are sales taxes, excise taxes, property taxes, license fees, fines, and so on. (Income, or corporate profit taxes are direct taxes, and it is assumed that they do not affect the price of the product.) Since indirect business taxes are included in the price of the product, the NNP is affected. However, no factor owners receive income from this portion of the value of the product, so indirect business taxes are subtracted from NNP to arrive at national income. For example, if a package of cigarettes retails for one dollar, the value of the product (NNP) is one dollar, but if the sales and excise taxes are forty cents, the suppliers of services and materials to the cigarette industry would earn only sixty cents (national income) per pack.

Subsidies Less Current Surplus of Government Enterprises

A *subsidy* is a payment by government to producers, whereas a *transfer payment* is a payment to nonproducers. With a subsidy, income earned in the production process is greater than the value of the product produced. For example, suppose the market price of peanuts is ten dollars per bushel, and the farmer is paid a one dollar subsidy per bushel. The farm income from the production of one bushel of peanuts is $11 (national income), but the value of the output is just $10 (NNP). Thus, subsidies are added to NNP to arrive at national income.

The surpluses of government enterprises are combined with subsidies in the national income accounts because they are, in a sense, opposites. A good example is the Tennessee Valley Authority (TVA) and the sale of electricity. The electricity is sold at its market value, but the income earned in its production is only wage income. The TVA does not pay interest, rent, or profit to the public. The difference between the TVA's receipts from the sale of electricity and its wage bill and payments to other firms is absorbed by the U.S. government. Thus, the surplus of government enterprises is subtracted from NNP to arrive at national income.

PERSONAL INCOME

For some purposes, a somewhat different concept of income than the one we have been using is valuable. This concept, called *personal income* by the Department of Commerce, is described as income *received* by households. Recall that national income is income earned in current production. This means that personal income differs from national income to the extent that some income received by households is not earned in production during the current time period, and some income earned is not received. The items included by the Department of Commerce that are earned in current production (and therefore included in national income, NNP, and GNP) but not received by households are as follows: (1) *Contributions for social insurance* by both employers and employees are considered to have been earned by workers, but none of those earnings are received by the households during the accounting period. (2) Similarly, *wages accrued* (earned) during the current year, but not paid during the current year, are deducted from national income. This would arise, for example, if the last day of the year would fall on Thursday, and payday would be on Friday, or if there were a payments lag such that paychecks were based on income earned in the week or month preceding the current one. On the other hand, at the beginning of the year, the opposite situation would arise, so that this circumstance is always a trivial item.

The receipts of households during the current accounting period that have not been earned in this period are *transfer payments by government and by business*. Thus, these two items are added to national income to get personal income.

Profit and interest present somewhat more complex situations. Dividends are the portion of corporate profits that are received by stockholders. The difference between corporate profits and dividends is the amount not received by households (that is, undistributed profits and corporation income taxes) although it has been earned. Thus, the BEA (Bureau of Economic Analysis) subtracts *corporate profits* and adds *dividends* when calculating personal income from national income.

Personal interest income includes interest received by households from business and government. Part of this is made up of transfer payments (for example, interest on the national debt and interest on consumers' debt to business). The account *net interest* is interest paid by business firms on debt presumed to be incurred in adding productive facilities. For this reason, net interest is included in national income (as well as NNP and GNP). The BEA adds personal interest income to national income and subtracts net interest (since it is already included in national income) to get the transfer payment portion of interest, which is then added to national income to arrive at personal income.

Table 6-6 summarizes the relationships among GNP, NNP, national income, personal income, and one additional concept, *disposable personal income*. Disposable personal income is simply personal income minus personal tax and nontax payments, a concept of considerable interest in analyzing consumer behavior.

GROSS DOMESTIC PRODUCT (GDP)

We have stated that the national income and the national product are conceptually identical amounts. However, some of the income earned in production within a country accrues to foreign workers or suppliers of other factor services. Thus the output in a country may differ from the income earned by its residents.

This is the basis for the distinction between the concepts of the Gross National Product and the Gross Domestic Product (GDP). While GNP is based on the output and earnings attributed to the *residents* of the nation (whether in the country or in other countries), GDP is based on the output and income of the geographic territory of the country

Table 6-6

Relation of GNP, NNP, National Income,
Personal Income, and Disposable Income, 1989
(In Billions of Dollars)

Gross national product		5,233.2
Less:	Capital consumption allowances with capital consumption adjustment	552.2
Equals:	Net national product	4,681.0
Less:	Indirect business tax and nontax liability	416.7
	Business transfer payments	31.8
	Statistical discrepancy	−23.4
Plus:	Subsidies less current surplus of government enterprises	9.1
Equals:	National income	4,265.0
Less:	Corporate profits with inventory valuation and capital consumption adjustments	298.2
	Net interest	461.1
	Contributions for social insurance	479.3
	Wage accruals less disbursements	0.0
Plus:	Government transfer payments to persons	600.3
	Personal interest income	657.8
	Personal dividend income	112.4
	Business transfer payments	31.8
Equals:	Personal income	4,428.7
Less:	Personal tax and nontax payments	648.7
Equals:	Disposable personal income	3,780.0

Source: *Economic Report of the President, 1990*. Data are preliminary.

(whether the income and production are attributed to residents or foreigners). In other words, GDP is GNP minus the production originating in other countries.

For example, if you are an American working in Saudi Arabia, your output and income would be included in the GNP of the United States. However, it would not be included in the GDP of the United States. Similarly, if you own stocks or bonds of a British corporation, the dividends or interest payments you receive would be included in this country's GNP but not in its GDP. Of course, the inverse also holds, namely, that incomes earned by foreigners in the form of wages, rents, interest, and profits are not counted as part of the U.S. GNP, but are included in the U.S. GDP.

In the United States, the difference between the GNP and the GDP is quite small. However, in other countries of the world, the distinction can be considerable. For an extreme example, in 1984, the GNP of Kuwait was 58 percent larger than its GDP, due to its large earnings from investments abroad.[3] Whereas the U.S. Department of Commerce does virtually nothing with the concept of GDP, for most international agencies such as the United Nations, the International Monetary Fund (IMF), the World Bank, and the Organization for Economic Cooperation and Development (OECD), the GDP figures are most frequently used.

WEALTH

Despite the great importance of wealth in influencing activity in an economy and its value as a measure of welfare, no adequate estimates of wealth on a national or sectoral level are constructed.[4] The practical difficulties of measurement are immense. Nevertheless, the idea of wealth is extremely important, and economists regularly use proxy (substitute) variables to approximate wealth or changes in wealth.

The definition of wealth is simple: wealth is defined as any tangible thing of monetary value. It must be tangible because wealth is a stock (as opposed to a flow) concept. It must have monetary value in order to be measured.

The nature of any piece of wealth (its particular characteristics, its special productive capabilities, and the like) depends on what has occurred in the past—how intensely and in what ways the wealth has been used, the changes that have been made over time, and so on. At the instant of measurement, however, the piece of wealth is whatever it is at that moment, and its value depends strictly on expectations regarding future prospects. The original cost of production is completely irrelevant. (This is one of the most difficult of all lessons in economics.) The value of anything is the anticipated future net benefits to be derived from its ownership discounted to the present moment to reflect that (1) future benefits (which might be money earnings, but could be subjective utilities with monetary values placed on them) are worth less than the same benefits at present, and (2) the further into the future the benefits are, the less their value. This calculation, which is called

---

3. Calculated from data in the World Bank publication, *World Development Report, 1984* (New York: Oxford University Press, 1984), pp. 219, 223.

4. Martin Gainsbrugh stated, "The lack of a current and continuing set of wealth and balance sheet estimates is perhaps the most serious omission in our current system of economic intelligence," in "Measuring the Nation's Wealth," *The Economic Accounts of the United States: Retrospect and Prospect*, a supplement to the *Survey of Current Business* (Washington, D.C.: United States Government Printing Office, July 1971), pp. 72–73.

Table 6-7

Hypothetical Personal Balance Sheet

Assets			Liabilities and Net Worth		
Financial assets	Cash (currency, coin, demand deposits)	$ 1,000	Mortgage on home	$ 40,000
	Savings accounts	$ 6,000	Broker's loan	$ 3,000
	Gov't. bonds	$ 4,000	Dept. store debt	$ 700
	Corporate bonds	$ 2,000	Auto loan	$ 2,000
	Common stock	$ 14,000	Total liab.	$ 45,700
	Insurance (surrender value)	$ 20,000		
Real assets	Home	$ 60,000		
	Furnishings	$ 9,000	Net worth	$338,300
	Automobiles	$ 5,000		
	Other personal items	$ 13,000		
	Present value of myself	$250,000		
			Total liabilities and net worth	
	Total assets	$384,000		$384,000

the present value determination, is demonstrated more rigorously in Chapter 9.

For most analytical purposes, the economic value of human beings (human capital) should be included as a part of the individual's wealth and, therefore, also as a part of national wealth. The reason for sometimes excluding human wealth is that, in general, it is not marketable. All income flows from wealth, either human or property wealth. On the other hand, wealth arises out of income (production) that has not been consumed—what earlier was called investment (which is equal to saving)—and, as noted, the value of wealth depends on expected future income. The measurement of wealth starts at the level of the household or individual. The individual's balance sheet might resemble Table 6-7.

An individual's wealth is his or her net worth. For the individual, wealth includes financial assets and real assets; for the society as a whole, however, only real wealth (plus net claims on other societies) is included. The reason, of course, is that financial assets owned by individuals are offset by financial liabilities of other individuals. Corporations are intermediaries. The net worth of a corporation is already included in the assets of the individuals who own the shares of the firm. Thus, the sum of the net worth of all individuals would be equal to the value of all the real wealth of the society—the land, the buildings, the capital equipment, inventories, and household goods.

A question that has not been completely resolved in the calculation of wealth is whether money should be included. If the society uses a full-bodied money, that is, a commodity such as gold, silver, or wheat, there would be no question that it would be wealth. However, the question would still remain of whether it should be valued at its value as a commodity or at its value as money. To the individual owning any kind of money, it is surely wealth, but fiat money (noncommodity money) is a liability of either the government, the central bank, or private commercial banks. Most economists conclude that money that is a liability of the government or central banks (called outside money) is a part of wealth. Their reasoning is that while this money is a liability, it need never be paid off nor (usually) must interest be paid. Demand deposits in commercial banks (called inside money) are usually not included in wealth.[5]

Money performs such tremendously important functions in the economic system that its real value must also be great. But if the stock of money were to double, for example, would we all be better off in real terms? Money has total utility, but its marginal utility may be nil. It may be best to act as if the real value of money is already embodied in the real value of all the physical wealth of the society.

In some analyses, economists separate the private sector from the government sector, noting that while the government has liabilities that are ultimately the public's, the public acts as if the liabilities were not its concern. On the other hand, the individuals or firms who hold these government liabilities as assets treat them as they would any other assets. For example, when the government issues a bond, this establishes the necessity of interest payments and repayment of principal in the future, possibly requiring higher taxes in the future. Thus, while the bond is a part of the bondholder's wealth, the expected increase in future taxes reduces everyone's current net worth. The point here is that people do not act as if their liabilities had increased, but rather as if their assets had increased because they have more government bonds and feel they are not directly responsible for interest or repayment.

---

5. Among economists who do include demand deposits as part of wealth are Boris Pesek and Thomas Saving. See *Money, Wealth, and Economic Theory* (New York: The Macmillan Company, 1967).

PRICE LEVEL COMPLICATIONS

The national income and product accounts and their component parts must be measured in dollar values in order for any summations to be made. Everyone recognizes that some distortion of the significance of the figures can occur if changes in the price level take place. For example, if it is observed that GNP has increased, it cannot be known whether the increase was entirely due to (1) a change in the output of goods and services, (2) a change in their prices, or (3) some combination of changes in output and prices.

Price indexes are attempts at measuring the degree to which prices in general (or prices in a grouping of commodities) have changed. If an estimate of the price level change can be made, then an estimate of the amount of change in the real variables can be made.

Before discussing the construction of price indexes, it may be advisable to mention some of their shortcomings, since misinterpretation seems to be rampant in the world, especially with respect to the media's reporting of price index changes. While it is valuable to have a good price index, a perfect one is inconceivable. Any price index should, therefore, be used with caution, and an awareness that "the price level" may not be accurately reflected by the price index.

One significant problem with price-level estimations is that all the commodities in one time period are never exactly the same as the commodities produced, purchased, and used in another time period. This is known as the quality change problem, and it becomes more serious with the length of the time period over which an index is used. For example, although we may use the same words to describe certain goods our parents bought (such as automobile, razor blade, or paint), the vast majority of those same goods are quite different today. Since most manufacturers constantly strive to improve their products, we should expect continual quality enhancement. In many cases, the changes are subtle, qualitative improvements that defy any attempts to rigorously quantify; yet, we would know that if we currently pay the same price for a gallon of paint as we paid five years ago, the price per quality unit of paint has therefore gone down.[6] Where it is possible to quantify quality improvements (or quality deterioration), the constructors of index numbers do attempt to make those adjustments.

---

6. An interesting experiment has been suggested that you might like to try: Get a copy of a mail order catalog, such as that of Sears, Roebuck & Co., of ten years ago and ask yourself whether you would prefer to make all of your purchases from that catalog at prices listed there or from the current issue at current prices.

Two opposing approaches can be taken to the quality problem. One approach is to insist upon using the identical or nearly identical product whose price is to be included in the index. The problem with this method is that buyers will tend to purchase the product with improved quality, and over time, the product in the index may become one that is no longer significant in the consumers' budgets. In addition, the products replacing it are not included in the index.

The second approach is to continually change the composition of the commodities included in the index so that the ones currently more important are in it. The difficulty with this approach is that comparisons of the prices of essentially different goods and services at two different points in time become practically meaningless. Besides, this approach would be prohibitively expensive. Therefore, the Bureau of Labor Statistics is forced to compromise and use both approaches. Most economists seem to agree that the quality issue and its handling lead to an upward bias in the price index with the degree of bias estimated at 0.5 to 1.5 percent. In other words, if the Consumer Price Index rose 0.5 percent to 1.5 percent in a year, the conclusion would be that, excluding all other factors, the price level had remained approximately constant.

Another significant problem with price indexes that also results in an upward bias is the fixed weight problem. Since prices of different commodities vary at differing rates and in different directions, even when prices in general move in one direction, relative prices change. It is an article of faith with economists that when relative prices change, buyers will demand more of the products whose relative prices have fallen and less of those whose relative prices have risen. Thus, more importance or weight should be given to the lower-priced (larger quantity) goods and less weight to those whose prices have risen. This is not done, however, when the weights are fixed at earlier base-year figures; using the end-of-period weights eliminates this element of the problem.

As a simple example, consider two substitute commodities with the same base weights, such as butter and margarine. Suppose the price of one rises 50 percent, and the price of the other falls 50 percent. The index including these two goods would show no change, but the true price level has fallen, since people would shift heavily to the lower-priced spread and get more utility with the same income.

The degree of the upward bias caused by changing relative prices in a fixed-weight index is difficult to gauge, since factors other than relative prices determine quantities demanded; but it too has been estimated to range from 0.5 percent to 1.5 percent per year.

A problem that is quite severe at times yet minimal at other times is that of getting data on the actual prices at which exchanges take place. Anyone who has shopped for a new automobile with a trade-in involved will recognize one dimension of the problem. When certain prices are illegal (under price control, for example), it is again difficult to know what prices really are. Secret price concessions, discounts, tie-in sales, and the like all occur at times to bias in some way the price index.

In recent years, an additional obstacle to any attempt to measure general price-level movements has taken on serious proportions. Much of current production is being sold at zero price, and the cost of production is being borne by some marketed good or service. For example, if you were to pay $50 per month for electricity (generated by coal but equipped with anti-pollution devices), you would really be buying some electrical service and some units of cleaner air, water, and landscape. You would also be buying statistical information for the government and a number of other services for yourself and for others. Hence, if the price of the electricity had increased by 10 percent, for example, it would not be clear whether the price of the electricity plus the other services had gone up at all.

This particular bias of price indexes has been important in making the appearance of inflation greater than the fact, especially during the 1970s. The bias is relevant, however, only during the time period that the events (usually, laws) are being phased into the economy. Once they are incorporated into the productive process, no index bias would appear. Another point to note is that no value judgment has been made about the worth of the zero-priced products—the cleaner environment, better health, better information, and so on. Clearly, judgments would differ on the particulars of such goods and services.

USE OF INDEX NUMBERS

One important use of a price index is to interpret the national income accounting figures as to whether any changes are real or simply attributable to price-level changes. The real GNP is equal to the GNP at current dollars divided by the price index. Similarly, real (or constant dollar) consumption is equal to nominal (that is, current dollar) consumption divided by the price index and so on for any economic variable measured in dollar terms.

The GNP in constant and current dollars is shown in Figure 6-1, page 153, for the years 1967–1988 and in Table 6-8 for the years 1950–1988. From these, the reader can discern the degree to which the growth in the nominal GNP has overstated the real increase in economic activity.

In developing index numbers for production or prices, several problems require solutions. One problem is determining the items that are to be included in the index, since it is impossible to include more than a fraction of the universe being studied. A decision must also be made concerning the sources from which the data are to be collected and the methods of collection to insure accuracy and uniformity over a period of time. It is also necessary to determine the relative importance of the various items that have been selected for inclusion in the index and then to assign proper weights to those items. Furthermore, a decision must be made concerning the base year or period for the index. A fairly recent year or period that is reasonably representative of the years covered by the index should be chosen.

It is also necessary to select the method of computing the index number. Two basic methods are available—the aggregative and the average of relatives. A simple example will be used to illustrate the basic principles involved in calculating indexes. Each year, a fruit merchant sells twenty bushels of apples and 500 pounds of bananas. Prices change over the next three years as follows:

Year	Average Price	
	Bushel of Apples	**Pound of Bananas**
1	$1.50	$0.04
2	1.20	0.12
3	0.75	0.16

To obtain a weighted aggregative type of index, the average annual price of each fruit is multiplied by the quantity weight. These products are then added. The values for the second and third years are expressed as percentages of the first or base year, taken as 100. These figures become the index numbers.

Year	Apples	Bananas	Total	Index Number
1	$30	$20	$50	100
2	24	60	84	168
3	15	80	95	190

The same result may be achieved by an alternative method known as the average of relatives type of index number. The first step is to state

Figure 6-1   GNP in Current and Constant (1982) Dollars, 1967–1988

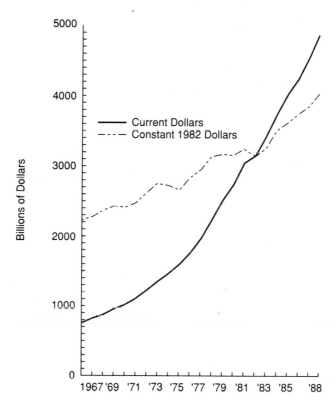

Source: *Economic Report of the President, 1990* (Washington, D.C.: US Government Printing Office, 1990).

the price for each year as a percentage of the price in the base year as is shown below.

	Price Relatives	
Year	**Apples**	**Bananas**
1	100	100
2	80	300
3	50	400

These relatives are then weighted by multiplying them by the total value of each commodity in the base year; that is, $30 for twenty bushels of apples at $1.50 and $20 for 500 pounds of bananas at $.04. The value for the base year is again taken as 100, and the values for subsequent years are expressed as a percentage of the base year.

Table 6-8

Gross National Product
in Current and Constant Dollars, 1950–1989
(Billions of Dollars)

Year	Current Dollars	Constant (1982) Dollars
1950	288.3	1,203.7
1951	333.4	1,328.2
1952	351.6	1,380.0
1953	371.6	1,435.3
1954	372.5	1,416.2
1955	405.9	1,494.9
1956	428.2	1,525.6
1957	451.0	1,551.1
1958	456.8	1,539.2
1959	495.8	1,629.1
1960	515.3	1,665.3
1961	533.8	1,708.7
1962	574.6	1,799.4
1963	606.9	1,873.3
1964	649.8	1,973.3
1965	705.1	2,087.6
1966	772.0	2,208.3
1967	816.4	2,271.4
1968	892.7	2,365.6
1969	963.9	2,423.3
1970	1,015.5	2,416.2
1971	1,102.7	2,484.8
1972	1,212.8	2,608.5
1973	1,359.3	2,744.1
1974	1,472.8	2,729.3
1975	1,598.4	2,695.0
1976	1,782.8	2,826.7
1977	1,990.5	2,958.6
1978	2,249.7	3,115.2
1979	2,508.2	3,192.4
1980	2,732.0	3,187.1
1981	3,052.6	3,248.8
1982	3,166.0	3,166.0
1983	3,405.7	3,279.1
1984	3,772.2	3,501.4
1985	4,014.9	3,618.7
1986	4,231.6	3,717.9
1987	4,524.3	3,853.7
1988	4,880.6	4,024.4
1989p	5,233.2	4,142.6

Source: *Economic Report of the President, 1990.* 1989 data are
preliminary.

	Apples	Bananas		
Year	Price Relatives × 30	Price Relatives × 20	Total	Index
1	3,000	2,000	5,000	100
2	2,400	6,000	8,400	168
3	1,500	8,000	9,500	190

In this simple form, these two methods of calculating index numbers give identical results. However, the methods may be modified in calculating more complicated indexes in which cases the results obtained will differ somewhat.

The method used here is an example of the *Laspeyres index*. The usual equation for a Laspeyres price index is:

$$PI = \frac{\Sigma p_t^i q_0^i}{\Sigma p_0^i q_0^i} \times 100 \qquad \begin{array}{l} t = \text{index year} \\ 0 = \text{base year} \end{array}$$

Table 6-9 shows the work sheet for its calculation. This index is special because the quantity weights are those taken from the base year, so that the index attempts to answer: how much more (or less) would it cost today (that is, in the index year) to buy the same basket of goods actually purchased in the base year? In the above example, we assumed the quantities remained the same in each year, but note that in calculating the Laspeyres index, actual quantities in the index years are irrelevant; they are not used in the calculation at all.

The *Paasche index* asks a somewhat different question; namely, how much more (or less) does it cost today to buy the basket actually bought today compared with how much that same basket would have cost in an earlier (base) year? This index's formula is:

$$PI = \frac{\Sigma p_t^i q_t^i}{\Sigma p_0^i q_t^i} \times 100 \qquad \begin{array}{l} t = \text{index year} \\ 0 = \text{base year} \end{array}$$

A difficulty with the Paasche index is that the quantity weights for the current period must be obtained. Collecting the quantity data can be extremely costly. Since the quantities are constantly changing over time, it is difficult to interpret a series of Paasche index numbers.[7]

---

7. Geoffrey Moore discusses the relative merits of fixed- versus variable-weight indexes, and in an experiment comparing the two approaches, concludes that as a practical matter the difference between the two is negligible. Geoffrey Moore, *Business Cycles, Inflation, and Forecasting*, 2d ed. (Cambridge, MA: Ballinger Publishing Co., 1983), Chapter 18.

Table 6-9

Calculation of a Laspeyres Price Index

Base year ($t=0$)

Good $=i$	Price $=p_0$	Quantity $=q_0$	Total expenditure $=p_0q_0$
Apples	$1.50/bu.	20 bu.	$30
Bananas	$0.04/lb.	500 lbs.	$20
			$\overline{\$50} = \Sigma p_0 q_0$

$$\text{Price index, base year}_0 = \frac{\Sigma p_0 q_0}{\Sigma p_0 q_0} \times 100 = \frac{\$50}{\$50} \times 100 = 100$$

Index year ($t=1$)

Good $=i$	Price $=p_1$	Quantity $=q_0$	Total expenditure $=p_1q_0$
Apples	$1.20/bu.	20 bu.	$24
Bananas	$0.12/lb.	500 lbs.	$60
			$\overline{\$84} = \Sigma p_1 q_0$

$$\text{Price index, year 1} = \frac{\Sigma p_1 q_0}{\Sigma p_0 q_0} \times 100 = \frac{\$84}{\$50} \times 100 = 168$$

Index year ($t=2$)

Good $=i$	Price $=p_2$	Quantity $=q_0$	Total expenditure $=p_2q_0$
Apples	$0.75/bu.	20 bu.	$15
Bananas	$0.16/lb.	500 lbs.	$80
			$\overline{\$95} = \Sigma p_2 q_0$

$$\text{Price index, year 2} = \frac{\Sigma p_2 q_0}{\Sigma p_0 q_0} \times 100 = \frac{\$90}{\$50} \times 100 = 180$$

Bureau of Labor Statistics Producer Price Index

Several indexes are available for measuring changes in prices. One of the most comprehensive is the Producer Price Index of the Bureau of Labor Statistics, formerly called the Wholesale Price Index. This index is based on prices of about 2,800 commodities that are classified into major product groups and numerous subgroups by stage of processing, by durability, and by other special groupings. The Producer Price Index measures price changes in primary markets, that is, at the level of first commercial transaction for each commodity.

For almost all of the items in the monthly index, three or more price quotations are averaged. Detailed specifications are drawn up for each item on which prices are collected. Some of the prices are obtained by mail from individual reports, others from trade journals, a few from boards of trade or commodity markets, and several from federal and state agencies.

Each price used in the index applies to only one day each week, but the day varies for different commodities. The monthly price is the average of the four or five one-day-a-week prices that fall within the month. Indexes for the subgroups are first computed and then the total index is developed from these indexes. When necessary, adjustments are made because of major changes in the specifications of commodities, shifts in the relative importance of sales to different types of purchasers or by different types of sellers.

In using the index, several limitations should be borne in mind. It is not a measure of the general price level or of the purchasing power of the dollar, since it does not include changes in the price of real estate, securities, services, and so on. It does not cover transactions at all levels of marketing. In addition, prices used in computing the index are those prevailing in national markets and are therefore not effective in any specific locality.

Bureau of Labor Statistics Consumer Price Index

The best known and most widely reported index is the Consumer Price Index, or CPI, of the Bureau of Labor Statistics (BLS). Beginning in January 1978, the BLS now publishes two CPIs, one in which the population included is "all urban consumers," and the other that covers "urban wage earners and clerical workers." The all-urban index includes, in addition to wage earners and clerical workers, groups that historically were excluded from CPI coverage such as professional, managerial, and technical workers; the self-employed; the unemployed; and retirees and others not in the labor force. The more comprehensive index is new; the urban wage earners and clerical workers index was initiated during World War I.

The CPIs are published monthly and attempt to measure changes in prices paid for goods and services by the population of consumers included in constructing the index. Table 6-10 shows the indexes from 1970 to 1988 with the major categories as indicated. The BLS publication, *Monthly Labor Review*, publishes the details of price changes for the individual goods and services included in these categories. Additionally, indexes are published for major metropolitan areas.[8]

---

8. For further information about the CPI, a very helpful publication is Alan S. Blinder, "The Consumer Price Index and the Measurement of Recent Inflation," *Brookings Papers on Economic Activity* (Washington, D.C.: The Brookings Institution, Inc., 1980), pp. 539–572.

Table 6-10

Consumer Price Index, 1970–1989 (All Urban Consumers)
(1982–84 = 100)

Year	All Items	Food and Beverages	Housing	Apparel and Upkeep	Transportation	Medical Care	Entertainment	Other Goods and Services	Energy
1970	38.8	40.1	36.4	59.2	37.5	34.0	47.5	40.9	25.5
1971	40.5	41.4	38.0	61.1	39.5	36.1	50.0	42.9	26.5
1972	41.8	43.1	39.4	62.3	39.9	37.3	51.5	44.7	27.2
1973	44.4	48.8	41.2	64.6	41.2	38.8	52.9	46.4	29.4
1974	49.3	55.5	45.8	69.4	45.8	42.4	56.9	49.8	38.1
1975	53.8	60.2	50.7	72.5	50.1	47.5	62.0	53.9	42.1
1976	56.9	62.1	53.8	75.2	55.1	52.0	65.1	57.0	45.1
1977	60.6	65.8	57.4	78.6	59.0	57.0	68.3	60.4	49.4
1978	65.2	72.2	62.4	81.4	61.7	61.8	71.9	64.3	52.5
1979	72.6	79.9	70.1	84.9	70.5	67.5	76.7	68.9	65.7
1980	82.4	86.7	81.1	90.9	83.1	74.9	83.6	75.2	86.0
1981	90.9	93.5	90.4	95.3	93.2	82.9	90.1	82.6	97.7
1982	96.5	97.3	96.9	97.8	97.0	92.5	96.0	91.1	99.2
1983	99.6	99.5	99.5	100.2	99.3	100.6	100.1	101.1	99.9
1984	103.9	103.2	103.6	102.1	103.7	106.8	103.8	107.9	100.9
1985	107.6	105.6	107.7	105.0	106.4	113.5	107.9	114.5	101.6
1986	109.6	109.1	110.9	105.9	102.3	122.0	111.6	121.4	88.2
1987	113.6	113.5	114.2	110.6	105.4	130.1	115.3	128.5	88.6
1988	118.3	118.2	118.5	115.4	108.7	138.6	120.3	137.0	89.3
1989	124.0	124.9	123.0	118.6	114.1	149.3	126.5	147.7	94.3

Source: Department of Labor, Bureau of Labor Statistics.

These indexes are based on the average of 1982–84 as 100. Weights are based on surveys of family expenditures determined by an extensive study of family consumption. Prices are gathered by part-time and full-time employees by means of shopping trips and personal interviews. A few prices, such as those for fuel, are obtained directly from dealers, and electric power rates are obtained from the Federal Power Commission.

Implicit Price Indexes

What index should be used if one is interested in the general price level or the value of the dollar? Most of the readily available price indexes are more or less specific; that is, they measure the price behavior of a particular class of commodities or services, such as farm products, transportation, lumber, or consumer goods. While it is usually the case that when general inflation is taking place, these indexes will also be rising, it is not necessarily so. We need an index that reflects price movements in all segments of the economy.

The best index for overall price movements is constructed by the Department of Commerce and is called the implicit GNP deflator. The deflator itself is found very simply by dividing the actual GNP (GNP in current dollars) by real GNP (GNP in constant dollars) and multiplying by 100. For example, in Table 6-8 on page 154, we have shown GNP in current and constant (1982) dollars. In 1988, actual GNP was $4,880.6 billion and real GNP was $4,024.4 billion, which means the implicit price deflator was 1.213(100), or 121.3. In other words, the general price level rose 21.3 percent from the 1982 average to 1988.

The important thing to understand is the method in which the Department of Commerce constructs the series of GNP in constant dollars. This series is extremely important in its own right, being our best estimate of what we are interested in: namely, the total output of goods and services corrected for price-level changes.

The GNP is broken down into the smallest groupings for which specific price indexes are available. The total output of the particular commodity or group of commodities is then corrected to reflect the price changes in those specific commodities. This yields a figure of output in constant dollars or in base-year prices. If this is done for all the components of GNP, all categories corrected for price changes can be summed to the corrected GNP. The deflators used for the various subgroups are also available in the *Survey of Current Business*.

There are still some shortcomings in this price index. Some gaps remain in that more refined subgroup indexes could be used. Estimates in the government sector, the service sectors, and the construction industries are thought to be particularly subject to error. The index is available only quarterly, and with a lag, so it is not usable for month-to-month or other short-run purposes. Despite these weaknesses, the implicit price index is still clearly superior to any other available index in measuring general price movements.

Another widely used implicit price index is the Personal Consumption Expenditure (PCE) deflator, which, in recent years, has become quite popular due to considerable criticism of the CPI. The quantity weights in the CPI are those of the base period (1982–84), whereas the PCE deflator employs current quantities. It is implicit that in periods of inflation, a baseweighted index will overemphasize the degree of inflation while the current-quantity-weighted index will underemphasize the degree of inflation.[9] The PCE deflator is analogous to the GNP deflator and is simply the PCE in current dollars divided by the PCE in constant (1982) dollars.

Federal Reserve Board Index of Industrial Production

The National Income and Product Accounts figures, when deflated to adjust for price level changes, give some indication of the total volume of production in the economy. A somewhat different and narrower, but more timely and greater detailed, approach is found in a measure of industrial production.

The Federal Reserve Board of Governors has developed the Index of Industrial Production, which includes manufacturing, mining, and utilities. The index is computed for all three areas from 1947 to the present and for manufacturing and mining only from 1919 to 1947. It is available on three base periods: 1957–1959, 1967, and 1977. This index is used extensively by many analysts of business conditions.

The items in the index are grouped by industry and by market. The first industry grouping is by manufacturing, mining, and utilities. Manufacturing is divided into two major subgroups, durable and nondurable manufacturers. Each group is further subdivided as shown in Table 6-11. Index numbers are available monthly for each subgroup, both with and without seasonal adjustment.

---

9. Moore, *Business Cycles*, p. 292.

Table 6-11

Major Groupings in the Federal Reserve Board Index of Industrial Production and Their Relative Importance

Industry Grouping	1977 Proportion		Market Grouping	1977 Proportion
Total Index	**100.00**	1	**Total Index**	**100.00**
1 Mining and utilities	15.79	2	Products	57.72
2 Mining	9.83	3	Final products	44.77
3 Utilities	6.06	4	Consumer goods	25.52
4 Manufacturing	84.21	5	Equipment	19.25
5 Nondurable	35.11	6	Intermediate products	12.94
6 Durable	49.10	7	Materials	42.28
Mining			*Consumer goods*	
7 Metal	.50	8	Durable consumer goods	6.89
8 Coal	1.60	9	Automotive products	2.98
9 Oil and gas extraction	7.07	10	Autos and trucks	1.79
10 Stone and earth minerals	.66	11	Autos, consumer	1.16
		12	Trucks, consumer	.63
Nondurable manufactures		13	Auto parts and allied goods	1.19
11 Foods	7.96	14	Home goods	3.91
12 Tobacco products	.62	15	Appliances, A/C and TV	1.24
13 Textile mill products	2.29	16	Appliances and TV	1.19
14 Apparel products	2.79	17	Carpeting and furniture	.96
15 Paper and products	3.15	18	Miscellaneous home goods	1.71
16 Printing and publishing	4.54	19	Nondurable consumer goods	18.63
17 Chemicals and products	8.05	20	Consumer staples	15.29
18 Petroleum products	2.40	21	Consumer foods and tobacco	7.80
19 Rubber and plastic products	2.80	22	Nonfood staples	7.49
20 Leather and products	.53	23	Consumer chemical products	2.75
		24	Consumer paper products	1.88
Durable manufactures		25	Consumer energy	2.86
21 Lumber and products	2.30	26	Consumer fuel	1.44
22 Furniture and fixtures	1.27	27	Residential utilities	1.42
23 Clay, glass, and stone products	2.72			
			Equipment	
24 Primary metals	5.33	28	Business and defense equipment	18.01
25 Iron and steel	3.49	29	Business equipment	14.34
26 Fabricated metal products	6.46	30	Construction, mining, and farm	2.08
27 Nonelectrical machinery	9.54	31	Manufacturing	3.27
28 Electrical machinery	7.15	32	Power	1.27
		33	Commercial	5.22
29 Transportation equipment	9.13	34	Transit	2.49
30 Motor vehicles and parts	5.25	35	Defense and space equipment	3.67
31 Aerospace and miscellaneous				
transportation equipment	3.87		*Intermediate products*	
32 Instruments	2.66	36	Construction supplies	5.95
33 Miscellaneous manufactures	1.46	37	Business supplies	6.99
		38	General business supplies	5.67
Utilities		39	Commercial energy products	1.31
34 Electric	4.17			
			Materials	
		40	Durable goods materials	20.50
		41	Durable consumer parts	4.92
		42	Equipment parts	5.94
		43	Durable materials n.e.c.	9.64
		44	Basic metal materials	4.64
		45	Nondurable goods materials	10.09
		46	Textile, paper, and chemical materials	7.53
		47	Textile materials	1.52
		48	Pulp and paper materials	1.55
		49	Chemical materials	4.46
		50	Miscellaneous nondurable materials	2.57
		51	Energy materials	11.69
		52	Primary energy	7.57
		53	Converted fuel materials	4.12

Source: *Federal Reserve Bulletin* (June 1989), pp. A49 and A50.

Table 6-12

Federal Reserve Board Index of Industrial Production
by Industry Groupings, 1988
(1977 = 100)

Industry Grouping	1988 avg.
MAJOR INDUSTRY	
1 Mining and utilities	107.5
2 Mining	103.5
3 Utilities	114.0
4 Manufacturing	142.8
5 Nondurable	143.9
6 Durable	142.0
Mining	
7 Metal	93.6
8 Coal	138.2
9 Oil and gas extraction	93.0
10 Stone and earth minerals	140.0
Nondurable manufactures	
11 Foods	142.7
12 Tobacco products	105.4
13 Textile mill products	116.4
14 Apparel products	109.1
15 Paper and products	150.2
16 Printing and publishing	183.8
17 Chemicals and products	152.0
18 Petroleum products	96.0
19 Rubber and plastic products	174.4
20 Leather and products	59.4
Durable manufactures	
21 Lumber and products	137.6
22 Furniture and fixtures	162.0
23 Clay, glass, and stone products	122.6
24 Primary metals	89.4
25 Iron and steel	78.2
26 Fabricated metal products	120.9
27 Nonelectrical machinery	170.7
28 Electrical machinery	180.1
29 Transportation equipment	132.2
30 Motor vehicles and parts	117.4
31 Aerospace and miscellaneous transportation equipment	152.4
32 Instruments	154.4
33 Miscellaneous manufactures	107.1
Utilities	
34 Electric	131.9

Source: *Federal Reserve Bulletin* (January 1990), p. A50.

The first market grouping is by final products and materials. Final products are divided into two groups, consumer goods and equipment (including defense equipment). Consumer goods are further divided into automotive products, home goods, clothing, and consumer staples. Materials are divided into durable goods materials, nondurable goods materials, and energy materials. Each of the subgroups is further divided as shown in Table 6-11. Monthly indexes are available for each of these groups and subgroups, both with and without seasonal adjustment.

Figures for the Index of Industrial Production by industry groupings in 1988 are shown in Table 6-12 on page 162. In weighting the various factors to be included in the index, the importance of the individual series is measured by the value added by manufacture as shown in the Census of Manufactures and Minerals and by annual census surveys and other benchmark data.

Whenever possible, physical production units are used as the basis for measuring changes in production. In about half of the industries included in the index, however, changes are measured by the use of series on worker-hours worked in each field. In order that these series may measure changes in production, it is necessary to adjust them for changes in the output per worker-hour. The use of worker-hour series makes it possible to get a better measure of changes in such fields as machinery, furniture, chemicals, baking, canning, and shipbuilding, where quantity figures are not too meaningful, because the product is not homogeneous, and there is no convenient unit in which output can be directly expressed.

OPTIMUM PERFORMANCE OF THE ECONOMY

Finally, we take up the question of the degree to which the economy is operating at the optimal level. That optimum usually is thought to occur when the human factor of production is employed in the numbers wishing to work, that is, full employment. Thus, the concepts of employment, full employment, unemployment, and their measurements are very important. Another way of looking at the issue is to ask what the capital stock level of utilization is. Here, both the notion of full capacity and the capacity rate become important.

Both the unemployment level and the unused capacity figures are significant from the point of view of the economy producing less than it is capable of producing, and both may be of importance in gauging the degree of inflationary pressures from any increase in aggregate demand. One difference between the two concepts is that the loss of productive activity by humans cannot be captured later, whereas, in some part, the loss of use-time of capital can be made up later.

A much more important difference, of course, is that workers are also human beings who may suffer severe psychological distress from the fact of unemployment, the feeling of worthlessness, familial problems, crime, alcoholism, the feeling associated with accepting charity or welfare, and many other very human concerns, as well as the loss of employment skills and attitudes resulting from disuse.

In summary, when the economy is performing at less than its potential, output is lost and the incomes of both workers and capital owners are reduced or eliminated. In addition, the social impact on the unemployed persons and on the society may be an even more serious consequence of this situation.

EMPLOYMENT, FULL EMPLOYMENT, AND UNEMPLOYMENT

The Bureau of Labor Statistics is an agency within the U.S. Department of Labor. The BLS gathers statistics on the many dimensions of the labor force; its composition in terms of sex, age, race, and other demographic characteristics; the skill and industry composition; and the employed-unemployed status.

The *labor force* is made up of the employed and the unemployed. Considerable debate surrounds the definition of the unemployed. At present, according to BLS rules, persons aged sixteen and over are *unemployed* if they:

1. Did not have a job and thus performed no work at all in the survey period (a full week). (Any work at all classifies a person as employed, regardless of any job-seeking activity.)
2. Actively looked for work sometime during the prior four weeks, as evidenced by the use of one specific job-search method (visited a public or private employment office, visited an employer directly, and so on). Persons on layoff or waiting to start a new wage or salary job within thirty days need not meet the job-seeking requirement.
3. Are currently available for work (excluding temporary illness).[10]

---

10. John E. Bregger, "Establishment of a New Employment Statistics Review Commission," *Monthly Labor Review* (March 1977), p. 15.

There is probably no ideal way to define unemployment statistically. It may depend on the purpose for which the figure is to be used. Thus, if the goal is to measure the hardship suffered by the unemployed, or the need for assistance to individuals or localities, a different definition may be needed than one that is used to judge the impact of fiscal or monetary policy on inflation or aggregative economic activity. In the current measurement, people who have quit looking for work because of despair of not finding a job ("hidden unemployment") are not counted as unemployed nor as a part of the labor force. There are also persons working at jobs below their capacity, such as a graduate engineer pumping gas ("underemployment"). There are many other such issues that indicate that no single concept will be completely satisfactory.

The unemployment figure is often used as the measure of how well the economy is performing, but frequently this is misleading.[11] For example, during the decade from 1967 to 1976, unemployment grew from 3.8 percent of the labor force to 7.7 percent of the labor force; yet, during that same period, employment grew from 74 million to 87 million people. The relevant population grew over this period by about the same percentage (17 percent) as the growth in jobs, but the growth in the labor force was about 20 percent. In other words, the economy was generating new jobs for the new population, but the labor force was growing more rapidly as people who were not previously in the labor market joined it. These new workers were primarily women, whose employment grew from 27 million in 1967 to 35 million in 1976, an increase of 30 percent.

This pattern continued through 1988 and into 1989. Over the decade 1979–1988, the noninstitutional population of the United States increased by 14.2 percent, the labor force increased by 18.2 percent, and employment increased by 18.6 percent, the labor force increased by 18.2 percent, and employment increased by 18.6 percent. Thus, even though unemployment grew from 5,963,000 in 1979 to 6,701,000 in 1988, employment increased by 18,024,000 over the same period, and the unemployment rate fell from 5.8 to 5.5 percent. To keep things in perspective, it should be noted that when the unemployment rate

11. An excellent discussion of the major reasons for the misleading nature of employment-unemployment figures is contained in Stewart Schwab and John J. Seater, "The Unemployment Rate: Time to Give It a Rest?" the Federal Reserve Bank of Philadelphia's *Business Review* (May-June 1977), pp. 11–18.

is 5.5 percent, the employment rate is 94.5 percent. The two rates necessarily sum to 100 percent.

Full employment is an elusive concept that does not have a rigorous definition. Most economists and others consider a condition where about 4 or 5 percent of the labor force is not working as full employment. Even in the most ideal situation, some of the labor force will not be at work during the survey period. Some will have quit a job or been laid off or fired, some will be new entrants or reentrants into the labor market, and some will prefer the alternative of some kind of welfare to gainful employment.

There will inevitably be a period of time during which a worker will be unemployed while looking for a position. The individual looking for employment would want to find the most attractive job in terms of pay, working conditions, challenge, and so on. Since no one has perfect knowledge about the openings available, the unemployed person will have to engage in a time-consuming search process. During this time, the searcher is counted as unemployed even though that person could have had a job. In economic theory, the individual job seeker is viewed as making the marginal comparison between the expected marginal benefits (higher pay, better work situations) and the marginal costs (primarily loss of income during the search). As economic conditions change, the average length of time the search for work continues will also change; and as this time changes, so does the "natural" unemployment figure.

Capital Stock Utilization

The unemployment rate is a measure of the degree of excess capacity of human capital. In general, the higher the unemployment rate, the larger the gap between potential output and actual output. Therefore, the unemployment rate is also a measure of the need for improvement in economic performance.

In a similar way, data on excess capacity in the stock of physical capital measure the rate of unemployment of the existing stock of plant and equipment. Full utilization of either the labor force or the capital stock limits the potential output at any point, but, of course, both the labor force and the stock of capital are expandable over time.

Every month, the *Federal Reserve Bulletin* publishes a table titled "Output, Capacity, and Capacity Utilization," which gives monthly and quarterly seasonally adjusted data for those three variables. The capacity utilization rate is a particularly important factor studied by economic analysts. It not only is one measure of the intensity of depressed or buoyant economic conditions, but also can indicate, along with other information, the likelihood of near-term investment expenditures.

QUESTIONS

1. Explain why the value of final goods production in the whole economy is equal to the sum of the "values added" in all of the producing units of the economy, and in turn, is equal to the incomes earned by all the factors of production.
2. How does the accounting concept of national income differ from gross national product?
3. Explain how each of the following is related to personal income:
   (a) Personal income taxes
   (b) Personal and real property taxes
   (c) Personal saving
   (d) Contributions for social insurance
   (e) Net interest paid by the government
   (f) Government payments to veterans
   (g) Corporate contributions to the American Red Cross
   (h) Dividend payments
   (i) Corporate income taxes
4. Explain how wealth and income are related.
5. Consider whether each of the following is included as a part of wealth of an individual and of the whole society. Explain your reasoning.
   (a) Corporate bonds
   (b) Government bonds
   (c) Corporate common stock
   (d) Houses
   (e) Money
   (f) The shoes you are wearing (if any)
   (g) The shoes in a department store
6. Discuss the difference between "the price level" and a price index.
7. What is the difference between the "cost of living" and the "standard of living" (not discussed in text)?
8. Describe the construction of the GNP deflator.
9. Explain what is meant by the cost of unemployment.

READINGS

Barro, Robert J. *Macroeconomics*, 2d ed. New York: John Wiley & Sons, 1987. Chapter 1.

Sheffrin, Steven M., et al. *Macroeconomics: Theory and Policy*. Cincinnati: South-Western Publishing Co., 1988. Chapters 1–3.

Sommers, Albert T. *The U.S. Economy Demystified*. Lexington, MA: Lexington Books, 1985.

U.S. Department of Commerce, Bureau of Economic Analysis, *Fixed Reproducible Tangible Wealth in the United States, 1925–85*, Washington, D.C.: United States Government Printing Office, 1987.

Young, Allan H. "Alternative Measures of Real GNP." *Survey of Current Business* (April 1989).

Young, Allan H., and Helen Stone Tice. "An Introduction to National Economic Accounting." *Survey of Current Business* (March 1985), pp. 59–76.

CHAPTER

7

CLASSICAL AGGREGATE ECONOMICS

For several centuries, attempts have been made to understand the functioning of the economy, and it is stimulating to realize that there is a great deal yet to be learned. Anyone who is likely to contribute to our further understanding will be a person who has knowledge of the history of economics. A number of past economists were brilliant scholars whose ideas deserve serious study.

This chapter will present the outline of a body of aggregate economic thought known as the "classical model." It is not necessarily a true representation of the views of any individual economist. Rather, it is a synthesis of orthodox economists' theories prior to the publication of John Maynard Keynes' *General Theory*.[1] Many contemporary economists feel that the classical model provides an extremely valuable framework for the analysis of current problems.

In the years following World War II, economic policy decisions demonstrated a growing acceptance by economists, politicians, and the general public of the basic ideas underlying Keynesian thought. The Reagan administration came into office largely on the basis of the disillusionment with those Keynesian prescriptions. The fundamentals of the Reagan economic policy proposals reflected a return to greater acceptance of neoclassical economic thought. The keystones of "Reaganomics" were called "monetarism" and "supply side economics," and these were to be made more effective by minimizing governmental interference with the workings of the economy. As should become very clear in the reading of this chapter, these are ideas consistent with classical aggregate economics.

---

1. John Maynard Keynes, *The General Theory of Employment, Interest, and Money* (New York: Harcourt, Brace & World, 1936).

FUNDAMENTALS OF CLASSICAL THOUGHT

Classical economists held certain fundamental beliefs about the nature of the economy; most importantly, the pervasiveness of competition and the law of diminishing returns. They also assumed that households seek to maximize their utility, and business units consistently seek to maximize their profits.

From these assumptions the following conclusions were reached:

1. Prices and wages are flexible and respond readily to changes in demand or supply conditions.
2. Money is a veil that makes it necessary to look behind activities expressed in money terms to discover the fundamental behavior underlying them. Relative prices are important in directing the activity of the economy.
3. The quantity theory of money explains how the stock of money determines the absolute level of prices—the only important variable determined by money.
4. The total demand for the output of the economy will be equal to the amount of goods and services produced (Say's law).
5. Full employment of labor is assured in the sense that anyone wishing to work at prevailing wages is able to do so.
6. The interest rate is determined by the willingness of households to save and of business firms to invest.
7. The rate of growth of the economy is related to the rates of saving and investment.
8. The size of the population of an area is related to the ability of its economy to support the populace.
9. The economic role of government should be minimal. The government's use of resources can occur only at the expense of private use.

In the pages that follow, the theoretical structure that produces these conclusions will be explained and the ramifications discussed.

SAY'S LAW

Because of the confining interpretation of Say's law, the mainstream of classical economic thinking was not directed toward the study of business fluctuations. The usual explanation of Say's law is that "supply creates its own demand." This means that the total value

of goods produced during a period of time (supply) is an amount sufficient to purchase (demand) all that was produced during the period.
Our national income accounting is based on this law, although in that
connection we usually state it in a slightly different way; namely, the
total income earned in a period by the factors of production is equal
to the total value of all the goods and services produced by those factors
of production. Thus, we speak of Say's law as a truism; supply of and
demand for the total output of the economy are equal by definition.

There is an exciting question that is raised by Say's law: Does the
amount of goods and services that producers wish to produce and sell
equal the amount of goods and services buyers want to buy? Since this
question involves people's intentions, it certainly is possible that supply and demand in this sense are not necessarily equal. In fact, their
equality is a condition of equilibrium. Classical economists, with their
basically hedonistic view of the nature of human motivation, believed
that departures from equilibrium would be transitory and of only short
duration. Their argument was that saving (abstaining from present
consumption) was unpleasant or onerous. Since present goods were
more highly valued than future goods, a reward or premium would
have to be paid to induce the public to save. This reward is the interest
paid to those who save, and the higher the interest rate, the more
people will be willing to save. While high interest rates encourage saving (thrift) and low interest rates discourage saving, just the opposite
is true of investment. A high interest rate makes it more costly to borrow or to use one's own funds for investment purposes, whereas a low
rate of interest lowers the cost and stimulates more investment. Briefly,
then, the savings function, that is, the supply of resources available for
investment, is positively sloped with respect to interest, and the investment demand for these resources is negatively sloped with respect
to interest. Interest rate adjustments assure the equality of savings and
investment and, hence, assure equilibrium of aggregate demand and
supply.

To understand the classicist viewpoint, consider the implications
of disequilibrium in Figure 7-1. At the present rate r_a, which stands for
any interest rate above the equilibrium rate, saving of S_a is greater than
investment of I_a. Since investors are willing to invest (or pay r_a to use
saved resources) in just the amount I_a, some savers would be unable to
lend their surplus funds at all, and therefore, their reward for saving
is zero. Rather than accept this state of affairs, the disappointed savers
would offer to lend at lower interest rates, but the lower interest rates

Figure 7-1   Saving and Investment Determination

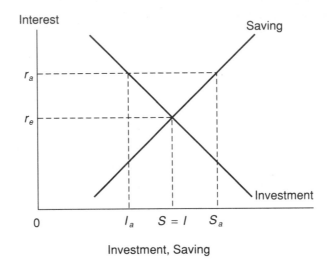

would encourage investors to invest more and induce some savers to save less. In this way, saving and investment come into equality and the interest rate falls toward r_e.[2]

If you were to question this analysis, as later economists did, by noting that people might be willing to forgo the interest income from saving by holding money instead of making it available to investors, the classicist would have made two counterarguments. First, the assertion probably would have been made that there is no advantage in holding money; therefore, no one would be willing to do it. After all, if one holds money, one is giving up the income that could be earned if the funds were shifted into real goods, bonds, or stocks. Second, even if there were such a thing as a demand for money to hold in idle balances, the only result on the macro level would be lower commodity prices and a redistribution of goods and services from the foolish money holders to the more reasonable members of the society who want money only because it can be used to purchase things.

David Ricardo (1772–1823) was the strongest adherent of Say's law, and the power of his logic was so great that few economists were bold enough to challenge it. One who did was his contemporary and friend, the Reverend T. R. Malthus. Ricardo was interested in demonstrating

---

2. We resist the temptation to explain the forces at work if the interest rate is below equilibrium so the reader can use this case as an exercise in understanding.

the nature of the forces included in Adam Smith's "invisible hand," the forces that ensured equilibrium in all economic activity.[3] His fascination with this study made Ricardo impatient with observations that the real world did not always coincide with his description of it. His interest was in the long run, not in the temporary aberrations. Malthus, on the other hand, lived in the short run. He observed and wanted to explain unemployment and overproduction, even though according to Ricardo's theory neither could exist.

Malthus was not convinced that all the resources being saved were automatically flowing into investment demand. In fact, he thought over-saving was a chronic problem in an economy where the demand for capital building was limited by the decisions of private entrepreneurs. Excess saving, according to Malthus, resulted from the unequal distribution of income. The wealthy landlords and other property owners were able to save large amounts while the working class remained poor and unable to save. Malthus's solution to the problem was to advise the wealthy to spend more on nonproductive or intangible output, such as the services of armies, clergy, teachers, and other retainers whose output was not storable.

Although Malthus's position was not accepted by any considerable number of economists, his was one respected (based on his other writings) voice questioning the unquestioned acceptance of Say's law. Malthus's questions opened the way for others to attempt explanations for fluctuations in economic activity.

REAL OUTPUT AND EMPLOYMENT LEVELS

The study of the determination of national income involves an analysis of supply and demand in the total economy. It is an important characteristic of the classical school that major emphasis is placed on the supply side or the output of goods and services; because of Say's law, demand is expected to be sufficient to purchase all that has been produced. Furthermore, since real income (that is, output) is used as a measure of the welfare of the people, the classicists devoted most of their effort to the analysis of the behavior of the supply side in aggregate economics.

The Austrian school of economists classified the economic factors of production as land, labor, capital, and entrepreneurship. Associated with these were rent as the payment for land, or "nature" (the non-

---

3. Adam Smith, *An Inquiry Into the Nature and Causes of the Wealth of Nations*, edited by R.H. Campbell and A.B. Skinner (Indianapolis, IN: Liberty Classics, 1981).

augmentable or God-given resource); wages, the payment for human effort; interest, the reward for waiting or saving embodied in capital goods; and profit, the return to the risk-taker and organizer of business activity. While there is no rigorous way to distinguish among these factors, as there is no way to demonstrate the correspondence between classes of factor payments and the individual factors, we have continued to use the terminology as a matter of convenience.

In the long run, or in a growth context, the total volume of output of goods and services the economy is capable of producing depends both on the quality and on the quantities of all these factors: the endowment of natural resources, the nature and the quantity of capital goods, the quality and characteristics of the labor force, and the entrepreneurial spirit. These, together with the know-how or technology available ("state of the arts"), dictate the potential level of output of goods and services. At the moment, our analysis is focused on the short run where, given both the state of the arts and the nonhuman resources as fixed, real national output depends on the level of employment.

The law of diminishing returns implies that if all other resources are constant, the total product will increase at a decreasing rate as employment increases. This means that the marginal physical product of labor declines as hours worked increase, both at the level of the firm and at the level of the total economy. Figure 7-2 shows the application of this important principle. The upper portion of the graph shows the aggregate production function where real output y depends on the amount of labor used N. The law of diminishing returns is reflected in the declining slope of the curve (concave from below). The same thing is shown in the lower half of the diagram since the line labeled MPP_L, the marginal physical product of labor, is precisely the slope of the production function.

The *marginal physical product of labor* is defined as the change in total output per unit change in the input, labor. Mathematically, it is the first derivative of the production function, $\frac{\partial y}{\partial N}$. Note carefully that the vertical scale of the upper portion of the graph may be many millions of times larger than the scale on the vertical axis of the lower portion. Thus, if total production in the economy were the equivalent of 1.5 billion bushels of wheat per year ($y_1 = 1,500,000,000$), the marginal physical product of labor might be the equivalent of 2,000 bushels per worker year ($MPP_1 = 2,000$) when N_1 workers are employed. If employment increased to N_2, total output might be y_2 or 2 billion (bushels of wheat equivalent), and the marginal physical product of labor might be MPP_2, or 1,200 (bushels equivalent).

Figure 7-2   Application of Law of Diminishing Returns

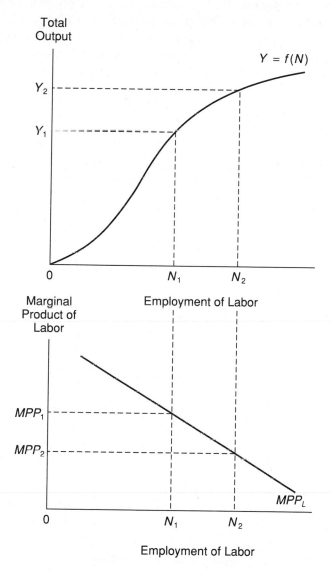

The Demand for Labor

We will continue the hypothetical example of the preceding paragraph to show that the marginal physical product of labor becomes the
demand for labor curve. For this, we must turn to the individual firm.
This particular firm (farm) finds that its output is 25,000 bushels of
wheat when it employs ten workers full time for the year, along with

particular amounts of land, seed, equipment, and other resources. If the manager determines that by employing eleven workers (and not changing anything else) the output will increase to 27,000 bushels, the marginal physical product of labor is estimated to be 2,000 bushels for those conditions. (MPP_L is 27,000 bushels minus 25,000 bushels divided by one worker, or 2,000 bushels.) If the expense (wages) of hiring the eleventh worker is less than the additional revenue to the firm from the sale of the 2,000 bushels, it would be profitable to employ the additional worker.

The law of diminishing returns implies that if this manager continues to add workers, the increase in the total product will be smaller each time another worker is added. Thus, if the wage per year per worker were the value equivalent of 2,000 bushels of wheat, the farm would employ not more than eleven workers. In fact, the farm would maximize profit by employing exactly eleven workers. On the other hand, if the wage were equal to 1,200 bushels of wheat, this farm would maximize profit by employing twenty workers, if the output increased by 1,200 bushels when the twentieth worker is added to the work force.

For this business unit, the demand curve for labor is its marginal physical product curve, because whatever the wage, the number of workers the firm will wish to employ is that number at which the wage and the marginal physical product of labor are equal.

Extending the analysis to the whole economy, the marginal physical product curve derived from the aggregate production function is society's demand for labor. This is also the summation of the individual firms' demand for labor curves.

The Supply of Labor

Similar to the demand for labor function, the explanation of the supply of labor is found in microeconomic theory foundations. Every potential worker is viewed as having a preference function relating the conflicting desires for income and the things it will buy on the one hand and leisure on the other. The point of this is that to get the income, the worker will have to expend effort and tolerate the onerousness of work, but to enjoy the leisure, some income will have to be given up.

The form of the function implies that the more one works in any given period of time, such as a week or a year, the more distasteful work becomes, the more attractive an additional hour of leisure becomes, and the less utility is attached to any additional income. It can be inferred from this that the utility-maximizing individual will be willing to work more hours per time period only at a higher wage rate. Some individuals enter the labor force only when wage rates reach a certain level, so that the higher the wages, the larger the labor force will be. This seems to be particularly characteristic of younger people (especially students), older people who remain in the labor force longer before retiring, and homemakers. In a completely open society, higher wages would also attract workers by way of immigration.

The upshot of all this is the assertion that the supply of labor curve is upward sloping. Many economists, however, believe that at some relatively high wage, any further increases in wage rates will decrease the total hours of labor offered. This proposition, called the backward bending supply curve, seems plausible by the observation that when wages are high, family income becomes large enough so the family can "afford" to enjoy the choice of sending the children to college and having the homemaker remain at home rather than work for wages.

It would appear to be unquestionable that the supply curve of labor for a particular firm, industry, or occupation is positive since workers would be attracted from other firms, industries, or occupations as the wages of one grew while others did not. It would, of course, be fallacious to infer that this necessitates a positive aggregate labor supply curve. Nevertheless, empirical evidence seems to support the positive supply function hypothesis, and in any case, classical economists accepted it. Indeed, all economists treat the "backward bending" portion as an exceptional case.

Wage and Employment Determination

A fundamental tenet of classical economics is that both the demand and supply of labor depend on the real wage rather than the money wage rate. The real wage is defined as the money wage divided by the price level, $w = \dfrac{W}{P}$. Real wages change when there is a change in the money wage rate or in commodity prices; real wages remain the same if both money wages and the price level change in the same direction and proportion. Real wages rise if the rate of increase in money wages exceeds the rate of rise in the general price level or if prices fall more rapidly than wage rates fall. Similar observations are pertinent to the case of declining real wages.

The equilibrium real wage and the amount of employment are determined simultaneously at the point where labor supply and demand are equal, as shown in Figure 7-3.

Figure 7-3   Demand and Supply of Labor, and the Real Wage

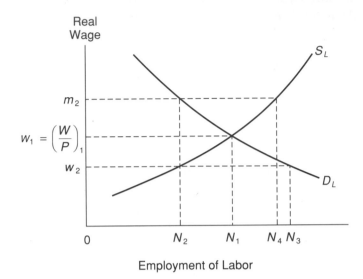

Employment of Labor

If both parties in the labor market are price takers, that is, if competition prevails, the wage will be $w_1 = \left(\frac{W}{P}\right)_1$, and employment will be N_1. N_1 represents one concept of full employment; it does not, however, agree with employment statistics. N_1 is full employment in the sense that everyone who wishes to work at the prevailing wage $\left(\frac{W}{P}\right)_1$ can do so. If the demand curve were to shift continuously to the left, the equilibrium level of employment would continuously decrease, but we would still be at full employment. Fewer people would be working because fewer would wish to work at the lower wages.

As long as the wage and employment combination is on the supply curve, the labor force is in equilibrium. Laborers will be at their optimum if the wage is $\left(\frac{W}{P}\right)_1$, or at any lower wage. For example, at a wage of w_2, workers would wish to work at the level N_2. Since there is nothing to prevent them from being employed at that level, they are in equilibrium—in fact, they are doing what they wish to do, *given the real wage.*

At any wage below w_1, it is the employers who are out of equilibrium. Employers *wish* to employ N_3 if the wage is w_2, but since workers will only supply N_2 amount of labor, the employers will be unable to employ as many as they wish. In this circumstance, it is evident that some producers would be willing to raise wages since, at N_2 employment, the marginal physical product of labor (m_2) is greater than the price of labor (w_2). As the wage rises, two things happen: (1) workers are induced to increase their provision of labor (moving upward on the supply curve), and (2) the marginal physical product decreases (moving down on the demand curve). Whereas at wage w_2 employers wish to employ N_3, at the wage w_1 they wish to employ N_1, which is exactly the amount of employment workers wish to offer.

At all wages above w_1, the business units would be at their optima, since they would be able to employ the number of workers they wish to employ (N_2 if the wage were equal to m_2). However, the workers would not be in equilibrium. More of them would wish to work (N_4) than employers would be willing to hire. The unemployed workers would then be expected to offer to work at lower wages. Lower wages would then increase the number of workers that business would employ and, at the same time, reduce the labor time offered by, at least, some workers.

Thus, given the demand and supply curves as drawn in Figure 7-3, the wage will be w_1 and employment will be N_1. As an exercise in understanding this system, visualize an ongoing process of inflation in which workers and their employers are raising wages faster than the prices of commodities are rising. The real wage will go above w_1, resulting in unemployment. This situation could persist, bringing about inflation and unemployment concurrently; a situation that seemed so perplexing to many people in the 1970s, referred to as stagflation. Of course, one would expect that the pressure of unemployment would slow the rate of increase in money wages and restore equilibrium.

Suppose the opposite situation was in effect; that is, inflation of commodity prices was more rapid than increases in money wage rates. In this circumstance, where prices are rising faster than wages, the real wage would fall below w_1, employers would be unable to employ as many workers as they would like, and they would thus offer higher money wages. The real wage would then return to w_1, and employment again would be N_1.

We must emphasize that the labor market as discussed has the greatest significance to the classical school, since it is here that the real national income and output are determined. Remember that once the amount of labor employed has been determined, all other things remaining constant, total output as shown by the aggregate production function has also been determined. (Refer back to Figure 7-2.) Neither the money supply nor fiscal policy nor saving and investment have any effect on the labor market. Although all three are somewhat important, none determine real national income or product. The roles these variables do play in the classical model will now be discussed.

MONEY IN THE CLASSICAL SYSTEM

The role of money in classical economics is simply to determine the absolute price level. By absolute price we mean the price of a commodity in terms of the unit of account. For example, if a loaf of bread costs $.50, and a particular shirt has a price of $5.00, these are the absolute prices. Their relative prices are determined by supply and demand and are one to ten, and ten to one, with respect to each other. At another time, the absolute prices of these same goods might be, respectively, $1.00 and $10.00, in which event their relative prices have not changed. The classical economist would say that the really important prices are the relative prices and that money has no influence on them.[4] The absolute price level is the weighted average of the prices of the included commodities.

The quantity theory of money is the classical explanation of the general price level or, in other words, the value of money. The quantity theory is the oldest, and also perhaps the newest, monetary theory. Of course, it has evolved with greater sophistication. Its earliest statement was based on the simple observation that when currency in a country increased, the prices of commodities also increased; and when currency flowed out of the country, prices fell. Later versions introduced refinements that involved the rapidity with which the money was spent and the volume of production.

The equation that is the starting point of any discussion of the quantity theory is called the *equation of exchange*: $MV = Py$. In the equation, M stands for the stock of money, V stands for the velocity of circulation of that money, P stands for the general price level, and y is a measure of the amount of goods and services produced and sold.

There is never any debate over whether the equation is true. If the components are carefully defined, it is a tautology, a truism, or an identity. Looking at the left side, we multiply the number of units of money by the average number of times each unit was spent to buy the things

---

4. This dichotomy in the classical system between the determination of absolute and relative prices has been the subject of considerable debate. For a convenient summary of the issues involved, see Robert L. Crouch, *Macroeconomics* (New York: Harcourt Brace Jovanovich, Inc., 1972), Chapter 15.

included in y during a specified period of time. MV, then, is the total spending of that money for those things that were purchased in that period. If y is the total number of units of goods and services sold, and P is their average price, then Py is the total value of those goods and services. There is no question that total spending for a particular group of commodities is equal to the total money received from the sale of those same commodities. In itself, this is a good disciplinary device. We must be careful not to say anything that contradicts a true statement. We can choose any set of goods, such as those that are included in the gross national product, or all goods and services, to define y. But once y has been defined, for the equation to be true, P and V must have reference to the same set.

An alternative statement, called the Cambridge equation, that involves the same variables is $M = kPy$. The only new symbol introduced here is k, and the only one not included is V. The relationship between V and k is very simple. From $MV = Py$, it can be seen that $V = \frac{Py}{M}$. From $M = kPy$, obviously $k = \frac{M}{Py}$. Thus, $V = \frac{1}{k}$ and $k = \frac{1}{V}$. For example, if $V = 4$, it means that, on the average, each unit of money is spent four times per period (assume it to be one year). In that event, $k = \frac{1}{4}$, which means that, on the average, each piece of money is not spent on y for one fourth of the year, or three months. Another way of looking at k is to observe that it is the portion $\left(\frac{1}{4}\right)$ of annual spending (Py) that is held in cash balances (M).

Looked at in this way, $M = kPy$ can be viewed as a demand for money function. But if it is that, it no longer is a truism; and if it is no longer a truism, we need a new definition of k. Now, instead of k being the portion of total spending held in the form of money, it is the portion of total spending that economic units wish or desire to hold in the form of money. To see the difference, let us take an example in which the monetary system determines the money supply originally at $100 billion; the money value of national income is in equilibrium at $400 billion. Since equilibrium exists, k of the identity (call it k') is the same as k of the equation (call it simply k). Both have a value of $\frac{1}{4}$, that is, $100 = \frac{1}{4}(\$400)$.

Now, suppose the operations of the monetary system act to double the money supply to $200 billion. The truism reads: $\$200 \equiv \frac{1}{2}(\$400)$.

k' has doubled from $\frac{1}{4}$ to $\frac{1}{2}$ because people are holding one half of total spending in the form of money. Since the money exists, someone must hold it. Our demand for money equation, however, says that people wish to hold only $100 billion when income is $400, so $200 $\neq$ $\frac{1}{4}$($400)—a disequilibrium condition. Economic units are holding twice as much money as they wish to hold, and we would expect them to take steps to reduce their money balances until they hold the desired amount. But by our assumption that only the monetary system can control the money supply, any individual can reduce cash balances only by inducing others to increase their balances. This can be accomplished by buying more things at the old prices or paying a higher price for the same number of things. In other words, either y or P will increase. If everyone holds rigidly to their original judgment on the portion of their income, they should hold in money balances, and if no change in income distribution occurs, Py will continue to rise until it reaches $800. Only then will equilibrium exist where both k and k' are $\frac{1}{4}$: $200 = $\frac{1}{4}$($800). Notice that if real output remained constant so that all of the expansion were accounted for by the increase in the price level, then the real value of money holdings would not change, even though more money was held. The real value of money balances is defined as $\frac{M}{P}$, and since M and P both doubled in our example, the ratio is the same after M and P increased as it was at the original equilibrium.

The example we have just covered is, of course, too extreme. No contemporary quantity theorist believes that k is quite as rigid as the one in our example. There is the opposite extreme view that is characteristic of those whom we might call antiquantity theorists, who believe that in certain circumstances, notably in a severe depression, k will change proportionately with any change in the money supply, so that money supply changes have no effect on national income. Going back to our example, where the original equilibrium situation was $100 = $\frac{1}{4}$($400), a doubling of the money supply would cause both k and k' to become one half, $200 = $\frac{1}{2}$($400). This demonstrates that people are willing to hold any additional amounts of money the monetary system creates and that they will not increase their rate of spending because of these increased amounts.

These two examples should make it clear that the usefulness of the quantity theory depends upon the degree of stability of k or its reciprocal, V, and, even more importantly, upon their independence of M. This is not as simple to determine as it might appear, since k itself cannot be measured directly. Statistically, we can measure only k', and even in the example above, where k was rigidly fixed, k' did vary. Quantity theorists, especially Irving Fisher, believed that the size of cash balances was mainly mechanically determined by institutional arrangement for payments in the economic system. Thus, the frequency of receipts and disbursements and the degree of correspondence between them would be important, as would the efficiency of the transportation and communication systems, the degree of specialization and integration of industry, population changes, habits of thrift and hoarding, and the use of trade credit. These are all factors that would change only slowly over time and, furthermore, would not seem to be related in any systematic way to the money supply. A modern critic might point out that several important influences have been neglected, such as expectations of future price levels and interest rate changes and the relative attractiveness of substitutes for money, such as savings accounts, bonds, and potential borrowing sources.

It would be consistent with classical thought to include the interest rate as an argument in the demand for money relation, even if the transactions motive is the only reason for holding money. The point is that the (opportunity) cost of holding money is the interest income forgone. Thus, the higher the interest rate, the greater will be the incentive for more efficient cash management, that is, the holding of less money per unit of transactions. At lower interest rates it would not be profitable to incur the costs of economizing on cash balances.

For the moment, if k is assumed to be a constant, then an increase in the money supply must increase Py proportionately; however, the question remains, will P increase, or will it be y, or might both increase? To the rigid classicist, the answer has to be that P alone will increase since y is always at its practicable maximum through the efficiency of the free market system and is determined in the labor market (as discussed earlier in this chapter). Real income, of course, would be expected to rise secularly as the state of the arts advances and as capital and population grow; however, in the short run, these could be assumed to be fixed. For this reason, the quantity theory was, above all, the explanation of the absolute level of prices and was a supplement to the explanation of relative prices through micro supply and demand analysis. To some business cycle theorists, however, the quantity theory was used to explain variations in both output and prices. In contemporary analysis, the point is usually made that the closer the economy is to full employment or "full capacity," the less y can change, so that increases in M result in significant changes in P; but when large-scale unemployment or "excess capacity" exists, the increase in M can increase y with negligible effects on P.

The graphic analysis in Figure 7-4 ties together some of the ideas developed so far in describing the classical system. Part (a) graphs the strict quantity theory. If the stock of money is M_0, the nominal level of national income will be $(Py)_0$. The slope of the line is the value of V, the income velocity of money, or the reciprocal of k. Thus, if $V = 4$, Py is simply four times as large as the money supply. If the quantity of money in the economy is increased by \$10 billion, the money value of national income (nominal income) will increase by \$40 billion.

Part (b) shows the combination of y's multiplied by P's to give the product $(Py)_0$ [as determined in Part (a)]. The curve is a rectangular hyperbola. For example, if y_0 times P_0 equals $(Py)_0$, which is \$400 billion, then any other pair of y and P values on the $(PY)_0$ curve when multiplied together must also equal \$400 billion. Thus, y_1 times P_1 equals $(Py)_0$.

Part (c), the aggregate production function, was explained earlier. Here, given employment of N_0, the level of real national income is y_0. If the volume of production of goods and services is y_0 and [from Part (a)] Py is $(Py)_0$, then Part (b) shows that the price level must be P_0.

The level of employment is derived in the labor market (also explained earlier) and is shown as Part (f). The real wage is seen to be the money wage (W) divided by the price level (P). This real wage $\left(\dfrac{W}{P}\right)_0$ is consistent with an infinite number of combinations of money wages and price levels, but since the price level was determined (in our figure) in Part (b), only one money wage is possible. This is shown in Part (e). The curve $W = W_0$ shows the points of w and P_0 consistent with the money wage W_0, which is also a rectangular hyperbola.

To complete the picture that is usually described as the classical system, we have repeated the saving-investment graph (with the axes reversed) as Part (d). Since the total real output is shown to be y_0 in Part (c) and investment is i_0 in Part (d), the production and sale of consumption goods and services is $y_0 - i_0 = c_0$.

Many of the implications of the classical system can be shown with the aid of this set of diagrams. Notice that one can trace the effects of

Figure 7-4   The Classical Aggregate System

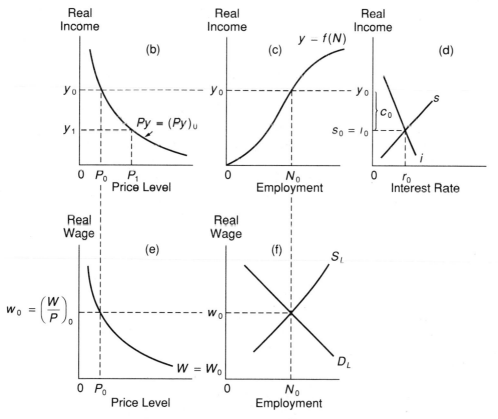
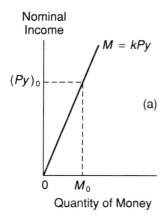

changes in any of the variables on all the others. These can be listed in the following way:

From Part (a)

1. M can change—move left or right on the abscissa.
2. k (or V) can change—rotate the function clockwise (if V falls) or counterclockwise (if V rises).

From Part (c)

3. The production function can shift upward (if productivity increases) or downward (if productivity decreases) as the quantities and/or qualities of the nonlabor factors change or as the quality of labor changes.

From Part (d)

4. The investment function can shift or rotate as the expected profitability of capital changes because of innovations or by changes in the quantities or qualities of the other factors of production.
5. The saving function can shift or rotate as the public changes its relative preferences between present and future goods.
6. If government is included in the model, the s function can incorporate taxes, and the i function can incorporate government spending, thus shifting either of the functions whenever government spending or taxation changes.

From Part (f)

7. The relative preferences of the population among work, leisure, and income change; or the population changes via immigration or increased or decreased birth and death rates; or a change in the age composition of the population, causing the supply of labor curve to shift and/or rotate. (Note that the demand for labor curve can change only if the production function changes as mentioned in 3 above.)

A complete taxonomy would require us to perform two further tasks. First, we should list all of the possible real world events that could cause the variables to change as specified above, and secondly, we should trace the implications of each variable shift on the total system. Since this would be a lifetime of analysis, we will have to be content with an example or two.

Changes in the Supply of or Demand for Money

Our first example is designed to trace the impact of a change in either the supply of money or the demand for money on the various endogenous variables included in this analysis. The conclusion is reached that the nominal variables (that is, those expressed in money prices, namely nominal income, nominal consumption, nominal savings, nominal investment, the price level, and the nominal wage) change, but that the real variables (output, real wage, employment, the interest rate, real consumption, real saving, and real investment) all remain the same. The explanation of this conclusion follows.

In Part (a) of Figure 7-5, nominal national income is caused to be increased to $(Py)_1$ by either an increase in the stock of money to M_1 or with the same amount of money a decrease in the demand for money (a decrease in the numerical value of k to k_1, which is an increase in V). A decrease in the demand for money is shown as a rotation of the $M = kPy$ function to the left.

Since the money value of national income has increased, a new higher rectangular hyperbola has been drawn in Part (b) and labeled $(Py)_1$. Production of goods and services (y_0) has not changed so the price level must increase to P_1. Our problem is to find out if y will change.

If the money wage remains at W_0, the real wage will fall to $\left(\dfrac{W}{P}\right)_1$, as shown in Parts (e) and (f). But, at that real wage, the demand for labor (N_h), exceeds the supply of labor (N), and employers will need to raise the money wage to get all the workers they wish to employ. Clearly, the money wage will rise until the real wage returns to $\left(\dfrac{W}{P}\right)_0$. That money wage will be W_1, a new rectangular hyperbola, as shown in Part (e). The money wage had to increase in exactly the same proportion as the price level for the ratio $\dfrac{W}{P}$ to remain the same.

Since the real wage did not change (because of the originating change in the money supply or demand), the level of employment did not change. Therefore, real output (y) did not change either, which is what the classicists wished to prove. The real system is not affected by the money system; money is a veil.

Figure 7-5   Monetary Changes and the Classical System

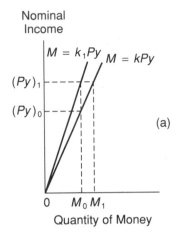

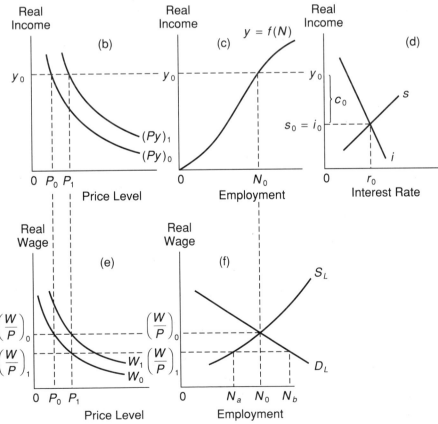

Changes in the Productivity of Labor

Figure 7-6 shows how changes in the productivity of labor brought about by (for example) changes in the amount of capital with which laborers must work affect the variables in the system.

In Part (d), we show a positive amount of investment occurring, which means that in the next time period, the stock of capital goods will be larger than it was. Any given amount of labor employed should produce a larger amount of output than before. As shown in Figure 7-6, the aggregate production function of Part (c) has shifted upward, as has the demand for labor in Part (f) shifted upward to D'_L.

From our previous arguments, we know that the real wage will need to go to the new equilibrium of $\left(\frac{W}{P}\right)_1$ and employment to the larger level of N_1. Real output then increases to y_1 on Part (c). Since nothing has happened to cause any change in Py on Part (a), the price level will fall in the same proportion as y increased. In the particular case drawn here, the money wage has fallen, but it might have risen or remained the same. The new money wage curve in Part (e) must intersect the point determined by the coordinates of the new real wage and the new price level.

CLASSICAL THEORY OF ECONOMIC GROWTH

Economic growth theory is covered more substantially in Chapter 12. At this point, we merely wish to present the basic elements of the classical analysis of growth. Referring again to the set of diagrams in Figure 7-6, economic growth is a process of rising national output over time, shown by an upward shift of the production function in Part (c) and/or a movement to a higher point on the same aggregate production function.

The discussion that follows is restricted to the growth that is unquestionably desirable, that is, growth in per capita real national income. This means that we are dealing with an upward shifting production function that, in turn, implies an upward shifting demand for labor function as in Part (f).

Such shifts are expected to arise via expansion of the stock of capital, that is, positive investment. Since investment can only occur to the extent that saving takes place, economic growth requires the willingness of people to abstain from present consumption. The rate of growth, then, depends on the saving propensities of the population and on the productivity of capital. Each individual is viewed as de-

Figure 7-6   Effect of an Increase in Labor Productivity on the Economic
                   System

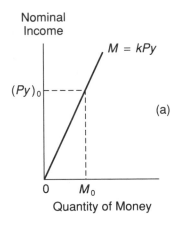

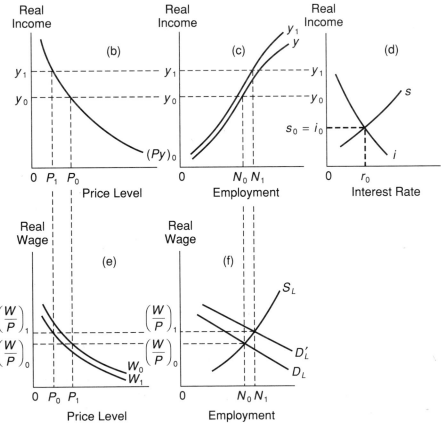

ciding his or her personal growth plans. The interest rate is determined in the total market so the individual takes the interest rate as given. The individual determines that at the given rate of interest, a certain amount of current income will be saved, and a larger amount of purchasing power will be received in the future. The individual will receive the larger future income as payment for having made resources available to business units (by buying bonds or stock or by direct investment) who use them for productive investment.

It would seem that in the classical paradigm, there is no role for government to play in the growth process other than assuring that society possesses the necessary social capital, such as transportation and communications systems, a legal environment conducive to the encouragement of business activity, a stable government, and so on. The "right" rate of growth depends solely on the conditions governing the productivity of resources used for investment and the rate of savings of the population *in toto* as determined by individual decisions.

Classical economists stressed the economic growth associated with population growth, but their conclusion was that while aggregate income increased with population, per capita income declined. The reason for this, once again, is that pillar of the classical school, the law of diminishing returns. The pessimistic view of Ricardo and Malthus on the implications of population growth superseded Adam Smith's principle that economic activity becomes more efficient as specialization and division of labor develop in response to the expansion of the market as population grows.

The Ricardo-Malthus analysis is summarized in Figure 7-7. The horizontal axis shows population, or what amounts to the same thing, the labor force. Real output appears on the vertical axis, and the curve drawn shows the declining marginal physical product of labor.

As explained earlier in this chapter, if the population is N_0, the real wage will be w_0. If the population increases, the real wage, which really stands for the standard of living, will fall along the curve MPP_L. In this analysis, the population will grow until the wage falls to the subsistence level, w_0. Were the population to increase beyond the point consistent with the subsistence wage, the standard of living would be so low that the population-labor force would decline through ill health, earlier deaths, fewer births resulting from later marriages, higher infant mortality, and so on.

Thus, if w_0 is the subsistence level, any wage higher than this (such as w_a, which would exist if population were N_a) will encourage growth in population and the labor force through better health, longer life,

Figure 7-7   Population Growth and Wages

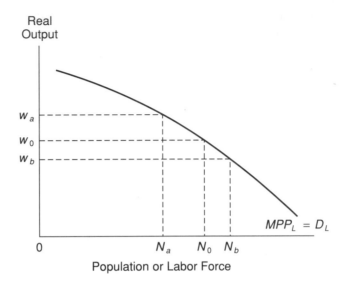

more births, earlier marriages, lower infant mortality, and so on. Since a wage of w_b would cause a reduction of the population from N_b toward N_0, there would be a tendency for the population always to move toward that level at which the wage would be at the subsistence level, and population would be N_0.

An important issue in this analysis is the connection between population growth and economic well-being as represented by per capita national income. Empirical evidence does seem to support the hypothesis that the two are indeed related, though the correspondence is not as close as implied by the theory. An immediately related consideration involves the meaning of the term "subsistence wage." Does the concept imply some physiological minimum standard of life sustenance? If so, the evidence in the developed economies contradicts the expectations derived from the theory, though in underdeveloped societies, the analysis does not appear to be an unreasonable description.

If we abandon the absolute notion of subsistence, the subsistence wage can be defined simply as that real wage at which population would be constant—or in equilibrium. This could be a relatively high wage in some societies where, if the wage fell below the equilibrium, the people would make the conscious decision to reduce the population by lowering the number of children per family, by reducing the number of families by later marriage, or by restricting immigration or

Figure 7-8   Labor Force Growth and Productivity Changes

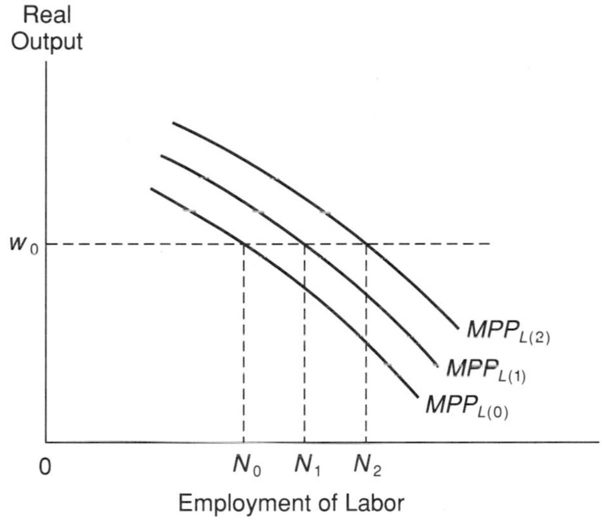

increasing emigration. In other words, the population and labor force would not decline because of the inadequacy of diets, housing, medical care, and so forth, but because of the judgment that the marginal benefits of additions to the population are less than the marginal costs.

The later classical economists, called neoclassicists, rejected the hypothesis of population as a function of real per capita income; they considered the growth rate of population to be exogenously determined for the purpose of analysis. The problem lies in the relationships among the rate of growth in the labor force, the rate of growth of the productivity of capital, and the rate of saving.

If the labor force is growing at the rate of n $\left(n = \frac{\Delta S_L}{S_L}\right)$ and S_L stands for the supply of labor, the real wage will fall unless the rate of growth of national income m $\left(m = \frac{\Delta y}{y}\right)$ is equal to or greater than n. As shown in Figure 7-8, for the standard of living (real wage) to remain at the current level (w_0), as the labor force increases from N_0 to N_1 the marginal physical product of labor schedule will need to shift to $MPP_{L(1)}$. For this to happen, the stock of capital must increase in the same proportion as the increase in the labor force (with no change in the average productivity of capital); that is, $\frac{\Delta K}{K}$ must also equal $n = m$. But ΔK is investment and so the rate of saving must be equal to ΔK. Thus, for a steady state of growth, the rate of increase in saving must equal the rate of growth in investment, which, in turn, must equal the rate of growth in the labor force.

Any independent change in any of these growth rates necessitates adjustments by the others. We will not be able to get involved in all the possible adjustments and repercussions of these changes. Suffice it at this point to observe that, according to the reasoning of the neoclassicist, since the rate of population change is fixed, the other variables will ultimately return to equality with that rate.

GOVERNMENT IN CLASSICAL ECONOMICS

The role of the state in classical economics was very limited. In general, the proposition was that the system, left alone to operate as a system, produced results that were superior to any results that could be foreseen from governmental interferences with the free market forces. The economy was viewed as having a host of self-adjusting mechanisms that produced harmony in the world of commerce. The price system was seen as a way of resolving conflict peaceably.[5]

However, a set of "rules of the game" was necessary. A framework was considered necessary, and it was thought to be a proper function of government to provide the legal framework detailing the meaning of private property and human rights. Classical economists frequently have been maligned as hardhearted, laissez-faire advocates, but in point of fact, most of them were compassionate persons, very concerned about the well-being of their fellow humans. They were quick to propose laws making consumer fraud illegal, to favor regulations to control monopoly, and to suggest protective labor legislation.[6]

Aside from establishing the legal environment for the operation of the economic system, the classicists determined other legitimate functions of government, which we shall now briefly review.

Public Goods

National defense may be the outstanding example of a public good. It is indivisible. If one person or group buys defense for itself, it is impossible to exclude others from the enjoyment of that service, and it is

---

5. See Armen Alchian and William Allen, *University Economics*, 3d ed. (Belmont, CA: Wadsworth Publishing Co., Inc., 1972).
6. See Warren J. Samuels, *The Classical Theory of Economic Policy* (Cleveland: World Publishing Co., 1966).

impossible to charge for the service what it is worth to the recipients. This might be called the "freeloader" principle. The individual would need to be compelled to pay through the power of the state if the service is to be provided. Adam Smith specifically charged the state with the responsibility of protecting society from external and internal threats of violence.

Externalities or Neighborhood Effects

A principle familiar to students of microeconomics is that an individual is advised to purchase an item if the marginal utility or benefit exceeds the marginal cost. There are some goods or services where the benefits to other people, or the society, are large in addition to the utility of the decision maker. In this case, it might be advantageous to the whole community to bear, at least, some of the cost. Immunization from communicable diseases and some categories of education are outstanding examples of this situation. These are called "neighborhood effects" or external benefits.

Conversely, there are instances when the market cost to the individual making the decision does not reflect all the costs involved in providing the good or service. Dramatic examples are provided by all forms of pollution where costs are imposed on individuals without regard to the amount of their consumption of the product. These too, are referred to as "neighborhood effects" or external costs and may provide justification for governmental interference with the free market system.

Public Works

Classical and neoclassical economists also felt that there was a category of public works proper for government to establish, even though it would be feasible for private enterprise to do so. Private enterprise did not because of the great capital requirement, the high risk involved, or the expense of collecting the price. A network of streets and highways might involve all these reasons for private firms not to undertake such a project. The Tennessee Valley Authority is often cited as an example of a project that the federal government initiated, because private firms seemed unlikely to be capable of providing such a service because of the great amount of capital required (in addition to the contention that great social benefits would be a concomitant).

The private sector will not produce where the probability of profit is not present. In some instances (where externalities are significant), the public sector should provide goods or services, rather than have the community do without them. This argument is often used in support of public transit systems.

Monopoly

Where one firm can operate profitably, but two or more firms in the industry could operate only at a loss, a monopoly situation usually arises. This is often due to decreasing costs as output is expanded within the range of the demand for the product, though it sometimes occurs by virtue of ownership of certain unique factors of production, including patents and other forms of governmental protection. Three possibilities in response to such circumstances are possible, and classical economists, as well as others, have differed in their decisions as to the best approach. The three possibilities are mentioned here without elaboration. They are: (1) to socialize, that is, to accept public ownership and control; (2) to allow private ownership regulated by a governmental authority as we do in our public utilities; and (3) to allow private ownership unfettered by government in the hope that competitive products or services will develop over time.

Taxation

Government, to be able to perform its functions, must finance its expenditures, and normally this will be done through taxation. The principle of a balanced budget was generally viewed as a virtue until the mid-1930s. Taxation was not thought of as a positive force for influencing aggregate economic activity, but as a necessary evil. Indeed, since real income was determined in the labor market, and nominal income was determined by the money supply and velocity, government spending could occur only at the expense of private expenditures. The idea is that since the total pie is fixed in size, if one sector takes a larger slice, there will be less available to the remaining groups.

QUESTIONS

1. Explain the difference between Say's law viewed as an identity and Say's law viewed as a condition of equilibrium. Why is this distinction important?
2. Using classical interest rate theory, explain why the interest rate would rise if it were below the intersection of the saving and investment curves. It is

not enough to say that aggregate demand is greater than aggregate supply, although that is true.

3. Show that a firm should employ the number of workers at which the marginal physical product of labor is equal to the additional expense of hiring one more worker.

4. The general proposition is that the supply of labor offered in the economy increases as the real wage increases. Explain why this statement seems plausible.

5. What would be the impact on the classical labor market situation if some outside agent forced nominal (money) wages to be higher than the equilibrium wage rate? Demonstrate graphically that, in this case, the problem could be cured by the inflation of prices of other goods and services.

6. Explain the difference between relative prices and absolute prices. What is the importance of each concept?

7. Some writers state the Cambridge form of the equation of exchange as $\frac{M}{P} = ky$. Review the meaning of the terms, and interpret this equation.

8. "Labor unions (or monopolies) are the cause of inflation." Using the tautology $MV \equiv Py$, what arguments would be necessary to defend such a statement?

9. Graph the complete classical system, and show that an autonomous increase in investment (or government expenditures) will redistribute the output of the economy, but (in the absence of any change in the money stock or in velocity) will not increase real output or the absolute price level.

10. Write an essay explaining why you think classical economists minimized the role of government in the economic system, and explain what principles were used to justify government involvement.

READINGS

Ackley, Gardner. *Macroeconomic Theory and Policy*. New York: The Macmillan Co., 1978, Part II.

Blaug, Mark. "Classical Economics." *The New Palgrave Dictionary of Economics*. London: The Macmillan Press Ltd., 1987, Vol 1, pp. 434–444.

Froyen, Richard T. *Macroeconomics: Theories and Policies*, 2d ed. New York: Macmillan Publishing Co., 1986. Chapters 3–4.

Green, Roy. "Classical Theory of Money." *The New Palgrave Dictionary of Economics*. London: The Macmillan Press Ltd., 1987, Vol 1, pp. 449–451.

Harris, Donald J. "Classical Growth Models." *The New Palgrave Dictionary of Economics*. London: The Macmillan Press Ltd., 1987, Vol 1, pp. 445–448.

Heilbroner, Robert L. *The Worldly Philosophers*, 5th ed. New York: Simon and Schuster, 1980.

Miller, Merton H., and Charles W. Upton. *Macroeconomics: A Neoclassical Introduction.* Homewood, IL: Richard D. Irwin, Inc., 1974.

Pigou, Arthur C. *The Theory of Unemployment.* London: Macmillan and Co., Ltd., 1933.

———. *Employment and Equilibrium*, 2d ed. New York: The Macmillan Co., 1952.

———. "Some Considerations on Stability Conditions, Employment, and Real Wage Rates." *Economic Journal* (December 1945).

Samuels, Warren J. *The Classical Theory of Economic Policy.* Cleveland: World Publishing Co., 1966.

Thweatt, William O., ed. *Classical Political Economy: A Survey of Recent Literature.* Norwell, MA: Kluwer Academic, 1988.

THE BASIC FRAMEWORK OF NATIONAL INCOME ANALYSIS

The next five chapters develop the modern theory of national income analysis. This chapter begins with some comments on the contributions of Lord Keynes, who was mainly responsible for initiating interest in this form of analysis, and then continues by presenting the basic framework of the theory. Chapter 9 extends the analysis by integrating the market for goods and services, develops the theory of investment, and includes a presentation of a multiplier-accelerator model that shows how business cycles can occur because of the form of the investment demand function. Chapter 10 develops a theory of the money supply process and a Keynesian-type demand for money analysis. These two relationships are used to develop the L-M function, which is then combined with the I-S function of Chapter 9 to determine the equilibrium levels of national income and the interest rate. Chapter 11 is concerned with the distinction between real values, such as physical quantities of goods and services, their nominal or dollar values, and the connection between them, namely, the level of prices. Chapter 12 concludes this part with some important topics in national income analysis.

THE KEYNESIAN CONTRIBUTION

The expression "Keynesian Economics" is employed in recognition of the influence of John Maynard Keynes in contributing an alternative approach to that of the classical aggregate economic analysis. While Keynes was a member of the neoclassical school as a professor at Cambridge University, he became dissatisfied with certain aspects of neoclassicism. He has had great influence both as an academic economist and as an adviser on public policy. Few, if any, economists, at least since the days of Adam Smith, have had as pronounced an effect on economic theory as did Keynes. In his *General Theory of Employment, Interest, and Money*, he analyzed what he considered to be the weaknesses of classical economics and presented a new set of tools for aggregate economic analysis and a new formulation of the factors that determine the level of employment of labor and other resources. As is the case with any new approach to a problem, Keynes' work generated a great deal of discussion and controversy, some of which continues to this day. Those who refused to accept his general approach to economic analysis were forced to reexamine their concepts and to define them more accurately and more clearly. His followers were given the tools that led them to develop a greatly increased understanding of our economy, especially the factors that determine the level of consumption, saving, investment, and interest rates.

Not only did Keynes attain a standing as an economist held by few individuals, but he also achieved a place as an adviser on public policy in the economic area, which has seldom, if ever, been equaled. In his early twenties, Keynes was an adviser on financial matters to the government of India; in his early fifties, governments in all parts of the world sought his advice on matters of economic policy. In his last years, he was one of the leading advisers responsible for the agreements that led to the establishment of the International Monetary Fund.

Another reason for devoting so much space to the work of J.M. Keynes is that he analyzed the factors determining the level of investment and consumption and developed the relationships between them in a fuller and different way from that of earlier cycle theorists. Since Keynes' analysis of these factors has become the wellspring of modern aggregative economic analysis, we use this chapter as the introduction to the basic elements of national income determination theory. By mastering the material in this chapter the reader will be able to comprehend the later developments in macroeconomic theory and contemporary business cycle thought, as discussed in the chapters that follow.

AGGREGATE DEMAND

In Chapter 7, where classical macroeconomics was discussed, we had little need for the analysis of *aggregate demand*. The classicists, in accordance with Say's law, reasoned that whatever the rate of output might be in an economy, there would always be sufficient aggregate demand. In stark contrast, Keynes' position was that the demand side was the active determinant of how much would be produced. It may be simplifying too much to put the matter as bluntly as this, but the general emphasis is valid to say that the classical school of thought was that when you determined how much would be produced, you knew how much would be demanded; whereas, Keynes said that if you knew how much would be demanded, you would know how much would be produced.

Aggregate demand is the sum of final goods and services that decision-making units intend to buy. The usual procedure is to group the decision-making units into the various sectors of the economy. In general, it has been found helpful to use the categories of households, business, government, and the rest of the world. There are three reasons for this particular breakdown: (1) the decision-making process is somewhat different for each of the categories or, at least, is handled differently in the theory explaining their behavior; (2) the impact of the expenditures of the various sectors on the future may be different; and (3) value judgments about the welfare effects of the expenditures of the several sectors may differ.

The Household Sector

Households include all the human beings in the domestic economy. The *raison d'être* of the economy is to improve the welfare, in some sense, of this sector. Consumption takes place to satisfy the desires of households, so that in the fundamental meaning of the term, only households consume. A large and well-developed theory of household behavior exists in the literature where each consuming unit is viewed as an expected utility maximizer. A household is at its consumption optimum when the marginal utilities of all commodities relative to their prices are equal; that is, $\dfrac{MU_A}{P_A} = \dfrac{MU_B}{P_B} = \ldots = \dfrac{MU_N}{P_N}$.

Macroeconomic theory does not concern itself significantly with the allocation of buyers' income among commodities, but it does concern itself with the allocation of income between present goods as a group and future goods as a group. In other words, in aggregative economic theory, the decision of households to spend a portion of current income on present consumption implies a decision to save the remainder. On partial equilibrium grounds, then, households are in equilibrium when the marginal utilities of all present goods relative to their prices are equal to the marginal utilities of all future goods relative to their current prices.[1] An increase in a consumer's income would be expected to increase the consumer's demands for both pres-

---

1. The future price of commodities is, of course, unknown. If the price level were expected to remain constant, then the interest rate could be used in calculating the current price ratios of present and future goods. Similarly, the future marginal utility of future goods is unknown; our reference must be to the present utility of future goods, which, too, involves a forecast.

ent and future goods. The precise manner in which a change in income will influence this decision is the subject of considerable controversy, as will be seen in our review of consumption function studies. To the extent that households opt for more saving, they have, at once, increased the demand for future goods and made resources available for production of goods for future use.

All income from production accrues to the household sector in the sense that all factors of production are owned by members of that sector, either through personal, direct ownership, or indirectly through the intermediary of a corporation or government. In national income accounting, reference is made to business saving and government saving, but even in these instances where retained corporate earnings or government surpluses exist, total saving will occur only to the extent that consumers acquiesce in the decision.

It stretches credulity too much to declare that consumption and household spending are identical. What should be included in consumption spending is the spending on those goods and services normally destroyed in value during the period under analysis. The purchase of a new home or new automobile, for example, should be excluded since the largest part of the expenditure is not for current consumption but for future use. Thus, spending for these items should be included in investment demand. Such spending should also be included in the category of investment, because the decision to purchase is based on the same elements as the process of decision making by business firms. Since investment is the act of adding to the stock of capital, the purchase of a home or auto is an act of investment that increases the supply of future income (the future income being the services of the house or car). In fact, the Commerce Department does treat the purchase of a new house as an investment, although the purchase of a new automobile is treated as a consumption outlay.

The Business Sector

In the circular flow analysis, all productive activity takes place at the level of the business sector. Business firms employ the services of the factors of production owned by the households. Microeconomic theory asserts that business units utilize resources in such proportions as to maximize expected profits. The optimum resource mix for a firm occurs when an additional dollar spent on any given resource is expected to yield a return equal to that of a dollar spent on any other resource. In the manner of price theory textbooks, $\dfrac{MP_A}{P_A} = \dfrac{MP_B}{P_B} =$

$\ldots = \dfrac{MP_N}{P_N}$, where MP is the marginal product of the factors of production A, B, $\ldots$, N, and P is the per unit price of factors A, B,
$\ldots$, N. This means that the employment of any resource will increase if its productivity increases or if its cost decreases.

From the side of aggregate demand, the most important decision of
the business firm is the amount of investment it will undertake. The
investment decision is based on the expected returns from dollars invested compared with the expected cost of engaging in the investment.
Chapter 9 contains a lengthy discussion of this principle.

If investment takes place, the stock of productive resources, that is,
capital increases and the ability of the economic system to produce
goods and services in the future has increased. In the case of investment in inventory, the physical supply of goods available for future
consumption has increased directly. The type of investment that takes
place makes a great deal of difference to future employment and to future price prospects. If the investment is primarily in increased inventories of finished consumer goods, in finished producer goods, in raw
material stocks, or in the many types of plant or equipment, the implications for the future are clearly different. It is easy to conceive of
cases in which the investment expenditures would be of the type that
would put pressure on wages to move in one direction and prices of
finished goods to move in the other direction. On the other hand, the
investment might be of a kind that created an unemployment problem,
or it might create an imbalance between agricultural versus industrial
production. Such problems are discussed in greater detail at later
stages of our study.

A major question may arise in the reader's mind concerning the
demand for replacement expenditures and for maintenance and repair
of the existing capital stock. Some aggregate economic models do include gross investment rather than net investment, as we shall do.
These economists argue that replacement expenditures generate a demand for workers and other resources just as much as do expenditures
for increasing the capital stock. Since that is true, one should be aware
of the situation involving the rate of actual destruction and deterioration in the capital stock compared with the actual amount of replacement. At certain times, during wars and depressions, for example, the
capital stock is allowed to deteriorate without replacement. At most
other times, but particularly in the aftermath of wars and in the recovery stage of the business cycle, for example, replacement expenditures
will be in excess of the current rate of capital consumption. Net in-

vestment is the concept that takes these issues into consideration. Therefore, if our concern is with national income as a measure of welfare, we want net investment as the business sector's contribution to aggregate demand. On the other hand, for short-run analysis of employment and price-level behavior, gross investment may be the more useful figure.

The Government Sector

The theory of government behavior has not been as well developed nor as generally accepted as has the body of theory on the private sector. On one hand, we have the welfare-oriented theory that states, in general terms, that marginal social benefits should be equal to marginal social costs. The problem of determining what these benefits and costs are to a society composed of individuals with different preference patterns is, of course, controversial. Theoretical analysis of actual government behavior runs the gamut from the extremely naive to the extremely cynical. One approach, which has attracted a number of adherents, runs in terms of votes gained from a particular action weighed against the number of votes lost by the action. It is at least conceivable that the two approaches lead to the same action, although at this stage in the development of the analysis, it cannot be proved nor disproved.

The place of the government sector in the circular flow depiction of the economy is to absorb purchasing power from the household sector by taxation and to direct this purchasing power to the business sector (including government employees) as governments purchase goods and services.[2] Some government expenditures will result in current utility to the public (thus being consumption-type expenditures), and some expenditures increase the wealth of the society by producing highways, buildings, and so on (thus being investment-type expenditures). Classification of particular government spending into either category would involve us in serious philosophical debate, so we restrain ourselves. It should be noted, however, that the question that needs to be answered is whether the expenditures have the effect of increasing the stock of wealth of the society or simply increasing current goods and services and, therefore, having long-run implications.

---

2. Government also distributes funds to some households without requiring any current goods and services in exchange. This is what is meant by "transfer payments," and we include transfer payments as negative taxes, since the amount of taxes offset by transfer payments constitutes no net outflow from the household sector.

For purposes of short-run analysis of national income behavior, it is insignificant whether government spending is classified as consumption or investment. All such spending acts as an injection of demand for the output of the economy and becomes income for the owners of the factors of production responsible for the production of the goods and services.

The main reason for handling the government sector apart from the others is that its behavior is subject to political control, and its taxing and spending can be adjusted to bring about what are believed to be desirable goals. Ultimately, the most important reason that the federal government differs from the other sectors is that it has the sovereign power, which makes its receipts from taxes different from the receipts of units that must sell a product or service; its borrowing power is unlimited, as long, of course, as the general public has confidence in the monetary system.[3]

The Foreign Sector

Exports of goods and services result in an injection of demand by other economies for the output of the domestic economy and an increase in the incomes of the factors that produced the commodities. Imports into this economy can be looked upon as an outflow or withdrawal from the income stream, since these expenditures do not return purchasing power to our business sector. The international transactions are almost always handled as a net figure called *net foreign investment* or net exports of goods and services, which is the difference between what our nationals sell to foreigners and the amount foreign nationals sell to citizens of this country.

Selling goods or services to peoples of other countries is akin to other investment activities, since it increases the future consumption abilities of our nationals, while purchasing goods from the rest of the world decreases our ability to consume in the future. Another important reason for dealing with the net amount by which exports exceed imports is that it is impossible for us to measure directly the amount of foreign as opposed to domestically produced goods and services bought by our households, government, and our business sector. Many goods said to be "made in America" may actually contain raw materials

---

3. This statement may sound shocking, but it must be remembered that issuing money is the prerogative of all national governments, and money is a noninterest-bearing form of debt. We are not yet ready to discuss whether, or under what conditions, government should borrow at interest or at no interest.

from foreign countries, or perhaps, foreign machines were used to produce the raw materials in this country.

The demand to import goods and services depends primarily upon national income and the prices of foreign goods as represented by the exchange rates among currencies. The demand for exports depends on the incomes in other countries and the exchange rates. In addition to these factors, exports and imports are heavily influenced by various governmental policies, such as quotas, tariffs, taxes, subsidies, and many others usually designed to encourage exports and discourage imports of the country.

THE CIRCULAR FLOW

The process by which income is generated through production and sales, and sales are made possible by income, is called the *circular flow*. Business firms receive receipts from the sale of goods and services to all the four sectors we have just described: households; governments; the rest of the world; and the business firms themselves, which buy or inventory whatever was not sold to the other three sectors. It is important to understand that what business units buy may be voluntary purchases by one firm from another, or the producing firm may not sell as much as it had intended, so that its inventory of its own product will increase. This increase in inventories may be intentional or unintentional. Such unintentional investment is critically important in the study of national income, because when it occurs, business units can be expected to attempt to reduce the unplanned accumulation by decreasing production, and therefore incomes, or by maintaining the old level of sales by lowering prices and thus also reducing incomes. Unintended real investment also can take place when a firm uses up less of its capital equipment than it had planned, because output was less than intended, while planned investment remained the same.

The receipts of business units accrue as income to household owners of the factors of production. Households allocate their incomes among the following uses: purchasing goods and services directly from business units (consumption); paying taxes to governments; purchasing goods from other countries (imports); or if the households do none of these, we say they have saved (personal saving). This saving is a definitional residual, that is, it is the difference between income and consumption, taxes and imports, $(S = Y - C - T - Im)$. Whatever else might be done with the money does not alter the fact that saving took place.

Like investment, saving can be viewed as taking place either voluntarily or involuntarily. Involuntary saving might occur because earners of income during a period do not receive it until some future period. The payment lag is quite short for wage earners, but for property income recipients it might be considerable. Franco Modigliani has pointed out that the strictly Keynesian analytical framework implicitly assumes that consumers have their way so that intended saving is always the same as actual saving and that unintended saving never occurs.[4] This assumption has the logical corollary that the impact of a disequilibrium income is always on the business sector and always appears as a condition where unintended investment or disinvestment exists. These statements will be made clearer when we demonstrate the income equilibrating mechanism.

Symbolically, the circular flow can be described in the following identity:

$$Y \equiv C + G + I_B + (Ex - Im) \equiv C + T + S_p$$

where

Y = income	Ex = exports
C = consumption	Im = imports
G = government spending	T = taxes
I_B = business investment	S_p = personal saving

Some further explanation of the net export $(Ex - Im)$ demand is needed. It is often impossible to determine which portion of any commodity was made domestically and which portion was produced outside the United States. Therefore, it is not possible to tell the exact amount of consumption of domestically produced goods and services. The same thing is true for investment, government purchases, and exports; they all include some output produced in other countries. If we measure total C, I_B, G, and Ex, we would be overstating our GNP or NNP by the amount of the foreign production. So, what is done is to simply subtract the total amount of imports from the exports.

As a first approximation, it is convenient to reduce $G + I_B + (Ex - Im)$ to I = injections (into the income stream) and $T + S_p$ to S = savings or withdrawals (out of the income stream). In this way, a simpler model can be constructed where the supply side or value of goods and services produced is equal to $C + S$, and the demand side is $C + I$.

---

4. F. Modigliani, "Liquidity Preference and the Theory of Interest and Money," *Econometrica* (January 1944).

The condition of equilibrium is that supply=demand; that is, $C+S=C+I$. It is necessary to see why equilibrium exists only if aggregate supply and demand are equal. First, suppose the total value of goods and services produced is greater than the demand for them. In that event, unintended inventories accumulate and business will attempt to reduce them by laying off workers and buying fewer materials and services from other firms. In other words, if income is greater than the equilibrium level, income will fall. If, instead of reducing production, firms with excess inventory lower the prices of the unsold goods, the profits of the sellers (which are their incomes) will fall. In later production, the incomes of the other factors of production will also fall.

In the preceding paragraph, the case of aggregate supply exceeding aggregate demand was discussed. Now, consider the case where demand is greater than supply: $C+I>Y$, or $C+I>C+S$. Since $C=C$, it follows that $I>S$. It is also true that since purchases of goods and services $(C+I)$ are greater than the value of goods and services produced $(C+S)$, some of the goods sold must have been produced in prior time periods. In other words, the stock of capital, most importantly, inventories, must have been reduced. This is described as involuntary disinvestment or negative investment. In this situation, where business is, in fact, investing less than it intended to invest, we can expect the firms to try to build back their inventories to the desired level. This will necessitate the employment of additional workers and other resources or an increase in the prices of goods and services as well as factor prices. Thus, when income is less than the equilibrium level $(C+I>C+S$, and $I>S)$, income will rise.

Parenthetically, it is worth noting that even in the disequilibrium situations where $S>I$ or where $I>S$, it is still the case that *actual* saving and *actual* investment are exactly equal in amount. In this framework, it is usually assumed that savers do save the amount they intend to save. If this is so, then when $S>I$, involuntary investment in the amount $S-I$ must take place; and conversely, when $I>S$, involuntary disinvestment in the amount $I-S$ must take place.

The Simple Algebraic Model

What has just been verbalized can also be put in the form of a formal model. Certain propositions can be more easily demonstrated with such a model; but more importantly, more complete models or models closer to reality simply cannot be handled, or cannot be handled efficiently, verbally.

The first model to consider is the simplest that can be constructed. It is composed of the following three equations containing three unknowns:

$$Y = C + I$$
$$C = a + bY$$
$$I = I_0$$

The first equation is the condition of equilibrium. Our goal is to solve for Y, that is, to find the equilibrium value of Y in terms of the knowns—a, b, I_0.[5] The second equation is the *consumption function*. It is a behavioral equation, which is to say that it describes the expected behavior of households that consume specific amounts at specific levels of income. The third equation asserts that the amount of investment is exogenously determined. For purposes of this model, investment is not to be explained. We derive the value of I_0 from some other theory, or we simply ask all business people their intentions. For our present purpose, it is most important to observe that intended investment does not depend on the level of current income.

Now solve for Y by substituting into the first equation. First, the unknown C can be replaced by $a + bY$ and the unknown I can be eliminated by using the known I_0.

Thus: $Y = a + bY + I_0$

Subtract bY from both sides of the equation: $Y - bY = a + I_0$

Factor out Y from the left side: $Y(1-b) = a + I_0$

Divide both sides by $(1-b)$: $Y = \dfrac{a + I_0}{1 - b}$

We now have one equation and one unknown (Y). In other words, we have the solution or the reduced form of the model. If we know the values of the known parameters, we can determine the value of the unknowns.

Thus, if a = $80 billion, b = 0.8, and I_0 = $120 billion, then:

$$Y = \frac{\$80 + \$120}{1 - 0.8} = \frac{\$200}{0.2} = \$1,000 \text{ billion} = \$1 \text{ trillion.}$$

Since $C = a + bY$, $C = \$80 + 0.8(\$1,000) = \$80 + \$800 = \$880$ billion. No equation for S was given, but we know that $S = Y - C$, so we can derive the equation for S by substituting $a + bY$ for C.

Thus: $S = Y - a - bY$, and by factoring: $S = -a + (1-b)Y$, and $S = -\$80 + (1-0.8)\$1,000 = -\$80 + \$200 = \$120$ billion. Since $I = I_0 = \$120$ billion, $S = I$.

---

5. The meaning and significance of these terms are detailed later.

Figure 8-1   Basic National Income Determination

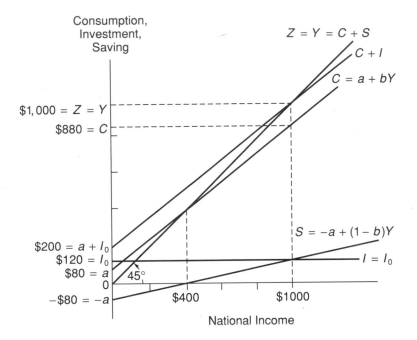

The Geometry of the Simple Model

This model can now be demonstrated graphically (see Figure 8-1). In general, the geometric approach is not as powerful as the equation approach, since the charts get cluttered up quite quickly when many refinements are added. It is, however, a very handy method for attacking certain problems.

Each line on the graph is now to be explained. First consider the Z line (Figure 8-2). It is drawn at a 45° angle from the origin, so that triangles such as $0YX$ and $0XZ$ are identical right triangles. This is significant in that it assures that $0Y = 0Z$. In this way, distances measured along the horizontal axis can be compared with distances measured along the vertical axis, since the equation for any straight line is a constant, which measures the intersection of the line with the vertical axis [call it α (alpha)], plus another constant, which is the slope of the line [call it β (beta)], times the value on the horizontal axis. For the Z line we have drawn, its equation is: $Z = \alpha + \beta y$ but $\alpha = 0$ and $\beta = 1$, so $Z = Y$. We know that $\beta = 1$, because the slope can be measured by any triangle,

Figure 8-2   The Z Function

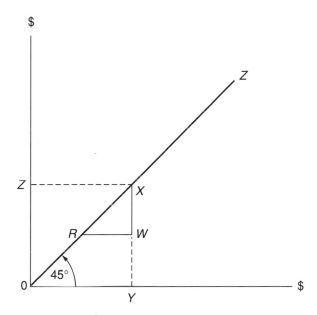

such as RWX. It is $\dfrac{XW}{RW}$, but $XW = RW$ (by construction, again) so $\dfrac{XW}{RW} = 1$, and the equation for the Z line collapses to $Z = Y$.

The Consumption Function

The C line (Figure 8-3) has the equation $C = a + bY$, which makes it a straight line. The consumption function is the heart of the Keynesian system. Some theorists feel that it is Keynes' most important contribution to the methodology of aggregate economic theory.

The C line is drawn on the basis of the past behavior of consumption and income. It is the line that represents the best single estimator of what consumption was at various levels of income. Statistically, it is the least-squares simple regression of consumption on income. When income is Y_1, the best prediction for consumption is C_1; and when income is Y_1, the best prediction for consumption is C_2. Furthermore, the line shows that if income is expected to increase from Y_1 to Y_2 (that is, by ΔY), consumption would be expected to increase from C_1 to C_2 (that is, by ΔC).

Figure 8-3   The Consumption Function

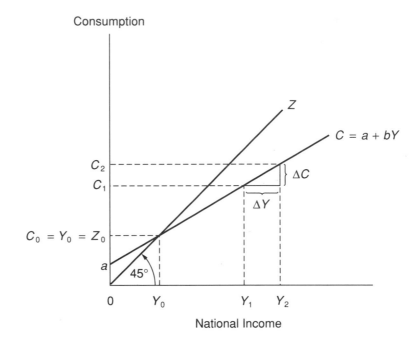

The ratio $\frac{\Delta C}{\Delta Y}$ is a very important element in the analysis. It is the *marginal propensity to consume*, the slope of the consumption function, and is equal to b of our equation. In a straight line, the slope is a constant; that is, it is the same wherever it is measured. Keynes reasoned that the marginal propensity to consume would get smaller as income gets larger; that is to say, he thought a curved line, rather than a straight line, would be a closer approximation to the real world consumption function. More will be said about the realism of the function in the next chapter.

Less important than the marginal propensity to consume is the *average propensity to consume*, defined as $\frac{C}{Y}$. On a linear consumption function, the marginal propensity to consume (MPC) is constant, but the average propensity to consume (APC) declines as income gets larger. For this to be true, the intercept, a, must be positive. This is easy to see. Since $APC = \frac{C}{Y}$, and $C = a + bY$, $APC = \frac{a + bY}{Y}$.

If a were equal to zero, the APC would be equal to $\dfrac{bY}{Y} = b$. With positive values of a and very small incomes (Y), the APC would be dominated by a. At that level of income at which $C = Y$ (Y_0 in Figure 8-3), of course the $APC = 1$. At all smaller incomes, $C > Y$, so $APC > 1$, and at all incomes larger than this, $Y > C$, so $APC < I$ and falls as income rises.

It should be clear how important the consumption-income relation is to the entire analysis. In all economies, consumption is, by far, the largest component of national income; thus, if income is to be accurately forecast, consumption must also be predictable. The analysis collapses if the consumption function is not relatively stable or if the shifts in it are not predictable.

A word of warning: Students are frequently tempted to argue that a somehow represents the minimum standard of living for the economy. It does not! We have no idea how much consumption there would be if income were, in fact, equal to zero. We have had no experience with such low levels of income. Thus, a should be thought of simply as the factor that establishes the height of the consumption function on the chart. Changes in the value of a can occur because of government restrictions on consumption or because of changes in the Social Security system or because of taxes and a number of other things; but this says nothing about what consumption would really be if income were zero.

The Saving Function

The saving function is derived from the definition of saving as the difference between national income and consumption. Since the 45° line labeled Z is equal to Y, we can subtract the C line from the Z line (Figure 8-4). At $Y = 0$, $S = Y - C = Y - (a + bY)$, but if $Y = 0$, $S = -a$. At $Y = Y_0$, $Y = C$, so $S = Y - C = 0$. At incomes to the left of Y_0, $C > Y$, so $S < 0$ by the vertical distance between C and Z. At incomes greater than Y_0, $Y > C$, so $S > 0$ by the amount of the vertical distance between Z and C. Thus, on the graph, $S_a = S_a$, $S_b = S_b$, and so forth.

It has already been shown that the equation for S is $S = -a + (1 - b)Y$. Thus, the intercept is $-a$, and the slope of the S function is $1 - b$. Therefore, if b, the MPC, is 0.8, the slope of the saving function is $1 - 0.8 = 0.2$.

In this example, if income were to increase by 20, consumption would increase by 16, and saving would increase by 4. Analogously to

Figure 8-4   Consumption Saving Relationship

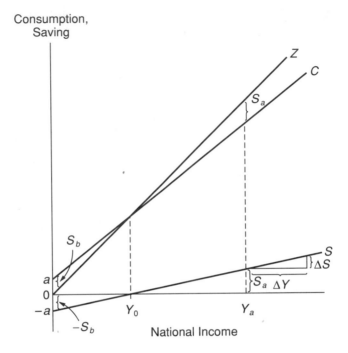

the consumption function, the slope of the saving function $(1-b)$ is the *marginal propensity to save* (MPS) and is defined as $\dfrac{\Delta S}{\Delta Y}$.

Another way to demonstrate this is to start with the definition of $S = Y - C$, and observe that it is also true that $\Delta S = \Delta Y - \Delta C$. Now, dividing through by ΔY gives $\dfrac{\Delta S}{\Delta Y} = \dfrac{\Delta Y}{\Delta Y} - \dfrac{\Delta C}{\Delta Y}$; so, $\dfrac{\Delta S}{\Delta Y} = 1 - \dfrac{\Delta C}{\Delta Y}$, which shows that the $MPS = 1 - MPC$.

The Investment Function

The investment function used in our present model is $I = I_0$, which appears graphically as a straight line parallel to the horizontal axis. Its intercept is I_0, a constant amount of investment. It has a slope of zero, which means that investment does not change as income changes. There are two reasons for adopting this functional form. First, logically, current income should be irrelevant in the decision to invest. A decision to purchase investment goods for future production should be based on expected future income, which may only be influenced by present income. A theory of investment behavior using this proposition will be developed in the next chapter. Second, there exists a statistical problem of discovering the investment income relationship. If a regression of the actual amounts of investment and income were computed, the resulting function would be the same as our saving function, because measured saving and investment are identical amounts. The justification for claiming that the regression is, in fact, the saving function and not the investment function lies in the belief that intended saving is relatively less volatile than intended investment, that investment is the active agent for change, and that saving is relatively passive.

THE MULTIPLIER

The concept of the multiplier, the notion that a given increase in investment or government spending would result in a multiplied effect on national income, was one of the most startling conclusions drawn from the Keynesian revolution. It is hoped that the following section will dispel any notions that any magic is involved and that what happens to bring about this result is actually quite ordinary behavior by quite ordinary people. The procedure here will be to demonstrate the multiplier algebraically, graphically, and in tabular form.

The Algebra of the Multiplier

We begin by defining multipliers in general as the change in a dependent variable per unit change in the independent variable. In aggregative economic analysis, the principal dependent variable is national income, so we shall derive income multipliers. In our simple model, income would change if I changed, if a changed, or if b changed. What is usually referred to as the *investment multiplier* is the amount by which income changes when investment changes, that is, $\frac{\Delta Y}{\Delta I_0}$. Recall the model presented earlier:

$$
\begin{aligned}
Y &= C+I \\
C &= a+bY \\
I &= I_0
\end{aligned}
$$

and the solution, or reduced form:

$$Y = \frac{a+I_0}{1-b}$$

Now, if this same economy experiences an increase in the rate of investment of ΔI_0, the model appears as follows:

$$Y' = C' + I'$$
$$C' = a + bY'$$
$$I' = I_0 + \Delta I_0$$

The solution to this system is:

$$Y' = \frac{a+I_0+\Delta I_0}{1-b}$$

We want to know the change in income (ΔY) that resulted from the change in investment (ΔI_0).

$$\Delta Y = Y' - Y = \frac{a+I_0+\Delta I_0}{1-b} - \frac{a+I_0}{1-b}$$

Subtracting: $\Delta Y = \frac{\Delta I_0}{1-b}$. If we now divide both sides of this statement by ΔI_0, we have discovered the multiplier: $\frac{\Delta Y}{\Delta I_0} = \frac{1}{1-b}$. Remembering that $1-b = MPS$, we can say that this multiplier is the reciprocal of the marginal propensity to save.

Using the same numerical values of the parameters as before: $a = \$80$ billion, $b = 0.8$, $I_0 = \$120$ billion, and adding $\Delta I_0 = \$40$ billion, we get the following results:

$$Y = \frac{a+I_0}{1-b} = \frac{\$80+\$120}{1-0.8} = \$1{,}000 \text{ billion}$$

$$Y' = \frac{a+I_0+\Delta I_0}{1-b} = \frac{\$80+\$120+\$40}{1-0.8} = \$1{,}200 \text{ billion}$$

$$\Delta Y = Y' - Y = \$200 \text{ billion}$$

$$\frac{\Delta Y}{\Delta I_0} = \frac{200}{40} = 5 = \frac{1}{1-b} = \frac{1}{1-0.8} = 5$$

The change in income of $200 billion is composed of the $40 billion of added new investment and $160 billion of added consumption. Our consumption function, $C=a+bY$, tells us that the original amount of consumption was $\$80+0.8\,(1,000)=\$880$, and at the new equilibrium, it is $\$80+0.8\,(1,200)=\$1,040$. Since the MPC is 0.8, we can determine immediately that a change in income of $200 billion would induce 0.8 of $200 billion of additional consumption, or $160 billion. The change in saving (ΔS), we know, must be 0.2 of $200 billion or $40 billion, which is the amount necessary for saving to equal investment. The change in investment (ΔI_0) of $40 billion is thus equal to the change in saving (ΔS) of $40 billion.

The Graphics of the Multiplier

Now, we will show the same events graphically. Figure 8-5 is the same as Figure 8-1, but with the addition of the new, larger investment function.

The original position of equilibrium income is at $1,000 billion, with consumption of $880 billion, and saving and investment equal at $120 billion. Now, the demand by business for investment increases by $40 billion per period. This means that aggregate demand is $1,040 billion, still $880 billion of consumer demand plus the $160 billion of investment demand, whereas the current production of goods and services totals just $1,000 billion. Y is no longer an equilibrium income. The increased demand for investment creates new income, the recipients of which will increase their demand for consumption. In turn, this new demand for consumption generates new income that again stimulates further consumption. This process continues as long as demand $(C+I')$ exceeds output $(C+S)$. It will stop when demand and output are equal at $Y'=\$1,200$, which is where the Z line intersects with the $C+I'$ line and where $S=I'$.

That the multiplier is the reciprocal of the slope of the saving function can be seen directly from Figure 8-5. Remembering the definition of the multiplier as $\frac{\Delta Y}{\Delta I_0}$, ΔY is the distance between the new and the old levels of equilibrium income $(Y'-Y)$, and ΔI_0 is equal to ΔS, that is, $(I'-I)$. The MPS is $\frac{\Delta S}{\Delta Y}$, which is the reciprocal of $\frac{\Delta Y}{\Delta S}$, or $\frac{\Delta Y}{\Delta I_0}$.

If the S line is drawn very flat, that is, with a very low MPS and hence, a very large MPC, the change in income would be very large. Conversely, a steep S function generates only a small change in Y. This is easily seen in Figure 8-6, where the same change in investment (ΔI_0) generates a very large change in income when the saving function is

Figure 8-5   The Multiplier Graphics

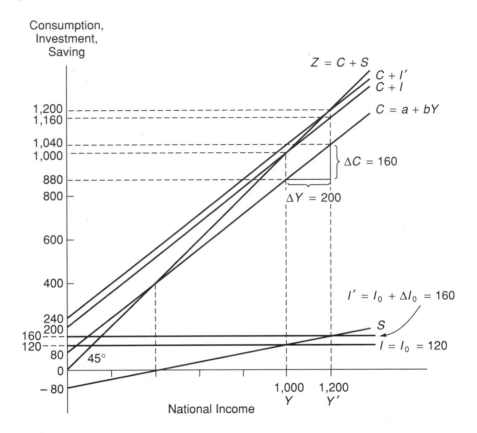

S''' and a very small change in income when the saving function is S''. In each case, the change in saving is the same ($\Delta S = \Delta I$), but the change in income needed to bring about that change in saving varies with the slope of S.

The Movement to a New Level of Income

It can be very helpful to study Table 8-1 to understand the dynamics of the movement of national income from one equilibrium to another when autonomous investment is increased. The table assumes a marginal propensity to consume of 0.8 and a marginal propensity to save of 0.2. It also assumes a *production lag*, which is to say that when demand increases, production does not increase in that same period.

Figure 8-6 The Change in Income Depends on the Slope of the S Curve

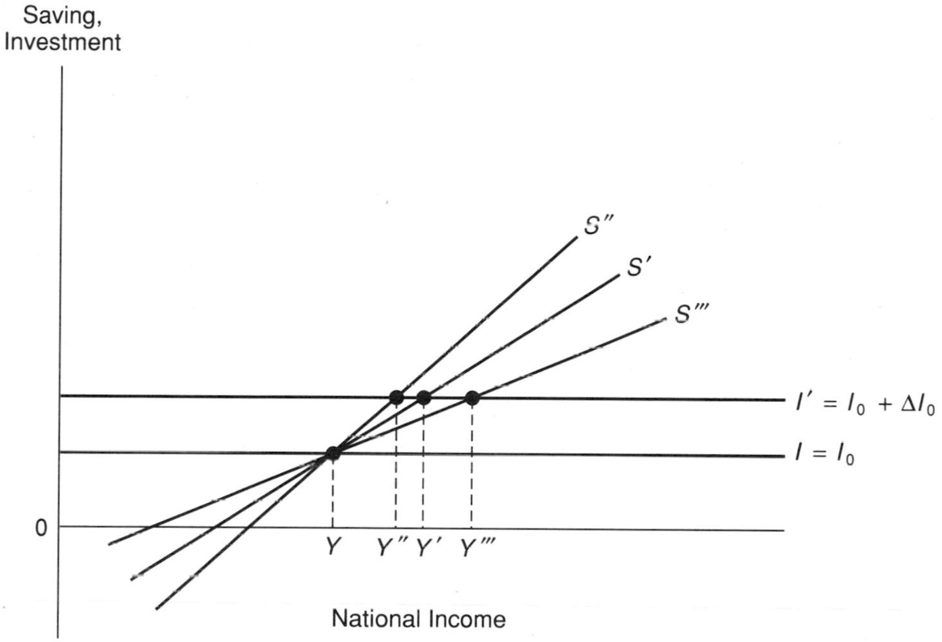

Period 0 and period n are the initial and final equilibrium periods. The process starts in period 1 when the only change is an increase in investment demand of $40, from a rate of $120 per period to $160 per period. Total production in period 1 is still $1,000, since that was the amount of total demand (sales) in period 0, but total sales in period 1 have increased by $40. Since sales were greater than production by $40, inventories must have decreased by $40; that is, the reason why actual investment is $40 less than intended investment.

Consider period 2: Income from production is $1,040, because demand (sales) in period 1 was $1,040. Consumption is $912, because the consumption function is $C = \$80 + 0.8Y$ [$\$80 + 0.8(\$1,040) = \$912$]. Intended saving is $S = -\$80 + 0.2Y = \$128$ [$-\$80 + 0.2(\$1,040) = \$128$]. Actual saving is the difference between income in the period ($1,040) and consumption in the same period ($912), so actual and intended saving are equal. Again, actual investment is the difference between production and consumption, and the discrepancy between actual and intended investment is the unintended decrease in inventory of $32. Sales of $1,072 minus production of $1,040 equals $32.

Table 8-1

Income Adjustment to a Change in Investment

Period	Production $Z=C+S$	C	Intended I	Intended S	Actual I	Actual S	Sales $Y=C+I$
0	1000	880	120	120	120	120	1000
1	1000	880	160	120	120	120	1040
2	1040	912	160	128	128	128	1072
3	1072	937.6	160	134.4	134.4	134.4	1097.6
4	1097.6	958.1	160	139.5	139.5	139.5	1118.1
5	1118.1	974.5	160	143.6	143.6	143.6	1134.5
.	.	.	.	.	.	.	.
.	.	.	.	.	.	.	.
.	.	.	.	.	.	.	.
n	1200	1040	160	160	160	160	1200

Source: Hypothetical data used in chapter.

Notice that income increases by 0.8 times the previous increase in income and that consumption increases by 0.8 times the change in income, since once investment demand has increased, the change in consumption is the only change in income. Note also that the actual saving and actual investment are always equal. From the initial equilibrium to the final equilibrium, income, consumption, saving, and actual investment all approach their equilibria asymptotically. At equilibrium, and only at equilibrium, $C+S=C+I$, and $S=I$. On the other hand, it is also worth pointing out that even at all disequilibrium points $C+S=C+I$, where the variables are defined as actual magnitudes.

Paul Samuelson has taught us the wisdom of checking up on our model in this way to be sure that the movement of the system is, in fact, toward the equilibrium position.[6] It would be a good exercise to test your understanding of this analysis by graphing a model in which the investment function has a steeper slope than the saving function. Now, shift the investment function upward, and find the new equilibrium. The next part of the exercise would be to construct a table similar to Table 8-1.

6. This involves what Samuelson calls the correspondence principle. See Paul A. Samuelson, *Foundations of Economic Analysis* (Cambridge, MA: Harvard University Press, 1947).

QUESTIONS

1. Explain the concept of the sectoral demand components of total demand for the output of the economy in the circular flow.
2. Explain why income will move toward the equilibrium level when total demand exceeds total supply and when total demand is less than total supply.
3. Consider the following model:

    $C = a + bY$ a = \$50 billion
    $I = I_0$ b = 0.9
    $Y = C + I$ I_0 = \$100 billion

    (a) What are the equilibrium values of Y, C, S, and I?
    (b) What is the numerical value of the investment multiplier?
    (c) What would be the equilibrium values of Y, C, and S if I_0 became \$120 billion?
    (d) What would be the equilibrium values of Y, C, and S, and I if a became \$60 billion? (Assume $I_0 = \$120$ billion.)
4. Draw question 3 on graph paper.
5. Construct a table for question 3 comparable to Table 8-1 in the text.

READINGS

Dornbusch, Rudiger, and Stanley Fischer. *Macroeconomics,* 4th ed. New York: McGraw-Hill Book Co., 1987. Chapter 3.

Gordon, Robert J. *Macroeconomics,* 4th ed. Glenview, IL: Scott, Foresman and Company, 1987.

Hall, Robert E., and John B. Taylor. *Macroeconomics,* 2d ed. New York: W. W. Norton and Co., 1988. Chapter 3.

Hicks, J. R. "Mr. Keynes and the 'Classics': A Suggested Interpretation." *Econometrica* (April 1937).

Keynes, John Maynard. *The General Theory of Employment, Interest, and Money.* New York: Harcourt, Brace & Co., Inc., 1936.

Modigliani, F. "Liquidity Preference and the Theory of Interest and Money." *Econometrica* (January 1944).

Ritter, L. S. "The Role of Money in Keynesian Theory," *Banking and Monetary Studies,* edited by Deane Carson. Homewood, IL: Richard D. Irwin, Inc., 1963.

Sheffrin, Steven M., et al. *Macroeconomics: Theory and Policy.* Cincinnati: South-Western Publishing Co., 1988. Chapter 3.

Wachtel, Paul. *Macroeconomics: From Theory to Practice.* New York: McGraw-Hill Book Co., 1989.

INVESTMENT AND THE *I-S* FUNCTION

In Chapter 8, we presented the basic framework of the modern approach to national income determination. That model demonstrated nothing about the role of money, and investment demand was simply assumed to exist. In this chapter, a theory of investment behavior is developed that then permits us to present the analysis of equilibrium in the market for commodities in a framework called the Hicks-Hanson *I-S* function. Within that same framework, the market for money and bonds is built up into an equilibrium relation called the *L-M* function (discussed in Chapter 10).

THE GOODS MARKET

A modern economy is made up of a large number of different markets; a market being any situation in which demand and supply relations can be distinguished. In macroeconomics, we aggregate many markets to reduce the number to a manageable few in order to generalize about large classes of events. The markets generally utilized in macro models are the goods market, the money market, the bond market, and the labor market. All markets are interrelated as noted in the frequently used statement, "In economics, everything depends on everything else." More formally, Walras' law states that if three of the markets mentioned above are in equilibrium, the fourth is also in equilibrium; or alternatively, if one of the markets is not in equilibrium, then at least one of the others is also in disequilibrium. As the analysis proceeds, some of these interrelationships should become clear.

What is called the *goods market* is the market in which goods and services are exchanged for money, but money is merely the vehicle by which the exchange is effected. What is actually involved is the exchange of goods and services for other goods and services. Productive goods and services are purchased by producing units and are converted into final goods and services, which, in turn, are sold to those whose incomes were derived from the sale of the productive services.

On the supply side of the goods market lies the production of the great variety of commodities available from the business sector. The demand side includes the demand for goods and services by households, governments, foreign nationals, and the business sector itself. Equilibrium in this market occurs when all of these buyers wish to buy all of the commodities the business units wish to sell. As shown in Chapter 0, this happens when saving (or aggregate withdrawals from the income stream) is equal to investment (or aggregate injections into the income stream). All of this is incorporated in the *I-S* function. However, before the *I-S* curve is explained, a theory of investment must be considered first.

The Marginal Efficiency of Capital and the Theory of Investment

It is now appropriate to ask the question: What will cause the investment function to shift upward or downward? This can be answered only if there is a theory of investment behavior, which we will now develop.

Decisions to invest are made by individual business units, not by business as a whole. Thus, the theory explaining investment expenditures must be based on the micro theory of the business firm. The firm's decision to invest in a physical asset will be affirmative if that asset is expected to yield a return greater than the return on alternative uses of funds. Presumably, business people would be able to rank the opportunities available to them at any moment according to their expected yields.

In this comparison, it is necessary to evaluate assets with differing expected lifetimes. For example, how would one choose between an asset expected to return $100 per year for 5 years with an asset expected to yield $20 per year for 30 years, if they both cost the same amount of money? This brings up the more basic question of how one values any asset, the returns of which are to be received in the future. The answer depends upon what future returns are worth at the time the decision is made—in general, today.

What, for example, is the value at this moment of $100 that is to be received one year from now, or of $100 to be received 30 years from today? The value of $100 one year from today is $\dfrac{\$100}{(1+r)}$, where r is the interest rate, and the value of $100 thirty years from today is $\frac{\$100}{(1+r)^{30}}$. This says that if the interest rate remains at r, the present value of a sum of money in the future is the amount needed today to produce that sum in the future. For example, if the interest rate is 10 percent, the present value of $100 to be received one year from today is $90.91— the amount you would have to deposit today in order to get $100 one year from today. If the interest rate were 5 percent, the comparable figure would be $95.24. On the other hand, at an interest rate of 10 percent, $100 to be received 30 years from today is worth only $5.70 today and, at an interest rate of 5 percent, is worth $23.10.

We can look upon any physical asset as the present embodiment of returns that will accrue in the future. Its worth in the present, then, is the discounted value of all of its expected future returns. The usual formula for the determination of present value is:

$$PV = \frac{a_1}{1+r} + \frac{a_2}{(1+r)^2} + \frac{a_3}{(1+r)^3} + \ldots + \frac{a_n+S}{(1+r)^n}$$

where

- PV is the present value of any durable (or financial) asset
- $a_1, a_2, a_3, \ldots, a_n$ are the expected annual returns in dollars in the designated year
- r is the interest rate used to discount those returns
- S is the expected value of the asset at some time in the future (usually at the end of the "lifetime" of the asset, that is, in period n), or the salvage value

For most physical assets, the expected returns, $a_1, a_2, \ldots, a_n$, are different, and they are also, in some degree, uncertain. Each a is calculated as the expected net return from owning the asset over not owning the asset. This means that the additional revenue and additional costs must all be estimated for all future periods. One important cost to be included, from the point of view of the development of the theory, is the cost of uncertainty. This cost of risk must include a subjective estimate on the part of the firm's decision makers, but, in part, it can be scientifically computed.[1] For our purposes, we will not include explicitly in our calculations the risk premium or the cost.

---

1. There are a number of ways that risk can be handled in these calculations, but it would take us too far afield to develop any of them properly.

There is often a question about which rate of interest to use as the discounting factor. We have avoided this problem by including all the risk and other costs in the numerators of the equation so that the interest rate should be the pure rate, reflecting only time preference. In the real world, probably the closest we can get to this is the rate on short-term Treasury bills. The interest rates that are theoretically relevant are those expected in all future time periods. This injects another serious uncertainty component, so that most practitioners explicitly use an average rate over the entire period and implicitly make a qualitative adjustment for this feature.

We have just seen how the value of any asset can be calculated. The firm will find it profitable to invest in any asset whose value to the firm is greater than its cost. It is now to be demonstrated that where the value is greater than the cost, the marginal efficiency of capital is greater than the rate of interest.

The *marginal efficiency of capital* (MEC) is to be defined with reference to the following equation:

$$C = \frac{a_1}{(1+m)} + \frac{a_2}{(1+m)^2} + \frac{a_3}{(1+m)^3} + \ldots + \frac{a_n+S}{(1+m)^n}$$

where m is the *MEC*, the a's and S are defined exactly as before, and C is the price to the firm of the asset being considered—what Keynes called the supply price of capital. In principle, this equation can be solved for the value of m, which equates the right hand side to the left. It should be obvious that since the a's are the same for a given asset, if *PV* is greater than C, then m is greater than r. This leads to the assertion that firms will find it advantageous to purchase a unit of capital as long as the *MEC* is greater than the rate of interest.

The following paragraphs will develop the analysis of the investment decision by individual firms and then expand the theory and its application to the aggregate economy.

The Investment Decision

The firm has a demand for capital goods derived from its demand for the productive services of capital. The demand for the services of capital can be thought of as being completely analogous to the producer's demand for labor services. The price of a unit of labor service is a person's wage per hour or other time period. The price of a unit of capital service is the cost (or rent) per hour or other time period of a machine. Both human workers and machines are extremely heterogeneous categories, so it is a gross simplification to speak of a unit of labor or a unit of capital. We will, nevertheless, have to think of "standard" units of labor and capital and mentally make adjustments for differences in productivity of different specific units.

Labor and capital are complements in the productive process but are, in greater or lesser degree, substitutes for each other as well. From microeconomic theory we know that if the price of one service increases relative to the other, the firm will employ more of the lower-priced one and less of the more costly service. In the following discussion, we will assume the real wage of labor to remain constant. This analysis presumes that the determination of the anticipated level of output has already been made. Clearly, the higher the level of output expected, the greater the amount of all input factors that will be employed.

Because of the law of diminishing returns, the marginal product of capital services declines as the quantity of such services increases. We would further expect that as a firm increases its use of capital, it would proceed by choosing the most productive forms of capital first and use less and less productive types as it expands. In Figure 9-1, we show the marginal physical product curve declining as the stock of capital (and, therefore, the services of capital) increases.

This curve, the MPP_K curve, is simultaneously the basis of the demand for capital services and the demand curve for the stock of capital. The assumption is made that all of the other factors of production and the state of technology are given because any change in these would cause the curve to shift. For example, if the level of output changes, the MPP_K curve will shift; upward if planned output is larger and downward if output were expected to decrease. This is due to the fact that if output were to increase (decrease), more labor and other factors would have to be increased (decreased), so that for any given stock of capital the proportion of capital to the other factors would be less, which means that MPP_K would increase.

For example, if a firm owns or rents twenty machines, the total output per year is 400,000 widgets. An additional machine would increase the annual output to 406,000 widgets. In this case, the marginal physical product of capital (MPP_K) would be 6,000 widgets. Suppose the price of a widget is $2.00. Then, the value of marginal product of capital (VMP) is $12,000 per year. If the firm were able to acquire the machine for a net cost of less than $12,000 per year, it would pay the firm to do so; and, of course, if the cost were greater than $12,000 per year, it would not pay to use the twenty-first machine.

The rental cost (which could be the same whether the firm rented the machine from another firm or owned the machine and, in effect,

Figure 9-1   Productivity of Capital

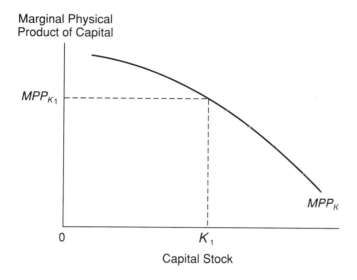

rented it from itself) depends upon the price of the machine, the durability of the machine, and the interest rate. For example, if each machine lasts three years and is worthless at the end of that time, the rent (or annual cost) would be $12,000 per year, if it costs about $29,842 with an interest rate of 10 percent to acquire the machine. This can be seen from the present value formula explained earlier.

$$PV = \frac{\$12{,}000}{(1+0.10)} + \frac{\$12{,}000}{(1+0.10)^2} + \frac{\$12{,}000}{(1+0.10)^3}$$

$$= \$10{,}909.09 + \$9{,}917.36 + \$9{,}015.75$$

$$\approx \$29{,}842$$

Thus, the $12,000 annual return would be sufficient to replace the machine (or repay the debt if the money were borrowed) at the end of the three years and still yield the required 10 percent interest return. Put another way, the value of the marginal product per machine per year is equal to the interest cost per year of $2,984.20 (0.10 x $29,842) plus the depreciation cost per year of $9,015.71.[2]

2. The depreciation figure is the amount that would have to be set aside each year and invested at 10 percent interest, in order to have $29,842 to buy a new machine at the end of the three years.

Summarizing this example, VMP_K, the value of the marginal product of capital, is \$12,000 per machine. Expressed as an annual rate per dollar's worth of capital, it is $\dfrac{\$12,000}{\$29,842}$, or 40.2 percent. Annual depreciation is \$9,015.71, which, expressed as an annual rate per dollar's worth of capital, is $\dfrac{\$9,015.71}{\$29,842}$, or 30.2 percent. The annual interest cost is $\dfrac{\$2,984.20}{\$29,842}$ or 10 percent.

Since 10 percent plus 30.2 percent equals 40.2 percent, this is an equilibrium situation. The marginal cost of buying a unit of capital (the interest rate plus the depreciation rate) is equal to the additional revenue from adding that unit of capital, which is the rate of the marginal product of capital.

If the rate of interest were to change, the required return on investment set by the firm would also change, as would the optimal stock of capital. An increase in the interest rate would increase both the cost of borrowing to acquire the machine and the rate of return required on the investment. This would lower the present value of the expected returns, and fewer machines would be desired. In order to decrease the stock of capital, the firm would allow some machines to wear out without replacing them. On the other hand, if the interest rate were to fall while other things remained the same, it would be profitable to add machines.

Notice that the rate of investment does not depend on the rate of interest (though it does depend on the change in the rate of interest), but that the stock of desired capital is determined by the level of the interest rate. This is due to the fact that whatever the interest rate, once the firm has the amount of capital it wishes to have, there is no need for investment or disinvestment. (Remember that investment is the act of adding to the stock of capital.) Investment takes place only after the interest rate has fallen, and the firm is in the process of expanding its capital stock. Once the capital stock has reached the desired level, investment would again be zero. The firm would be at its optimum with respect to the size of its stock of capital, and only the replacement expenditures (equal to depreciation) would take place.

What would happen if the price of capital goods increased? In that event, the firm would want fewer machines and would substitute labor for capital. The marginal efficiency of capital (the marginal product of capital minus depreciation, both expressed as a ratio to the price of capital) would then be less than the rate of interest. Referring once again to the present value formula, this implies that the machines are worth less than they cost.

Anything that would increase the marginal productivity of capital would increase the demand for capital. This would happen if the quality of the capital itself were improved, if its durability were increased, if the quality or the quantity of other factors of production were enhanced, or if the technology of production were somehow improved.

To this point, we have assumed that the discrepancy between the desired stock of capital and the actual stock of capital will be made up in a single period, for instance, one year. Some capital expansion plans, however, might take several or many years to accomplish efficiently. Thus, the rate of investment per year might be considerably less than the difference between the desired and the actual stock of capital.

Aggregate Investment

The discussion thus far has dealt with the decision process involving the demand for capital and the resulting act of investment by the individual firm. We turn now to the study of investment behaviour in the aggregate economy.

It is usually assumed that a single business unit is not large enough to perceptibly change the price of the product it produces by changing its output, nor is it able to change the price of its inputs when it changes its purchases of them. This is what differentiates the micro from the macro approach; since if all firms change their output, the price of the products sold will change, as will the prices of the resources used.

We can construct a demand relationship for capital as a function of the price of capital goods by aggregating or summing the demand curves of individual firms. Recall that these were derived from the marginal product of capital curves. Figure 9-2 shows the aggregate demand for capital curve where K is the total amount of capital desired at all possible prices of capital (P_K). The curve has a negative slope because (1) the marginal product per unit of capital service would decline as the capital stock is enlarged; and (2) the price of the goods produced by this capital would decline as the amounts produced are increased.

At a price of capital goods of P_{K_1}, the amount of capital all firms wish to have is K_1. At equilibrium, firms would, in fact, have the amount of capital they wish to have. If the price were just a little higher, say P_{K_2}, less capital would be desired. How would they adjust to the new higher price? Presumably, they would reduce their capital hold-

Figure 9-2   The Demand for Capital

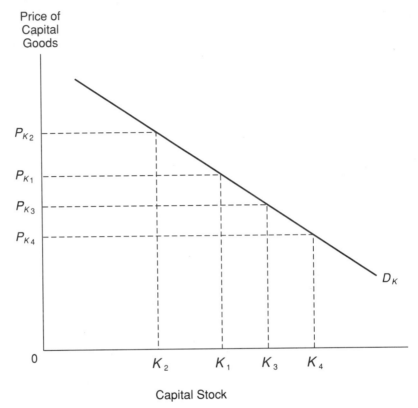

Capital Stock

ings to K_2 by allowing some machines to depreciate without replacement, or they would be willing to sell the amount $K_1 - K_2$. The demand for machines to add to the stock of capital, as a function of the price of capital, is therefore negative; that is, the demand for investment is negative in the amount $K_1 - K_2$.

At prices below the equilibrium price P_{K_1}, the demand for new capital (investment) would be positive. Thus, at price P_{K_3}, K_3 amount would be desired. In order to increase capital from K_1 to K_3, new machines would have to be purchased from the producers of such machines. There would then be demand to buy new capital in the amount $K_3 - K_1$. At a still lower price, say P_{K_4}, the demand for investment would be the difference between the desired stock of capital (K_4) and the actual stock of capital (K_1). This is shown as the amount $K_4 - K_1$ in Figure 9-2. In this fashion, we can construct the demand for (net) investment

Figure 9-3   A Shift in the Demand for Capital Due to a Decrease in the
Interest Rate

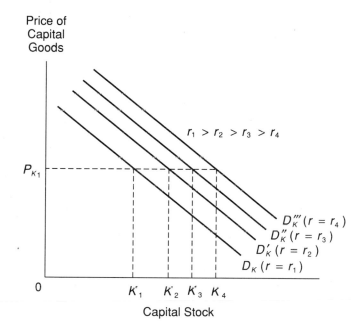

as a function of the price of capital. The D_K curve can be thought of as
the demand to *hold* or to own capital.

Keep in mind that we have been talking about the demand for capital. We now need to discuss the demand for investment, that is, the
demand to increase the stock of capital. As will be shown, investment
demand is a function of the interest rate and the level of expected
output.

If the interest rate were to fall, the present value of the machines
would rise. In that event, the firms would demand a larger number of
machines at any given price of machines. This is shown in Figure 9-3,
where, at the original interest rate, the quantity of capital desired, and
at equilibrium actually purchased, is K_1 when the price per unit of capital is P_K; and at the new lower interest rate, the firms would wish to
have K_2 amount of capital. The difference between the desired stock K_2
and the actual stock K_1 is the desired investment quantity. Thus, the
lower the rate of interest, the greater the demand for investment; and
conversely, the higher the rate of interest, the lower the demand for
investment.

Figure 9-4   The Supply of Capital

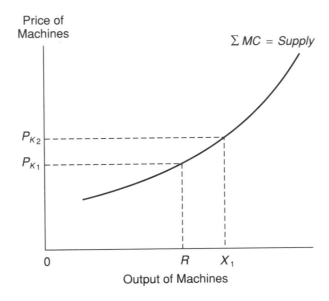

Since the situations we are considering are supposed to be general throughout the economy, a decrease in the interest rate (or an increase in output) would leave the business community with a smaller stock of capital than desired, so we presume that the firms will order more capital goods. We know that the machine-producing firms, too, are subject to the law of diminishing returns, so that the marginal cost of producing machines increases as output increases. Micro theory also shows that the sum of all the marginal cost curves of the individual firms becomes the supply curve for the industry. Figure 9-4 graphs the supply curve of the machine-producing industry.

Starting from a position of equilibrium where all firms have the number of machines they wish to have, the machine-producing industry will be producing just the number of machines needed to replace those that are wearing out. In Figure 9-4, this is designated as 0R. The equilibrium price is $0P_{K_1}$ when 0R is the rate of output of machines.

When the machine-using firms want more machines because the interest rate has fallen, the additional output of machines will force the price of machines to rise. For instance, if the demand for machines increases such that the total output of machine producers is $0X_1$, the price per machine would have to go up to $0P_{K_2}$. The number of new machines added to the existing stock per time period would then be

RX_1. Gross investment would be $0X_1$, and net investment would be RX_1. In summary, a decrease in the interest rate caused an increase in investment demand, but since the price of capital goes up as the output of capital expands, the amount of investment will be somewhat less than originally planned.

The increased prices of capital goods reduces the yield per dollar spent on them. In other words, the marginal efficiency of investment is lessened as investment increases, because the price of capital increases as the output of the capital goods industry increases.

Reverting to our numerical example, let us assume that the interest rate falls from the earlier rate of 10 percent to 8 percent. The rate of return the firm requires falls also, and the present value of the machines rises to PV_1.

$$PV_1 = \frac{\$12,000}{1.08} + \frac{\$12,000}{1.08^2} + \frac{\$12,000}{1.08^3}$$

$$= \$11,111.11 + \$10,288.07 + \$9,526.07$$

$$\cong \$30,925$$

If the price of the machines stays at the original level of $29,842, the firm will buy more machines. As the number of machines increases, however, the value of the marginal product will decline. The number of machines the firm will wish to add to its stock will be that number at which the *VMP*, when discounted to the present by the 8 percent interest rate, will equal the price of the machines. Thus,

$$C = \frac{VMP}{(1+r)} + \frac{VMP}{(1+r)^2} + \frac{VMP}{(1+r)^3}$$

$$\$29,842 = \frac{VMP}{1.08} + \frac{VMP}{1.08^2} + \frac{VMP}{1.08^3}$$

$$VMP = \$11,580.13$$

But since all the firms would be demanding more machines, the price of the machines will go up. As the price of the machines rises, the return on the investment, or the marginal efficiency of capital, declines. Thus, if the machine price were to rise to $30,500, the firm would buy the number of machines at which the *VMP*, discounted at the 8 percent rate of interest, would equal $30,500.

Figure 9-5   Investment Varies as Income Varies

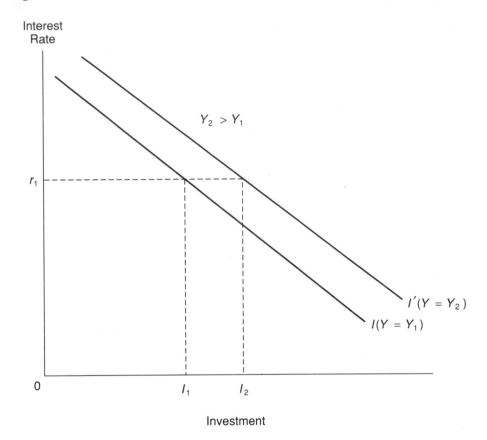

$$\$30,500 \;=\; \frac{VMP}{1.08} \;+\; \frac{VMP}{1.08^2} \;+\; \frac{VMP}{1.08^3}$$

$$VMP \;=\; \$11,835.47$$

Thus, the rate of investment depends on the price of capital and on the interest rate. Figure 9-5 is the graph of the investment function in which investment is dependent on the rate of interest. We have also pointed out that investment depends on the level of output firms plan to produce in the future. Figure 9-5 shows the effect of an increase in planned output on the investment demand relation. It simply demonstrates that at any given rate of interest, investment will be larger the greater is planned output.

Investment is a dynamic process. In a static equilibrium, whatever the rate of interest or whatever the level of national income, firms would have adjusted the stock of capital to the desired level and no investment would take place. Investment occurs only when the interest rate, the level of income, or other determinants change or are expected to change. Therefore, it is not true that investment will be larger the lower the interest rate; however, it is true that investment will increase as the interest rate falls. Gross investment will be larger the lower the interest rate, since a low interest rate implies a larger stock of capital and, hence, a larger rate of capital consumption and replacement expenditure.

The investment demand schedule is one of the most volatile functions with which economists have to deal. Knowledge of the kinds of events that will cause the schedule to shift upward or downward is indispensable to the business conditions analyst. The subject is far too large for an exhaustive discussion here, but we can mention certain classes of events that would shift the function.

The most important category in this connection is innovation in the broad Schumpeterian sense. Innovations may increase the physical productivity of capital by lowering the cost of production or affect the value of the output by increasing the demand for it. Outside events, such as changes in tax provisions, in other governmental policies, or in the business environment, also will have an effect in one direction or another.

The class of events that projects uncertainty into future forecasts of profits has often been emphasized, particularly by Keynes and his followers, as a basis for shift in the investment demand schedule. Greater uncertainty leads to a higher risk premium being included in costs and so, a downward shift. Pure optimism or pessimism, even if the cause for it cannot be found, will also shift the function. The major reason historically, for the function to shift, however, probably has been the change in expectations of changes in income and output.

GOVERNMENT AND THE NATIONAL INCOME

In this section, government expenditures and taxation will be introduced into the theory of national income determination. Part 5 discusses the national policies used to promote full employment, price stability, economic growth, and other goals; at this juncture, our concern is with the analytical framework rather than with the evaluation of such policies. Taxation, of course, is also a very important aspect of the government's impact on national income, but its effect is by way of altering consumption behavior. For that reason, the subject of taxation is covered in Chapter 12, where the consumption function is explored at some length.

Government and Aggregate Demand

Purchases of goods and services by government are a portion of the total demand for the national output. They may be on capital account or on current account; by state and local units or by the federal government. From the point of view of their impact on the level of national income, these distinctions can be ignored. In using the theory as a framework for forecasting, however, they are quite important.

State and local governmental units do not have the spending flexibility of the federal government. Borrowing is often restricted by provision of their constitutions or charters and is otherwise more difficult to accomplish. The federal government has the power to create money, but the smaller units do not have this power. Thus, the state and local levels of government are necessarily more closely tied in their decisions to spend by their ability to tax.

The ability to tax is more restricted for state and local units than it is for the federal government. The smaller the taxing jurisdiction, the easier it is for the public to avoid the taxes by moving to another jurisdiction. The type of taxation available to the smaller levels of government is also usually quite limited. As a rule, they are forced to depend more on taxes based on property rather than income.

The many difficulties involved in acquiring funds by the smaller governmental units force their spending patterns to be dictated by their receipts rather than by considerations of their counter-cyclical effect. It would probably be correct to consider state and local spending a positive function of national income.

Spending by the federal government is such a large portion of aggregate demand that changes in its volume have an important impact on the national income. The national government must be concerned with the effect of its expenditures upon the economy, and we are concerned here with what that effect will be. Since it is a matter of policy, government expenditures are usually handled as an exogenous factor. The G function is, therefore, autonomous, or not a function of income; however, in a broader context, government outlays are influenced by the stage of the business cycle.

Figure 9-6   Government Expenditures Multiplier

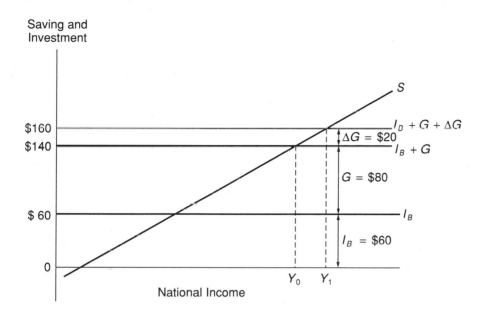

In Figure 9-6, government expenditures for goods and services have been added to business investment (I_B) to become the injections function ($I_B + G$). A new, higher rate of spending by the government is indicated by adding ΔG to create a new total amount of injections. The multiplier is operative on the new spending demand in exactly the same way as it was for new investment demand. The government expenditures multiplier is defined as $\dfrac{\Delta Y}{\Delta G}$, and it would be derived exactly as the investment multiplier was in Chapter 8. Graphically, it can be seen that income would increase from Y_0 to Y_1 when government spending was increased by ΔG, so

$$\frac{\Delta Y}{\Delta G} = \frac{1}{\dfrac{\Delta S}{\Delta Y}} = \frac{1}{1 - \dfrac{\Delta C}{\Delta Y}}$$

In other words, in the mechanics of income determination, government spending can be handled in exactly the same manner as is investment. Since no new principles are involved in introducing government expenditures into the model, we shall delay its incorporation into an algebraic model until we have also brought in the taxation component.

The *I-S* Curve

The purpose of the *I-S* curve development is to bring together all of the elements of the demand for goods and services in the total economy and to relate them to their fundamental determinants, namely, the rate of interest and national income. In this discussion of the *I-S* curve derivation, the interest rate is assumed to have been established. In the following chapter, we will discuss how the interest rate is determined.

The supply of national income is the rate of production of commodities by the business sector, and in the Keynesian type of analysis, this will be sufficient to meet the demands of buyers for these commodities. The demand categories are classified as demands by households for consumption expenditures, by the business community for investment, by the government for the expenditures it wishes to make, and as the net difference between the demand by foreigners for our goods and our demand for theirs, which we term net foreign investment.

In the following discussion, government expenditures and net foreign investment will be considered to be independent of both interest rates and national income, or exogenous variables. This is shown in Figure 9-7 (d) where $\overline{G}_0 + \overline{F}_0$ are at their given levels, no matter what the rate of interest happens to be. In the preceding section, the argument was presented that the lower the rate of interest, the greater the spending on new plants, equipment, and inventories by business firms. For example, if the interest rate is r_1, government spending will be $\overline{G}_0$, net foreign investment will be $\overline{F}_0$ and investment will be I_1. The sum of the three demands is shown on the $G+F+I$ function.

A fall in the interest rate to r_2 has no effect on G nor on F, but does increase investment to I_2, and the sum of the three demands would then be $\overline{G}_0 + \overline{F}_0 + I_2$, as shown.

Our analysis in Chapter 8 showed that national income is in equilibrium when supply of national output is equal to the demand for goods and services, that is, when $C+S_p+T=C+I+G+(Ex-Im)$. Since the supply and demand for consumption are equal, this condition reduces to $S_p+T=I+G+(Ex-Im)$. In the diagrams of Figure 9-7, $S=S_p+T$ and $Ex-Im$ is labeled $\overline{F}_0$. Thus, national income is shown to be in equilibrium in Figure 9-7 where $S=\overline{G}_0+\overline{F}_0+I$. Diagram (b) of Figure 9-7 is simply a 45° line that allows us to "turn the corner" so that $\overline{G}_0+\overline{F}_0+I$,

Figure 9-7   Derivation of the *I-S* Function

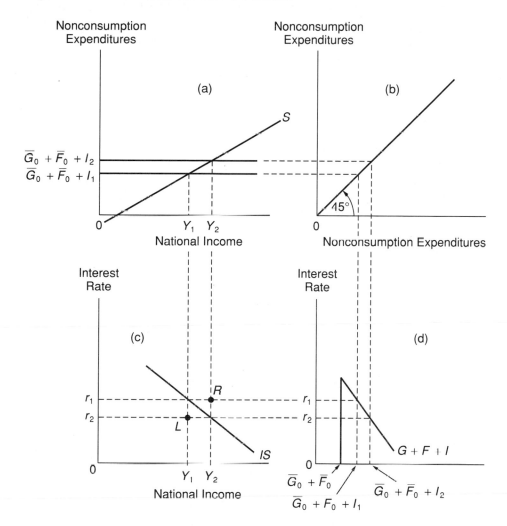

determined horizontally in diagram (d), can be converted to a vertical measurement and then projected to diagram (a). For an interest rate of r_1, the level of $\overline{G}_0 + \overline{F}_0 + I_1$ is found in diagram (d). For $S = \overline{G}_0 + \overline{F}_0 + I_1$, national income will have to be Y_1 in diagram (a). In diagram (c), we show the conjuncture of interest rate r_1 and national income Y_1 as an equilibrium situation. Now, if the interest rate falls to r_2, $G + F + I$ will be $\overline{G}_0 + \overline{F}_0 + I_2$ and income must rise to Y_2 in order for S to increase to equal $\overline{G}_0 + \overline{F}_0 + I_2$.

Two points on the I-S curve have been derived. The curve is a locus of such points at which the equilibrium condition holds that the aggregate supply of goods and services is equal to the aggregate demand for goods and services; or what amounts to the same condition, saving $(S_p + T)$ is equal to investment $(I + G + F)$. Putting it still another way: at any point on the I-S curve, nonconsumption demands equal the supply of goods and services not consumed.

What would happen if the economy had an interest rate of r_1 and income were at Y_2, that is, at point R, to the right of the I-S curve? Since r_1 is a high rate of interest, investment would be curtailed to a level of I_1. At income Y_2 saving is greater than $\overline{G}_0 + \overline{F}_0 + I_1$, so either actual saving is less than intended saving, or actual investment is greater than intended investment. In either case, we know that income must fall. In this case, it would fall to Y_1, which is a point on I-S. Conversely, of course, at a point to the left of the I-S curve, such as L, intended injections $[(\overline{G}_0 + \overline{F}_0 + I_2)$ from Figure 9-7(d)] would exceed intended saving $[(\overline{G}_0 + \overline{F}_0 + I_1)$ from Figure 9-7(a)] and income would rise to Y_2.

MULTIPLIER-ACCELERATOR INTERACTION

In this chapter, we have looked at the foundations of investment behavior from a study of the decision processes of the firms demanding capital and those supplying capital goods. This theory makes investment depend on changes in the interest rate, given any level of national income. The acceleration principle makes investment depend on changes in the level of national income, given any interest rate. In a complete theory of investment, both ideas would seem necessary.

The acceleration principle has been seen to produce cyclical behavior in certain industries. The same sort of forces are operative on the macro level of analysis. The theory that is outlined here as the multiplier-accelerator interaction theory has become an important contemporary explanation of business cycles.

The multiplier process is capable of explaining why income and expenditures rise in a cumulative fashion once an expansive act occurs, or why economic activity declines cumulatively in response to some contractive action. The theory itself does not explain the turning points of business cycles. Other theories must be introduced for that purpose, such as Keynes' psychologically caused shifts in the marginal efficiency of capital.

The essential features of introducing the acceleration principle into the theory is that cycles are generated as a part of the response mechanism of the economy. The basic difference between a "multiplier-type" model and a model that incorporates the accelerator lies in the nature of the investment function.

A multiplier-type investment function either makes investment independent of income or associates larger investment with larger levels of national income. This implies that if income were constant at some high level, investment would also be constant at a high rate. In a business firm, one would expect that if the level of production were constant, the firm would have no need for new equipment except to replace that which wears out or becomes obsolete, neither of which are a part of net investment. A firm would purchase additional capital only to meet expected increases in its rate of production.

An accelerator-type investment function takes this reasoning into account, making investment depend on the change in national income and not on the level of income.[3] This implies that if national income is constant, no matter what the level, investment expenditures will be zero. But if income increases, investment will be positive no matter what the level of income. The accelerator, then, is a dynamic theory where time plays an important role.

The easiest way to see why the accelerator generates cycles and why multiplier-type investment relations do not is through the use of an example. First, compare the investment functions themselves.

$$I = \bar{I} + iY \text{ (multiplier-type investment function)}$$

$$I' = \bar{I}' + A\Delta Y \text{ (accelerator-type investment function)}$$

In these two equations, $\bar{I}$ and $\bar{I}'$ are autonomous investment parameters, the portion of investment that is not related to income.

A study of Tables 9-1 and 9-2 should highlight the distinction being made between a multiplier-only model and a model that incorporates both the multiplier and the accelerator. Table 9-1 is the multiplier model constructed from the following equations and parameter values:

$$Y_t = C_t + I_t$$
$$C_t = a + bY_{t-1}$$
$$I_t = \bar{I}_t + iY_{t-1}$$
$$a = 30, b = 0.8, \bar{I}_0 = 50, \bar{I}_1 = 60, i = 0.1$$

3. Frequently, writers relate investment to a change in consumption rather than in income, which sometimes leaves the impression that this is the distinctive feature of the accelerator. It is not! Whether making changes in consumption or income, the independent variable has no effect upon the cycle-generating capability of the model.

Table 9-1

Multiplier Model

Period	Y	C	$\bar{I}$	$I_i = iY$	I
0	800.00	670.00	50.00	80.00	130.00
1	810.00	670.00	60.00	80.00	140.00
2	819.00	678.00	60.00	81.00	141.00
3	827.10	685.20	60.00	81.90	141.90
4	834.39	691.68	60.00	82.71	142.71
5	840.95	697.51	60.00	83.44	143.44
6	846.86	702.76	60.00	84.10	144.10
7	852.18	707.49	60.00	84.69	144.69
8	856.97	711.75	60.00	85.22	145.22
9	861.28	715.58	60.00	85.70	145.70
10	865.16	719.03	60.00	86.13	146.13
.	.	.	.	.	.
n	900.00	750.00	60.00	90.00	150.00

The first row is found by solving for equilibrium income in period 0, as follows:

$$Y_0 = \frac{a + \bar{I}}{1 - b - i} = \frac{30 + 50}{1 - 0.8 - 0.1} = 800$$

$$C_0 = a + bY_0 = 30 + 0.8(800) = 670$$

$$I_0 = \bar{I}_0 + iY_0 = 50 + 0.1(800) = 50 + 80 = 130$$

The succeeding rows are completed by first finding consumption as a function of income in the preceding period, then finding induced investment (I_i) also as a function of the preceding income, and adding $C + I$ to find Y.

In this table, Y will always increase, because once the rate of autonomous investment has increased, consumption and investment must both increase. Increases in consumption and investment are increases in income that, in turn, mean that consumption and investment in the following period must increase. Each of the increases is smaller than the one that went before it, and all variables will approach new equilibria as shown in period n.

Table 9-2 shows the accelerator in action and was constructed from the following:

Table 9-2

Multiplier Model with Accelerator

Period	Y	C	$\bar{I}$	$I_A = A\Delta Y$	I
0	800	700	100	0	100
1	810	700	110	0	110
2	828	708	110	10	120
3	850.4	722.4	110	18	128
4	872.72	740.32	110	22.4	132.4
5	890.50	758.18	110	22.32	132.32
P 6	900.18	772.40	110	17.78	127.78
7	899.82	780.14	110	9.68	119.68
8	889.49	779.85	110	−0.36	109.64
9	871.26	771.59	110	−10.33	99.67
10	848.78	757.01	110	−18.23	91.77
11	826.55	739.03	110	−22.48	87.52
12	809.02	721.25	110	−22.23	87.77
T 13	799.70	707.23	110	−17.53	92.47
14	800.45	699.77	110	−9.32	100.68
15	811.12	700.37	110	0.75	110.75

$$Y_t = C_t + I_t$$
$$C_t = a + bY_{t-1}$$
$$I_t = \bar{I}_0 + A(Y_{t-1} - Y_{t\ 2})$$
$$a = 60,\ b = 0.8,\ \bar{I}_0 = 100,\ \bar{I}_1 - 110,\ \Lambda = 1$$

Equilibrium income is found from $Y_0 = \dfrac{a + \bar{I}_0}{1 - b}$ at which income $C_t = a + bY_{t-1} = 60 + 0.8(800) = 700$. Investment is 100, which is the autonomous portion ($\bar{I}$) only. Induced investment (I_A) is zero because income is at equilibrium and is therefore constant, so $Y_0 - Y_{0-1} = 0$.

Table 9-2 has been carried out to fifteen periods to show that with these particular values of the *MPC* ($b = 0.8$) and "the relation" ($A = 1$), a cycle is indeed operating with a peak, or upper turning point, in period 6 and a trough, or lower turning point, in period 13. Other values of b and A would produce different behavior. This particular set creates a slightly explosive or divergent cycle; another set (different values of A and b) would lead to damped or convergent cycles; in other cases, the multiplier effect would swamp the accelerator so that income would move only in one direction.[4]

The acceleration principle is a good example for being wary of too mechanistic an approach to determining cause and effect. On the basis of the statistics alone, one might conclude that, since investment declined earliest (period 5), this was the "cause" of the ensuing depression. But why did *I* fall? The answer is that the increase in income from period 4 to 5 was less than the increase from period 3 to 4. Why was this true? We already know that the reason for the cycle is the relative sizes of the response mechanism and the structure of the economy. In this case, at least, a purely statistical search for direct cause and effect would be fruitless.

The accelerator relation (A) can be related to the productivity of capital by observing that $A = \dfrac{I_t - \bar{I}_t}{Y_{t-1} - Y_{t-2}}$ or if we ignore the exogenous portion: $A = \dfrac{I_t}{Y_{t-1} - Y_{t-2}}$. (In this model, A is also equal to the capital-output ratio.) Recalling that investment is the change in the stock of capital goods, and $Y_{t-1} - Y_{t-2}$ is the change in output, or income, A is almost the reciprocal of the national average of the marginal product of capital. The marginal product of capital is defined as the change in total output per unit change in the stock of capital, with all other factors held constant. The important difference between the two ideas is that in the accelerator concept, the change in income is the independent variable, and the change in capital (I) is dependent, whereas in the marginal product concept, income (or output) change is dependent upon the change in the stock of capital.

The marginal product of capital is a technological relation between capital input and the product output. In the theory of the firm, after some refinements, the marginal product schedule becomes the demand curve for the factor of production. In the case of capital, interest is the relevant price or wage. The accelerator, too, should be considered as an element of the demand for capital; here, the quantity demanded varies as income varies. Higher or lower interest rates would be assumed to alter the size of the accelerator coefficient.

The speed with which business managers react to an increase in the demand for their product and the length of time required to construct new capital are also important elements in the determination of

---

4. For more precision, see the frequently quoted article by Paul A. Samuelson, "Interaction between the Multiplier Analysis and the Principle of Acceleration," *Review of Economic Statistics* (May 1939).

the size of A. The time lag involved in the model (such as that of Table 9-2) must be determined by the consumption lag, that is, the length of time for consumers to adjust their spending to their new income. Suppose the consumption lag to be one month, so that $Y_{t-1} - Y_{t-2}$ is the change in the rate of income within one month. If all businesses immediately ordered new equipment, and producers of this equipment were able to produce it in less than a month, the accelerator would be very large. This is not very realistic for most industries. It would seem more likely that many investors would hesitate to evaluate immediately the permanence of the increased demand and would also require time to arrange financing. Furthermore, the cost of production of capital often dictates that a long period of time will be taken to produce it. The response will also depend, in part, upon the current degree of utilization of existing capital. If much excess capacity exists, firms need not increase their capital stock significantly when demand increases so A would be relatively small. On the other hand, if the capital goods-producing industry is at or near full capacity, it may take a relatively long time to supply new equipment to the users of the equipment—again, a low value of A would exist.

On technological grounds, underdeveloped economies are likely to exhibit lower A values than are the well-developed industrial societies, because the marginal product of capital relative to that of labor and land is quite high. This can partially be used to explain the observed phenomena that the business cycle is a greater problem in the well-developed systems than it is in the less industrialized systems.

This discussion would seem to indicate that the acceleration coefficient is complex. The lag is probably distributed over several periods. The numerical value of the relation fluctuates over a period of time, especially over the business cycle, and varies in different industries or geographic areas. Although we can find many qualifications to the simple theoretical system, it is nevertheless an important contribution to business cycle analysis.

QUESTIONS

1. Refer to the example on page 227. Figure the machine's worth if the interest rate were 4 percent. Figure its value if the interest rate were 6 percent.
2. Using the present value formulas, comment on the investment action of a firm
   (a) if the price of a machine it uses falls;

    (b) if the machine is improved to add a year to its productive life;

    (c) if the firm's product price increases.

3. Derive the government expenditure multiplier.

4. Choose a point to the left of the *I-S* function, and explain why the point would have to move to the *I-S* curve.

5. Without a numerical example, explain why a multiplier-type investment relation can produce only single-direction movements of national income, while the accelerator relation generates cyclical responses to the same shock.

6. Would you expect the accelerator to operate differently when the capital stock is being used only partially and when it is being used near capacity?

7. Continue Table 9-1 through the 15th period. Will there be a turning point?

8. Continue Table 9-2 through the 21st period. Is there another turning point?

9. Derive graphically the shift in the *I-S* function caused by

    (a) a shift to the right of the investment demand schedule,

    (b) an upward shift of the saving function.

READINGS

Dernburg, Thomas F. *Macroeconomics: Concepts, Theories, and Policies*, 7th ed. New York: McGraw-Hill Book Co., 1985. Chapter 6.

Glahe, Fred R. *Macroeconomics: Theory and Policy*, 3d ed. San Diego, CA: Harbrace, 1985.

Gordon, Robert J. *Macroeconomics*, 4th ed. Glenview, IL: Scott, Foresman and Company, 1987. Chapters 4 and 14.

Hirshleifer, J. *Investment, Interest, and Capital*. Englewood Cliffs, NJ: Prentice-Hall, Inc., 1969.

Jorgenson, Dale W. "The Theory of Investment Behavior." *Determinants of Investment Behavior*, edited by Robert Ferber. Urbana, IL: Bureau of Economics and Business Research, 1966.

Patinkin, D. "Price Flexibility and Full Employment." *The American Economic Review* (September 1948).

Pigou, A. C. "Economic Progress in a Stable Environment." *Econometrica*, New Series (August 1947).

Samuelson, Paul A. "The Simple Mathematics of Income Determination." *Income, Employment, and Public Policy: Essays in Honor of Alvin Hansen*, edited by Lloyd A. Metzler, et al. New York: W. W. Norton & Co., Inc., 1948.

———. "Interactions between the Multiplier Analysis and the Principle of Acceleration." *Review of Economic Statistics* (May 1939).

Witte, James G. "The Microfoundations of the Social Investment Function." *Journal of Political Economy* (October 1963).

Wonnacott, Paul. *Macroeconomics*, 2d ed. Homewood, IL: Richard D. Irwin, Inc., 1980. Chapter 14.

MONEY AND THE *L-M* CURVE

We begin this chapter with the construction of a basic theory of money supply behavior. We then develop the demand side by discussing the liquidity preference theory that was introduced by Keynes to supplement or supplant the quantity theory and to act as an alternative to classical and neoclassical interest rate theories. This allows us to construct a curve of interest rate and income levels in which the supply of and demand for money are in equilibrium. Since the interest rate and income are also important in establishing equilibrium in the market for goods and services, the *I-S* curve of Chapter 9 is combined with the money market equilibrium curve to determine the interest rate and national income.

MONETARY AND CREDIT SYSTEM

Money and credit are profoundly important in determining the nature of business fluctuations in an economy. For this reason, we discuss this facet of our economic system somewhat more thoroughly than other institutional factors.

Monetary System

Money has traditionally been defined as anything generally accepted in payment for goods and services or in discharge of debt. This definition stresses the role of money as a medium of exchange. Money has other important functions—as the standard of value and as a store of value—but its uniqueness lies in its use as the means of effecting economic transactions. The closest empirical counterpart to this concept of money is the Federal Reserve's M1 balances, which are made up of currency and coin, travelers' checks, demand deposits in commercial banks, and other checkable deposits. The checkable deposits include negotiable order of withdrawal (NOW) accounts, automatic transfer service (ATS) accounts at banks and thrift institutions, credit union share draft balances, and demand deposits at mutual savings banks.

The U.S. monetary system comprises the U.S. Treasury, the Federal Reserve System (FRS), the system of commercial banks, and other financial institutions that offer checkable deposits to the public. All of these institutions have one feature in common that no other units of the economy have: they are capable of both creating and destroying money. These institutions are peculiar in that they have money as a liability. The bulk of our money supply is in the form of demand and other checkable deposits, which are liabilities of commercial banks and certain thrift institutions. Our hand-to-hand money is made up of coins (a liability of the Treasury) and currency (a liability primarily of the Federal Reserve Banks, but also, to a minor extent, of the Treasury).

The stock of money at any time depends mainly on the actions of the members of the monetary system, on the constraints placed on them by the law and its administration, and on the actions of parties not included in the monetary system, such as households, business units, and the rest of the world. The significance of variation in the money supply is discussed later. Here, however, the purpose is to show how the variation comes about. In the analysis of business conditions, it is not merely the currency supply that is important, but the total money supply. If the money supply were, for instance, $500 billion, it would make very little difference whether it were $500 billion of currency or $500 billion of checkable deposits. It is simply a matter of convenience for the nonmonetary system (the public) to have both kinds of money. The monetary system accommodates the public by dividing the total money supply into the proportions wanted by the public. In restricting our attention to the stock of money, defined in the narrow sense of checkable deposits plus currency and coin, we are not denying the importance of near monies. Near monies are assets that do not possess the medium of exchange property because they have to be converted into money to be used to make payments, for example, savings and time deposits or government bonds. These items are important, but in our approach, their effect is considered separately from the effect of money itself.

A *commercial bank* is a firm that has the power to accept accounts that are subject to immediate withdrawal by check. Commercial banks are either FRS members or nonmember banks. All national banks—

banks that receive their charters from the Comptroller of the Currency of the U.S. Treasury—must be member banks. State banks, chartered by state governments, may become member banks if they meet certain standards on capital and agree to abide by FRS laws and regulations. The distinction between the two categories of banks has become relatively insignificant.

Member banks must keep a legally prescribed minimum amount of reserves as deposits with the district Federal Reserve Bank or as vault cash. Nonmember depository institutions offering "transactions accounts" are required to hold reserves either directly with the Federal Reserve, in the form of deposits with a Federal Reserve Bank, or as vault cash; or indirectly with a Federal Reserve Bank, on a pass-through basis with certain approved institutions.[1] The definitions of reserves and the reserve requirements have changed occasionally, causing variation in the money stock.

The distinctions made among member bank, nonmember bank, commercial bank, and thrift institution have become blurred and are less significant since the enactment of the Depository Institutions Deregulation and Monetary Control Act (DIDMCA) of 1980.[2] This act became law on March 31, 1980, when signed by President Carter. The act makes all depository institutions (commercial banks, savings and loan associations, savings banks, credit unions, agencies and branches of foreign banks, and the Edge corporations) subject to the same reserve requirements as member banks.

Table 10-1 shows the reserve requirement regulations after implementation of the Monetary Control Act. In addition to the controls shown in the table, the Federal Reserve Board of Governors has the authority to impose a supplemental reserve requirement of up to 4 percent on total transactions accounts. This authority is hedged somewhat, but it is interesting that these additional reserves will earn a return for the depository institutions amounting to the average return earned by assets held by the Federal Reserve. In the past, the Federal Reserve was not permitted to pay interest on reserves of member banks. The law specifies, however, that the supplemental reserve requirements may be imposed only for monetary policy purposes.

---

1. Board of Governors of the Federal Reserve System, 71st Annual Report, 1984, p. 240.

2. For a complete description of other provisions of the law, see "The Depository Institutions Deregulation and Monetary Control Act of 1980," by Charles R. McNeill, *Federal Reserve Bulletin* (June 1980), pp. 444–453.

Table 10-1

Reserve Requirements of Depository Institutions[1]
Percent of Deposits

Type of Deposit, and Deposit Interval[2]	Depository Institution Requirements after Implementation of the Monetary Control Act	
	Percent of Deposits	Effective Date
Net transaction accounts[3,4]		
$0 million—$40.4 million	3	12/19/89
More than $40.4 million	12	12/19/89
Nonpersonal time deposits[5]		
By original maturity		
Less than 1½ years	3	10/6/83
1½ years or more	0	10/6/83
Eurocurrency liabilities		
All types	3	11/13/80

1. Reserve requirements in effect on Dec. 31, 1989. Required reserves must be held in the form of deposits with Federal Reserve Banks or vault cash. Nonmember institutions may maintain reserve balances with a Federal Reserve Bank indirectly on a pass-through basis with certain approved institutions. For previous reserve requirements, see earlier editions of the *Annual Report* or the *Federal Reserve Bulletin*. Under provisions of the Monetary Control Act, depository institutions include commercial banks, mutual savings banks, savings and loan associations, credit unions, agencies and branches of foreign banks, and Edge corporations.

2. The Garn–St. Germain Depository Institutions Act of 1982 (Public Law 97–320) requires that $2 million of reservable liabilities (transaction accounts, nonpersonal time deposits, and Eurocurrency liabilities) of each depository institution be subject to a zero percent reserve requirement. The Board is to adjust the amount of reservable liabilities subject to this zero percent reserve requirement each year for the succeeding calendar year by 80 percent of the percentage increase in the total reservable liabilities of all depository institutions, measured on an annual basis as of June 30. No corresponding adjustment is to be made in the event of a decrease. On Dec. 20, 1988, the exemption was raised from $3.2 million to $3.4 million. In determining the reserve requirements of depository institutions, the exemption shall apply in the following order: (1) net NOW accounts (NOW accounts less allowable deductions); (2) net other transaction accounts; and (3) nonpersonal time deposits or Eurocurrency liabilities starting with those with the highest reserve ratio. With respect to NOW accounts and

other transaction accounts, the exemption applies only to such accounts that would be subject to a 3 percent reserve requirement.

3. Transaction accounts include all deposits on which the account holder is permitted to make withdrawals by negotiable or transferable instruments, payment orders of withdrawal, and telephone and preauthorized transfers in excess of three per month for the purpose of making payments to third persons or others. However, MMDAs and similar accounts subject to the rules that permit no more than six preauthorized, automatic, or other transfers per month, of which no more than three can be checks, are not transaction accounts (such accounts are savings deposits subject to time deposit reserve requirements).

4. The Monetary Control Act of 1980 requires that the amount of transaction accounts against which the 3 percent reserve requirement applies be modified annually by 80 percent of the percentage change in transaction accounts held by all depository institutions, determined as of June 30 each year. Effective Dec. 19, 1989 for institutions reporting quarterly and Dec. 26, 1989 for institutions reporting weekly, the amount was decreased from $41.5 million to $40.4 million.

5. In general, nonpersonal time deposits are time deposits, including savings deposits, that are not transaction accounts and in which a beneficial interest is held by a depositor that is not a natural person. Also included are certain transferable time deposits held by natural persons and certain obligations issued to depository institution offices located outside the United States. For details, see section 204.2 of Regulation D.

Source: *Federal Reserve Bulletin* (January 1990), p. A8.

Credit Expansion

Credit expansion refers to the process by which banks increase the money supply.[3] One should distinguish between credit expansion and money supply expansion. Money supply expansion points to the lia-

---

3. To the extent that other types of financial institutions create liabilities that serve as media of exchange, the principles described in this section apply to them also.

bility side of the balance sheets of the members of the monetary system. Credit expansion points to the asset side of bank balance sheets and emphasizes the fact that bank credit normally increases as demand deposits grow. The purpose of this section is to review credit and money expansion as it takes place through the activities of commercial banks.[4]

If a customer deposits either currency or coin in a bank, the full amount is immediately included as reserves, since vault cash is counted as legal reserves. If a deposited check is drawn on the receiving bank itself, neither its total deposits nor its legal reserves are affected. If a check drawn against another bank is deposited, the check will be sent for collection, and the collection will take the form of an increase in the bank's deposit account with the Federal Reserve Bank of its district. Although it may take a day or two for the collection to occur, when it does, the full amount is added to the bank's legal reserves.

The bank receiving the deposit has 100 percent of its new deposit backed by reserves. If its reserve requirement were 10 percent, it could allow its reserves to fall by 90 percent of the new deposit and continue to operate within the legal minimum. The bank could expect that if it made a loan or purchased securities in the amount of the 90 percent, the borrower or the seller of the security would write checks on the created balance and thus withdraw the deposit, and the bank's reserves would be reduced. The bank then would have the original deposit as its liability, the 10 percent remaining in reserves as assets, and the 90 percent as earning assets (loans or investments). But the bank on which the original deposited check was written would have lost reserves and deposits in the check's amount. Its required reserves would have decreased by 10 percent of the amount of the withdrawal, so it must now take steps to acquire 90 percent of the check amount in reserves. The bank will allow loans to expire or sell other earning assets in this amount so that the expansionary action by the bank receiving the check is exactly offset by the contractionary action of the bank whose deposits were withdrawn.

The key to most of the analysis of credit and money expansion or contraction is whether or not an offsetting action exists elsewhere in the system. If, for example, currency that had been in circulation for some time was returned to the banking system, there would be an in-

---

4. Although we tend to speak of expansion, the reader should realize that the contractionary process is equally important in business cycle analysis. The steps involved in the contraction are just the reverse of those cited for the expansion.

crease in reserves of the bank receiving the deposit without a corresponding loss by another bank. Similarly, if the Federal Reserve bought securities, or if the Treasury paid off some of its debts or spent some money out of its account at the Federal Reserve, some banks would receive new reserves while no other commercial bank would lose reserves.

Let us assume that the Federal Reserve buys $100 million worth of Treasury bills on the open market. The sellers will receive checks drawn against the Federal Reserve Banks and will deposit them in commercial banks, which will have new reserves as soon as the checks are sent to the Federal Reserve Banks. Since no commercial bank loses reserves in this transaction, there is a net increase of reserves in the banking system and of deposits of $100 million for the sellers of the bills. The affected banks now have excess reserves of $90 million (assuming a 10 percent reserve requirement). Each bank could lend or purchase other earning assets by the amount of its excess reserves, unless it wished to hold additional excess reserves. For example, if banks, on the average, had a demand for excess reserves equal to 5 percent of their demand deposits, they would expand earning assets by $85 million rather than the $90 million that legally could be added. Borrowers would spend the proceeds by writing checks, and those who received these checks would deposit them in their own commercial banks. In this process, we might expect a currency drain to take place, since, as the money supply is expanding, it is likely that the public will demand more of both kinds of money, that is, currency and coin as well as demand deposits.

To the extent that currency and coin are drawn into circulation, the banks are losing reserves. If we assume that the currency drain is 10 percent of deposit expansion, the public will withdraw $10 million since demand deposits have increased by $100 million. This means that of the $85 million of earning asset expansion by banks, $75 million will be deposited to become new reserves for depositors' banks. These banks, in turn, will have $63.75 million available for loans and investments (deposits and reserves increased by $75 million; required reserves went up by $75 million × 0.10 = $7.5 million; desired excess reserves increased by $75 million × 0.05 = $3.75 million). This process of banks making loans and losing reserves and deposits to other banks and to currency in circulation will continue until all the original $100 million is absorbed into required reserves, desired excess reserves, and currency in circulation. The interesting question in monetary theory is how much the money supply will increase.

To answer this question, it is necessary to discover the size of the monetary expansion multiplier. This multiplier is the number by which the monetary base must be multiplied to equal the size of the money stock; that is, $M=KB$ where $M=$ the amount of money in the economy, $K=$ the multiplier, and $B=$ the monetary base, which is currency in circulation plus bank reserves held at the Federal Reserve.

The Simple Multiplier

If we were to introduce all, or even most, of the complications in the real world, the model would become extremely complex. In view of this, we will present first the simplest possible multiplier and then develop one that is adequate for the analysis we will need in this book.

1. $M=KB$
2. $B=R$ where R is the amount of legal reserves held by the banking system.
3. $R=rD$ where r is the reserve requirement and D is the amount of demand deposits in the banking system.
4. $M=D$ which states that in this model, the only kind of money is demand deposits.

Solving for K:

$$K = \frac{M}{B} \text{ from (1)}$$

$$K = \frac{D}{R} \text{ from (2) and (4)}$$

$$K = \frac{D}{rD} \text{ from (3)}$$

$$K = \frac{1}{r}$$

Thus, the simple multiplier is the reciprocal of the reserve requirement. If the reserve requirement is 0.20 (or 20 percent), the value of K, the multiplier, is 5. This means that if reserves are $20 billion, the money supply will be $5 \times \$20$ billion, or $100 billion; and if R is increased by $100 million, the money stock will increase by $500 million.

A More Complete Multiplier

To use the simple model as a forecasting tool would obviously be absurd; other things would have to remain constant, and we can be quite certain that some very important things would not remain constant. For example, if the reserve base were increased and the amount of demand deposits were increasing, the public would be expected to increase their demands for currency and time deposits, and the banks might want more excess reserves. Our next problem is to incorporate these factors into a model. Note that there are still a number of important variables that have not been included.

1. $M = KB$
2. $B = R + C_b + C_c$ where R is deposits of banks in Federal Reserve Banks, C_b is vault cash, and C_c is currency in circulation.
3. $R + C_b = rD + eD + r'T$ where e is the desired excess reserve ratio, r' is the reserve requirement on time deposits, and T is time deposits.
4. $C_c = aD$ where a is $\dfrac{C_c}{D}$, the ratio of currency to demand deposits that the public wishes to hold.
5. $T = tD$ where t is $\dfrac{T}{D}$, the ratio of time deposits to demand deposits the public wishes to hold. (T includes only those time deposits subject to reserve requirements, namely, nonpersonal time deposits.)
6. $M = D + C_c$ The money supply is made up of demand deposits and currency in circulation.

Solving for K:

$$K = \frac{M}{B} = \frac{D + C_c}{R + C_b + C_c} \quad \text{from (6) and (2)}$$

$$K = \frac{D + aD}{rD + eD + r'T + aD} \quad \text{from (3) and (4)}$$

$$K = \frac{D(1 + a)}{D(r + e + r't + a)} \quad \text{from (5)}$$

$$K = \frac{1 + a}{r + e + r't + a} \quad , \text{and}$$

$$M = \frac{1 + a}{r + e + r't + a} \quad (B)$$

To demonstrate the value of this type of model, let us assign some values to the parameters and observe the resulting consolidated balance sheet of the banking system:

$$a = 0.20 \qquad r' = 0.05$$
$$r = 0.15 \qquad t = 0.60$$
$$e = 0.02 \qquad B = 100 \text{ (in billions of dollars)}$$

Now we can insert these values into the equation for K:

$$K = \frac{1+a}{r+e+r't+a} = \frac{1+0.20}{0.15+0.02+0.05(0.60)+0.20} = \frac{1.2}{0.40} = 3$$

Thus, the money supply multiplier, K, is 3, and since $M-KB$, $M = 3 \times \$100$ billion $= \$300$ billion. Now that the money supply is known, its division into currency in circulation and demand deposits can be determined. Since $M = D + C_c$ and $C_c = aD$, $M = D + aD$ or $M = D(1+a)$ or $D = \frac{M}{1+a} = \frac{\$300}{1+0.20} = \$250$ billion. Currency in circulation is the difference between the money supply and demand deposits; that is, $C_c = M - D$, or $C_c = \$300$ billion $- \$250$ billion $= \$50$ billion. To check that result, compare it with (4), which is $C_c = aD$. Thus, $C_c = 0.20 \times \$250$ billion $= \$50$ billion. The consolidated balance sheet of the banking system would appear as follows:

Banking System (Billions)

$R+C_b$	$ 50	D	$250
Earning Assets	350	T	150
Total Assets	$400	Total Liabilities	$400

Reserves, including deposits with the Federal Reserve plus vault cash, were found by multiplying the reserve requirement r of 0.15 times D of $250 billion, and the desired excess reserve ratio e of 0.02 times D, and r', the time deposit reserve requirement (0.05) times T. T was found from equation (5): $T = tD = 0.60(\$250$ billion$) = \$150$ billion. Earning assets are the difference between total liabilities and nonearning assets (cash); that is, $350 billion $= \$400$ billion $- \$50$ billion.

If $1 billion is added to the base (B) through open-market purchases of government securities by the Federal Reserve, the changes in the consolidated balance sheet of the banking system would be as follows:

Banking System (Billions)

$R+C_b$	+$0.5	D		+$2.5
Earning Assets	+ 3.5	T		+ 1.5
Change in Total Assets	+$4.0	Change in Total Liabilities		+$4.0

The new balance sheet of the banking system now looks like this:

Banking System (Billions)

$R+C_b$	$ 50.5	D		$252.5
Earning Assets	353.5	T		151.5
Total Assets	$404.0	Total Liabilities		$404.0

The money supply increased by the multiplier $(K=3)$ times the change in the reserve base $(B=+$1$ billion), or $3 billion ($0.5 billion of currency in circulation and $2.5 billion of new demand deposits). While the money supply increased by $3 billion, credit expansion was $3.5 billion (change in earning assets), and liquid assets of the public $(D+T)$ increased by $4 billion, which is partly offset by the fact that the public's liabilities to the banks increased and/or their holdings of other assets (such as government securities) were reduced.

We have demonstrated here a theory of the money supply determination process. For such a model to be useful as a predicting tool, the values of the various parameters would have to be determined through econometric methods. The results of such an exercise could then be compared with the empirical measure for the money expansion multiplier calculated by simply dividing the proper money supply measure by the current size of the monetary base, that is, $K=\frac{M}{B}$. The Federal Reserve Bank of St. Louis computes this figure on a weekly basis. In recent years, the multiplier has hovered around the 2.6 mark, when M1 is defined as the money stock.[5]

Money and Business Fluctuations

In this section, we shall demonstrate the way the model that has just been presented can be helpful in the analysis of money's role in business fluctuations and in evaluating monetary policy. Later chapters develop these topics in more detail.

---

5. The Federal Reserve Bank of St. Louis employs the "adjusted base" for its calculations, which is adjusted for changes in reserve requirements.

In Chapter 2, we gave a brief account of the events leading up to the crisis of 1929 and the severe depression that followed in the 1930s. Here, we can examine the impact on the money supply of some of the attitudes and reactions to the situation existing at the time. A quite dramatic example can be seen in the behavior of a, the currency/demand deposit ratio, which was approximately 0.16 in June of both 1928 and 1929 and rose to about 0.33 in the same month of 1933. If we insert these figures into our model, holding all other values constant, the money supply would decline by some 22 percent! Of course, other factors also changed. The ratio of time deposits to demand deposits (t) decreased from 1.28 in June 1928 to 1.00 in June 1933, which by itself would have increased the money supply by about 3 percent. The excess reserve ratio (e) increased over this same period from 0.002 to 0.026, sufficient to cause a 6-percent decrease in the money supply. It was after 1933 that the great increase in bank demand for excess reserves took place to put greater contractionary pressure on the stock of money. The excess reserve ratio of member banks rose to 0.136 in 1936 and continued to 0.214 in June 1940.

Monetary policy also can be evaluated by means of our model. It probably is reflected in all of the variables, but the most direct relationship is in the reserve requirement parameters and in the monetary base.

Reserve Requirements

The Federal Reserve Board of Governors has some authority to vary the reserve requirements of depository institutions,[6] hence, r and r' are under the control of the Federal Reserve System. The size of the multiplier, the money stock, and bank credit rise when r or r' is decreased and fall when r or r' is increased.

Member bank reserve requirements were unchanged from 1917 until 1936, when they were increased by approximately 50 percent. They were raised again in 1937; and on May 1, 1937, they were increased to their legal maxima and were kept at that level for some years and at relatively high levels afterward. Since the late 1930s was a period of depressed economic conditions and large-scale unemployment, one might wonder why reserve requirements were kept so high. After all,

---

6. Specifically, the range permitted under the DIDMCA of 1980 is between 8 and 14 percent for the portion of transactions accounts in excess of $41.5 million. For deposits up to $41.5 million, the requirement is fixed at 3 percent. (The 41.5 figure is that for 1989; it has and will change over time.) No reserves are required on personal time deposits not subject to immediate withdrawal. On other time deposits, required reserves can vary between zero and 9 percent.

we have seen that an increase in r is contractionary to the money and credit supply! Some very eminent economists have also questioned this action. Defenders of Federal Reserve policy argue that it was desirable to lower the value of the multiplier because of the growth in the monetary base that was taking place during these years. There was also a great fear in the FRS of what would happen if e were suddenly to decrease; that is, if banks were to decide to significantly expand their earning assets, the money supply could explode. Detractors of Federal Reserve policy respond that if the money supply were to expand at too rapid a rate, open-market operations could be used to effectively dampen the rate of growth.

Open-Market Operations

The impact of open-market operations is directly on B, the monetary base. No matter what is happening within the multiplier, the effect can be offset by changes in B. Thus, if one of the components of the multiplier is changing in such a way as to cause an increase in the money supply, and the Open-Market Committee (the policy-making body of the FRS) finds this undesirable, the open-market agent can be told to sell enough securities to counteract the expansion. On the other hand, if additional expansion is deemed warranted, the orders will be to purchase securities.

There is no possibility of open-market operations failing to affect B. If the Open-Market Committee buys or sells, someone must sell to them or buy from them. Since all the firms who deal directly with the Open-Market Committee are large dealers in government securities, the checks received in payment or the checks they pay for the securities immediately result in an increase or a decrease in some banks' reserves held at the Federal Reserve Banks. These new reserves, of course, spread pervasively throughout the system of banks.

Discount Rate

Another policy tool of the Federal Reserve that affects the monetary base is the *discount rate*, which is the rate of interest at which depository institutions may borrow from the Federal Reserve Bank of the district. When a bank borrows from the Federal Reserve Bank, it takes payment in the form of deposits at the Reserve Bank. Since no other bank has lost reserves by this act, total reserves and B have increased by the amount of the loan. The borrowing is at the initiative of the individual bank, but granting the loan is at the discretion of the Federal Reserve

Bank and, therefore, is not under the precise control of the monetary authority. The Federal Reserve can encourage borrowing by lowering the discount rate and can discourage borrowing by raising the rate.

Many writers and practitioners of central banking have concentrated their attention on what is called the "announcement effect" of discount rate changes, arguing that an increased rate is taken as a signal that the Board of Governors views the current situation as one where contractionary action is in order and that the banks ought to be more cautious in their lending policies. In terms of our model, the expectation (or hope) is that e, the excess reserve ratio, will rise somewhat, causing a slight decrease in the size of the multiplier as well as decreasing B by decreasing bank indebtedness to the Federal Reserve.

Other Factors Affecting the Monetary Base

Federal Reserve policy is not the only determinant of B. There are other important sources of variation, but the reader should keep in mind that if these other sources cause undesired changes, the Federal Reserve's policy can neutralize them, although it has not always done so.

One continuously perplexing feature of the U.S. monetary system is that both the Federal Reserve System and the U.S. Treasury have powerful ability to affect the money base. Although this is consistent with the political philosophy of checks and balances, it makes for divided responsibility, inconsistent policy actions, and, sometimes, a stalemate. Both the Treasury and the Federal Reserve System are capable of completely offsetting the effects of the policy actions of each other.

The Treasury causes member bank reserves to vary inversely as its own deposit balances at the Federal Reserve Banks vary. A decrease in the Treasury's balance means that it has paid out money for the purchase of goods and services, transfer payments, or the retirement of its debt; the recipients have cashed the checks; and member banks have received new reserves. Reserves decrease when the Treasury's balance at the Federal Reserve increases, because the reserve balance falls when the Treasury directly transfers funds from its deposits at commercial banks, and when tax collections or the proceeds of government security sales are placed in its balance at the Federal Reserve Banks. The Treasury also adds to the base by issuance of currency and coin.

Another important source of variation in the monetary base arises out of the flow of monetary gold. Purchase of gold bullion by the Treasury results in the receipt by the seller of the gold of a check drawn against the Treasury's balance at the Federal Reserve. The Treasury's balance may then be replenished by the issuance of gold certificates. In this way, the reserves of banks are increased without a decrease in the Treasury's Federal Reserve Bank balance.

An additional item in determining the monetary base is the "Special Drawing Rights (SDR) certificate account." These certificates are broadly comparable to the gold certificates mentioned above. The Treasury is authorized to issue the SDR certificates to the Federal Reserve, which then allows the Treasury to use the funds to pay for the SDRs or to engage in foreign exchange stabilization operations.[7]

Monthly, the *Federal Reserve Bulletin* publishes tables entitled "Reserves of Depository Institutions and Reserve Bank Credit" and "Reserves and Borrowings, Depository Institutions" with which one can see the various factors that have caused changes in the monetary base.

Table 10-2 is a restructuring of the tables in the *Federal Reserve Bulletin* to conform with the monetary base scheme being used here. The table shows very clearly that government securities held by the Federal Reserve Banks explain the bulk of the monetary base at the present time. They come into being primarily through net purchases over time in the open market. Treasury currency has grown quite steadily, but slowly, and so presents no serious problem. The gold stock is the next largest item, but it is now less than half of what it was in the 1940s and 1950s. Some of the items are important mainly in their short-run volatility, such as loans (reflecting the discount policy of the Federal Reserve and money market conditions), float (reflecting variations in clearing and collection time, the volume of activity, and the availability schedule), and Treasury deposits at the Federal Reserve (reflecting the mechanics of Treasury cash flows).

In understanding the reasons for changes in the money supply, the starting point is an analysis of the behavior of the components of the monetary base. Then, if one analyzes the sources of change in the base, and also determines the causes of variation in the parameters of the money multiplier, one necessarily has the explanation for changes in the money stock. This must be the case since the statement $M \equiv KB$ is a truism. The value of such an exercise crucially depends upon the relevance of the structure of the multiplier model to the real world. A measure of that relevance, as suggested above, is the closeness of the

7. For a more complete explanation of Special Drawing Rights, see "SDR's in Federal Reserve Operations and Statistics," *Federal Reserve Bulletin* (May 1970), p. 421.

Table 10-2

Components of the Monetary Base, June 1989
(In Millions of Dollars)

Reserve Bank Credit Outstanding		$263,924
U.S. Government and Federal Agency Securities	234,442	
Loans and Acceptances	1,495	
Float	1,279	
Other Federal Reserve Assets	26,709	
+Gold Stock		11,061
+Special Drawing Rights Certificate Account		8,518
+Treasury Currency Outstanding		19,188
−Treasury Cash Holdings		−488
−Deposits, Other Than Reserve Balances		
with Federal Reserve Banks		−12,550
Treasury Deposits	−10,072	
Foreign Deposits	−251	
Service-Related Balances and Adjustments	−1,924	
Other Deposits	−303	
−Other Federal Reserve Liabilities and Capital		−8,101
=Monetary Base		$281,552
Currency in Circulation (includes bank holdings)		$247,860
+Reserve Balances with Federal Reserve Banks		33,692
=Monetary Base		$281,552

Source: Adapted from the *Federal Reserve Bulletin* (October 1989), p. A4.

multiplier computed by its component parameters and its measure by dividing the money stock by the base.

THE MONEY MARKET

In the preceding chapter, it was shown that the goods market is in equilibrium when aggregate savings and investment are equal, or in the expanded version $S_p + T = I + G + (X - M)$, and national income is determined at that point. In that analysis, the rate of interest was assumed to be given, that is, determined in some other market. For the model to be complete, the interest rate must be determined, that is, the reason the interest rate is what it is, and the kind of forces that will cause it to change must be explained. It is to the money market that we look for the theory of interest rate determination in the Keynesian model.

The Theory of Interest

The interest theory to be discussed now is called the *liquidity preference* theory. It was the theory Keynes advanced, although what is to be presented here also draws from the work of later contributors. According to this theory, interest is determined by the supply of and the demand for money. (Remember that money is defined to include checkable deposits and currency.)

Every dollar of the money stock must be held by someone, so there is no question of how much money people and business hold. They will hold exactly the amount of money that exists. The question asked by demand-for-money theory is: How much do they *wish* to hold?

The demand for money is divided into two basic categories. The first is referred to as working balance demand or active balances, and the second category is referred to variously as pure liquidity preference, speculative demand for money, asset demand for money, or inactive balances.

Demand for Money for Working Balances

The demand for money for working balance purposes is a function of the money value of national income, $M_W^D = f(Y)$. According to classical economists, the only reason for holding money is for transactions purposes. Every economic unit needs some cash to bridge the time span between receipts of money, during which time, outflows of funds occur. Everyone is familiar to some extent with this reason for holding cash. To operate effectively as a going concern or a household, one simply needs some money. How much one needs depends upon the nature of receipts and expenditures. However, it is probably a correct generalization to say that the larger the level of economic activity, the more money a household or business unit would need. This would seem to be true whether the increased activity is in increased physical output or in higher prices of the same output.

Figure 10-1 demonstrates the positive relation between the amount of money demanded for working balances and the level of national income. In it, income is the independent variable, and the demand for money is the dependent variable; that is, when income is Y_1, money demanded for working balances will be M_1. In the theory it is assumed that the amount of money people wish to hold for this purpose is the amount they actually do hold.

Figure 10-1   Relationship Between Income and Demand for Money

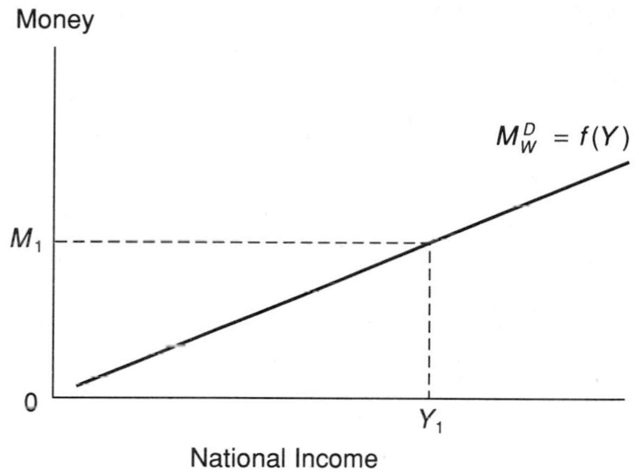

Money

$$M_W^D = f(Y)$$

M_1

0

Y_1

National Income

Pure Liquidity Preference

The term "liquidity preference" is meant to indicate that money held for the speculative motive is held in preference to other assets. This is also why some economists refer to these balances as asset balances. In some respects, money is superior to other assets, and in some respects, other assets are superior to money. The price of money is constant in terms of the unit of account and is, therefore, perfectly liquid. Its value, however, is variable in terms of what it will command in goods and services.

Debt instruments, which shall be referred to generally as bonds, are similar to money in that the legal obligation is stated in terms of the unit of account, so bonds and money share the quality of variability in value in terms of the goods and services they will buy. This means that if inflation is expected, both money and bonds would be expected to lose value; and if deflation is expected, bonds and money would both gain in real value. On this consideration alone, bonds would be preferred to money since an interest income is attached to the bonds.

There is a risk, however, involved in holding bonds rather than money. The risk is that interest rates will rise, because a rise in interest rates is equivalent to a decrease in the price of outstanding bonds. One would prefer to hold money if the expected loss in the capital value of the bond is greater than the interest income the bond yields over the relevant period of time. If the current interest rate is very high, two

Figure 10-2   The Liquidity Preference Function Shows the Relationship Between Interest Rates and the Demand for Money

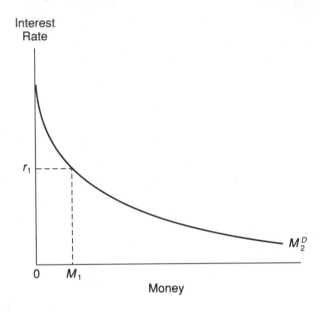

factors should be noted: (1) the interest income to offset any losses in bond prices is high, and (2) any given interest rate change (increase) will have a relatively small effect on the price of bonds. This leads to the conclusion that when interest rates are high, the demand for money in the expectation of rising interest rates will be smaller than when the interest rate is low.

A low current rate of interest induces more holding of money because the cost of holding it (the forgone interest income) is low. A given change in the interest rate has a relatively larger effect on capital value, and the earnings to offset such capital losses are small. Keynes and others have argued further that when interest rates are high, expectations are likely to be that they will fall, so less money would be demanded; whereas when interest rates are low, they would be expected to rise and thus induce more demand for money for the speculative motive.

All of this leads to the conclusion that the demand for money as an asset is a negative function of the current rate of interest. Its general shape seems to be that shown in Figure 10-2. An interest rate of r_1

would induce M_1 amount of money to be held for pure liquidity preference purposes.

An additional complication that we will not explicitly enter into
our model is that transactions balances are also, in part, dependent
upon the rate of interest. This is simply because when interest rates
are high, it pays firms and households to find ways of operating that
reduce the need for inventories of cash. At low interest rates most economic units find that some of these cash-minimizing methods are not
worth the effort. This complication reinforces the argument that the
demand for money is negatively related to the rate of interest.

The *L-M* Function

We can now combine the two types of demand for money and the
supply of money to form a new function, the *L-M* curve. In the derivation of the *L-M* function, it is convenient to start at the lower right-
hand part of Figure 10-3. Choose any income, such as Y_0, which indicates that the amount of money people wish to hold and, in fact, do
hold for working balance purposes is M_1. The total money supply is
shown on the lower left-hand part of Figure 10-3. There, a 45° line is
drawn from the total money supply measured on the horizontal axis
to the same amount measured on the vertical axis. Observe that $0M_1$ is
equal to $0\bar{M}^s - 0X_2$ (by right triangles) so that $0X_2$ is the amount of the
money supply not being used for working balances. This is the amount
that is available for holding for other purposes, namely, as speculative
balances.[8] The interesting thing is that this money, because it exists,
must be held whether or not people want to hold it. What makes them
willing to hold it is a particular rate of interest. The upper left-hand
part of Figure 10-3 shows that the public is willing to hold exactly $0X_2$
only if the rate of interest is r_0.

Point A on the upper right-hand part is a point of equilibrium at
interest rate r_0, given an income of Y_0. Likewise, point B is a point
showing that income Y_1 is compatible with interest rate r_1 and so on
for all other points on *L-M*. Any point on *L-M* represents a possible
condition of equilibrium in the money market where the supply of

---

8. Thus, $0M_1 = X_2E$. Triangle $X_2\bar{M}^sE$ is a right triangle since $\angle X_2 = 90°$ and $\angle E$ and
$\angle \bar{M}^s = 45°$. EX_2 is therefore equal to $X_2\bar{M}^s = 0M_1$. $X_2\bar{M}^s = 0\bar{M}^s - 0X_2$. Looking at the situation the
other way, note that if $0M_1$ is used for transaction balances, the rest of the money supply
$(0M^s - 0M_1)$ is available for speculative balances. $0M^s - 0M_1 = M_1E$ because triangle M_1EM^s is a
right triangle. Therefore, $0X_2 = M_1E$ is the part available for speculative holdings that is transferred to the graph.

_____

Figure 10-3   Derivation of the *L-M* Function

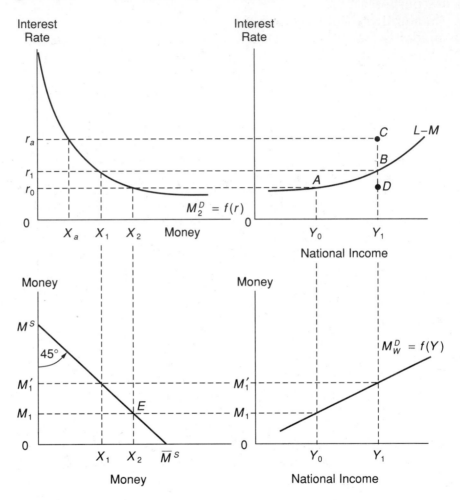

money and the demand for it are equal. As with the *I-S* function, any shift of the functions making up the *L-M* function will cause a shift in the *L-M* curve.

Suppose the system is not in equilibrium. What is the nature of the forces at work in the economy to drive interest rates and/or income to the position we have called equilibrium? We know immediately that income cannot adjust in this, the money market, since income is determined in the market for goods and services. Take a point such as *C*, a point above the *L-M* curve. Income is Y_1, so the amount of money demanded for working or transaction purposes is $0M'_1$, which means that $0X_1$ is available for speculative holdings. Point C interest rate is r_a; but if the interest rate is r_a, the amount of money people wish to hold is just $0X_a$, which is less than the amount they must hold. Now, if more money is held than the holders wish to hold, we would expect them to try to get out of money and into bonds. The offers to buy bonds would drive the price of bonds up, thus driving current yields on the bonds and, hence, current interest rates down. Therefore, if interest rates are above equilibrium, competitive pressures in the bond markets will push the interest rates downward toward equilibrium.

To help reinforce the reader's understanding of this analysis, prove that if the interest rate and income were at the point labeled D on Figure 10-3, that is, any point below the *L-M* curve, the forces operative in the system would move interest rates upward toward *L-M*.

Both the *L-M* and the *I-S* curves represent possible points of equilibrium of income and interest rates. But there is an infinity of points on both curves, so equilibrium can exist only at that point common to both curves, that is, at their intersection. Figure 10-4 shows this situation.

A good exercise to see why income would really be Y_e, and why the interest rate would really be at r_e is to ask the question: What would the economic environment be like if a different combination of income and interest existed? To do this, select a point such as A on Figure 10-4, which is on neither the *L-M* nor the *I-S* curve. Take the analysis in steps. First, since A is above the *L-M* curve, by the reasoning we used above, the interest rate would have to fall to point B. Point B, however, is to the right of the *I-S* curve, and by our argument in Chapter 9, income would fall to the level represented by point C. C is above the *L-M* function, so the interest rate would fall to the point represented by D; but since D is to the left of the *I-S* curve, income would rise to point E.

As you can see, if this "cobweb" mechanism were continued, interest and income would oscillate in the direction of the equilibrium levels where the *L-M* and *I-S* functions intersect. Our approach here has been very mechanistic. The real world does not operate exactly in this step fashion, which we adopted for pedagogical reasons. A spiraling approach toward the equilibrium point might be more realistic. The exact path by which the forces at work operate to move income and interest toward equilibrium is dependent upon several time lags. In truth, we still have a great deal to learn about these lags. Professor Hicks, who first advanced the cobweb theorem in this context, proposed some rather complicated lags in both the money and the goods

Figure 10-4   *I-S—L-M* Equilibrium

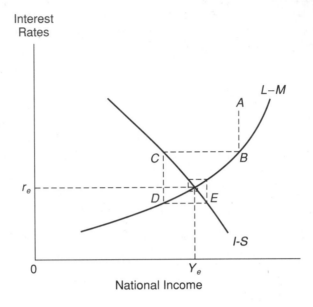

markets. It takes time for consumption spending (or saving) to react to changes in income; for investment spending (or saving) to react to changes in income; for investment spending to change when interest rates change; and for the adjustment of money balances as income and interest rates change.[9]

It is difficult to evaluate the relevance of the Keynesian monetary theory to the contemporary economy. This has become more evident in very recent years as innovations in the financial system have accelerated due primarily to progress in the communications and the computer industries and to changes in the regulatory environment.

First, the theory presumes bonds to be the only alternative to the holding of money. Even if one excludes the alternative of holding real, or physical, assets, the range of financial instruments available is extremely wide and diversified. Close substitutes for money include money market funds, NOWS and Super NOWS, ATS savings accounts, negotiable certificates of deposit, sweep accounts, Treasury bills, and other government securities.

9. J. R. Hicks, *A Contribution to the Theory of the Trade Cycle* (Oxford, England: Oxford University Press, 1950), Chapter 11.

At the very least, one should distinguish between debt instruments whose price varies inversely with the interest rate and financial instruments whose price does not vary with interest rate changes. Savings accounts, for one example, maintain their nominal value as market rates of interest change. Thus, in terms of liquidity preference theory, if an individual expects interest rates to rise, he or she would find it wise to reduce holdings of variable-price instruments (such as marketable bonds) but would not necessarily want to hold more money. Instead, savings deposits, or any other instrument whose price did not vary with interest rates, would give the same protection from capital loss as money does and still yield a positive return. To the extent that this is a serious shortcoming of the liquidity preference theory, it would appear that what the theory explains is the differential between interest rates on fixed-price and variable-price debt instruments.

QUESTIONS

1. The text does not define "the financial system." What do you think should be the important elements in such a definition? Explain how "the monetary system" differs from your definition of "the financial system."
2. Using the complete multiplier model on pages 254–256, show the final balance sheets of the commercial banking system and the money supply in each of the following events:
    (a) Reserve requirements on demand deposits (r) increase to 35 percent.
    (b) Reserve requirements on time deposits are eliminated altogether.
    (c) Currency in circulation increases significantly, so that the value of a becomes 0.50.
    (d) The monetary base decreases by $2 billion.
3. Discuss the events that will increase or decrease the monetary base. Organize your answer according to the agency responsible for the change, that is, the Treasury, the Federal Reserve, and "other."
4. Refer to Figure 10-4 on page 268. Explain why a point below the L-M function and to the left of the I-S function would not be an equilibrium point. What are the forces that would cause movement of the interest rate and income in the direction of the intersection of the L-M and I-S curves?
5. Graphically derive the shift in the L-M function caused by
    (a) an increase in the money supply,
    (b) a downward shift in the M_W^D function,
    (c) a shift to the right of the liquidity preference function.

6. Given the following conditions, when would it be advisable to hold bonds? (Assume that the bonds available are all perpetuities and can be exchanged only on one date each year.)

   (a) The current interest rate is 1 percent, and you forecast that the rate next year will be 2 percent.

   (b) The current interest rate is 2 percent, and you forecast that the rate next year will be 1 percent.

   (c) The current interest rate is 30 percent, and you forecast that the rate next year will be 31 percent.

   (d) The current interest rate is 10 percent, and you forecast that the rate next year will be 11 percent.

   (e) The current interest rate is 10 percent, and you forecast that the rate next year will be 12 percent.

7. How would you qualify your conclusions in question 6 if the forecast of future interest rate behavior was clouded with a great deal of uncertainty?

READINGS

Brunner, Karl, and Allen Meltzer. *Monetary Economics*. Cambridge, MA: Basil Blackwell, Inc., 1989.

Burger, Albert E. *The Money Supply Process*. Belmont, CA: Wadsworth Publishing Co., Inc., 1971.

Dow, Sheila C. *Macroeconomic Thought*. New York: Basil-Blackwell, 1985.

Federal Reserve Bank of Boston. Controlling Monetary Aggregates. 2 vols. 1969, 1972.

Friedman, Milton. "A Monetary Theory of Nominal Income." *Journal of Political Economy* (March/April 1971).

Gertler, Mark. "Financial Structure and Aggregate Economic Activity: An Overview." *Journal of Money, Credit, and Banking*, Part II (August 1988), pp. 559–588.

Gordon, Robert J. *Macroeconomics*, 4th ed. Glenview, IL: Scott, Foresman and Company, 1987, Chapters 4 and 5.

Hicks, J. R. *A Contribution to the Theory of the Trade Cycle*. Oxford, England: Oxford University Press, 1950.

Laidler, David E. W. *The Demand for Money: Theories and Evidence*, 2d ed. New York: Harper & Row, Publishers, 1978.

Patinkin, Don. *Money, Interest, and Prices: An Integration of Monetary and Value Theory*, 2d ed. New York: Harper & Row, Publishers, 1965.

Sorkin, Alan L. *Monetary and Fiscal Policy and Business Cycles in the Modern Era*. Lexington, MA: Lexington Books, 1988, Chapter 6.

Tobin, James. *Asset Accumulation and Economic Activity*. Chicago: University of Chicago Press, 1982.

AGGREGATE DEMAND AND SUPPLY AND THE PRICE LEVEL

The discussion of the *I-S–L-M* analysis in Chapter 10 was ambiguous in the definition of some of the variables by not explicitly stating whether the variables are in nominal or real terms. It is uncertain from this structure if any given change, in income, for example, is caused by an increase in real output or is partly or wholly a change in the price level. Since this question is of considerable interest, and since price level changes may have independent significance, many economists treat all variables in the framework adjusted for price level.

THE DETERMINATION OF THE PRICE LEVEL

The following discussion will consider what impact there is on real variables as the price level changes. Lower case letters c, i, g, ex, im, m, s, and t will be used to stand for real consumption, real investment, real government expenditures, real exports, real imports, the real value of money, real saving, and real taxes, respectively. The corresponding nominal values are C, I, G, Ex, Im, M, S, and T, each one being the real value multiplied by the price level P. Therefore, the real values are also the nominal values divided by the price level P. For example, $c = \dfrac{C}{P}$ and $C = cP$.

The discussion will distinguish between an expected change and an actual change in the price level. Expectations will be considered, but at this time, it is the actual change in the price level that is being incorporated into the analysis. References to price level changes are abstracted from changes in relative prices; thus, if the price level changes by 5 percent, it is assumed that all prices have changed by that same rate.

Investment and Government Expenditures

It is usually agreed that real investment depends on the real rate of interest and real income. The real rate of interest is the nominal or market rate minus the expected rate of inflation. A firm would invest the same amount if the rate of interest were 7 percent, and no inflation were anticipated, as it would if the market rate of interest were 16 percent and 9 percent inflation were expected.

Business decision makers are judged to be sufficiently sophisticated to be aware of the implications of price level changes, so that if the demand for total output were to increase (given a constant interest rate) only because of an increase in prices, their investment decisions would not change. In other words, no money illusion is assumed in the market for capital goods. That is, $\frac{I}{P} = f(\frac{Y}{P}, r) = i = f(y)$.

Consumption and Personal Saving

Our primary concern is with the real system, the actual goods and services produced, consumed, and so on. If the price level is constant throughout the time of the events included in the analysis, this would constitute no problem. If, for instance, national income in value terms increased by 10 percent, real national income would also increase by 10 percent. At very high levels of unemployment and great excess capacity of productive facilities, this situation is likely to be closely approximated. At the other extreme, that is, full employment and near capacity utilization of capital, any change in the money level of national income is likely to be almost completely a change in the price level, since real output is near its maximum.

Classical economic theory concluded that full employment was the equilibrium to which the system would always adjust. Therefore, any increase in aggregate demand, caused by increases in either the money supply or in the velocity of money, would not affect total output, but would influence price-level behavior. Classical economists' concern with saving and investment was directed at the impact of saving and investment on future production rather than their role in the determination of current income.

If the economy exhibits unemployment, it signifies that the total demand for output is less than the potential output. A classical economist would contend that unemployed workers and the owners of other unused factors would lower the prices of their services, thus making it economical for more of them to be reemployed.

Most classical theorists mistakenly handled this question with the tools of partial equilibrium theory. They reasoned that the lower wages resulting from the pressure of unemployment would shift the firm's marginal cost curve downward, leading to increased output and lower product price. The increased output would absorb the unemployed resources, and the pressure for falling wages would continue until full employment was reached.

The Swedish economist, Knut Wicksell, was probably the most adamant critic of this approach. He pointed out that in the total economy, the income earned by laborers and other resource owners was what they used to demand the output. Thus, the demand curve for the product of a firm could be held constant while the marginal cost curve shifted owing to lower wages paid by that firm. However, it is completely erroneous to do so for the entire economy.

Keynes, too, adopted this position. He believed that wages in particular, and prices, generally, were not flexible. While the upward movement of nominal wages would take place quite easily, Keynes said that workers would vigorously resist the lowering of their nominal wages. Furthermore, he argued, lower nominal wages would be effective in stimulating increased output only if the real wage, that is, the money wage divided by the price level, were also lowered, and that workers and their unions could have an influence only on the money wage rate.

Another way to see the issues involved is to observe that if labor agrees to lower the money wage rate such that the marginal cost curves of all firms decrease, the demand curve for the output of the firms will also decrease. According to Keynesians, there is no reason to believe that the marginal cost curve would shift more than the demand curve. The result of lowering money wages is shown in Figure 11-1.

The situation depicted is what Keynes referred to as "the doomsday case," with wages and prices falling continuously while employment and production continue at a depressed level. The classical response to this argument was offered by A. C. Pigou; in fact, it has been titled "the Pigou effect."

Pigou said that as prices are falling in the manner just described, there is an important reason for believing that the demand curve for the firms' output will not fall as much as the supply curve does when wages fall. When the demand curve falls less than the supply curve does, the quantity of output, and therefore the level of employment, will increase. The reason for this is that holders of money become wealthier in real terms without anyone else becoming less wealthy.

Figure 11-1   Result of Lowering Money Wages: "The Doomsday Case"

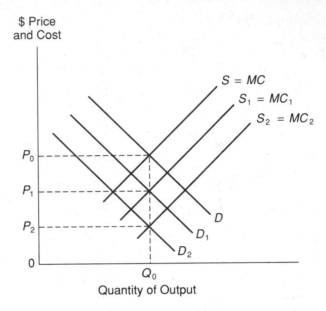

With debt instruments other than money, the creditors become wealthier and would thus be expected to increase their real demand for goods and services. However, that increase in demand would be approximately offset by the decrease in demand of debtors who become less wealthy as prices fall, and the real burden of their debt becomes more severe. The government and the banks are the debtors in the case of money outstanding, and neither would be expected to react to an increase in the real value of their debt as would other debtors. However, the important characteristics of money as debt are that there is no interest paid by the debtor, and money is a perpetual debt so the principal need never be repaid. When there is deflation, holders of money become wealthier and increase their demand, while the issuers of money do not decrease their demand. By this reasoning, the economy exhibits an automatic corrective to the problem of unemployment.

Another way to look at the significance of the Pigou effect is to consider the Keynesian national income analysis in real rather than money-value terms. According to this theory, national income is determined at the intersection of the saving and investment functions, and Keynes said that this intersection could occur at a level insufficient to provide full employment. Adding the Pigou effect, however,

Figure 11-2   The Pigou Effect and Full Employment

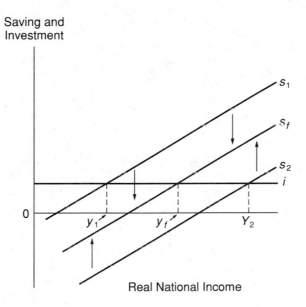

amounts to saying that saving and consumption depend not only on current income but also on wealth. Falling prices have no effect on the real value of goods nor on the aggregate real value of financial instruments, except money. The real value of money would increase, increasing total real wealth, causing real consumption to increase and, therefore, causing real saving to decrease.

The Pigou effect can be included in the theory by using as the saving function: $s = f(y, m) = \dfrac{S}{P} = f(\dfrac{Y}{P}, \dfrac{M}{P})$, where $\dfrac{M}{P}$ is the money supply divided by the price level and, hence, is a measure of the real value of money holdings. If P falls while M is constant, or if M rises when P is constant, real balances increase and s falls. On our familiar saving and investment graph, the classical system includes the proposition that the saving function will shift downward as long as unemployment exists.

Consider the situation shown in Figure 11-2. Income is at the Keynesian equilibrium of y_1 where s and i are equal. The Pigou effect is included to cause s to shift in the direction of s_f, at which point the economy would be in equilibrium at Y_f, full employment national income.

Figure 11-3   Effect of Price Level on Real Income Demand

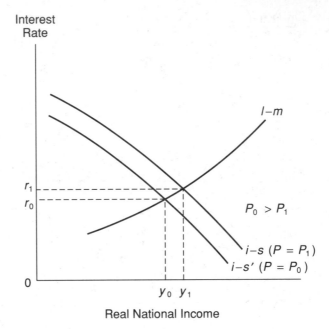

Real National Income

The analysis would presumably apply also in the case of rising wages and prices as well. If, for example, the saving curve were to the right of (below) the s_f curve, such as s_2, so that national income were greater than the full employment level, inflation would be in process. Rising wages and prices would reduce the real value of money balances $(\frac{M}{P})$ so that economic units would attempt to increase their holdings of money by increasing their rate of saving. In other words, the real saving function shifts upward whenever the price level increases and shifts downward whenever the price level decreases. This, of course, implies that the real consumption function shifts downward for increases in the price level and upward for decreases in the price level.

If we translate this to the i-s relation, plotting real income (y) on the horizontal axis and interest on the vertical axis, the i-s function moves further to the right as the price level falls. Thus, in Figure 11-3 the i-s function with the higher price level ($P=P_0$) is to the left of the i-s function with the lower price level ($P=P_1$). Then, given any l-m curve, the lower the price level, the greater the real demand.

How strong this effect is, that is, how much and how fast the curve would shift, has not been finally determined. It may take a large change in the price level to affect a relatively small change in real consumption and saving. Logically, it should assure full employment, but the time required might very well be unacceptably long.

Real Money Balances

When the price level falls, if the nominal stock of money remains the same, the real value of the money stock rises. Less of the nominal stock would be needed for transactions purposes, so more would be available for speculative holdings, thus causing the interest rate to fall. This is demonstrated in Figure 11-4, where the decrease in the price level is shown as an increase in the real money stock in diagram (c), causing the l-m function to shift to the right and indicating that at any given level of real income the interest rate will be lower. This lower interest rate will then induce additional investment to be initiated. The new equilibrium would then settle at y_2, with the new equilibrium interest rate somewhere between r_1 and r_2.

We have two reasons to expect that aggregate demand is larger when the price level is lower, and conversely, the higher the price level, the lower the level of aggregate demand: the Pigou effect and the real balance effect. To explain movements along the aggregate demand curve, we ask the question: what will happen to the total demand for the output of the economy when the price level changes? The answer is that if a change in the price level causes either the l-m or the i-s curves to shift, total demand will change. Thus, we have just seen that the real balance effect is reflected in a shift in the l-m curve, and the Pigou effect reflects a shift in the i-s curve. We now consider whether the other elements of aggregate demand, namely i, g, t, ex, or im will shift the i-s curve because of changes in price levels.

Investment

We conclude that real investment is not affected by different price levels. The reason for this is that we have been assuming that all prices vary proportionally, which means that while the prices of the goods being produced would increase by 10 percent if the price level increased by 10 percent, so would the costs of production. Therefore, nominal profit would also increase by 10 percent, but the real profit rate would remain constant.

Figure 11-4   Real Money Balances

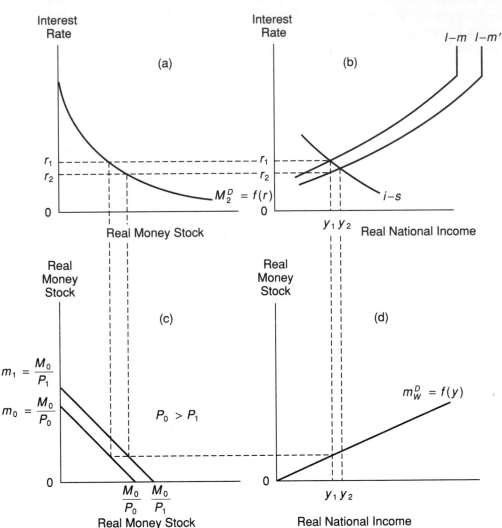

Foreign Trade

At any given level of real national income, a changing level of prices of domestic goods and services alters the relative prices of foreign versus domestic commodities. If our prices rise while foreign prices do not, as long as exchange rates are fixed or less than completely flexible, the demand for domestically produced goods will fall relative to foreign-made products. Our exports will fall and imports will increase so that $(ex - im)$ decreases. Thus, again, the i-s curve shifts to the left as domestic prices rise and to the right as our prices fall, and real aggregate demand varies inversely with the price level.

Government Spending and Taxes

Taxes are collected not on real income but on the basis of nominal personal income. If our tax structure is progressive, an increase in the price level (and therefore an increase in nominal income earned) will cause the tax liability to increase by a larger proportion than the increase in income, so that the real tax will increase when the price level increases, even though real income remains the same. Consequently, if real consumption depends on real disposable income, consumption will decline as the price level rises. This is an additional reason to believe that the i-s curve shifts to the left at higher prices and to the right at lower price levels, and that real aggregate demand is negatively related to the price level.

This decrease in private consumption demand could, of course, be offset by an increase in real government spending, which could neutralize the impact of real tax changes on aggregate demand. Whether government spending will increase when real tax collections increase is simply uncertain. It depends on the political forces extant at the time. It is even possible that the administration and Congress might elect to offset the increase in real taxes by lowering tax rates. In the short run, it may be that changing neither spending nor taxes is feasible, given the cumbersomeness of the governmental decision-making processes.

THE AGGREGATE DEMAND FUNCTION

Figure 11-5 is a graphic representation of the aggregate demand function. It simply shows the inverse relationship between price levels and the quantity of real goods and services demanded in the whole economy in conformance with the preceding discussion.

As usual, if such a tool is to be valuable, the causes of shifts in the function must be explained. Only the changes that shift the AD function upward from AD_1 to AD_2, for example, will be discussed, leaving downward shift analysis to the reader. These are the reasons the real

Figure 11-5   Aggregate Demand Function

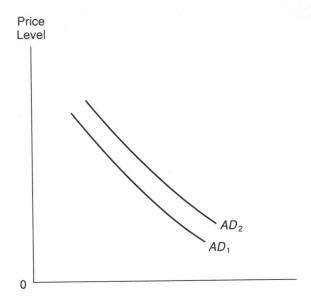

i-s or the real l-m functions can shift to the right. If either of these functions shifts to the right, the aggregate demand curve also shifts to the
right, indicating that at a constant level of prices, demand for goods
and services will be larger. Changes that shift the AD function upward
are:

1. An increase in the money stock shifts the aggregate demand curve
    by causing the interest rate to fall, inspiring an increase in the de-
    mand for national output for investment purposes and, perhaps,
    an increase in consumption demand (by reducing desired saving).
2. Autonomous decreases in the demand for money for either trans-
    actions or speculative purposes shift AD upward by decreasing in-
    terest rates and, as above, increasing investment and consumption
    demand.
3. An autonomous increase in the consumption function, the in-
    vestment function, government spending, or export spending, or
    autonomous decreases in taxes or imports are all expected to shift
    the AD curve upward.

AGGREGATE SUPPLY

The above points are a summary of the construction of an aggregate demand curve and the factors that might cause it to shift. In the following paragraphs, we will discuss the aggregate supply curve, which shows the quantity of real output firms will wish to supply at all possible price levels.

In considering the classical model in Chapter 7, it was shown that changing price levels would have no effect on output. Thus, in the purely classical case, the aggregate supply curve is a perpendicular line; that is, output is inelastic with respect to the price level. This is because wages and prices are both considered completely flexible, and both the demand for and supply of labor depend on real wages $(w = \frac{W}{P})$. Any change in the price level would be matched by a proportional change in money wage rates so the real wage would not change, and hence, the quantity of labor employed would remain the same. Since output depends only on the amount of labor used, given that other factors of production and technology remain constant, real production would be unchanged. The classical case can be seen simply in Figure 11-6. Here, nominal (or money) wages are shown on the vertical axis, and the employment level on the horizontal axis. An increase in the price level from P_0 to P_1 shifts both the supply and the demand for labor functions proportionally upward, leaving the real wage and employment as they were. Since employment remained constant, so does real national income, which means that the aggregate output does not change when the price level changes.

If the assumptions of the classical case are changed, the aggregate supply curve can take on different shapes. First, if wages are less flexible than prices of commodities, a change in the price level will result in a change in real wages. For example, assume that wages are fixed in nominal terms, and the price level increases. Real wages would fall, and workers would be willing to supply fewer hours of work so output would decline. On the other hand, if the price level decreases, and money wages do not change, the real wage will rise and employers will want to employ fewer worker-hours, and again, output will fall. Thus, if wages are completely rigid, any change in the price level, whether upward or downward, will decrease employment and production. Indeed, the same conclusion is reached if nominal wages are only more rigid than commodity prices.

Many people have concluded that, in fact, money wages are rigid

Figure 11-6   Aggregate Supply in the Classical Model

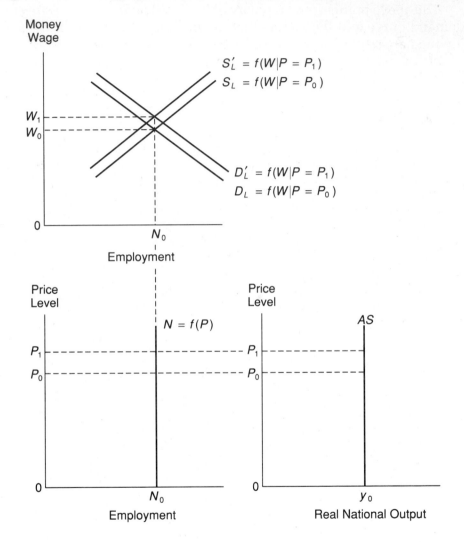

only in the downward direction but are flexible in an upward direction. If this is true, then lower price levels will reduce employment and output; however, higher price levels will be matched by higher nominal wages, and employment and production will remain the same.

If employment decisions of workers are made on the basis of the nominal wage and not on the basis of the real wage as assumed by the classicists, then the supply curve of output, with respect to the price level, will be positively sloped. Under these conditions, if the price level increases, the demand for labor will increase, because the real wage paid to workers will decrease; in other words, for any given number of workers employed, the money value of the contribution of an additional worker (the value of the marginal product) will be greater than it was before the price of the product increased. At the existing money wage, firms will wish to employ more workers, so the money wage will rise. Therefore, according to the assumption that the supply of labor depends on nominal wages only, more employment, and thus more output, will be forthcoming. Figure 11-7 illustrates this case.

While this assumption is quite unrealistic and insulting to the intelligence of workers, it is quite plausible to say that workers might be more conscious of their own wages in dollar terms than they are aware of the prices of the multitude of commodities they buy. So while the "money illusion" of the labor force may not be as complete as assumed by a labor supply curve based strictly on money wages, as long as there is any degree of money illusion, the labor supply curve and, hence, the aggregate supply curve, will be positively sloped. Money illusion exists in this direction, as long as the increase in labor supplied per unit increase in the nominal wage is greater than the decrease in labor supplied per unit increase in the price level. Figure 11-8 shows a case where money illusion exists but is less than complete.

Here, both the demand for and the supply of labor curves shift upward because of an increase in the price level, but the supply curve shifts less than the demand curve. Again, the aggregate supply curve is positively sloped but is less elastic than in the pure money illusion case.

If we can accept these ideas, the aggregate supply curve (AS) is derived as shown in Figure 11-8. The original equilibrium is shown with the 0 subscripts; that is, employment is N_0, nominal wage is W_0, real national product is y_0, and the price level is P_0. If the price level increases to P_1, the quantity of labor demanded increases to N_2 at the current wage W_0; but since the supply of labor curve has shifted upward because of the price level increase, employment will go to N_1 rather than to N_2 as the money wage rises to W_1. (Notice here that the real wage has fallen since the money wage did not rise as high as W_2.) Since employment has increased, output will rise to y_1 on diagram (c) of Figure 11-8.

The AS curve will shift if the supply of labor curve shifts or because the demand for labor curve shifts. The supply curve will shift because laborers changed their attitudes toward work versus income or because

Figure 11-7   Aggregate Supply Where Labor Supply Depends on Money Wages

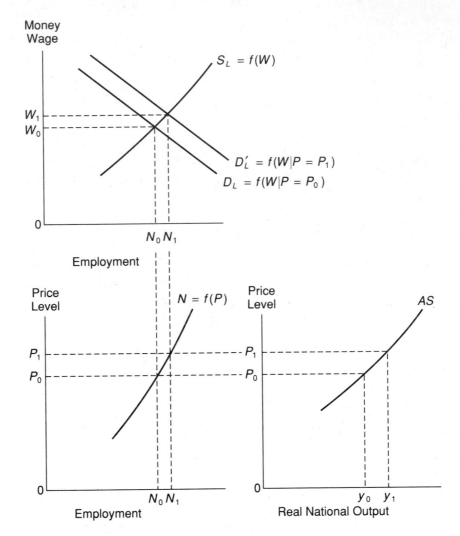

the labor force changed. The demand for labor curve will shift if the productivity of labor changes, thus changing the production function and, hence, the marginal product of labor.

The aggregate demand and the aggregate supply relationships have now been explained, so they can be combined to show the mutual determination of the price level and the level of national income or product. According to this framework of analysis, inflation can occur only

---

Figure 11-8   Aggregate Supply Where Labor Supply Depends on Money
Wages More Than on Price Level

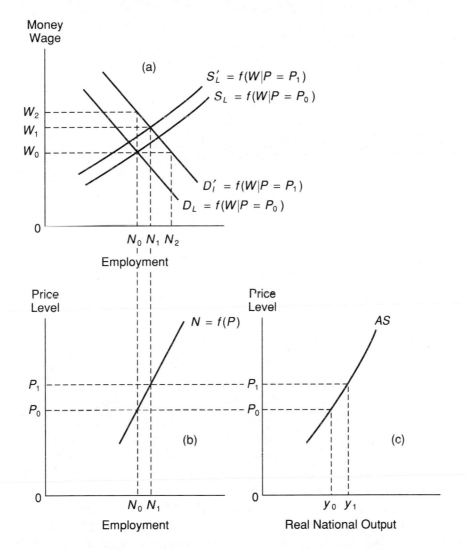

if aggregate demand increases or if aggregate supply decreases. In the
analysis leading up to this point, all of the events that can cause either
AD or *AS* to shift have been described. The underlying relations that
determine the slopes of the two functions have also been discussed in
regard to what will determine whether the price level or output will
change in response to any shift in one of the relations.

Figure 11-9   Aggregate Supply and Demand Determine Price Level and
Output

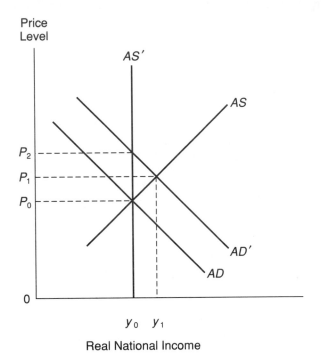

Real National Income

Figure 11-9 shows the AS and AD curves determining the price
level at P_0 and real national output at y_0. The AD curve shifts to AD' if
any of the functions making up the i-s curve shift the i-s curve to the
right, such as an increase in government spending, or if any of the functions making up the l-m function shift the l-m function to the right,
such as an increase in the money stock.

If we use the classical assumption of (1) flexible wages and prices
and (2) labor supply determined by real wages, the supply curve will
be AS', and the shift in the demand curve will cause prices to rise with
no increase in output. If the assumptions of flexible wages and prices
and of labor supply determined by money wages are made, then AS is
the aggregate supply curve, and both output and prices will increase
in response to the increased aggregate demand.

An example may be helpful in demonstrating what is involved in
the model as it is now composed. The model starts from a condition
of equilibrium in all aspects of the economy, then changes any variable

Figure 11-10   Shift in Aggregate Demand

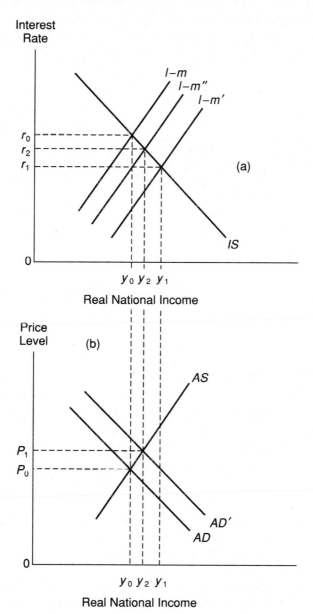

Real National Income

that shifts the i-s or l-m function and thus the AD curve, and traces the impact on the other variables. Alternatively, one of the variables that shifts the AS curve can be changed and the effects then traced.

An increase in the money stock shifts the l-m curve to the right, reducing interest rates and increasing demand for real national income. Investment and consumption demand both increase because of the lower interest rate. This point is seen as r_1, y_1 in diagram (a) of Figure 11-10. Looking at diagram (b), we interpret this by noting that if the price level remained at P_0, the aggregate quantity of commodities demanded would be y_1. Thus, the AD curve has shifted to AD' and excess demand in the amount of the difference between y_1 and y_0 would show up. This causes the prices of products to go up because the demand has increased more than the costs of production by way of wage increases. This brings us to a price level of P_1 on diagram (b) and an equilibrium national income and output of Y_2.

Since prices have gone up, the real value of money balances has decreased; since this amounts to a decrease in the real money stock, the l-m curve will shift upward to l-m'', bringing the interest rate to r_2. This increase in the interest rate reduces investment and consumption compared with what they would have been had the interest rate stayed at r_1, which is the reason that income moves to y_2 rather than y_1.

PRICE EXPECTATIONS

All the factors considered thus far lead to the conclusion that falling price levels increase the quantities demanded of the economy's output and that rising price levels decrease quantities demanded. However, if falling prices generate the expectation in people's minds that prices will fall further, then they might very well hold off on some of their expenditures. Similarly, inflation may precipitate expectations of further price-level expansion, and economic units may decide that it is advisable to shift into more goods and out of monetary assets. When price level movements generate expectations of this sort, it cannot be said with any confidence that aggregate demand is inversely related to the price level.

The market interest rate is another variable significantly influenced by price expectations. The liquidity preference theory concludes that an increase in the money supply will decrease interest rates. However, we have observed that an increase in the money stock has normally been followed by an increase, not a decrease, in rates of interest. The apparent explanation is that the increase in the money stock generates expectations of inflation, which, in turn, induces borrowers to be willing to pay higher market rates of interest and lenders to demand higher rates.

Rational Expectations

The persistent inflation of the 1960s and 1970s inspired economists to devote a great deal of attention to the issue of expectations of changes in price levels and the effect of those expectations on the behavior of consumers, investors, and suppliers of the factors of production. Two basic approaches have developed. One is called "rational expectations," where the view is that the public has some understanding of what causes inflation, and as they see changes in the causal factors, they forecast the rate of price-level changes. Thus, if the public believes that lowering taxes and raising government expenditures cause inflation, no amount of "jawboning" by government officials will convince them otherwise, and their consuming and investing behavior will reflect these beliefs. Rational-expectations theorists assume that the public has the information at any point in time to make predictions about future price levels and to act accordingly. The theorist naturally assumes the public's theory of price-level determination is the same as that of the theorist. For example, a quantity theorist postulates that expectations of inflation depend on the rate of change in the money supply or in the monetary base. The rational-expectations hypothesis has been an important part of the argument for steady growth in the money supply, as opposed to a policy of fine tuning, and is said to account for the persistence of inflation and the "failure" of Keynesian economic policy.

Adaptive Expectations

The second approach used to treat the issue of expectations is called "adaptive expectations" or "error adjustment models." In this method, the forecast of future price-level changes depends strictly upon the past behavior of the price level, the more recent past having more influence than earlier times. No theories about why the price level changes are involved.

To get some of the flavor of the analysis, let us start from a situation of equilibrium where the price level has been constant, and the public forecasts no inflation for period one. Now, suppose prices actually increase by 4 percent in the first quarter. Because there has been an error in forecasting, the assumption is that an adjustment will be made in the forecast for the second quarter. We will assume the error adjustment factor is one half ($\beta = 0.5$). Thus, for the second period, the public will forecast an inflation rate of 2 percent. Suppose the actual inflation rate in period two remains at 4 percent. Then, the forecast for period three will be 3 percent; that is, the error adjustment will be one half the difference between the actual and the forecasted rate.

Symbolically[1]:

$$(1)\ \dot{P}^e = \dot{P}^e_{-1} + \beta(\dot{P} - \dot{P}^e_{-1})$$

where

- $\dot{P}^e$ is the currently held expectation of the value of the inflation rate next period,
- $\dot{P}^e_{-1}$ is the preceding period's expected value of the inflation rate for the current period,
- $\dot{P}$ is the current value of the inflation rate, and
- $0 < \beta < 1$.

Equation (1) can be put into a more convenient form:

$$(2)\ \dot{P}^e = \beta\dot{P} + (1-\beta)\dot{P}^e_{-1}$$

The procedure then is to lag Equation (2) to form:

$$(2')\ \dot{P}^e_{-1} = \beta\dot{P}_{-1} + \beta(1-\beta)\dot{P}^e_{-2}$$

which is substituted for $\dot{P}^e_{-1}$ in Equation (2). Successive lagging and substituting periods -2 and $-3, \ldots , -n$ yields:

$$(3)\ \dot{P}^e = \beta\dot{P} + \beta(1-\beta)\dot{P}_{-1} + \beta(1-\beta)^2\dot{P}_{-2} + \ldots + \beta(1-\beta)^n\dot{P}_{-n}\ .$$

Therefore, the expected inflation depends only upon past rates of inflation, with the most recent experience having more influence than more remote periods. If the actual rate of increase in the price level stays at some constant figure, expectations will, over time, approach that same figure. The parameter β can be looked upon as a measure of how rapidly the public's adaptation to inflation is. If β were large (say, 0.9), this would mean that people are very sensitive to changes in the price level and change their expectations accordingly. This is more

---

1. The dot over a symbol indicates rate of change, that is, $\dot{P} = \dfrac{1}{P} \times \dfrac{\Delta P}{\Delta t}$. Also, see Laurence H. Meyer, *Macroeconomics: A Model Building Approach* (Cincinnati: South-Western Publishing Co., 1980), pp. 362–363.

likely to be the case when there has been a great deal of experience with inflation than if the price level behavior had been fairly stable. After a long period of stability of prices, the β is likely to be small, and expectations will be adjusted slowly.

Price Expectations in Macroeconomic Theory

It is difficult to know how price expectations should be treated in our economic analysis. Classical economists generally made the assumption of static expectations; that is, the assumption that the current price level will also be the expected future price level, or that the current rate of inflation is expected to be the rate that will prevail in the future. Such forecasts might be accurate for individuals who feel completely uncertain about future price-level behavior or who have no knowledge of economic theory. However, almost everyone has some information and some knowledge of economic theory, no matter how incomplete or naive it might be.

One solution to the problem of incorporating price expectations into our models is to despair of ever discovering systematic relationships among economic variables and expectations and treat expectations as exogenous variables. For empirical applications, one can then make use of the reports of agencies that conduct public-opinion polls (for example, those of the Survey Research Center at the University of Michigan's Institute for Social Research) to determine the current state of price expectations.

The importance of the issue of incorporating price expectations into macroeconomic theory is in evaluating stabilization policy. The discussion is broadened and put into this context in Chapters 21 and 22.

QUESTIONS

1. Draw a set of seven graphs showing the equilibrium interest rate and real national income determined by the intersection of the *i-s* and the *l-m* curves. The *l-m* curve is to be *derived* from the demand and supply of money as shown in Figure 10-3 and the *i-s* curve is to be *derived* from the saving and investment analysis as shown in Figure 9-7. (Note that the two figures are presented in nominal terms, while the analysis here is in real terms.)

2. Having completed question 1, show graphically the effect on both the interest rate and real national income of an increase in the stock of money

caused, for example, by a decrease in reserve requirements. Now, using the aggregate demand and aggregate supply graph, show what happens to the price level.

3. State what happens to the *i-s* or the *l-m* function and, therefore, to the equilibrium rate of interest and income from the following events:

   (a) a decrease in the demand for money for transactions purposes caused, for example, by the elimination of the fee for credit card use.

   (b) a decrease in the demand for money for speculative purposes caused, for example, by a reduction in economic uncertainty after a presidential election.

   (c) an increase in autonomous consumption spending caused, for example, by the event mentioned in (b) above.

   (d) an increase in demand for investment spending caused, for example, by the realization that large profits could be achieved through exploitation of a significant innovation.

   (e) an increase in spending by the federal government.

   (f) a decrease in the average rate of taxation.

   (g) an increase in exports.

   (h) a decrease in imports.

4. Explain why the Pigou effect would not be expected to operate on corporate bonds, whereas it would be operative on Federal Reserve notes.

5. Give as many reasons as you can to explain why aggregate demand for the output of the economy will rise as the price level falls.

6. Give as many reasons as you can to explain why aggregate supply of goods and services will rise as the price level rises.

READINGS

Boyes, William J. *Macroeconomics: Intermediate Theory and Policy*, 2d ed. Cincinnati: South-Western Publishing Co., 1988. Chapter 8.

Lucas, Robert E., Jr. "Expectations and the Neutrality of Money." *Journal of Economic Theory* (April 1972), pp. 103–124.

———, and Thomas Sargent. *Rational Expectations and Econometric Practice.* Minneapolis: University of Minnesota Press, 1981.

Patinkin, Don. *Money, Interest, and Prices: An Integration of Monetary and Value Theory*, 2d ed. New York: Harper & Row, Publishers, 1965.

Pesaran, M. Hashem. *The Limits to Rational Expectations.* Cambridge, MA: Basil Blackwell, Inc., 1989.

Shaw, G. K. *Rational Expectations: An Elementary Exposition.* New York: St. Martin's Press, 1984.

Tobin, James. *Asset Accumulation and Economic Activity.* Chicago: University of Chicago Press, 1982.

CHAPTER 12

TOPICS IN NATIONAL INCOME ANALYSIS

In this chapter the topic of aggregate consumption theory is pursued in some depth, beginning with the influence of taxes on consumer spending. The discussion presents a hypothesis called the stagnation thesis, which, while having fallen out of favor somewhat as a forecast for the U.S. economy, is still very useful for illuminating certain economic principles. It also serves as an introduction to the last segment of the chapter on the theory of economic growth.

TAXATION

Whereas government expenditures are included among the injections into the income stream, receipts by government are looked upon as a withdrawal from the income stream. Government has the ability to absorb purchasing power from the rest of the economy by its legal power to tax. Usually, the taxing authority first sets the tax rate and other laws affecting tax payments and then forecasts the amount of collections.

Since taxes are withdrawals, they are not a part of aggregate demand. Instead, they are a part of aggregate supply but influence aggregate demand. Some taxes or rules for computing taxes will have their impact on the marginal efficiency of capital. Others will affect the net foreign investment figure. The most important classes of taxes, however, are those that reduce the disposable income of households and thus influence the consumption function. These are the taxes that now will be introduced into our national income model.

The new consumption function that is to be utilized here is $C = \alpha + \beta Y_D$. We have switched from English to Greek letters for the parameters simply to indicate that this function is the after-tax consumption function. Y_D is disposable income, equal to national income (Y) minus taxes (T_x). (Recall that T_x is equal to total tax collections minus transfer payments.)

For our example, a linear tax function is used: $T_x = \bar{T}_x + tY$. This relationship is similar to a proportional tax in that a change in income results in a proportional change in the tax payments; that is, $\frac{\Delta T_x}{\Delta Y} = t$ is constant. However, $\frac{T_x}{Y}$ is not constant. It is declining; so in that sense, it is a regressive tax. A strictly proportional tax function would have both $\frac{\Delta T_x}{\Delta Y}$ and $\frac{T_x}{Y}$ constant, which would be true only if $\bar{T}_x$ were equal to zero. This tax function relates to national income, not to personal or individual incomes; therefore, we can say very little about the tax rate structure that applies to individuals. As national income changes, so may its distribution. Formally, our model looks like this[1]:

$$
\begin{aligned}
Y &= C + I_B + G \\
C &= \alpha + \beta Y_D \\
Y_D &= Y - T_x \\
T_x &= \bar{T}_x + tY \\
I_B &= \bar{I}_B \\
G &= \bar{G}
\end{aligned}
$$

And its solution can be shown in the following way:

$$
\begin{aligned}
Y &= C + I_B + G \\
Y &= \alpha + \beta Y_D + \bar{I}_B + \bar{G} \\
Y &= \alpha + \beta(Y - T_x) + \bar{I}_B + \bar{G} \\
Y &= \alpha + \beta Y - \beta T_x + \bar{I}_B + \bar{G} \\
Y &= \alpha + \beta Y - \beta \bar{T}_x - \beta tY + \bar{I}_B + \bar{G} \\
Y - \beta Y + \beta tY &= \alpha + \bar{I}_B + \bar{G} - \beta \bar{T}_x \\
Y(1 - \beta + \beta t) &= \alpha + \bar{I}_B + \bar{G} - \beta \bar{T}_x
\end{aligned}
$$

$$
Y = \frac{\alpha + \bar{I}_B + \bar{G} - \beta \bar{T}_x}{1 - \beta + \beta t} \quad \text{or} \quad Y = \frac{\alpha + \bar{I}_B + \bar{G} - \beta \bar{T}_x}{1 - \beta(1 - t)}
$$

A tax multiplier can be constructed if it is defined as $\frac{\Delta Y}{\Delta \bar{T}_x}$. The meaning of $\Delta \bar{T}_x$ here is that whatever the level of national income, the amount of the tax will be $\Delta \bar{T}_x$ larger than before. Notice, however, that

---

1. For simplicity we have left international trade out of the model. Therefore, the model is called a "closed system."

it does not indicate that taxes will be $\Delta \bar{T}$ larger than before the additional tax was imposed. Since the change in taxes will change the national income, taxes will also change because income changes. The derivation of this multiplier can be accomplished by comparing the equilibrium income of the latest model with the income found to be equilibrium when the tax function includes $\Delta \bar{T}_x$. Thus, in place of $T_x = \bar{T}_x + tY$ use $T'_x = \bar{T}_x + tY + \Delta \bar{T}_x$.

The new equilibrium income Y' is then:

$$Y' = \frac{\alpha + \bar{I}_B + \bar{G} - \beta(\bar{T}_x + \Delta \bar{T}_x)}{1 - \beta + \beta t} = \frac{\alpha + \bar{I}_B + \bar{G} - \beta \bar{T}_x - \beta \Delta \bar{T}_x}{1 - \beta + \beta t}$$

Our goal is to find $\dfrac{\Delta Y}{\Delta \bar{T}_x}$. ΔY is $Y' - Y$. Subtracting the equation for Y above from the equation just found for Y' gives $Y' - Y = \Delta Y = \dfrac{-\beta \Delta \bar{T}_x}{1 - \beta + \beta t}$. Then, dividing both sides of this equation by $\Delta \bar{T}_x$ we get:

$$\frac{\Delta Y}{\Delta \bar{T}_x} = \frac{-\beta}{1 - \beta + \beta t} \text{ , or } \frac{-\beta}{1 - \beta(1 - t)} \text{ , which is the tax multiplier.}$$

The tax multiplier is negative. Since $\Delta \bar{T}_x$ is positive, ΔY must be negative; that is, an increase in taxes results in a decrease in national income.

Figure 12-1 shows how to develop a consumption function when taxes are imposed in the form described by the tax function $T_x = \bar{T}_x + tY$. Y_2 is disposable income (that is, $Y - T_x$) when national income is Y_1 ($T_1 = Y_1 - Y_2$). We make the assumption that households will spend the same amount on consumption if national income is Y_2 and no taxes are paid, or if national income is Y_1 and taxes of T_1 make disposable income equal to Y_2. For example, a person with an income of \$150 and taxes of \$50 would consume the same as if income were \$100 with no taxes to pay; or, in other words, the person acts on the basis of take-home pay rather than gross pay.

By this assumption we are able to draw an after-tax consumption function: $C' = a + bY$. At a given level of income, it is below the pretax function ($C = \alpha + \beta Y_D$) by β times the amount of the tax at that income. The individual's disposable income has been reduced by the amount of the tax, so we expect the consumer to reduce consumption by the marginal propensity to consume times the reduction in income. Also, given this particular tax function, b is the marginal propensity to con-

Figure 12-1   Before- and After-Tax Consumption Function

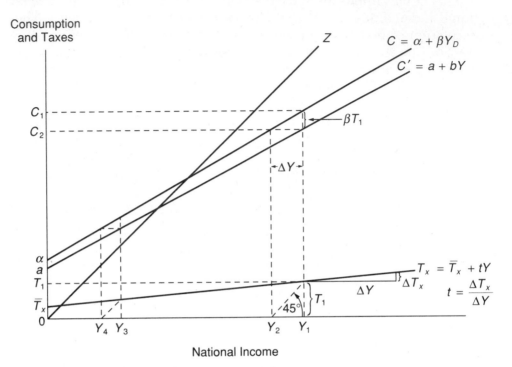

National Income

sume national income. It will be a little smaller than β, the marginal propensity to consume disposable income. A little algebra will show that $b = \beta - \beta t$ or $b = \beta(1-t)$. With the given tax function, C' is the relevant consumption function. The C function is needed to derive C', so it is kept in the diagram.

Now that taxes have been incorporated, aggregate leakages or withdrawals (S) include both personal saving and taxes: $S = S_p + T_x$. $S = Y - C'$, so $S_p + T_x = Y - C'$. Therefore, $S_p = Y - C' - T_x$. The aggregate saving curve can be derived by simply subtracting the C' line from the Z line. Then the S_p line can be found by $S_p = S - T_x$. Alternatively, the S_p line can be constructed by the same reasoning by which the C' curve was derived in Figure 12-1. Then S_p and T_x sum to S.

As before, equilibrium income occurs at that level at which aggregate saving $(S_p + T_x)$ is equal to aggregate investment $(I_B + G)$. An increase in government spending of ΔG will cause income to increase by that amount (ΔG) times the reciprocal of the slope of the S function $\left(\dfrac{1}{1 - \beta + \beta t}\right)$.

Figure 12-2   Balanced Budget Situation

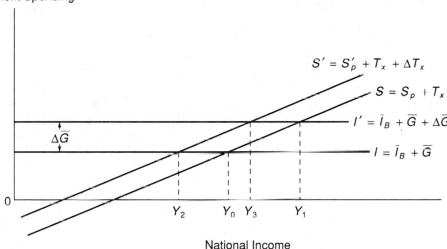

Saving, Investment,
Taxes, and
Government Spending

$S' = S'_p + T_x + \Delta T_x$

$S = S_p + T_x$

$I' = \bar{I}_B + \bar{G} + \Delta\bar{G}$

$I = \bar{I}_B + \bar{G}$

$\Delta\bar{G}$

0

Y_2 Y_0 Y_3 Y_1

National Income

A decrease in taxes by a given amount will result in an increase in income, but the increase will be somewhat less than that resulting from the same increase in government spending. Likewise, if government expenditures and taxes were both increased by the same amount, national income would not be constant—it would increase. The reason for this asymmetry of taxes and spending is that while government purchases of goods and services become a part of national income, a decrease in taxation increases consumption by less than the full amount of the tax. The change in taxes of $\Delta\bar{T}_x$ shifts the consumption function by $\beta\Delta\bar{T}_x$ and the aggregate saving function by the same amount but in the opposite direction. The shift of the saving curve can be viewed as a composite of the shift in the personal saving function and the shift in the tax function. For example, suppose the increase in the tax is $10 billion ($\Delta\bar{T}_x = \$10$ billion) and the MPS disposable income is 2/10. The tax function then shifts upward by $10 billion, and the S_p function shifts downward by $2 billion—a net increase in the S function of $8 billion.

Figure 12-2 shows a balanced budget situation where taxes and government spending were both increased by an amount equal to $\Delta\bar{G}$. If only government expenditures had been increased, income would

Figure 12-3   Effect of Equal Government Spending Increases and Tax Decreases

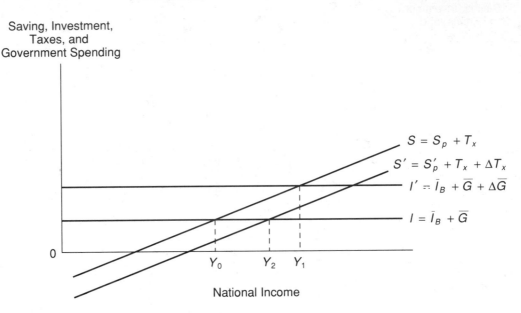

Saving, Investment,
Taxes, and
Government Spending

$$S = S_p + T_x$$

$$S' = S'_p + T_x + \Delta T_x$$

$$I' = \bar{I}_B + \bar{G} + \Delta \bar{G}$$

$$I = \bar{I}_B + \bar{G}$$

Y_0 Y_2 Y_1

National Income

have risen to Y_1. If only taxes had been raised, income would have fallen to Y_2. Since both were raised, the net effect is for income to rise to Y_3.

Figure 12-3 compares the effect of an increase in G and a decrease in T_x of equal amounts. Clearly, the increase in G has a larger impact on national income than does the decrease in T_x.

CONTRIBUTIONS TO THE THEORY OF CONSUMPTION

The statistical correlation between annual real personal consumption expenditures and annual real disposable personal income is extremely high. With the exception of the war years 1941–1945, virtually all the points from 1929 to the present fall on the regression line that has a slope of about 0.90, which seems to confirm the empirical relevance of the kinds of consumption functions we have been using.

Our confidence in the function is shaken considerably, however, if we go through the same procedure using quarterly or monthly data. Here the correlation is not nearly so impressive, since the points appear to be scattered almost haphazardly. Some significant errors in forecasting consumption on the basis of income have inspired many economists to probe more deeply into the nature of consumer behavior. This can be done by studying individuals or groups of individuals with different characteristics—such as age, urban versus rural, wealth, and education—or it can be done by a more sophisticated theoretical attack on the aggregative level. Research economists are continuously using both the micro and the macro approaches to learn more about forecasting consumer behavior. The answers are not yet all in.

The significant errors in the short-run empirical consumption function suggest that factors other than disposable income contribute importantly to the consumption decision, some of which will be discussed here. Some empirical evidence on them will be taken up in the chapters on forecasting.

Expectations of Changes in Income, Employment, and Prices

Households in any given income bracket would be expected to increase their current consumption if they anticipated a considerable increase in income in the near future. Such expansion of spending out of a given income is usually possible through the reduction of saving, spending out of assets accumulated during the past, or borrowing against future income. If a person fears the possibility of unemployment, his or her spending behavior will probably become more conservative. If the feeling is widespread, the consumption function would shift downward.

We would expect that uncertainty in and of itself would be an important reason for saving, so anything creating uncertainty in the minds of the family decision makers would shift the consumption function downward. Closely connected to this idea, but independent of it, is the reasoning that volatility of income would alter consumption behavior. Imagine two families whose incomes over a long period of time would be equal, but one family had a constant income from an annuity, and the other had an income that greatly fluctuated on a monthly or quarterly basis. The short-run consumption function for the two families might be quite different, even though the longer-run functions might be identical. The aggregate consumption function would probably be higher and more stable as uncertainty and volatility of income were diminished. This is one of the expected effects of the expansion of Social Security and certain other governmental economic policies.

The Survey Research Center of the University of Michigan has engaged in extensive research into consumer expectations and behavior, stressing particularly the psychological and sociological elements of the study. In general, their findings support the view that pessimism with respect to income and employment, as well as the vague feeling that "things are going to get worse," results in diminished consumer spending. The converse also seems to be true: an attitude of optimism about future income, employment, and the general economic and political climate acts as a stimulus to consumption expenditures.[2]

One would certainly anticipate that consumers who expect prices to rise would take advantage of the current lower prices and increase their spending. Conversely, consumers would curtail present consumption as much as possible, if they expected prices to fall in the future. Apparently, consumer psychology is more complex than this. It seems that when prices are rising and expected to rise further, they are already higher than they were, and consumers are reluctant to increase their purchases at what they believe to be "high" prices.

Expectations of the future price level will affect the demand for some goods more than others. For example, if prices are expected to fall in the near future, families will probably choose to get by with their present automobile or household appliances, whereas their consumption of less durable items may remain about the same.

Prices

Rational consumer behavior implies that if all prices (and, hence, incomes) increased proportionally, consumption valued in current prices should also increase by the same proportion, so that real consumption would remain constant. Households frequently suffer from a type of myopia encountered earlier in the labor-supply context; economists call this the "money illusion" in the goods market. This means the consumer might emphasize a rise in nominal income without realizing that prices have also increased. Others might be so conscious of the higher prices of goods and services that they seemingly are unaware that their incomes have also increased. Economists do not generally agree as to whether a money illusion exists in a form dependable enough to include the hypothesis in their analysis.

---

2. Most of the Center's publications are pertinent to this discussion. See also, for a recent example, Richard T. Curtin, "Slow Economic Progress Dims Consumer Optimism," *Economic Outlook USA* (Spring 1981), pp. 32–35. Older but still relevant is G. Katona, *The Powerful Consumer: Psychological Studies of the American Economy* (Westport, CN: Greenwood Press, 1977).

We have previously seen that the major effect of price-level changes on consumer behavior came through the Pigou effect, where increases in the general level of prices reduced the real value of money balances and thus inspired consumers to attempt to add to their money holdings by reducing their consumption. The Pigou effect assumes that the money illusion is not operative. In fact, it assumes a high degree of awareness of the "real" effects of price-level changes, unclouded by any veil of money illusion.

Historically, inflations and deflations have not been characterized by proportional price changes. Rather, some prices change very readily, while others are termed "sticky." This fact alone can be quite important in generating business fluctuations as described by W. C. Mitchell. (Mitchell's theory is discussed in Chapter 13.) We don't know enough to make empirically meaningful generalizations about the effect of nonproportional price variability on aggregate consumption spending. We can, however, observe that if it were true that price volatility was characteristic of goods whose income elasticity of demand was high, and if price rigidity were true of goods with low income elasticity, then a general rise in price level would reduce consumption. Of course, such statements are only hypotheses until a great deal more research on the problem is complete.

There are other similar considerations that can be observed. For example, a general increase in prices, even if proportional, will result in a shift of real income from the private sector to government, where a progressive income tax is in effect. Assume all prices to increase by 10 percent, so that all money incomes also increase by 10 percent. Since the income tax is progressive, the increase in tax payments will be more than 10 percent, and real disposable income will have declined. In this instance, we should expect real consumption to be reduced.

Another possible source of a change in consumption could come through a systematic redistribution of income by price level changes from those with a high marginal propensity to consume to those with a low marginal propensity to consume, or vice versa. First, however, we would need to know that inflation does have this redistributional effect on particular classes of consumers and that classes so affected do, in fact, have different marginal propensities to consume. Inflation could also cause a shift from the consumption of domestically produced goods to foreign-produced goods as their relative prices changed.

Interest

In a number of connections, it has been pointed out that classical economists relied on the interest rate to explain the division of income into its consumption and saving components. In the logic of utility maximization, an increase in interest rates should cause households to save more and consume less out of any given level of income. A saver whose goal is to accumulate a particular sum of wealth at a particular future date, however, would save less when interest rates rise, since the same sum could be accumulated by that date with smaller periodic additions. In some instances, this may describe some households' behavior, but it is inconsistent with utility maximization and, therefore, somewhat suspect as a part of the theory.

The other side of the role of interest rates on saving-consumption behavior is the effect on borrowing for consumption purposes. High interest rates discourage spending on consumer durables, such as automobiles, furniture, appliances, as well as home purchases. Lower consumption of these items implies an increase in saving.

Income Distribution

Many schemes to promote economic expansion are based on the belief that the marginal propensities to consume of low-income groups are higher than those of high-income groups. Consumption and national income would increase if income were taken away from the low MPC households and given to high MPC households. The hypothesis seems to be so intuitively appealing that many have accepted policy proposals based upon it. There are several fallacies incorporated into this position, quite aside from the most fundamental one: because an act has one desirable outcome, it should be done.

The simple error of confusing the marginal propensity to consume with the average propensity to consume is often discovered. It is quite well-established that the APC of high-income families is significantly lower than that of low-income families. The evidence on the MPC by income class, however, is an entirely different matter. It is very difficult to measure, and most attempts to do so seem to indicate that the differences in the marginal propensities to consume of the various income classes are not significant. One reason for this surprising conclusion is that low-income families might have debts to pay or cash balances to build up. There are many nonconsumption uses for added income.

Even if it were discovered that low-income households had high marginal propensities to consume, it would be advisable to determine whether some other factor might be the fundamental reason, rather than the level of income. For example, young families seem to have a high *MPC* and are more likely to be lower on the income scale. Certainly, there are groups in the low-income category that may have low marginal propensities to consume, such as farmers and certain immigrant groups. The source of income seems to have some influence on consumption behavior. Profit recipients behave differently than do wage earners and interest and rent receivers. These considerations ought to give us pause before we recommend income redistribution as the preferred solution to a slumping economy. This is not to say that income redistribution may not be defended as a worthwhile goal, but its defense must rest on other grounds.

Wealth

The relationship of wealth to consumption behavior is difficult to ascertain. For one thing, wealth and income are so highly correlated that it is difficult to determine their individual effect upon consumption. Another difficulty is that wealth ownership may actually indicate that the owners have saved large portions of income and are thus motivated differently than those with less wealth. Again, considering any given level of income, wealth holding is likely to be concentrated in the older age group whose spending patterns differ from those of younger people.

Different kinds of wealth may have different effects on consumer spending. Some consumer wealth requires additional spending, if its value is to be maintained and services received. Automobiles and household appliances are in this category. On the other hand, the services of some kinds of consumer wealth substitute for new consumer goods and services. Thus, to some extent, a VCR may reduce spending on other forms of entertainment, and ownership of an automobile reduces spending on other forms of transportation.

The influence of financial wealth on consumer spending habits is the more serious question. It has been suggested that the unexpectedly high levels of consumption following World War II can be partially explained by the rapid accumulation of financial assets in the hands of consumers during the war years. It does seem plausible that of two families with the same income, the one with the larger holdings of financial assets would spend more on current consumption. Undoubtedly, the most important consideration is the level of wealth relative to the family's aspiration level. Unfortunately, this is not directly measurable.

Consumer Credit Terms

Consumption can be accomplished without regard to current income, either by allowing the stock of assets to vary or by varying the amount of indebtedness over a period of time. The terms on which consumers can borrow are altered periodically. The interest rate is of some consequence in these terms, but other conditions may be of equal or even more importance. Among these conditions are the down-payment requirement, the length of the repayment period, and the credit standards imposed by the lenders. The easing of these terms stimulates consumer borrowing and spending, and their tightening discourages new borrowing and spending. The major impact, of course, is on durable consumer goods, but revolving-type charges, involving the purchase of "soft goods," are also affected.

Short-Run Versus Long-Run Consumption Functions

The statistical evidence on the consumption-income relation suggests that the consumption function over short periods of time has a positive intercept and a relatively small slope. The long-run function derived from empirical evidence is approximately proportional; that is, it is linear and its intercept is close to the origin.[3] These apparently contradictory findings demand an explanation. In fact, any explanation of consumer behavior must be consistent with these observations. Figure 12-4 is drawn to serve as the basis for discussing the problem.

The consumption function labeled C_L represents the long-run consumption-income relationship. Kuznets found remarkable stability in the average propensity to consume when he used decade figures from 1869 to the beginning of the great depression in 1929. During the 1930s, the APC increased significantly when disposable income fell well below what it had been. During the years of World War II, the APC was very low as incomes again grew very rapidly. After the war, the APC again returned to figures comparable to the long-run historical norms.

---

3. The study on which these statements are based is Simon Kuznets, *National Income: A Summary of Findings* (New York: National Bureau of Economic Research, Inc., 1975).

Figure 12-4   Consumption-Income Relation

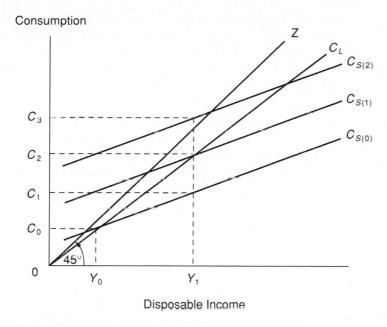

The short-run consumption functions of Figure 12-4 have the sub-script s, and represent the consumption behavior in response to in-comes in relatively short time periods. The argument is that the short-run consumption function has been shifting upward because of some basic changes taking place in the economy, such as developments of new consumer goods, accumulation of wealth, education to new de-sires, the growth of urban populations, and so on.

Start with income Y_0, at which level of income consumption is C_0. If income increases to Y_1 within a short period of time, consumption would increase to C_1; but if the above-mentioned changes occurred over a longer time period, such that the consumption function shifted to $C_{s(1)}$, consumption would increase to C_2. Many years later, Y_1 might be a severe depression level of income, but since the consumption function had shifted upward considerably during that time, consumption would be at C_3. Arthur Smithies showed that the statistical evi-dence was consistent with this explanation of consumer behavior.[4]

---

4. Arthur Smithies, "Forecasting Postwar Demand," *Econometrica* (January 1945).

But, as we shall see, a number of other explanations are also consistent with the evidence.

Relative Income Hypothesis. One of these explanations is the "relative income hypothesis" of James Duesenberry. Where Smithies felt that the basic consumption relation was the short-run function, and the long-run proportional function showed up as shifts in the short-run functions, Duesenberry believes that it is the proportional function that is the fundamental one.[5] In other words, if income were to continuously increase, consumption would increase proportionally; but since income fluctuates, consumer response is nonproportional.

This argument is based on the view that consumption is determined not simply by one's current income but, to an important extent, by one's position in society, which in turn depends partly upon one's own past income and the income of one's neighbors. Thorstein Veblen, in his penetrating discussion of consumption, emphasized the degree to which people consume to impress others via "conspicuous consumption," and how socially approved consumption patterns were set by the higher ranking or higher income groups, a phenomenon called "pecuniary emulation."[6] Persons whose income is low relative to their neighbors' will spend a larger proportion of their income, whereas those with relatively large incomes can consume smaller proportions of their income. Thus, the least wealthy of the "jet set" may have a higher *APC* than the wealthiest persons living in a very poor neighborhood.

Duesenberry's description of consumption behavior is based on the dynamics of fluctuations and growth in income. Figure 12-5 can be used to explain the hypothesis. Consumption would be equal to C_1 if income were Y_1, and if income grew steadily, consumption would follow the C_L line, so that as income increased to Y_2, consumption would increase to C_3. But when income hits a peak of Y_2 and declines, consumption would follow the $C_{S(1)}$ line down, so that if the income fell all the way back to Y_1, consumption would be C_2 rather than C_1. The reason given for making the short-run (nonproportional) function the relevant one when income falls is that households, having once reached a high standard of living (as represented by C_3), will relinquish it only very reluctantly. They will allow their savings to decline rather than give up the level of consumption attained during the boom. How-

5. J. S. Duesenberry, *Income, Saving, and the Theory of Consumer Behavior* (Cambridge, MA: Harvard University Press, 1949).

6. Thorstein B. Veblen, *The Theory of the Leisure Class: An Economic Study of Institutions* (New York: Penguin Books, 1979).

Figure 12-5   Duesenberry's Hypothesis of Consumption Behavior

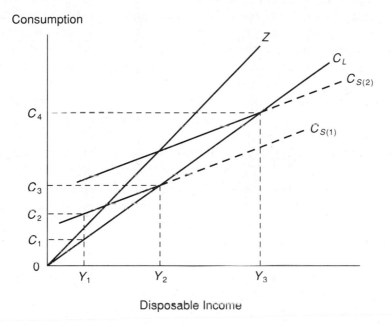

Disposable Income

ever, as income reaches its trough, say, at Y_1, and begins to rise again, consumption will also increase, but again along the $C_{S(1)}$ line. Thus, when one has grown accustomed to the lower standard of living represented by C_2, the desire to save seems more urgent when income rises. But when income again reaches Y_2 and continues to increase, consumption will again increase according to C_L, until income reaches a new peak at, say, Y_3, at which point if income falls, consumption behavior will follow a new short-run function $C_{S(2)}$.

Permanent Income Hypothesis. Economist Milton Friedman approached the problem of the consumption-income relation in a novel way.[7] The underlying motivation and attitudes of consumers are similar to those described by Duesenberry, but Friedman makes consumption depend explicitly on what he calls "permanent income." The term "permanent" should not be taken too literally. It is measured as a weighted average of incomes of the recent past and can be viewed as an approximation of an individual's expected future income. This is a long step toward making consumption depend on current wealth rather than

7. Milton Friedman, *A Theory of the Consumption Function* (Princeton, NJ: Princeton University Press, 1957).

on current income, since if expected future incomes are discounted to the present, the resulting figure is the present value of wealth. This wealth figure would include both human and nonhuman wealth.

Actual income differs from permanent income by an amount called "transitory income." Friedman believes, and his statistical evidence supports his belief, that consumers will not respond to an increase in income by a proportional increase in consumption; but if that income continues for several years, they will consume virtually all of it.

Friedman's theoretical statement is that the marginal propensity to consume out of permanent income is one, and that the marginal propensity to consume transitory income is zero. Transitory income is in the nature of a windfall gain or loss and, therefore, is not incorporated into the consuming units' budget. Instead, people tend to use transitory income to pay off debts or to accumulate assets for future use when income might fall or when heavy expenses might arise.

It is important to keep in mind when evaluating the permanent-income hypothesis that the consumption variable is not synonymous with consumer outlay or spending, but is a measure of current household use of resources for utility. Thus, if an individual were to receive a significant windfall, part of it may very well be spent to purchase an automobile. Consumption, however, would be increased only to the extent that the new car provided more or better service than the old one during the income period.

Another observation that is consistent with the permanent-income hypothesis is that people with fluctuating incomes do not alter their consumption patterns to conform with the variation in their incomes. Someone with a great amount of wealth might in a particular year have a very small or even negative income. Such an individual would not be expected to drastically reduce consumption. Conversely, persons whose income is very stable and who can forecast that their future income will be roughly the same as their current income tend to consume most of their income continuously.

The Life Cycle Hypothesis. Another theory explaining consumption behavior of individuals from which an aggregate consumption function can be derived is the "life cycle hypothesis."[8] In this theory, the individual is viewed as wishing to maximize lifetime utility from

8. The earliest presentation of this theory was in Franco Modigliani and R. E. Brumberg, "Utility Analysis and the Consumption Function: An Interpretation of Cross Section Data," in *Post-Keynesian Economics*, edited by K. K. Kurihara (New Brunswick, NJ: Rutgers University Press, 1954). Another important contribution came in Albert Ando and F. Modigliani, "The 'Life Cycle' Hypothesis of Saving: Aggregate Implications and Tests," *American Economic Review* (March 1963), pp. 55–84.

consumption on the basis of expected lifetime income. As in Friedman's hypothesis, short-run changes in income would not be expected to seriously alter consumption behavior. Wealth, in the sense of present value, rather than current income dominates the consumption-saving decision process.

Over an individual's lifetime, a certain pattern of income receipts can be expected. Typically, income is very small during the earliest years, rises in the middle years, reaches a peak, and then declines with a sometimes precipitous drop upon retirement from the labor force. If lifetime utility is to be maximized, consumption will have to be rationally allocated. The consumption pattern need not closely follow expected income flows. Imagine two contrasting extreme cases of income recipients. A young man who has just graduated from college, but who happens to be the best basketball player in the country, will have an extremely high income for a relatively short number of years. If he were to consume during those years commensurate with his salary, his ability to consume in the future would be quite low. A young woman may know that in twenty years she will be the recipient of a very large inheritance. She would not be expected to deny herself the pleasures of consumption in the years prior to the receipt of the inheritance. Both young people might have identical spending patterns over their lifetimes, with the basketball player saving in the early years and during those years making the resources available for use by others, and the heiress being a borrower (and dissaver) during the early years.

Most people are somewhere between these extremes but would exhibit the same sort of propensities. Whatever the expected income pattern may be, a person will also have a utility function relating expected utility from consumption in the present and in all future periods. In noneconomic terms one would say that very young children have fewer needs than adults, that people in their child-raising years have more needs, and that older people have fewer needs. If this sort of pattern reflects an individual's views of future utility potentials, that person might equate a dollar's worth of present spending with a dollar and a half of spending ten years from now. An important part of this decision is that the further into the future the projection is made, the lower the probability that the person will be alive to enjoy the future consumption. On the other hand, some people may have powerful psychological fears of not having purchasing power when they get older, or others may have a strong desire to leave an estate to their heirs.

Whatever the motivation, the life-cycle hypothesis predicts that consumption behavior in the aggregate will be less variable than income. Saving, of course, will then need to adjust, being large when income is unusually large and being small or negative when income is small.

A large proportion of the low income earners are either quite young or quite old. According to the life-cycle hypothesis, both groups would have low average saving (or even dissaving), whereas the large proportion of high income earners are those in their middle years who have a higher average propensity to save. Thus, the life-cycle theory predicts a relatively flat cross-section consumption function. It also demonstrates that saving and consumption depend partly on the age distribution of the population.

The life-cycle theorists stress that current income depends on wealth and that current wealth is the result of saving in the past. This means that even though the marginal propensity to consume current income is relatively low, over the long run, the average propensity to consume increases as wealth increases. The underlying rationale for this observation is that a change in current income has relatively little impact on wealth and thus relatively little influence on current consumption, but in the longer run, the stock of wealth increases as income increases, and therefore, by hypothesis, consumption will increase proportionately.

Clearly, the explanation of consumption behavior is not a simple thing. Many economists, besides those mentioned, have made important contributions to the study, and the research continues. In particular, much of the work discussed here involves consumption rather than household expenditures. For forecasting and employment analysis, the steps of developing an expenditure theory from a consumption theory are still "in the works."

ECONOMIC GROWTH AND FLUCTUATIONS

Let us now move into the study of long-run economic problems. We can visualize the situation by means of Figure 12-6. First, we observe that the equilibrium levels of income where $s = i$ are only short-run equilibriums, because if investment is a positive amount, it means that the stock of capital is increasing each period during which this situation holds. For short periods of time, this may not be very significant, because the amount of investment may be a relatively small fraction of the total stock of capital. But if this short-run equilibrium exists for many periods, the stock of capital grows by i amount each period and must become a significant proportion of the total.

The growth of the capital stock must have some impact because capital is productive. At this point, it is necessary to be clear on

Figure 12-6   Saving, Investment, and Full Employment

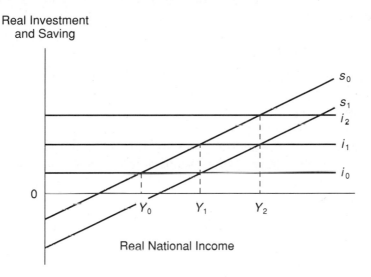

whether we are speaking of real or money-valued national income. If y_0 is real national income, then factors of production other than capital must be unemployed as investment takes place, since the given level of output can be produced with the larger amount of capital goods and a smaller amount of labor. The severity of the unemployment of labor depends upon the nature of the new capital or how productive it is in terms of the displacement of labor.

Presumably, under these conditions, prices and wages would continuously fall, and if the Pigou effect is operative, the saving function would decline, causing real income to increase to absorb the unemployed. In this context, the question is: would the saving function shift downward at a rate fast enough to exactly compensate for the increased contribution of capital to total output caused by the increase in the amount i?

To be more explicit, refer to Figure 12-6. If study would indicate that when i_0 amount of investment took place, income would have to increase to y_1 in order for employment of labor to remain constant, would the saving function shift to precisely the position represented by s_1? The answer depends most importantly on the degree of flexibility of prices and wages and on the responsiveness of the public to these price changes in their saving behavior via the Pigou effect.

Since a downward-shifting saving function is one solution, government policy directed at achieving this end also is frequently suggested. While it can be accomplished in a number of indirect ways, the direct method would be by either lowering income taxes or increasing transfer payments.

Domar's Growth Theory

In the preceding section, it was pointed out that a positive amount of investment would lead to unemployment of labor unless income continuously increased. Excess capacity of capital might also occur, which would discourage any further investment. In that event, national income would decline. We are forced to the conclusion that Schumpeter was correct (refer to Chapter 14) in saying that the only complete static equilibrium is one in which saving and investment are both zero.

Growth theorists search for another kind of equilibrium: a dynamic equilibrium where savings and investment will be equal at growing levels of income. The first growth theory to be presented is that of Professor Evsey Domar.[9]

Central to the Domar model is the concept of the increase in productive capacity of the economy caused by an increase in its capital stock. Domar uses the symbol σ (lowercase sigma) to represent the ratio of the change in the amount of output that can be produced in the system (Δy^*) divided by the increase in the stock of capital that brought about the increase in potential output. The letter k represents the total amount of capital goods in the system, so Δk (the change in that stock) is by definition the amount of investment (i). Thus, $\sigma = \dfrac{\Delta y^*}{i}$. If $\sigma = 0.25$, the ability of the system to produce goods and services will increase by $25 per time period for every $100 of new investment (in constant dollars).[10]

To demonstrate the principle involved, Domar uses a very simple national income model. It is the same as the first model we presented in Chapter 8, except that he assumes that the long-run consumption function, and, therefore, also the saving function, are proportional. The model is:

---

9. Evsey D. Domar, *Essays in the Theory of Economic Growth* (New York: Oxford University Press, 1957). Essay IV is a straightforward, nonmathematical treatment. The same model with the mathematical derivations is found in Essay III.

10. The value of σ incorporates the fact that some of the old capital may be retired early by virtue of the introduction of the new. In other words, the new investment might be capable of producing $30 of new output per period, but since some old capital was retired, the net increase in output per $100 of investment might be $25.

$$y = c + i$$
$$c = by, \text{ which implies that } s = (1-b)y \text{ or } s = \alpha y$$
$$i = \bar{i}$$

If $b = 0.88$, $1 - b = \alpha = 0.12$, and $\bar{i} = \$18$, $\dfrac{\bar{i}}{\alpha} = \dfrac{\$18}{0.12} = \$150$.

Since $\alpha = 0.25$, the addition to the stock of capital of $18 means that, in the next period, potential output (Δy^*) will be $0.25 \times \$18 = \$4.50$ larger than it had been. If "full employment" of capital is to continue, national income or aggregate demand must also increase by $4.50. Since the multiplier in this model is $\dfrac{1}{\alpha} = \dfrac{1}{0.12} = 8.33$, investment must increase by $0.54 (that is, $\Delta y = \dfrac{1}{\alpha} \times \Delta i = 4.5 = 8.33 \times 0.54$). If investment increases by $0.54, saving will also increase by $0.54 because $\alpha = \dfrac{\Delta s}{\Delta y} = \dfrac{12}{100} = \dfrac{0.54}{4.5}$.

The increase in investment of $0.54 means that investment (and saving) in the second period will be 18.54, which implies that productive capacity (Δy^*) and aggregate demand (Δy) must both increase (by an equal amount) in the following period. To maintain full employment, $\Delta y^* = \Delta y$.

Since $\Delta y^* = \sigma i$, and $\Delta y = \Delta i \dfrac{1}{\alpha}$, and $\sigma i = \Delta i \dfrac{1}{\alpha}$, multiply both sides of the equation by α: $\alpha \sigma i = \Delta i$, and divide both sides by i: $\alpha \sigma = \dfrac{\Delta i}{i}$.

The right-hand side is the rate of change of investment necessary to keep the change in potential output equal to the actual change in output or income; that is, $\Delta y^* = \Delta y$. The left-hand side tells us what this rate of growth must be. In our example, $\alpha = 0.12$ and $\sigma = 0.25$, so the rate of growth in investment per period needed to maintain the full use of capital is $0.12 \times 0.25 = 0.03$, or 3 percent.

In this example, income must also increase by 3 percent.[11] Our original income was $150 and increased by $4.5 ($\dfrac{4.5}{150} = 3$ percent). This can be seen directly by observing that the rate of change of income can be expressed as $\dfrac{\Delta y}{y}$, and $\Delta y = \dfrac{\Delta i}{\alpha}$, and $y = \dfrac{i}{\alpha}$; thus, $\dfrac{\Delta y}{y} = \dfrac{\Delta i / \alpha}{i / \alpha} = \dfrac{\Delta i}{i} = 0.12 \times 0.25 = 3$ percent.

---

11. This result depends upon the assumption used here that the marginal propensity to save and the average propensity to save are the same.

The reader should not take all of this too literally: our economy is much too complex to be represented by this model. However, the model does indicate that both the productivity of capital, as expressed in σ, and the habits of the population with respect to saving (and consumption), as expressed in α, influence the degree to which income must grow in order to avoid a recession.

Moreover, if aggregate demand increases at too rapid a rate relative to the growth of productive capacity, inflation will result. Thus, according to this theory, economic growth must proceed at a particular rate to maintain full employment and stable prices. A faster rate results in inflation; a slower rate results in unemployment and/or deflation. This problem has been described as the "tightrope" or "knife-edge" problem. We look more closely at this aspect in Harrod's growth model.[12]

Harrod's Growth Theory

In the Domar model, investment or the change in investment was treated as exogenously determined. Domar's problem was to show the change in the rate of investment required to achieve an equilibrium rate of growth in national income. Sir Roy Harrod, on the other hand, uses a version of the accelerator as the equation explaining investment: $i = A\Delta y$. In order to switch to Harrod's symbols, we note that what we have called A, Harrod calls C_r: in his words, the "capital requirement."

In our discussion of the acceleration principle, we pointed out that the equation could be looked upon both as a behavior relation and as a technical production relation. Harrod uses both meanings. As a behavior relation, $i = C_r \Delta y$ is the demand by business for new capital. If income increased in the last period, investment would be positive in the current period; however, if income fell, investment would be negative as businesses failed to replace worn-out capital. As a behavior relation, the equation expresses the intentions to invest and may, therefore, be different from the actual amount of investment. In the Harrod model, the burden of adjustment in a disequilibrium situation is entirely on investors, since Harrod assumes that savers actually save the amount they intend.

---

12. Sir Roy Harrod, *Towards a Dynamic Economics: Some Recent Developments of Economic Theory and Their Application to Policy* (Toronto: Macmillan Co. of Canada, Ltd., 1948).

The rationale behind Harrod's acceleration-type investment demand function is that the change in income from the last period to the present serves as a forecast of aggregate demand in the next period. In order to produce goods and services sufficient to supply the amount demanded, new plant and equipment will be needed. Hence, new investment will be proportional to the change in income—the proportion being determined by the productivity of capital; that is, $i = C_r \Delta y$.

Like Domar, Harrod uses a proportional long-run saving function without a time lag: $s_t = sy_t$. The concept of the warranted rate of growth is central to his analysis. It is the rate of growth in national income that keeps saving and investment equal and is labeled G_w. Since (1) $i_t = C_r(y_t - y_{t-1})$ and (2) $s_t = sy_t$, the equilibrium condition $i_t = s_t$ implies $C_r(y_t - y_{t-1}) = sy_t$. Dividing both sides by s gives (3) $y_t = \dfrac{C_r}{s}(y_t - y_{t-1})$. The value of $y_t - y_{t-1}$ is the change in income from one period to the next (call it Δy). The rate of change in income is $\dfrac{\Delta y}{y}$. From Equation (3) we find that $\dfrac{\Delta y}{y} = \dfrac{s}{C_r}$. This is the warranted rate of growth (G_w).

If income grows at precisely this warranted rate, the amount of goods and services demanded will be exactly enough to employ all new capital as well as the previously existing stock of capital. Entrepreneurs who planned the investment expenditures made the right decisions and will continue planning to increase their investments in accordance with the forecasting procedure previously used.

While income is growing at the warranted rate, income increases by just enough to generate the amount of saving needed to supply the resources for investment. To summarize the growth process described by the warranted rate of growth, output measured by consumption plus saving exactly balances with the demand for the output by consumers and investors.

Harrod finds no reason to believe that the economy would actually grow at the rate prescribed by the warranted rate, and herein lies the difficulty. If the actual growth rate (G) is greater than G_w, income will grow at a still faster rate, diverging farther and farther from G_w. For instance, suppose the propensity to save should suddenly decline to a figure less than equilibrium requires, which, of course, means that consumption demand would increase. This would mean that the output forecast on which investment expenditures were based was too small. Inventories would decline (unintentionally). Capital equipment would wear out faster than expected. In other words, intended investment would be greater than actual investment, so in the next planning period, businesses would increase their demands for investment; however, this would further aggravate the problem, leading to a greater rate of growth of actual income.

If income expands faster than it should to maintain G_w, output has not increased as much as has aggregate demand. The reverse case, that is, where output increases faster than aggregate demand, will occur when $G < G_w$. A higher rate of saving or a lower demand for investment would bring about this result. An increase in saving (a decrease in consumption) or a decrease in investment demand would mean that output would exceed sales, inventories would build up (unintentionally), and capital would not be fully utilized. Actual investment, in this case, would be greater than intended investment, which would, in turn, reduce demand for capital still further and income would decline. In this case, too, the actual growth rate would get continuously farther away from the warranted rate.

Harrod's warranted rate of growth is the rate that will assure the full utilization of the capital stock of the economy and thereby assumes the condition of equality of saving and investment. But Harrod also points out that if population and the labor force are also growing, there must be some rate of growth that will absorb all additions to the labor force into employment. The rate of growth needed to maintain exactly full employment—neither unemployment nor over-full employment—he terms the natural rate of growth. The situation is complicated in that not only does the labor force grow but the productivity of labor also increases through the growth of capital and its quality and by the improvement of the labor force itself through education and training.

Harrod finds no systematic reason for believing that the rate of growth appropriate to both the growth of capital and labor will be the same. Indeed, he finds it highly unlikely that they would be close enough to avoid difficulties. What does happen when the natural rate and the warranted rate differ?

The actual rate of growth in output is restricted by the growth of the labor force and its productivity. Thus, if the natural rate is less than the warranted rate, actual income will grow too slowly and chronic stagnation will result. As we have just seen, under these conditions where $G_w > G$, actual investment, including unintended investment in capital and inventory, will exceed planned or intended investment.

The opposite case occurs when the labor force is growing fast enough to cause the natural rate of growth to be higher than that warranted by the need to keep capital utilized. In such a situation, $G_n >$ G_w and $G > G_w$, which would lead to continuously expanding output as actual investment would be below intended investment.

QUESTIONS

1. Graph and explain the construction of an after-tax consumption function where consumption is a linear function of disposable income and taxes are an upward curving function of national income.
2. List the attributes of families or individuals whom you would expect to produce a high level of consumption relative to income.
3. List the attributes of families or individuals whom you would expect to produce a low propensity to consume.
4. Show that a high *APC* could be consistent with a low *MPC*, and vice versa.
5. Consider how various types of consumer wealth might increase and/or decrease consumption out of current income.
6. Develop the thesis that the true consumption function is based on expected lifetime income rather than on current income. Remember that borrowing, lending, and repayment are always possible, and that expected future income and expenses can be discounted to the present to give a present value estimate.
7. Using the Domar growth model, determine the rate at which income would need to grow to maintain full employment of capital if the marginal (and average) propensity to consume were 0.8 and if the ratio $\Delta y^*/i$ were 0.2.
8. Explain the following of Harrod's terms: (a) warranted rate of growth, (b) actual rate of growth, (c) natural rate of growth.

READINGS

Domar, Evsey D. *Essays in the Theory of Economic Growth*. New York: Oxford University Press, 1957.

Dornbusch, Rudiger, and Stanley Fischer. *Macroeconomics*, 3rd ed. New York: McGraw-Hill Book Co., 1984, Ch. 6.

Duesenberry, J. S. *Income, Saving, and the Theory of Consumer Behavior*. Cambridge, MA: Harvard University Press, 1949.

Ferber, R. A. *A Study of Aggregate Consumption Functions*. New York: National Bureau of Economic Research, Inc., 1953.

Friedman, Milton. *A Theory of the Consumption Function*. Princeton, NJ: Princeton University Press, 1957.

Harrod, Sir Roy. *Towards a Dynamic Economics: Some Recent Developments of Economic Theory and Their Application to Policy.* Toronto: Macmillan Co. of Canada, Ltd., 1948.

Houthakker, H. S., and L. D. Taylor. *Consumer Demand in the United States.* Cambridge, MA: Harvard University Press, 1970.

Juster, F. Thomas. " What do we know about saving behavior?" *Economic Outlook USA,* (Fourth Quarter 1986).

Katona, G. *The Powerful Consumer: Psychological Studies of the American Economy.* Westport, CT: Greenwood Press, Inc., 1977.

————, and E. Mueller. *Consumer Expectations, 1953–1956.* Ann Arbor, MI: University of Michigan Institute for Social Research Center.

Kotlikoff, Lawrence J. *What Determines Savings?* Cambridge, MA: The MIT Press, 1989.

Reid, Gavin. *Classical Economic Growth.* Cambridge, MA: Basil Blackwell, Inc., 1989.

Veblen, Thorstein B. *The Theory of the Leisure Class: An Economic Study of Institutions.* New York: Penguin Books, Inc., 1979.

BUSINESS CYCLE THEORIES

Part 3 presents various aspects of cycle theory, beginning with theories that explain the cyclical behavior of some forces outside the economy. There is no attempt to analyze all possible theories, nor are the theories presented in the chronological order of their formulation. The major types of theories are considered to emphasize the role in the cyclical process of the main points stressed by each group of theorists. These theorists give us insights into the workings of the whole economy and how particular events or developments lead to responses of economic factors that produce fluctuations in total activity.

PART 3

Most of the authors mentioned in these two chapters wrote a long time ago, but it is interesting to read analysts of contemporary business conditions and discover that the analysis leans heavily upon the work of the earlier business-cycle theorists. In fact, one seldom finds anything in present-day reports that was not developed by the authors reviewed in Chapters 13 and 14. An eclectic process has gone on, so that current analysis incorporates what has been judged to be correct in all past analysis, and of course, some ideas have been rejected by contemporary economists.

AN INTRODUCTION TO BUSINESS CYCLE THEORIES

In the next two chapters we focus on theories of the business cycle. Before doing so, it would be beneficial to explain why we take the time to study different, and even conflicting, theories rather than devote all our effort to the presentation of *the* theory of the business cycle. Fluctuations in economic activity are far too complex to be incorporated into a single universal theory applicable to every historical period. There is a great deal to be learned from each theory that is relevant to today's student, even though the theory might have been developed many years ago. Each theory stresses certain forces or aspects of the economy and necessarily slights others. A complete theory would need to incorporate all of these important causal factors in a systematic way. Even those ideas that may be considered errors of past writers are valuable, because they teach us to not make the same mistakes and point out which alleys are blind.

Virtually all economic theory has been developed with the concept of equilibrium at its core. Movement or changes in any variables are viewed as returns to equilibrium (to either a new or old one) following some exogenous, or outside, change. It is very difficult to break out of this method of comparative statics to the kind of theory needed to explain the continuity of successive rises and falls in economic activity that result in cyclical behavior. This has been one of the stumbling blocks to the development of a satisfactory theory of economic fluctuations.

In Chapter 5, the "cobweb theorem" was explained as an example of the way equilibrium analysis can be made dynamic, thus explaining fluctuations. It is also an example of a "specific cycle" as opposed to the "general cycle" on which we spend most of our time. Other specific cycles discussed were the building cycle, hog and cattle cycles, the coffee cycle, and seasonal cycles in a number of industries. In contrast to these, the general cycle is measured by variations in more aggregated variables, such as GNP, employment, unemployment, and price levels.

There are three general observations required for the understanding of the phenomenon of business cycles. It might be helpful to keep these in mind as we discuss the various explanations advanced in the pages that follow. The first has been mentioned in connection with the cobweb theorem and the acceleration principle, namely the requirement of the existence of time lags. There could be no business fluctuations if economic activity did not take time. The length of the time lags and their nature are important determinants of the duration and the severity of business cycles, as should become evident from the study of the theories we take up. The second fundamental prerequisite for cycles is the interdependency among the firms making up the economy. There would be no business cycles in a self-sufficiency system; it is in the interrelationships among economic units where we look for the causes of the cycle. The third basic underlying feature is the fact of uncertainty, which is very closely related to the first two conditions. If the future were certain, errors would not be made. Producers would produce exactly the amounts that buyers would wish to buy. All economic units would always be in equilibrium. The nature of these three features of economies are continuously changing and are different for different economies, and account for the variations we observe in historical business cycles.

This chapter begins with a summary statement of a number of theories that have been advanced to explain the phenomenon of general business cycles. The classification of theories will be the one suggested by Gottfried von Haberler in the third edition of his definitive study, *Prosperity and Depression* (Geneva: League of Nations, 1941).

OUTSIDE-FORCE THEORIES

Theories in which the cyclical nature of business activity is explained by the cyclical behavior of some outside force are known as outside-force theories or exogenous theories of the business cycle. Determining what an exogenous or outside variable is can be difficult. We might all agree that the economic system has no influence on sunspot activity, but what of war, or the discovery of gold, or innovations? A Marxist would probably consider wars to be endogenous (or internal) to the economy, as something to be explained by the economist. Gustav Cassel argued that gold discovery was an endogenous variable in that lower prices and costs would encourage the prospecting for and mining of gold, the value of which would be high when other prices were low.[1] Joseph Schumpeter's theory depends heavily upon the argument that the volume of innovations is strictly dependent upon the stage of the business cycle and therefore is endogenous.[2]

Thus, there is no exact rule that tells us whether factors are exogenous or endogenous. Such determination depends completely on the theory or the theorist. In general, the procedure is to agree that there is no way for us to know which variables are really exogenous, so we adopt the convention that if the value of a variable is to be explained by the theory, it is endogenous; and if we are not concerned with explaining the behavior of the variable, we call that variable an exogenous one. A variable may actually be both exogenous and endogenous in the same theory. For example, government spending might be increased for political reasons, in which case the economist will consider that to be an exogenous change; whereas, if the increased spending were caused by an increase in national income, it would be considered as endogenous.

The appeal of exogenous explanations of the business cycle is easy to understand. We observe fluctuations in business activity. Business activity responds to outside forces. If an outside force behaves cyclically, cycles in business are explained by the cycle in the outside force. Even today, many people are involved in the search for statistical series that are so highly correlated to business conditions that they can be used as forecasting guides. If the movement in the series is not explained by theory, this amounts to an exogenous theory of the business cycle. In an earlier day when agriculture dominated the economy and variations in crop yields were dominated by the weather, it was natural to look for cycles in weather to account for cycles of good and bad trade.

Changes in Agricultural Yields

Some students of cycles claim to have found a high degree of relationship between cycles in agricultural yields and business cycles. In particular, British economist W. Stanley Jevons[3] and Henry L.

1. Gustav Cassel, *Theory of Social Economy* (New York: Harcourt, Brace & Company, Inc., 1932).

2. Joseph Schumpeter, *Theory of Economic Development* (Cambridge, MA: Harvard University Press, 1934).

3. W. S. Jevons, *Investigations in Currency and Finance* (London: Macmillan and Co., Ltd., 1884).

Moore[4] searched for periodicity in meteorological phenomena consistent with the periodicity in business fluctuations. Jevons found such periodicity in sunspot activity while Moore found it in the peculiarities of the orbit of the planet Venus. Both went on to explain the connection between weather and agricultural activities and between agricultural activity and general business conditions.

Other scholars, however, have come to exactly opposite conclusions, and in several cases, shortcomings were found in the statistical techniques used to establish the relationship between agricultural and business cycles.

This is not intended to imply that changes in agricultural production do not affect business conditions. For example, when crops are bountiful, prices of agricultural commodities drop, and costs in the industrial fields using them as raw materials are reduced. If prices are not reduced in the same proportion, profits increase, and higher profits tend to stimulate further capital investment. If prices are reduced and the demand for the product is elastic, consumers buy larger quantities of such goods and thus industrial activity in that field expands. Higher agricultural prices resulting from small crops have just the opposite effect.

Changes in agricultural yields also may affect the income of agricultural areas. The income of agriculture is not changed at the same rate as the change in agricultural yields, because prices of most farm products increase sharply when crops are small and drop markedly when crops are large. In those cases in which the demand for a product is quite elastic, however, farmers may get a larger total income in periods of large crops than they do when crops are small. This is especially true when crops are large in a year in which consumer income in general is increasing. More money is also paid to operators of farm services, such as combine crews for harvesting wheat when crops are large, and railroads and trucking companies get more revenue for hauling the products to market.

If exports are increased materially when crops are large, there is also a tendency for business activity to increase. Exports will reduce, in part, the price decline that would occur if all of the crop had to be marketed at home, and so the total income in the domestic economy is increased. As foreign funds flow into the country to pay for the larger

---

4. Henry L. Moore, *Generating Economic Cycles* (New York: The Macmillan Company, 1923). See also his earlier *Economic Cycles: Their Law and Cause* (New York: The Macmillan Company, 1914).

exports, there is also a tendency for money supplies to increase and for interest rates to decline. This lowering of interest rates has a stimulating effect on business activity. Conversely, when crops are small and exports are reduced, the opposite effect takes place.

However, modern records of agricultural production and business fluctuations do not make clear that such relationships between total agricultural yields and general business activity exist. This situation can be accounted for in several ways. First, agricultural production does not move up and down as a unit. In the same year, there may be a good cotton crop and a poor corn crop. The effects on business in general of a large crop of one commodity may thus be offset by the effects of a small crop of another commodity.

There also have been some farmers, especially those who operate on a large scale, who have held their crops in storage in years of low prices and sold them later when prices have been more favorable. This storing has helped to mitigate the effects of changes in crop yields. Since the early 1930s, until quite recently, this practice of storing crops has been done on a large scale by the U.S government.

As our industrial economy has expanded, agriculture has accounted for an increasingly smaller proportion of total income, so that its influence on business has continuously diminished.Therefore, its role in initiating changes in economic activity also has become less important. Changes in agricultural yield cannot alone explain the cycle, since such changes do not correspond to the regularly recurring cycles of recession and recovery in business.

Sunspots

One of the earliest of the outside-force theories of the cycle and, in fact, one of the earliest explanations offered for business cycles, was the sunspot-cycle theory proposed in 1875 by W. Stanley Jevons. From the available data on major British business cycles and from fragmentary data on sunspot cycles, Jevons reasoned that sunspot cycles must cause changes in agricultural yields and, in turn, these cause business cycles. This thesis was refuted when research showed that the sunspot cycles were longer than Jevons thought and that changes in agricultural yields did not correspond closely to business cycles.

The sunspot idea, however, occasionally continues to find support. Different measurements have been made of solar activity, especially of the total area of "bright spots" on the sun, and in recent years, claims of a high correlation between such measurements and business activity have been made. An explanation of the relationship is that sunspot changes cause changes in the quantity of ultraviolet rays reaching the earth and that this affects the emotional responses and general health of human beings. The transference to business cycles is obvious.

A quite sophisticated chain of analysis was forged by Henry L. Moore relating the conjunctures of the sun, Venus, and the earth to the weather conditions on earth, particularly in the amount of rainfall.[5] The cycle of favorable and unfavorable weather conditions results in a cycle of high and low crop yields, which, in turn, generates a cycle in the prices of basic raw materials, which then produces a cycle in industrial production and general economic activity.[6]

War Cycles in Population

Some students of cycles, particularly in Germany, have reasoned that major cycles can be traced to changes resulting from major wars, especially changes in population. Heavy war casualties, especially in the wars preceding World War II, were primarily among young men, which thus reduced the size of the labor force. The birth rate also was reduced while the men were on the fighting fronts, but it increased sharply when the war ended. Such changes in the number of births affect the birth rate a generation later, because many young people marry at about the same time, have some effect two generations later, and then gradually disappear.

Some geopolitical theorists have carried the analysis further by arguing that this growth in population exerts such pressure on the limited national territories of some countries that their governments seek relief by attempting to claim the territory of other nations, which precipitates new wars. Thus, war itself is a periodic phenomenon and produces cyclical economic responses.

The effect of wars on population seems well established, and the high birth rates in the years after World War II will affect the American economy for some time to come. The time intervals involved, however, are too long to account for business cycles in general, and certainly this factor cannot account for past American cycles.

---

5. In many languages, the term "conjuncture" is used to describe business cycles.

6. Recently developed statistical techniques designed to determine the direction of causality of economic variables have been used to test the sunspot theory. The absurd conclusion has been reached that business-cycle activity causes sunspot cycles! This may say something about the techniques or something about the phenomenon. See R. G. Sheehan and R. Grieves, "Sunspots and Cycles: A Test of Causation," *Southern Economic Journal* (January 1982), pp. 775–777.

UNDERCONSUMPTION THEORIES

Underconsumption theories of the cycle are about as old as the discipline of economics. These theories have appeared in various forms and have frequently been expounded by writers who lacked formal training in economics. The theories are often used to justify such political schemes as the depression-inspired Townsend Plan of large pensions for the elderly. The views of many underconsumption theorists do not actually constitute a complete theory of the cycle, since most have attempted only to explain the downturn of the cycle and the depression period. A complete analysis of the cycle cannot be based upon such underconsumption theories.

Another difficulty in describing these theories is that the term "underconsumption" is not used in the same sense by all theorists. Some use underconsumption to mean that the economic system does not pay out sufficient funds to purchase all the goods that are produced, which we know from national-income accounting cannot be true. This point of view should be distinguished from a periodic hoarding of money or slowing down of the velocity of money, which are integral parts of a monetary theory of the cycle. Others use underconsumption to describe a situation in which too large a proportion of income is saved in relationship to the amount that is spent on consumption.

Underconsumption as Oversaving

If we were tracing the chronological history of underconsumptionist thought, we would probably start with Malthus (recognizing his roots in Adam Smith's *Wealth of Nations*) and end with the theory of John Maynard Keynes. We could go further by including a later Keynesian economist such as Alvin Hansen, late of Harvard. The most important stop between Malthus and Keynes most likely would be John A. Hobson, the British economist who presented a persuasive case both for underconsumption as the cause of depression and for a theory of cyclical instability based on underconsumption principles.

Hobson challenged Say's law directly, asking why, in a world in which human wants are said to be insatiable, large amounts of unsold commodities appear at the beginning of a business downswing. One part of his answer is that a kind of cultural lag exists. Consumption is, according to Hobson, a very conservative activity. Tradition, custom, and habit dominate. Most consumption is done in private and, contrary to Thorstein Veblen's hypothesis concerning conspicuous consumption, the pressures to increase consumption when income increases are relatively mild.[7]

Productivity, on the other hand, increases in modern times at a relatively rapid rate. There are no important deterrents to instituting new production methods or innovations that will increase the rate of output. Competition in capitalistic systems forces producers to introduce production-enhancing methods as quickly as possible. Society is faced with the problem of rapidly increasing powers of production with lagging willingness or ability to consume the increasing output.

From this point of view, if production and income are increasing faster than consumption, savings are growing. This would seem to present no problem, if there is sufficient investment demand to absorb this additional output capability. But if all the additional savings go into new productive capacity by way of investment, the problem becomes still more acute when this new capital begins to add more goods and services to the aggregate supply. Unless one can conceive of a world in which capital goods are continuously being produced to produce more capital goods, a crisis must be pending. The additional productive capacity must result either in inventories of goods unsalable at current prices or in drastic price reductions. In either case, the demand for investment will decline sharply, and total production will be reduced to a level that can be sustained by consumer demand. This means idle workers and plants—thus, a recession.

We can see in Hobson the beginnings of a dynamic theory of growth not unlike that of Harrod and Domar, as discussed in Chapter 12. The rate of savings must be the right amount necessary to add to the capital stock the productive power to produce increased goods and services at the rate of increase that consumers will demand. As we have just seen, if the rate of savings is greater than this, a recession will inevitably ensue. When will the downward movement stop? The answer is when excess capacity has been eliminated by depreciation or capital consumption, and when consumers have learned to consume a larger portion of their income, which will happen as incomes fall.

Typically, underconsumption theorists argue that the problem can only be eliminated by a redistribution of wealth and income. Hobson pointed out that most economists believe that the average level of saving is high for high-income groups and low for low-income goups. This means that a redistribution of income away from the high-saving, high-

---

7. Thorstein B. Veblen, *The Theory of the Leisure Class* (New York: Penguin Books, 1979).

income recipients in favor of low-saving, low-income workers would result in a lower ratio of savings to spending or income. Therefore, there must be some distribution of income that would produce a rate of savings compatible with the rate of increase in productivity. Hobson recognized that if the redistribution were carried too far in the direction of equality, the rate of savings could be so low that economic progress would be impeded. On the other hand, he pointed out that progress was also slowed down by the intermittent periods of depressed business conditions under the present income distribution.

It must be conceded that the underconsumption theory, as presented by its most capable adherents, is highly convincing. It is not something out of the dead past. It is present doctrine for many, and some of its aspects are accepted by virtually all economists. New Deal policies of the 1930s, as well as many current governmental policies, imply the acceptance of the basic hypothesis. Those who believe that our economy would be in serious difficulty if the defense budget were slashed are agreeing with the underconsumption theorists.

As expressed in Chapters 8 through 12, the relationship between saving, consumption, and income is not as straightforward as it seems in the underconsumptionist theory. Some of the intuitively plausible propositions on savings and income turn out to be a confusion between marginal and average propensities. In particular, the evidence Hobson relied upon was the observation that the average propensity to save increased as income increased. We now know that even though the average may be increasing, the marginal may not be, and it is the marginal propensity to consume or save that is important in redistribution of income schemes.

Outline of the Underconsumption Cycle

The expansion phase of the business cycle is characterized by underconsumption theorists as a period when, as income rises, wages tend to lag behind the growth in other incomes, especially the profit component. Since it is contended that wage earners spend a larger proportion of their income on consumer goods than do the higher-income profit recipients, saving grows at an increasing rate during the upswing of the business cycle. The rate of growth in saving must reach a point where it is in excess of the amount of investment that can feasibly be justified on the basis of the current amount of consumption. This brings about the crisis or upper turning point.

During the resulting contraction phase, incomes fall, but now, profit incomes fall more rapidly than the incomes of wage earners.

Since profit earners have high saving to income ratios relative to wage earners, saving declines more rapidly than consumption and income. In the early stages of the downswing, the supply of capital is large relative to the need for it, as expressed by the demand for consumption. For this reason, investment will fall off very sharply and will remain depressed until the forces of depreciation reduce the stock of capital to a level consistent with the current rate of consumer-goods output. The downswing is supposed to stop when consumption stabilizes, and consumption will stop falling as income is transferred from the low consumption group of profit recipients to the high consumption group of laborers. The stage is then set for a reversal of direction of economic activity, which will happen when investment increases.

PSYCHOLOGICAL THEORIES OF THE BUSINESS CYCLE

We will now discuss the theories of economists who consider psychological factors as the dominant forces causing oscillations in economic activity. The reader should not get the impression from this that other economists ignore the psychology of decision makers in their theories. Since any economic decision has its psychological aspects, every economist is concerned with them to some degree. Those who are not included as psychological theorists, however, generally take the state of mind of the economic unit as given. Their usual reaction is that changes in psychology are very important, but that they have no ability to predict the cause of these changes beyond what is already incorporated in their theory. When prices have been rising for some time, for example, some people will expect them to continue to rise; others will feel that since they have gone up so long they are sure to fall soon. It is relatively easy, after the fact, to say that expectations were such and such. It is very difficult, if not impossible, to say what they are or what they will be.

In the study of economics, most of the important decisions that are analyzed involve forecasts. If the period of time is relatively long, the outcome depends on many possible events that simply cannot be accurately forecast at the moment the decision is made. The business person, or the homemaker, or the government official is forced to fall back on a judgment as to whether important innovations will occur, whether war or peace will be the environment, whether depression or prosperity will characterize the period, or whether more or less government intervention will take place. Pessimism and optimism will bias the judgment when few objective grounds are available on which to base a forecast.

The economist who is best known for placing emphasis upon emotional responses in business decisions is Arthur C. Pigou, and it is his theory that we will summarize.[8] Wesley Clair Mitchell, founder of the National Bureau of Economic Research, quoted Pigou approvingly in this regard and is, himself, considered an adherent of the psychological theory. The key features of Keynes' explanation of business fluctuations are also psychological in origin. According to Keynes, the depression of the 1930s was so difficult to solve because of the collapse of the marginal efficiency of capital, owing to continued pessimism in the business community. Likewise, the liquidity-preference function is largely psychologically based. Though these economists subscribe to the general thesis that the psychological reactions of business people are important causal factors in the cyclical process, they do not ignore other important objective events. They hold, however, that even though changes in the supply of and demand for the factors of production can bring about fluctuations in economic activity, those changes are not sufficient to bring about business cycles in the absence of psychological factors.

These economists believe that the causal factors in the cyclical process can be found in the ways in which changes in real underlying factors cause changes in the attitudes of business people. Pigou, for example, recognized five real causes of business change: (1) changes in agricultural yield, (2) changes in the rate of investment, (3) discovery of new mineral resources, (4) industrial disputes, and (5) changes in consumer tastes. Changes in the first three have similar effects, since they lead to an increase or a decrease in supply with no change in labor input, or they lead, at least, to a change in the supply per unit of labor expended. The impact of any of these three factors on the economy may be illustrated by considering the effect of a change in agricultural yield. Changes in agricultural yield are believed to stimulate or retard business activity, since an increase in yield promotes business expansion, while a decrease in yield discourages expansion or may even lead to a contraction. If there is an increase in the yield of an agricultural commodity, and if the demand for that product is such that the total amount spent on it is larger than before, total demand for all goods will tend to be increased. Farmers will have more money to spend, and this fact will lead to increased sales and production of the goods they demand. A decrease in agricultural yield will have the opposite effect. Such changes lead to fluctuations in business activity, but not to a business

---

8. A. C. Pigou, *Industrial Fluctuations* (London: Macmillan and Co., Ltd., 1927) and *The Theory of Unemployment* (London: Macmillan and Co., Ltd., 1933).

cycle. The same follows for increased production caused by the discovery of new resources or by inventions that reduce costs.

The last two of the real causes, namely industrial disputes and net changes in consumer tastes, are not considered important factors causing business fluctuations. Industrial disputes in basic industries, if prolonged, could lead to a downturn in the economy; but this does not happen very often, if at all, and net shifts in consumer tastes are not likely to be important enough in the short run to affect the economy seriously. These two factors should probably be looked upon as exogenous shocks.

Errors of Business People

When any of these real changes occur, there will be a dual effect. There will be the direct effect of the change that has taken place as well as an indirect effect caused by the reactions of business people to the change. These reactions will not always be consistent with the facts, because they may be based on errors in evaluating the situation. The scope or range of the errors of business people will be determined primarily by two basic factors: the capacity of business forecasters and the accessibility of information.

In a capitalistic system, with its interdependent processes of production, forecasting is a difficult procedure. The economic response of business people to real changes will partially depend upon the skill developed in forecasting the effects of these changes. Some error, however, will always be involved in such forecasts.

Sources of Errors. Probably more important as a source of error is the lack of information about all the factors that will be affected by the change. Under a competitive system, individual producers have no real way of knowing what the demand for their product or the supply of productive factors will be in the future. Each producer endeavors to supply a part of the market without knowing the portion of the increased demand that other producers are preparing to meet. The result is that producers tend to overestimate the quantity they can sell and the price at which they can sell their output during an expansion period and to underestimate these same items during a period of declining business. They likewise underestimate the costs of production during the upswing and overestimate them during the contraction. This is also true in regard to the cost of capital, that is, the interest rate.

A second reason for the lack of adequate knowledge on the part of business people is the tendency to order more goods than are really wanted during periods of rising prices to insure the receipt of at least those quantities that are needed. Such duplication of orders makes it impossible to know what the true state of demand is and causes producers to turn out goods in excess of the quantity demanded at current prices. Additionally, if rising prices lead to expectations of further increases, stockpiling of goods may be encouraged.

A third reason is the large geographic area of the market. Raw materials are frequently purchased from various parts of the nation as well as from foreign countries. Production is also carried on for regional, national, and international markets. Under such conditions, it is difficult to properly appraise future supply and demand conditions.

The basic reason for the lack of satisfactory knowledge of the market is the length of time required to produce a commodity, especially a capital good. Pigou placed great emphasis on what he called the *period of gestation*, which is the length of time required for the new output to come on the market after the decision to increase production has been made. Different commodities have different gestation periods. Very long gestation periods would characterize commodities that are produced with large amounts of complex capital goods. If capital goods are produced without the expansion of bank credit, normally nothing happens that should give rise to any serious errors. If, as actually occurs, an expansion of bank credit takes place during the gestation period, however, there is an overall increase in purchasing power without a corresponding increase in the volume of consumer goods. This excess purchasing power leads to higher prices until the capital goods are completed and the output of consumer goods increased. As a result, business decision-makers are misled about the real demand for their products. As the gestation period ends, and the new consumer goods begin to flow onto the market, the errors come to light. The length and severity of the expansion phase of the cycle are dependent upon the length of the gestation period.

Mutual Generation of Errors. These errors can only lead to a cyclical process if they are predominantly in the same direction. If they are made on a more or less random basis, they will tend to neutralize each other as errors of optimism are canceled out by errors of pessimism. The latter situation does not occur because business people tend toward common action.

Several factors cause errors of either optimism or pessimism to become general throughout the business world. One such factor is that during the course of business as well as in meetings of business organizations, people tend to influence each other's thinking and thus spread feelings of optimism and pessimism on a continual basis. Furthermore, errors in forecasts of business conditions tend to create their

own justification. An error on the optimistic side by one producer results in an increased demand for goods and services, thus brightening
the prospects of other businesses. Thus, the errors of some producers
lead other producers to commit errors in the same direction.

The debtor-creditor relationship also disperses errors through the
various parts of the business system. If one optimistic business person
makes credit more easily available to customers or relaxes terms of
credit, this, in turn, stimulates others to do likewise so as not to be at
a competitive disadvantage.

The cycle occurs because errors on the optimistic side inevitably
lead to errors of pessimism, and these, in turn, to errors of optimism,
and so on in a continuous cycle. In a period of expansion, errors of
optimism do not become apparent during the period of gestation, because the creation of credit and the length of time required to produce
various goods prevent the realization that part of the demand is ficti-
tious and that the shortage of consumer goods is only temporary. When
the errors of optimism are revealed at the end of the period of gestation,
the expansion comes to a halt and a recession begins. Optimism then
gives way to pessimism, as firms realize that their forecasts of the situation were wrong, and as business turns downward, errors of pessimism spread. As expenditures are curtailed, there is an oversupply of
consumer goods, and as a result, producers underestimate the real demand for their products. As capital goods again need replacement, the
errors of pessimism come to light and the stage is set for revival. This
process by which errors of optimism lead to errors of pessimism and
errors of pessimism to those of optimism is referred to as the *mutual
generation of errors*.

Evaluation

Even though the psychological theorists have stressed psychological factors, their explanation of the cycle includes many factors that
relate to investment and bank-credit creation. They have made a valuable contribution to business-cycle theory by showing how waves of
optimism can lead to waves of pessimism and these in turn to waves
of optimism. Since these are based upon real changes that have taken
place in the economy, however, it can hardly be maintained that the
cycle is due entirely to psychological factors. These factors help explain the cumulative nature of expansion and contraction, but are of
little or no help in explaining turning points. Psychological factors
should be considered in a complete explanation of the cycle, but they
should not be given the only position of importance.

SERIES OF OUTSIDE FACTORS

Some economists contend that the cycle is caused by the many outside forces that are continually affecting the economy. These include not only weather changes, cycles in farm yields, wars, and war-induced changes in population, but also new inventions and discoveries. Since these occur in a more or less random fashion, they lead to cycles of different time intervals. Occasionally, several factors occur at about the same time and thus lead to more severe cycles. Even though such outside influences do affect business activity, they alone cannot account for the cycle, because they cannot explain the cumulative nature of the expansion and contraction. These explanations must be sought in the operation of the economic system itself. More recent work in this field involves the creation of formal economic models that incorporate the behavior relations of the economic system. When random disturbances or "shocks" are introduced into such a system, the response of the economy is to generate cyclical movement. The theories of Wesley Clair Mitchell attempt to explain the cumulative nature of expansion and contraction.

MITCHELL'S THEORY OF THE CYCLE

In his classic volume, *Business Cycles* (Berkeley, CA: University of California Press, 1913), Mitchell presented a synthesis of cycle theory based on the evidence available to him at that time. He also founded the National Bureau of Economic Research, where he made the study of business cycles an empirical science. It was Mitchell's profound belief that the study of business cycles was no less than the study of the total operation of the capitalist system. Understanding the cycle phenomenon was not based on broad general aggregates but on the complex interrelationships among all parts of the economy.

Using this principle, Mitchell examined over eight hundred time-series, observing that when the preponderance of the individual production and price series were rising, a business expansion was in progress. Likewise, a general contraction was made up of contractions in most individual industries. But not all series behaved alike; some series of data tended to lead general activity, some usually followed, and some activities varied inversely to the business cycles. Mitchell looked for clues to the explanation of the cyclical nature of business in these diverse movements.

Mitchell concluded that there were some features that seemed to be common to all the cycles he was able to study, but that each cycle was unique. Thus, one does not find dogmatic assertions in the writings of Wesley Mitchell about what happens during business cycles. His last book, published posthumously and summarizing the work of many years, still described the results as "tentative and subject to change as the investigation proceeds."[9] The remainder of this chapter is a brief overview of Mitchell's conception of the nature of the business cycle.

Upswing

According to Mitchell, a revival in business activity begins with a legacy from the depression period. Prices during a depression are low in comparison with prices during prosperity. Business costs have been drastically reduced, profit margins are narrow, bank reserves are liberal, the policy in regard to the extension of credit is conservative, stocks of goods are moderate, and buying is cautious. The upturn is slow at first, but the process is cumulative. It often has been accelerated by some propitious event, such as unusually profitable harvests, large government purchases of goods, or a large increase in exports.

The revival initially begins in a small sector of the economy but then soon spreads to all fields. This is true because those concerns experiencing an increase in business buy materials from other enterprises, who buy from still others, and so on. As incomes increase, expansion increases in a cumulative fashion. Price increases and the expectation of future price increases lead to an increase in orders to beat the price rise, and this accelerates the upward spiral.

This would be of little interest if all prices rose in the same proportion. For instance, if the price of the product a firm sells were to increase by 10 percent, and the prices of all the services and materials that go into the product were also to increase by 10 percent, the profit rate would be as it was before the price increase. Mitchell's statistics indicated, however, that finished-goods prices rise more rapidly during the business expansion than do the prices of those items entering into costs of production, particularly wage rates, rents under leases, and interest on bonds. Thus, profits increase and investment expenditures are encouraged, which lead to further expansion of the physical volume of production, thus putting additional pressure on prices.

---

9. Wesley C. Mitchell, *What Happens During Business Cycles: A Progress Report* (New York: National Bureau of Economic Research, 1951), p. 5.

Downturn

This cumulative process also sets in motion stresses that undermine prosperity. The lag in supplementary costs ceases when the limit to the business that can be handled with the present equipment of a firm is reached. A rise in costs begins when the expiration of contracts forces renewals at higher rates of interest, rent, and salaries. Simultaneously, other costs rise rapidly because less efficient equipment is brought into use, more overtime is paid, and prices of raw materials rise faster than selling prices on the average. Waste and inefficiency occur and increase the cost of doing business.

Stresses also develop in the investment and money markets as the supply of funds available fails to keep pace with the rapidly swelling demand. Tensions in the money markets are unfavorable to the continuance of prosperity. This is true because high rates of interest reduce prospective margins of profit and thus reduce the demand for additional capital goods for further expansion. As new orders fall off and as old contracts are completed, there is a serious reduction in the volume of production of capital goods, and thus, workers are laid off in this field.

Increases in prices at different rates also lead to an imbalance in the system. Some prices cannot be raised sufficiently to prevent a reduction in profits, because they are set by public commissions, by long-term contracts, or by custom. Consumer demand does not remain the same in all fields as nominal income increases, and as a result, prices rise faster in some fields than in others. In some cases, prices do not rise as fast as costs, and profit margins are reduced. As profits decrease, cautious creditors fear for the safety of their loans and stop making new loans and refuse to renew old ones as they mature. Thus, prosperity ultimately brings about a liquidation of the huge credits piled up during expansion.

Just as expansion was cumulative, so, too, is the process of contraction. The same factors that work to increase business on the upswing are also at work depressing business activity during the downswing. Depression spreads over the whole field of business and grows more severe as it spreads.

The rapid decline in business, however, sets into motion the very factors from which a revival will emerge. Prices fall, but again not uniformly in all fields. Wholesale prices drop faster than retail, the prices of producer goods faster than those of consumer goods, and the prices of raw materials faster than those of manufactured goods. Not only are the day-to-day costs of doing business reduced, but supplementary costs are also reduced by the reduction in rents, the refunding of loans, the charging off of bad debts, and the writing down of depreciable properties. Accumulated stocks left over from prosperity are gradually exhausted, after which current consumption requires current production. Consumer and producer durable goods wear out and must be replaced and, as population continues to grow, more food, clothing, and shelter are needed. The environment for investment also becomes more favorable as pessimism gives way to cautious optimism. New methods of production are developed, and these call for additional capital investment. As a result, revival begins and the cumulative cyclical process is once more under way.

This synthesis by Mitchell is still a reasonable explanation of the cyclical process. However, it does not give sufficient emphasis to the factors at work in the investment process. In the next chapter, we consider the theories that place primary emphasis on the role of investment in the business cycle. This prepares the way for the later study of the contributions of Keynes and his followers.

QUESTIONS

1. What is the basic difference between an exogenous and an endogenous theory of the business cycle?
2. Explain the conflict between the acceptance of Say's law and the development of business-cycle theory.
3. Explain the relevance to Mitchell's theory of the business cycle that some categories of prices react more quickly than others to changing economic conditions.
4. According to the underconsumption theory, what makes the collapse of an economic expansion inevitable?
5. Explain why a business-cycle expansion would be of long duration if the gestation period for key commodities is long.
6. What do you see as the principal difficulty in constructing a theory of the business cycle based on waves of optimism and pessimism?

READINGS

American Economic Association. *Readings in Business Cycle Theory*, Vol. III. Homewood, IL: Richard D. Irwin, Inc., 1965.

Clark, John J., and Morris Cohen (eds.). *Business Fluctuations, Growth and Economic Stabilization, A Reader*. New York: Random House, 1963.

Estey, J. A. *Business Cycles, Their Nature, Cause, and Control*. Berkeley, CA: University of California Press, 1941.

Ezekiel, Mordecai. "The Cobweb Theorem." *Quarterly Journal of Economics* (February 1938).

Gabish, Gunter, and Hans-Walter Lorenz. *Business Cycle Theory: A Survey of Methods and Concepts*, 2d ed. New York: Springer-Verlag Publishers, 1989.

Haberler, Gottfried von. *Prosperity and Depression*, 3rd ed. Geneva: League of Nations, 1941.

Hansen, Alvin H. *Business Cycles and National Income*. New York: W. W. Norton & Company, Inc., 1964.

———, and R. W. Clemence. *Readings in Business Cycles and National Income*. New York: W. W. Norton & Company, Inc., 1953.

Jevons, W. S. *Investigations in Currency and Finance*. London: Macmillan and Co., Ltd., 1884.

Kaldor, Nicholas. *Essays on Economic Stability and Growth*, 2d ed. New York: Holmes and Meier, 1980. Part 2.

Mitchell, W. C. *What Happens During Business Cycles: A Progress Report*. New York: National Bureau of Economic Research, 1951.

———. *Business Cycles*. Berkeley, CA: University of California Press, 1913.

Moore, Henry L. *Generating Economic Cycles*. New York: The Macmillan Company, 1923.

———. *Economic Cycles: Their Law and Cause*. New York: The Macmillan Company, 1914.

Pigou, A. C. *Industrial Fluctuations*. London: Macmillan and Co., Ltd., 1927.

———. *The Theory of Unemployment*. London: Macmillan and Co., Ltd., 1933.

Schumpeter, Joseph. *Theory of Economic Development*. Cambridge, MA: Harvard University Press, 1934.

CHAPTER 14

MONETARY AND INVESTMENT THEORIES OF THE CYCLE

The structure of the monetary and credit system of the economy has an important influence on the nature of business fluctuations. In fact, since Say's law would be true in a barter economy, business cycles as we know them could not exist. The important role of monetary factors led early business-cycle theorists to give them major emphasis when analyzing the causal factors at work in the cycle. One group of monetary theorists held that changes that occur in this system are sufficient in themselves to produce cycles. Another group thought that the interaction of the monetary system with changes in investment activity leads to cyclical fluctuations. Most of the writers who held these theories were quantity theorists, as were almost all economists of their day. Chapter 7 includes a review of the quantity theory, so it will not be repeated here.

In this chapter, we will also consider those theorists who hold that the basic cause of the cycle is found in the process of investment rather than in the operation of the monetary system. One group of investment theorists has stressed a shortage of capital followed by an excess as the basic cause of the cycle; another, fluctuations in the investment process that are produced by innovations; and a third, changes in consumption that lead to magnified changes in the demand for producer goods and thus lead to imbalance.

THE PURELY MONETARY THEORY

Considering the pervasive role of money in modern economic systems, it would be strange indeed if it were not included in an important way in the explanation of business fluctuations. In fact, the only disagreement lies in the particular way and the degree of importance attached to money in generating business cycles. Even those theories that are called nonmonetary implicitly require the necessary response

341

of the money supply to bring about the cycles described. These theo-rists argue that the initiating or causal force is something other than monetary, whereas the monetary theories place the monetary system in this critical position. The purely monetary theory takes the polar position that variations in money are the necessary and sufficient con-ditions for variations in economic activity. This is essentially the po-sition taken by Ralph G. Hawtrey, a British economist whose name is virtually synonymous with the purely monetary theory.[1]

Without question, the kinds of cycles that have occurred in the economies of industrial nations could not exist in an economy with an inelastic monetary system. Under such a monetary arrangement, an increase in business activity could not develop in a cumulative fashion for any period of time. As the demand for goods increased in some sectors of the economy, more money would be used to make sales in these fields. With inelastic money and credit, this would leave fewer funds for other fields of business activity and prices would fall in these areas. Velocity could increase to some extent, but a simultaneous cu-mulative expansion of sales in many fields would be impossible.

Such cumulative expansions and contractions of sales, however, are major characteristics of the cycle in the United States and other industrial countries. During prosperity, normally, both the volume of goods sold and the prices of goods expand. On the upswing, the quan-tities of goods sold expand somewhat faster than do the prices at which they are sold. During the downswing, both the prices of goods sold and the quantities sold usually contract.

The usual situation in the case of individual products or services is that the quantities sold increase as prices are lowered and decrease as prices are raised. Prices of goods and quantities sold can only move together in the upswing and downswing of a cycle, because the total supply of purchasing media is expanding and contracting as business goes up and down. This change in the supply of purchasing media is due primarily to a change in the volume of demand deposits that are expanded and contracted as borrowing from the banking system in-creases and decreases during the cycle.

The Upswing

Hawtrey's theory is a good example that in cycle analysis, it is not unusual to have the turning points effected by the conditions created

---

1. Ralph G. Hawtrey has written many books and articles detailing his view of the cycle. Two representative books are: *Trade and Credit* (London: Longmans, Green & Co., Ltd., 1928) and *Capital and Employment* (London: Longmans, Green & Co., Ltd., 1937).

in the phase just preceding them. The period of downswing develops a situation of the banking system accumulating excess reserves and bankers becoming more eager to make loans. Accordingly, interest rates fall, and other credit terms and standards for borrowing are eased. The depression has also gone on long enough to eliminate any excess inventories that might have existed early in the downswing. Weaker firms may have been eliminated, so that even though general business conditions are depressed, conditions for the remaining business units are, at least, stabilized. Lower interest rates obviously make borrowing more attractive, but the firm must expect the borrowed funds to add enough to its earning power to more than cover the costs of the borrowing.

Who will borrow during the depths of a depression? The business person who overcomes the pessimism of the times and anticipates an imminent period of good times will do so. Most economists would expect borrowing to increase even during the downswing, if innovations create expectations of improved sales or lower costs. The general opinion has been that lower interest rates have the greatest effect on borrowers whose use for funds is very long term. Hawtrey, however, concentrates his attention on the short-term end of the market and on merchants who have the carrying of inventories as a major expense. Since a large portion of the variable cost of maintaining inventories is the interest payment, any lowering of interest rates reduces these costs. We would expect any lowering of costs of maintaining inventories to induce merchants to add to their holdings. Larger stocks of inventories provide greater selection for customers, quicker service, and more certain delivery of large orders. Thus, even if aggregate sales are low, an individual seller can gain some competitive advantage by increasing the company's inventory.

So, in Hawtrey's version of the monetary theory of the "trade cycle," as he calls it, the upswing begins when excess reserves in the banking system build up sufficiently for interest rates to fall enough to cause merchants to borrow to increase their inventories. For the new orders to be additions to total demand, the purchasing power must come from new or idle money that would not decrease demand elsewhere. The new demand produces added income for the producers, and the upswing is in progress.

After the process of expansion has been started, it is cumulative for a period of time. As more goods are ordered, more are produced, more income flows into the hands of consumers, and consumer expenditures are increased. Retailers, finding their stock of goods decreased because of the growth in sales to consumers, increase their orders for merchandise, which, in turn, increases production, consumer income, and consumer outlay. As this cumulative process develops, there is a rise in the general level of prices because output in certain areas cannot be increased readily, owing to a scarcity of plant capacity, labor, or intermediate inputs. That is to say, bottlenecks arise at key points in the production process. The rise in prices adds further impetus to the expansion that is underway, since it increases the profits of entrepreneurs and, therefore, makes them willing to increase the amount of borrowed funds used in their business. This credit expansion accelerates the expansion process and, in turn, adds to the pressure on prices and reinforces the upward movement.

According to Hawtrey, the expansion is reinforced by the expectation of rising prices that causes people to reduce the size of their cash balances relative to the amount of their transactions—that is, that k in the equation $M = kPy$ falls (or alternatively, velocity in the equation $MV = Py$ increases) during the expansion, if rising prices are expected.

The Contraction

Prosperity ends when banks restrict the expansion of credit. Banks take such action because their excess reserves are being depleted by the increase in loans and deposits and by the withdrawal of cash for hand-to-hand circulation. The central banks could continue to supply additional credit, but they have usually felt that it was their function to prevent excessive expansion and, therefore, have generally refused to do so.

Some monetary theorists believe that if the restriction of credit did not occur, the expansion phase of the cycle could be continued indefinitely, although that would mean an indefinite rise in prices. The continuous increase in prices leads to an increasing demand for cash for hand-to-hand circulation, for till cash and petty-cash funds by business concerns, for working cash balances by financial institutions, and for cash needed in day-to-day operations of banks. These increased demands for cash drain reserves and cause banks not only to stop expanding credit but also to contract the amount outstanding.

According to Hawtrey, the upper turning point is brought about because of a lag between the growth in bank deposits and the outflow of currency into circulation. While Hawtrey was referring to a gold standard system in which gold served both in the capacity of reserves for the banking system and as circulating currency, the general ideas are applicable to our present system. At the time expansion begins, the skeleton balance sheet of the banking system might look something like this:

Commercial Banking System

Gold (reserves)	$ 20	Demand deposits	$150
Earning assets	$130		

British banks did not have legal reserve requirements, but tradition did dictate a minimum reserve ratio. For purposes of our example, let us assume this to be 10 percent of deposits, so that in our initial situation the amount of excess reserves is $5 billion. At this stage, the banks, being anxious to increase their loan portfolios, are lowering their interest charges, and merchants begin to borrow for the purpose of adding to their stocks of inventory. Bank earning assets increase, and at the same time, demand deposits are increasing in step. While this is happening, the incomes of workers who are producing the goods are growing, although with a lag. In Hawtrey's time, workers kept their cash balances in the form of currency rather than demand deposits, so a currency drain is in progress.

Not only is there a flow of gold into active domestic circulation, but the system of international trade leads to a second reason for gold to leave the banks. If one country is expanding credit faster than other countries, prices will rise faster in that country, leading to more imports and fewer exports. Gold would therefore flow out of the banks of the first country and into those of the other countries. This flow also has, according to Hawtrey, a considerable time lag. Thus, gold specie will be accumulating in the hands of the workers and in the vaults of foreign banks, hence leaving the domestic banks. The balance sheet of the banking system might approach a position like this:

Commercial Banking System

Gold (reserves)	$ 18	Demand deposits	$180
Earning assets	$162		

At the 10 percent reserve ratio limit, the banks are loaned up at this point; but because of the lag, gold will continue to flow into circulation, which throws the banks into a deficient reserve position. This, of course, will force the contraction of the banking system's earning assets. Interest rates will rise to encourage borrowers to get out of debt to the banks and discourage new borrowing. Some forced liquidation of inventories will be imposed. Merchants will find the interest costs high enough to induce them to decrease the size of their inventories. Now the contraction is in progress.

When bank credit is curtailed, business firms must reduce their stocks of goods in order to acquire the funds to retire bank loans, and thus they place orders for a smaller amount of goods than they are selling currently. This starts business on a downward movement, which is cumulative just as the upward movement was. As prices begin to fall, merchants expect them to fall further and, therefore, try to reduce their stocks. As producers receive smaller orders, they cut down production; consumer income is cut as are consumer expenditures; so, the reduction in stocks will be less than intended. The same lags that were observed in the expansion appear in the contraction phase. Income reductions of workers lag behind the reduction in loans and demand deposits, and the inflow of currency into the banks that becomes bank reserves lags behind the decline in incomes. If people expect the continuance of the price declines, the velocity of money will fall and cash balances will increase, accentuating the downswing.

Periodicity

According to the purely monetary theory of the business cycle, there are pronounced business cycles rather than minor oscillations around a level of equilibrium because of the cumulative, self-sustaining nature of the processes of expansion and contraction. These processes go on for a period of time, because the expansion of bank credit and the use of the increased cash balances of the community are not instantaneous. It takes time for economic activity to expand to the point where increased cash balances are needed and for this loss of cash by the banks, along with increased borrowing, to put pressure on bank reserves. Likewise, during contraction, it takes time for these cash balances to return to the banking system and to increase bank reserves above normal levels.

When most of the commercial nations of the world were operating on the gold standard, this process took place with some regularity, since the central banks acted to maintain the gold reserves. Since the abandonment of the automatic gold standard, however, the regular periodicity is no longer apparent, because the intricate mechanism that produced regular periods of expansion and contraction has been materially altered.

Evaluation

Monetary factors are certainly active factors in the cyclical process. It is difficult, however, to agree that the cyclical phenomenon is entirely a monetary one. Changes in economic activity may be due to changes in demand, new inventions, changes in the cost structure, changes in the methods of doing business, and so forth, which are not monetary factors but which, of course, affect monetary factors. The monetary theorists have well described the cumulative processes of expansion and contraction that such factors set into motion. Their explanation of the turning points, however, is not a completely satisfactory one.

It is highly doubtful that business people generally are as sensitive to small changes in interest rates as the monetary theorists maintain. The most important factors affecting investment decisions generally are present and prospective levels of sales, and price, cost, and profit expectations rather than minor variations in interest rates. Under any given state of expectations, some firms may indeed gain by increasing inventories and are encouraged to do so by lower interest costs, but this is not likely to be quantitatively important in bringing about an expansion, unless expectations are favorable for increased business activity. A complete explanation, then, must also account for changed expectations. The explanation of the upper turning point is likewise not fully satisfactory. Historically, turning points have occurred when bank credit was easily available, and prosperity periods have continued even when credit was severely restricted.

THE MODERN MONETARIST THEORY

The monetary theory of the business cycle has made a comeback in recent years, after the period of the 1930s, 1940s, and 1950s when the majority of economists felt that money really wasn't very important. The resurgence can be attributed to the keeping of the flame at the University of Chicago, mainly by Professor Milton Friedman. The majority of economists today have been persuaded that money does matter. Debate revolves around questions such as how much money matters and the nature of the transmission mechanism by which money stock changes are translated into changes in other economic magnitudes.

In recent years, a great amount of empirical work has been done to assess these questions. The evidence of close correspondence between money and general economic activity is impressive. Friedman and Schwartz found that over a period of almost one hundred years, the stock of money generally increased during both expansion and contraction phases of the business cycle.[2] However, during the most severe contraction periods, the stock of money did decline absolutely. They found not only that the rates of change in the money stock were closely associated with general business conditions, but that the severity in the rate of change in money stock and the magnitude of cyclical movements in business were highly correlated.

The money series normally leads the general business cycle, but the length of the lead varies. This variability in the presumed response of the economy to changes in the quantity of money has not been entirely adequately explained, and until it has been explained, the skeptics will have some justification for their doubts.

It is recognized, of course, that the fact that two statistical series vary together is not proof that one causes the other. An explanation is needed for the monetarist case to show that the direction of causation is from money to business activity, and that, while it is recognized that feedbacks from economic activity to variations in money stock exist, it is the money stock variation that triggers the change.

Modern Quantity Theory

Friedman and Schwartz visualize the basic process in the following way. Suppose the economy proceeds in a moving equilibrium in which real income per capita, real wealth per capita, the money stock, and the price level are all increasing at constant rates. The example they use assumes that the income elasticity of the demand for money (8) is 1.5; that is, if real income increases by 2 percent, the demand for money will increase by 3 percent. Thus, if the rate of growth of real income (a_y) is 2 percent per year, and the rate of growth of the nominal money stock (a_M) is 4 percent per year, the rate of growth of the price level (a_p) will be 1 percent per year: $a_p = a_M - \Delta a_y = 1\% = 4\% - 1.5(2\%)$.[3]

---

2. Milton Friedman and Anna J. Schwartz, "Money and Business Cycles," *The Review of Economics and Statistics* (February 1963), pp. 32–64.

3. Ibid., p. 59. Friedman and Schwartz state that the values given here are approximate averages over the ninety years between 1870 and 1960.

Now, if the Federal Reserve were to engage in open-market operations and cause the rate of growth in the money supply to go to 5 percent per year, the price level would increase at the rate of 2 percent annually. Thus, an increase of 1 percentage point in the rate of money-stock growth resulted in a 1 percentage point increase in the rate of price-level growth.

How do we move from increased open-market purchases by the Federal Reserve to the increased growth in the price level? First, the open-market agent buys (for example) from a government securities dealer who deposits the check received into a commercial bank. The dealer has more money and fewer securities now. Presumably, the dealer's inventory of securities would be replenished by purchasing other securities from customers who might be financial institutions, other corporations, or individuals. Security dealers try to buy at lower prices and sell at higher prices. This buying activity, first by the Federal Reserve and then by the dealers, has the effect of somewhat raising security prices (and, hence, lowering the interest yield).

In the meantime, the reserves of the commercial banks will have been increased by the open-market purchase, and the banks will have more excess reserves than desired, so they too will be in the market for securities and/or loans to local customers. This also forces financial asset prices to rise, and as banks expand their assets, the money supply increases. Most of the entities who have received money in exchange for their assets, or who have borrowed from the banks, will have uses for the money other than simply holding it dormant. Some of this money will be spent for bonds to replace those that were sold; some will be spent for real goods, such as plants and equipment, homes, and automobiles. Some of the spending will be for equity securities, the prices of which are also bid up, encouraging firms to increase real capital and causing the price of real capital to increase.

In summary, the open-market purchase and the response of the banking system to the purchase increase the amount of money and decrease the financial assets held by the nonbank public. Portfolios are out of adjustment until prices of financial and nonfinancial assets rise. The adjustment process describes the expansion phase of the business cycle. The forces would be reversed, if the initial impulse were a reduction in the growth rate of money stock.

This theory implies that the stock of money must provide the expansive and the contractive impulses that propel the business cycle. After study of the major business cycles in the United States, Friedman and Schwartz conclude that each cycle can be explained by such monetary forces, but its systematic character is elusive. Each significant change in the growth rate of the money stock is accounted for in a different way.

Rational Expectations

A new economic hypothesis concerning expectations was developed in the early 1960s by John F. Muth. The idea is called "rational expectations" and states that people base their expectations on the best economic theory available as they understand the basic relationships involved.

Robert E. Lucas, of the University of Chicago, applied the rational expectations view to the influence of the stock of money on the business cycle. If the price level depends on the stock of money, as Friedman and Schwartz conclude, people will catch on to this relationship. If the money supply is expanding, businesses and individuals will rationally expect prices to increase and will raise prices now. Therefore, these expected changes in the money supply will not affect real output. According to Lucas, Robert Barro, and others who share the rational expectations view, it is unanticipated or unexpected changes in the stock of money that are the basis for changes in real output and business cycles.

THE NONMONETARY OVERINVESTMENT THEORY

One group of investment theorists stresses overinvestment as a basic cause of the cycle and assigns only a subordinate role to monetary factors. Therefore, their theory has been referred to as the nonmonetary overinvestment theory.[4]

Over the course of the business cycle, investment spending fluctuates more severely than do the other major components of total spending in the economy. This can be explained either as the response of investment to other forces at work in the system, as it was in the purely monetary and the psychological theories, or as the causal factor that provokes the other elements to behave in a cyclical fashion. The nonmonetary overinvestment theory focuses upon investment as the factor that has an inherent tendency to fluctuate and causes the whole economy to react in a cyclical manner. These economists describe the

---

4. For an excellent survey of the overinvestment school of theorists, see Alvin Hansen, *Business Cycles and National Income* (New York: W. W. Norton & Co., Inc., 1951).

monetary system as a passive agent in the cycle, expanding during the upswing and contracting during the downswing. In other words, the money supply is not an originating force but a response variable. Changes in the money supply are a necessary but not a sufficient condition for cycles.

The earliest writer of this group we have called the nonmonetary overinvestment theorists was Tugan-Baranowsky.[5] In his version, the most important feature of the cycle was the conversion of free capital into fixed or real capital during the expansion and the opposite movement of fixed into free capital during the contraction. Free capital, which today we would call loanable funds, is converted into fixed capital, or capital goods, by the act of investment. Fixed capital is converted into free capital by the capital producing the receipt of funds, which are not used to replace the depreciating machine but are available for future spending. Free capital also builds up during the downswing because of people on fixed incomes whose savings accumulate without acceptable outlets for the use of these funds. Of course, investment in plant and equipment absorbs these funds during the expansion phase. A downswing comes to a halt, and the direction of the economy is reversed, when free capital has accumulated in amounts large enough that great pressure to employ these funds is felt, and the fixed capital, which was too large at the beginning of the downswing, has been reduced by way of depreciation in use over this time. The low interest rate in effect is further encouragement to the initiation of investment activity. The upper turning point is explained by the absorption of all the available free capital by real capital. Investment must stop, because there are no longer funds to pay for the new equipment and buildings.

Arthur Spiethoff improved upon Tugan-Baranowsky's explanation of the overinvestment theory, especially with regard to the turning points.[6] Spiethoff agreed with Tugan-Baranowsky that the lower turning point would be initiated by the push of free capital, but Spiethoff also believed that the pull of fixed capital might be a more powerful force. This demand for capital goods would arise from innovations that would open up new profit possibilities. Spiethoff's addendum to the theory of the upper turning point is to observe that the expansion will stop if society runs out of loanable funds, as Tugan-Baranowsky sug-

---

5. Michel Tugan-Baranowsky, *Les Crises Industrielles en Angleterre*, 1913.

6. Arthur Spiethoff, *Business Cycles*, International Economic Papers, No. 3 (New York: The Macmillan Company, 1953).

gested; but it will also come to an end if the investment possibilities inherent in the innovations are exhausted. Thus, Spiethoff has added the force of the pull of investment or fixed-capital demand at both the upper and lower turning points to the reliance that Tugan-Baranowsky had made on the push of free capital.

It remained for Joseph A. Schumpeter to explain why innovations would occur with sufficient regularity to explain the periodicity of the business cycle.[7] The Schumpeter schema will be considered immediately after we have summarized the events of the cycle according to the nonmonetary overinvestment school.

The Upswing

The nonmonetary overinvestment theorists describe the upswing and the cumulative process of expansion in the following way. After a period of depression, there are, again, profit possibilities and an increase in investment activity. This revival of investment generates income and purchasing power, which leads to an increase in the demand for capital goods and also for consumer goods. The increased demand for consumer goods stimulates further investment, and the increase in profits arising from larger volumes of business and a rising price level provide a psychological stimulus for further expansion. Thus, prosperity arises out of this cumulative process of expansion.

To describe the maladjustments, which develop in the expansion period, theorists in this group divide goods into four categories: nondurable consumer goods, durable and semidurable consumer goods, durable capital goods, and materials used to produce durable goods. Disequilibrium arises among these categories of goods during the upswing of the cycle. What actually occurs is a simultaneous shortage and abundance, since there is too much of one type of good and too little of another. Because of the development of new types of durable capital goods that can be used to reduce costs of production, a larger proportion of the factors of production are allocated to the making of durable capital goods and the materials used to produce such goods. As a result, insufficient resources are available for the consumer-goods industries that are counted on to use the new capital goods.

Also contributing to the imbalance is the long interval between the start of construction of a plant or factory and the time when it begins

---

7. Joseph A. Schumpeter, *Business Cycles*, Vol. I (New York: McGraw-Hill Book Company, 1939); also his *Theory of Economic Development* (Cambridge, MA: Harvard University Press, 1934).

to produce. This situation makes a correct forecast of demand very difficult. Additional income is being paid to workers and capital owners in the field of producer goods, and this increased income leads to more demand for consumer goods. The increased demand cannot be satisfied until the new producer goods go into production and, as a result of this excess demand, prices rise. This rise in prices is temporary to the degree that the supply of new producer goods will increase to an extent large enough to meet demand. It is difficult for individual producers to determine the industry's increase in capacity as well as the prices that will exist after production is in full swing. The higher prices may also lead to some expansion projects based on profit expectations at these prices, which will turn out to be unsound when supply is increased and prices return to lower levels.

The development of new durable consumer goods may also attract the factors of production to this field and away from the production of nondurable and semidurable consumer goods. The imbalance among the various types of production cannot be corrected because to do so would require additional labor and additional consumer goods to satisfy the total demand. Since all resources are in use, the additional labor and consumer goods are not available.

The Downturn

The expansion continues until either a shortage of loanable funds develops, which forces investment to decrease, or because of the virtual completion of profitable investment projects. The capital-goods industry becomes depressed, and the downswing is under way. After a long period of high activity and high incomes, the people who receive their incomes from this industry find their incomes, and hence their ability to purchase consumer goods, reduced at about the same time that the new plants and machinery are ready to turn out larger volumes of consumer goods. Now it can be seen that overinvestment has taken place. Projects—which would have been profitable had they been available when incomes were rising and resources were being devoted to capital building rather than consumer goods—are now excessive when large amounts of resources are available for the production of consumer goods, and incomes are insufficient to buy them at the expected or earlier prices. Prices of consumer goods fall and a cumulative contraction is under way.

During the downswing, conditions are being created that make the lower turning point possible. The capital wears out over time and is not replaced so the stock of capital is reduced. Excess inventories are eliminated. The costs of building capital equipment are lowered, wages are reduced, prices of raw materials are cut, and interest rates are lowered as loanable funds accumulate in the system. The contraction will continue until investment is again stimulated by these conditions and/or until the occurrence of an innovation that requires capital expenditures.

Evaluation

This form of the overinvestment theory is hardly satisfactory as a complete explanation of the business cycle. Nevertheless, it has made a contribution by pointing out that imbalances can occur among different categories of consumer goods as well as between producer and consumer goods. The most basic imbalance taking place during the cycle, however, is that between saving and investment. As the overinvestment theorists see the matter, saving is a steady, nearly constant activity, whereas investment is strong during the expansion and very weak throughout the contraction phase of the cycle. In other words, investment calls the tune. This saving and investment analysis is an important precursor of the more complete explanation later developed by Keynes. The overinvestment school had a fair understanding of the process of the multiplier without having the technical tools developed by Keynes and later economists. There is no completely satisfactory explanation given of the reasons for the imbalances among the different categories of goods. The minor emphasis on monetary factors cannot be fully accepted, since changes in the monetary system have played an active role in many past cycles. The explanation of the factors that initiate an upswing after business has declined during a recession period is inadequate in that it does not sufficiently explain why innovations occur at just the right time to produce the regularity of the business cycle. For this we turn to the work of Professor Schumpeter.

INNOVATIONS

The most thorough analysis of the role of innovations and the process by which they generate economic fluctuations was developed by Joseph A. Schumpeter. Changes in economic activity may be initiated by external factors, such as war, changes in tariffs, damage caused by earthquakes, and changes in agricultural yield. Such external influences disturb economic equilibrium, but they do not of themselves lead to cyclical fluctuations of business activity. Fluctuations may also be due to internal changes in the economic system, such as changes in consumer tastes, changes in the quantity or quality of factors of production, and innovations in the ways of producing commodities.

The movement is cyclical because of the cumulative process that takes place. Conditions in a period of prosperity become unbalanced and therefore lead inevitably to depression; and, in turn, conditions in the depression become favorable to a revival of investment. Thus, the cycle continues in a regular fashion. After there has been an initial boom in capital construction, replacements tend to assume a cyclical character, since much of the equipment must be replaced at about the same time in the future.

Crucial to the understanding of the Schumpeterian analysis is the distinction between inventions, or discoveries, and innovations. New methods of production, new products whether consumer or capital goods, and the discovery of new markets or new sources of raw materials are the major categories of inventions. These would seem to happen at any time, even in a random fashion. The presumption is that individuals and organizations engaged in research to discover or invent do so at a fairly continuous rate, but there is no regular pattern to the actual occurrences. Innovations are the economic exploitation of these inventions or discoveries, which is the introduction of them into the economy so that they are effective in causing the system to respond as it does in the business cycle. Innovations are introduced because a few business leaders see possibilities that are not generally seen by the rank and file. At first, they must strive hard to overcome inertia and introduce the innovation. After a time, others see the prospects for profits, and they too get into the new field. Since the initial innovator has demonstrated the feasibility and, indeed, the profitability of the new development, it is relatively easy to convince bankers to grant credit to the imitating followers, as well as to those firms coming into existence to supply the intermediate needs of the new industry.

Schumpeter used the construct of the "stationary state" or "static flow," an idealized situation of equilibrium that is as complete an equilibrium as can be imagined. In it there is no uncertainty, because there are no changes, and no changes because there are no innovations. There is no reason to invest except to replace worn-out equipment, so there is no saving. All output and all spending are on consumption. The lack of uncertainty assures that no profit will exist. Management, having no risk to take, simply repeats what was done in the past and so receives only its wages. There would be no borrowing or lending between households and business because capital would earn no net return. Everything else is constant, including the money supply, the velocity of money, prices, output, and full employment.

Into this euphoric environment rides the dynamic entrepreneur, Schumpeter's hero. The entrepreneur is the risk taker, the innovator, the creator of change and uncertainty. Inventions or discoveries that may have been made in the past are introduced by this entrepreneur.

Since this analysis starts with an economy that is in a state of equilibrium and has no unemployed factors of production, any new production must be financed by bank credit. This introduction of bank credit causes prices to rise, as well as an increase in money income.

If most of the great obstacles to change are conquered and the innovation is successful, profit will arise and hosts of imitators will be attracted into the new field and into peripheral areas. This expansion of investment will be paralleled by credit and monetary expansion, and savings will be forced to increase to equal the investment.[8] Since the expansion started from a condition of full employment, there can be no net increase in total output. As a result, when more labor and capital are devoted to the production of additional capital goods, output of consumer goods must fall. At the same time, the demand for consumer goods will increase as the additional money arising through bank credit is paid out in wages, thus putting additional pressure on prices.

This situation is changed as soon as the capital goods have been produced and the new consumer goods arising from putting them into production flow into the market. Since the innovations are more efficient than the processes they replaced, the volume of consumer goods will be greater than it was before the process began. Old plants will be either modernized to compete with the efficient plants or forced out of business. The turning point in this process will come when entrepreneurial activity in introducing innovations ceases. This slowing down in the activity of the entrepreneurs will cause uncertainty in business, and for a time, new projects will not be planned. This process, however, is not cyclical in the sense in which business cycles have occurred in our economy. It describes the disturbance from equilibrium and the expansion and then the return to equilibrium. The return to equilibrium is a period of the adjustment of industry to the new environment created by the innovations. Some old firms will go out of

---

8. The process of "forced saving" is detailed in the next section on the monetary overinvestment theory.

business as they are unable to compete with the new. Others will curtail the scale of their activity or in other ways readjust their output or ways of production. Some of the old firms whose products are complementary to the new innovation will adapt by expansion or other adjustments.

The cycles we have experienced in the past are described as due to a secondary wave of speculation. When business is in the process of readjustment because innovations are being introduced, many feel that the boom being produced, especially in the capital goods industries, will be permanent. As a result, the already-established firms borrow money to increase their operations, and consumers also go into debt to buy additional goods. General expansion of inventories also takes place, owing to expected price increases. The excessive indebtedness built up during this speculative wave causes trouble.

When the additional goods and services that are made possible by the new capital equipment enter the markets, prices gradually drop. This leads to difficulties for businesses and consumers who have gone into debt, because they contracted their obligations under the impression that the boom would be permanent. When prices and wages fall, many cannot meet their obligations and a depression results. During the expansion, overoptimism and overextension of debt took place. During the downswing, overpessimism takes over and forced liquidation of inventories and indebtedness continue. This situation can easily lead to a panic.

THE MONETARY OVERINVESTMENT THEORY

One group of theorists stresses deviations in the structure of production that are caused by an expansion in economic activity initiated by monetary factors. These theorists, including F. A. Hayek, are referred to as the Austrian school of economists. During a boom, a basic maladjustment occurs in the structure of the economy. Not only is there a shortage of bank credit, but also the production of capital goods is increased to a larger extent than is justified by the demand for consumer goods.[9]

The structure of production that exists at any period of time is not an accidental or arbitrary one. It has been built up by entrepreneurs who have invested in plant and equipment for the purpose of produc-

---

9. For an excellent presentation of this point of view, see F. A. Hayek, *Monetary Theory and the Trade Cycle* (New York: Harcourt, Brace & World, 1933), and *Prices and Production* (London: George Routledge & Sons, Ltd., 1935).

ing those goods that consumers demand. This includes all of the many intermediate servicing industries. The amount and types of machinery used depend, in part, upon the stage of technology in the economy. Also of primary significance is the amount of savings available for investment in business plant and equipment and the rate of interest that must be paid to get the holders of savings to invest them. The relative costs of capital and labor are also significant, because firms combine these factors of production so as to achieve the best possible combination from a cost standpoint.

To keep the economy in equilibrium, it is necessary that the factors of production be utilized so as to produce a pattern of production that corresponds to the pattern of consumption. The pattern of consumption is, in a general way, determined by the decisions of the population to spend or save its income and by the decisions concerning the distribution of expenditures among various types of goods. If, as production increases, the division between the making of new producer goods and of new consumer goods does not correspond to the division of income between saving and spending on consumption, a vertical maladjustment occurs. If the pattern of production of consumer goods of various types does not correspond to the pattern of consumer expenditures for such goods, there is a horizontal maladjustment.

The terms "vertical maladjustments" and "horizontal maladjustments" are used because of the nature of the relationships of the industries to each other. Consumer-goods industries are considered as being on one plane, and producer-goods industries are thought of as being on a higher plane. There are also stages in the producer-goods field, since some plants produce consumer goods directly, some produce machinery for such plants, some produce machine tools needed to make production machinery, some the basic metals for the tools, and so on. The stages closest to the consumer have been referred to by the monetary overinvestment theorists as the "lower stages of production"; those further removed, as the "higher stages of production."

Central to the monetary overinvestment theory of the cycle is the concept of the natural rate of interest. This is the rate at which the demand for loan capital (investment) is just equal to the supply of loan capital (savings). It should be distinguished from the money or market rate, which is the actual going rate of interest at any time. If banks lower the market rate below the natural rate, the demand for credit will rise and exceed the available supply of savings. The supply of credit is supplemented by the creation of bank credit, which leads to inflation. If the market rate is above the natural rate, the demand for credit will fall,

and, as a result, part of the supply of savings will not be used and deflation will occur.

The Upswing

The monetary overinvestment theorists have stressed an important
economic phenomenon called "forced saving." Hayek, in particular,
has made great use of the concept and feels that this is the essence of
the expansion process in the business cycle. To explain how forced
saving occurs, we shall first show in Figure 14-1 how investment can
increase without forced savings, that is, when savings are increased
voluntarily.

The original equilibrium condition is represented by the intersection of the savings and investment functions, where $S = I$ at the interest
rate r. Now, for example, we assume an increase in the demand for resources to produce capital goods because of (say) an important innovation. This increased demand means that business units wish to increase investment spending and are willing to pay higher interest costs
to do so. In this case, investors persuade savers to increase saving (that
is, reduce their consumption spending) by offering a higher reward for
saving in the form of a higher rate of interest. In fact, households voluntarily relinquish their right to use resources for consumption in
exactly the amount needed to satisfy the investors' demands. Saving
increases (consumption decreases) from S to S_1, and investment increases from I to I_1. The rise in the rate of interest from r to r_1 induced
the higher rate of saving and caused investors to invest less than they
would have invested had the interest rate remained at r. There is nothing disruptive in this process. Total income and output in the economy
will not change, since neither M nor V of the equation of exchange has
changed. Only the composition of output has been altered—more capital goods are produced, and in equal amount, less consumer goods are
produced. Austrian economists describe this alteration in output as a
lengthening of the stages of production. When it happens in the manner just presented, no business-cycle expansion occurs.

To demonstrate the contrast between the situation involved in Figure 14-1 and what happens in a business cycle, the monetary overinvestment theorists use the Wicksellian analysis. That analysis involves
the notions of the market rate of interest and the natural rate of interest.[10] The natural rate is the rate that equates savings and investment

---

10. Knut Wicksell, *Interest and Prices* (London: Macmillan & Co., Ltd., 1936).

Figure 14-1   Investment Increase and Voluntary Saving

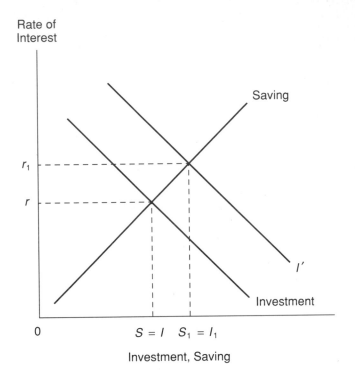

Rate of
Interest

and maintains equilibrium of the price level. In Figure 14-1, the market rate, which is the rate actually in existence, is the same as the natural rate. Divergence between the two occurs if an increase or decrease in hoarding, that is, a decrease or increase in velocity, V, or an increase or decrease in the money supply takes place. An increase in the money supply or the release of funds from "hoards" can make resources available to buyers of capital goods just as surely as if the resources were derived from saving.

Figure 14-2 includes on the supply side, savings plus changes in the money supply. For simplicity we have not incorporated increases in velocity, but the analysis would be basically the same. (That is, the supply curve would be farther to the right to the extent that velocity increased.) To start the analysis, we can take $S_e = I_e$ at interest rate r_n (natural rate) as the original equilibrium position, and some event causes the banking system to find itself in a position of having excess reserves that bankers want to lend. To get all the available funds bor-

Figure 14-2   Investment Increase and Forced Saving

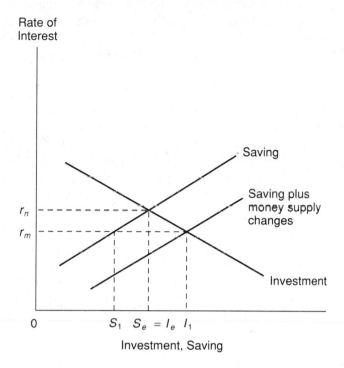

rowed, the interest rate will fall to r_m, the market rate of interest. Now, the market rate is below the natural rate. Investors can command resources valued at I_1 amount. Of this total, S_1 is supplied by savers and $I_1 - S_1$ is supplied by the expansion of the money supply by way of bank lending. Notice the difference between this case and the case depicted in Figure 14-1. When investment increased in Figure 14-1, saving increased; that is, the use of resources for consumption purposes decreased. In Figure 14-2, when investment increased, planned saving actually decreased, which is to say that consumption demand increased at the same time that the quantity of investment demanded increased. In other words, aggregate demand has increased.

We must point out that Hayek assumes that we started from a position of full employment so that the total supply of output cannot increase. This being the case, if investors are successful in increasing the output of capital goods, they must lure resources away from their current employment in the production of consumer goods. This can be done only by raising factor prices and, therefore, also the prices of final goods. In other words, consumers are forced to decrease their real consumption by way of price inflation. This is what is meant by the term *forced saving*. Actual saving is equal to I_1, even though desired or intended saving is just S_1.[11]

The market rate of interest will continue to be below the natural rate, as long as the money stock continues to expand; and as long as the rates differ in this way, the upswing of the business cycle will persist. But what happens when the source of expansion of the money supply dries up? Then, again, the supply of loanable funds will be limited to the desired amount of current saving, and the market rate of interest will rise to become equal to the natural rate. At this point, in the Austrian terminology, a shortage of capital exists. Investment projects, which were expected to be profitable when evaluated in terms of the lower market rate of interest, cannot be justified at the higher rate. It is now the households whose desires are fulfilled. They will save the amount they wish to save, and investors will be able to invest just that amount. Investment must decline to I_e, and savers will plan to increase their saving to S_e. Since both investment and consumption demands have decreased, there is a decrease in aggregate demand, and nominal national income will fall.

The Downturn

According to the overinvestment theory, the process of monetary expansion and heavy investment must always end in a collapse. Let us review very briefly the sequence of events of the expansion leading to this collapse. The artificial lowering of the interest rate causes business firms to invest in capital equipment at a rate that cannot be maintained because it is out of balance with consumer demand. The effective demand for consumer goods is reduced by forced savings at the same time that additional capital is invested to produce consumer goods. In other words, the structure of production has become top heavy, since it is now out of balance with too many facilities in the higher stages of production in the capital-goods field.

Forces that tend to reverse this pattern are then set in motion. As money is paid out to laborers, who are producing capital goods, the

---

11. This description should be qualified to observe that new investment demand would be expected to drive up prices of resources used in both consumption and capital-goods industries, so that some forced reduction of investment will take place as well as some reduction in consumption. The amount of the reduction in each industry will depend largely on the length of the lag in receipts of wages and other income payments behind money-supply expansion.

demand for consumer goods rises, and the consumer-goods industries become more profitable. This, in turn, entices the factors of production away from the higher stages of production back to the production of consumer goods. This demand for the factors of production in all fields causes an increased demand for bank credit, and increases the money supply, which creates further inflation.

The immediate cause of the breakdown of the boom is almost always the inability or unwillingness of the banking system to continue the process of credit expansion. This is due to monetary reasons, that is, either to the pressure on the reserve requirements of individual banks or to central bank policy.

When pressure develops on bank reserves and bank credit is restricted, the producers of capital goods can no longer obtain the funds to pay the higher prices and wages needed to bid raw materials and labor away from the consumer-goods field. Moreover, increased costs force these producers to charge higher prices for their products. These higher prices of capital goods lower the return to be received from investment in capital equipment at the same time that interest rates are rising, because banks have used up most of their excess reserves and are no longer anxious to increase their loan volume. This combination of factors leads to reduced activity in the capital-goods field. As workers are laid off, total income is reduced and the downward spiral sets in. The real cause of the collapse, however, is the shortage of real capital. It is not merely a shortage of investment funds but a real shortage of capital in the lower stages of production, which is needed to achieve a new balanced pattern of production in line with the additional investment in the higher stages.

During the depression, the structure of production is again brought into balance. This is a lengthy and painful process of readjustment during which workers are thrown out of work in the higher stages of production and gradually reabsorbed in the lower stages as a new pattern of equilibrium is developed. The depression is intensified by the general deflation that accompanies the decrease in the velocity of circulation brought about by hoarding on the part of businesses and households. Now, the market rate of interest will rise above the natural rate because of the increase in hoarding and the possible decrease in the money supply. If total output did not decrease, something like "forced consumption" would take place, because the price level would decrease, and since investment has decreased, consumption would have to increase. While this is apparently the assumption that Hayek makes, a more realistic position would be that unemployment does occur, and total output falls and results in a decline in both investment and consumption during the contraction phase of the cycle. The depression ends when the money supply ceases to decline and when the pessimism that caused the hoarding dissipates. At this point, the natural rate and the market rate would again come into equality, and the stage would be set for another expansion phase that would take place whenever the banking system again finds it profitable to create more money.

Evaluation

There are several shortcomings to this theory as the sole explanation of the cycle. The thesis that credit, which is created when the market rate of interest is below the natural rate, goes to the higher stages of production and leads to an imbalance between consumption and investment would be generally true under conditions of continuous full employment. However, the upswing of the cycle usually starts at a time when the economy has unused resources, and the production of both producer goods and consumer goods can be expanded before full employment of resources is reached. At full employment, if credit continues to be expanded to meet the demands of producers, forced saving and imbalance result. But imbalance also results if credit is created to meet the demands of either consumers or government.

The stress upon changes in interest rates as a determinant in the investment process may also obscure other factors that are at work. Investment decisions are based upon the interaction of the demand for funds with the supply and cost of funds. The demand for funds at various stages in the cyclical process is affected materially by changes in prospects of sales and profits. An analysis of the reasons for the changes in these prospects is an integral part of an understanding of the cyclical process.

Answers to this question supplied by a group of theorists stressing changes in investment activity will be considered in the next section. The monetary overinvestment theorists have stressed an important factor in their analysis of imbalance during the cycle between producer and consumer goods and between different types of producer goods.

THE ACCELERATION PRINCIPLE

In Chapter 9, we looked at the modern incorporation of the acceleration principle into macroeconomic models under the head, "Multiplier-Accelerator Interaction" (page 240). Our purpose here is to show the historical development of the concept, as well as to consider its microeconomic foundations.

Both the monetary and the nonmonetary overinvestment theories, as well as the innovation theory, hold that the initiating force in the cyclical process comes from the investment sector of the economy. There is, however, a point of view that has been used in explaining the cyclical process, which holds that the initiating impulses come from changes in consumer demand. According to this point of view, changes in consumption expenditures can lead to a cycle, because slight changes in the demand for consumer goods can produce much more violent fluctuations in the demand for investment goods. This principle, known as the *acceleration principle*, has been used by many theorists as part of their explanation of the cycle, notably by French economist Albert Aftalion, American economist J. M. Clark, and British economist R. F. Harrod.[12]

In its broadest aspect, the acceleration principle states that changes in the absolute rate of change in the demand for and production of finished goods and services tend to give rise to much more pronounced changes in the demand for and production of the producer goods that are needed for their production. This principle applies not only to finished consumer goods but to all intermediate goods with respect to their preceding stages of production. It also applies to changes in demand resulting from other factors than changes in final demand, such as changes in technology calling for the use of more machinery to produce a given level of output. To a certain degree, it holds true in the production of durable and semidurable consumer goods as well.

Producer Goods

The relationship in the case of producer durable goods may best be illustrated by means of a hypothetical example. Let us suppose that in a given economy, 1,000 units of consumer goods are produced in a year and that it takes 100 units of producer durable equipment to turn out the consumer goods. If the producer equipment lasts ten years, there is an average demand for ten units of equipment each year to replace those that are wearing out, so as to keep the stock of equipment intact.

Let us suppose further that there is an increase of 10 percent in the demand for this particular consumer good, so that 1,100 units are now

---

12. Harrod made use of the acceleration principle in his analysis of the business cycle, but following his own terminology called it "the relation."

desired by consumers. To produce these additional 100 units, it will be necessary to have ten more units of equipment. Even though this equipment will be useful for a period of ten years, it is immediately needed. As a result, there is now a demand for twenty units of equipment, the ten needed for replacement and the ten additional units needed to take care of the increased consumer demand. Thus, an increase of 10 percent in the demand for consumer goods has been magnified into an increased demand of 100 percent in the producer-goods field.

The degree of this acceleration in the derived demand for capital goods depends upon the life of the capital equipment. If the machines in our example lasted only five years, there would be a normal demand for replacement of twenty per year. In this case, a 10-percent increase in the demand for consumer goods would result in a 50-percent increase in the demand for producer goods, since ten additional machines would be needed, and twenty are being regularly produced. On the other hand, if the machines lasted twenty years, the normal replacement demand would be only five per year, and the 10-percent increase in the demand for consumer goods would lead to a 200-percent increase in the demand for producer equipment.

At the one extreme, if a machine would last indefinitely and was capable of producing an unlimited number of commodities, there would be no activity in the replacement business, and so any increase in primary demand would result in an increase in the demand for new equipment only. In that case, the total demand for equipment would be represented in Table 14-1 by our column headed "Demand for New Equipment." There would be no demand for replacement. This is the most volatile case. At the other extreme, suppose the durability of the machines was just one period, that is, capable of producing only ten units of commodity output. In that case, the replacement industry would be producing the existing stock of capital each period, and any increase in primary demand would result in exactly a proportional increase in total demand for equipment. These examples demonstrate the proposition that the greater the durability of the capital involved, the more extreme the fluctuations will be.

It is possible for the demand for new equipment to slow down while the demand for consumer goods is still increasing. If the demand for the consumer goods increases from 1,000 to 1,100 units, the demand for equipment increases by ten, or 100 percent. However, while the demand for the consumer goods continues to increase to 1,150 units, the total demand for equipment has already been cut to sixteen

Table 14-1

Changes in the Demand for Producer Goods Resulting from Changes in Consumer Goods Demand*

Period	Commodity Demand	Equipment Stock (Beginning of Period)	Demand for Equipment for Replacement	Demand for New Equipment (Net Investment)	Total Demand for Equipment (Gross Investment)
1	1,000	100	10	0	10
2	1,100	100	10	10	20
3	1,150	110	11	5	16
4	1,150	115	11.5	0	11.5
5	1,000	115	11.5	-15	-3.5

*Assumptions:
1. Commodity demand figures are arbitrarily selected.
2. One piece of equipment produces at the rate of ten units of the commodity per period.
3. The equipment has a life of ten periods; that is, its depreciation rate is 10 percent per year.
4. No depreciation occurs in the year in which equipment is added.

units, a reduction of 20 percent. If, in the next period, the demand for the commodity remains constant, the only equipment demand is for replacement, and as a result, demand falls still further. This can be seen clearly from the example in Table 14-1.

Thus, it can be seen that increases in the absolute rate of change in demand for consumer goods when an industry is at or near capacity will lead to an accelerated derived demand for producer goods, but this demand will be sharply curtailed as the rate of increase slows down.

Durable and Semidurable Consumer Goods

The second case of the principle of acceleration is similar to the first, except that it pertains to durable and semidurable consumer goods. The same example can be used with modifications in terms. Instead of the production of a consumer good, it is necessary to substitute the service received from it (as, for example, the service received from a house) and to substitute the supply of houses for the equipment used to produce consumer goods. An increase in the demand for housing accommodations leads to a greatly magnified demand for new houses, because houses last for a long period of time.

The same situation is true in the automobile field, where the basic demand is for transportation service. Since cars last for several years, there is a basic demand for automobiles for replacement, and an increase in the demand for transportation service leads to an accelerated increase in the demand for new cars. This relationship will be elaborated on more fully in a discussion in Chapter 20 of the methods of forecasting the demand for consumer durable goods.

Inventories

The third case of the acceleration resulting from derived demand occurs in the case of inventories. Let us suppose that it is the practice of a retailer of business suits to adjust the store's inventory to sales in such a way that the usual stock on hand is about equal to two months' sales, and that sales are normally 100 suits a month. Because of an increase in demand, sales rise to 110 suits a month. As a result, it is necessary to increase orders for suits by more than the increase in sales, if the regular relationship of inventory to sales is to be maintained. If the increased demand for suits is permanent, twenty extra suits must be added to the stock to maintain past inventory relationships.

This principle works on the downturn as well as on the upswing, although it is subject to some very definite qualifications. It is by no means clear that a relatively fixed relationship will always be maintained between sales and stocks, especially in the short run. In addition, the volume of stocks is subject to speculative changes that may easily overshadow any changes owing to the acceleration principle.

Evaluation

The acceleration principle has been used as part of the explanation of the cycle by various theorists. There is another factor that explains the accelerated increase in demand in the upswing of the cycle. It is especially significant in a highly developed economy in which large amounts of capital equipment are in use, with much of the equipment having a long period of usefulness. As has already been demonstrated, the longer the life of the equipment, the greater the acceleration due to derived demand. Since some of the new capital equipment is financed out of credit expansion, the additional credit intensifies the upswing. The acceleration in demand for durable goods and in demand for inventories also offers a further explanation of the factors leading to the cumulative nature of the expansion.

The acceleration principle adds a new possibility for an explanation of the downturn. Instead of being caused by a shortage of money or equipment, the downturn may occur because the rate of increase in the demand for consumer goods has slowed down, thus reducing the demand for new equipment and leading to unemployment in the producer-goods industries. This further reduces the demand for consumer goods, which still further reduces the demand for producer goods. As this cumulative process of contraction takes place, the boom must come to an end.

Attempts to verify the acceleration principle statistically have not always met with success. This is to be expected since it is only a greatly simplified statement of a principle, not an explanation of a phenomenon that happens in precisely that way in the real world. In the case of producers' durable equipment, for example, it is very unlikely in an economy that experiences marked fluctuations in demand that there will be any regularity in the replacement of equipment. Most replacement is likely to occur in prosperity periods when the demands for new equipment must also be met. Furthermore, when an expansion of business begins, there is usually unused capacity in an industry, so that the first effect of an increased demand for consumer goods is a fuller utilization of existing capacity. As demand expands further, it is also possible in many plants to utilize existing equipment more fully by adding additional shifts of workers. Beyond that point, it becomes necessary to place orders for new equipment, which will show the accelerated effect of derived demand.

As the economy approaches full employment of workers and other resources, however, it is no longer possible to increase production in all fields. The major result will be a bidding up of prices, especially those of basic raw materials utilized in both the producer- and consumer-goods fields. Thus, the acceleration principle cannot hold completely as full employment of labor and resources is achieved. This explanation is harmonious with the record of business fluctuations as developed by the National Bureau of Economic Research. The most rapid rate of increase in the production of capital goods occurs early in the cycle, but the most rapid rate of increase in price does not occur until the last segment of expansion. This relationship is much too complex to be measured effectively in all of its ramifications, and therefore it is not surprising that the evidence on this point is at variance. It is, however, an integral part of the explanation of the cyclical process, especially the more pronounced fluctuations in demand for durable goods of all kinds rather than for nondurable goods.

QUESTIONS

1. Show the balance sheet changes of the commercial banking system over a complete business cycle as implied in Hawtrey's analysis. Use successive T-accounts. The only items needed are reserves, earning assets, and demand deposits. Assume a 10 percent customary or required reserve ratio.

2. Trace the development of a full business cycle according to the purely monetary theory within the framework of the equation of exchange, either $MV = Py$, or $M = kPy$.

3. What weakness in Tugan-Baranowsky's theory did Spiethoff correct? What was Schumpeter's contribution to this same problem?

4. Would the nonmonetary theory of the cycle be an acceptable theory if the money supply were held completely constant? Defend your answer.

5. In the overinvestment theories, the upper turning point is associated with a decrease in investment. Why, then, are the theories called "overinvestment"?

6. Explain how inflation of the general price level operates to produce the phenomenon called "forced saving."

7. Explain why the acceleration principle is more pronounced the more durable the capital equipment.

READINGS

Blinder, A. S., and S. Fischer. "Inventories, Rational Expectations, and the Business Cycle." *Journal of Monetary Economics* (November 1981), pp. 227–304.

Bronfenbrenner, Martin. *Macroeconomic Alternatives*. Arlington Heights, IL: AHM Publishing Corp., 1979.

Hawtrey, Ralph G. *Trade and Credit*. London: Longmans, Green & Co., Ltd., 1928.

————. *Capital and Employment*. London: Longmans, Green & Co., Ltd., 1937.

Hayek, Friedrich A. *Monetary Theory and the Trade Cycle*. New York: Harcourt, Brace & World, 1933.

————. *Prices and Production*. London: George Routledge & Sons, Ltd., 1935.

Metzler, Lloyd A. "The Nature and Stability of Inventory Cycles." *Review of Economics and Statistics* (August 1941), pp. 113–129.

Schumpeter, Joseph A. *Business Cycles*, Vol. 1. New York: McGraw-Hill Book Company, 1939.

————. *Theory of Economic Development*. Cambridge, MA: Harvard University Press, 1934.

Spiethoff, Arthur. *Business Cycles*, International Economic Papers, No. 3. New York: The Macmillan Company, 1953.

Tugan-Baranowsky, Michel. *Les Crises Industrielles en Angleterre*, 1913.

Wicksell, Knut. *Interest and Prices*. London: Macmillan & Co., Ltd., 1936.

FORECASTING ECONOMIC ACTIVITY

One of the important reasons for studying the nature of business fluctuations and the causal factors that have produced them is to be able to determine the most probable future levels of economic activity. This is significant for developing governmental policies in the monetary and fiscal areas, and it is also extremely important to the business person who must develop plans in light of future prospects for the economy. Part 4 will deal with techniques and procedures currently used to forecast future levels of economic activity.

Chapter 15 considers various procedures for projecting the trend of activity in the economy for several years into the future and describes and analyzes various approaches to such forecasting. Chapters 16, 17, and 18 deal with short-run forecasting of economic activity for a year ahead and present procedures for building a model of gross national product for the next year. Chapter 19 discusses methods of predicting long-run price trends and of making short-run price forecasts.

Chapter 20 shows how forecasting is used in business to forecast sales. Many factors must be forecast in addition to sales, including costs, capital

PART 4

requirements, and labor requirements. The starting point in all of these forecasts is, however, a forecast of sales. To provide a basis for business planning, such forecasts need to be stated in dollars as well as in units.

To some degree, all business is affected by general economic activity. Therefore, before a forecast for an industry or an individual business is made, it is desirable to have a forecast of overall economic activity. This background is used to help develop a forecast for an industry, and an industry forecast generally is useful in developing a forecast for an individual business. The steps in developing a sales forecast are usually to forecast (1) general economic activity, (2) the level of sales in the industry, and (3) the sales of an individual business.

Because a great deal is still unknown about the causal factors at work in the economy and the reactions of the economy to such factors, a full science of prediction is not possible and a large area of judgment remains. At this stage of development, forecasts will therefore be subject to some error and, at times, may be completely incorrect. However, a forecast based on available techniques is, on the average, far superior to intuition, chart reading, and the like.

FORECASTING THE TREND OF ECONOMIC ACTIVITY

In light of the long-term trend in sales of any business, important decisions must be made. If sales are likely to be growing over a period of time, plans must be made for the expanded facilities necessary to handle the increased volume of business and for the necessary financing for such facilities. This planning must be done on the basis of the long-term trend of the total economy, of the industry of which this business is a part, and of the business itself.

Moreover, if the business is regional, the trend of economic activity in its region will affect its sales in the future. If the business is national, the trend of sales in different regions will influence the location òf future plant and distribution facilities. The business will want its facilities to be most economically located in relationship to raw materials, labor, and future markets.

PROJECTING THE GROSS NATIONAL PRODUCT TREND

The starting point for making a long-range projection of total economic activity is to project the level of gross national product, since this is the most comprehensive measure of economic activity in general use. Forecasting GNP is done by groups such as the National Planning Association, the Conference Board, and the Department of Commerce. These projections are not forecasts of the actual level of economic activity to be expected in the future but projections of long-run trends in the economy. They are made on the assumption of full employment in the forecasted year and in terms of prices current at the time the forecasts are made. Such projections are useful as a guide to the building of plant and equipment on the basis of the long-run demand for a product, not on the basis of the cyclical fluctuations.

Since trends change slowly, such projections can be made with reasonable accuracy for a number of years. As the period of time involved is lengthened, the projections become less reliable. Unforeseen factors can have considerable influence on future economic activity, and trends may change materially over time. Projections have been made for as many as fifty years ahead, but these are only rough, general estimates of the potentialities of the economy. Fortunately for planning most types of capital expenditures, projections in real terms for five to ten years are usually sufficient, and these can be made with reasonable accuracy.

Various procedures with different degrees of refinement may be used for projecting GNP. The simplest technique is to project the trend for the past few years either freehand or using the line of least squares to develop an equation to forecast future GNP. Since the line of least squares is based on the notion of a linear trend, another possibility would be to consider nonlinear trends and use the method of least squares to develop an equation. A more complex approach is based on a determination of the number of persons likely to be in the labor force and of the most likely output per employed worker in the forecast year. This approach can be refined by determining the most likely distribution of employees by fields and also the most likely output per worker in each field. Each of these procedures will be considered more fully.

Line of Least-Squares Trend

In projecting the trend, it is necessary to consider which time period will be used as the basis for such a projection. GNP, for example, grew very rapidly from the depths of the depression in 1933 through the early post-World War II period. The period since then has not been affected by these abnormal developments, and GNP has grown much less rapidly. Prices have risen since World War II, but this effect is largely eliminated by using GNP in constant dollars as a basis of projection. This is done because increases in real output are to be projected, not price changes. Table 15-1 gives GNP figures from 1967 through 1987 in terms of 1982 dollars. The formula for the line of least squares applied to these data is:

$$Y = 2,982.7 + 76x \text{ (x is the forecast year minus 1977)}$$

The projected 1993 GNP in 1982 dollars is $4,198.7 billion ($Y_{1993} = \$2,982.7 + 76(1993 - 1977) = \$4,198.7$). Adjusting this figure to 1987 prices (by multiplying it by the 1987 GNP price deflator of 117.5) gives a GNP figure for 1993 in 1987 dollars of $4,933.5 billion.

Table 15-1

Gross National Product for 1967–1987
(Billions of 1982 Dollars)

Year	GNP	Year	GNP
1967	2,261.2	1978	3,115.1
1968	2,365.6	1979	3,192.3
1969	2,423.2	1980	3,183.2
1970	2,416.2	1981	3,248.7
1971	2,484.8	1982	3,466.0
1972	2,608.5	1983	3,279.1
1973	2,744.0	1984	3,501.4
1974	2,729.3	1985	3,607.4
1975	2,695.0	1986	3,713.2
1976	2,826.3	1987	3,821.0
1977	2,958.6		

Source: *Survey of Current Business*, various issues.

Extending Average Rates of Growth

An alternative and somewhat superior method of projecting GNP is to extend the average rate of growth in a past period into the future to the forecast year. Selecting a relevant base period is also important when calculating average rates of growth.

The average rate of growth of GNP in real terms for the period from 1967 through the 1986–1987 period was about 2.7 percent per year. The rate of growth dropped in the 1980 and 1981–1982 recession periods but increased again in 1983. Extending the 2.7 percent rate of growth to 1993 from the 1987 level of real GNP of $3,821.0 billion gives a value of $4,483.2 billion in 1993. Adjusting this figure to reflect 1987 prices yields a nominal GNP for 1993 in 1987 prices of $5,267.8 billion.

Nonlinear Trends

In the previous section, the real GNP forecast for 1993 was based on compound growth; that is, real GNP in 1993 was projected at $4,483.2 billion, which equals $3,821.0(1.027)^6$. The forecast was based on an obvious nonlinear assumption—one of compound growth. This material can be extended to include different types of nonlinear trends that can be made linear through transformations, and thus, least squares can be applied.

In the following, let Y = the actual data, the variable to be forecasted, such as real GNP. Let X = the time variable, the trend. Here are some examples of nonlinear trends that can be made linear by using transformations. Once made linear, then the method of least squares can be used.

- Inverse linear $\qquad\qquad Y = a + b/X$
- Exponential curve $\qquad\quad Y = ae^{bX}$
- Compound growth $\qquad\; Y = ab^X$
- Modified exponential $\quad\; Y = aX^b$
- Logistic $\qquad\qquad\qquad Y = 1/(K + ab^X)$

The parameters to be determined by least squares are a and b. The constant e represents the base of natural logarithms.

The various trend equations can be matched with different trend growth or decline scenarios; see Figure 15-1.

1. Great expansion
    exponential curve with b positive
    compound growth, $b > 1$, $a > 0$
    modified exponential, $b > 1$, $a > 0$
2. Expansion leveling
    inverse linear with b negative
    modified exponential, $0 < b < 1$
3. Decline leveling
    inverse linear, b positive
    exponential, $b < 0$
    logistic, $0 < b < 1$, $a > 0$, K constant
4. Decline getting worse
    compound growth, $a < 0$, $b > 1$

These nonlinear trend equations can be made linear by using transformations. For example, consider the compound growth equation, $Y = ab^X$. Take the natural logarithms of each side of the equation, and this gives $\ln(Y) = \ln(a) + \ln(b)X$ or $Y' = A' + B'X$. This is linear and A' and B' can be calculated. By working backwards we can then determine values for a and b.

Estimating GNP from the Supply of Factors of Production

A more refined approach is to project GNP from the basis of the ability of the economy to supply goods and services. This is done by

Figure 15-1   Examples of Nonlinear Trends

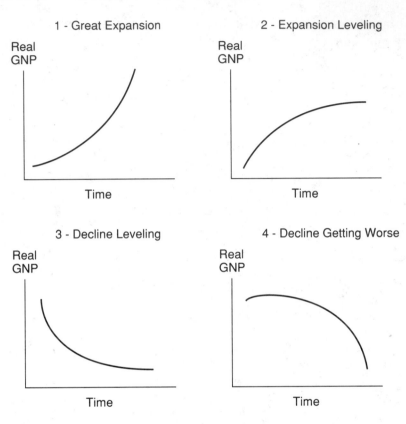

estimating the most likely level of the labor force and the GNP output per worker. The GNP output is total output of GNP arising from the combination of labor itself and the other factors of production. This procedure also projects GNP in terms of current prices. Furthermore, it assumes full employment in the forecast year. This means that results will be somewhat higher than projections based on extending past growth from a period in which significant unemployment existed in some years. This will be true in the 1964–1987 period, since there was unemployment of some magnitude above frictional unemployment from 1975 through 1986.

Population and Labor Force. The first step in this procedure for projecting GNP is to estimate the population at the future date selected for the forecast. This step requires a study of the trend of population

Table 15-2

Population and Employment, 1940–1987

Year	Population (Millions)	Total Labor Force[a] (Millions)	Labor Force Participation Rate[b]	Unemployment Rate[c]
1940	132.6	56.2	42.4%	14.6%
1950	152.3	63.4	41.6	5.2
1960	180.7	71.5	39.6	5.4
1970	205.1	84.9	41.4	4.8
1971	207.7	86.4	41.6	5.8
1972	209.9	88.8	42.3	5.5
1973	211.9	91.2	43.0	4.8
1974	213.9	93.7	43.8	5.5
1975	216.0	95.5	44.2	8.3
1976	218.0	97.8	44.9	7.6
1977	220.2	100.7	45.7	6.9
1978	222.6	103.9	46.7	6.0
1979	225.1	106.6	47.4	5.8
1980	227.7	108.5	47.7	7.0
1981	229.8	110.3	48.0	7.5
1982	232.1	111.9	48.2	9.5
1983	234.2	113.2	48.3	9.5
1984	237.0	115.2	48.8	7.4
1985	239.8	117.2	50.0	7.1
1986	241.6	119.5	49.5	6.9
1987	243.8	121.6	50.0	6.1

[a]Labor force including resident armed forces; in millions of persons.
[b]Total labor force as a percent of total population.
[c]Unemployed as a percent of total labor force.
Source: Bureau of Labor Statistics data.

and a projection of this trend into the future. Such estimates are made by the Bureau of the Census of the Department of Commerce, as well as by individuals and private agencies. Table 15-2 shows the increases in population since 1940, the total labor force, the labor force participation rate, and the unemployment rate.

After the size of the population has been estimated, then the number of individuals who will be in the labor force must be estimated. Projections are based upon a study of the long-term trend of the labor force in relationship to the total population and the population of working age. From 1900 until about 1950, when compared with total population, the labor force participation rate was growing. It began a slow decline that continued until the early 1960s. In the mid-1960s, it began to increase again as more married women entered the labor force. The labor force participation rate has been rising faster since 1969, as babies born during the post-World War II baby boom have entered the labor force, and the rate of population increase has slowed down. Now that the post-World War II population "bulge" is part of the labor force, the labor force participation rate has leveled off at between 49 to 50 percent. All these factors must be considered in estimating the total labor force from an estimate of population. The Census Bureau estimates the size of the labor force and its probable distribution as to sex and age groups.

Assume that the population in 1993 will be 258 million, which is near the center of the range of estimates for that year. As more married women enter the labor force, the labor force participation rate will probably continue upward. If we assume 51.0 percent participation rate, the labor force estimate for 1993 is 131.6 million workers.

Estimates of GNP are usually based on production of goods and services by the civilian labor force. Therefore, the number of people likely to be in the armed forces must be subtracted. For several years, it had been gradually decreasing before it increased in the summer of 1966 as a result of the Vietnam War. In 1987, it had decreased to about 1.7 million.[1] Let us assume it remains at 1.7 million in 1993. Our estimate of the civilian labor force is then 129.9 million workers, whereas it was 121.9 million in 1987.

After the size of the civilian labor force in the forecast year has been projected, the amount of frictional unemployment must be estimated. *Frictional unemployment* includes unemployed workers who are entering the labor force for the first time and workers who are currently between jobs. Even in years of high business activity such as 1929, 1948, 1966, 1973, and 1979, unemployment did not drop below 3 to 4 percent of the civilian labor force, and in some prosperous years in the 1960s and 1980s, it has been over 6 percent. Therefore, 5 percent can be used as an approximation of frictional unemployment. The above estimate of the civilian labor force for 1993 was 129.9 million workers. If approximately 5 percent, or 6.5 million workers, are unemployed, civilian employment in 1993 will be about 123.4 million.

---

1. Bureau of the Census, Publication P-25.

Production. After the size of the employed civilian labor force in the forecast year has been determined, the volume of goods and services that will be produced must be estimated. This estimate depends upon the number of hours that will be worked and the rate of output per hour. The long-run trend of the number of hours worked has been decreasing. In 1987, the average hours worked per week were about 34.8. The downward trend in this series seems to have slowed considerably, so it would seem reasonable to assume for our projection of GNP that in 1993, the average number of hours worked per week will be 34.5.

The next step is to estimate the amount of GNP likely to be produced for each hour of civilian employment in the forecast year. The rate of increase in GNP per worker-hour since 1957 has been about 3.0 percent per year. From 1957 to 1960, it was below the postwar average, and this was again true in the 1966–1969, 1973–1974 periods and in 1980–1982, but in other years, it was well above the average. From 1977 to 1981, growth in productivity was measured near zero, which has been of real concern to many economists. However, some improvement has been observed since then.

Let us assume that it will be 3 percent per year between 1987 and 1993. In 1987, GNP per hour of civilian employment was $18.60— GNP of $3,821.0 billion/205.4 billion hours of work (34.5 hours average work week × 52 weeks × 114.5 million civilian employees). At an average annual rate of increase of about 3 percent per year, GNP per civilian worker-hour will be $22.21 in 1993. Gross national product in 1993 is then based on the following factors:

- Civilian employment: 123.4 million workers
- Average hours of work per week: 34.5
- GNP per hour of civilian employment: $22.21

The average hours of work per year per worker is 1,794 (52 × 34.5), and the total number of hours of work in the year is 221.4 billion (1,794 × 123.4 million workers). Multiplying by an average projected rate of output of $22.21 per worker-hour gives a 1993 GNP of $4,917.29 billion in 1987 dollars.

In this exercise, it is important to keep in mind that we have been using GNP in 1987 prices, so the figure for 1993 is what that year's GNP would be, if the price level remains constant between 1987 and 1993. In other words, we have not made a forecast of changes in the price level over the six-year period. Note also that we have made no forecast of cyclical unemployment by assuming that only frictional unemployment exists, and thus, there is no cyclical unemployment for forecast year 1993.

More Refined Estimates of GNP

Estimates of GNP based on expected employment levels and expected output per worker may be refined by making separate estimates for major sectors of the economy and totaling these to arrive at an estimate of GNP. One such refinement is to estimate separately the private sector and governmental contributions to GNP. This is done because it is difficult to measure trends in productivity in government employment, since government services are not sold in the marketplace. Another reason for doing so is that trends in wage rates in government and private employment have not always been the same.

The private contribution to GNP is found by determining private employment, hours worked per year, and output per hour. Output can be projected on the basis of trends of productivity in general, or by separately figuring trends in productivity of labor and capital. The governmental contribution is developed from figures on the number of workers and the average pay per worker. The number of workers in government employment is determined from past trends and a qualitative evaluation of the factors likely to affect employment in the future. An example of factors that affect employment would be the fewer teachers required in the 1970s to educate the smaller number of school-age children because of decreased birth rates in the 1960s. The average wage per governmental worker is likewise determined from the trends of wages as well as from a consideration of qualitative factors.

A further refinement calls for separately estimating output in major fields of private-sector employment. This is, at times, done only for agricultural and nonagricultural production because of varying rates of productivity and hours of work in these fields. At other times, nonagricultural employment is further subdivided.

The Bureau of Labor Statistics (BLS) publishes historical data on average weekly hours, average hourly earnings, and average weekly earnings in mining; construction; manufacturing; transportation and public utilities; wholesale trade; retail trade; finance, insurance, and real estate; and services. Two Department of Labor publications, *The Monthly Labor Review* and *Employment and Earnings* publish BLS data. In addition, projections of employment are available. For ex-

Table 15-3

U.S. Employment by Sector, 1983–2005
(Millions of Jobs)

	1983	1990	1995	2000	2005
TOTAL	106.9	123.1	131.6	136.3	143.3
Farm	3.9	3.9	3.8	3.8	3.7
Nonfarm	103.0	119.2	127.7	134.6	139.6
Private	84.3	100.1	108.4	114.9	120.6
Agricultural Services	0.8	1.1	1.3	1.4	1.5
Mining	1.0	1.1	1.2	1.3	1.3
Construction	5.1	6.3	6.7	7.0	7.3
Manufacturing	18.8	21.8	22.7	23.3	23.7
Nondurable	7.8	8.4	8.5	8.6	8.6
Durable	11.0	13.4	14.2	14.7	15.2
Transportation, Communications, and Utilities	5.3	6.1	6.6	7.0	7.3
Wholesale Trade	5.6	6.6	6.9	7.2	7.6
Retail Trade	17.3	20.2	21.9	23.2	24.9
Finance, Insurance, and Real Estate	6.2	7.5	8.3	8.9	9.2
Services	24.2	29.5	32.9	36.5	37.8
Government	18.7	19.0	19.3	19.8	20.0
Federal Civilian	3.0	3.0	3.1	3.2	3.2
Federal Military	2.6	2.6	2.6	2.6	2.6
State and Local	13.1	13.4	13.6	14.0	14.2

Sources: U.S. Department of Commerce, Bureau of Economic Analysis, *OBER Regional Projections*, Vol. 1 (Washington, D.C.: U.S. Government Printing Office, 1985).

ample, the Bureau of Economic Analysis of the Department of Commerce has divided the economy into the fields shown in Table 15-3 and provides estimates of employment figures for selected years.

The change in the structure of industry in the United States from manufacturing, or goods-producing, industries to the service-producing sector has made productivity estimates more difficult to make. Employment in the goods-producing industries declined slightly from 1980 to 1987 (from 25,855,000 in 1980 to 24,884,000 in 1987), whereas employment in service industries grew from 64,802,000 in 1980 to 77,228,000 in 1987, a gain of 19.2 percent. In spite of the relative changes in employment in the two categories, the share of manufacturing in the gross domestic product has remained generally the same over the past thirty-five years. The implication of this is, of course, that over these years, productivity in manufacturing has considerably increased.

ESTIMATING GNP FROM THE DEMAND FOR GOODS AND SERVICES

Gross national product can also be estimated from the demand side by making an estimate of each of the major categories of GNP in the forecast year. This is done by estimating personal consumption expenditures, gross private domestic investment, governmental purchases of goods and services, and net exports of goods and services. These categories are estimated from past trends in each of its major subdivisions, from an analysis of qualitative factors, and from past relationships between them. The procedure is similar to that described in Chapters 17 and 18 for making a short-run forecast.

More refined estimates may be made by estimating receipts and expenditures in each major sector of GNP and determining the excess of receipts or expenditures in each sector. The total of these must, of course, balance *ex post*, and estimates should be evaluated and, if need be, modified. An imbalance between total receipts and disbursements may indicate that some of the estimates are not accurate or that they have not been made consistently. It may also indicate that the economy will tend to behave in this way, but that forces will be put in motion to adjust the lack of *ex ante* balance between savings and investment. These factors are considered more fully in Chapters 17 and 18.

Estimates of GNP made from the supply and demand sides also can be compared and differences analyzed. If the supply figure is above that from the demand side, unemployment is likely to exist; if the demand figure is the higher, inflationary pressures will exist. In making a final forecast, it is necessary to consider the most likely actions by government, business, and labor if deflation or inflation exists and to estimate the effect of these actions on GNP.

The National Planning Association has long been estimating future levels of GNP. These estimates have been made by using various approaches to projecting GNP and developing the most likely figures on the basis of the judgment of the economists making the estimates. The size of the labor force and the most likely output per hour of employment are used as one approach. Estimates are also made of the demand for GNP from purchases of goods and services by consumers, for domestic investment, by government, and from net international purchases. In developing the estimate for each sector, disposable receipts, as well as purchases, are estimated, and the projected excess or deficit of receipts is determined for each sector and for the balance for the total economy.

PROJECTING DISPOSABLE PERSONAL INCOME

In many areas of economic decision making, and especially in projecting consumer expenditures, it is necessary to have a forecast of disposable personal income as well as a forecast of GNP. The amount of income individuals have remaining after taxes have been deducted is one of the major factors determining the level of many consumer expenditures. The following adjustments must be made to GNP to get disposable personal income:

- Subtractions
    Capital consumption allowances
    Indirect business tax and nontax liability
    Current surplus of government enterprises
    Corporate profits and inventory valuation adjustment
    Contributions for social insurance
    Excess of wage accruals over disbursements
    Personal tax and nontax payments
- Additions
    Government transfer payments
    Net interest paid by government and consumers
    Government subsidies to business
    Dividends

To develop a forecast of disposable personal income, each of these items must be estimated in the forecast year. Minor items, such as the surplus of government enterprises and government subsidies to business, are usually ignored. An estimate of capital consumption allowances requires estimates of the year-by-year increases in plant and equipment and their depreciation. Also needed are estimates of losses of capital by destruction and of capital expenditures charged to income currently. These estimates are made on the basis of past relationships and the qualitative factors in the present situation.

Indirect business taxes, mainly sales and excise taxes, must also be estimated and subtracted, since they are not available for consumer expenditures. These taxes are usually estimated by applying present tax rates to estimates of future increases in business and adjusting the figures for expected tax changes.

Corporate income taxes and retained earnings are not available for consumer expenditures. Except during recession years, corporate profits after taxes had a fairly stable relationship to GNP. This past relationship can be used along with present and projected tax rates and qualitative factors to estimate corporate income taxes. Estimates of retained earnings and dividend payments also can be made from an analysis of past trends in the division of profits after taxes between dividends and retained earnings.

Deductions for estimates of Social Security contributions can be estimated from past trends and any expected changes in Social Security tax rates, as well as from projected levels of employment and increases in the income of workers.

Personal taxes must be estimated and subtracted to determine disposable personal income. This is usually done first by assuming that current tax rates will continue, and then by making adjustments for expected changes in tax rates.

Government transfer payments must also be added to arrive at disposable personal income. These can be projected from past trends and from a thorough study of present programs for veterans, for Social Security, and the like. Another important item to be added is personal interest income, which involves a projection of interest rates and the levels of governmental and consumer debt. The level of the debt can be developed from a study of probable surpluses or deficits in governmental budgets and from trends and current developments in consumer borrowing. The estimate of interest rates involves a study of supply and demand factors.

An alternative approach to estimating disposable personal income starts with a projection of national income. This is built up by projecting the trend of the various payments to the factors of production—essentially, wages, interest, rent, and profits. Then, the various items that must be added to and subtracted from national income to arrive at personal income must also be estimated. These items, as well as the various payments making up national income, are described in Chapter 6.

PROJECTING THE TREND FOR AN INDUSTRY

Several steps are involved in making long-range estimates of sales in various fields. One step for many consumer items is to find the relationship to disposable personal income. Sales of some items bear a more or less constant relationship to disposable personal income; some items are growing more rapidly than income; some are growing at a slower rate. If the relationship to disposable personal income follows a regular pattern, that relationship and a forecast of disposable personal income can be used as a basis for a projection for five or ten years in the future.

In making such a projection, the trend of sales in the industry itself should also be considered. It may be helpful to study the trend of consumption on a per capita basis. The trend is difficult to project in the early stages of an industry, when sales may be growing rapidly and also irregularly. In the early stages of growth, a nonlinear trend may be useful. When an industry has become well established, however, and sales are growing primarily in response to changes in such factors as income, population, and price changes, projections based on past trends can be made more confidently. Qualitative factors, such as the development of substitute products or changes in consumer tastes or habits must be carefully considered. Consideration must also be given to trends in exports and imports, if they are significant.

The Department of Commerce analyzes trends in many industries and publishes such data in an annual publication called *U.S. Industrial Outlook*. This volume analyzes past trends and makes a forecast for the next year and a projection for a period some five to ten years in the future.

The soft drink industry may be used as an example of the types of projections that are made. In recent years, the sale of soft drinks had been growing somewhat less rapidly than disposable personal income. Figure 15-2 shows relative changes in the value of soft drink shipments, disposable personal income, and the wholesale price of soft drinks for the 1975–1987 period.

One explanation of the somewhat smaller increase in soft drink shipments than in disposable personal income is that, in relative terms, the population has been getting older. Furthermore, the industry was successful in introducing new products in the early part of this period. But these new products have started to reach maturity in the mid- to late 1980s. Exports and imports are insignificant and can be ignored in long-range projections. The value of soft drink shipments grew in line with disposable income from 1975 through 1982. The increase in sugar prices in 1980 caused producers to shift to greater use of high fructose corn syrup, causing shortages and higher prices for that substitute input. Consumers adjusted by reducing the quantity of soft drink purchases, but dollar purchases increased slightly.

Sales can be expected to grow at a slower rate than disposable per-

Figure 15-2   Value of Soft Drink Shipments, Producer Price Index for Soft
Drinks, and Disposable Personal Income, 1975–1987

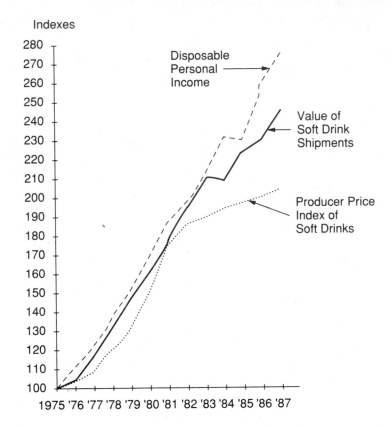

sonal income, since many of these factors that have led to the slower
rise of soft drink sales are expected to continue. It is unlikely, however,
that sales will continue to grow at the rate of the late 1970s, especially
since the number of teenagers will not be increasing as rapidly as it did
in that decade, and the price of soft drinks has gone up more rapidly
than consumer prices.

    In projecting the long-term sales trend of an industry, the best pro-
cedure is to correlate sales with projected disposable personal income,
farm income, or GNP, whichever is most applicable. The future growth
of the industry in question, considering all qualitative factors, must
also be studied. The basic idea would be to assume that Sales = f(GNP).
After collecting data on company sales and GNP, the next step would
be to estimate the slope and intercept of the equation by using the
method of least squares.

$$\text{Sales} = a + b(\text{GNP})$$

Earlier in this chapter, methods for obtaining GNP projections were presented. With forecasts for GNP and the line of least squares, projections for sales can be obtained. On the basis of this information, a tentative estimate may be made of the long-term trend of the industry; the reader must remember, however, that this trend can be altered by changes in any of the factors that determine the trend.

REGIONAL FACTORS

In developing the trend for a particular business, it is necessary to consider trends in the region and in the state or states in which the business is conducted. For national businesses, such trends are also important in deciding on plant location in relationship to future markets and labor supply, as well as sources of raw materials. Periodically, the Department of Commerce makes studies of trends in income payments by regions and states and compares income for years in which economic activity was at about the same stage in the cycle. The Department of Commerce also divides longer periods into subperiods to determine if there is a continuity of trend.

According to a study done by the Department of Commerce, there has been a relative shift in income from New England, the Middle East, and the Great Lakes area. This shift is based, in part, on relative shifts in population from the Northern and Central Regions to the Southwest and Far West. Since 1950, population has grown much more rapidly in the Far West than in any other region of the country. The Department of Commerce makes projections of shares of population and personal income by region. Figures for 2000 and some earlier years and estimates of growth rates of personal income and population are presented in Table 15-4.

The projections shown in Table 15-4 indicate that the Southern and Western Regions will continue to increase their shares of personal income relative to other regions. However, the rates of growth in their relative shares of income will be slower than in the 1973–1983 period.

For many economic decisions, an important variable is per capita personal income rather than total personal income in a region. Table 15-5 shows regional per capita personal income as a percent of the national average. The Mideast, Far West, and New England Regions of the United States generally have per capita personal income above average. The Rocky Mountain, Southeast, and Southwest Regions have lower than average per capita income. Note that there is a clear tendency of those areas with low per capita income to experience growth

Table 15-4

Regional Shares of Personal Income and Population

	1973	1983	1990	2000	Average Annual Growth Rate 1973–1983	Average Annual Growth Rate 1983–2000
PERSONAL INCOME U.S. Total*	1,001,799	1,280,180	1,603,313	1,970,899	2.5	2.6
		Percent of National Total				
Fast-Growing Regions†	49.40	55.37	56.79	58.61	3.7	2.9
Rocky Mountain	2.48	2.86	3.04	3.28	4.0	3.4
Southwest	7.52	9.69	10.15	10.63	5.1	3.1
Far West	14.46	16.33	16.66	17.14	3.7	2.9
Southeast	18.88	20.54	20.98	21.52	3.4	2.9
New England	6.06	5.95	5.96	6.04	2.3	2.7
Slow-Growing Regions	50.60	44.63	43.21	41.39	1.2	2.1
Plains	8.11	7.21	7.16	7.03	1.3	2.4
Great Lakes	20.33	17.50	16.98	16.10	1.0	2.1
Mideast	22.16	19.92	19.07	18.26	1.4	2.1
POPULATION U.S. Total‡	211,349	234,023	249,203	267,464	1.0	.8
		Percent of National Total				
Fast-Growing Regions†	52.47	56.70	58.13	59.79	1.8	1.1
Rocky Mountain	2.62	3.04	3.19	3.42	2.5	1.5
Southwest	8.51	10.02	10.43	10.90	2.7	1.7
Far West	13.40	14.76	15.33	15.98	2.0	1.3
Southeast	22.33	23.52	23.75	23.98	1.6	.9
New England	5.71	5.36	5.39	5.51	.3	1.0
Slow-Growing Regions	47.53	43.30	41.87	40.21	.1	.3
Plains	7.87	7.44	7.28	7.13	.5	.5
Great Lakes	19.38	17.72	16.92	16.04	.1	.2
Mideast	20.28	18.14	17.67	17.04	−.1	.4

Source: *Survey of Current Business* (May 1985).
*In millions of 1972 dollars.
†Includes Alaska and Hawaii.
‡In thousands of persons.

in the future and areas with high per capita income to have slower than average growth in per capita income. Thus, a convergence has been occurring, at least, from 1929 to the present, and is projected to continue well into the future.

In using such analyses of the trends in income for the purpose of forecasting the sales trend of a particular business, it is again necessary to look at the qualitative factors to see why these trends have been tak-

Table 15-5

Regional Per Capita Personal Income

	Percent of National Average				Percent Change in Relation to National Average	
	1973	1983	1990	2000	1973– 1983	1983– 2000
Fast-Growing Regions[a]	94	98	98	98	4.3	0.0
Rocky Mountain	95	95	95	96	0.0	1.1
Southwest	89	97	97	98	9.0	1.0
Far West	108	110	108	107	1.9	-2.7
Southeast	85	87	8	90	2.3	3.4
New England	105	111	110	110	5.7	-0.9
Slow-Growing Regions	107	103	103	103	-3.7	0.0
Plains	103	97	98	99	-5.8	2.1
Great Lakes	105	99	100	100	-5.7	1.0
Mideast	109	110	108	107	0.9	-2.7

[a]Alaska and Hawaii included in Far West total.
Source: *Survey of Current Business* (May 1985), p. 42.

ing place. This means that the sources of the relative gains or declines in regional income must be analyzed to determine whether they arose from shifts in manufacturing, agriculture, trade, service, government, and so on. It is also necessary to see whether they are based primarily upon shifts in total population or upon per capita variations in income. The reasons for the changes in each individual field must then be analyzed, and estimates of the future course of each field made in light of future economic developments.

A Department of Commerce study[2] is based on such an analysis. This study projected data on employment and on total personal income for the year 2000 for each region and for each state in a region. It also projected total earnings for major sectors of the economy in agriculture, mining, construction, manufacturing, transportation and utilities, trade, finance, services, and government. Constant study of all these factors is required, since to some degree, past trends are always changing and, at times, even abruptly.

---

2. "Regional and State Projections of Income, Employment, and Population to the Year 2000," *Survey of Current Business* (May 1985), pp. 39–67.

On the basis of the national and regional trends of the industry, the future trend of sales in an individual business may be determined. The first step is to find the trend of sales of the business and to compare it with the industry trend. Since trends differ in various regions of the United States, the trend of sales of the business should be compared with industry sales on a region-by-region basis. The next step is to explain any differences in rates of company and industry growth; for example, little sales effort may have been put into some regions, or high transportation costs may have cut down sales. On the bases of industry trends, of past relationships to industry trends, and of future sales policies, it is possible to develop projected sales for the company in each region and in total.

Regional and Local Indicators

The NBER was a pioneer in the development of leading, lagging, and coincident economic indicators for the national economy. Recently, this same idea has been applied to the development of economic indicators for regions and localities.

One of the nation's largest banks, headquartered in Detroit, has developed an activity index for the Michigan economy. The index is based on a weighted average of the stock-market price of large business firms headquartered in Michigan. Over time, this index has proven to be a leading indicator for Michigan economic activity. The Federal Reserve Bank of Dallas has researched both coincident and leading indicators for the Texas economy. The coincident indicators consists of real gross state product, Texas industrial production index, Texas real personal income, Texas nonfarm employment, and Texas unemployment rate. Variables used in the index of leading indicators for Texas involve state, national, and international data. The state data cover average weekly hours of production workers in manufacturing, help-wanted index, real Texas 77 stock-market index, new unemployment claims, real retail sales, number of oil-well permits issued, and the real price of oil. The national and international variables include national index of leading indicators and Texas-weighted real value of the dollar. Similarly, Pennsylvania State University has developed a composite leading indicator for the Pennsylvania state economy.

Economic data for local areas is more difficult to come by and, if available at all, only with long time delays. This makes construction of timely local indicators more troublesome. Some recent research has provided one possible direction to explore in the construction of local indicators. Paul J. Kozlowski has published data on indicators for Metropolitan Statistical Areas (MSA) in Michigan. The local variables included in the indexes cover labor market data, construction activity, and banking data. A leading economic indicator that covers the Flint, Michigan MSA is reported monthly. The composite indicator is an average of average weekly production hours, local checking and saving balances (in a sense, money supply). The average lead time for the index has been six months. Thus, if regional and local data are available, it is possible to develop regional and local indicators.

QUESTIONS

1. On what assumption is a projection of the trend in economic activity based?
2. Outline the steps involved in projecting GNP by
   (a) projecting the line of least squares,
   (b) extending past average rates of growth,
   (c) estimating the number of employed workers and the output per worker.
3. What problems are involved in projecting the size of the labor force?
4. How are trends in output per hour of employment determined?
5. Why is projection of GNP made by estimating the labor force and output per worker likely to give somewhat higher results than projecting the trend of GNP?
6. Outline several procedures for making more refined estimates of future levels of GNP.
7. Describe the National Planning Association procedure for projecting GNP.
8. Outline the procedure for developing estimates of disposable personal income from estimates of GNP.
9. Describe a procedure for estimating consumer expenditures in total and for major categories of expenditures from estimates of disposable personal income.
10. How do varying regional growth trends affect long-run business decisions?
11. How have population, personal income, and per capita personal income by regions shifted since 1973?
12. What changes are expected in the relative shares of personal income by regions and in per capita personal income by regions?
13. Outline a procedure for projecting sales on a regional basis.

READINGS

Ellis, Dennis F. "Leading Indicator Flint Area." *Flint Marketing Journal* (May 1981), pp. 1–3.

Kendrick, John W., and Eliott S. Grossman. *Productivity in the United States: Trends and Cycles*. Baltimore: The Johns Hopkins University Press, 1980.

Kozlowski, Paul J. *Business Conditions in Michigan Metropolitan Areas*. Kalamazoo, MI: The Upjohn Institute for Employment Research, 1979.

Long-Range Economic Projection, Studies in Income and Wealth, Vol. 16. Princeton, NJ: National Bureau of Economic Research, 1954.

"Midwest Manufacturing Index." *Economic Perspective*, Federal Reserve Bank of Chicago (September/October 1987).

Newbold, Paul, and Theodore Bos. *Introductory Business Forecasting*. Cincinnati: South-Western Publishing Co., 1990.

Pennsylvania Business Survey. University Park, PA: Pennsylvania State University (November 1988).

Phillips, Keith R. "New Tools for Analyzing the Texas Economy: Index of Coincident and Leading Economic Indicators." *DallasFed*, Federal Reserve Bank of Dallas (July 1983), pp. 1–13.

"Regional and State Projections of Income, Employment, and Population to the Year 2000." *Survey of Current Business* (May 1985), pp. 39–67.

Sivia, Timothy B. *U.S. Regional Projections 1980–2000*. Washington: National Planning Association, 1981.

U.S. Department of Commerce, Bureau of Economic Analysis, *OBER Regional Projections* (Washington, D.C.: U.S. Government Printing Office, 1985).

Valentine, Lloyd M. "The Economy of 1984." In *Environment 1984: Interfacing with Management and Business* by Henry G. Baker. Columbus: Grid, Inc., 1975.

SHORT-RUN FORECASTING OF GENERAL BUSINESS ACTIVITY

Since forecasting is still much more of an art than it is a science, economists use varying approaches in making forecasts. This is especially true in making short-run forecasts of general economic activity. Most forecasters also use several approaches to forecasting, since none of them is completely accurate at this stage of development. This eclectic attitude is especially useful when economic activity is believed to be near an upper or lower turning point. The major approaches to short-run forecasting of overall economic activity will be considered in this chapter.

FAVORABLE AND UNFAVORABLE FACTORS

A simple, but valuable, starting point to forecasting is to list all the favorable and unfavorable factors in the situation under study. Favorable factors are those whose effect is likely to keep the level of overall economic activity expanding, while unfavorable factors are those that have a tendency to cause a slowing down or decline in economic activity. The analyst must also understand the factors that are likely to lead to further expansion or to contraction. It is true that what is considered a favorable factor by one analyst may be considered to be unfavorable by another. It depends upon the analysts' understanding of the operation of the economy, that is to say, upon the theory used. Better theorists make better forecasters.

Events or conditions that might be considered favorable in and of themselves might very well be unfavorable in conjunction with other existing circumstances, so one should not get into the habit of labeling a particular factor as either favorable or unfavorable in isolation.

Factors to be considered in check-listing short-run favorable and unfavorable circumstances or events include:

- new products or methodologies taking hold
- newly discovered raw materials sources
- demographic changes that are in process
- the stage of the building cycle
- the current interest rate and apparent pressures for its change
- relative changes in demand for major commodities such as autos, housing, recreation, communication, and transportation
- foreign competitive forces
- balance of payments situation
- foreign exchange rates, relative rates of inflation
- interest rates in foreign versus domestic markets
- political positions of administration in office *vis à vis* economic issues
- federal, state, and local budget deficits or surpluses
- philosophical-economic stance of the Federal Reserve Board concerning interest rate versus money stock control
- attitude of labor leaders and rank and file
- current rate of inflation and prospects for its change
- degree of political and economic uncertainty
- business leaders' view of prospects for profit in the future that influences investment decisions
- households' views influencing saving decisions
- inventories relative to sales balance
- costs of production versus commodity prices
- wholesale versus retail price trends

This method is valuable because it requires a thorough analysis of the current situation. After all factors are listed, the forecaster's judgment is used to decide what the impact of all these factors in combination will be on the economy. This is especially difficult after economic activity has expanded for a time and unfavorable factors develop in greater number.

CONSENSUS OF OBSERVERS

Because forecasting is so important to many businesses and governmental units, as well as being subject to error, it is natural to want the opinion of other analysts who have studied the economic outlook. Therefore, getting the consensus of qualified observers is part of the program of almost every forecaster. For some, it is the major approach to forecasting.

Several sources of such opinions are available. At the turn of each year, financial papers and journals, as well as the financial sections of many daily newspapers, publish the opinions of leaders in government, industry, and education. The Conference Board, Inc., holds a discussion meeting on the outlook, which is attended by prominent economists engaged in forecasting, and publishes the proceedings in a pamphlet called the *Business Outlook*. Every six months, the First National Bank of Chicago publishes the opinion on the outlook for their industry by leaders in many fields. Magazines such as *Business Week*, *Fortune*, and *Dun's* have articles on the economy in almost every issue. Two publications, *The Journal of Business Forecasting*, and the *Quarterly Domestic & Global Forecasts of Key Economic Indicators*, present a quarterly consensus forecast that covers important economic variables. In these two publications, a survey is taken of financial economists/forecasters associated with bank, insurance companies, and security dealers and money managers. The procedure is to contact, by telephone or in writing, the forecasters and get their projections for the upcoming four quarters. The consensus is the average of individual forecasters. Information also is provided on the standard deviation, so that the reader of the forecasts can obtain information on the variation of the individual projections.

"Are Economic Forecasters Worth Listening To?" is the title of a study done by Peter L. Berstein and Theodore H. Silbert.[1] The study is based on a consensus forecast of principal economic variables as found in *Blue Chip Economic Indicators*. Robert J. Eggert, chief economist for *Blue Chip*, surveys 48 broadly based economic forecasters and collects information on the expected year-over-year changes in each economic variable. Comparing the consensus projections for real GNP and the inflation rate, as measured by changes in the GNP deflator, the authors conclude:[2]

> At one time or another, every professional forecaster is wrong. Taken as a group, however, forecasters have a good record, this article asserts. Reliance on a consensus outlook can at least keep you aware of signs that current trends are changing. These kinds of signals can help the corporate executive avoid victim-

---

1. Peter L. Bernstein and Theodore H. Silbert, "Are Economic Forecasters Worth Listening To?" *Harvard Business Review* (September–October 1984), pp. 32–40.
2. Ibid., p. 32.

ization by the ups and downs of business cycles—such as being fully stocked and expecting more materials to come into inventory, just as the economy takes a nose dive.

LEADING AND LAGGING SERIES

Economists have searched for years for a series that would signal changes in economic activity by turning upward and downward before the overall economy turned. No single series has had such a relationship on a regular basis. Several series usually lead at turning points, however, and others usually lag. An analysis of a group of such series has been used to get an indication of the direction of economic activity.

The most complete studies of cyclical leads and lags have been made by the National Bureau of Economic Research. Geoffrey H. Moore and Julius Shiskin have chosen 88 indicators from the large number of series studied by the NBER, 36 of which they have placed in a leading group, 25 in a roughly coincident group, 11 in the lagging group, and 16 in a group unclassified as to timing. These series cover a wide range of economic processes representing all sectors of the economy.

Since 1957, the Department of Commerce has become heavily engaged in the collection and analysis of data series for the study of economic indicators. The work is now housed in the Bureau of Economic Analysis, which publishes the *Survey of Current Business* monthly. In this publication, the behavior of data series can be followed for their conformity to business cycles. Short lists of leading, coincident, and lagging indicators are studied particularly closely, and composites of each grouping are made available regularly. After considerable theoretical and empirical study, the makeup of these short lists periodically changes. The current series included in the composites are shown in Table 16-1, and Figure 16-1 shows the indexes of the composite of leading, lagging, and coincident composite indicators from 1952 through early 1988.

It is interesting to examine the recent behavior of these series. The leading series foreshadowed the upturn in 1958, the downturn in 1960, and the upturn in 1961. However, in 1962 and in 1967, they gave false signals of recession. These periods were only retardations in the forward advance of economic activity, although, in 1967, the retardation was more serious than it was in 1962. The leading indicators did, however, foreshadow the 1969–1970 recession.

All three composite indexes performed in near-textbook fashion in the three and one half cycles since 1970: the leading series turning be-

Table 16-1

Short List of Economic Indicators

Leading Indicators (11 series)

Average weekly hours of production or nonsupervisory workers, manufacturing
Average weekly initial claims for unemployment insurance, state programs
Manufacturers' new orders in 1982 dollars, consumer goods and materials industries
Vendor performance, percent of companies receiving slower deliveries
Contracts and orders for plant and equipment, 1982 dollars
New building permits, private housing units (index: 1967 = 100)
Change in manufacturing unfilled orders in 1982 dollars, durable goods industries,
   smoothed
Change in sensitive materials prices
Stock prices, 500 common stocks (index: 1941–1943 = 100)
Money supply, M2, 1982 dollars
Index of consumer expectations

Coincident Indicators (4 series)

Employees on nonagricultural payrolls
Personal income less transfer payments, 1982 dollars
Industrial production, total (index: 1977 = 100)
Manufacturing and trade sales, 1982 dollars

Lagging Indicators (7 series)

Average duration of unemployment
Ratio, manufacturing and trade inventories to sales, 1982 dollars
Change in index of labor costs per unit of output, manufacturing, smoothed
Average prime rate charged by banks
Commercial and industrial loans outstanding, 1982 dollars
Ratio, consumer installment credit outstanding to personal income
Change in consumer price index for services, smoothed

Source: *Business Conditions Digest.*

fore the business cycle turns; the coincident series turning at almost the precise time of the business cycle; and the lagging series always reaching their turning points after the business cycle has done so. In addition, no serious false signals were recorded during the 1970–1988 period. The peak in several indicators expressed in nominal terms came somewhat late, although, when expressed in real terms, the peaks came earlier, thus giving a longer lead. This was true in the 1973–1975 and the 1980 recessions and their respective recoveries.

Although one would expect that the leading-series indicators would be most useful for forecasting turning points, there are some economists who feel that there is a superior indicator, which is the

Figure 16-1   Indexes of Composite Leading, Coincident, and Lagging Indicators

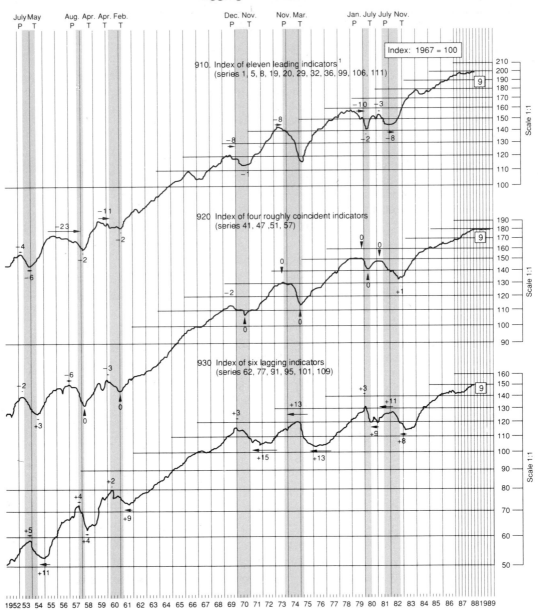

NOTE: Numbers entered on the chart indicate length of leads (−) and lags (+) in months from reference turning dates.
[1]Values of this index prior to January 1984 include a twelfth component, series 12, which has been suspended from the current index. Current data for these series are shown on page 60.

Source: *Business Conditions Digest* (November 1989), p. 10.

ratio of the coincident series to the lagging series. This particular ratio, published irregularly in the *Survey of Current Business*, has consistently given a longer warning signal of impending downturns than has the leading indicator series.

DIFFUSION INDEXES

Economic time series do not all move uniformly up or down in any stage of the business cycle. Therefore, diffusion indexes are used at times to gauge the relative strength of the forces of expansion and contraction over a time span. The diffusion index is the percentage of the series in any group being studied that is expanding in any period of time, such as a month or a quarter. For example, if out of a group of fifty series, thirty series, or 60 percent, are expanding in a month, the diffusion index is 60; if thirty-five series, or 70 percent, are expanding, it is 70; and so on. Various time spans are used ranging from one to twelve months, and at times, a six- or nine-month time span and a one-month span are used together. A diffusion index fluctuates between 100 percent when all components are expanding and zero when all are declining. When the index is at 50, it is implied that there is no change in the aggregate series. This would, of course, only be true if all the component series had the same relative importance. A diffusion index also takes no account of the magnitude of change in the component series. An index of 80 may at one time be associated with a 10-percent rate of increase in the aggregate series and, at another time, with a 5-percent increase.

Even though diffusion indexes have limitations, they can be useful in predicting turning points in the aggregate series. Both the level and direction of change of a diffusion index must be considered. When a diffusion index is rising in the 50- to 100-percent range, it implies that the aggregate series is increasing at an increasing rate. An index that is falling at a rate between 50 percent and zero implies that the aggregate series is declining at an increasing rate, and one that is rising at a zero to 50-percent rate implies that the series is declining at a decreasing rate. These changes may be seen in Figure 16-2.

Business Conditions Digest publishes the data and graphs for diffusion indexes of the leading, the coincident, and the lagging indicator components. The graphs for these three indexes are shown in Figure 16-3. This is, of course, what is happening in the "real world" as opposed to the picture shown in Figure 16-2, so things are not so neat. Business-conditions analysts spend considerable time studying the

Figure 16-2   Properties of a Diffusion Index

Aggregate Series

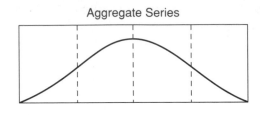

Diffusion Index

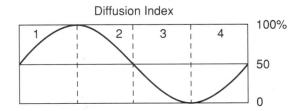

Stage	a diffusion index that is	implies that the aggregate series is
1	rising (50% - 100%)	increasing at an increasing rate
2	falling (100% - 50%)	increasing at a decreasing rate
3	falling (50% - 0)	declining at an increasing rate
4	rising (0 - 50%)	declining at a decreasing rate

Source: *Economic Review*, Federal Reserve Bank of Cleveland (January 1971), p. 6.

past and the present status of all three series. Maturity of judgment comes from this sort of study.

Also included in Figure 16-3 is the diffusion index of industrial production. It is made up of series of industrial production in twenty-four industries and is one of the components included in the coincident diffusion index. *Business Conditions Digest* publishes the data and graphs for a large number of these individual diffusion indexes.

You might try the following exercise to get a feel for using these series for forecasting business cycles, as well as for determining the current situation in the economy. In the leading series diffusion index, find the date the series reaches 50 percent from above, and note the length of time before the peak is reached. Then, find the date the series reaches 50 percent from below, and note the length of time before the trough is reached. Do the same for the coincident and the lagging series. Also look at those times on the graph when the series approach

Figure 16-3 Diffusion Indexes of Leading, Coincident, and Lagging Indicators for Components and Industrial Production

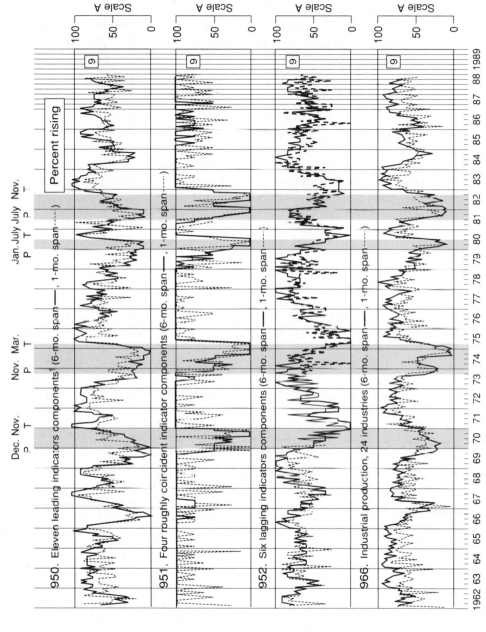

¹Values of this index prior to January 1934 include a twelfth component; series 12, which has been suspended from the current index.
Source: *Business Conditions Digest* (October, 1988), pp. 36-37.

100 percent expanding, and observe the stage of the business cycle at those points. Do the same for the times when the indexes approach 100 percent contracting.

With this kind of study, you will find that as a forecaster, you probably would have been fooled on several occasions, but on the other hand, you would never have missed forecasting the turning points that did occur. The leading indexes have indicated every turn in general economic activity in the post-World War II period. They have also turned for a short period when no turn in the business cycle took place. Therefore, the indexes cannot be used alone as a forecasting device or without judgment. They also do not tell the exact timing of turning points or the intensity of changes in business activity.

QUANTITATIVE FORECASTING WITH LEADING INDEX INDICATOR

Geoffrey Moore has suggested a quantitative method of forecasting with the composite leading series.[3] While the method is very simple and the data are readily available, the results are competitive with many forecasting techniques of much greater complexity, sophistication, and cost.

A simple linear regression is estimated from the equation:

$$Y = a + bX$$

where

1. Y = percentage change in GNP, or employment, or industrial production, or any other economic aggregate from one calendar year to the next.
2. X = percentage change in the average of the index of leading indicators from one fiscal year to the next; the fiscal year is defined as June 30 to June 30.

For example, the change in GNP of calendar year 1987 to 1988 is the dependent variable, when the independent variable is the change in the average of the leading indicator index from June 30, 1986, to June 30, 1987, and June 30, 1987, to June 30, 1988. This gives the forecast a six-month lead. A longer lead time can be had by using the first quar-

---

3. Geoffrey Moore, "Forecasting Short-Term Economic Change," *Journal of the American Statistical Association* (March 1969). Reprinted in Moore, *Business Cycles, Inflation and Forecasting*, 2d ed. (Washington, D.C.: NBER, Inc., 1980), Chapter 25.

Table 16-2

Forecasting Percentage Changes in GNP from Percentage Changes in the
Index of Leading Indicators, 1951–1984

Independent Variable	Dependent Variable				
	Percentage Change in GNP from Calendar Year to Calendar Year in Constant (1972) Dollars				
Percentage Change in Leading Indicators Index	r	a	b	t	MSE
From fiscal year to fiscal year	0.90	1.79	0.39	11.45	1.33
From fiscal year to the 3d, 4th, and 5th quarters	0.87	1.93	0.41	9.87	1.68
From fiscal year to the 3d and 4th quarters	0.83	2.02	0.46	8.04	2.26
From fiscal year to the 3d quarter	0.75	2.03	0.54	6.26	3.08

Note: r = coefficient of correlation, a = intercept constant, b = slope estimate, t = t statistic for b, MSE = mean square error.
Data source: *Business Conditions Digest*.

ter of the fiscal year (that is, the third quarter of the calendar year), at
an annual rate as if it were the figure for the entire year. The same thing
can be done using the averages of the first two or the first three fiscal
quarters as proxies for the entire fiscal year. As would be expected, the
fiscal year to fiscal year data for the independent variable produced
better results than when three quarters of data were used, which, in
turn, was better than using two quarters of data.

A recent study following Geoffrey Moore's methodology is summarized in Table 16-2.[4]

RELATIONSHIP OF NEW ORDERS, INVENTORIES, SALES, AND PRODUCTION

Another method used for short-run forecasting involves the relationships between sales and inventories and sales and new orders and,
in turn, the effect of changes in such relationships to changes in pro-

---

4. The study referred to was conducted by Thomas Fisler, James Leigh, and Charles Parker,
three graduate students in author Lloyd Valentine's course, "Business Conditions Analysis." Dividing the data into two periods, 1951–1967 and 1968–1984, these students found that the b
coefficients were nearly identical in the two cases, but a downward shift in the function was
evident. When current-dollar GNP was used as the dependent variable, their results were not
nearly so impressive, the coefficient of correlation ranging from 0.42 to 0.50.

duction. The ratio of inventory to sales for the manufacturing field as a whole and for major sectors of it, such as durable-goods manufacturing, often gives an indication of turning points in production. During the upswing of a cycle, inventories are first reduced as sales rise faster than expected and are then increased to realign them with sales. In the past, inventories have been increased too much, which led to a downturn. As sales declined, inventories became even greater in relationship to sales until substantial inventory liquidation has occurred. These changes were clearer and more pronounced in serious recessions, such as 1957–1958, than in the mild recessions of 1960–1961 or 1969–1970.

The relationship of inventories and sales during the recession of the early 1980s and the expansion of the late 1980s is shown in Figure 16-4. In early 1980, sales fell off sharply and inventories grew at a rapid pace. The ratio of inventory to sales increased throughout the first half of 1980 because of the drop in sales. The economy was able to recover only after these redundant inventories had been liquidated. When sales picked up in the latter half of the year, production was kept level to again decrease the inventory-sales ratio. As the economy started to expand in 1983, sales grew and the level of inventories declined— along with a drop in the inventory-sales ratio. Late in the 1980s, both sales and inventories increased at about the same rate, and the ratio of sales to inventories remained relatively stable. By studying such relationships of inventories to sales, it is possible to predict turning points in production. Since the leads are not uniform and the ratios give some false signals, the forecaster's judgment is still required to pinpoint changes.

An analysis of new orders and of new orders in relationship to sales and production can also be used as an indication of turning points. For example, the turning point in new orders during a recovery period is preceded by a slowdown in the rate of decrease in new orders. When new orders turn up, the turning point in production is usually only several months away.

Some economists forecast production for one to two quarters by studying patterns of new orders, unfilled orders, inventories, sales, and production in the major sectors of durable and nondurable goods production. From past relationships and typical time intervals between new orders, production, sales, and inventory levels, it is possible to forecast future production. However, such forecasting cannot be done purely mechanically, because relationships change and factors such as threatened strikes alter the business decisions made about inventories and production.

Figure 16-4   Manufacturers' Inventories and Sales

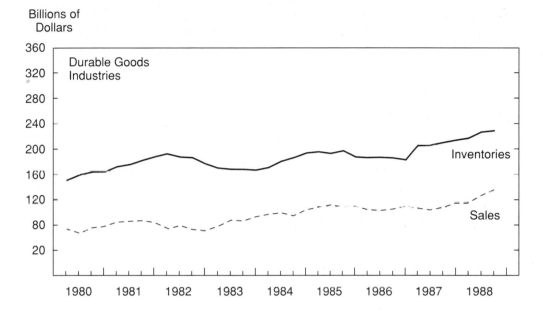

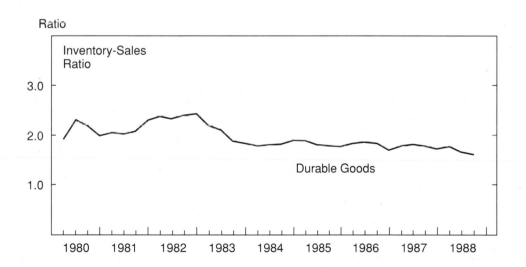

Source: *Survey of Current Business*, various issues.

SERIES ON EXPECTATIONS AND EXPENDITURE PLANS

It is often thought that the course of aggregate economic activity can be influenced by shifts in anticipation and expectations about the future. Forecasting may be improved by using anticipatory information. Surveys of expectations do not try to explain the structure of the economy or theory of demand, rather their usefulness depends on how well they predict.

One such approach to forecasting is to try to develop data on expectations of future business conditions by business executives whose decisions determine the economic outlook. The approach has been expanded to include expectations and expenditure plans for most of the major spending sectors of the economy. Dun and Bradstreet publishes a quarterly survey that is based on interviews with a sample of over 1,500 business executives regarding their expectations for their respective businesses. The executives are asked if there will be an increase, a decrease, or no change in net sales, net profits, selling prices, the level of inventories, and the number of employees, compared with the same quarter a year ago. Data are presented for all concerns and also separately for manufacturers, wholesalers, and retailers.

The National Association of Purchasing Management, Inc. (NAPM) obtains the reaction of some of its members to business conditions through a monthly survey of a committee selected to reflect both regional and industrial diversification. These members are asked to indicate whether production, new orders, commodity prices, inventories of purchased raw materials and purchased finished materials, employment, and their level of buying were higher than a month ago, lower, or the same. The questionnaire also asks for specific commodity price changes and the reasons for them, for items that are in short supply, for business changes in the member's area, and for general business factors that may affect purchasing policies. A summary and an analysis of the answers of the purchasing agents in the Survey Committee are published in the Association's bulletin.

The NAPM surveys are valuable gauges of monthly changes in business conditions, since the results are accurate and available within two weeks or less after the questionnaires are filled out. In the period since 1947, the NAPM surveys have forecast downturns several months in advance, but were not always accurate on the magnitude of changes in business.

A major problem with the NAPM and Dun and Bradstreet's surveys is that they sometimes show changes in sentiment when general business conditions do not experience a turning point. They give signals of changes when overall activity changes, but they also give false signals and, therefore, cannot be used alone to predict changes in the economy. They are, however, valuable to the forecaster because they provide a check on forecasts obtained by other methods.

Another way to use data on expectations is to get information on expenditure plans by major spending sectors in the economy. These plans are available for many of the major categories of expenditures into which GNP is divided. Surveys of consumer-buying plans were begun in 1946 by the Survey Research Center of the University of Michigan. The Center does quarterly interviews of a nationwide sample of about 2,000 families. Their answers provide information on consumer intentions to buy durable goods, including automobiles, furniture and appliances, and new houses. The Conference Board sponsors a monthly survey and publishes it in the *Conference Board Record.*

Generally, the consumer surveys have been accurate in predicting changes in expenditures, that is, downturns and upturns. They have not, however, been accurate on a regular basis in predicting the magnitude of the changes in purchases of durable goods. These surveys provide no data concerning plans for expenditures on nondurable goods and services. However, nondurable expenditure plans do not change much in the short run and, hence, may not be very helpful in predicting turning points in the economy.

Data on plans for spending by the federal government are available in the budget, which is presented by the President almost nine months before the beginning of the new fiscal year. This is generally a good guide to the direction of change in expenditures, if any, but it cannot be used without analysis and revision as an estimate of the amount of change. To date, no series exists on the expenditure plans of state and local governments. The same is true of exports and imports; but until relatively recently, the net figure, which is all that is included in GNP, was small enough that it did not need to be seriously considered. This situation has changed dramatically in the past few years, and effort could be profitably spent in developing expectations and plans series on exports and imports.

Series on expenditure plans exist for most components of gross private domestic investment. The Department of Commerce and the McGraw-Hill Book Company survey plans of business executives for expenditures on plant and equipment, which have been accurate in predicting turning points in expenditures. Series on building permits can be used to show future changes in the volume of new building.

Changes in plans for the level of inventories can be obtained from surveys performed by the NAPM and the U.S. Department of Commerce.

Thus, there are series on expenditure plans for every major sector of spending, except state and local governmental expenditures, foreign trade, and consumer expenditures on nondurables and services that have not abruptly changed direction in the past. A study of all these series can be used to judge the direction of business. When all the expenditures are moving in the same direction, as they are in the early stages of recovery, this procedure is relatively easy and effective. Later in prosperity, the expenditures of some sectors may show increases and others a leveling off or decreases; thus making it difficult—if not impossible—to judge future business from changes in direction of spending alone, which would require estimates of the magnitude of changes that are made in model building. (Chapters 17 and 18 present a technique for building a model of GNP by the expenditure approach.)

CYCLES AND TRENDS

Some attempt has been made to forecast economic activity by projecting the cycle and trend. If a regular cycle with uniform duration and amplitude existed, this would be the only procedure needed for accurate forecasting. Since such a cycle does not exist, however, this procedure cannot be used with any degree of assurance of success. Some analysts have tried to develop a cyclical pattern in GNP or industrial production by developing a multiple correlation relationship with a series of factors that they consider to be most significant in determining the course of the cycle, such as prices, interest rates, and unit labor costs. Such techniques must be viewed with skepticism, since it is possible to recreate the movement of a series, such as the GNP or industrial production, with formulas relating the past behavior of the variable to the future behavior of that same variable. The correlation method is called *autocorrelation*, and the technique based on it is called *autoregressive forecasting*.

Some forecasters have used cycles and trends to develop a general picture of the pattern of economic development for five or ten years in the future. This may be done, for example, by using a future cycle pattern based on the average duration and amplitude of postwar cycles. Such a pattern is easy to develop and can serve a useful purpose in business planning and in assessing the possible effects of cycles on plans, but it cannot be used to make forecasts. The outstanding characteristic of cycles is their variability.

ECONOMETRIC MODELS

The development of econometric models was discussed in Part 2 of this textbook in the section concerning the theory of national-income determination. Past relationships are used to determine the endogenous variables in such models from known levels of exogenous variables. The procedure by which this is done is known as *regression analysis*. In some respects, regression is similar to trend analysis; but instead of using time as one variable, other series are used as the independent variables.

In a strict sense, the changes in the dependent variable should be caused by changes in the independent variable or variables. However, such a strict causal relationship seldom, if ever, holds in economic analysis. Usually a whole series of forces are at work, even though one or two may be dominant. However, unless a relationship exists that has remained fairly stable over time and is likely to continue to do so, the use of measures of regression can lead to serious errors in prediction. The only situation in which a statistical measure of regression analysis can be reliably used in forecasting is when theoretical analysis leads to the conclusion that the changes in the variables are related.

The period used to develop a regression relationship should cover more than one complete cycle, because it is desirable to establish the validity of the relationship. Generally, the effects of price changes also should be removed by putting value series in real terms. This is sometimes essential when relating a value series with a physical volume or other nonprice series.

In developing regression relationships between time series, it is often desirable to use year-by-year changes in the series rather than the original data. The trend of many time series is so strongly upward that a high degree of relationship exists because of this factor alone. If a significant relationship exists in the year-by-year changes in each series, it is frequently more useful for prediction than the relationship between the series themselves.

The development of a regression equation is similar to the determination of the trend in that it is a curve-fitting operation. The line of relationship is usually developed in one of two ways. The line of least squares may be used just as it is for the trend. The straight-line relationship between two variables is expressed by the formula $y = a + bx$, where x is the independent variable instead of time. When used to develop the relationship among variables rather than the relationship of one variable over time, the method of least squares is called regression analysis.

Frequently, a relationship exists between a series and two or more other series. Such a multiple regression relationship should be developed mathematically, but as a first step, it may be done graphically. A regression line is developed between the dependent variable and the most important independent variable. Deviations from this line are plotted against a second independent variable and a regression line developed from these relationships. The relationships between these factors must then be expressed by the appropriate equations.

The relationship between a series and two or more series may, at times, still be best expressed by a straight line. But the relationship is often a more complex one and may require more complex mathematical formulas. It may be useful to express the factors in the form of logarithms, because certain nonlinear relationships become linear in log form.

A form of multiple regression is one in which time is one of the variables that is used in developing the relationship. If technological, population growth, or other factors have affected the relationship so as to introduce a time trend, the deviations from the first line of regression may be plotted year by year on a second chart to determine if a consistent pattern appears. This is true in the case of consumer expenditures on clothing and shoes in constant dollars that show a relationship to disposable personal income, but one that has been decreasing gradually for some years. When there is a trend in the relationship over time, a formula must be used in which time measured from a base year is introduced as a factor.

Example of an Econometric Model. As suggested above, an econometric model uses mathematics and statistics to derive and estimate relationships suggested by economic theory. As an illustration of what an econometric model might look like, consider a simplified "classical" macro-model as put forth in Chapter 7.

1. Demand for Labor. As suggested in that chapter, the real wage is a function of the labor demanded:

$$\frac{W}{P} = a + bN$$

W = the money wage $w = \dfrac{W}{P}$ = the real wage

P = the price level N = quantity of labor

By using regression analysis the coefficients a and b could be estimated.

2. Supply of Labor. The quantity of labor supplied is assumed to be a function of the real wage:

$$N = a + b\left(\frac{W}{P}\right)$$

3. Output Equation. Real output (GNP) is a function of labor input, as suggested by a production function:

$$y = a + bN$$
$$y = \text{real output}$$

4. Demand for Real Balances. Demand for real money balances is a function of real output:

$$M/P = ky$$

M = nominal money supply

k = a constant to be estimated by least squares

5. Central Bank Policy. It is assumed that the nominal money supply is exogenous; determined by central bank policy:

$M = \bar{M}$, a given as set by the central bank

The above model is a simplified description of the economy in that we have only three sectors—a labor input sector, an output production sector, and a money sector. In this model, the variables W, P, $\left(\frac{W}{P}\right)$, N, and y are endogenous, and $M = \bar{M}$ is exogenous. The parameters a, b, and k would be estimated by regression analysis.

The internal workings of the econometric model can be seen in the flow chart presented in Figure 16-5. The flow of the model is such that equilibrium in the labor market determines the real wage $w = \frac{W}{P}$, and the quantity of labor, N. Having determined N, the production equation allows for the determination of real output, y. The central bank sets policy and determines the nominal money supply $\bar{M}$. Knowing $\bar{M}$ and y, the demand for real balances determines the price level, P. The definitional identity of the real wage equaling the money wage divided by the price level, $w = \frac{W}{P}$, allows for the determination of W, since w and P were determined earlier.

Projections could be made with this econometric model by first projecting central bank policy, that is, projections for the nominal

Figure 16-5   Flow Chart for a Simple Econometric Model

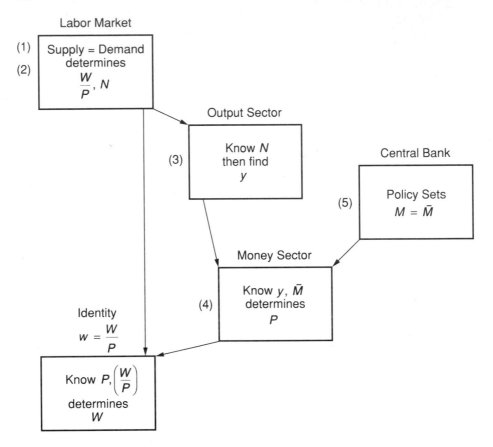

money supply in the future. Using these forecasts for $\bar{M}$, and using the estimated relations suggested by the model, forecasts for w, W, P, N, and y can be calculated. Needless to say, an econometric model describing the U.S. economy would need to involve more sectors, more equations, and thus, more variables.

Econometric Models in Practice. With the aid of computers to handle the huge amounts of data and calculations, econometric models have been used with increasing success as a basis for forecasting GNP and its major components. The Research Seminar on Quantitative Economics at the University of Michigan has been making forecasts for some time with the Klein-Goldberger model.[5] The

5. L. R. Klein and A. S. Goldberger, *An Econometric Model of the United States 1929–1952* (Amsterdam: North Holland Publishing Co., 1955).

model has been regularly revised and improved since it was first used to make forecasts in 1953. In most years, the results have been good so far as total GNP is concerned, but not as good on individual components.[6]

The Bureau of Economic Analysis of the Department of Commerce has done research and experimentation with a quarterly economic model of GNP that is based on a variant of the model developed by economist Lawrence Klein. The model is based on sixty-three equations on each of the major components of GNP and on factors such as prices, the labor force, income to the factors of production, monetary factors, taxes and transfers, and output and capacity utilization. In most years, the error in total GNP was $3 billion or less, but errors in the components were larger than in GNP, as is generally true of all forecasts. Turning points were generally forecast within one quarter plus or minus the actual turning points.[7] The model has been used by the Bureau of Economic Analysis as one of its forecasting tools since 1965. Its record has been comparable to other models, especially when the judgment of the forecasters is used along with the model rather than using the model mechanically. Recently, a large number of additional econometric models have been developed, including a number of proprietary models such as those of Chase Econometrics, Inc., Data Resources, Inc., and Wharton Econometrics.

An analysis of the forecasts of econometric models for the postwar period made under the sponsorship of the NBER concluded that they have not been able to forecast the levels of aggregate economic activity as well as some forecasts that are based on more general methods. The errors have resulted primarily from the forecasts of price movements that have often been wide of the mark. The forecasts of changes in economic activity, which exclude price movements, have been about as accurate as the better forecasts made by other methods.[8]

The NBER has continued to analyze the results of forecasts made by various methods. It has cooperated with the American Statistical Association (ASA) in conducting a quarterly survey of forecasts of ASA members who are professionally engaged in a continuing analysis of the economic outlook. An analysis of the surveys led the NBER to

6. Daniel B. Suits, "Forecasting and Analysis with an Econometric Model," *American Economic Review* (March 1962), pp. 104–132.

7. Maurice Liebenberg, Albert A. Hirsch, and Joel Popkin, "A Quarterly Econometric Model of the United States: A Progress Report," *Survey of Current Business* (May 1966), pp. 13–41, and Albert A. Hirsch, Maurice Liebenberg, and George R. Green, *The BEA Quarterly Economic Model* (Washington, D.C.: U.S. Department of Commerce 1973), pp. 1–5.

8. *Fifty-Fifth Annual Report* (New York: National Bureau of Economic Research, Inc., 1975), p. 38.

Figure 16-6   How Reliable Are Economic Forecasts?

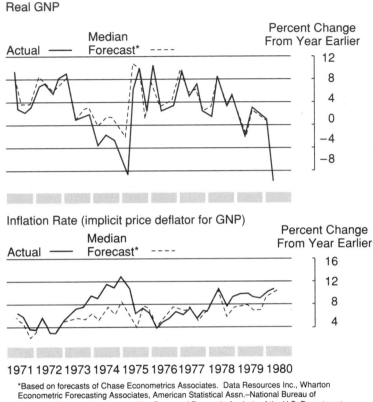

Real GNP

Inflation Rate (implicit price deflator for GNP)

1971 1972 1973 1974 1975 1976 1977 1978 1979 1980

*Based on forecasts of Chase Econometrics Associates. Data Resources Inc., Wharton Econometric Forecasting Associates, American Statistical Assn.–National Bureau of Economic Reasearch survey, and the Bureau of Economic Analysis of the U.S. Department of Commerce.

Data: Federal Reserve Bank of Boston

conclude that no systematic differences appeared between the accuracy of the forecasters who principally used the informal GNP model, an econometric model, or the leading indicator approach.[9]

For some perspective on how accurate the forecasts of some respected forecasting groups have been in the recent past, study Figure 16-6. The analysis emphasizes the point that external or exogenous shocks that cannot be foreseen are the major reasons for serious errors in the forecasts of the formal econometric models employed by these

---

9. *Fifty-First Annual Report* (New York: National Bureau of Economic Research, Inc., 1971), p. 67.

groups. In times when economic relationships remain fairly stable, the forecasting errors are relatively tolerable.[10]

The reader should not get the impression that the sole value of econometric models is to forecast future economic activity. A very important function of such models is simulating an economy's performance under conditions imposed by the operator. As an example, the simple classical econometric model described earlier could be used to ask such questions as: "What if central bank policy becomes very tight?" Or: "What would happen if wage-price controls were established?" Government policymakers need an estimate of the quantitative impact on many aspects of the economy of any particular change in the law or policy. In other words, with a good econometric model, an action can be tested in its theoretical representation before being tried out in the real world.

MONETARY FACTORS AND MODELS

Monetary factors can be used to give some indication of future changes in business conditions, because in the past, changes in the money supply have led to changes in business activity. This holds true whether the money supply is defined as demand deposits plus currency adjusted for seasonal variation, or defined in the broader concept to include time deposits. A good leading series is the M1 measure of the money supply expressed in constant 1982 dollars. Its record in postwar cycles is shown below.[11] (Like all leading indicators, this series also turned down during the period of retardation in the rate of growth in 1952 and in 1966–1967, so it must be used with care.)

Recession	Lead at Peaks (In Months)	Lead at Troughs (In Months)
1949	5	4
1953–1954	2	7
1957–1958	16	1
1960	9	8
1970	10	9
1973–1975	10	1
1980	24	6
1981–1982	9	8

10. Ronald A. Krieger, "Economists: What Can They Offer?" *The Chase Economic Observer* (January/February 1981), pp. 6–8.

11. *Business Conditions Digest* (May 1975), p. 12, (March 1982), pp. 13, 31, (June 1985), p. 31, (September 1988), p. 31.

The Federal Reserve Bank of St. Louis has developed a model of the economy based on the monetarist approach to economic analysis. The model is designed to provide information on the most likely course of development of strategic economic variables in response to monetary and fiscal actions. It is not designed to provide exact information on quarter-by-quarter changes in economic activity, but on the effect of money and monetary aggregates on spending, output, and prices. According to this model, total spending is determined by monetary and fiscal actions. Fiscal actions are defined as federal spending financed by taxes or borrowing from the public. The change in total spending is combined with potential output at full employment to provide a measure of demand pressure. Anticipated price change, which depends on past price changes, is combined with demand pressure to determine the change in the price level. The changes in total spending and in the price level can be used to find the change in output. The model also can be used to predict market interest rates and the unemployment level. The workings of this model are summarized as a flow diagram in Figure 16-7.

The change in total spending in this model is a function of two key exogenous variables. One variable is current and past changes in the money stock defined as demand deposits and currency held by the nonbank public. The other variable is current and past changes in high-employment federal expenditures defined as expenditures on goods and services plus transfer payments adjusted to remove the influence of variations in economic activity on unemployment benefit payments. The period from 1960 to 1984 has been used to develop the relationships. The pattern of coefficients of relationship for this period indicates a large and rapid influence of monetary actions on total spending, when compared with that of fiscal actions.

The St. Louis model succeeded in providing good indications of the changes in real product, prices, unemployment, and interest rates during the recession period of 1969–1970 and the recovery period of 1971. It did not work well in the period before the 1973 recession primarily because price controls obscured the effect of monetary factors. For the period 1975–1984, the model had a relative degree of success in following actual changes in real output and inflation. It nevertheless should be included in the forecaster's kit and used with other tools.

JUDGMENT MODELS

At this stage of knowledge of the economy, it is impossible to use an econometric model to develop a completely accurate forecast.

Figure 16-7   A Monetarist Model of the Economy

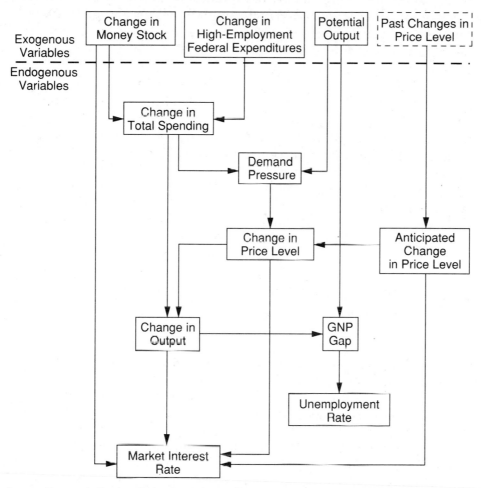

Source: *Economic Review*, Federal Reserve Bank of St. Louis (April 1970), p. 10, (October 1986), p. 49.

Therefore, models are also built that use the judgment of the forecaster to determine the most likely figure for each sector in the model. Such models have been developed primarily for GNP and industrial production. A GNP model is generally developed by the expenditure approach. All available data are gathered on each major sector of GNP, including expenditure plans, analysis of supply and demand factors using formulas based on past experience, monetary factors, and leading series. A preliminary figure is developed for each spending sector based on the best judgment of the forecaster. These figures are then checked for consistency based on past relationships among them and, if necessary, revised. A step-by-step approach to such model building to forecast GNP by the expenditure approach is presented in the next two chapters.

At times, a judgment model of GNP is developed from the income or receipt-of-money-flow approach. Although this approach is a more complex procedure and involves many more estimates, it adds several valuable items of information. First, it provides forecasts of income payments for wages, interest, rent, and profits. Because the federal government's major sources of revenue are personal and corporate income taxes, the Treasury Department needs the information this approach provides when it forecasts budget receipts for the year. In addition, a judgment model of GNP developed from this approach is helpful as a cross-check on a model developed from the expenditure approach.

Models also are developed from the Federal Reserve Board Index of Industrial Production. The divisions of the index itself can be used to build up a model. They are at times reclassified into groups that have similar factors affecting them. One such classification uses the following groups:

Consumer perishable goods	Capital goods
Consumer semidurable goods	Fuels
Consumer durable goods	Materials and supplies
Construction materials	

A judgment figure is developed for each sector using techniques similar to those used to build up a GNP model by the expenditure approach. When adequate productive capacity exists, the major emphasis is put on demand factors.

An alternative approach, which is often used at the same time as an analysis of changing demand factors, is a study of new orders and production in each sector of the economy into which the model is divided. Time lags that occur between changes in new orders and production are studied for a period covering several of the most recent cycles. In some cases, it is easier to get data on new orders and on sales or expenditures than it is on production. Changes in new orders can then be used to predict changes in production based on past relationships. A study must continually be made of any past relationships that have tendencies to change.

QUESTIONS

1. Describe and evaluate the use of a listing of favorable and unfavorable factors as a method of forecasting.
2. How may the consensus of qualified observers be used in forecasting?
3. Describe how the leads and lags in forecasting can be used.
4. Evaluate the recent record of the NBER's statistical indicators.
5. What is a diffusion index? How may it be used in forecasting?
6. How are new orders, inventory, production, and sales series used in forecasting?
7. How may expectations about future business conditions be used in forecasting?
8. Describe and evaluate the use of series on spending plans as a method of forecasting.
9. Of what value is a projection of cycles and trends in forecasting and in business planning generally?
10. What is the record of econometric models as forecasting devices?
11. Discuss the use of monetary factors as a means of forecasting income.
12. Describe the St. Louis model for forecasting total spending, prices, and output.
13. Using the St. Louis model, give three "what if" questions that could be approached with this model.
14. What is a judgment model? How is it developed?

READINGS

Bernstein, Peter L., and Theodore H. Silbert. "Are Economic Forecasters Worth Listening To?" *Harvard Business Review* (September–October 1984).

Carlson, Keith M. "A Monetarist Model for Economic Stabilization: Review and Update." *Review*, Federal Reserve Bank of St. Louis (October 1986), pp. 18–28.

———, and Leonall C. Anderson. "A Monetarist Model for Economic Stabilization." *Economic Review*, Federal Reserve Bank of St. Louis (April 1970), pp. 7–25.

Conference Board, Inc. *Business Outlook*, annually.

Curtin, Richard T. "The Crash and the Consumer." *Economic Outlook USA* (Winter 1987–88), pp. 20–23.

"Diffusion Indexes and Economic Activity." *Economic Review*, Federal Reserve Bank of Cleveland (January 1971), pp. 3–17.

Economic Outlook USA. Ann Arbor, MI: Survey Research Center, quarterly.

Eggert, Robert J. "Consensus Forecasts of Financial Institutions." *The Journal of Business Forecasting: Methods and Systems*. Flushing, NY, quarterly.

————. *Blue Chip Economic Indicators*. Alexandria, VA, monthly.

Ellis, Dennis F. "U.S. Macroforecasts." *Quarterly Domestic & Global Forecasts of Key Economic Indicators*. Flushing, NY, quarterly.

Granger, Clive W.J., and Paul Newbold. *Forecasting Economic Time Series*, 2d ed. New York: Academic Press, 1986.

Hirsch, Albert A., Maurice Liebenberg, and George R. Green. *The BEA Quarterly Economic Model*. Washington, D.C.: U.S. Department of Commerce, 1973.

Katona, George. *Psychological Economics*. New York: Elsevier, 1975.

Klein, Lawrence R., and Richard M. Young. *An Introduction to Econometric Forecasting and Forecasting Models*. Lexington, MA: Lexington Books, 1980.

McLaughlin, Robert L. *Forecasting Techniques for Decision Making*. Cheshire, CT: Micrometrics, Inc., 1984.

Newbold, Paul, and Theodore Bos. *Introductory Business Forecasting*. Cincinnati: South-Western Publishing Co., 1990.

Oppenlander, Karl Heinrich, and Ganter Poser, eds. *Leading Indicators and Business Cycle Surveys*. New York: St. Martin's Press, 1984.

Pindyck, Robert S., and Daniel L. Rubinfeld. *Econometric Models and Economic Forecasts*, 2d ed. New York: McGraw-Hill Book Co., 1981.

"A Psychological Approach to Understanding the Economy: A Survey of Consumer Attitudes." *The Research News*, The University of Michigan (August-September 1985), pp. 14–19.

U.S. Department of Commerce. *Business Conditions Digest*, monthly.

"What Businessmen Expect." *Dun's*, quarterly.

Also see the "Business Roundup" section of *Fortune* and the "Business Situation" section of the *Survey of Current Business* for current analyses of inventories, sales, and new orders.

SHORT-RUN FORECASTING OF GNP BY BUILDING AN EXPENDITURE MODEL

This chapter will consider the procedures involved in forecasting GNP by estimating governmental purchases of goods and services, personal consumption expenditures, and net exports of goods and services. Chapter 18 will consider the procedures for forecasting gross private domestic investment and for checking and refining the overall forecast.

In forecasting GNP, it is necessary to bear in mind the major factors that cause shifts in economic activity. Money flows through the economy in a circular fashion, since expenditures of one group are income for another. Changes in economic activity occur because individuals, businesses, private institutions, and governmental units change the amount of their spending or change the relationship of such spending to the amount of income received. Changes may also occur because the spending units decide to spend their income in a pattern different from that in which goods are being produced, and as a result, demand exceeds supply in some fields and is less than supply in others. Since labor and capital are not completely mobile, and prices are not everywhere flexible, these changes lead to shifts in the level of economic activity.

The circular flow of economic activity may appear to create a problem in forecasting, since there is no clear-cut starting or stopping point. However, since time elapses between various economic activities, such as an increase in production owing to an increase in sales with consumers receiving income from such production and the resultant additional increase in sales, it is possible to break into the process at any point and to determine what is likely to happen during a future period. As long as the proper time relationships between the variables are considered, it makes little difference at what point in the economic cycle forecasting is begun.

Forecasts of GNP for a year ahead can be made by estimating expenditures by consumers, business, government, and foreigners. Such forecasts must include factors resulting from the trend and the business cycle. Seasonal variations do not affect the annual forecasts, and quarterly forecasts are usually made at seasonally adjusted annual rates. Therefore, the effect of the seasonal variations can be ignored in a GNP forecast.

Before this analysis is begun, the general state of the economy and the direction of economic activity should be studied. The analyst also should check the relationship of economic activity to the economy's capacity to produce goods and services by comparing the current level of activity with an estimate of full employment GNP.[1] It is also desirable to check unemployment levels and the indexes of manufacturing capacity utilization to determine if there is any slack in the economy. The trend of prices in the recent past also should be studied, along with trends in the growth of the money supply and the full employment deficit or surplus in the federal government's budget, to become familiar with price trends and price pressures.

The factors involved in estimating governmental purchases of goods and services for the next year will be analyzed first, because they are, in part, based on decisions that are not related to the circular flow of economic activity. The level of these items, nevertheless, materially affects general business activity.

GOVERNMENTAL PURCHASES OF GOODS AND SERVICES

Since 1929, governmental purchases of goods and services have fluctuated widely. However, since, to a large extent, they are not dependent upon the general level of business activity, and since the democratic process requires a great deal of time, especially when money is being appropriated, it is possible to forecast governmental expenditures with a reasonable degree of accuracy for a year ahead. Attention will first be directed to federal expenditures and then to state and local governmental expenditures.

Federal Governmental Purchases of Goods and Services

The level of governmental purchases of goods and services can be forecast by analyzing the budget of the federal government and political and international factors in the current and future situation. The

---

1. Refer to Chapter 15 for procedures in estimating full employment GNP.

U.S. government uses a fiscal year that runs from October 1 to September 30. The fiscal year is designated by the number of the calendar year in which it ends; thus, fiscal 1989 ran from October 1, 1988, to September 30, 1989.

The President must submit a budget to Congress in January of each year. The budget as submitted is in great detail and involves a large amount of work by the U.S. Office of Management and Budget (OMB). The salient features of the budget are contained in a pamphlet called *Budget in Brief*, which is available as soon as the budget is transmitted to Congress. Some aspects of the budget are analyzed in a companion volume to the budget entitled *Special Analyses Budget of the U.S. Government*. The economic implications of the budget are analyzed a few days later in the *Economic Report of the President*. The budget and its economic implications are also analyzed in the February issue of the *Survey of Current Business*, and budget progress is periodically reviewed in later issues.

The federal budget process was significantly revised by the Congressional Budget Act of 1974, which set up new congressional budget procedures. The early stages are still the same: calling for the President to submit a budget in January, based on budgets proposed by the various agencies; reviewed in detail by the OMB; and modified to conform to overall outlay and receipt levels considered appropriate by the President. The Budget Act sets up new House and Senate Budget Committees and requires them to receive reports on individual budget requests by the various agencies from congressional committees. They also receive a fiscal-policy report by April 1 from the Congressional Budget Office. By May 15, Congress must adopt a concurrent resolution that sets budget targets. Congress then works on bills providing budget authority and, on September 15, passes a second concurrent resolution on budget ceilings. By September 25, Congress must reconcile appropriations to conform to the second concurrent resolution ceilings.[2]

Budget authority is voted by Congress; this total, however, is different from outlays for the year, because the budget authority for major projects covers the full cost when a project is started, even though funds may be spent over several years. This is also true for many loan, guarantee, and insurance programs, as well as for some trust funds that are used, as needed, over a period of years. New authority is therefore

---

2. This step has been eliminated in recent years, so the first budget resolution holds.

divided into outlays for the current year and funds to be spent in future years. Part of the unspent authority from prior years also will be spent in the current year. The Office of Management and Budget (OMB) provides estimates of the amount to be spent in the current year from new and unspent obligational authority.

Types of Budget Data. In working with the contribution of the federal government to overall economic activity, three sets of budget figures must be distinguished. These are the unified budget, the national income accounts budget, and the full employment budget.

The *unified budget* is the government's financial operating plan. It includes total spending, lending, and financing activities.

The *national income accounts budget* is more useful than the unified budget in making economic forecasts, since it is consistent with the general national income and product account framework. Financial transactions and lending activity are excluded, since they make no direct contribution to economic activity. In the national income accounts budget, governmental receipts are generally recorded on an accrual basis, that is, when the tax liability is incurred, except for personal income taxes, which are recorded when payment is received. On the expenditure side, most purchases of goods and services are recorded when delivery is made, but other expenditures, including transfer payments, are recorded on a cash basis. Although in the unified budget all receipts and expenditures are recorded on a cash basis, it is planned for the future to put them on an accrual basis.

The *full employment* (or high employment) *budget* is the budget as it would be if the economy were operating at an assumed level of full employment, generally considered to be a level based on a 5-percent unemployment rate. The main difference between the national income budget and the full employment budget is on the revenue side, since in the full employment budget, revenues are estimated on the basis of GNP at full employment. The only difference on the expenditure side is for unemployment compensation, which is estimated on the full employment basis.

Forecasting Governmental Purchases of Goods and Services. The figures in the unified budget are not in the same form as in the national income accounts, owing to such items as different handling of geographic coverage, netting differences in financial transactions, and timing differences. National income account figures are also on a calendar-year basis. The *Survey of Current Business* usually shows such relationships in its February issue. Table 17-1 shows such relationships for fiscal years 1987, 1988, and 1989.

Table 17-1

Relation of Federal Government Expenditures in the National Income and
Product Accounts to the Unified Budget
(Billions of Dollars)

| | Fiscal Year | | |
	1987	1988	1989
Unified budget outlays	1,004.6	1,055.9	1,094.2
Less: Coverage differences:			
Geographic	5.5	5.7	6.0
Other	−1.4	0.1	−0.4
Financial transactions:			
Net lending	10.4	10.3	8.6
Other	−4.0	−0.9	−1.4
Net purchases of land:			
Outer Continental Shelf	−1.6	−0.7	−1.2
Other	0.2	0.2	−3.1
Plus: Netting differences:			
Contributions to government			
employees retirement funds	35.5	38.9	41.5
Other	13.7	16.4	18.4
Timing differences:			
National defense purchases	7.4	3.0	−0.5
Other	2.9	−1.7	1.0
Miscellaneous	0.2	0.1	0.0
Equals: Federal governmental			
** expenditures, national**			
** income, and product**			
** accounts**	1,055.1	1,098.1	1,145.9

Source: *Survey of Current Business* (February 1988), p. 21.

The forecast of governmental purchases of goods and services
should begin with an analysis of the budget for the remainder of the
current fiscal year and for the next fiscal year. The budget review can
be used to get the final figures for the current fiscal year. As early as
the first part of December, the size of the budget to be proposed to Con-

gress is usually reported in the press. When the budget is available, it cannot be taken as presented as a forecast of what will happen, because Congress is unlikely to concur with all items, and because there is some bias in the budgetary process itself. Expenses of items included in the purchase of goods and services are usually somewhat overestimated, especially on new programs. In the postwar period, final expenditures have usually been within 10 percent of the President's final budget and, in most years, within 5 percent. More accurate estimates are possible if based on an analysis of the budget along with an analysis of the current situation.

One factor that should be considered is an analysis of appropriations for new programs or agencies. When a new agency is set up or appropriations are made for a new program, in the early stages, expenditures are often below the budget. This is due to such factors as overestimating the speed with which a new program can be set up, delays in getting the proper employees, delays in getting equipment, and the like.

To forecast the appropriate figure for governmental purchases of goods and services, it is necessary to adjust budget figures on the basis of an analysis of the major items of equipment to be produced, the overall military situation, and the use of judgment. It is possible to use data on new obligational authority as a lead series to gauge the future trend of expenditures.

Two members of the staff of the Board of Governors of the Federal Reserve System, Harvey Galper and Edward Gramlich, developed models using regression techniques for forecasting defense spending. They estimated the lag between awards and expenditures so as to show variation of the lag in response to measures of supply bottlenecks, demand urgency, and the mix between short-lag and long-lag items. Supply bottlenecks are measured by the Federal Reserve index of the capacity utilization rate, and demand urgency is measured by the rate of growth or decline of the armed forces. This model has had a good measure of success in predicting spending on equipment and appears to be a promising aid in short-run forecasting in this field.

In addition to considering the effects on spending of new programs or agencies and of purchases of major items of equipment, requests for changes in governmental expenditures should be considered carefully, in light of the present and prospective political and international situation. Adjustments should be made in the budgeted figures for items the analyst feels Congress will raise or cut, especially when the analyst believes Congress will not follow the budget recommendations for military spending or for pay rates of federal government employees.

Therefore, the budget expenditure figure as presented should be adjusted for three types of factors:

1. Bias in estimates of spending when new programs are introduced.
2. Other cases in which spending on purchases of major items may not be as great as estimated by the OMB.
3. Estimates of changes Congress will make in the President's budget.

State and Local Governmental Purchases of Goods and Services

If data and resources were available, it would be possible to forecast state and local government expenditures in the same way as federal government expenditures. However, there are well over 100,000 such governmental units; many do not publish budget figures, and others have little classification of items in their budgets. Since 100 of the largest spending units account for about half of all spending at the state and local level, an analysis of their budgets can be made to get some idea of what is happening. This may be supplemented by analyzing a sample of the budgets of smaller spending units.

The most generally used approach in recent years has been to extend the trend of the last several years into the future for one year. This trend line may be modified if recent elections and political trends have shown a tendency to either defeat or pass tax increases, new bond issues, and so on. This procedure is likely to be reasonably accurate for some years to come.

State and local government expenditures are showing up in some econometric models using per capita income, school populations, and per capita federal grants-in-aid as independent variables. Until some research organization develops figures on state and local government expenditure plans, the average analyst must rely on a projection of recent trends that, when necessary, are modified by an analysis of qualitative factors.

PERSONAL CONSUMPTION EXPENDITURES

The forecast of the major sectors of GNP also includes forecasting personal consumption expenditures. Estimates of consumer expenditures can be made by collecting recent expenditure data and analyzing how they will be affected by foreseeable changes in current conditions. The analysis can be done for all individual categories that form the twelve major subdivisions of consumer expenditures used in national income accounting, but it becomes a formidable undertaking. A common practice is to develop separate forecasts for expenditures on durable goods, nondurable goods, and services.

Consumer Durable Goods

The surveys of consumer buying intentions discussed in Chapter 16 are helpful in forecasting expenditures on durable goods, since they have generally gauged accurately the changes in the direction of consumer expenditures. Studies have been made to determine which factors cause consumer purchases to vary from intentions.

Some analysts calculate a normal volume of automobile sales by figuring a total of expansion demand and replacement demand. Expansion demand can be calculated from the trend in the number of cars in use over the last several years. The trend must be modified to account for significant changes in the number of households and the number of households adding a second and third car. Replacement demand can be calculated from the trend in automobile scrappage for five or more years in the past.

This procedure, however, will not in itself give an accurate year-by-year picture of automobile demand, although it does give a fairly good picture of average demand over a period of years. Replacement in any one year is determined, to a large extent, by changes in income and psychological factors. When more new cars are purchased, more used cars are available, thus depressing prices on the used-car market, which drops the value of older used cars to the point where selling them as scrap is the most profitable course. Thus, years of high car sales are also years of high scrappage.

In developing forecasts of new car sales, the sales picture of the last few years should be analyzed, especially in relation to long-run demand. The effect of probable changes in income must then be considered. The Department of Commerce has found that, on the average, an increase of 1 percent in real disposable income has been associated with a rise of 2.5 percent in automobile sales. Prices of automobiles must be considered, since a change in auto prices, in comparison with general consumer prices, has led to a greater percentage of change in car sales.

Sales figures must also be adjusted for psychological factors. Major changes in new models have a stimulating effect on sales. The extent, of course, depends on consumer acceptance. The general attitude of optimism or pessimism on the part of consumers also has an effect, and in any model year, car manufacturers can push sales and get dealers to move cars as was done in 1955, in 1973–1974, and in 1985. For the next year or two, this may reduce sales below long-term levels.

Some of these ideas about forecasting sales of durable goods, especially autos, can be summarized in what is called a "stock adjustment" model. That is, there may be certain kinds of equations that may be useful in estimating, by regression analysis, demand for durable goods, such as automobiles. The rationale for the stock adjustment model follows. It is assumed that there is some stock of goods that is desired by consumers. This desired amount depends upon price and income. That is,

(1)
$$X_{Dt} = a + by_t + cP_t$$

where

$$
\begin{aligned}
X_{Dt} &= \text{ desired stock at period } t \\
y_t &= \text{ real income at period } t \\
P_t &= \text{ relative price at period } t.
\end{aligned}
$$

A second assumption of the model is that changes in the actual stock are some proportion of the difference in the desired stock and the actual stock. This is expressed in the following equation:

(2)
$$X_t - X_{t-1} = K(X_{Dt} - X_{t-1})$$

where

$$
\begin{aligned}
X_t &= \text{ actual stock in period } t \\
X_{t-1} &= \text{ actual stock period in } t-1 \\
K &= \text{ constant adjustment coefficient.}
\end{aligned}
$$

Using the first equation and substituting in for X_{Dt} in the second equation, we find (after combining terms):

$$X_t = aK + bKy_t + cKP_t + (1 - K)X_{t-1}.$$

The stock of goods is a function of real income, relative price, and the stock last period. The parameters a, b, c, and K can be estimated by regression analysis. The stock adjustment model has been used to estimate demand for automobiles and housing.[3] Projections for y and P,

---

3. Gregory C. Chow, "Statistical Demand Functions for Automobiles and Their Use in Forecasting," pp.149–178, and Richard F. Muth, "The Demand for Non-Farm Housing," pp. 29–98; both in *The Demand for Durable Goods*, Arnold C. Harberger (ed.) (Chicago: University of Chicago Press, 1960).

and knowledge of X this period would allow one to forecast X next period.

The sales of other durables depend, to a large degree, on the trend in the number of households and disposable income and on changes in disposable income. Thus, expected income changes are a major factor in forecasting changes in demand and sales. Years of major increases in home building are also likely to show more than normal increases in sales of home furnishings and appliances. In determining sales levels, increases in prices resulting from cost increases must be considered.

In making a forecast of demand for all consumer durables, the financial position of consumers must be considered. Years in which consumer debt has increased markedly are followed by years of a smaller increase as consumers get into a more liquid position. The total of consumer expenditures on durables and personal saving that includes net repayments on consumer credit is more stable than either series alone. Thus, when consumers go into debt at an unusually rapid rate, a slowdown in new debt as well as durable goods sales is to be expected as consumers plan their finances. This factor must be considered in making the forecasts of automobile and other consumer durable goods sales.

The general availability of credit also has an effect on the purchase of durable goods. The staff of the Federal Reserve has developed a model for projecting expenditures on automobiles and parts and also one for other durables, both of which use a vector of interest rates, income, and the price of durables relative to other consumer goods and service prices as demand factors.

Nondurable Goods and Services

Forecasts of demand for nondurable goods and services are the easiest to make. The volume of these purchases is little affected by small changes in income. Even in years of severe depression, the effect is negligible, until economic activity has been declining for a year or more. Such sales have increased in the postwar period in line with changes in real income, population, and the price level. These factors can be analyzed separately, or the trend of several years in the past can be projected. When this is done, allowance must be made for expected price changes different from the average for the last few years. Some upward adjustment also is desirable because of a recent above-average increase in expenditures on household operation. Above average expenditures

Table 17-2

Expenditures on Nondurable Goods and Services in Relationship to
Disposable Personal Income, 1968–1988
(Billions of Dollars)

Year	Disposable Personal Income	Nondurable Goods Spending	Services Spending	Total Spending	Percentage of Income
1968	609.6	235.0	236.4	471.4	77.3
1969	656.7	252.2	259.4	511.6	77.9
1970	715.6	270.3	284.0	554.3	77.5
1971	776.8	283.3	310.7	594.4	76.5
1972	839.6	305.1	341.3	646.4	77.0
1973	949.8	339.6	373.0	712.6	75.0
1974	1,038.4	380.9	411.9	792.8	76.3
1975	1,142.8	416.2	461.2	877.4	76.8
1976	1,252.6	452.0	515.9	967.9	77.3
1977	1,379.3	490.4	582.3	1,072.7	77.7
1978	1,551.2	541.8	656.1	1,197.9	77.2
1979	1,729.3	613.2	734.6	1,347.8	77.9
1980	1,918.0	681.4	831.9	1,513.3	78.9
1981	2,127.6	740.6	934.7	1,675.3	78.7
1982	2,261.4	771.0	1,027.0	1,798.0	79.5
1983	2,428.1	816.7	1,128.7	1,945.4	80.1
1984	2,668.6	867.3	1,277.8	2,145.1	80.4
1985	2,838.7	911.2	1,345.6	2,256.8	79.5
1986	3,013.3	942.0	1,449.5	2,391.5	79.4
1987	3,205.9	998.1	1,591.7	2,589.8	80.7
1988	3,477.8	1,052.3	1,727.6	2,779.9	79.9

Source: *Business Conditions Digest.*

are likely to continue in years when high levels of residential building
are maintained.

Since expenditures on nondurable goods and services do not fluctuate unduly but move in relationship to changes in total economic
activity, they can also be forecast on the basis of other factors for which
forecasts are available. Expenditures on nondurable goods and services bear a more or less linear relationship to disposable personal income, but one that has a declining trend. The relationship since 1968
may be seen in Table 17-2. This relationship can be projected for the
year being forecast from annual trends and quarterly figures for the last
seven or eight quarters.

Table 17-3

Relationship of Gross National Product, Personal Income, and Disposable
Personal Income, 1968–1988
(Billions of Dollars)

Year	GNP	PI	PI/GNP	DPI	DPI/PI
1968	892.7	707.2	79.2	609.6	86.2
1969	967.9	772.9	80.2	656.7	85.0
1970	1,015.5	831.8	81.9	715.6	86.0
1971	1,102.7	899.0	81.5	776.8	86.4
1972	1,212.8	981.6	80.9	839.6	85.5
1973	1,359.2	1,101.7	81.0	949.8	86.2
1974	1,472.8	1,210.1	82.2	1,038.4	85.8
1975	1,598.8	1,313.4	82.1	1,252.6	86.3
1976	1,782.8	1,451.4	81.4	1,252.6	86.3
1977	1,990.5	1,607.5	80.8	1,379.3	85.8
1978	2,249.7	1,812.4	80.0	1,551.2	85.6
1979	2,508.2	2,034.0	81.1	1,729.3	85.0
1980	2,732.0	2,258.5	82.7	1,918.0	84.9
1981	3,052.6	2,520.9	82.6	2,127.6	84.4
1982	3,116.0	2,670.8	85.7	2,261.4	84.7
1983	3,405.7	2,838.6	83.3	2,428.1	85.5
1984	3,772.2	3,108.7	82.4	2,668.6	85.8
1985	4,014.9	3,325.3	82.8	2,838.7	85.4
1986	4,231.6	3,526.2	83.3	3,013.3	85.5
1987	4,526.3	3,777.6	83.5	3,205.9	84.9
1988	4,880.6	4,064.5	83.3	3,477.8	85.6

Source: *Business Conditions Digest.*

Disposable personal income, in turn, has a predictable relationship
to personal income. Since 1968, it has fluctuated between 84.0 and
87.0 percent of personal income, as can be seen from Table 17-3. Although there is some evidence of a declining trend, the rate of decline
is not rapid. Figures for the last several years and quarterly figures for
the past seven or eight quarters can be used to project the relationship
for the next year.

Personal income also has a predictable relationship to GNP. As can
be seen from Table 17-3, the median figure is approximately 82 percent, which can be used in a forecast, although greater accuracy is possible if cyclical deviations are considered. In a period of moderate expansion, the figure will generally be in the 79- to 80-percent range. In

the recession period of 1973–1975, it was above 82 percent in 1974, 1975, and 1980. Lately, the ratio has been above 83 percent. Past figures and a general indication of the state of the economy in the forecast year can be used to derive a percentage figure for that year.

These relationships can be used to relate expenditures on non-durables and services to GNP as follows:

$$\frac{PI}{GNP} = x \qquad \frac{DPI}{PI} = y \qquad \frac{C_{NS}}{DPI} = z$$

Then $C_{NS} = xyzGNP$

And $GNP = G + I + F + C_D + xyzGNP$

or $GNP - xyzGNP = G + I + F + CD$

or $GNP = \dfrac{G + I + F + CD}{(1 - xyz)}$

where

GNP	=	Gross national product
PI	=	Personal income
DPI	=	Disposable personal income
G	=	Government expenditures on goods and services
I	=	Gross private domestic investment
F	=	Net export of goods and services
C_D	=	Consumer expenditures on durables
C_{NS}	=	Consumer expenditures on nondurable goods and services

x, y, and z are relationships projected for the forecast year.

All the factors are available to find GNP in the equation above. And GNP times xyz is equal to the forecast for expenditures on nondurable goods and services.

NET EXPORTS OF GOODS AND SERVICES

Net exports of goods and services traditionally have been a relatively small item in the GNP. Even sizable errors in forecasting net exports would have a negligible effect on the total GNP forecast. Throughout the post-World War II period the net export figure for the United States had generally been positive, but never more than 1.7 percent of GNP. In early 1984, the net export figure turned negative, reaching its lowest point in the fourth quarter of 1987 at −2.7 percent of GNP. None of this is meant to denigrate the importance of correctly forecasting the change in net exports. The change in net exports is sometimes a significant percentage of the change in GNP and, in that respect, is similar to the change in business inventories.

There are many reasons to forecast the behavior of net exports other than to estimate the future course of the aggregate economy. International trade activity can significantly impact the financial system, the balance of payments, interest rates, the price level and relative prices, exchange rates, employment and output in diverse industries, and so on. For many purposes, accuracy in forecasting aggregate exports and aggregate imports is of greater concern than is the accuracy of the forecast of the difference between them. In any case, net exports are usually forecast by studying imports and exports individually.

Imports

The Department of Commerce breaks down import and export categories into great detail. It regularly publishes data in the *Survey of Current Business* on the value of imports and exports by geographic regions, by leading countries, and by commodity groups and principal commodities.

The volume of merchandise and service imports is related to the volume of domestic business activity. It is affected by the level of overall economic activity in the United States, since raw materials and materials used in production are imported as well as are finished goods. The volume of merchandise and service imports also is affected by the relative prices to buyers of domestic and imported goods. In the period from 1968 to 1973, imports generally fluctuated between 5.0 and 7.4 percent of GNP. Since 1973, the percentage has risen steadily, until 1987, when it was 12.5 percent. Relationships since 1968 are shown in Table 17-4.

In general, imports have grown somewhat more rapidly than GNP in periods of rapid growth. For example, in the years after 1965, inflation in the United States made imports more desirable from a price standpoint. Domestic prices rose more rapidly during the Vietnam War than prices in many foreign countries, and thus, the dollar became overvalued. Costs were increasing in many fields on a long-run basis, because labor in some fields in the United States was getting wage increases at a faster rate than increases in productivity. Consumer preferences in many fields had shifted to foreign-made goods. During the

Table 17-4

The Relationship of Merchandise and Service Imports to GNP, 1968–1988
(Billions of Dollars)

Year	GNP	Merchandise and Service Imports	Percentage of Imports to GNP
1968	892.7	48.7	5.0
1969	963.9	54.0	5.6
1970	1,015.5	59.9	5.9
1971	1,102.7	66.4	6.0
1972	1,212.8	79.2	6.5
1973	1,359.3	100.0	7.4
1974	1,472.8	137.3	9.3
1975	1,598.8	132.7	8.3
1976	1,782.8	162.1	9.1
1977	1,990.5	193.8	9.7
1978	2,249.7	229.9	10.2
1979	2,508.2	281.6	11.2
1980	2,732.0	330.0	12.1
1981	3,052.6	362.2	11.9
1982	3,116.0	349.3	11.3
1983	3,405.7	371.3	10.9
1984	3,772.2	455.7	12.1
1985	4,014.9	460.7	11.5
1986	4,231.6	498.5	11.8
1987	4,524.3	565.3	12.5
1988	4,880.6	621.3	12.7

Source: *Business Conditions Digest.*

early 1980s, when inflation in the United States declined relative to that in the trading-partner countries, the percentage of imports to GNP declined. This occurred in spite of the general impression that the U.S. dollar was seriously overvalued in foreign markets. In 1985, the value of the dollar started a long decline, and the percentage of imports to GNP slightly dropped. In 1987, as the value of the dollar leveled off, imports relative to GNP slightly grew.

A forecast of merchandise imports should begin with an analysis of trends of imports to GNP. Modification of recent figures should be based on the expected growth in GNP and on the relative price trends of domestic and imported goods. Other qualitative factors, such as overstocking in some fields, which may lead to price cuts and, thus, tend to lower foreign purchases, should also be considered.

In peacetime, governmental purchases of items for military establishments and troops abroad do not change rapidly. Such purchases can be forecast from the past trend and modified by expected changes in the number of troops abroad. Some attention should also be given to pressure by Congress and U.S. manufacturers to supply troops and military establishments abroad with more American goods, since this may cut direct expenditures.

Income from foreign investments in the United States can be forecast by projecting the trend. Any factors that might lead to significant short-run changes in foreign investment, as well as significant changes in the trend of dividend rates, should be considered.

Payments for services, except for tourist expenditures, are largely related to the import of merchandise and can be forecast by applying to them the same percentage by which merchandise imports are expected to change. Tourist expenditures should be handled separately and can be forecast by projecting the trend of the past several years. This trend should be modified if economic conditions are expected to be materially better or worse, since personal expenditures on travel are made from discretionary income and are easy to defer.

Exports

Merchandise exports depend on business conditions in foreign countries and, to a large degree, fluctuate in relationship to the industrial production in such countries. To analyze demand factors in every country is an almost impossible task; therefore, analysis generally is restricted to Canada, France, Italy, Japan, the United Kingdom, and West Germany.

Prospective changes in foreign production are used as a basis for projecting changes in export purchases. Past relationships must be modified, if relative prices are expected to change materially. *Business Conditions Digest* publishes monthly charts on industrial production and consumer prices in each of these countries or groups of countries. Some analysts study exports by commodity groups and their trends and use projections on a commodity-group basis to check forecasts made on an area basis. In recent years, exports of agricultural products have been large and must be analyzed separately to get a good picture of the projected level of exports. Transfers under military agency sales can be forecast by projecting the trend, which should be modified if military aid programs are likely to change in the coming year. Legislative and budgetary action in Congress can be used as a guide to such potential changes.

Receipts of income from U.S. investments abroad can be forecast by projecting the trend modified by significant business changes expected in the next year. Foreign dividend policies are more erratic than those in the United States, so a check of business trends is more important on the export side than it is on the import side. Services can be forecast in a manner similar to imports.

Econometric forecasting models that incorporate exports and imports have appeared in recent years. A classic article in this category is one written by H. S. Houthakker and Stephen Magee in which imports and exports are both made functions of income and relative prices.[4] Estimates of the responsiveness (that is, elasticities) of exports and imports to changes in income and prices are made for fourteen important trading nations. For example, the equations for the United States state that a 1-percent increase in income is associated with a 1.5-percent increase in imports, and an increase of 1 percent in the price of foreign-traded goods and services relative to U.S. prices is associated with a 0.5-percent decline in U.S. imports.

Exports in the Houthakker-Magee study also depend on incomes and relative prices, but in this case, income is a weighted index of the GNPs of twenty-six importing countries, and the relevant relative price is an index of this country's export prices divided by an index of the export prices of twenty-six other exporting countries. The export equation for the United States yields elasticities of exports with respect to income of 0.99, which means that a 1-percent increase in the incomes of other nations results in approximately a 1-percent increase in U.S. exports. The elasticity of U.S. exports with respect to relative export prices is -1.51, meaning that if U.S. export prices rise by 1 percent, relative to other exporters' prices, U.S. exports will fall about 1.5 percent.

Forecasting a nation's exports is analogous to forecasting a firm's sales or share of market, since in the international realm, a country is one of many competing countries, just as in the business world, a firm is one of many competing firms.

---

4. H. S. Houthakker and Stephen P. Magee, "Income and Price Elasticities in World Trade," *The Review of Economics and Statistics* (May 1960).

QUESTIONS

1. Describe the relationship between the circular flow of economic activity and forecasting.
2. Describe the preliminary analysis that should be made before beginning to build a judgment model of GNP by analyzing major sectors.
3. Describe the budget process of the federal government.
4. Distinguish between the unified budget, the national income accounts budget, and the full employment budget.
5. How are the expenditures for defense systems and other major equipment items handled in the federal government budget?
6. Describe procedures for forecasting the effect of defense expenditures on governmental purchases of goods and services.
7. Explain the role of new and unused obligational authority in the budget process.
8. Describe the adjustments needed in federal budget figures to be able to use them as a basis for developing a forecast.
9. Explain how a forecast of federal governmental purchases of goods and services may be developed from adjusted budget figures.
10. Explain a procedure for forecasting state and local governmental purchases of goods and services.
11. In the stock adjustment model, the equation to be estimated is $X_t = A + BI_t + CP_t + DX_{t-1}$. How would you estimate a, b, c, and K?
12. How may durable-goods sales be forecast?
13. Describe the process for forecasting nondurable goods and service expenditures directly.
14. How can relationships between GNP, personal income, disposable personal income, and consumer expenditures for nondurable goods and services be used to forecast expenditures for nondurable goods and services?
15. Explain a procedure for forecasting each major sector of imports of goods and services; of exports of goods and services.

READINGS

"Business Investment and Sales Expectations." *Survey of Current Business*, annually in March issue.

Butler, William F., Robert Kavesh, and Robert B. Platt (eds.). *Methods and Techniques of Business Forecasting.* Englewood Cliffs, NJ: Prentice-Hall, Inc., 1984.

Carlson, Keith M. "Federal Fiscal Policy Since the Employment Act of 1946." *Review*, Federal Reserve Bank of St. Louis (December 1987), pp. 14–25.

———. "How Much Lower Can the Unemployment Rate Go?" *Review*, Federal Reserve Bank of St. Louis (July/August 1988), pp. 44–57.

The Federal Budget—Its Impact on the Economy. New York: Conference Board, Inc., annually.

Federal Budget Trends. Federal Reserve Bank of St. Louis, quarterly.

Frumkin, Norman. *Tracking America's Economy.* Armonk, NY: M. E. Sharpe, Inc., 1987.

Galper, Harvey, and Edward Gramlich. *A Technique for Forecasting Defense Expenditures.* Washington, D.C.: Board of Governors of the Federal Reserve System, 1968, and *The Review of Economics and Statistics* (May 1968).

Granger, Clive W. J. *Forecasting in Business and Economics*, 2d ed. New York: Academic Press, 1986.

Hansen, Alvin H. *Business Cycle Theory: Its Development and Present Status.* Westport, CT: Hyperion Press, 1979.

Jayne, Edward R. "The Economic Impact of Defense." *Business Economics* (October 1988), pp. 31–37.

"Manufacturers' Inventory and Sales Expectations." *Survey of Current Business.* Washington, D.C.: Department of Commerce, annually in March and later issues.

Moore, Geoffrey H. *Business Cycles, Inflation and Forecasting*, 2d ed. Cambridge, MA: Ballinger Publishing Co., 1983.

Penner, Rudolph G. (ed.). *The Congressional Budget Process After Five Years.* Washington, D.C.: American Enterprise Institute for Public Policy Research, 1981.

18

BUILDING AN EXPENDITURE MODEL

This chapter concludes the procedures for developing an expenditure model of gross national product. First, we will consider gross private domestic investment, which includes residential and other construction, producers' durable equipment, new plants and equipment, other capital items, and the change in business inventories. The last section of this chapter discusses the steps involved in developing the final forecast of GNP.

GROSS PRIVATE DOMESTIC INVESTMENT

The most volatile component of GNP is gross private domestic investment, which includes new construction, producers' durable equipment, and the net change in business inventories. Only the value of private construction is included in gross private domestic investment. Government construction is included under governmental purchases of goods and services.

For forecasting purposes, private building is usually divided into several categories, as follows:

- Residential building, nonfarm
- Nonresidential building, nonfarm
- Farm construction
- Public utility construction
    Railroads
    Telephone and telegraph
- Other public utilities
    Local transit
    Petroleum pipelines
    Electric light and power
    Gas

Residential Construction

The level of residential construction may be estimated by using various methods. One method that was developed by the Bureau of the Census is based upon data on building starts. Since 1959, building starts have been measured directly rather than estimated from building permits. These data cover all residential buildings both in areas requiring permits and in those that do not. The estimate is subject to sampling error, since it is based on sample data. The Bureau of the Census also develops data on the value of housing under construction. Figures are available for single-family and for multi-family units and are published monthly by the Department of Commerce in the *Construction Review*.

In developing patterns of construction from permit data, it is necessary to work with single-family and multi-family units separately, since the factors affecting them are different. The availability and cost of financing also may be different in the short run for different types of housing, as may be the pattern of construction expenditures. The first step in developing an estimate of construction volume for single-family dwellings is to develop patterns of construction spending from the housing starts and permit value data. A study of past construction activity will show the average expenditures over the period of construction for various types of projects. For example, a project costing $80,000, which is begun in January, may typically involve expenditures of $8,000 in January, $16,000 in February, $32,000 in March, $16,000 in April, and $8,000 in May. In making such estimates, it is necessary to consider qualitative factors, such as a shortage of materials or labor, or work stoppages resulting from strikes, or excellent weather, that may prolong or, perhaps, speed up activity. Some analysts prefer to work with data that are not seasonally adjusted, because the weather may differ in some years such that average seasonal patterns do not hold. For example, a mild February may allow housing starts to begin early in some sections of the country and, therefore, make seasonal adjustments misleading.

Estimates of expenditures for multi-family units based on starts are not very helpful, because there are very few actual "starts" in large projects. Therefore, estimates must be developed from permit data. These estimates are not as accurate as estimates based on single-family units, because the quantity of data is not as great for multi-family as for single-family units. Although in recent years the proportion of multi-family units has been increasing, the length of time for which data are available is not as great as for single-family units. Also, figures may need to be adjusted on the basis of value of multi-family housing under construction, because past patterns may not develop owing to strikes, material shortages, financing problems, or slow sales. Some analysts prefer to use data on permits and starts to gauge direction of movement, and thus develop some indication of volume changes, rather than developing a detailed forecast.

The demand for residential construction also may be forecast from an analysis of the most significant demand and supply factors. The starting point in such a forecast is an estimate of net family formation and net household formation. Net family formation can be accurately forecast for a year ahead, since the age at which persons marry and the percentage of persons of marriageable age who marry change slowly. To develop estimates of net household formation, it is necessary to make allowances for changes in the doubling up of families in one housing unit, as well as for the net change in single-member families and nonfamily households. The Bureau of the Census publishes projections of up to twenty years for the number of families and households.

New houses may be demanded for reasons other than new household formation. Houses may be demolished as a result of accidents, such as fires and tornados, as a result of slum clearance to make way for housing projects, or to clear areas for commercial centers, highways, and the like. However, because population continually shifts (for example, from rural to urban areas in the post-World War II period), vacant houses are found in some sections, while new houses are needed in others. A small housing demand also exists for second houses. These factors may be summarized as follows:

Net family formation
>   + or − Undoubling or doubling
>   + or − Changes in single-member and nonfamily households
>   = Net household formation
>   + or − Net change in vacancies
>   = Housing units required based on demand changes
>   + Replacement demand
>   + Net demand owing to population shifts
>   + Net demand owing to an increase in two-house families
>   = Total housing units required
>   − Forecast for mobile home sales
>   = Permanent housing units required

The unit forecast for permanent housing units can be put on a dollar basis by a fairly simple procedure. To calculate the average cost per house, the dollar value of housing for the past year is divided by the number of houses built. To arrive at an average unit cost and total cost for the forecast year, this figure can be adjusted for expected changes in construction costs and the size of houses.

A preliminary forecast of housing expenditures based on demand must be adjusted in light of qualitative factors on the demand side, as well as on the basis of supply factors. Individuals buy houses more easily when income is rising than when it is falling. Housing demand is increased significantly when occupancy rates are higher than normal because building in the past has not kept up with demand. Housing demand increases when credit terms on government-underwritten mortgages are favorable and financing is easily available, and it drops when credit is harder to get. Housing demand is increased when monthly payments are less than rentals for comparable units. Housing demand is slowed somewhat by rising costs of new houses. Some indication of the effects of changing rental rates and construction costs may be obtained by comparing rates of change in the rent-index section of the consumer price index and a residential construction cost index. Housing demand also will be slowed when demand is close to, or somewhat ahead of, available supplies of building materials, which has a tendency to slow construction and thus reduce the number of houses built in a year. The effect of these factors cannot be put into quantitative terms, but the analyst must judge whether to raise or lower the forecast in light of the analysis of these factors.

The effect on housing of the cycle in housing construction must also be considered, especially in the short cycle, as discussed in Chapter 5, in which housing activity has been almost countercyclical. To a large degree, this pattern is based on the availability of financing and, to some degree, on the shift of labor from other construction. Therefore, a complete analysis of the financial markets and prospects for housing credit must be made and their effect on prospective housing used to modify a forecast based on demand factors and other qualitative factors. If the forecast for other construction shows a decline, the analyst should also consider the effect of shifts of resources to housing. The analyst must study both current and new programs for housing credit, since these programs modify the shortage of housing funds as the economy expands and will thus change the housing cycle.

The effect on demand for a permanent type housing, as a result of competition from sales of mobile homes, must also be considered.

Some mobile homes are used for second homes, but the vast majority are used for low-cost housing. In 1972, a record number of such homes were sold when the total reached 575,000, compared with just over 100,000 in 1960. The number in 1973 was almost as large, but then dropped in 1981 to 230,000 units as a result of the housing slump that began in 1980. A near-term high was reached in mobile home purchases in 1984 as interest rates moderated and mobile home values improved, relative to other housing options. Since then, sales have trended down—1988 sales totaled 220,000 units.[1] Mobile homes are bought primarily by people in the mid-twenties to mid-thirties age range whose family incomes are generally considerably below-average incomes. Almost all new housing units sold in the under $20,000 price range are mobile homes.

A sum must be added to the forecast of expenditures for new houses to account for additions, alterations, and new structures involving existing homes. This is an increasing category in which complete data have only recently become available. These expenditures probably respond closely to changes in consumer income, to the cost of remodeling work, and to the ease of getting it done.

Forecasts prepared from analysis of demand, permit data, and the index of consumer purchase projections for single-family housing can well be compared to determine to what extent they are harmonious. Any significant differences call for a thorough analysis of all factors in the forecasts and any revisions that seem necessary to bring the forecasts into agreement. The analyst will also want to check other forecasts such as that published usually in the November issue of *Construction Review*.

Other Construction

Private nonfarm, nonresidential building may be forecast in much the same way as is done for housing from the contract data provided by the Dodge division of McGraw-Hill, Inc. To use this data as a basis for a forecast, several adjustments must be made. Dodge reports cancellations or corrections in the month in which they are ascertained. It is necessary to adjust the data for the month in which the contracts were reported. The Dodge data include permits for offices, warehouses,

---

1. *U.S. Industrial Outlook 1982* (Washington, D.C.: U.S. Department of Commerce), p. 6, and *U.S. Industrial Outlook 1989*, pp. 1–9.

and other buildings constructed by public utilities that are usually estimated separately and must therefore be excluded.

The same pattern that was used for residential construction can be used to forecast nonresidential construction from a record of permits. A study of the progress of past projects of various types, such as the construction of retail establishments, office buildings, schools, hospitals, and churches, is used to determine the rate at which building is likely to take place. Qualitative factors are again considered and these, along with the past patterns, are used to develop the final forecast. Since construction of most of the structures in this category takes a relatively long period of time, forecasts may be made on the basis of general relationships between permit data and construction data, without analyzing construction spending patterns in detail. Some analysts use a different technique for forecasting construction of retail establishments. Since these have followed residential construction with only a short lag, they have used forecasts of residential construction to develop retail construction forecasts. A general demand factor is sometimes used to help forecast the demand for office buildings. Since office buildings are used primarily to house white-collar employees, there is a relationship between trends in such building and trends in white-collar employment. A projection of such past relationships is used to arrive at a demand for office building. Such a demand forecast must be modified, however, for added demands owing to shifts in centers of employment or a trend toward new, more modern buildings. The relationship of the level of industrial construction to the Federal Reserve Board Index of Industrial Production is also used at times to develop a demand factor for new industrial structures. But shifts in production patterns and processes and the trend toward greater efficiency make such demand projections of limited usefulness.

Estimates of farm construction are developed from forecasts of farm income. In the past, there has been a high degree of relationship between the trend of cash farm income and the amount of building done on farms. Some analysts prefer to use the relationship between farm construction and net farm income per farm. This may prove to be more useful in the future as farming becomes more a business and less a way of life. By using the past trend and studying qualitative factors, such as the relationship of building costs to farm prices, it is possible to forecast farm building.

Forecasts of the level of construction activity by railroads and public utilities are made somewhat differently. The Interstate Commerce Commission prepares monthly estimates of expenditures for all Class

1 railroads. These must be adjusted upward on the basis of past experience to make allowance for expenditures by smaller railroads. From developments in the past year or so and from a study of plans of the major railroad systems, it is possible to project construction levels for a year ahead with reasonable accuracy and a quarter ahead with a fairly high degree of accuracy.

Data for capital expenditures of electric light and power, gas, and petroleum pipeline companies are published quarterly by the Securities and Exchange Commission (SEC). Since such projects often take several years to complete, changes do not occur quickly. By studying both the figures for the past five or six quarters and the expansion plans that are made several years ahead, it is possible to arrive at reasonable forecasts.

Producers' Durable Equipment

Forecasts of private construction include only business plants, not expenditures on producers' durable equipment. The latter are treated as a separate subcategory of gross private domestic investment and must be projected independently, if a separate figure is to be developed for both plant and equipment. The next section discusses techniques for forecasting expenditures on plant and equipment together.

The late C. F. Roos of the Econometric Institute developed a statistical method of forecasting the demand for domestic producers' durable equipment by studying the factors that influence business executives to invest in such equipment. There is an incentive to invest in equipment when the expected return from that equipment in relationship to its supply price is greater than the interest rate. Since it is impossible to accurately determine the future rate of return, Roos believed that most executives solve this problem by projecting the present rate of profit, and therefore, he used current profits in his calculations. To determine a measure of the interest rate that is significant in business decisions, Roos worked with both AAA bond yields and a combination of AAA bond yields and short-term interest rates, since some capital equipment is financed by short-term borrowing. Because Roos found that adding short-term rates made little difference in the accuracy of his forecasts, he used only AAA bond yields.

No index is available to show changes in the supply price of capital assets. Its closest approximation is an index of machinery and machinery-products prices. Unfortunately, this index is not available for a period long enough to make an adequate study; but for the period for which it is available, the index fluctuates in much the same manner as does the Bureau of Labor Statistics index of the price of metals and metal products. Therefore, Roos used this index as a proxy for changes in the supply price of capital assets.

Furthermore, he found that changes in real wage rates influence the demand for investment goods. This relationship may well be two-fold, since as real wages go up, there is a greater demand for capital equipment to cut production costs. At the same time, increases in wages also lead to an increase in the demand for consumer goods and, thus, in the derived demand for capital equipment. Because there was no index available to measure changes in real wage rates, Roos used the Bureau of Labor Statistics index of nonfarm prices as the best ap-proximation of such changes. The relative prices of consumer goods to producer goods also influence the level of demand for investment goods; a high level of consumer-goods prices to producer-goods prices encourages investment, whereas a low level discourages it. From these data, Roos calculated capitalized profits based upon corporate profits and the supply price of capital assets and adjusted them for changes in nonfarm prices. This capitalized relative-profits factor is calculated as follows:

$$X = \frac{\text{Corporate profits}}{\text{AAA bond yields}} \times \frac{\text{Nonfarm prices}}{\text{Price of metals and metal products}}$$

This factor is then correlated with producers' durable equipment six months later.

The lag in the production of producers' durable equipment is to be expected, since some time must elapse between the decision to invest in new equipment and the fabrication of this equipment. The formula that expresses this relationship is as follows:[2]

$Y = 0.021X + \$2,500$ million, where
$Y = $ Producers' durable equipment six months in the future

Thus, from this formula it is possible to make a preliminary forecast six months ahead with some degree of accuracy. Forecasts for a year ahead can also be made fairly accurately, since it is necessary to fore-cast the four factors involved in capitalized relative profits for only six months in the future.

---

2. Charles F. Roos, "The Demand for Investment Goods," *American Economic Review* (May 1948), pp. 314–316.

Roos found that the demand for producers' durable equipment is greater than that which would be expected from past relationships when the economy is operating at or near capacity levels. At such times, upward adjustments must be made in the figures to take the effects of this capacity "squeeze" into consideration.

Some analysts develop their forecasts of producers' durable equipment by following new orders, unfilled orders, inventories, and shipments. This is the method frequently used to forecast the Federal Reserve Index of Industrial Production, which was discussed in Chapter 16.

New Plant and Equipment

The value of new construction and producers' durable equipment is often broken down differently for forecasting purposes than it is in national income statistics. As a rule, business firms do not clearly differentiate in their planning between new buildings and new equipment. Therefore, business expenditures on new plant and equipment are often projected as one unit. This reduces the number of classes of new construction that must be separately projected to the following:

- Capital outlays by business
- Residential construction
- Nonresidential construction for nonbusiness purposes, such as institutions and private schools
- Farm construction

Expenditures on farm machinery and equipment must also be projected separately, since they are included in producers' durable equipment, but not in business expenditures on plant and equipment. The same is true of expenditures on professional equipment and expenditures for private institutions.

In the post-World War II period, the Department of Commerce and the SEC have surveyed business plans for expenditures on new plant and equipment. The SEC gathers data on plans of all corporations registered with the SEC under the Securities Acts, and the Department of Commerce uses a large sample of businesses in order to obtain data from nonregistered corporations. Beginning in 1972, the Bureau of Economic Analysis of the Department of Commerce assumed responsibility for all aspects of the survey. A Department of Commerce forecast for 1988 is illustrated in Table 18-1.

Table 18-1

New Plant and Equipment Expenditures, 1986–1988
(Billions of Dollars)

	Actual 1986	Actual 1987	Planned 1988	Percentage Change	
				1986 to 1987	1987 to 1988
ALL INDUSTRIES	379.47	384.67	430.95	2.7	10.6
Manufacturing	142.69	145.90	163.56	2.2	12.1
Durable goods	69.14	71.01	78.06	2.7	9.9
Nondurable goods	73.56	74.88	85.50	1.8	14.2
Nonmanufacturing	236.78	243.78	267.39	3.0	9.7
Mining	11.22	11.39	12.62	1.5	10.8
Railroad	6.66	5.92	7.05	−11.1	19.1
Air transportation	6.26	6.53	7.61	4.3	16.5
Other transportation	5.89	6.40	6.91	8.7	8.0
Public utilities	46.38	44.88	46.47	−3.2	3.5
Communication & other	160.38	168.65	186.74	5.2	10.7

Source: *Survey of Current Business* (September 1988), pp. 18–19.

McGraw-Hill also conducts a similar survey and publishes the results in *Business Week*. It is based on a smaller sample that is somewhat less representative, since it concentrates, to some extent, on larger concerns.

These surveys have established a good record in anticipating the change in investment expenditures. The Department of Commerce-SEC annual surveys from 1947 through 1975 had a median deviation from actual expenditures of only 3 percent. In twenty of the twenty-nine years for which the annual survey was conducted, anticipated expenditures have been within 3 percent of actual expenditures.

In the fall of 1956, the Conference Board introduced a new survey, which is published quarterly in the Conference Board publication *Investment Statistics*. The data gathered is based on a survey of capital appropriations of the 1,000 largest manufacturing companies. The survey gives data on newly approved capital appropriations and total outstanding capital appropriations. The difference between spending plans and new appropriations is analogous to that between new appropriations and expenditures in the government budget. Thus, the

Conference Board survey gives additional information that should prove useful in projecting capital spending more accurately several quarters ahead.

Economists at the Federal Reserve Bank of Cleveland have developed relationships between new capital appropriations and expenditures on plant and equipment. The procedures are similar to those for defense spending based on new authorizations and for construction expenditures based on permit data. The basis for these relationships is a seven-quarter relationship between appropriations and expenditures. Estimates for spending for each quarter are based on some portion of new appropriations for that quarter and for each of the previous six quarters. In manufacturing, for example, during the 1961–1969 period, 14 percent of new appropriations was spent in the first quarter, and this amount accumulated as follows:

Within Quarter	Cumulative Percentage of New Appropriations Spent
1	14
2	35
3	56
4	74
5	86
6	92
7+	100

In utilities, however, only 6 percent was spent in the first quarter and only 62 percent in six quarters.[3]

The figures reported in the surveys of expenditures on plant and equipment should be analyzed in light of conditions in the economy and revised, if necessary. It is impossible to check these figures quantitatively with building permit data, but an analysis of such data for several quarters will show whether the surveys conform with future building as shown in permits. The same kind of check can be made with the Department of Commerce series on new orders and order backlogs in the durable goods manufacturing industries. If these series have been moving in the same direction as the expenditure surveys indicate that expenditures on plant and equipment will move, they help substantiate the survey figures. If not, the series raise serious

---

3. *Economic Review*, Federal Reserve Bank of Cleveland (October 1970), p. 9.

questions about the figures in the survey, and consequently, some revision of them may be necessary.

The survey figures should also be checked for feasibility, from both a physical and a financial point of view. If the construction and equipment industry is operating at or near full capacity, additional spending plans cannot be fully met on time, and the figures should be adjusted downward. If there are indications that money will become extremely tight, some downward revision may also be necessary. Large concerns usually can obtain the funds needed to carry out plans for the current year, but some of the smaller firms may have to postpone some expenditures because of difficulties in financing. The effects of tight money are felt primarily in making plans for the next year and not in completing those for the present year. Downward revision may be necessary if stock prices are dropping or have dropped significantly, since this will cause some businesses to defer new financing.

Expenditure plans may need to be changed because the analyst believes sales and profits will be substantially different from those that business executives expected at the time of the survey. Minor changes in sales do not significantly affect spending decisions, but a sharp drop in sales and profits will. There is, however, a lag of three or four quarters before significant changes occur. The Department of Commerce report asks business executives about sales expectations and thus provides the analyst with information on the sales picture for the year.

Other Capital Items

After expenditures on plant and equipment have been forecast from surveys of business plans, it is necessary to estimate the levels of the remaining items. Capital outlays charged to the current account fluctuate in about the same way as capital outlays in general. They are usually forecast by adjusting the figure for the past year by the same percentage by which the expenditure survey shows that spending on plant and equipment will change. (Methods of forecasting residential construction, nonresidential construction for nonbusiness purposes, and farm construction have already been discussed.)

Expenditures on farm machinery and equipment show a reasonable degree of correlation with cash farm income or net income per farm and, therefore, can be forecast by adjusting levels in the past year by expected changes in these factors. Expenditures on professional equipment are not a large part of total investment expenditures and do not change rapidly. They can be estimated from expenditures during the past year and trends over the past five years.

Change in Business Inventories

The last item in the gross private domestic investment group to forecast is the net change in business inventories. This has often been the most volatile series and so, in many ways, the most important one to forecast accurately, especially in minor recessions. It is also one of the most difficult to forecast.

In analyzing inventory changes, it is well to bear in mind the adjustments that companies try to make in inventory levels. In the retail and wholesale fields, and in major segments of the manufacturing field, goods are no longer made to order but kept in stock and sold out of stock. The competent business manager knows the optimal relationship of inventory to sales. Inventory acts as a cushion for unexpected changes in sales levels, since it is depleted in an upturn as sales increase more than expected and, conversely, is allowed to increase when sales decrease in a downturn.

In such fields as the production of major types of industrial equipment, goods are still made to order. In these industries, for example, in machine tools, sales and production are almost the same. The cushion is in unfilled orders, because new orders are above sales in an upswing and below sales in a downturn. In most other manufacturing industries, although some goods are made to order, enough are kept in stock so that inventories perform a major cushioning function.

The attempt to adjust inventories to sales has been reasonably successful, but there is usually a lag. In those industries in which sales are made primarily out of finished-goods inventories, production lags behind sales when there are unexpected changes in sales. Unexpected increases in sales are limited in the short run by the availability of inventories.

Total inventories in manufacturing and trade cannot be changed rapidly, because concerted efforts to build or to liquidate stocks are, in part, self-defeating. If a retailer wants to increase inventory because less inventory than planned is available as a result of higher sales than expected, he or she orders more inventory from wholesalers and manufacturers, which, in turn, reduces their stocks. The result has been a lag of several months between sales and inventories in manufacturing and trade. The change in the book value of inventories in manufacturing and trade is, however, a leading series, as is to be expected from

Figure 18-1   Relationship of Inventory to Average Monthly Sales in
Manufacturing and Trade, 1964–1988

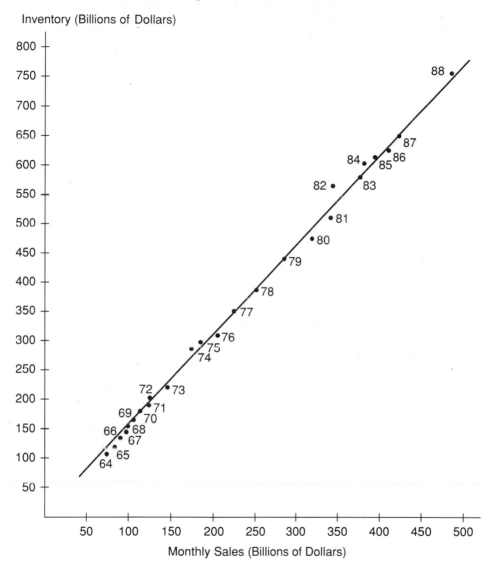

Source: *Business Conditions Digest.*

attempts by business executives to adjust planned inventory levels to
planned levels of future sales.

  In recent years, the relationship of inventories to sales has remained stable. There has been a trend toward lower inventories in re-

lation to sales, owing to better methods of inventory control and higher costs of financing inventories. A close relationship exists between average monthly sales in manufacturing and trade and the book value of inventory (see Figure 18-1). This relationship holds for retail-trade inventories and for the volatile durable-goods sector of manufacturing, as well as for nondurable goods.

The relationship of inventories to average monthly sales on an annual basis is effective for showing the ratios that businesses would like to have when they consider stocks to be normal. Quarterly figures show variations around these levels as inventories move out of balance and are realigned.

Forecasting Inventories

The first step in forecasting inventories is to develop an estimate of the level of inventories expected from past relationships and to compare these with current levels to determine the size and direction of changes that are likely to occur.

Forecasting such changes involves an analysis of the cyclical and price factors that have affected inventories in the past several quarters. The analysis of optimal inventory policy in Chapter 4 shows that inventories tend to increase more rapidly than sales in the early expansion phase of a cycle. This is especially true when significant price rises are expected and when raw materials and parts are expected to be short. The opposite tendency holds in a downturn; that is, inventories decrease less rapidly than sales. The result is that inventory-to-sales ratios rise rapidly in recession periods and drop significantly in the early stages of recovery periods. If such changes are occurring or are likely to occur on the basis of the overall forecast being developed, they must be considered in projecting changes in inventories from past relationships. Such adjustments are significant when a recession is in progress or is being forecast, or when an upturn is being forecast or is in its beginning stages. The price situation should also be considered when the economy is in a period of rapid price rises in the materials stage that have not as yet been fully reflected in finished-goods prices. In such a situation, the book value of inventories may, for a time, rise faster than past relationships would indicate.

The GNP figures on nonfarm business inventories are somewhat more inclusive than manufacturing and trade inventories, although the two series move together. Therefore, the percentage change expected in manufacturing and trade inventories can be applied to nonfarm business inventories. Changes in farm inventories then remain to be forecast; they are small and the change generally can be forecast from an extrapolation of the trend during the past seven or eight quarters. This trend projection should be adjusted up or down, if an analysis of qualitative factors indicates that unusual factors are at work.

Such forecasts of inventory changes should be compared with manufacturers' inventory and sales expectations as reported in the quarterly survey by the Department of Commerce. This survey shows manufacturers' expectations for changes in inventories and sales for the next two quarters. It also gives manufacturers' evaluations of their inventories as about right, too high, or too low, as well as an estimate of the net amount and percentage of inventory imbalance. If the analyst is expecting a level of sales different from that expected by manufacturers, appropriate changes can be made in the inventory figures. The data on the condition of inventories also will help to adjust a forecast of inventory levels based on past relationships, since it will show any tendency to change inventory-sales relationships.

Econometric models are used by some analysts to help forecast inventory investment. A simple model correlates the book value of inventories with sales in the second preceding quarter. More complex models use such factors as the change in inventory investment from the preceding period, the change in final-product sales in the preceding period, the change in plant and equipment outlays from the preceding period, and the change in manufacturing and unfilled orders from the preceding period. Such models have proved helpful, but results generally have not been as good as those based on less formal procedures or those using a combination of procedures.

Before making a final forecast of the change in inventories, inventories in major fields should be examined. It is especially significant to study the inventory situation in the automobile and steel fields, because significant changes often take place here. This has been especially true in years in which a steel strike threatens or in which sales have not been up to expectations. In periods following a major build-up in the defense field, it also is necessary to look at prospective changes in defense inventories. (The relationship of such inventories to government purchases was described in Chapter 17.) For example, as the Vietnam War heated up, defense inventories more than doubled during the 1965–1968 period. They were reduced by about 15 percent between the third quarter of 1969 and mid-1971 as war goods were delivered in large quantities and defense spending was cut.

Econometric Studies for Investment Forecasts

The reason why firms invest has been the subject of many econometric studies, and new research is periodically made. Because of their number, we will make no attempt to be complete in describing the econometric studies, but will describe them sufficiently to demonstrate their use in forecasting. We will concentrate on two propriety models, Wharton Econometrics, and the latest version of the University of Michigan Model.

In the Wharton Econometric Model, investment spending is divided into different categories—business purchases of plant and equipment, residential construction, and inventory accumulation—just as presented earlier in this chapter. Each category is modeled separately and is represented by a different equation.

Business investment in plant and equipment is modeled on the assumption that executives build their stock of machines and buildings on the needs for changing production capacity and the user cost of capital. The surrogate for the cost of capital is the long-term interest rate adjusted for tax incentives and tax credits.

Residential construction is influenced by different economic variables. The equation for residential construction is influenced by the need for new housing, the cost of financing, and the availability of mortgage funds. In the Wharton Model, the availability of funds is captured by the differential between long- and short-term interest rates. It is believed that this difference reflects whether funds flow into mortgages or flow into short-term investments.

The last equation describes the most highly volatile component of investment—inventory accumulation. In this equation, the variables influencing inventory are current sales, inventory sales ratio, and the carrying cost of inventory, as measured by the interest rate.

In the Michigan Model, business fixed investment is disaggregated into two categories—producers' durable equipment and structures. Equations for producers' durable equipment are modeled by drawing heavily on standard capital theory and investment theory. Investment in production equipment is modeled using a "stock adjustment" type model. Expenditures for production equipment depend upon both the actual stock and the desired stock of equipment. The desired stock of equipment is a function of real output, the user cost of capital, and the price of equipment. Using the stock-adjustment idea and the equation for the desired stock, the model arrives at an equation describing equipment investment.

In the Michigan Model, other types of fixed investment are essentially functions of real GNP, interest rates, and components of taxes relevant to capital investment.

DEVELOPING THE FINAL FORECAST OF GNP

After figures for each sector of GNP have been developed, the resulting product will not necessarily be the final forecast of GNP; in fact, it is very unlikely to be. The whole forecast should be cross-checked and revised, as needed. The first step calls for a comparison of the total of GNP with the level of activity considered most likely when such sectors as residential construction and consumer-durable-goods purchases were forecast. If it appears that total economic activity will be greater or less than originally expected, these estimates should be revised.

The forecast can then be cross-checked in several ways by using past relationships. One such check uses the relationship between real disposable income and real consumer expenditures on goods and services. Price developments may be such that prices will rise or fall more than was assumed as forecasts were made. The effect of various factors on the general price level and methods of forecasting prices are considered in Chapter 19. These factors and past relationships can be used to revise consumer-expenditure forecasts, which, when revised, are a first approximation. Past relationships of real durable sales, nondurable sales, and service expenditures to real disposable income can be used to divide the adjustments among these categories. These relationships are discussed more fully in Chapter 20.

A second approximation calls for an adjustment in other factors, such as capital-goods expenditures, that are likely to be affected as the levels of consumer sales change. These changes affect GNP and, in turn, call for more revision of consumer expenditures. This process could last indefinitely, but rather than do it mechanically, the analyst should use his or her best judgment and make all revisions in one step.

A last check is worthwhile before the forecast is accepted as final, which involves an analysis of the excess of receipts or expenditures for each sector of the economy. The sum of these must, in actual fact, balance out to zero. The procedure used by the Council of Economic Advisers, as published in its annual report, is a good one to follow.

At this stage, the analyst has most of the figures necessary for making a final check, and those figures not available are reasonably easy to forecast. Interest paid by persons can be forecast from past trends and developments expected in the durable-consumer-goods field. Transfer payments to foreigners are small and can be forecast by projecting the trend. Governmental tax and nontax receipts can be forecast from budget data and from past relationships to personal-consumption expenditures. Government transfers can be forecast from budget data and past trends, and the same holds true for interest payments, if the trend of debt and interest rate developments is also considered.

The only complex item to forecast is business-retained earnings, which involves a forecast of profits, corporate income taxes, and dividend payments. Dividends change slowly and can be forecast from trends for the past seven or eight quarters. Profit is a volatile factor that bears some relationship to GNP and has a pronounced cyclical pattern. Past relationships and the stage of the cycle can be used to develop a preliminary forecast. This can be adjusted for qualitative factors such as the trend of costs and prices, governmental attitudes and policies, and the labor situation. Corporate-profits taxes can be forecast from past relationships to profits and any prospective changes in tax rates.

Any significant lack of balance of the excess of receipts or disbursements calls for adjustments, since the economy will set forces into motion that will balance them. However, no set rules can be given for doing this. The analyst must make needed adjustments based on his or her knowledge of the economy, past cycles, and the causal factors at work in the cycle.

Such cross-checking helps refine a forecast to make it internally consistent. At this stage of knowledge of the cycle, the forecaster cannot assure accuracy because the economy does not always react as it has in the past. To a large degree, even though the amount of guesswork is being reduced, forecasting remains an art.

QUESTIONS

1. Outline a division of private building for forecasting purposes.
2. Describe, step-by-step, two alternative procedures for forecasting the volume of residential construction.
3. How do developments in the mobile-home field affect a housing forecast?
4. Explain how other nonresidential construction may be forecast.
5. Explain a procedure for forecasting the volume of producers' durable equipment.
6. How is the Department of Commerce series on new plant and equipment related to the construction and producers' durable equipment series?

7. What has been the record of the Department of Commerce series on projected expenditures on new plant and equipment?
8. Explain a procedure for forecasting expenditures on new plant and equipment using the Department of Commerce series.
9. Describe the use of the series on new appropriations as a forecasting device.
10. How are the remaining capital items forecast?
11. Explain a procedure for forecasting inventory investment.
12. Using the stock adjustment idea and the Michigan Model, formulate an equation for investment in production equipment.
13. Describe the process of checking a forecast for consistency and revising it in light of such checks.

READINGS

Adams, F. Gerard. *The Business Forecasting Revolution*. New York: Oxford University Press, 1986.

Fazzari, Steven M. "Tax Reform and Investment: Blessing or Curse." *Review*. Federal Reserve Bank of St. Louis (June/July 1987), pp. 23–33.

Shapiro, Harold T., and George A. Fulton. *A Regional Econometric Forecasting System*. Ann Arbor, MI: The University of Michigan Press, 1985.

For additional readings see those cited at the conclusion of Chapters 16 and 17.

FORECASTING PRICE CHANGES

A forecast of probable price changes is an integral part of a forecasting program. It may be necessary as a basis for converting a dollar forecast into a unit forecast. Conversely, if the basic forecast is in units, a price forecast is needed to put it on a dollar basis.

The government uses price forecasts in formulating monetary and fiscal policy. Such forecasts are needed to estimate both expenditures and revenue in governmental budgets, especially those of the federal government. Price forecasts are also used in planning programs in the agricultural area. Federal price forecasts often provide a basis for action to prevent an unfavorable situation from arising.

Price and unit forecasts are specially valuable in business—the unit forecast to plan production and the dollar forecast to plan finances. Data on prospective price changes are also useful in other phases of business operations. Price forecasts are necessary to set prices months ahead for inclusion in a catalog; they are useful in planning raw materials purchases. A forecast of changes in the general price level is often used in bargaining with labor on wages. Data on long-term price trends aid in effective long-range planning of capital expenditures. Thus, a price forecast is an integral part of any forecasting program.

Methods of determining price trends and forecasting price changes are considered in this chapter. Consideration will be directed first to projecting the trend of prices, since short-run price forecasts are affected by the general direction in which prices are moving. Then, the factors involved in forecasting short-run changes in the general price level are discussed. This presentation is followed by an analysis of the factors involved in forecasting prices of specific commodities. A final section will consider some of the schemes that purport to forecast common stock prices. Forecasting in this area is all but impossible because of the changing psychological reactions of a changing group of investors.

ANALYZING AND PROJECTING PRICE TRENDS

In projecting price trends, it is necessary to consider the basic factors that affect prices in the long run and the effect those factors have had on price levels over the years. Several factors seem to indicate that the long-run price level in the United States should have a downward bias. Prices should move downward gradually, because cumulative increases in technology and in the skills of the labor force and of management are making it possible to produce increased quantities of goods and services at a lower per unit cost. A study of long-run price movements, however, fails to show such a downward trend because factor prices have not remained stable.

During the major wars, prices rose substantially and have not in all cases dropped to prewar levels before new forces have caused them to rise again. Since 1900, prices have materially increased, primarily as a result of the inflationary financing of World Wars I and II. Even at the low point in the 1933 depression, prices were well above prosperity levels in 1900. After World War II, there was no tendency for prices to decline because of the government's inflationary policies. New demand pressures and supply problems also pushed prices upward.

Factors Determining Long-Run Prices

As was pointed out earlier in the description of the salient features of the American economy, there are several important sources of new money in the U.S. monetary system. The stock of money is supplied by the Treasury, the Federal Reserve System, and the system of commercial banks and thrift institutions. The bulk of it is in the form of demand and other checkable deposits that are liabilities of depository institutions; coins are provided by the Treasury and currency by the Federal Reserve Banks. The size of the money supply depends on the actions of these agencies and is partially determined by the constraints placed upon them by laws and by the procedures developed to administer their programs. The money supply also depends on the actions of governmental units, households, business units, and the rest of the world in demanding credit to meet their needs. The potential for monetary expansion depends on excess reserves that are available in the banking system and on the monetary expansion multiplier.

As discussed in Chapter 7, changes in the money supply can lead to changes in the price level. The cash balances that spenders desire to hold or the level of goods and services that are produced, or both, may also change. The institutional arrangements on which cash balances depend, to a large degree, are not likely to change rapidly; but the desire to hold cash is also affected by such factors as expectations of changes in the price level and interest rates, the relative attractiveness of near money substitutes, such as money market accounts, and the ease of credit. If the desire to hold cash balances or its reciprocal, the velocity of money, does not change, either the general price level or the output of goods and services must change. Output is likely to increase in part, at least, as long as there are unused resources. But as full utilization of plant and equipment and full employment are approached, the major impact of an increase in the money supply will be on the price level.

This has happened during wartime when the money supply has been increased by the creation of credit for the government in the form of credits to the Treasury checking accounts arising out of bank purchases of government bonds with excess reserves or newly created reserves. When government deficits are financed in this way (monetized), the effect on the economy is potentially inflationary, because the money supply is increased without increasing the supply of goods. This type of action was used, in part, to finance World War II expenditures. Prices were held in check by price control laws, but the basis was laid for an increase in the price level. The money supply was increased about threefold between 1939 and 1947, while physical output rose somewhat less than 50 percent. In other words, the supply of money rose over twice as fast as the supply of goods. Prices rose by only about 75 percent by 1947, since the velocity of money had fallen. When the velocity of money increased in 1948, 1949, and 1950, the full impact of the increased money supply was brought into play. Much the same pattern can be seen in the Vietnam War period and its aftermath.

Projecting Price Trends

A projection of price trends involves projections of the money supply, the velocity of circulation of money, and also the level of output of goods and services. The level of output can be projected several years ahead by the methods described in Chapter 15. The projection of the money supply involves an analysis of many factors. The level of coins and currency in circulation can be projected from past trends, and to a large degree, this is also true of the level of demand and other checkable deposits held by businesses and households. Other factors, such as the general state of the money markets and the level of interest rates, must be considered, since these also affect the degree to which businesses and some individuals invest idle short-term funds in short-term obligations. Policies of the Treasury and the Federal Reserve must be analyzed, and the effect of likely changes must be projected. Changes in the velocity of circulation of money can be projected from past trends. These projections must be modified by an analysis of the factors that may lead to a change in desired cash balances, such as the relative attractiveness of short-term obligations like commercial paper; the attractiveness of keeping liquid funds in other institutions, such as money market funds; and the ease of obtaining credit in emergencies.

So many variables are involved that it is difficult to work with all of them at one time. Part of the difficulty may be overcome by working with rates of change in two basic series, that is, the output of goods and services and the money supply, since the velocity of money circulation does not change materially except in unusual periods, such as World War II and the early postwar period when controls were phased out. Data on all these variables are published in the *Federal Reserve Bulletin*, and information on rates of change of many monetary and related series is available in *Monetary Trends*, a monthly publication of the St. Louis Federal Reserve Bank.

This method of estimating changes in the general price level involves many broad estimates and cannot be expected to give completely accurate results. It can determine the level of prices in a general way by a comparison of the trend of output with the trend in the size of the supply of purchasing media. The analyst must be on the alert constantly for changes in other factors, such as velocity, which could occur in a period of price controls, or as in the late 1970s and early 1980s, when the menu of financial instruments that serve as substitutes for money increased markedly and caused velocity to increase substantially.

Effect of Production Costs on Prices

A rise in the price level may also be caused by an increase in the costs of production. Historically, increases in productivity have reduced total costs, especially in manufacturing. In some industries, however, organized labor has had sufficient bargaining power to win wage increases at a rate greater than increases in overall productivity. The expected result from this is increased costs to the industry employing the unionized labor and increased prices of the products. The higher factor expense and the higher product price would be expected to lead to less employment and lower output in the effected firms. If there are rigidities (which there are) preventing the unemployed workers and other resources from moving quickly to other areas of the economy, the result is an increase in prices and a decrease in aggregate output. This is one possibility in a class of events referred to as *cost-push* or *administered-price inflation*. In terms of the equation of exchange ($MV = Py$), MV has remained constant and the changes in P and y have offset each other.

Inflation generated through this cost-push mechanism is typically accommodated by the monetary authority allowing the money supply to increase, thereby permitting real output (y) to rise to its original level. Thus, it would appear that M and P have increased in approximate proportionality, with V and y remaining essentially unchanged.

There are many other examples of cost-push (a better term would be *supply-side inflation*) factors that have led to overall price increases in recent years. Among them are the higher cost of imported resources, such as oil, and the greater amount of resources needed to produce energy from domestic sources, governmental rules on environmental concerns, rules on occupational safety and health, the outlawing of a number of inputs (and outputs), such as DDT, low auto and truck speed limits, and increased governmentally required record keeping. The number of examples could be expanded, but the important point to remember is that each has its impact by shifting production functions downward, such that for any given level of labor employment, a smaller total output will be produced. Again, in terms of the equation of exchange, if real output (y) falls, and MV remains constant, P must rise.

SHORT-RUN PRICE FORECASTING

The direction of prices in the short run may be determined in a fashion similar to that for projecting long-run price developments. In the long run, it is usually sufficient to know the general direction of prices and to have some idea of the average rate at which they are moving; whereas in the short run, it is often desirable to have more definite information about future prices.

Use of Supply and Demand Factors

General measures of supply and demand are called for in forecasting the level of prices. The supply of all goods is determined by the supply of the factors of production, that is, "raw" materials, real property, capital goods, and labor. The supply of real property is not a significant variable, since for all practical purposes it remains constant in the short run. The capacity of capital equipment to turn out goods is, however, an important variable. It is almost impossible to arrive at a general measure of the productive capacity of all plants and other capital improvements used in producing goods and services. An index is available, however, of manufacturing capacity utilization based on 1977 output as 100.[1]

Measuring Supply and Demand Factors. The supply of labor is continually measured by the Bureau of the Census, and figures on the size of the labor force and on unemployment are regularly published by the Bureau of Labor Statistics. The measure of manufacturing capacity utilization and figures on the labor force and unemployment thus provide a measure of the use of these factors of production. Changes in these measures will show the degree to which pressure on price is changing because of the rate of utilization of labor and capital.

It is very difficult to find an accurate measure of the aggregative demand of the community. It is, however, possible to use GNP figures to show changes in demand that have occurred, since the demand for goods is translated into expenditures. Many analysts prefer real GNP figures, which can be especially important in a period in which significant price changes are taking place. Some analysts maintain that it is better to use the Federal Reserve Board Index of Industrial Production as a measure of past changes in demand. Production in the manufacturing sector is adjusted rather quickly to changes in demand; therefore, changes in the Index of Industrial Production provide a reasonable measure of current changes in demand. If goods are being produced for inventory rather than for sale, total demand is increased, which results in pressure on prices; but if stocks are being depleted, the situation is reversed. Changes in real GNP or in the Index of Industrial Production provide a fairly good measure of changes in the aggregate demand for goods.

Monetary Factors. The third group of factors that must be considered are changes in the monetary factors that affect the general price level. These could be measured in detail, but such a procedure adds too many factors for practicable forecasting. Therefore, changes in the money supply and in the velocity of circulation have been used as a general measure of monetary influences on prices.

---

1. For a description of this index, see the *Federal Reserve Bulletin* (November 1966), pp. 1605–1615, and (October 1971), pp. 779–781.

Many studies have shown the very close relationship between the long-run growth in the money stock and the rate of inflation.[2] For example, during the entire period from 1960 through 1984, the average growth rate of the money stock and the average rate of inflation were nearly identical. Forecasts of short-run changes in prices, however, require the inclusion of other influences. Money growth alone does not have adequate explanatory power over periods as short as one quarter.

Forecast Procedure. The first step in developing a forecast of prices from these supply, demand, and monetary factors is studying the past relationships of these factors. One technique for doing this is to plot supply, demand, and monetary factors on ratio paper and analyze past relationships between them and wholesale prices as changes in the various series occur. Another possibility is to develop a multiple correlation relationship between producer prices and supply, demand, and monetary factors.

The next step is to forecast each of the major factors that affect prices. Methods of forecasting GNP, industrial production, the size of the money supply, and the velocity of circulation have already been considered. The size of the labor force changes slowly, and factors affecting it are continually studied by the Bureau of Labor Statistics. Forecasts of the size of the labor force are made regularly by the Bureau of the Census. The index of manufacturing capacity changes slowly, but not necessarily at a regular rate. Changes can be forecast from past trends and from data on plans for capital expenditures in manufacturing. Forecasts of each of these factors for several quarters in the future can be used to arrive at a preliminary forecast of wholesale prices.

Factors other than those considered in studying past relationships between supply, demand, and monetary factors also have an effect on prices. Thus, the preliminary forecast must be adjusted in light of these other factors. (In formal econometric models these events are treated as "random shocks.") Some specific examples are foreign aid programs that stimulate exports and wartime price controls and materials allocation. Also included would be general increases in costs, such as increases in raw material prices resulting from import restrictions and increases in labor costs resulting from general wage increases that are greater than increases in productivity. Therefore, before making a final forecast of wholesale prices, it is necessary to study all qualitative fac-

---

2. The classic study on this topic is Milton Friedman and Anna Schwartz, *A Monetary History of the United States, 1867–1960* (Princeton, NJ: Princeton University Press, 1963). See also Keith M. Carlson, "The Lag from Money to Prices," *Review*, Federal Reserve Bank of St. Louis (October 1980), pp. 3–10.

tors. Continual study of the relationships among the basic forecasting factors should also be done, since past relationships among so large a group of variables can readily change.

The St. Louis Model

The economic model of the St. Louis Federal Reserve Bank, as described in Chapter 16, is designed to measure changes in the price level as well as changes in total spending and changes in output. The general nature of this model can be seen from Figure 16-7 on page 419. It estimates price changes on the basis of current and past demand pressure, anticipated price changes, and the relative price of energy. To measure demand pressure on prices, the change in total output is related to the potential change in output, that is, full employment GNP in constant prices. The use of these two variables provides a measure of the total demand for goods and services in relation to the capacity of the economy to provide such goods and services. The change in prices is in part a positively related linear function of this measure of demand pressure. Demand pressure, D_t, is defined as:

$$D_t = \dot{X}_t - \{[(XF_t/X_{t-1})^4 - 1]100\}$$

where

$\dot{X}_t$ =   annual rate of change in real GNP in 1982 prices in quarter t
XF_t =   full employment GNP in 1982 prices in quarter t
X_{t-1} =   real GNP in the previous quarter

The factor $[(XF_t/X_{t-1})^4 - 1]100$ is the potential for growth at an annual rate, that is, the percentage that full employment GNP in quarter t at 1982 prices is of previous quarter actual GNP. This potential for growth is then compared with the actual annual growth in real GNP, $\dot{X}_t$.[3] If the potential for growth is given, the larger the change in real GNP, the greater will be the spillover into higher prices. If the change in real GNP is given, the larger the potential for growth, the greater the expansion of output, and the less the spillover into higher prices.

The price equation includes past measures of demand pressure as well as current values. This allows for lags in the response of prices to changes in output and for changes in demand resulting from changing input prices and costs of production.

---

3. Carlson, Keith M., "A Monetarist Model for Economic Stabilization," *Review*, Federal Reserve Bank of St. Louis (October 1986), pp. 18–48.

The other variables in the price equation are the rate of change in anticipated prices, and the rate of change in the relative price of energy. Anticipated price changes are included, because anticipation of future price changes has an effect on current price decisions. There is no observable measure of price anticipation so one needs to be constructed. To do so, past changes in prices are used as a weighted average in order to arrive at anticipated price changes. Lagged values for the relative price of energy are included in order to incorporate the impact of supply-side energy inflation. The price equation, omitting scripts for time periods and lags, is:

$$\dot{P} = f(D, \dot{P}A, \dot{P}E)$$

where

$$
\begin{array}{rcl}
D & = & \text{demand pressure} \\
\dot{P} & = & \text{annual rate of change in the GNP deflator} \\
\dot{P}A & = & \text{anticipated price change[4]} \\
\dot{P}E & = & \text{change in the relative price of energy}
\end{array}
$$

R. W. Hafer, while an economist at the Federal Reserve Bank of St. Louis, achieved good regression results by making the rate of change in the price level depend on the rate of change in the money stock with a one-year lag and the rate of change in the relative price of energy with a distributed lag.[5]

Other Methods

Leading series and series on expectations may also be used in short-run price forecasting either independently or in conjunction with forecasts based on supply, demand, and monetary factors. One of the leading series is the sensitive crude materials price index, a subgroup of the Producer Price Index.[6] This index usually leads the Producer Price Index, but the time period of the lead is not uniform. Price increases in sensitive crude materials that are rapid or sustained tend to be followed by price increases in other industrial materials and these, in

---

4. Ibid., p. 20.

5. R. W. Hafer, "Examining the Recent Behavior of the Inflation," *Review*, Federal Reserve Bank of St. Louis (August/September 1984), pp. 21–39.

6. The sensitive crude materials prices index includes iron and steel scrap, nonferrous metals, lumber, plywood, wastepaper, rubber, hides, leather, textile fibers and intermediate products, and residual fuel oil.

turn, by price increases in finished goods. The daily spot price index of thirteen raw industrials may also be used as an indicator of present and future price developments. This index must be studied for basic underlying movements, since it is subject to erratic movements on a day-by-day basis. This index, like all leading series, must be considered along with other factors in the situation, since it often gives false signals.

Price diffusion indexes may also be used to help gauge future price developments. When a diffusion index moves above 50 percent, price increases are outnumbering price decreases, and this is usually an indication that the aggregate price index will rise. Diffusion indexes can be used to gauge the direction of price changes, but they cannot be used to determine the timing or magnitude of such changes. One such index is based on the National Association of Purchasing Management, Inc.'s monthly survey of price developments. The index shows the percentage of purchasing agents reporting higher prices from the previous month, plus one half of the percentage reporting unchanged prices. When this index has fallen below 50 percent, the industrial section of the Producer Price Index has declined or shown weakness; when it has passed 50 percent, prices have firmed or risen. Another diffusion index, which is published by the Department of Commerce, is that of industrial commodities prices based on the Index of Industrial Commodities Prices of the Bureau of Labor Statistics. This index also has foreshadowed major price movements, but it must be used with care, since it can give false signals.

Another approach to price forecasting is the use of series on price expectations. In Dun and Bradstreet's quarterly survey, over 1,500 executives are asked what they expect will happen to prices in the next quarter in relation to the same quarter a year ago. The net percentage of those executives expecting price increases, that is, the percentage expecting increases minus the percentage expecting decreases, gives some indication of future price developments. These executives are more often right than wrong about future price changes. But this series must be used with care, since expectations sometimes lag behind price developments, especially in periods when prices are declining.

FORECASTING THE PRICE OF AN INDIVIDUAL COMMODITY

In forecasting the price of an individual commodity, such as a farm product, it is necessary to consider the same three groups of factors—supply factors, demand factors, and monetary factors. The specific items used are different from those for the general price level because only one commodity is involved.

As far as the supply is concerned, the most important variable is the volume of production. If the commodity sells primarily in the domestic market, only U.S. production needs to be analyzed; but if it has a world market, foreign production must be included as well. Inventories also have an effect when they are unusually large or small, especially in the case of agricultural raw materials.

Disposable income is one of the basic demand factors. Other demand factors are consumption in the United States and, for a product having a world market, consumption outside the United States. It is often desirable, especially for farm products, to use consumption per capita.

Monetary factors can be measured, as was done in the forecasting of the general level of prices, by determining the degree of credit expansion. For commodities having a worldwide market, it is necessary to study monetary and credit expansion in the major trading nations of the world. For individual commodities that have a largely domestic market, it is usually sufficient to use disposable income as a measure of such changes, since such changes reflect the monetary factors that have been at work. Thus, disposable income should be a significant factor in forecasting the prices of many individual commodities, because it is related to both demand factors and monetary factors.

Agricultural Prices

The first step in forecasting annual price changes in agricultural commodities is to decide upon the dating of the year to be used. For a commodity that is produced continually throughout the year, such as butter, the calendar year may be used. For crops such as wheat, which are produced only once a year, it is best to use the crop year, beginning with the month in which the new crop is harvested. For livestock, there is a fairly distinct marketing year that should be used.

Selection of Factors for Study.   The next step is the selection of the supply, demand, and monetary factors to be analyzed. As has already been indicated, consumer disposable income is one of the most important of these factors. Next in importance is the annual variation in supply. This variation may be analyzed as one factor, that is, current production plus carryover, or the two may be treated separately. If the amount of carryover has a significant influence upon price, it should be considered as a separate factor. Consumption may also be considered as one of the factors in the analysis. If most of the product is consumed in the United States, domestic consumption may be used. If not, a separate measure of consumption outside the United States may be needed.

To determine which factors to use in correlation analysis, it is usually best to plot separately on a graph several of the most significant factors, plotting at the top past price variations of the commodity and the related factors beneath. The two or three factors that fluctuate most similarly to the price in question should be selected for correlation. In forecasting individual prices, it is seldom practicable to use more than the three related factors and two are often sufficient.

Past Relationships of Selected Factors. The past relationships between these factors may be determined by multiple-regression analysis. However, graphic-correlation analysis can also be used quite effectively with about the same degree of accuracy, as well as having the added advantage of visual presentation. The period selected for correlation analysis should be long enough to cover several business cycles so that almost any conceivable combination of factors that may affect prices is included. If graphic correlation is to be employed, the factor fluctuating most similarly to the price being forecast should be used first and deviations from it then plotted against the factor having the next closest variation. In this way, it is usually possible to explain past variations by two or three variables, usually disposable personal income and some measure of production or consumption or both. In those cases in which stocks are extremely important in determining price, it may be advantageous to use disposable personal income, production, and inventories or stocks as the three variables to be correlated.

Forecast Procedure. After past relationships have been established, it is necessary to forecast the related factors to obtain the price forecast. Methods of arriving at disposable personal income have already been considered. For basic agricultural raw materials, the Department of Agriculture and private organizations make continuous crop forecasts. Changes in consumption may be estimated from past changes in relationship to disposable personal income, and future stocks of goods may be estimated from the differences between estimated production and consumption. Qualitative factors in the situation, such as governmental controls and changes in them, unusual demands owing to war, and shifts in consumer tastes, should be continually studied and forecasts modified in light of these studies.

After annual prices have been forecast, it is necessary to superimpose onto them a forecast of seasonal movements to describe prospective price changes during the year. Seasonal variations in raw material prices may be determined by using the method described in Chapter 3, watching carefully for changes in seasonal patterns. This is important because changes such as the gradual introduction of improved methods of cold storage have materially affected the seasonal variations of some prices. More significantly, however, are different seasonal patterns that occur under different conditions. For example, there may be one seasonal variation in years following a small crop of a commodity and another variation in years after a large crop. There also may be different variations in years in which national income is increasing or decreasing.

The relationship in some fields may be still more complex. Since the price of corn is related to the price of hogs, when the major price trend of hogs is downward, there are different patterns in the years following a large corn crop and those following a small corn crop; and other patterns following large and small crops when the major hog-price trend is upward. Some of the most accurate price forecasting on a seasonal basis has been done by a very careful study of the different seasonal patterns under different conditions. Of course, the use of too many seasonals will limit the number of past examples of each type, and the patterns will not be representative.

Manufactured Goods Prices

In forecasting the price of manufactured goods in which administered prices hold to some degree, it is necessary to forecast not only the price of the basic raw materials used but also changes in labor costs and overhead costs. This involves estimates of wage increases to be granted and also a study of internal business costs. Past patterns between costs and prices can be used to arrive at preliminary price forecasts from future cost estimates. This procedure will indicate the prices that businesses would like to charge. Whether or not they can depends upon the prospective demand for their product. A forecast of demand and a study of past relationships between the level of demand and prices in relation to costs can be used to make the needed adjustments in the price forecast.

Paul H. Earl and Nancy E. Kennedy have applied this type of analysis in their econometric studies of price increases.[7] The basic procedure in their research is to view prices of individual commodities by

7. Paul H. Earl and Nancy E. Kennedy, "A Disaggregated Approach to Forecasting Prices," in Paul H. Earl (ed.), *Analysis of Inflation* (Lexington, MA: Lexington Books, 1975), pp. 129–155.

stages of process; that is, the price is built up by the cost and prices that cover the inputs used in producing the commodity. In their analysis, short-run profit maximization is the foundation for deriving a price equation whose parameters could be estimated by regression techniques. The profit equation for an individual firm is:

$$PRF = PQ - [TFC + AHE(Q)(1/PRO) + PMAT(MAT)Q]$$
$$PRF = PQ - TFC - AHE(Q)(1/PRO) - PMAT(MAT)Q$$

where

$$
\begin{aligned}
PRF &= \text{profit} \\
P &= \text{price} \\
Q &= \text{output} \\
TFC &= \text{total fixed cost} \\
AHE &= \text{average hourly earnings} \\
PRO &= \text{productivity} \\
PMAT &= \text{input material prices} \\
MAT &= \text{material input per unit of output}
\end{aligned}
$$

Profit maximization for this individual firm leads to the following price equation:

$$P - AHE(1/PRO) + PMAT(MAT)$$

Earl and Kennedy also assume that changes in marginal costs are equal to changes in unit variable costs (material and labor), then the change in price, ΔP, is given by:

$$\Delta P = \Delta AHE(1/PRO) + AHE[\Delta(1/PRO)] + \Delta PMAT(MAT) + PMAT(\Delta MAT)$$

Any long-run analysis may include some capital costs.

But the change in price is also influenced by the output market. That is,

$$\Delta P = f(QD - QS)$$

where

$$
\begin{aligned}
QD &= \text{quantity demanded} \\
QS &= \text{quantity supplied}
\end{aligned}
$$

So, a price equation to be estimated by regression analysis might look like:

$$P = a + bAHE + cPRO + dPMAT + eSD$$

where

$$AHE = \text{average hourly earnings}$$
$$PRO = \text{productivity}$$
$$PMAT = \text{input material prices}$$
$$SD = \text{market measures}$$

a, b, c, d, and e are parameters to be estimated

Average hourly earnings (AHE) are represented by indexes appropriate to labor in retail, wholesale, durable and nondurable goods, depending on the type of commodity price to be forecasted. Material prices ($PMAT$) in each processing stage are represented by output prices from the previous stage of the production process (perhaps, various components of the Producer Price Index). These material prices represent an important force in price movements, because changes in prices at lower stages of processing feed into prices/costs at higher stages. Data for productivity (PRO) can rely on Bureau of Labor Statistics productivity measures. However, often the PRO term is omitted and included in the constant term. Market measures (SD) vary by market structures and timing relations. The analyst may find lags at the various stages of processing. Surrogates for the market measures might include output, inventories, capacity-utilization index, unemployment rate, or the employment rate.

One of the authors, Dennis Ellis, has used this disaggregate approach to price forecasting in making projections for costs escalation in military aircraft. The basic components of any aircraft are airframe, avionics, and engines. A price/cost total for each component is derived by viewing the price of each component by stage of processing. For example, the price/cost of an airframe is built up from labor cost (average hourly earnings in the aircraft industry), material costs (prices for aluminum sheets, nuts, bolts, wires, and other materials), and overhead costs (administration). Future values for these input variables give a future value for the airframe price.

FORECASTING COMMON STOCK PRICES

The value of a share of stock should theoretically be the present discounted value of a stream of earnings expected over a period of years. It is easy to develop the theory but difficult to measure the variables and the relationships among them. The stream of earnings is very difficult to forecast, since it depends on factors in the economy at large and in the business in question. The time period itself also presents a difficulty, since it cannot be infinite and earnings in the near future are worth more than they are in later years. Economists talk of earnings to the "period of the horizon," but this period cannot be precisely determined and probably is different for different investors. The interest rate at which to discount earnings is also indefinite, and different analysts use different rates. In addition, expectations of future conditions play a large role in the investors' decisions. Therefore, all that can be done on the basis of the factors involved is to make general observations. Current profits have a positive impact on the stock market and have the impact with some lead time. Interest rates also have an impact, but it is an inverse one, since, when the rate used to discount expected future income is higher, the value of a share of stock is less and vice versa. It is all but impossible, however, to determine reliable relationships in more than a general way.

Nevertheless, no phase of economic activity has received as much study as the fluctuations in the security markets. Spurred on by a desire to make profits in the stock market, a large number of individuals and institutions have attempted to forecast the future course of stock prices. Many of the forecasting services have proved to be of little value, and some individuals have sold forecasts that were not even based on a study of stock market behavior. For example, in 1947, in New York, an individual who had a large number of clients for his forecasting service was arrested. The authorities became suspicious because he claimed to have inside information. Upon checking, they found that he claimed that he obtained his information through his sister who insisted that she had contacted the spirits of some of the great speculators of the past and that they had given her the secret of the security market. According to this source of information, the market was rigged every day, and clues to the security market could be found in the Maggie and Jiggs cartoon (a newspaper comic strip popular at that time). The amazing thing about this situation was that many of the clients of this forecasting service maintained that it had an unusual degree of accuracy. Forecasters do develop strong and loyal followings, which can be illustrated by the huge number of people who, in 1981, sold their stock holdings after receiving a sell recommendation issued by Joseph Granville, a popular stock market analyst.

It should be recognized that a forecaster could be right a number of times purely on a chance basis. For example, if 100 people are forecasting the direction of the market, fifty could be right the first time purely by chance. Of those fifty, twenty-five could be right the second time, twelve the third time, six the fourth time, three the fifth time, and at least one the sixth time, purely by chance. About eleven of the forecasters would be expected to be correct at least five times out of the six chances, even if they were all to flip coins to make their choices. Therefore, a system must not be accepted that forecasts the market on its record of calling four or five turns correctly without a study of the scientific basis underlying it. To demonstrate that chance relationships can exist, one analyst (with tongue in cheek) found a high degree of relationship for the 1970–1976 period between year-end prices of the Dow-Jones Industrial Index stocks and the number of times players on the New York Mets baseball team struck out each season.

Numerous attempts have been made to forecast the security market by finding a number of economic series that, when combined over a past period, have moved in conformity with an average of stock prices. For example, one such service was inaugurated in 1948 on the basis of a study of the market from 1919 through 1947. By combining several series, a line was developed that gave buy and sell signals that had been correct in practically every case over the past test period. The hypothetical results if money had been invested beginning in 1919 and held through 1947 were phenomenal, since a fund would have increased by over six hundred times. In the first year in which the line was used to make actual forecasts, however, it gave a major sell signal at a point below the last buy signal and several false indications in between.

This has happened frequently, because by combining several series and weighting them properly, it is possible to pass through or near almost any series of points. In fact, it can be shown mathematically that a combination of three curves properly weighted can be made to pass through or near ten points chosen almost at random. Therefore, little faith should be placed in any forecasting service in which the series chosen and the weights used in combining them are not based upon a logical study of the movements of the market but only upon the excellence of past fit.

Other approaches to forecasting the level of stock prices are based on the technical approach that assumes that a relationship exists between prices in one period and prices in another period. This assumption has been questioned, and some have suggested that stock price movements are more like a random walk, that is, that past price behavior is no indicator of future price behavior. A major statistical study to test this hypothesis has been carried on at the Center for Research in Security Prices at the University of Chicago.

One study was designed to test two of the major theories of market behavior. The chartist approach holds that past market behavior gives information on future behavior because price patterns develop and such patterns tend to recur. If this is true and the patterns can be identified, it should be possible to develop a forecasting technique based on past developments. The random-walk approach holds that no regular pattern exists and that the future of prices is no more predictable than the path of a series of random numbers that have been cumulated. In other words, successive price changes are independent, random variables with no identifiable pattern. To test these hypotheses, the daily prices of each stock in the Dow-Jones Industrial Average were used. The time periods were usually from the end of 1957 to September 26, 1962. For each of the thirty stocks in the Industrial Average, there were between 1,200 and 1,700 observations. The price changes were found to be distributed in a frequency distribution that was similar to that based on chance, but had a long tail, because there were more scattered large increases in price than small ones. These data thus supported the random-walk hypothesis, since this is the shape of frequency distributions of most economic series that are not causally related to each other.[8]

Dow Theory

Some techniques that are used to forecast the security markets have met with some degree of success. The best known of these is the Dow theory. The Dow theory was named after Charles H. Dow, who was the founder of Dow-Jones & Company and the original editor of *The Wall Street Journal*. Dow wrote a series of articles in *The Wall Street Journal* in which he analyzed and attempted to explain past actions in the stock market. William P. Hamilton, who was an assistant to Dow and succeeded him as editor, continued these studies in his *Wall Street Journal* column, "The Stock Market Barometer." Various individuals have elaborated on the writings of Dow and Hamilton and have stressed different phases of their work or have added their own interpretations so that there is really no one Dow theory.

---

8. Eugene F. Fama, "The Behavior of Stock Market Prices," *The Journal of Business* (January 1965), pp. 34–105.

From a study of stock market averages developed by the Dow-Jones Publishing Company beginning in 1885, Dow recognized that there were three major movements in the security markets: the primary movement, which has varied from less than a year to several years in duration; the second reaction, which has lasted from three weeks to three months or more and has retraced from one third to two thirds of the preceding primary swing; and the day-to-day fluctuations. This observation was based on averages of railroad stocks and industrial stocks. Today, practically all Dow theorists still work with the Dow-Jones Industrial Average and the Dow-Jones Transportation Average.

Forecasting by the Dow theory is based upon the study of the primary fluctuations and the secondary reactions. Usually, a primary upward movement has had two or more secondary reactions, and a primary downward movement has had two or three upward reactions. According to the Dow theory, stocks should be bought on a primary upswing when the high point of the last secondary reaction has been exceeded. Since it is impossible to accurately forecast the low point of the cycle, the best policy is to wait for a secondary reaction to run its course so as to clearly establish that the primary trend is up. When the market, after a secondary reaction, passes the high point from which this reaction began, it is an indication to Dow theorists that the primary movement is upward and that a new bull market is in progress. For a positive signal to buy, it is necessary for this to happen in both the rail and the industrial averages. Figure 19-1 shows such buy signals.

To sell at the high point of the cycle is also impossible, since the peak cannot be forecast. Therefore, under the Dow theory, the investor takes no action on the first downturn in prices when the primary trend is reversed because it is not possible to be sure that this may not be another secondary reaction on the upswing. When the market has moved substantially downhill for a period of three or more weeks, has revived and moved upward from one third to two thirds of its previous drop, and has again turned downward, indications are that a secondary reaction on the downswing is in progress. When the market on the downturn exceeds the low point from which the last secondary revival began, a sell signal is given. The determination of the point of such a sell signal is also shown in Figure 19-1. It is again necessary for the two averages to corroborate each other for a positive signal.

When followed in major market swings, this technique has often been used quite successfully. The Dow system, however, has given many false signals, especially in more recent years. In a market in which wide swings occur, it provides a method for an individual to

Figure 19-1   Dow Theory—Major Buy and Sell Signals

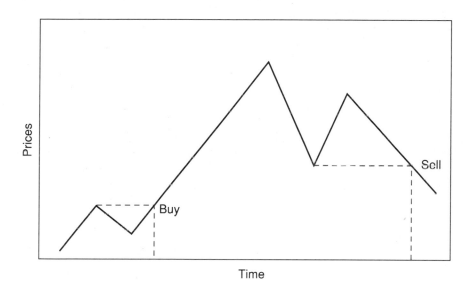

buy stocks at relatively low prices and to sell them at relatively high prices without trying to forecast the exact tops or bottoms of the market. It cannot work, however, when the market is not subject to large up-and-down movements, since it is easily possible in such a case to have a buy signal at a higher point than a subsequent sell signal. The system has also, in part, defeated itself, since it has had many adherents and their actions have influenced the course of the market at times.

Since the Dow theory has given false signals, Dow theorists have also used other market factors in conjunction with it. For example, some of these theorists are on the alert for a line being formed in the market, which occurs when, for a period of several weeks, both the rail and the industrial averages fluctuate within narrow limits of about 5 percent. According to Dow theorists, if both of the averages break out above the line, there is an indication of higher prices. If they break out below the line, the indication is for lower prices. There does not appear to be much logical basis for this phase of the Dow theory, and it has given many false signals.

More recently, stress has been placed on the relationship of volume to price movements. For example, according to this theory, a market that has been overbought becomes dull on rallies and develops activity on declines; and bull markets tend to terminate with excess activity after beginning with a comparatively low volume. There is undoubtedly something to the relationship between volume and price, since these factors are important in determining the total demand for stocks, but little of true forecasting value has been developed to date.

Other Techniques

A large number of other services that attempt to forecast prices in the security markets have appeared. One such service is based on the principle that in a strong market, there will be not only an increase in the averages but also a large number of individual stocks advancing in price. When the number of stocks advancing declines while the market averages are continuing upward, or vice versa, there is an indication of a reversal in movement.

Other services have tried to use odd-lot data, that is, data on sales of less than a round lot, as a basis for forecasting. When odd-lot sales are moving in a direction different from that of the general market, bullish or bearish signals are given. When in a market upswing or downswing the odd-lot traders significantly change their behavior and switch from buying to selling or vice versa, this is a signal to do the opposite. The main difficulty with this system is not only that it has given wrong signals, but that it has also given no signal when a signal has been called for. It will, as a rule, give a dependable signal to sell in those speculative markets in which the general public has done a large amount of speculative buying, but such markets have not often existed.

Some analysts have used a confidence index to try to gauge the general direction of the stock market. One such index is calculated by dividing high-grade bond yields by lower-grade bond yields. For example, the yield on Aaa bonds may be divided by the yield on Baa bonds or Ba or B bonds. The basic idea is that the smaller the spread, the greater the level of investor confidence in the future of the economy. A rise in this index indicates that stock prices will go up; a decline indicates that they will fall. This is again too simple a device to be used alone, since many factors other than investor confidence affect the market, and the change in relative bond yields may be due to factors other than changes in investor confidence.

Other forecasters have gauged future price movements by using the ratio of the number of new highs to new lows of stocks on the New York Stock Exchange. An increase in the ratio of highs to lows is bullish; a decrease is bearish. Some analysts believe that if the number of new lows exceeds the number of new highs, it is a signal of the end of a bull market. The basic idea of this technique is similar to that of a diffusion index, but it is too simple a technique to be used as the sole forecasting device and can serve only as one of several factors to gauge general price movements.

Some analysts base their forecasts of stock prices for individual firms on the stock market activities of the firm's officers and other employees who are called "insiders." These activities must be publicly reported under SEC rules. According to these analysts, the timing and size of insider purchases or sales of a firm's stock indicate the future direction the stock price will take.

There have been some attempts at econometric studies of the stock market. While the econometric approach can be used to project stock averages, the major usefulness of this research is in the understanding of the market.

As stated earlier, stock prices are determined by the present discounted value of the stream of earnings expected in the future. Although this is the ultimate determinant of stock prices, the critical question is, what economic variables interact together to influence stock prices? An econometric model developed several years ago by Michael W. Keran shows what economic variables influence stock prices.[9]

In Keran's model, there are four exogenous variables, full-employment output, which is not a policy variable, and three policy variables: the corporate tax rate, fiscal policy, and changes in the nominal money supply. Fiscal and monetary policy affect stock prices in two ways: (1) they influence total spending, and this, combined with the corporate tax rate, affects earnings; and (2) policy changes will influence spending. This spending, compared with full-employment output, influences prices and expectations of future price changes. Expectations of inflation and real growth impact interest rates, which, in turn, have a negative influence on stock prices.

Attempts to forecast stock price changes will no doubt continue. These prices, however, are among the most difficult to forecast because, to a large extent, psychological factors influence them. From time to time, also, the uninitiated enter the market and accentuate price swings. The average investor would do well to base any purchase of

---

9. Michael W. Keran, "Expectations, Money, and the Stock Market," *Review*, Federal Reserve Bank of St. Louis (January 1971), pp. 16–31.

common stock on an analysis of the worth of individual stock based on forecasts of the future prospects of particular companies rather than on price forecasts of the stock market in general. In this way, the investor is assured of a reasonable return and relative safety, irrespective of market movements.

QUESTIONS

1. Discuss the factors that lead to price changes in the long run.
2. Describe a procedure for projecting price trends.
3. What effect do costs have on price trends?
4. Describe and evaluate the use of supply and demand factors for forecasting prices.
5. Describe the St. Louis model for forecasting the general price level. Relate it to the analysis of the quantity theory in Chapter 7.
6. Describe procedures for forecasting prices based on leading series, expectations, and diffusion indexes.
7. Describe the procedures used to forecast prices of agricultural commodities.
8. How may monthly price forecasts for such commodities as cotton be developed from annual price forecasts?
9. Describe how the price of a durable good might be forecasted using the stages of processing approach.
10. Describe the chartist and the random-walk theories of stock price movements. What are the implications for the investor of the random-walk theory?
11. Describe the workings of the Dow theory for forecasting stock prices.
12. Under what conditions would the Dow theory work reasonably well?
13. Discuss several other methods for forecasting stock price changes.

READINGS

Bosworth, Barry P., and Robert Z. Lawrence. *Commodity Prices and the New Inflation*. Washington, D.C.: The Brookings Institution, 1982.

Cragg, John G., and Burton G. Malkiel. *Expectations and the Structure of Share Prices*. Chicago: University of Chicago Press (an NBER Monograph), 1982.

Earl, Paul H. *Inflation and the Structure of Industrial Prices*. Lexington, MA: Lexington Books, 1973.

———, (ed.). *Analysis of Inflation*. Lexington, MA: Lexington Books, 1975.

Eckstein, Otto. *Core Inflation*. Englewood Cliffs, NJ: Prentice-Hall, Inc., 1981.

Ellis, Dennis F. "Uses of Commercial Forecasting Models—Price Forecasting." *Business Economics* (January 1979), pp. 44–46.

Fama, Eugene F. "The Behavior of Stock Market Prices." *The Journal of Business* (January 1965), pp. 34–105.

Friedman, Milton, and Anna J. Schwartz. *Monetary Trends in the United States and the United Kingdom*. Chicago: University of Chicago Press (an NBER Monograph), 1982.

Hall, Robert E., ed. *Inflation: Causes and Effects*. Chicago: University of Chicago Press (an NBER Research Project), 1983.

Handbook of Agricultural Charts. Washington, D.C.: U.S. Department of Agriculture, annually.

Karnosky, Denis S. "The Link between Money and Prices: 1971–1976." *Review*, Federal Reserve Bank of St. Louis (June 1976), pp. 17–23.

Malkiel, Burton G. *A Random Walk Down Wall Street*, 2d College Edition. New York: W. W. Norton & Co., 1981.

Moor, Roy E. "Economics of Financial Markets." *Business Economics* (April 1985).

Rhea, Robert. *Dow's Theory Applied to Business and Banking*. New York: Simon and Schuster, Inc., 1938.

Waugh, Frederick V. *Demand and Price Analysis*. Washington, D.C.: U.S. Department of Agriculture, 1964.

FORECASTING SALES

In addition to a forecast of general economic activity, it is often useful to have forecasts of the volume of sales in major industries. Industry forecasts can help cross-check forecasts of total business activity. They also are valuable in helping to determine if unemployment is likely to occur in an industry, to decide if additional workers must be recruited, and to estimate the amount of additional new capital that may be required. The managers of a business will find a forecast of industry sales helpful in forecasting sales of their business and in planning operations for the next several quarters.

FORECASTING INDUSTRY SALES

When forecasting cyclical movements in an industry, it is necessary to study the factors that have been responsible for past changes. The *first step* in this process is the careful selection of the specific product(s) that are to be analyzed. It is necessary to decide whether the sales should be analyzed as a whole or divided into subcategories. The latter should be done if different factors affect different classes of sales. For example, in analyzing the factors that have affected sales in the clothing industry, better results are obtained by studying women's, men's, and children's clothing separately, since trends are different in each segment. Also, changes in birth rates affect the last category materially.

The *second step* is to select the measure of aggregate economic activity that is most closely related to changes in sales of the product(s) being analyzed. In some cases when a good is sold to consumers, producers, and the government, the most important factor to study is the relationship to GNP. In other cases when a product is sold primarily to consumers, it is probably the relationship to disposable personal income or, in rural areas, to cash farm income. In still other industries, such as construction hardware, the volume of construction activity may be the most important factor, and in some manufacturing industries, the Federal Reserve Board Index of Industrial Production may be the best measure. The forecaster must determine the best variable data to use by employing correlation analysis, whether simple or multiple. Consideration should be given to the availability of the needed data, whether the data can be received in time to be useful, and whether the cost or effort to acquire the data justifies their use.

The *third step* in forecasting cyclical movements in an industry is to analyze the trend of sales over the past ten to fifteen years. This trend should be compared with trends in GNP, industrial production, disposable personal income, or other appropriate measures to see how sales have been growing and how they have fluctuated relative to changes in total economic activity. A thorough analysis should be made of factors that have affected the trend of sales, especially in periods in which activity in the industry may not have been following the trend.

The *fourth step* is to develop a preliminary forecast based on the relationships of industry sales to general economic activity and other factors that affect the sales of the product. Any business can easily list fifteen to twenty factors that affect sales in its industry. It is seldom practicable, however, to work with more than three or four of the most important variables on a quantitative basis. It is extremely important in selecting these variables to work only with those that are logically related to the series being studied and as nearly as possible directly related causally. Variables that are often useful include changes in the level of income from the past year and earlier years, changes in price, changes in the expected life of the product, and changes in population.

After selecting the most important variables, it is necessary to consider the nature of the relationships that have already occurred by graphing the relationships or by using regression analysis. The regression approach has the advantage of being definite, since, once the general formula is chosen, any analyst will arrive at the same specific formula. The graphic approach, however, is simpler and is easier for most business people to comprehend.

To use relationships involving general measures of economic activity as a basis for forecasting industry sales, it is, of course, necessary to have a forecast of the aggregate measures. Basing a forecast on general measures is feasible for a business, because private organizations and governmental agencies have spent millions of dollars in developing such forecasts. Many of these are available at little or no cost, and even those bought from research organizations cost far less than it would cost to develop forecasts by the firm itself. Another reason for using relationships of aggregate measures is that they are often easier to develop than sales forecasts for industries using other methods.

The basic procedure needed to complete step four is to relate sales to national business activity. That is, one could consider sales as a function of GNP; sales = $f(GNP)$. To forecast sales in the future we need forecasts for GNP in the future. (Chapters 15, 16, and 17 discussed ways of making a GNP projection.) Or, one could rely on projections for GNP available commercially, such as the proprietary econometric models (for example, Data Resources Inc. or Wharton Econometric Forecasting Associates), or surveys (*Blue Chip Economic Indicators* or *The Journal of Business Forecasting*). By substituting these future values for the independent variable (GNP) in the estimated functional relation, and making the needed computations, a forecast for sales can be obtained.

As an example, we will use historical data to develop a simple regression relation between sales and some aggregate economic variable, such as current dollar GNP. Suppose the regression relation is:[1]

$$Sales_t \;=\; 257.82 + 0.88 GNP_t$$

where

$$
\begin{aligned}
Sales_t &= \text{current dollar sales at time } t, \text{ measured in thousands} \\
GNP_t &= \text{current dollar } GNP \text{ at time } t, \text{ measured in billions}
\end{aligned}
$$

Next, complete your GNP projection for the next two quarters (or you could use GNP projected by a commercial model). For our example, the forecast for next quarter $(t+1)$ is \$5,231.2 billion, and for the following quarter $(t+2)$ is \$5,319.8 billion. Thus, projected sales for next quarter, and the following quarter would be:

$$
\begin{aligned}
Sales_{t+1} &= 257.82 + 0.88(\$5,231.2) \\
&= \$4,861.276 \text{ billion or } \$4,861,276 \\
Sales_{t+2} &= 257.82 + 0.88(\$5,319.8) \\
&= \$4,939.244 \text{ billion or } \$4,939,244
\end{aligned}
$$

A *fifth step* is to analyze all of the qualitative factors in the past,

---

1. Dennis F. Ellis, "How to Use Macroforecasts in Sales Forecasting," *The Journal of Business Forecasting* (Fall 1987), pp. 19–21.

present, and future to determine if past relationships will continue. In general, consumer buying habits do not deviate radically from the pattern of the past in the short run, nor do methods of business operation change rapidly in the absence of marked technological innovations. Changes do take place, however, and it is necessary to study the effects of changes in governmental policies, technological innovations, and the like before deciding that past relationships will continue into the immediate future.

A *sixth step* (or in some cases, an alternative to steps two, three, four, and five) is to develop a forecast by end-use analysis. This technique starts by grouping products or services by end uses, such as for direct personal consumption, as a material or part for further manufacture in a specific industry, or as a product or service sold to the federal government. Then, the relationship of activity in the end-use industries to sales in the industry being forecast is determined.

The *seventh step* is to forecast the level of sales in each of the end-use industries and use that information, and past relationships, to develop an industry forecast. This method is practicable only if end-use is distributed over only a few major industries. It is used, for example, in the industrial chemical industry in which most of the sales go to a limited group of users. Detailed information on the end-use of industry products is available in input-output tables, which are discussed later in this chapter. In cases in which it is practicable, industry forecasts should be made using both end-use analysis and relationships to aggregate measures of economic activity, and the two forecasts used as a cross-check on each other. If the two methods have given similar results in the past and now give significantly different results, it is an indication that all factors need to be carefully analyzed. Chances are good that some significant factors have been overlooked or that past relationships are changing.

The *final step* is to be aware of the degree of error that is inherent in any forecast. No relationship based on the past can be expected to work perfectly in the future, since there are scores of factors other than the variables used that affect sales, and since new factors also come into play. The effects of these other factors may tend to balance out in most years, but, at times, there may be an unusual number of them working in the same direction so that the error may be greater than the average. The analyst will wish to learn from these errors. If the forecast is significantly different from the actual result, discovering the reason for the discrepancy may lead to improved specifications for future attempts at forecasting.

Forecasting Sales in Consumer Nondurable Goods and Services Industries

Sales of consumer nondurable goods are usually easier to forecast than that for consumer durable goods, because the former are usually purchased more frequently, and because they do not last for long periods of time; therefore, the purchases cannot be transferred to the future to any great extent.

The Department of Commerce has developed a relationship between disposable personal income and personal consumption expenditures for detailed categories of nondurable goods and services. The sensitivity of personal consumption expenditures to disposable personal income is expressed by a ratio showing the average change in expenditures compared to changes in income. (See Table 20-1.) For example, the ratio for gasoline and oil for the post-World War II period is 1.6, indicating that expenditures on gasoline and oil have changed on the average 1.6 times as fast as changes in incomes. Some Department of Commerce ratios for the prewar and postwar period for the major categories of consumer expenditures are shown in Table 20-1. This table shows the sensitivity of expenditures in real terms based on 1957 dollars, thus eliminating the effect of price changes.

A study by the Harvard Economic Research Project under a contract with the U.S. Bureau of Labor Statistics has also developed relationships based on past data that are helpful in forecasting consumer expenditures. This study developed the relationships, in constant dollars of expenditures, of eighty-two categories of personal consumption expenditures to total consumption expenditures. This was done using 1929–1964 and 1946–1964 data. The study concluded that relationships based on the two time periods were better than those for the postwar period alone, because many postwar series had a persistent upward movement. Also, the results were largely due to the trend rather than changes in personal income for eleven broad expenditure groups used by the Department of Commerce based on data for the 1929–1964 period. Some of the Harvard sensitivity ratios are also shown in Table 20-1.[2]

During the pre-World War II period, the changes in sales of most nondurable goods were determined largely by changes in disposable personal income. The high degree of correlation between sales of non-

---

2. H. S. Houthakker and Lester D. Taylor, *Consumer Demand in the United States: Analyses and Projections* (Cambridge, MA: Harvard University Press, 1970), pp. 189–190.

Table 20-1

Sensitivity[a] of Personal Consumption Expenditures
to Changes in Disposable Personal Income

Group	Prewar	Postwar[b]	Both[c]
	Based on Constant (1957) Dollars		
Total personal consumption expenditures	**0.8**	**1.0**	
Durable goods	2.1	1.2	
Nondurable goods	0.7	0.9	
Services	0.5	1.0	
Automobiles and parts	2.8	1.1	1.5
Furniture and household equipment	1.6	1.0	1.3
Clothing and shoes	0.9[d]	0.5[f]	0.9
Food and alcoholic beverages	0.8[e]	0.8[f]	0.9
Gasoline and oil	0.6[d]	1.6[f]	1.9
Household operation	0.9	1.5	—
Housing	0.2	1.3	2.0
Transportation	1.0	0.3	0.4

Source: *Survey of Current Business* (March 1959), p. 25; and H.S. Houthakker and Lester D. Taylor, *Consumer Demand in the United States: Analyses and Projections* (Cambridge, MA: Harvard University Press, 1970), pp. 189–190.
[a]Based on least squares using $C=aI^a(1+r)^t$ for the period 1929–1940 and $C=aI^a$ for the postwar period where C=personal consumption expenditures, I=disposable personal income, and t=time. The exponent a derived from the data is an approximate measure of the income sensitivity of the expenditure items.
[b]In the case of total goods and services, durable goods, nondurable goods, and services, the sensitivity coefficients in this column were based on the twenties and the postwar period.
[c]From the study by Houthakker and Taylor for the period 1929–1964.
[d]Based on period 1929–1940 and postwar years including income and time as factors. The postwar relations using income alone give a coefficient of 0.5 for clothing and 2.0 for gasoline.
[e]Based on period 1933–1941 and postwar years.
[f]Based on current dollars.

durable goods and disposable personal income was somewhat disturbed during World War II because of shortages, especially of gasoline. In the early postwar periods, sales of nondurables were above the level indicated by prewar relationships, but many have returned to prewar levels. Personal consumption expenditures for services have grown more rapidly than personal consumption expenditures for durable and nondurable goods. Expenditures on housing and household operation also have shown a marked upward shift from the prewar to the postwar period. When forecasting the most likely sales levels, societal changes that have taken place or are in progress must be studied.

Forecasting Sales in the Consumer Durable Goods Industries

Forecasting the sales of consumer durable goods is usually somewhat more complex than projecting the sales of nondurables. Sales change more rapidly and to a greater degree, and more factors must be considered because buying decisions are more complex. The most important influence on the sales of durable goods, just as in the case of nondurable goods, is disposable personal income. Since the purchase of a consumer durable good usually involves a larger expenditure than does the purchase of nondurable goods, the direction of change in income from the preceding year and earlier years is also important. Purchases from any given income tend to be greater when income has been rising from the level of the year previous than when it has been falling. Most likely, this is due, in part, to the optimism associated with rising income and to the pessimism associated with falling income, and to the lag that probably exists in adjusting expenditures for major items to changes in income.

Also important in forecasting the sales of many durable goods is the rate of population growth and the growth in the number of families. Demand is likewise affected by the relative price of the durable good in relationship to the general price level. A change in the length of the useful life of the good, such as an increase in length of life for autos, would also significantly influence current demand.

Purchasers of durable consumer goods, including autos, major appliances, and furniture, tend to be quite sensitive to interest rates as being the cost of borrowing. Durable-goods purchases can, and will, be postponed quite easily if interest rates, incomes, and/or prices are expected to be more favorable in the near future. In 1982, durable goods were hit hard in all three ways, since consumers expected lower interest rates, lower inflation, and lower incomes in the future.[3]

An important source of information for forecasting consumer durable goods is the University of Michigan Survey Research Center, which regularly publishes the results of household surveys on consumer attitudes about future expectations involving purchases of autos, houses, and household durables. The Center's Index of Consumer Sentiment provides a general indication of the current degrees of consumer optimism and pessimism.[4]

---

3. Richard T. Curtin, "Unemployment Adds to Interest Rate Distress," *Economic Outlook USA* (Winter 1982).

4. See current editions of Survey Research Center, Institute for Social Research, *Economic Outlook USA* (Ann Arbor, MI: University of Michigan, quarterly).

Forecasting Sales in Industries That Sell Goods Used by Producers, Consumers, and Government

Although the changes in sales for most nondurable goods used by consumers can be explained by changes in disposable personal income, it is better to use GNP, national income, or industrial production when measuring changes in the sales of products used by producers, consumers, and the government. For example, paper production in total (as an indicator of sales) shows a high degree of correlation with GNP. There is substantial demand for paper by consumers, retailers, wholesalers, manufacturers, and the government; in fact, by every segment of the economy. One finds a good relation when paper production is correlated with the Federal Reserve Board Index of Nondurable Goods Production.

On the basis of a forecast of GNP, it is possible to forecast paper production by using past relationships and by studying the current situation. Such a forecast can be cross-checked by a forecast of the Federal Reserve Board Index of Nondurable Goods Production and the past relationships of paper production to it.

Forecasts of total paper production are valuable to the producers of basic paper raw materials and diversified lines of paper products. Many individual producers, however, will need to study the demand for a particular type of paper, such as book paper, wrapping paper, tissue paper, container board, and various papers used by the building trades. In each sector, it is necessary to find the specific component of GNP or industrial production that most closely explains past changes in sales. It also may be necessary to analyze technological changes and price changes that have led to the substitution of one type of paper for another and/or to shifts in paper usage.

Just as the sales of paper fluctuate relative to economic activity, so do the sales of paperboard. Since paperboard is used primarily for packing manufactured products, it correlates best with industrial production. Until the middle 1950s, paperboard production was growing more rapidly than industrial production, since transport technology was shifting from the use of wooden containers to paperboard containers. After 1955, the growth of paperboard production was only slightly more than industrial production growth, and for a period of time in the mid- and late 1960s, the rate of growth was practically the same. Figure 20-1 shows the relative growth of paper and paperboard production compared to industrial production during the 1969–1987 period. A forecast of paper and paperboard sales might begin with an analysis of such past relationships. It is also necessary to study care-

Figure 20-1   Growth of Paper and Paperboard Production in Relation to
Industrial Production, 1969–1987

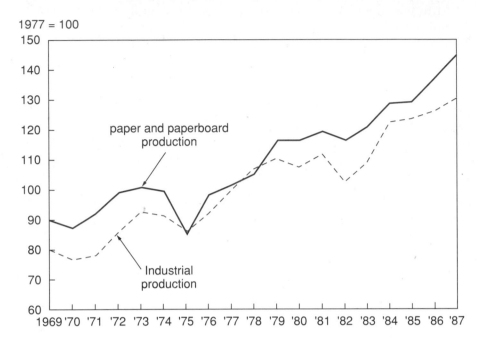

Source: Data from *Survey of Current Business* and *Federal Reserve Bulletin*.

fully all factors in the current and prospective situation as well as the
possibility of a change in past relationships.

Forecasting Sales in Producer Goods and Building Materials Industries

Many of the techniques discussed under other industries are used
in forecasting sales in the producer goods and building materials industries. Procedures for forecasting overall sales in these industries
were considered in forecasting GNP and industrial production. Since
the demand for producer goods is a derived demand, a basic approach
is to study sales of producer goods in relationship to changes in demand and production in the related consumer goods or service industry. Sales of some types of railroad cars, for example, is related to the
demand for transportation of freight by railroad and correlates with
industrial production. In a recession period, new cars are not needed
and railroads are reluctant to buy ahead of needs when profits are de-

clining. As an upturn proceeds, additional demand for cars exists and funds are available to finance these purchases. Past patterns of freight-car sales relative to industrial production, and a forecast of industrial production can be used as a basis for developing a forecast of sales of freight cars.

In some producer goods industries, pressure indexes may be used to indicate increases or decreases in the sales of a particular product. A *pressure index* shows the relationship between the production or output in an industry and the amount of capital equipment used to produce that output. Pressure indexes based on present usage give an indication of the demand in the near future for many types of durable producer goods. For example, the present rate of use of existing electric power-generating equipment gives some indication of demand for it at a future time; and the ratio of seasonally corrected car loadings to the number of cars owned by railroads gives a reasonable indication of the number of cars railroads will order six months to a year in the future.

In many individual industries, it is possible to employ use data on relationships between new orders, production, and inventory in a manner similar to that used in forecasting various measures of overall economic activity. The Department of Commerce has this kind of data series available for an increasing number of industries. Trade associations also gather and publish these figures for their particular industries.

In some industries, such as those that produce construction materials, it may be possible to arrive at reasonably accurate timing of the changes in sales from lead/lag relationships. For example, the sales of producers plumbing supplies have usually followed by three or four months the F. W. Dodge Company series on residential contracts awarded. Many of the items used in housing construction have a sales pattern that matches the actual use of these materials in building, since supplies are not stocked to any great extent. In looking for lead-lag relationships, only those with a logical basis should be considered, since spurious relationships may hold for a period of time. Continuous study is needed, even in the case of logically related series, since past relationships may change.

Outside the construction industry, there has been some research on developing industry economic indicators. One study was completed by Michael P. Niemra for the chemical industry.[5] Niemra found that a composite index of chemical industry production, employment, and

---

5. Michael P. Niemra, "Developing Industry Leading Economic Indicators," *Business Economics* (January 1982), pp. 5–16.

the real value of shipments gave a good determination of the peaks and troughs in the chemical industry. In other words, this composite was used as the indicator of an "industry cycle." The turning points of this composite industry indicator were roughly coincident with the U.S. reference business cycle as designated by the National Bureau of Economic Research (NBER). By using a composite index, Niemra found greater reliability in conforming to NBER reference cycles. Also, the use of several indicators in the industry index makes turning point dates less dependent on data revisions.

One question to ask is, because of the closeness of the industry cycle to the NBER reference cycle, why develop a distinct, special industry leading indicator? Niemra found that U.S. business cycles are widely diffused among U.S. industries. In other words, every industry is not affected in precisely the same way or the same degree in every business cycle. The industry economic indicator provides additional insight into the lead/lag relationship in an industry sector.

Use of Input-Output Data in Industry Forecasting

The Bureau of Economic Analysis (BEA) of the Department of Commerce is working on a major program that involves the periodic preparation of interindustry tables that can serve as a basis for industry forecasts. These tables provide a comprehensive picture of the interactions among the various industries and the final market demand in the economy. The input-output tables show final product flows and value added just as in the case with the National Income and Product Accounts. The final product flows are shown as sales by each industry to consumers, investors, government, and foreigners; and the value added is shown by the industry in which it originates. The input-output accounts also cover the flow of raw materials, semifinished products, and services among industries. The tracing of these flows is the major contribution of input-output accounts.

The tables that are currently available in detailed form are based on data for 1977 and cover 537 industries or products. Data are also available on eighty-five industry categories that are aggregates of the data for the 537 industries. Earlier input-output analyses are available for 1947, 1958, 1963, 1967, and 1972. The BEA has developed input-output data as a regular part of an integrated system of national accounts, although budget cuts have limited publication in recent years.

Input-output data are usually presented in a table in which each industry is represented by a row and a column, each final market by a column, and value added by one or more rows. The row for an industry shows the distribution of its output to itself, to other industries, and to final markets. These final markets are the familiar personal consumption expenditures, gross private domestic investment, net inventory change, gross exports, federal governmental purchases, and state and local governmental purchases. The column for an industry shows its consumption of goods and services from the various industries and the value it has added.

Five basic tables are prepared as part of the input-output accounts. They are:

1. The use of commodities by industries in dollar terms at producer prices. This table shows the value of each commodity used by each industry.
2. The make of commodities by industries in dollar terms at producer prices. This table shows the value of each commodity made by each industry.
3. Commodity-by-industry direct requirements per dollar of industry output at producer prices. This table shows the direct inputs required by an industry to produce a dollar of the industry's output (called "direct requirements coefficients").
4. Commodity-by-commodity total requirements, direct and indirect, per dollar of delivery to final demand at producer prices. This fourth table (a portion of which is shown in Table 20-2) shows the direct plus the indirect production of inputs required to produce a dollar's worth of some specified commodity (called "commodity-by-commodity total requirements coefficients").
5. Industry-by-commodity total requirements, direct and indirect, per dollar of delivery to final demand, at producers' prices. This table is similar to the fourth, except that it shows the requirements from industries to produce the specified commodity.[6]

To demonstrate how to read Table 20-2, consider petroleum refining and related industries (commodity number 31) as an example. To provide for the final demand from an additional $1,000,000 in expenditures on refined petroleum products, $1,102,190 of production by the industry itself ($1,000,000 × 1.10219 from column 31, row 31) is required. Continuing the example, $60,420 is required from the chem-

---

6. We are able just to touch on some of these. The interested reader will wish to study the article by the Interindustry Economics Division, "The Input-Output Structure of the U.S. Economy, 1977," *Survey of Current Business* (May 1984), pp. 42–84.

Table 20-2

Commodity-by-Commodity Total Requirements, 1977
(Total requirements, direct and indirect, per dollar of delivery to final demand, at producers' prices)

Each entry represents the output required, directly and indirectly, of the commodity named at the beginning of the row for each dollar of delivery to final demand of the commodity named at the head of the column

Commodity number	21 Wood containers	22 Household furniture	23 Other furniture and fixtures	24 Paper and allied products, except containers	25 Paperboard containers and boxes	26 Printing and publishing	27 Chemicals and selected chemical products	28 Plastics and synthetic materials	29 Drugs, cleaning and toilet preparations	30 Paints and allied products	31 Petroleum refining and related industries	32 Rubber and miscellaneous plastics products	33 Leather tanning and finishing
21 Wood containers	1.00883	.00104	.00060	.00013	.00008	.00006	.00010	.00010	.00020	.00011	.00004	.00024	.00043
22 Household furniture	.00003	1.00222	.00037	.00003	.00003	.00002	.00003	.00003	.00002	.00003	.00004	.00004	.00002
23 Other furniture and fixtures	.00005	.00005	1.00773	.00009	.00007	.00004	.00006	.00005	.00004	.00005	.00009	.00005	.00004
24 Paper and allied products, except containers	.03672	.01892	.01708	1.23393	.51626	.22657	.02489	.03646	.03686	.02274	.00909	.03723	.02216
25 Paperboard containers and boxes	.06174	.01700	.01636	.02138	1.05392	.01003	.00860	.01457	.02922	.01426	.00484	.01886	.02038
26 Printing and publishing	.00538	.00569	.00477	.00507	.00504	1.13135	.00540	.00464	.01037	.01095	.00259	.00421	.00673
27 Chemicals and selected chemical products	.02843	.04870	.04238	.08879	.07921	.05610	1.31548	.46903	.15933	.38224	.06042	.17874	.13272
28 Plastics and synthetic materials	.01255	.04004	.02155	.04560	.03319	.01390	.01880	1.07644	.01766	.08146	.00348	.21758	.00577
29 Drugs, cleaning and toilet preparations	.00088	.00151	.00101	.00358	.00206	.00142	.00763	.00880	1.07608	.00654	.00516	.00325	.03340
30 Paints and allied products	.00344	.01292	.01073	.00217	.00355	.00141	.00345	.00393	.00323	1.01551	.00178	.00234	.00135
31 Petroleum refining and related industries	.03414	.02852	.02616	.06386	.05065	.02747	.06707	.06092	.03476	.05707	1.10219	.04248	.03878
32 Rubber and miscellaneous plastics products	.00937	.06057	.05030	.03654	.02102	.01924	.01753	.02979	.04481	.01517	.00683	1.05995	.01170
33 Leather tanning and finishing	.00006	.00398	.00045	.00006	.00004	.00018	.00005	.00004	.00004	.00008	.00003	.00017	1.05690
34 Footwear and other leather products	.00019	.00015	.00010	.00013	.00011	.00012	.00018	.00015	.00013	.00016	.00011	.00025	.00013
35 Glass and glass products	.00132	.00729	.00316	.00141	.00098	.00101	.00191	.00200	.01811	.00273	.00107	.00700	.00859
36 Stone and clay products	.00832	.00948	.00877	.00684	.00527	.00306	.00670	.00580	.00383	.01658	.00688	.00788	.00563
37 Primary iron and steel manufacturing	.02295	.05328	.16150	.01371	.02237	.01038	.02940	.01999	.02175	.04281	.02060	.03017	.01373
38 Primary nonferrous metals manufacturing	.00892	.02662	.04501	.01329	.01733	.01014	.04400	.02581	.01826	.04437	.00963	.01814	.01118
39 Metal containers	.00106	.00198	.00256	.00211	.00194	.00148	.01307	.00971	.02526	.06168	.00489	.00333	.01642
40 Heating, plumbing, and structural metal products	.00377	.00244	.00226	.00283	.00244	.00157	.00335	.00277	.00194	.00243	.00481	.00286	.00179
41 Screw machine products and stampings	.00618	.01092	.02182	.00314	.00242	.00188	.00288	.00232	.00679	.00409	.00177	.00558	.00256
42 Other fabricated metal products	.01911	.06687	.04417	.01682	.01494	.00768	.01005	.00832	.01290	.01156	.01114	.01157	.00560
43 Engines and turbines	.00130	.00121	.00180	.00151	.00136	.00084	.00289	.00201	.00112	.00170	.00338	.00163	.00109

Source: *Survey of Current Business* (May 1984), pp. 68–69.

ical and selected chemical products industry (column 31, row 27), and $4,890 is required from the metal containers industry (column 31, row 39).

The rows in Table 20-2 can be used to determine the requirements for the product of an industry owing to final demand for the output of other industries. From row 31 for crude petroleum and natural gas, we can see that if a $1,000,000 increase in final demand for wood containers occurs, $34,140 of additional output by the petroleum industry would be required (column 21, row 31). Reading across row 31, it is clear that any additions to most other industries' final demand will result in significant increases in petroleum demand, as we would expect. Contrast this with row 21 for wood containers, where household furniture requires the only significant increase in wood container demand.

Many firms, academicians, and private forecasting organizations make use of these input-output tables as the core of their sales forecasting efforts. The tables can indeed be very helpful for this purpose, especially for a firm such as a specialty steel producer whose output is used as intermediate inputs of other firms rather than going directly into final demand. These tables do require, however, an awareness of the problem of the fixity of the coefficients. In the first place, new tables become available infrequently, and with a considerable time lag, and thus may be out of date. Second, microeconomic theory provides that coefficients of production change with changes in technology and with changes in relative prices. The petroleum products example would be viewed currently with some suspicion, after the extreme changes in prices in recent years caused producers to shift to substitutes for gas and oil and then shift back to gas and oil.

The BEA has also prepared a table showing the output attributed to final demand by major sectors of GNP for each industry. These data are shown in terms of producers' prices and purchasers' prices. This information can be used, along with a forecast of changes in major sectors of GNP, to get an approximation of changes in a particular industry arising from changes in GNP. A final forecast must, of course, be made only after an analysis of changes that may have occurred in relationships that held in 1977 and after a study of all factors that may affect demand.

As was pointed out earlier, all figures in the input-output table are in terms of producer prices, whereas figures in the National Income and Product Accounts are in terms of final-purchase prices. The differences are shown in input-output accounts primarily under two industry groupings, the transportation and warehousing industry and the wholesale and retail trade industry, and, in some cases, under the finance and insurance industry.

FORECASTING SALES FOR AN INDIVIDUAL BUSINESS

Forecasts of total economic activity and of sales in an industry are useful in determining the general business climate and the direction of sales. However, for setting sales quotas, scheduling production, and ordering raw materials, it is necessary to have a sales forecast for an individual business, and, if it is a multiproduct firm, for each of its major lines of products. General business and industry forecasts constitute a basis for making a sales forecast, but other important items must also be considered.

Product Classification

The first step in forecasting sales for an individual business is a classification of the products sold by that concern. The classification should group together products that would seem to have common factors affecting the level of sales. If a system of product classification is used for inventory and production control, many of the same classes can be used. Additional classifications needed for forecasting purposes often can be added to an existing system, or some of the classes in that system can be combined.

One of the first classifications required is the division between basic products and by-products, since the planned level of production of the basic product determines the prospective supply of the by-products that will have to be sold. If the demand for the by-products is elastic, adjustments can be made in price so as to move all of them. If the demand is not elastic, it will be necessary to develop a market for the projected volume of by-products.

Differences in demand may occur, because different types of consumers buy the products, or because a different set of factors motivates their purchases. For example, a manufacturer of electrical controls found that the basic classifications for the firm's products were heating controls and air-conditioning controls. Heating controls were further subdivided into controls for industrial and residential users. Each of these controls was further broken down into controls for gas, oil, and coal units. Significant variations, especially in gas heating, were found between controls for conversion burners and those for new units.

Whenever a study of past sales experience shows appreciable differences in demand determinants, it is necessary to set up a separate category for forecasting purposes. Other factors also affect the production and the sales of a product, and these should be noted and checked in grouping products for sales forecast purposes. A factor that is especially important when business is in a downturn is the degree to which purchases may be deferred. For example, the purchase of furnace controls for the repair and replacement market may not be deferred for any period of time, but purchases for new installations may be put off as disposable personal income decreases.

It is also desirable to make separate lists of those products for which production is based to a significant extent on contracts received in advance and those products that are sold from current stock. If firm contracts are received well in advance, it may not be necessary to forecast external factors. Even if contracts are received shortly before shipment is expected, or if trade practices permit cancellations or postponement of shipment, contracts can still be useful in developing a forecast.

The forecasting department should also have available information on the average volume of sale for each of its basic product categories. This information is necessary, because sales will tend to be more uneven if made to a few large accounts. The effect on sales of losing one or more of these accounts will be large.

Products should be analyzed according to the basic raw materials that are used in them so that different influences affecting the price and the availability of raw materials may be considered in forecasting.

Analysis of the Trend of Sales

After the products that are sold by the business have been grouped into categories that have about the same demand determinants, the trend of sales of these products for the last ten to fifteen years should be studied. This trend can be compared with trends in GNP, in disposable personal income, or in industrial production to see, in a general way, how sales have been growing relative to the growth in total economic activity.

The trend in sales should also be compared with that in the industry of which this product group is a part. This may be difficult if the industry is not homogeneous. For example, each major chemical company produces a different product mix, and the trends in sales of different products have been quite different. The sales of some plastics has been growing much faster than that for heavy chemicals, and some companies have divisions that are producing new drugs that have rapidly increasing sales. However, in those cases, it is usually possible to obtain sales figures for major products or groups of products from trade association or governmental sources and to compare company sales of these products in the past with sales nationally.

After the trend for the product group has been established and compared with trends in the economy and in the industry, the results must be analyzed. A thorough study should be made to determine the relationship between company policies and the trend of sales. Changes in pricing policies, sales policies, production policies, and the like may have caused company sales to grow slower or faster than industry sales.

Analysis of Cyclical Variations in Sales

In forecasting sales, past cyclical fluctuations in sales of each group of products should be analyzed. One of the first steps is to find the relationship between product sales and general business activity.

Relationship to General Business Activity. The basic procedure for finding the relationship between the sales of a company or of particular products and a logically related measure of general economic activity is the same as it is for an industry. At times, the relationship may not be as clear, however, since some factors affect the sales of an individual company to a much greater extent than they do those of the industry. This is true of such factors as strikes in individual plants, local shortages of materials or labor, changes in business policies, and the like. Nevertheless, it is worthwhile to see what past relationships have been and to study any deviations from typical patterns in the past.

In studying past relationships, changes in the sales of the company relative to changes in the related measure of economic activity must be considered carefully. A company in a growing industry, such as chemicals, may find that its sales are related to changes in GNP, but the rate of growth is much faster. In some cases, the most accurate relationships may be found by making the correlations after deflating both the sales of the product in question and the measure of aggregate income by appropriate price indexes to obtain the relationship in real terms.

Even if it is not necessary to deflate the series to obtain patterns of past relationships, it may be necessary to deflate the forecast of the dollar volume of sales to put it on a per-unit basis. If the firm has an index showing the changes in price of the product being forecast, this is, of course, the best index to use for deflation. If it does not have such an index, the appropriate subcategory of the consumer-price index or the producer-price index may be used.

In some situations, the best results may be achieved by means of correlation with the Federal Reserve Board Index of Industrial Production, or its durable or nondurable goods component, or one of the subdivisions of these. For the most accurate forecasting, it is worthwhile to make the correlation with the Index of Industrial Production, even if a close relationship has been found with disposable personal income or one of the other dollar measures of aggregate economic activity. A comparison can then be made between the value forecast and the quantity forecast to see if they yield similar results. If the two forecasts disagree, it is necessary to carefully study again all the factors in the situation. Indications are either that past relationships have changed or that factors that were of minor significance in the past are currently much more important.

As a quantitative example of the type of relationships discussed, consider a study by G. Fromm and E. Hyman developed by using the econometric model from Data Resources Inc. (DRI).[7] Fromm and Hyman argue that in cases where prediction is the only objective of the model, one need not be concerned with the reasonableness of the causal relation. The basic idea is to use appropriate sector or industry predictions from the DRI macro-econometric model as explanatory variables in forecasting company sales. The regression relation provides a mechanism in which changes in key economic variables can impact company sales through the DRI model.

The procedure is to develop a single regression equation that relates company sales to economic variables predicted by the commercial macro-model. The starting point is to examine the company's principal lines of business. The next step is to find closely related macroeconomic variables projected by DRI.

As an example of this procedure, the approach taken to forecast Sears, Roebuck and Co. sales was to relate sales to national consumption expenditures for clothing and shoes, consumption of other nondurables, and expenditures on durables except autos. The actual regression equation was:

---

7. G. Fromm and E. Hyman, "Econometric Models of Company Performance," paper presented at the 1971 meetings of The Econometric Society (December 1971). The details of the study are found in Jan Walter Elliott, *Economic Analysis for Management Decisions* (Homewood, IL: Richard D. Irwin, Inc., 1973), pp. 295–297.

$$S = -680.2 + 11.5(CDEA) + 29.6(CNCS + CNO)$$

where

S = dollar sales

$CDEA$ = $CD - CDA$

CD = personal consumption expenditures, durables

CDA = personal consumption expenditures, new and net used autos

$CNCS$ = personal consumption expenditures, clothing and shoes

CNO = personal consumption expenditures, other nondurables

As another illustration, a sales prediction equation was also developed for E. I. DuPont's sales. Explaining DuPont's sales gave the following equation:

$$S = 725.8 + 709.2\ (JFRB28) + 37.47(CDA) + 8.04(CHINVEAF)$$

where

S = dollar sale

$JFRB28$ = index of industrial production, chemicals and products

CDA = personal consumption expenditures, new and net used autos

$CHINVEAF$ = change in nonfarm business inventories

In both examples, the independent variables are forecasted by DRI, and thus, one can obtain a forecast for dollar sales.

Relationship to Industry Sales. A study also should be made of the relationship of the sales of the business or of its major product groups to those of the industry in the past. It may be possible to find a regular relationship between sales in the business in question and those in the industry and so devise a forecast from an industry forecast. This method is satisfactory if the industry consists of fairly homogeneous units, all producing an essentially similar line of products. This is true of large segments of the shoe industry in which factories produce a complete line of family shoes. A manufacturer of women's shoes alone will probably find, however, that the relationship of the firm's sales to those of the industry is not regular.

The relationship of the sales of the firm or of one of its product groups to those of the industry may follow one of several patterns. The firm may do a more-or-less constant percentage of the total sales in the industry. In other cases, the firm may be gaining a gradually increasing share of the industry sales or suffering a gradually decreasing share. If there is such a trend in this relationship, it usually can be found by plotting the percentage of business the concern does in the industry. In some cases, there may be cyclical divergences in the sales; that is, the percentage share of industry sales may be higher when business in general is rising, and, conversely, the percentage may be lower when business is in recession.

Other Factors. The individual business may develop reference-cycle patterns and specific cycle patterns of past sales as an aid to forecasting, following an NBER technique. Any constant reference-cycle leads or lags will aid in forecasting. Information thus obtained about the average duration of the cycle, amplitude of the cycle, and conformity to the reference-cycle pattern will also prove valuable. It may be possible to develop independently the patterns for major cycles and minor cycles and thus increase their usefulness as a forecasting device.

An analysis should also be made of cyclical variations in sales relative to the cycle in general economic activity or in a related segment of the economy. This should be done to determine if there is any tendency for cyclical variations in sales of the company to become more or less severe than those in the industry or in general economic activity.

Another factor that should be checked is the relationship of the trend of prices in the industry being studied to the general trend of consumer prices. In many consumer-goods industries, sales will be higher when prices in an industry are relatively more favorable than consumer prices in general and lower when the reverse is true. The effect of such divergent price trends may be studied as part of the correlation pattern and expressed on a numerical basis, or treated as a qualitative factor that is used to modify statistical calculations based on past relationships.

Forecast Based on Decomposition Technique. Recall from Chapter 3 that the assumption was made that the actual data, Y (say, sales), is composed of a trend factor, T; a seasonal factor, S; a cyclical factor, C; and an irregular factor, I. That is, sales $= Y = T \times S \times C \times I$. Also in chapter 3, the derivation of a linear trend equation was discussed. By using the ratio-to-moving average technique, seasonal indexes can be calculated (again, see Chapter 3). Dividing the actual data by $T \times S$ gives $C \times I$; that is, $(T \times S \times C \times I)/(T \times S) = C \times I$. So, it is possible to decompose the sales data into its components, T, S, and $C \times I$. In forecasting, the procedure is to "put the components back together" in the future.

Using the trend equation it is possible to obtain trend values in the future. That is:

$$Y = a + bX$$

where

$$
\begin{aligned}
Y &= \text{trend value of the data} \\
X &= \text{time trend variable}
\end{aligned}
$$

The seasonal indexes in the future are expected to remain the same as in the past. After all, the seasonal factor represents a regular and periodic influence on sales.

The last component to project is $(C \times I)$. Graphing the historical values of $(C \times I)$ is helpful. From this graph, and a feeling of where the sales cycle might be expected to go (as discussed earlier in this section), an analyst can plot and obtain future values for $(C \times I)$.

Future sale values can now be obtained by putting the components back together. That is, future sales = future $T \times$ future $S \times$ future $C \times I$. This sales forecast should be studied and possibly modified according to the suggestions in the next section.

Forecasting Sales

The first step is to forecast company sales on the basis of economic factors. A study of the factors affecting sales in the past, both over the long term and during past cycles, and an analysis and forecast of industry sales and of total economic activity serve as the basis for making this forecast of company sales. The forecast should then be modified by special information on sales, if any, that may be available from the sales department. Then, the sales forecast should be reviewed by high-level management. Management will alter the forecast, if it feels that policies should and will be followed that will change the forecast. These three stages, called the first approximation, the second approximation, and the forecast, will each be considered here.

The First Approximation. In developing the first approximation, the starting point is a forecast of total economic activity and industry sales. Past relationships can be used to develop a tentative forecast from industry and general economic forecasts. If the company's products have been separated into groups for forecasting purposes, a separate forecast should be made for each product group.

A complete survey must be made of all qualitative factors in the situation. Economic variables are continually changing, and these changes must be considered in developing a forecast from past relationships. A survey of this kind should include an analysis of the company's marketing activities and any planned changes in those activities. It should also analyze the effects of the marketing programs of competitors and the effects of any other actions or potential actions of competitors. Also included should be analysis of any changes in the competitive picture and any possibility of the development of substitute products.

In checking a forecast, it is usually worthwhile to study the trends of costs and profits in the industry as well as the business itself. If profit margins are being squeezed, the possibility of price increases and their effects on sales should be considered. Low profit margins are also likely to affect the potential for expansion of existing businesses and introduction of new concerns into the industry, and so affect future supply.

Before any forecast for a company selling its products to other businesses is complete, trends in each of the major industries using the company's product must be checked. When forecasting their sales, some companies make forecasts of sales in several of the major industries using their products. The conditions in each industry supplying raw materials to the company must also be studied. Any potential shortages or changes in prices of raw materials will affect the prices of the company's finished goods. Price changes will lead to changes in the quantity of goods demanded and sales forecasts.

The Second Approximation. A forecast of sales based on a study of past patterns of relationships and on an analysis of all qualitative factors must be adjusted to consider the special factors affecting the sales of the company. A major sales drive may be planned early in the year, which, from past experience, will raise sales 10 percent through June. It may be planned to eliminate a product, to change it materially, or to cut prices to move old stock quickly. All such programs must be considered and forecasts of specific product sales changed to meet expected results.

It is usually desirable to get once or twice a year an estimate of expected sales from the sales force. For a survey of the sales force to be most valuable, it must be carefully planned. The sales representatives should be allowed adequate time to study all plans for sales promotion during the time of the forecast. Figures should be supplied to the representatives for sales in the comparable period last year for all regions and all customers for whom forecasts are desired. A separate forecast should be requested for any region in a sales representative's territory in which sales experience has varied materially from the rest of the area as well as a separate forecast for each major customer. In cases where sales are expected to be different from those of the preceding year, the sales representatives should be asked to give their reasons.

Such information, if carefully developed, is extremely useful. The sales representatives know whether customers are moving into or out of a sales area. They also know whether major new accounts are likely or if some current accounts are likely to be lost. The representatives may also be able to report if inventory is piling up in the hands of some customers.

Some companies make a formal users' survey in determining the sales expectations of customers. Customers may be surveyed by mail, telephone, or personal interviews. To get a reasonable response, companies usually assure the respondents that the information provided will be kept confidential and that they will be given the results of the overall survey. Some companies have attempted to improve the accuracy of a users' survey by asking for responses from more than one official in a company, as, for example, the production manager as well as the purchasing agent. Again, to improve the response rate, it is generally better to ask how much of a product the customer plans to buy in total rather than just from the company making the survey. Past experience can then be used to estimate the company's share of the total.

The first approximation forecast should be adjusted to incorporate any changes that are discerned from the sales force or users' survey. The revised forecast becomes the second approximation, which is sent on for analysis by high-level management.

The Forecast. The second approximation forecast should be reviewed by a committee of high-level management, including representatives from each of the major functional areas. If the committee members conclude that the forecast is a proper basis for planning next year's business, they may accept it. If they feel the forecast calls for unattainable sales levels, they may reduce it. If the committee members determine the forecast is too low to meet the company's objectives for profit (and/or other factors, such as market position in the next year) they may develop promotional plans to raise the sales level. They will then adjust the forecast in line with such programs.

After the level of sales has been forecast for the year ahead, it is usually necessary to put it on a quarterly basis and a month-by-month basis for at least one or two quarters ahead. This projection requires the calculation of a typical seasonal pattern that shows the percentage of the year's business normally done in each month. Before any past seasonal pattern is used, a study should be made to determine if anything has happened that might change past patterns. The seasonal pattern is then used to break down an annual sales forecast into monthly and quarterly forecasts.

Review and Revision. Since the economic climate can change quickly, those responsible for forecasting should review the situation continually and, if necessary, recommend changes in the forecast. Except in unusual situations, it is sufficient in most businesses to revise a forecast quarterly. Before any major change is made, the sales force should again be consulted. In addition, the revised forecast should always be approved by the committee of high-level management that approved the original forecast.

The final step in any forecasting procedure is to evaluate the record of all past forecasts. When a forecast is inaccurate, every attempt should be made to ascertain the reason. The search for reasons will increase the analysts' awareness of unusual factors that affect sales. The procedure may also identify changing or new relationships that involve sales.

Forecasting by Statistical Smoothing

Perhaps the most frequently used method of short-run sales forecasting is some form of smoothing technique. Earlier, we demonstrated the moving average method, which is of not much value as a forecasting tool. There are many other forms of *exponential smoothing*. Here we will demonstrate a simple version. The data used for this example happen to be annual expenditures on plant and equipment in the United States, a particularly difficult series to forecast. The actual data are seen in Table 20-3, column 2.

The first step is to calculate the smoothed average, column 3. We use, for a starting point in 1980, the arithmetic mean of the three preceding years, that is, 219.3. For the remainder of the column, the formula for the exponential smoothing is:

Table 20-3

Forecasting Expenditures on Plant and Equipment by Statistical Smoothing

(1)	(2)	(3)	(4)	(5)	(6)	(7)	(8)	(9)
Period	Actual Expenditures (AE)	Smoothed Average (SA)	Smoothed Average Forecast (SAF)	Percentage Error (e_1)	Change in SA (Δ)	Trend Adjustment (T)	Final Forecast (FF)	Percentage Error of Final Forecast (e_2)
1977	185							
1978	218							
1979	255							
1980	282	219.3						
1981	315	244.4	219.3	−30.4	25.1	10.0		
1982	310	272.6	244.4	−21.2	28.2	17.3	259.4	−16.3
1983	304	287.6	272.6	−10.3	15.0	16.4	298.6	−1.8
1984	354	294.2	287.6	−18.8	6.6	12.5	312.2	−11.8
1985	387	318.1	294.2	−24.0	23.9	17.1	313.0	−19.1
1986	379	354.7	318.1	−16.1	36.6	24.9	343.8	−9.3
1987	389	364.4	354.7	−8.8	9.7	18.8	392.1	+0.8
1988			364.4				392.6	

(1) $$SA_t = \alpha AE_t + (1-\alpha)SA_{t-1}$$

where

SA_t is the smoothed average of expenditure in the same period
AE_t is the actual expenditure in the same period
SA_{t-1} is the smoothed average in the preceding period
α is the smoothing constant, and $0 < \alpha < 1$

The choice of the value of α is based on judgment, and makes considerable difference to the accuracy of the forecast. Forecasters will usually choose a number between 0.1 and 0.5. The smaller the value of α chosen, the less the weighting given to the more recent values of the data; and the larger the value of α, the greater the weight given to recent data. This is obvious from the equation since AE_{t-1} is the immediately preceding value of the actual expenditures, if α is close to 1, most of the effect on SA_t is felt there. $(1-\alpha)SA_{t-1}$ represents the influence of earlier data, and if α is large, $(1-\alpha)$ is small. Generally, the greater the volatility of the series, the larger the value of α which would be appropriate.

For our example, let us use $\alpha = 0.4$. For our initial value of SA, we have used the arithmetic average of the preceding three years' expenditures. Inserting the numbers into equation (1), we have

$$SA_{1981} = 0.4(282) + 0.6(219.3) = 244.4$$
$$SA_{1982} = 0.4(315) + 0.6(244.4) = 272.6$$

and so on for the rest of that column.

The forecast for any period, then, is simply the smoothed average of the preceding period, that is, $SAF_t = SA_{t-1}$.

If the smoothed average forecast were used to forecast expenditures on plant and equipment, the errors would be the difference between the forecasted expenditures and the actual expenditures (that is, column 4 minus column 2). The percentage the errors are of the actuals is shown in column 5. The smoothed averages are consistently less than the actuals, which indicates a strong trend, which is also obvious by inspection.

A method of making an adjustment for trend in this method is to calculate equation (2).

(2) $$T_t = \alpha \Delta_t + (1-\alpha)T_{t-1}$$

where

$$\Delta_t = SA_t - SA_{t-1}$$

Thus, $\Delta_{1981} = 244.4 - 219.3 = 25.1$, and
$\Delta_{1982} = 272.6 - 244.4 = 28.2$

and so on for the rest of column 6;

and $T_{1981} = 0.4(25.1) + 0.6(0) = 10.0$ (We assume no trend in 1980) and
$T_{1982} = 0.4(28.2) + 0.6(10.0) - 11.28 + 6.0 = 17.3$

and so on for the rest of column 7.

The final forecast from this method is found from equation (3).

(3) $$FF_t = SA_{t-1} + (1-\alpha)/\alpha \ T_{t-1} \text{ or } FF_t = SAF_t + (1-\alpha)/\alpha \ T_{t-1}$$

Thus, $FF_{1982} = 244.4 + 1.5(10.0) = 244.4 + 15.0 = 259.4$, and
$FF_{1983} = 272.6 + 1.5(17.3) = 272.6 + 26.0 = 298.6$

and so on for the rest of column 8.

It can be seen that the percentage errors in the final forecast, which makes an adjustment for trend in the series, are considerably smaller than those for the smoothed average alone. The average percentage error (ignoring sign) is 9.9 for the former and 18.5 for the latter.

Exponential smoothing is one form of autoregressive forecasting. In other words, it is the behavior of the variable itself over time, which is the only information used to forecast it. Therefore, it is a mechanical procedure; no economic analysis involving other forces is employed to make the forecast. The forecast can be accurate only to the extent that other relationships remain constant. In our example using data on expenditures on plant and equipment, no explicit account was taken of changes in interest rates, income, profit prospects, and so on. Thus, judgment and analysis are still necessary. The user of the autoregressive forecast should adjust the estimate for any changes in the economic environment that are important for the particular variable being forecast.

FORECASTING THE MARKET FOR A NEW PRODUCT

Economic analysis cannot be used as the basic tool for forecasting the sales of a new product. It can help, however, by indicating what general business conditions will be and by showing how similar products have fared in the past. Forecasting sales of a new product is primarily a project in market research and, therefore, will not be treated fully here. However, the general methods by which it may be done will be considered.

Sometimes, a new product replaces an old product in whole or in part, and forecasting can be done on the basis of data concerning the old product. For example, color television gradually replaced black and white television. Some idea of the demand pattern for color television was gained from the black and white television market in the past and, at the time the forecast was made, for color. Industry surveys of buyers' intentions helped gauge the speed of the shift.

Even when a product does not replace another, an industry survey will often help establish the demand for it. This may be done in the case of industrial products by showing drawings and specifications to prospective users, but actual samples are needed for most consumer products. In fact, it is usually best to offer a consumer product for sale in sample markets and then to estimate demand from the sales experience. In some cases, growth curves of similar products may be used as a general guide for sales. For example, the growth curve for refrigerators can be used to estimate the growth curves for other generally accepted appliances.

All sales forecasting is based on a series of estimates and projections and, therefore, cannot be completely accurate. The margin of error can be kept within reasonable limits for established products so that forecasts can be used as a basis for production planning, if revised quarterly. Forecasts of the sales of new products are less reliable, but, even so, they are better than basing production on hunches or guesses. Additional study of the factors affecting consumer expenditure patterns should help in time to improve sales forecasting.

QUESTIONS

1. Why is product classification important in developing a forecast?
2. Which factors must be considered in classifying products?
3. Why is the trend of sales important in a short-run forecast?
4. How may sales be studied relative to some measure of aggregate economic activity?
5. How can the relationship of the sales of a particular business to industry sales be used in forecasting?
6. What effect do sales promotions, actions of competitors, and the like have on sales forecasts?
7. How can users' surveys be used in a forecasting program?
8. Summarize the steps involved in forecasting sales for a particular business.
9. What Is involved in forecasting the sales of a new product?
10. Using the data on expenditures on plant and equipment in Table 20-3, and employing the same techniques, construct a similar table using a value of $\alpha = 0.3$ and a value of $\alpha = 0.6$. Are the forecasting results better or worse than those of Table 20-3? Why?

READINGS

Bails, Dale G., and Larry C. Peppers. *Business Fluctuations, Forecasting Techniques and Applications*. Englewood Cliffs, NJ: Prentice-Hall, Inc., 1982.

Farnum, Nicholas R., and LaVerne W. Stanton. *Quantitative Forecasting Methods*. Boston: PWS-Kent Publishing Company, 1989.

Granger, C. W. J. *Forecasting in Business and Economics*, 2d ed. New York: Academic Press, 1989.

Gross, Charles W., and Robin T. Peterson. *Business Forecasting*, 2d ed. Boston: Houghton Mifflin Co., 1983.

Montgomery, Douglas, et al. *Forecasting and Time Series Analysis*, 2d ed. New York: McGraw-Hill Book Company, 1990.

Newbold, Paul, and Theodore Bos. *Introductory Business Forecasting*. Cincinnati: South-Western Publishing Co., 1990. Chapter 5.

Rothermal, Terry W. "Forecasting Resurrected." *Harvard Business Review* (March-April 1982), pp. 139–147.

Sales Executives Club of New York. *Sales Forecasting: Time Saving and Profit-Making Strategies That Work* (prepared by Harry R. White). Glenview, IL: Scott, Foresman and Co., 1984.

Seitz, Neil. *Business Forecasting: Concepts and Microcomputer Applications*. Reston, VA: Reston Publishing Company, Inc., 1984.

Wheelwright, Steven C., and Spyros Makridakis. *Forecasting Methods for Management*, 5th ed. New York: John Wiley & Sons, Inc., 1989.

Willis, Raymond E. *A Guide to Forecasting for Planners and Managers*. Englewood Cliffs, NJ: Prentice-Hall, Inc., 1987.

PROPOSALS FOR ACHIEVING ECONOMIC GROWTH AND STABILITY

Major fluctuations in the level of economic activity and in price levels create some of our most serious economic, social, and political problems. In the present state of world affairs, a serious depression or a major period of inflation in the United States has serious repercussions not only in this country but also in most of the other nations of the world. Humanitarian concern for the plight of those afflicted by economic reversals, an awareness of both the international and the domestic political impact of fluctuations, and a faith in the efficacy of policy to cure economic ills have all combined to bring about increased attention toward devising means to stabilize economic activity.

Programs to stabilize economic activity affect all sectors of the economy, both in the short run and in the long run. In the long run, the goal of stability must

PART 5

be balanced with the goal of assuring a rising trend of real output and real income. Both long-run and short-run programs must be politically and socially acceptable to our society to be put into effect. To achieve stability but to simultaneously lose a significant measure of our freedom is to win a battle but lose the war. Thus, programs to achieve stability involve political decisions that are as important as or perhaps more important than economic decisions.

The first chapter in this part looks at the goals and some of the issues and problems in developing overall aggregate economic policies for growth and stabilization. The last chapter is a survey of the tools and methodology of the major approaches used, namely monetary policy and fiscal policy and their interrelationships.

PROBLEMS IN ECONOMIC POLICY FOR GROWTH AND STABILITY

Intelligent discussion of economic policy is possible only among those who have an understanding of how an economy functions. This is the reason our chapters on policy come at the end of the book rather than at the beginning, after a theoretical framework for understanding has been constructed and some insights from the historical record have been gained. In this chapter, we consider some of the major problems in developing governmental programs to promote growth and stability and the role of the private sector in that endeavor. Chapter 22 is devoted specifically to the primary tools of aggregate economic policy—monetary and fiscal policy.

THE NATURE OF ECONOMIC GROWTH AND STABILITY

Economic growth may be judged from the growth in total output of the economy as measured by annual increases in net national product in constant dollars. Although such a measure tells us how much the total economy is growing over a period of time, it tells us very little about changes in the standard of living. The more significant measure is the growth in real output per capita as measured by increases in real net national product divided by the number of people in the population. From 1900 to 1989, real per capita GNP has grown at the rate of approximately 1.8 percent per year, though, of course, not at a steady rate.

The Nature of Economic Growth

A rising level of real output per capita can be achieved in various ways. It may be done by using a larger quantity of the factors of production in proper combination or by improving these factors so that more output results from using the same quantity. The factors of production may also be combined more effectively so that a larger output results from their use. The role of each factor of production in achieving real growth per capita will be considered first; then, attention will be directed to the gains from a better combination of these factors. In the case of labor, growth can be achieved by using more labor as long as the amount of capital per unit of labor is not reduced in doing so. More labor may be used, because a larger percentage of the population of active working age is engaged in gainful employment. This may be achieved by having fewer people idle either voluntarily or involuntarily because of unemployment, sickness, or accident. It may also be achieved by lengthening the number of years individuals work during their life span. More labor may also be used by working more hours per week. This method has limited possibilities, because in many fields, as hours of work greatly increase beyond the present work week, output per hour drops rapidly.

Growth is also fostered by improving the skills of the labor force through formal education and on- and off-the-job training after a person begins to work. To obtain maximum growth, it is necessary to use the skills of all workers to the maximum, which requires the proper motivation to achieve the optimum output per worker. It also calls for proper job placement, including programs to promote labor mobility. Optimal labor productivity also means no discrimination because of race, sex, age, or national origin, which prevents using all available skills to the fullest.

Growth requires an adequate and balanced supply of labor to meet the needs of the expanding economy. The need for various types of skilled labor must be projected, and a program must be developed to assure the training of the needed workers. It is often found that even when unemployment is at high levels, some skill categories are in high demand and workers to fill these jobs are nearly impossible to find.

By far the most important way of assuring continued growth in the national economy is to increase investment in human capital! The investment starts at the level of the family unit, which means trying to raise children so as to maximize the probability of their attaining their potential. Improvement throughout the nation at all educational levels, but especially at the earliest stages, is vital to bring about increases in the value of human capital.

One of the major factors leading to growth is the use of more capital equipment, since machines provide many times the power of human beings. Most significant is the use of increasingly improved machines that turn out a greater number of goods in relation to the economic resources used to build and run them. Research and development are needed to produce the machines and the trained scientists and engineers to do such work. Computers and robotics are the most recent developments along these lines. The increasing use of machinery and equipment is possible only if sufficient resources are available for investment. This may necessitate programs to stimulate saving to make the capital available.

Significant, too, is the better utilization of natural resources. This may be done in such ways as getting more usable ore from a mine, finding ways to use low-grade ores, replacing scarce materials with those that are more plentiful, and using less material to do the same job. Growth requires an adequate source of raw materials to meet expanding needs. These needs are met through better exploration for materials, the conservation and replacement of present supplies, where this is possible, and the development of substitute materials for those that are scarce.

Growth also requires an adequate supply of trained managerial talent and is furthered by both better management methods and the more effective use of such methods by present and prospective managers. Management is responsible for combining the factors of production to achieve the greatest possible output with the given amount of resources or to produce a given amount of output with the minimum use of resources. Growth also occurs when more and better capital is made available to labor trained to use the capital. Growth can be achieved when labor and capital are used more optimally. Mobility of labor and capital helps to achieve the optimum combination.

The optimum combination may be achieved when procedures are developed to reduce material handling, expedite the flow of goods in a plant, and the like. These factors are as important in the field of distribution or marketing as they are in production. Equally important are more efficient procedures for handling work in planning, engineering, accounting, and other white-collar fields.

Stability

To achieve the maximum practicable rate of growth, it is necessary to have some degree of stability. This does not mean a perfectly smooth rate of growth, but one that is not interrupted by severe depressions or inflations. In other words, the optimum in stability means the end of the business cycle as we have known it. There would still be some changes in the rate of growth but no periods of sustained cumulative contraction in real economic activity.

To some economists, stability is impossible, since they believe that the business cycle is an integral part of the growth process in a free-enterprise economy. Historically, this has been the case, and some fluctuations in the rate of growth no doubt will always occur in a free economy. But the cumulative nature of the cycle is based on the reactions of individuals and groups to real changes and, therefore, is subject to modification.

The nature of economic development has also lessened the impact of individual changes. Innovations such as the canal, the steamboat, the railroad, and the automobile had a very great effect on the overall economy, but today, so many areas exist in which industry and the consumer use machinery and equipment that an innovation is likely to affect a smaller part of the economy. Research has led to so many innovations that their impact is more regular than it was in the past. Therefore, it may be possible to achieve a large measure of stability without hampering growth.

THE GOALS OF POLICY

The habit of assuming that we all agree on the goals of policy, or that the goals are obvious, is at the root of much of the debate on the wisdom of particular proposals. Economists are in agreement that a policy that leads to the result of more goods and services is preferred to one that results in fewer goods and services. Even here we recognize a degree of arbitrariness, since such policies may effect a change in the relative welfare of the individuals of the society. Being the richest poor person may be preferable to being the poorest rich person.

The economist, as an economist, is rigorously limited to the value judgments implicit in the concept called "Pareto optimality," named for the great Italian sociologist-economist, Vilfredo Pareto. *Pareto optimum* exists when it is not possible to make anyone better off without someone else being made worse off. Consensus is readily achieved in those instances where a particular policy leads to this optimal position. In other words, if a situation exists when a policy could be initiated that would improve the economic lot of some individuals without reducing the welfare of others, such action would probably be taken. Such instances present no problem. But major problems, in particular the kind considered under the heading of stabilization and growth policy, cannot lay claim to this solution. Still, we can use the Pareto criterion to make choices among alternative policies, not precisely, but in an acceptable or workable sense.

Evaluation of any policy involves the evaluation of all the effects of that policy. Most actions have elements that will be judged beneficial, but there will also be results that are undesirable. The question then becomes one of deciding, on the basis of the total impact, the relative merits and demerits associated with the proposal or program. Milton Friedman has often admonished us to remember that because a policy was instituted to bring about a certain result does not mean the policy accomplishes what was intended.

Economic policy always involves technical problems, which the economist is trained to answer, and questions of value judgments, which the economist is trained to discover, but not to answer. Suppose, for example, that economic analysis concludes that a particular tax reduction policy will reduce unemployment by one million workers, but that it will also result in a 5 percent increase in the price level. Would this policy be superior to the continuation of a constant level of unemployment and prices? A conscientious answer demands that one be aware of the costs of unemployment to the families of the unemployed as well as to the rest of society. Are there any benefits to society? Surely, everyone will agree that the costs of unemployment far exceed the benefits. But it is also necessary to analyze the impact of inflation. What difference does it make if we have a 5 percent growth in the price level? Who is hurt? Who benefits? Do these cancel out? Are there ramifications of price-level changes on production?

It is too simple to say that unemployment is bad and inflation is evil. Sometimes a choice must be made between the two, but this is too heavy a burden to put on economists. It must be left to society at large through its political processes. It is to be hoped that economists will be helpful in educating society to the nature of the choices it must make.

GOALS OF A GOVERNMENTAL PROGRAM FOR PROMOTING ECONOMIC GROWTH AND STABILITY

The pressure to attain economic stability in our economy is so strong that measures to promote stability have been established by law as a goal of national policy. At the end of World War II, after lengthy debate, Congress passed the Employment Act of 1946, thereby recognizing the relationship of the government to fluctuations in the economy. In this act, Congress declared that it was the continuing policy and responsibility of the federal government, with the assistance of industry, agriculture, labor, and state and local governments, to use all practicable means consistent with national policy and the free-enterprise system to promote maximum employment, production, and purchasing power. The Employment Act provides that, at the beginning of each regular session, the President shall submit to Congress a report on the current levels of economic activity and the levels needed to carry out the policy of high employment. The President is also to present information on current trends and on the present economic program of the federal government and its effects. In light of such data, a program is to be presented for carrying out the objectives of the full employment policy whenever there are indications that this will not be achieved otherwise.

A Council of Economic Advisers, composed of three members, was set up to aid the President in developing such a report, and a Joint Congressional Committee on the Economic Report has been established to provide economic information and analysis for Congress, especially for the use of other committees. Since the passage of this bill, unemployment on the scale of that of the 1930s has not been a problem, except for brief periods including 1969–1970, 1974–1976, and in 1981 and 1982, when it was of some concern. Most of the recent recommendations have dealt with methods of avoiding inflation, since that has been the major problem in the postwar period. Up to the present time, however, neither the Council of Economic Advisers nor the Joint Committee on the Economic Report has instituted any plans for coordinating governmental activities affecting the economy.

The Humphrey-Hawkins Full Employment Bill, which was passed in 1978, further advocates governmental responsibility for full employment by codifying into law the proposition that every American has the right to a job and that, as the employer of last resort, it is the government's responsibility to provide jobs. The Bill set a national unemployment-rate goal of zero percent by 1988, but did not state specific means to reach that goal.

Growth and stability are so closely related that the economic policy of the government should include both. It is desirable to develop goals to guide governmental policies in the economic sphere by discussing the basic issues carried on from the grass-roots level to the halls of Congress. Business and labor can plan on a long-run basis much more effectively if they know what to expect from government. Consumers can make long-run decisions more effectively, such as buying a home or planning a savings program, if they know what to expect in the way of economic policies. The development of a set of goals for governmental economic policy would, in itself, help promote growth and stability, since some amount of uncertainty might be eliminated.

In his 1955 Economic Report, President Eisenhower stated the goals of our national economic policy as follows:[1] "Our economic goal is an increasing national income, shared equitably among those who contribute to its growth, and achieved in dollars of stable buying power." Such a goal has several important elements: a rising trend of real income, full employment, stable prices, and the equitable sharing of a growing national income among those who have contributed to producing it. Most Americans will readily agree with these goals. There is some difference of opinion, however, as to the exact meaning of each goal and the degree to which it is desirable to achieve it.

Problems in Promoting Economic Growth

Let us first examine the goal of a rising trend of real income. There is some question about the rate of growth that should be achieved. Some economists feel that an annual rate of growth of about 3 percent in GNP is adequate, because this is in line with the trend since the turn of the century and has produced our present high standard of living. Others feel that it is not only possible to grow at a rate of around 5 percent per year but also essential in the present world situation. They argue that the growth of 5 percent per year that was achieved in several of the post-World War II years shows that such a goal is attainable. They also feel it is essential if we are to meet our worldwide military and economic commitments.

Desirability of Growth.   There is some disagreement about the possibility of achieving a rate of growth of 5 percent a year and at the same time achieving a stable price level. Some economists believe that such a rate of growth would make it all but impossible to keep prices stable, because demand would probably be constantly at or somewhat in excess of current supply. On the other hand, we remember Professor Hobson's hypothesis that consumption is a conservative art and, therefore, slower to change, whereas production is not so constrained.

The biggest disagreement exists about the role of the government in stimulating a high rate of growth. Some economists feel that gov-

---

1. *Economic Report of the President, 1955* (Washington, D.C.: U.S. Government Printing Office, 1955), p. 2.

ernment's role should be restricted to providing a favorable climate for growth and providing incentives through such steps as rapid amortization of new plant and equipment or other tax benefits. Other economists feel that government should increase its investment expenditures to a level needed to insure a high rate of growth. There is still considerable disagreement about governmental investment programs in many areas, such as public housing and federal funds for school construction.

At this point, we might ask the surprising question: Is growth, in fact, a desirable goal at all? This question obviously cannot be answered, because we would need to consider, for example, whether Americans in 1800 were happier or more prosperous than Americans today. Although most of us might judge that this was not the case, we do not know for certain.

In recent years, there has been a sizable and respectable minority of economists who have proposed that, along with zero population growth, we should deliberately establish a policy of zero economic growth. These economists, including E. J. Mishan of the London School of Economics and Ernest F. Schumacher, are concerned about the rate at which a growing economy uses up exhaustible and irreplaceable resources, such as fossil fuels. They also seem to feel that the quality of life deteriorates with economic growth as such concomitants as pollution, congestion, and ecological deterioration occur.[2]

Growth of per capita income requires capital expansion—improvements in the quality or quantity of capital goods and "natural" resources or in the quality of the contribution of the human factor. None of these can be achieved without cost. The nature of the cost is emphasized in the classical expression for saving, namely waiting or abstinence. In other words, we can have more goods and services in the future only if we give up goods and services in the present. This may not appear to be a very great sacrifice to an American student of the 1990s, but in many countries of the world, a significant increase in saving could be accomplished only with a serious shortening of the average life span as current consumption declined.

The key question for a well-developed society as well as for the underdeveloped is: Who should make the decision as to what should be the rate of economic growth? Should this be a collective decision, or should each individual determine a personal rate of asset growth

2. See E. J. Mishan, *Technology and Growth* (New York: Praeger, Inc., 1970); and Ernest F. Schumacher, *Small Is Beautiful* (New York: Harper & Row Publishers Inc., 1973).

and, thus, in the aggregate, determine the rate of growth of national income? Should industries that are engaged in growth-promoting activities be given special encouragement or subsidies, and should industries producing less urgent or even frivolous commodities be penalized in some way?

As a general proposition, most economists would argue in favor of allowing the free-market system to determine the rate of growth. If interference with the freedom of the individual to make choices is to be abridged, some quite powerful arguments must be marshalled. Are there such arguments?

There would appear to be two major justifications for attempting to induce a rate of growth faster than might be natural without a specific growth policy. First is the requirement that growth be sufficient to absorb into meaningful employment the additions to the labor force out of a growing population and to reemploy those who would otherwise be replaced by capital. The other justification is the political one of growing at a rate fast enough to continuously maintain the nation's military and political strength relative to any potential enemy nations.

Population Growth.   The most profound question in growth policy is what should be society's attitude toward population growth. Is a larger human population an absolute good? If not, is there an optimal rate of population growth? We know that serious problems arise if population grows at a faster rate than the rate of expansion of economic output. Many nations of the world, particularly in Africa, can attest to this side of the problem. On the other hand, the governments of many of our most mature economies have felt that the source of some of their most fundamental problems is that population has not grown at a fast-enough rate. Probably, the safest attitude for an economist to take on this subject is to accept the rate of population growth as a given and to suggest policies that move in the direction of maximizing the per capita income of the actual population.

In the previous paragraph, we raised the question of optimum population. One approach is that an increase in population is desirable if, on the average, any new entrant to the society could be expected, over a lifetime, to contribute more to the society than the individual would take from the rest of the society. If the individual's contribution were accurately measured by lifetime income (equal to production; that is, creation of value) and if the lifetime consumption (that is, destruction of value) could be accurately measured, then, proof that, on balance, an increase in population would be a positive contribution to the rest of the population could be inferred to the extent that people had positive wealth at the time of death over and above any inherited assets. This is so because an increase in wealth is, by definition, the difference between income and consumption. If the wealth of society were to decrease as population increased, this would be proof that the population was too large. Thus, the optimum population would be that population at which the expected wealth of society remained constant or if per capita wealth grew. For this approach to be useful, we would need to include all of the nonmarket benefits and costs as well as those with market prices. Disagreements over the nonmarket aspects naturally are quite severe. Some people hate crowds; some love crowds. Some people love children; some do not. We often cannot even agree on whether a particular development is a cost or a benefit, let alone measure it.

Full Employment

There is general agreement on the goals of full employment and stable price levels, but disagreement on the exact meaning of such goals. Full employment does not mean that no one is out of work in a free-enterprise economy. The *demand* for labor shifts from field to field, and workers must shift jobs. People may be out of work for a time when they first enter the labor force or change jobs voluntarily. A committee of the American Economic Association has developed the following workable definition of full employment:

> Full employment means that qualified people who seek jobs at prevailing wage rates can find them in productive activities without considerable delay. It means full-time jobs for people who want to work full time. It does not mean that people like housewives and students are under pressure to take jobs when they do not want jobs, or that workers are under pressure to put in undesired overtime. It does not mean that unemployment is ever zero.[3]

The amount of unemployment that is consistent with this definition of full employment is not a constant. It depends on the rigidities to employment adjustments, on the costs of information to employers and employees, on expectations about future employment conditions, and, in general, on the attitudes of workers about the trade-offs between

---

3. Committee of the American Economic Association, "The Problem of Economic Instability," *American Economic Review* (September 1950), p. 506.

employment and its alternatives. In recent years, U.S. figures usually ranged between 4 and 5 percent as the target for aggregate economic policy.

Increases in aggregate demand lead to the expansion of the money value of national income, but this will be beneficial to the society only if the real output increases and unemployment is reduced. If unemployment is very large, we expect any growth in national income to be primarily in real output and very little in the price level. It depends a great deal, however, on the nature of those who are unemployed. If all of the unemployed were very mobile geographically and flexible in their occupational skills, inflation would not be likely to occur until employment was nearly 100 percent of the labor force. The other extreme is also conceivable. Even if the unemployed were a very large percentage of the labor force, if they were unable or unwilling to move to new locations or other occupations, expansion of aggregate demand might result only in inflation rather than in the diminution of unemployment.

Another important element in the employment versus the inflation problem is the degree of wage flexibility. If, for example, the legal minimum wage were set at a rate well above the marginal revenue product of a large percentage of the labor force, a considerable amount of inflation of product prices would need to take place before these workers could find employment. Any other institutional rigidities imposed on money wages, such as union contracts or industry custom, would have the same effect.

It would be extremely valuable to us to have knowledge of the true relationship between levels of unemployment and price inflation. We would like to be able to answer such questions as the amount of inflation that would be required to reduce unemployment by a given amount if the rate of unemployment were 8 percent, 6 percent, 3 percent, 2 percent, and so on. Figure 21-1 shows a graph of such a relationship estimated by Samuelson and Solow from twenty-five years of American data.[4] Such a curve is usually called a Phillips curve after A. W. Phillips, who studied the inflation-unemployment relationship for the United Kingdom with such a chart.

The Samuelson-Solow estimate is that price stability in the United States could be achieved only at the cost of unemployment of about 5.5 percent. This is shown as point *A*. Point *B* can be interpreted as

---

4. Paul A. Samuelson and R. M. Solow, "Analytical Aspects of Anti-Inflation Policy," *American Economic Review* (May 1960), pp. 177–194.

Figure 21-1 A Phillips Curve

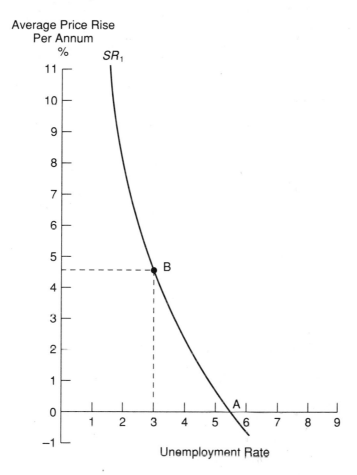

Average Price Rise Per Annum %

Unemployment Rate

saying that a rate of unemployment of 3 percent would cost about 4.5 percent in annual inflation. Improvement would be defined as a shifting of the function to the left, so that at any given level of unemployment, a lower rate of inflation would be experienced. Such gains can be achieved by increasing the mobility of labor through education and training, by improving information on employment sources, and by using other methods instituted by labor, management, and government.

In fact, during the years since the Samuelson-Solow estimate of the Phillips curve, the curve has apparently shifted to the right. Figure 21-2 shows the plotting of the annual unemployment and inflation data

Figure 21-2 Unemployment-Inflation Experience, 1960–1984

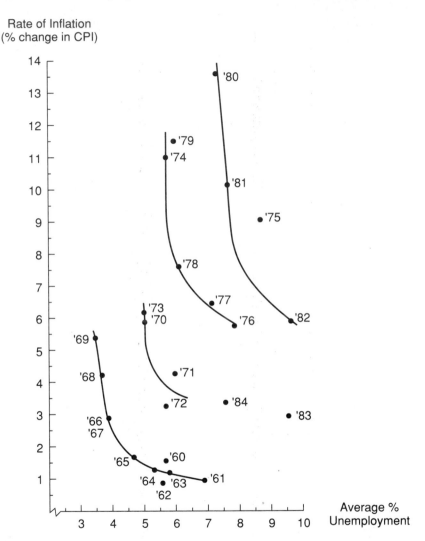

from 1960 through 1981. One interpretation of these data is shown by the lines drawn in—one approximating the curve for the period of the 1960s, one for 1970–1973, one for the 1974–1979 period excluding 1975, and one for the early 1980s. Something quite remarkable appears to have happened in the 1982–1985 period. Both the rate of inflation and the rate of unemployment have declined, suggesting that structural changes in the economy have occurred such that the Phillips curve has reversed its rightward movement and has shifted to the left. At the same time, interest rates have fallen by an average of 35 percent from 1982 to the middle of 1985, reflecting expectations of lower rates of inflation.

The experience from 1983 to 1989 does not fit the Phillips curve hypothesis very well. The inflation rate has averaged under four percent per year, while the unemployment rate has fallen from a high of almost eleven percent at the end of 1982 to just over five percent in early 1989. This might indicate that, among other explanations, the decline in unemployment and the corresponding increase in employment were encouraged by the relative stability of the price level.

However, one must be very cautious in interpreting this relationship. The connections between the level of real economic activity, the level of unemployment (proxy for excess demand), and inflation are extremely complex. Examples of the sorts of forces that may have generated the experience shown on this graph are the increasing numbers of women, minorities and other new entrants into the labor force (whose unemployment rates are usually higher), change in the alternatives to employment (unemployment compensation and welfare payments, retirement programs, and so on), changes in the minimum wage, and changes in the degree of responsiveness of output and labor to changes in prices and wages. Certainly, an aspect of this that must be very important, but is so difficult to explain theoretically, is the population's perception of inflation and the expectations of future inflation derived from it.

It has been argued that the long-run Phillips curve is a vertical line, its position set by the *natural rate of unemployment*. The natural rate of unemployment is the unemployment rate that would exist at a full equilibrium of the economy. Unemployment would consist only of frictional and structural unemployment; there would be no cyclical unemployment. In Figure 21-3, point A represents such a natural rate. Suppose the economy to be at that point and the monetary authority tries to reduce unemployment by increasing the money supply, which causes the inflation rate to increase from 0 to 4.5 percent. The system might move to point B where unemployment has fallen to 3 percent. This would seem to be a very happy result, but it depends on workers and consumers being unaware of the inflation. If expectations develop that inflation will continue at the 4.5 percent rate, everyone will adjust to it, and the short-run Phillips curve will shift to the right with unemployment rising back to the natural rate at point C. Attempts to reduce unemployment again by more inflation could move the system

Figure 21-3   The Long-Run Phillips Curve

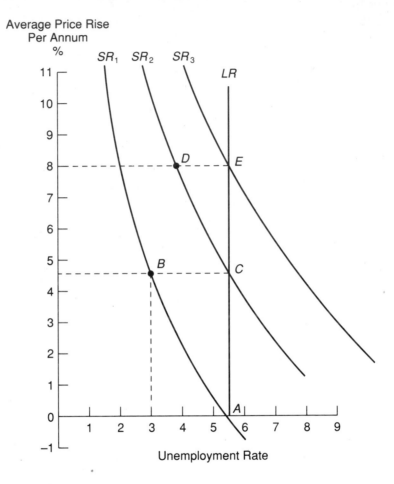

to *D* only temporarily until the short-run Phillips curve shifted right-ward again to establish the new point at *E*. Thus, in the long run, there is no trade-off between inflation and unemployment according to this theory.

Now, if the economy is at point *E* with unemployment at a very acceptable level, but an unacceptable level of inflation disinflating (that is, reducing the rate of inflation) would be a very painful process moving down the short-run curve (*SR₃*). A contractionary monetary-fiscal policy would decrease the rate of inflation but increase the un-employment rate. It would take time for the public to believe that prices will not rise as much in the future, so unemployment would get more severe until the curve shifted to the left again. This appears to be a plausible explanation of what happened in the United States up to the middle of 1982, after which the public seems to have had more faith that inflation had indeed subsided. To further complicate this situation, the high rate of inflation had pushed nominal interest rates to exceptionally high levels, reducing aggregate demand, and thereby decreasing the demand for labor. However, in the several years following 1982, the decline in the rate of inflation effected the lowering of interest rates and the reversal of the decline in aggregate demand. However, before actually happening, it was some time before the fall in the rate of inflation was reflected in lower interest rates.

Stable Price Level

The goal of a stable price level does not mean a completely fixed price level. Individual prices, of course, will and should fluctuate in response to changes in supply and demand, in both the short and long runs. Not all economists agree on a goal of price stability, however. Some favor a gradually rising price level, with prices moving up a maximum of 2 or 3 percent a year in boom years and remaining relatively stable in recession years. They feel that a gradually rising price level makes it easier to achieve full employment and an acceptable rate of growth, especially in an economy of strong labor unions, imperfect competition among large concerns, and administered prices. Others believe that any rate of inflation will generate expectations of its continuance, which means that the velocity of money will increase and cause further increases in inflationary pressures.

We have just seen that there may be a conflict between the two desirable goals of relative price stability and full employment. There is also, at times, a conflict between stable prices and stable interest rates. This was particularly evident during the latter half of 1966 when the pressure on rising prices was somewhat held in check by monetary policy that allowed interest rates to rise significantly. At that time, interest rates could have been held steady at low rates, but the tradeoff for low rates would have been considerably more inflation. The actual response of the monetary authority was a compromise: some inflation and some increase in interest rates. In the 1970s and early 1980s, while inflation was generally felt to be the most serious economic problem, market interest rates rose significantly. Had interest rates been held down, it is probable that inflation would have been even more severe than it actually was.

There is no final answer to the question of which route is superior. Inflation and high interest rates both are harmful to some people and helpful to others. If real output is the same in the two cases, the choice between high prices and high interest rates turns on the issue of the distribution of income and wealth and the equity thereof.

Equitable Sharing of National Income

The last goal, an equitable sharing of a growing national income among those who helped to produce it, is open to more debate. Opinions differ widely on what is equitable, and, of course, self-interest and group interest become involved. The extremes range from advocates of a return to more or less unregulated free enterprise, such as we had in the 1920s, to governmental programs of welfare economics to assure a "good life" for all groups. Most individuals agree that in developing a program to share the fruits of production equitably, the basic political freedoms must be preserved. This is also generally true of economic freedoms, including the choice of goods to be purchased, the field of labor to be entered, and the type of business to be established. Differences in this debate are largely based on differing social and political views and are only, in a small part, based on differences in the analyses of the economic effects of various programs affecting the economy.

Almost any important economic policy has some effect on the distribution of income and wealth. Some attempt to determine this effect should be made even if it is true that, as economists, we cannot say that one distribution is better or worse than another. There are extreme cases where virtual unanimity would exist. Almost all economists agree that there are extreme distributions of income that are unacceptable both from the standpoint of equity and from the standpoint of the viability of the economic and political systems.

Choices of Governmental Policies

At various points in previous sections, we have spoken of reasons for our economy behaving in an undesirable manner, creating unemployment, inflation, and many other problems. These are problems we do not expect to encounter in a world fitting our theoretical ideal of the purely competitive model. One approach then, it would seem, would be to have a series of governmental policies designed to make the real-world economy more closely approximate the theoretical one.

No one seriously believes that a perfect correspondence is possible, but there are many who feel that a great deal can be accomplished in this direction. At a minimum, current policies by government that prevent the operation of the free-price mechanism from making the necessary adjustments could be altered. Such programs as farm support prices, minimum wage laws, and many public utility regulations are grist for such criticism. Antitrust enforcement aimed at ensuring free entry into markets and flexible competitive price and wage behavior would be an important aspect of this type of structural policy.

It seems that almost invariably the arguments in favor of those governmental actions that distort the operations of the economic system are based on a criticism of the distribution of wealth or income in the system as it exists. Humane concern for the hardships suffered by the economically disadvantaged provides justification for relinquishing some of the benefits of a capitalistic economy. Thus, many economists who are defenders of free enterprise and yet sympathize with the plight of the underprivileged believe that governmental interference with the free operation of the system can be eliminated only if the income distribution problem can be solved first. To this end, the *negative income-tax plan* is often proposed. This plan would guarantee a minimum income for everyone and, at the same time, make it advantageous to work at whatever an individual is capable of doing.

Positive programs and policies aimed at increasing the mobility of labor and other resources, increasing and improving the flow of information to households and other decision makers, and encouraging persons to take risks in forming new businesses and undertaking innovations would be important elements of structural strategy. Presumably, this class of economic policies should be the continuing effort of government. To the degree to which they are effective, the macro-level policies will be less needed; and when macro-level programs are undertaken, they should be more successful in accomplishing their goals without undesirable side effects.

INCOMES POLICIES AND DIRECT CONTROLS

The category of policy actions referred to by the term *incomes policies and direct controls* is the antithesis of the structural policies discussed above. Incomes policies and direct controls are advocated by those who are skeptical about the real world ever being represented realistically by the theorists' model. Or they are favored by those who are impatient with the slow working of the system itself. They are particularly attractive to noneconomists who can appreciate the particular problem, such as inflation, but are unable to see the difficulties associated with direct controls on wages and prices. After all, from the noneconomist point of view, if rising prices cause hardship, why not pass a law making price increases illegal? If interest rates are "too high," pass a law saying they must be lower. If unemployment is high, have the government employ the people or pay businesses to employ them.

Incomes policies range from voluntary compliance and wage-price guideposts to the complete freeze on wages and prices imposed during World War II and again in 1971 by President Nixon. Are such programs effective in preventing inflation? The answer is that they are never completely successful, if strong pressures for price increases continue to exist. There seem to be an infinite number of ways for those who wish to avoid compliance to do so. Starkly illegal black markets spring up, and many other questionable practices develop. Where discounts might have been granted to purchasers before, full list price is charged. Where certain services were rendered without charge, a fee is imposed. The quality of products, and even the quantity of the unit product, will be reduced. Tie-in sales will be demanded. Anyone who has observed periods of price controls could enumerate a long list of such subterfuges to push up the effective price, while ostensibly keeping the official price unchanged. If the enforcement agents are large enough in numbers and have sufficient legal backing, many of these practices can be curtailed. But if workers are diverted to management of the controls, the output of desirable goods and services will be reduced, which, in itself, would inject more inflationary pressure.

There may be some beneficial results from overall price controls. Under certain circumstances, inflation will be fed by inflationary expectations; in which case, the dramatic announcement of a control program might lead people to revise their beliefs about the inevitability of increasing prices. Of course, the opposite result is at least conceivable, in which the imposition of controls would be viewed as an admission that the administration is unable to control price-level behavior through conventional tools, thus generating more firm convictions that price increases are due. A second possible positive result of direct controls would be the achievement of a breathing spell, wherein the pressures to supply the banking system with additional reserves would be relaxed and thus permit a slowing down of the growth of the money stock.

Suppose, for the moment, that controls are completely effective in preventing price and wage increases. Would our problems be solved? For a short period of time, they might seem to be; but as changes take place in the underlying conditions of supply and demand, new diffi-culties arise. When prices are allowed to vary, and the demand for a particular commodity increases, the price rises and encourages addi-tional output to satisfy the new demand. If the price is not permitted to rise, the added output will not be forthcoming and so shortages ap-pear, and resources will continue to be used to produce goods that are desired less. The other side of the problem occurs when conditions of supply change. Suppose, for example, that petroleum reserves are found to be reduced, or are more costly to recover. In a free-market sys-tem, the price of petroleum products would rise and their use would be curtailed by limiting consumption to more urgent needs, saving the resources for future needs. If the price is not allowed to rise, these re-sources will be used excessively, or producers will cut back production and, again, "shortages" will be evident.

In the environment of price controls, there will be fewer goods of many kinds than people wish to buy at the control price. Then, the question arises as to how the limited quantities should be allocated among the prospective buyers. It can be accomplished by any number of forms of favoritism—to the strong, to the attractive, to "good cus-tomers," to someone who has favors to grant to the seller, to whoever comes first, and so on. The government can decree who gets priorities, or can outlaw certain uses, or can allocate by means of ration coupons, in which case people with little desire for the product can get as much as those with a strong desire for it.

It is certainly relevant to ask whether the evils of inflation are more or less serious than the evils of the attempts at direct price control. A responsible answer requires knowledge of the consequences of both events. It becomes even more urgent to come to some conclusion on the question in time periods when knowledgeable observers talk about inflation as a chronic ill of the modern economy.

MONETARY AND FISCAL POLICY

The main burden of aggregate economic policy must fall either on monetary policy or on fiscal policy or on a combination of the two. In the next chapter, we will review the theory and the nature of the tools, and the techniques available in the two classes of policy actions. Here, we wish to take up the controversy described as the monetarist-fiscalist debate.

The polar positions, which very few economists would admit hold-ing, are, on the monetarist side, that only the money stock matters in determining the behavior of the national income and that fiscal policy is impotent; on the fiscalist (or post-Keynesian) side, exactly the reverse statements would be true. The debate has been productive. Fiscalists have been forced to study and to concede that money does matter and that the impact of fiscal policy is greatest when it is accompanied by alterations in the stock of money. On their side, the monetarists have been forced to study and to concede that the method by which the money stock changes is of some significance in evaluating the effect on the economy. For example, money created as a result of budgetary deficit may have a greater impact than money created through open-market operations.

The post-Keynesian interpretation of the impact of money on the economy is that when the money stock is increased by the action of the monetary authority, the public will readjust its portfolio holdings of money and bonds. In the process, the interest rate will fall as the price of bonds rises. Then, to the extent that spending on capital goods is sensitive to interest cost conditions, aggregate spending will increase. The monetarist views money stock changes as being more pervasive than this, arguing that if the money stock increases, *all* of the assets in the public's portfolio will need to adjust to reach a new optimum, and so, all forms of spending will increase, not just interest-sensitive categories.

Fiscalists consider governmental expenditure to be a powerful force on national income, because it is a direct contributor to aggregate demand, and taxes are important, because they influence consumer spending via changes in disposable income. The monetarist denigration of fiscal policy is based on the belief that if a deficit is financed by borrowing, without resort to a monetary expansion, interest rates would rise and resources would be diverted from private use. Thus, the increase in aggregate demand by government would be offset, at least in some degree, by a reduction in private demand. This is referred to as the *crowding-out effect*.

The difference between the monetarist and the fiscalist is often expressed as a difference in opinion about the slopes of the *I-S* and the *L-M* functions. Thus, if the *L-M* function is very flat (infinitely or very elastic with respect to interest rates), then the fiscalist case holds; whereas, if the *L-M* function is perpendicular (infinitely or very inelastic with respect to interest rates), the monetarist case is powerful. On the other hand, given an intermediate *L-M* curve, the more elastic the *I-S* curve, the stronger the monetarist case is; the steeper the *I-S* curve, the stronger is the fiscalist case. By the criterion of this paragraph, the dispute could conceivably be settled by empirical estimates of elasticities of the relevant relationships. Notice that the framework of this discussion has been the Keynesian one and, thus, the one favored by the fiscalists.

Monetarists are more likely to utilize some version of the quantity theory to appraise the relative merits of monetary versus fiscal policy. The issue then turns on the stability of cash balance demand or velocity. The monetarist case is strongest when velocity is unaffected by changes in the money stock, and the monetarist argument would collapse if V varied perfectly inversely with changes in the amount of money in existence. The fiscalist case would be verified if velocity varied directly with government expenditures and inversely with taxes.

Two monetarists, Milton Friedman and David Meiselman, conducted a study to determine whether the Keynesian multiplier or the velocity variable of the quantity theory would serve better as a forecaster of the movements of national income.[5] They did this by testing the stability of the two variables, reasoning that if the velocity of money is relatively stable, changes in the money stock would result in predictable changes in national income and would support the monetarist view. If the investment (or government expenditure) multiplier was more stable, it would indicate that a change in aggregate demand imposed by fiscal policy would result in a more predictable change in national income. The results were clearly in favor of monetary policy and the quantity theory, but the debate was not ended. Economists at the Federal Reserve Bank of St. Louis tested more directly the predictive power of changes in money versus changes in fiscal policy. Again, the evidence was in favor of monetary policy, but the debate was not ended. Post-Keynesians have not entirely accepted these findings, because they are critical of the methodology used, because they have a strong attachment to the logic of their own position, and lastly, because they have had considerable success in forecasting using econometric models built along Keynesian lines.

Where does all of this leave the reader? With an open mind, we hope. We don't have all of the answers in economics. We still need to be very cautious in our policy prescriptions. There is a good deal of talk about "fine tuning" the economy with just "the right mix" of mon-

---

5. Milton Friedman and David Meiselman, "The Relative Stability of Monetary Velocity and the Investment Multiplier in the United States, 1897–1958," in *Stabilization Policies, A Series of Research Studies Prepared for the Committee on Money and Credit* (Englewood Cliffs, NJ: Prentice-Hall, Inc., 1964).

etary and fiscal policy. It is, perhaps, a bit premature at this stage in our scientific development to take such talk very seriously.

QUESTIONS

1. What do you conceive to be the role of the economist in determining national economic goals and policies?
2. Compare the real costs in achieving economic growth of a relatively affluent society, such as the United States, with the costs to a society in which the majority of the population is at or near a subsistence level of income.
3. Explain how you would go about deciding for yourself what your "trade off" rate would be regarding the conflict between increased employment and inflation. Relate your discussion to the Phillips curve on page 529.
4. If policymakers must choose between inflation and higher interest rates, what would be the nature of the considerations that should be made?
5. Discuss the following policy issues with reference to Pareto optimality:
    (a) Tariff reductions.
    (b) Highway construction during periods of full employment.
    (c) Highway construction during periods of serious unemployment.
6. How do you react to the observation that the hurt caused some people by inflation is perfectly offset by benefits derived by others?
7. Explain the most important methods of promoting economic growth.
8. Can you construct a definition of optimum population or optimum growth of population? What would be the important elements in evolving such a definition?
9. This chapter and the following chapter stress policies of aggregate demand expansion to reduce unemployment. What other approach seems promising?
10. Many governmental policies to promote economic growth and stability have an impact on the distribution of wealth and income. Can you formulate criteria by which you can determine that one distribution is better than another? Is it possible to argue that change in the distribution is either good or bad?
11. Describe the purpose and basic provisions of the Employment Act of 1946.

READINGS

Andersen, Leonall C. "The State of the Monetarist Debate" with "Commentary" by Lawrence R. Klein and Karl Brunner. *Review*, Federal Reserve Bank of St. Louis (September 1973).

————, and Jerry L. Jordan. "Monetary and Fiscal Actions: A Test of Their Relative Importance in Economic Stabilization." *Review*, Federal Reserve Bank of St. Louis (November 1968).

Economic Report of the President. Washington, D.C.: USGPO, annually.

Friedman, Milton. "Nobel Lecture: Inflation and Unemployment." *Journal of Political Economy* (June 1977), pp. 451–472.

Garner, C. Alan. "How Fast Can the U.S. Economy Grow?" *Economic Review*, Federal Reserve Bank of Kansas City (December 1989).

Lipsey, Richard G. "Government and Inflation." *American Economic Review* (May 1982), pp. 67–71.

Phelps, Edmund S. *Inflation, Policy, and Unemployment Theory*. New York: W. W. Norton & Co., Inc., 1972.

Samuels, Warren J. *The Classical Theory of Economic Policy*. Cleveland, OH: The World Publishing Co., 1966.

Santomero, Anthony M., and John J. Seater. "The Inflation-Unemployment Tradeoff: A Critique of the Literature." *Journal of Economic Literature* (June 1978), pp. 499–544.

Schultze, Charles L. "Industrial Policy: A Dissent." *The Brookings Review* (Fall 1983).

Sorkin, Alan L. *Monetary and Fiscal Policy and Business Cycles in the Modern Era*. Lexington, MA: Lexington Books, 1988, Chapters 6 and 7.

Tobin, James. *Policies for Prosperity*. Edited by Peter Jackson. Cambridge, MA: MIT Press, 1989.

MONETARY AND FISCAL POLICIES FOR ECONOMIC GROWTH AND STABILITY

This chapter is devoted to an analysis of monetary and fiscal policies designed to promote economic growth and stability. Present programs and policies will be analyzed, and proposals for revisions or for new policies will be considered.

The question arises as to whether a clear-cut distinction can be made between policies that are to be termed "monetary" and those that are to be called "fiscal." Considerable ambiguity about these terms exists, which often leads to useless debate and confusion. No difficulty would arise if policies were purely monetary (those that have their impact directly on the quantity or cost of money) or purely fiscal (government spending and taxing programs). But any federal budget has some implications for the money supply. A budgetary deficit requires a decision about its financing, and this will have an impact on the supply or cost of money. A surplus requires a decision about its disposition—again, this will influence the supply or cost of money.

The point is not that we need rigorous definitions of monetary versus fiscal, but that we should recognize the interrelations between the policies of the same names. We should also be aware that many people use these words differently.

An often-used approach is one that declares arbitrarily that actions by the central bank (the Federal Reserve System in the United States) are monetary policies, and those by the Treasury are fiscal actions. This works fairly well for the United States, but it is hardly useful in those countries where the treasury and the central bank are under the control of the same officers.

Our organization of the discussion will be based on the proposition that Federal Reserve policy is mainly monetary and Treasury policy mainly fiscal. We, of course, will try to keep the interrelationships in proper perspective.

THE NATURE OF MONETARY POLICIES

The nature of our monetary system and the tools of monetary policy were described briefly in Chapter 10, and the theoretical framework was discussed in Part 2. It should be clear that any policy proposal must be based on some theory. There is no alternative. The hope is that the theory we choose is the most accurate picture available of the economy the policy will affect.

As discussed in Chapter 10, money supply theory concerns the relationship between the variables that can be directly determined by the monetary authority, the monetary base (B), which is mainly member bank reserves and currency in circulation, and the money supply (M). We used the expression $M = KB$, where K is the relationship called the money multiplier. Recall that K involved the behavior of the public and the commercial banks and incorporated the significance of reserve requirements that are controlled by the Federal Reserve Board of Governors.

Once we have a theory that explains how the money supply is affected by monetary policy, we then need a theory that explains how changes in the money supply influence the economy. We considered two basic approaches to this problem. The classical quantity theory approach concludes that changes in the money supply directly influence the level of absolute prices and, when unemployment exists, directly affect the level of real national income. The Keynesian approach concludes that the direct effect of changes in the money supply is on interest rates, which, in turn, affect the rate of investment and thereby, through the multiplier process, affect national income.

We should emphasize that the analytical apparatus used, classical or Keynesian, is not the source of differing opinion on the effectiveness of monetary policy. Rather, conclusions differ primarily because of differences in judgment about what the real world is like—the degree of flexibility of wages and prices, the degree to which interest rate changes influence the level of investment or saving, the degree to which money supply changes will change interest rates, and so on.

A new and very difficult problem for monetary policy discussions has arisen in recent years by virtue of the many financial innovations that make our concept of money ambiguous. In 1978, it became legal to allow savings accounts to be automatically transferred into checking accounts (ATS or automatic transfer service). Negotiable orders of withdrawals (NOW accounts) became legal nationwide in 1981. Repurchase agreements (repos or RPs) have become important in financial markets. Brokerage firms introduced money management accounts that paid attractive interest rates and were withdrawable on demand. These and other innovations are such good substitutes for demand deposits or currency that they either should be included as money or should be recognized as having dramatic effects on the velocity of the narrowly defined money stock.

Federal Reserve Policy

Robert V. Roosa divides the responsibilities of the Federal Reserve System into what he calls the defensive and the dynamic responsibilities.[1] *Defensive actions* are taken by the Federal Reserve System in response to changes in the reserve position of commercial banks caused by others. Defensive actions simply offset such reserve status changes. *Dynamic policy* aims at either increasing or decreasing the ability of commercial banks to expand the money supply and credit.

The major factors, not involving Federal Reserve action, affecting member bank reserves are gold flows and foreign transactions, currency in circulation, Treasury balances in the Federal Reserve Banks, and the float. In addition to these, the volume of required reserves changes as deposits shift among banks with different reserve requirements[2] and between time deposits and demand deposits.

If all these factors were to behave in such a way that the excess reserves in the banking system were to increase by, for example, $2 billion, the Federal Open-Market Committee in its defensive posture would sell $2 billion worth of securities. Selling less than that amount would amount to a dynamic action of promoting monetary ease and expansion. Selling more than $2 billion worth of securities would be a dynamic action of curtailing the ability of banks to expand or forcing them to contract money and credit.

In an economy where money was left to manage itself, serious instability would be generated by virtue of these changes in the reserve position of commercial banks. Indeed, in Chapter 14, we looked at the purely monetary theory of the business cycle where the basic cause of the cycle was the flow of reserves into and out of the banks in the form of currency movements and gold flows. Much of the instability expe-

---

1. Robert V. Roosa, *Federal Reserve Operations in the Money and Government Securities Markets* (New York: Federal Reserve Bank of New York, 1956).
2. This was once a very important consideration, but currently, reserve requirements differ among banks only based on the amount of deposits held.

rienced in this country during the time of the independent treasury system (from 1846 until the Federal Reserve System took over the fiscal agency function) was due to the flow of funds between the Treasury and commercial banks as the Treasury collected taxes in cash and paid for its expenditures from those accounts.

Very little controversy surrounds the defensive actions of the Federal Reserve System. For example, a serious snowstorm that would slow the mails and increase the amount of the float should not disrupt the money market and the economy. Similarly, the fact that the public uses more currency in the month or two before Christmas is not justification for a large contraction of the money supply. The important question at any time is whether it is appropriate to increase or decrease the money supply to counter the cyclical movement of the economy or to promote growth in real output. If something should be done, the questions of how much and what particular instruments should be used need to be considered.

Using the Instruments of Monetary Policy

The Federal Reserve System uses the various instruments of monetary policy at its disposal to help smooth out seasonal and cyclical fluctuations in economic activity and to meet the needs of the economy for growth. Seasonal variations in the reserves of member banks are principally offset by open-market operations. Some banks may offset seasonal pressures by borrowing from their Federal Reserve Banks, but this happens primarily when pressures on a bank or a group of banks are due to special or unusual seasonal fluctuations.

The provision of bank reserves to meet the needs of a growing economy is partly through open-market operations, partly through changing reserve requirements, and partly through lending to member banks. Reserve requirements are frequently lowered during a period of recession when long-run growth indicates the need for additional reserves. This is done to help provide the stimulus for expansion. Reserve requirements also may be changed when large international movements of gold need to be offset to keep reserves in line with the demands of the economy.

The role of the Federal Reserve in helping to stabilize cyclical fluctuations is carried on primarily through the use of open-market operations and by altering the ability or the willingness of commercial bank borrowing through the discount window. When economic activity is expanding rapidly and inflationary pressures develop, restraint on monetary expansion is called for to promote stability. Under such circumstances, the Federal Reserve resorts to open-market operations to provide banks with a smaller amount of reserves than needed to meet all demands for credit. The first reaction is for individual banks that are short of reserves to sell government bonds to obtain funds. Such sales provide funds for the individual bank, but do not increase the supply of reserves, since other banks lose reserves as checks are drawn against deposits to pay for the bonds. Banks deficient in reserves also borrow reserves from banks with excess reserves in the "federal funds market," but this, too, results in merely a shift in reserves and not an increase in the total available supply. In this situation, the federal funds rate increases as the total volume of excess reserves in the system decreases.

As the monetary authorities continue the policy of restraint, a greater number of banks grow short of reserves. This leads more banks to borrow from their Federal Reserve Banks to meet shortages in required reserves. As loans are retired and not renewed and funds are used to repay the loans from the Federal Reserve Banks, other banks experience a shortage of reserves. Thus, an increase in borrowing from the Federal Reserve Banks is a normal reaction to a restrictive monetary policy. This borrowing provides an offset to the reduction in reserves brought about by open-market sales, but it does not nullify the effects of monetary restraint. The borrowing will be offset by open-market operations to keep total reserves at the level desired by Federal Reserve authorities.

The cost of borrowing or the discount rate also will be raised to help discourage borrowing. Furthermore, banks in debt to their Reserve Bank use any reserves that they acquire to repay their loans and thus restrict credit expansion. Their lending policies also become more stringent, since they are under pressure to repay their indebtedness. Actions of one bank to free itself of indebtedness to the Federal Reserve, however, cannot correct a reserve shortage situation, because the reserves one bank gains are lost by others. As long as the Federal Reserve maintains pressure on bank reserve positions, member banks will remain conservative and even become cautious in their lending policies.

This process is simply reversed when economic conditions call for a policy of monetary ease. Reserves are supplied through open-market operations and, at times, through lowering reserve requirements when long-run expansion requires a larger volume of reserves. The first action of member banks is to reduce their debt to the Federal Reserve

Banks. When this phase has ended, excess reserves become available for bank loans and investments.

Effect of Monetary Policy on the Economy

When bank reserve positions are under pressure, banks sell government securities and thus reduce their supply of secondary reserves. As their reserves are reduced and they are forced to borrow from their Reserve Bank, banks become more conservative in their lending policies. The loan requests of marginal borrowers are either refused or reduced in amount. This forces business firms to spend less to increase inventory or plant and equipment. Banks are less willing to make loans on residential real estate and to consumers for purchasing durable goods. Banks are also less willing to lend to other financial institutions, such as sales finance companies, consumer finance companies, and mortgage loan companies. The lessened availability of credit puts a brake on spending. This is reinforced by the increase in interest rates that results when the supply of loanable funds is restricted while demand continues to increase.

The actions of banks also affect other credit markets. As banks try to increase reserves, they sell securities, which takes funds from the money markets at the very time when demand for funds is high and helps raise interest rates. Rising interest rates make borrowing less attractive, and marginal projects are canceled or postponed.

In periods of credit ease, the effect is largely the reverse. Banks have an adequate supply of funds and are willing to make funds available to other financial institutions. Lower interest rates also encourage investment and raise the price of existing securities and, in this way, make the sale of securities more advantageous.

When the new money comes into existence, the public will have more money than it had before, so adjustment to a new equilibrium position with respect to cash balances is necessary. As we have seen, this adjustment involves the attempts by money holders to shift into other things, securities or real goods. Through this process the prices of goods will rise and interest rates will fall, unless unemployment is serious, in which case, output will increase instead of the prices of securities, goods, and services.

Reduction of the money supply would be expected to have the opposite effect of money expansion, although there is the general belief that prices are less flexible downward. If this is true, the impact will be greater on output and employment rather than on prices.

Monetary policy has an indirect effect through its influence on the expectations of consumers and business people. If consumers feel prices are likely to rise, they will speed up purchases of durables; if they expect prices to decline, they will defer them. Business people react in a similar fashion to expectations of price changes, to difficulties in financing expansion projects, and to other changes in the economic outlook.

The Federal Reserve System has not always been clear about which monetary aggregate it wishes to designate as the primary target of its actions and has, on occasion, changed its target variable. This is partially due to the process of deregulation, which resulted in the many close substitutes for demand deposits or time deposits. For example, NOWs and money market deposit accounts have almost as much liquidity as demand deposits and yet yield an interest income as attractive as or more attractive than the interest earned on traditional savings accounts. The definitions of the monetary aggregates have changed several times over recent years, and yet, the definitions in use today are still met with dissatisfaction. A great deal of controversy continues over which measure should be the target. Some research is devoted to the development of an aggregate that includes deposit items that are weighted according to their importance as transactions deposits.[3]

Selective Versus General Monetary Controls

Up to now, the discussion of monetary policies has been in terms of general controls over the amount of credit available. Selective controls of various types also have been used periodically, and several of them are still in use. One selective credit control currently in the hands of the Federal Reserve is that over stock market credit. By changing margin requirements on stock purchases, the Federal Reserve is able to influence directly the amount of credit used in the stock market. This is a highly volatile type of credit affected by speculative activity in the market. Selective controls in this area moderate the degree of general credit action that is necessary to offset speculation and the use of credit in the stock market.

The payment of interest on demand deposits was prohibited by the Banking Acts of 1933 and 1935, which also authorized the establish-

---

3. Paul A. Spindt, "Money Is What Money Does: Monetary Aggregation and the Equation of Exchange" (Washington: Board of Governors of the Federal Reserve System, 1984), and R. W. Hafer, "Inflation: Assessing Its Recent Behavior and Future Prospects," *Review*, Federal Reserve Bank of St. Louis (March 1984), pp. 19–27.

ment of interest rate ceilings on savings and time deposits, which were effectuated in Regulation Q. The purpose of these rules was to prevent what was viewed as dangerous interest rate competition among banks. It was believed that in trying to attract deposits by paying high interest rates, banks would need to invest in excessively risky assets and thus put the whole financial system in jeopardy. As the fears generated by the experiences of the 1930s subsided, and as economists criticized the practice of governmentally mandated rates, support for the regulations weakened, and in 1973, early steps toward deregulation were taken. The Depository Institutions Deregulation and Monetary Control Act of 1980 provided for the gradual deregulation and the ultimate elimination of interest rate ceilings as well as the elimination of minimum balance requirements on most deposit accounts. After March 31, 1986, only the prohibition of interest payments on demand deposits remained.

The problem with the government setting legal maximum rates was that when free market rates rose above those rates, the public shifted its funds out of the regulated and into the unregulated sectors, a process called *disintermediation*. Disintermediation resulted in hardships for many financial institutions, especially savings and loan associations. The home mortgage market was hit particularly hard. Another result of the large gap between the market interest yields and the ceiling rates was the spurt in development of financial innovations aimed at getting around the regulations.

The Federal Reserve had power to control consumer credit during World War II, and again briefly in the postwar period, and for a time also had control over real estate credit; but these powers have not been renewed. Selective credit controls of a limited type are in operation, however, in other credit markets. The federal government has a number of credit granting and insuring agencies that can influence credit conditions by encouraging or discouraging activity in the home building and other industries.

Arguments Against Selective Controls. There is a basic difference of opinion about the role of selective credit controls as a permanent instrument for influencing economic growth and restraining inflationary pressures. Those economists who argue against selective credit controls do so largely on the basis of the efficiency of the free market mechanism. They believe that competitive markets can best determine interest rates and the allocation of resources to various lenders. Any governmental interference can, at best, produce results that are less desirable in the long run than those established in the market.

Another argument against selective controls arises out of their administration. In many cases, such controls are difficult to enforce, especially in the field of consumer credit. This is, in part, due to the large number of merchants and dealers involved in selling consumer durables on credit and to the difficulty of establishing true prices and down payments due to the widespread practice of giving inflated allowances for trade-ins as a means of cutting list prices.

One of the major arguments against selective credit controls is that they are not effective. Margin requirements in the stock market do not appear to have any significant influence on stock prices, the volume of stock trading, or even the amount of credit used in the stock market. To the degree, if any, that selective controls are effective in the segment of the economy in which they are imposed, they only shift the inflationary problem rather than solve it. The funds made idle in one segment of the economy are transferred to other segments, and price pressure thus develops.

Arguments in Favor of Selective Controls. The proponents of such controls argue that any monetary policy involves discrimination and that there is no real choice between general monetary controls and selective monetary controls from a free economy point of view. They feel that selective controls can prevent maladjustments that lead more easily to instability than do general controls. For example, if housing is in a boom while unemployment exists in other areas, these advocates feel that control of housing credit can prevent undue expansion and later collapse; whereas general credit controls are powerless, unless the whole economy is to be restrained at a time when such a policy is not required.

There also has been some advocacy of selective controls as a means of stimulating or retarding long-run growth in a sector of the economy to establish balanced patterns of growth. For example, under such a proposal, consumer credit could be used to increase or decrease automobile demand, if it were out of line with what the regulatory authorities believed to be balanced growth with the rest of the economy. Using selective controls this way would, of course, intensify the argument over control by regulation or market forces.

Analysis and Evaluation of Monetary Policy

There is considerable disagreement amongst economists about the efficiency of monetary policy in helping to promote full employment and a stable price level. Since economic forces are extremely complex and are based on many interrelated factors, it is difficult, if not impossible, to determine the real effect of any policy in isolation. Therefore, we cannot determine exactly what would have happened if monetary policies of a different type had been followed or if the timing of changes in monetary policy had been different.

Favorable Effects of Monetary Policy. Monetary controls have several advantages over other policies for stability. One important advantage is that monetary controls are impersonal; the monetary authorities determine the total volume of bank reserves, but not their distribution among banks, then, the banks ration the available credit. However, such controls do directly affect various groups. Since monetary controls affect the volume of and interest rates on bank loans and investments, bank profits are directly affected. Changes in interest rates also redistribute income between those who pay interest and those who receive it. Many individuals and organizations are able to determine whether they will be lenders or borrowers. This is, however, not universally true, nor is it true at all times, even for those for whom it is generally true.

Monetary policy can be very flexible. A powerful and immediate impact need not be instituted, but can be, if needed. This is particularly true of open-market operations where the impact can be spread out in any desired amounts without any change in laws and without any announcements of what it is doing. Indeed, very few in the general public are likely to even know what is happening. Reversal of the direction of policy can be accomplished very easily, if it is discovered that the initial action was erroneous.

It takes time for monetary policy to influence the economy. The time lag, however, is probably shorter than for most other policy actions, particularly those requiring action by both the Congress and the executive branch of government.

Many economists believe that monetary policy is more effective in combating inflation than it is in stimulating recovery from depressed conditions. The statement defending this opinion is that during inflationary periods, banks usually have negligible amounts of excess reserves, and therefore, they will be forced to contract earning assets and demand deposits following any contractionary actions by the Federal Reserve. On the other hand, during depressions, since banks usually hold larger amounts of excess reserves, any expansionary Federal Reserve policy will simply permit but not force the banks to expand.

In addition, as discussed earlier, Keynesians feel that the liquidity preference function is so elastic that any increase in the money supply during depressed periods will have virtually no effect on interest rates. Since the Keynesian analysis makes interest rates important only to the extent that they influence investment demand, if interest rates are not lowered significantly, the impact on investment and national income will be negligible. The other string to the Keynesian bow is the judgment that at the low interest rates that prevail during depressions, investment demand is not responsive to further rate reductions.

Since the people responsible for monetary policy throughout most of the Federal Reserve's existence seem to have accepted this argument, they have had little faith in the power of their tools to bring the economy out of depressions. Consequently, during such periods, expansionary monetary policy has been somewhat half-hearted; at least, so argue the defenders of monetary policy.

The negative side of the argument is countered point by point by those who do believe in the effectiveness of monetary policy. First, on the question of whether banks with large excess reserves will increase earning assets and, hence, the money supply, these economists contend that under the prevailing economic and banking conditions, equilibrium for banks requires a large volume of excess reserves. But if banks are provided with additional amounts, they will have more than the desired amount and will thus seek profitable outlets for their excess reserves. In particular, since large volumes of risk-free government securities are available for purchase, and if the monetary authorities act aggressively to promote expansion, it is felt that banks will not continuously allow nonearning cash to accrue.

A rebuttal to the interest rate and investment argument is that Keynesians have excessively stressed interest as a cost to investors. They have neglected to observe that at low interest rates, even a minute reduction in the rate has a large positive impact on capital values. For that reason, an increase in the money supply would be very expansionary, even if the interest rate effect were small. Ultimately, of course, the answers to these questions are not to be found in a priori speculation but must be found from empirical tests. Perhaps, we have never adequately tested the power of monetary policy in bringing about expansion from a serious depression.

In October 1979, there occurred a dramatic change in the operating procedures of the Federal Reserve. An announcement was made that interest rates would (within limits) be free to change as the free market dictated and that the Federal Reserve would put primary emphasis on the control of monetary aggregates. The intent was to target money supply rates of growth by controlling bank reserves. The earlier procedure of trying to control interest rates (specifically the Federal funds rate) led to the problem of continuing inflation. When the Federal Reserve attempted to prevent rising interest rates by injecting reserves into the system, the result was an increase in price levels, and the increase in inflation led to expectations of inflation, which, in turn, led to still higher interest rates.

The new policy apparently was successful in reducing the rate of growth in prices and some declines in interest rates, but unemployment became more severe, and the volatility of the money stock and of interest rates grew more pronounced. It has become very evident that trying to stop inflation is a painful and long-run process.

Unfavorable Effects of Monetary Policy. Major criticism of monetary policy lies in the area of timing. The tendency is not to act until it is clear that action is needed. This means that action is usually too late to do the most good and, in fact, may actually be counterproductive. For example, during the recovery period of a cycle, the Federal Reserve may hesitate to restrict credit for fear of reversing the recovery. When action is taken, inflationary pressures have already built up.

Another criticism of monetary policy is that it tends to slow down the rate of growth. In a period of tight money, financing new projects is more difficult than it is in a period of monetary ease. New businesses based on new ideas and growing small businesses, which are important sources of economic growth, find it harder to get funds. Although the forced saving that arises in the inflationary stage of a cycle may lead to short-run inequities, it promotes growth by increasing investment faster than would voluntary savings.

It is often argued that the high interest rates resulting from monetary restraint slow down investment. This is, of course, what they are designed to do. Price stability can exist only when investment takes place from voluntary saving, not from forced saving. In the long run, lower interest rates will stimulate investment, if they exist because the supply of funds for investment has been increased because of an increase in the saving function. When interest rates are kept abnormally low because of an expansionary monetary policy, prices will rise and offset much of the real effect on investment.

Monetary policy is also criticized because of the hardship it imposes on various groups in society. In a period of inflation brought about by monetary ease, monetary policy reduces the income of those trying to live on the earnings from bond investments and other fixed-income sources. Problems are created for financial institutions if their income from interest is cut. In a period of monetary restraint, other problems arise as a result of high interest rates. For example, the cost of financing a home increases, thus burdening young people who are trying to buy their first home. Small business finds it more difficult to obtain funds and, therefore, feels disadvantaged. Financing costs of state and local governments and private institutions, such as hospitals, rise. Those who must finance at the period of greatest monetary pressure are hardest hit. Such policy is, of course, designed to postpone projects, but some plans cannot be postponed without serious consequences.

Proposals for Changes in Monetary Instruments of Control

Various proposals have been made for changing the monetary instruments used for control of the economy; some would make relatively minor changes, others more drastic changes. Several such proposals will be considered briefly.

Discretionary Monetary Control.   First, consider the current major Federal Reserve tools. Open-market operations, per se, are almost never criticized. They can be as powerful as needed; they are flexible and impersonal, there are no "announcement effects," and the impact is quite predictable. Indeed, a number of monetary economists contend that open-market operation is so ideal a tool that the other methods are not needed and, in fact, are harmful. Changing the reserve requirements, it is said, is too upsetting to the banking system; the impact is less predictable, they are not flexible, and the announcement effects are dramatic and uncertain. Changing the discount rate is judged to be a weaker tool. With the development and growth of the federal funds market and other financial instruments, there no longer is any need for the discount facilities of the Federal Reserve Banks. Bank borrowing or repayments of loans to the Federal Reserve can offset the effects of open-market operations. Therefore, if open-market action takes away reserves, the member banks can get them back by borrowing, thus frustrating policy's intent. Defenders of the discount mechanism point out that that is the virtue of the tool; it allows for an escape valve and an orderly adjustment to a new reserve situation. Even those who advocate keeping the discount mechanism usually feel that it should be more closely attuned to market interest rates, rather than lagging seriously behind them, as has been the practice.

Automatic Monetary Control.   Some critics of discretionary monetary policy have proposed that it be eliminated. Several reasons are offered for this change. First, it is felt that the Federal Reserve's record in preventing the extremes of business cycle swings has been worse than what would have happened in the absence of any action. Second, and as a partial explanation of the first statement, the lags in monetary policy are believed to be so long that by the time the action takes effect, the economy may already have reversed direction and would need the opposite prescription. Advocates of automatic monetary policy further argue that discretionary monetary policy depends upon a degree of accuracy in forecasting that is beyond our present capabilities.

The proposal itself involves the rule that the money supply should be allowed to grow at approximately the same rate as the long-run rate of growth in productivity. The reason for choosing this rate of growth is to maintain relatively constant prices over the long term, although the particular growth rate chosen is not critically important to the proposal.

The basic reasoning behind the plan is that a constant rate of growth in the money supply will act as an automatic stabilizer. During an expansionary period when aggregate demand is increasing at a more rapid rate than is aggregate output, interest rates would rise, discouraging investment demand and, to some extent, consumption. It is felt that depressions could not become very severe or last very long if the money supply were to increase continuously. Aggregate demand would have to turn up when the money stock becomes large enough. In the depression, the interest rate would fall, which would then promote increased investment and consumption demand.

Some proponents of this type of plan advocate that Congress should establish the required rate of monetary growth and give the responsibility for the policy to elected officials. Other economists would advise the Board of Governors of the Federal Reserve System to establish the rate as a guide to policy, leaving some flexibility for unusual circumstances. Having such a clearcut rule of policy would eliminate one important source of uncertainty in the economy. Whereas discretionary policy requires planners to forecast what the monetary authorities will do, a rule requires planners to forecast only the more fundamental variables of the economy.

Of course, there are objections raised to this proposal. Advocates of flexible monetary policy feel that discretionary policy is needed to adapt to different growth conditions and changes in the world economic scene. They also argue that discretionary monetary policy has functioned well when given a chance to work. They feel that a fixed-growth rate that is subject to change by Congress would become a political football and would not achieve the advantages claimed for it, but would instead create new uncertainty in ascertaining what Congress would do.

A problem for monetary policymakers is the uncertainty about the behavior of the demand for money or its velocity. Early results of the research on this issue supported the proposition that velocity was relatively stable or, at least, predictable by forecasting models. Recent research, however, throws doubt on such a conclusion. The major reason usually given for the observed variation in velocity is the growth of the financial innovations introduced in recent years, which serve as substitutes for what has traditionally been counted as money. A second explanation is the degree of public uncertainty. From 1945 until 1982, M1 velocity increased at a steady, rather rapid rate (the demand for money falling). However, from 1982 through 1987, velocity fell noticeably, which is to say that the demand for narrowly defined money increased. This increase generally has been explained by an increase in uncertainty, much of which is being generated by the volatility of the money stock and interest rates.

The implication that stable growth in the money supply would lead to a more even rate of growth is also questionable. As discussed in Part 3, real changes take place in supply and demand, and these changes lead to changes in economic activity. The cycle would be different if the money supply were set at a fixed rate of growth, but it would not be eliminated.

FISCAL POLICY AND OTHER PROGRAMS FOR ECONOMIC GROWTH AND STABILITY

In this section, we will focus on fiscal and other governmental programs designed to promote economic growth and stability. These programs include measures to help stabilize disposable income, influence the propensity to consume out of a given level of income, and influence the level of all types of investment. This may be done indirectly by means of fiscal policy or by more direct controls, such as price and wage controls. Governmental policies also can be used to stabilize the level of economic activity arising out of international transactions.

Automatic Stabilizers

The workings of a free, frictionless economic system are characterized by a multitude of automatically stabilizing forces. When unemployment occurs, wages fall to restore full employment. Excesses or deficiencies of aggregate demand are self-correcting by rising or falling price levels. Imbalances in international transactions are automatically adjusted by international reserve flows or exchange rate fluctuations. Such equilibrating mechanisms are at the core of most economic theory. If these adjustment variables are fully operative, the need for economic policy by government is lessened considerably.

However, to the extent that rigidities in prices, wages, and interest rates exist, and to the extent that factors of production are not completely mobile, the automatic stabilizers of the economy fail to produce the precise results of competitive theory. One view of government's role in the economy is to break down the frictions that arise and restore, as much as possible, the self-adjusting economy. Other views are pessimistic about government's ability to bring about this result and, thus, call for more direct action to cure the resulting evils.

Still another approach is to design the federal government's receipts and outlays in such a way as to provide automatic stabilizers for the economy. To accomplish this function, receipts must fall and outlays rise when the economy is moving downward; and receipts must rise and outlays fall when the economy is expanding. Americans demand somewhat more than this of our fiscal policy, since our goal is not simply stability, but stability at a high (near full employment) level of activity.

A "pay-as-you-go" progressive income tax structure provides a most important automatic stabilizer in the sense that as income increases, the withdrawal of purchasing power from the private sector gets progressively greater; and, conversely, during periods of declining income, the withdrawals or taxes decrease more than proportionally. With the progressive income tax then, disposable income will increase and decrease as the GNP increases and decreases, but the variation in the former will be much less than in the GNP. For this reason, consumption demand is less volatile than it would be expected to be if taxes were less progressive; and if consumption expenditures are relatively stable, this situation will have a stabilizing influence on investment expenditures. The degree of progressivity of the U.S. income tax rates was reduced considerably by the 1986 Tax Reform Act when the number of tax rate brackets was changed from fifteen to three (15%, 28%, and 33%). If the personal income tax structure is indexed to eliminate increased taxes resulting from inflation, real taxes would be constant if real income remained constant. In that event, variations in disposable income will result from changes in real GNP, but not from changes in nominal GNP, which are due only to inflation. This reduces the automatic stabilization effect of progressive income taxes, but it also eliminates the distortions of decision making due to the taxes in an inflationary environment.

The corporate income tax also is an automatic stabilization force even though the rates are not progressive in any very significant way. The reason is that corporate profits themselves tend to increase more than proportionally when national income increases. In this way government withdraws spending power from the private economy progressively as income increases.

The best example of an automatic stabilizer in the complete sense is the unemployment insurance program, because it is tied directly to the social goal of full employment. As long as people are out of work, payments from the unemployment compensation fund will continue. Such payments are injections into the flow of national income—large when unemployment is great, small but still positive, even when unemployment is small. Contributions into the fund are withdrawals from the income stream and vary as income and employment vary. Thus, the entire program acts to stabilize disposable income and serves as a depressant to national income when full employment exists and inflation threatens. Conversely, it is a stimulant to national income whenever the economy is operating at less than full employment. The more severe the unemployment, the greater is the expansionary impact of the program.

Other governmental programs contribute stability to the economy automatically, such as the agricultural price support programs and the Social Security programs. However, none are as important as those we have already mentioned.

The Full Employment Surplus Concept. The Council of Economic Advisers has developed a very interesting technique by means of which one can evaluate and distinguish clearly those elements of governmental activity that are called the automatic stabilizers and those that are not automatic but are, instead, discretionary acts. This tool focuses on the surplus or deficit in the federal budget under the given set of laws and regulations and various levels of national income.

It was shown in Chapter 9 that a deficit financed by monetary expansion was multiplicatively expansionary to the national income and that a surplus, together with money contraction, was multiplicatively contractive to the national income. Since, as we have just seen, some government expenditures and some government revenues depend upon national income, the size of the deficit or surplus cannot be known unless the size of national income is known (see Figure 22-1).

Figure 22-1   Full Employment Surplus Budgets

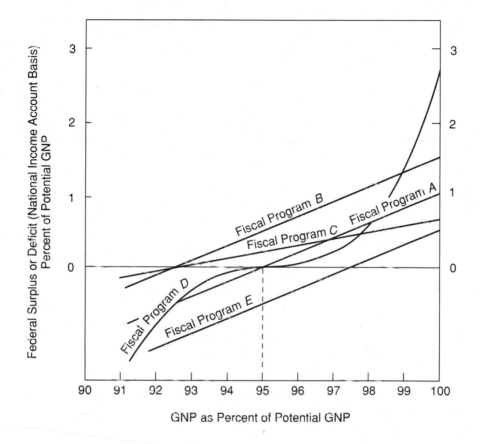

Figure 22-1 shows that under Fiscal Program *A*, a surplus of 1 percent of GNP will occur in the event that GNP is at its full potential, and a balanced budget will take place if GNP is 95 percent of potential GNP. At lower levels of actual GNP, budget deficits will occur.

Each of the fiscal programs charted reflects the tax and spending plans of a particular set of laws. The lines all have positive slopes because of the assumption that tax revenues and/or expenditures always vary positively with GNP. Since the horizontal axis is GNP as a percentage of potential GNP, we can compare the degree of "drag" on national income expansion of two budget plans at different times or places or, most significantly, of any two proposed fiscal programs.

Fiscal programs with steep slopes are powerful in their counter-cyclical effects. Falling incomes bring about rapid decreases in surpluses or increases in deficits; and rising incomes precipitate large decreases in deficits or increases in surpluses. In Figure 22-1, Programs A, B, and E all have the same slope; Program C is a weak countercyclical plan; and Program D is the extreme in its strong anticyclical impact, since surpluses and deficits increase at an increasing rate.

The line shifts upward whenever an increase in taxes is included in the budget or when a reduction of spending plans is programmed. Shifting the program lines is called discretionary fiscal policy. If, for example, the economy were operating at about 90 percent of its potential and Fiscal Program B were in effect, there would be great pressure to include new spending proposals and/or tax cuts to help stimulate the economy. The function would then shift to Program A or, if the action were still more dramatic, to Program E.

It is very important to realize that a change in spending or taxes that will produce a given increase in the size of the deficit at the current level of GNP will result in a much smaller deficit, since the action itself would be expected to increase GNP. What that actual deficit would be could only be forecast, which could be done in the manner of our models in Part 2, supplied with the statistical values of the parameters.

The point at which the fiscal program line crosses the balanced budget line presumably should be about at that point where it is estimated that further increases in GNP would be largely through inflation.

Balanced Versus Unbalanced Budgets. Since the 1930s, most economists have struggled to gain acceptance for the idea of planned divergences from the annually balanced federal budget. Many people think of deficits as immoral or, at least, as very poor and dangerous business practice. In the early 1980s, the Congress began to consider proposals requiring a balanced budget and, in 1985, passed the Gramm-Rudman-Hollings bill. This legislation requires successive annual reductions in the federal deficit until, in 1991, there should be a balanced budget. As a matter of fact, deficits can be very harmful, but so can budget surpluses and even balanced budgets. Under different business conditions, each budget situation can be appropriate.

The balanced budget principle does serve the important function of acting as a disciplinary device. At or near full employment, any use of resources by the federal government implies the giving up of desired goods or services by the private sectors of the economy. In this condition, two basic questions need to be answered. First, does governmental use render a greater "social" utility than private use? This question has an answer only through the democratic political process.

Second, are taxes the best way to induce the private sector to give up the necessary resources? It should be clear that there are alternatives.

The two alternatives to taxation as a means of financing government expenditures are (1) borrowing from the public by issuing interest-bearing bonds or other forms of indebtedness and (2) borrowing from the public by issuing noninterest-bearing debt, namely, money. How different are these two methods from each other and from taxes?

When government acquires its ability to command resources by taxation of individuals, the taxpayer's demand for goods and services is reduced. The balanced budget multiplier theory indicates that the public does not voluntarily give up quite as much as the government spends, so that at full employment, an increase in government expenditures matched by increased taxes will have some inflationary effect.

If government acquires its ability to command resources by the sale of bonds, it is not necessarily true that the bond buyers reduce their demand for goods and services at all. The buyers may simply shift from private security holdings to government security holdings, but the result will be a rise in interest rates, which will reduce demand by business for investment and may increase saving (decrease consumption demand). If an increase in government spending is matched by an increase in government debt without a change in the money supply, the result on aggregate demand is not greatly different from the increased tax case. There is a difference on the balance sheets of the public in that more government securities are outstanding, and this may influence future consumption behavior.

If increased government spending is made possible by an increase in the money supply, the situation is quite different from the tax and debt expansion methods. The money supply will increase if the Treasury borrows from the Federal Reserve System,[4] spends out of its past accumulation of deposits in the Federal Reserve, or issues new gold certificates or new Treasury currency. The money supply may or may not increase if the Treasury borrows from commercial banks, depending upon the reserve position of the banks. When the money supply does increase to allow the additional government spending, the public will give up resources, but it must be done by rising prices—the process we referred to earlier as "forced saving."

---

4. The Treasury does not normally borrow directly from the Federal Reserve, but the effect is the same if, as the Treasury is selling to the public, the Federal Reserve is buying from the public.

Inflation redistributes the use of resources from the private to the government sector just as does taxation or borrowing, but it does it capriciously. The people who pay may or may not be the people who society's principles would decree should pay. In particular, inflation strikes without reference to economic contribution, equity, ability to pay, or any other criterion.

The situation is considerably different if the economy is experiencing serious unemployment. Then, any action that increases aggregate demand can increase output without increasing prices. This is the reason for recommending a deficit and, if real impetus is needed, the reason for financing it in such a way as to increase the money supply. In less than full employment conditions, government may be able to increase its use of resources without the private sector giving up any because the resources might otherwise be unused.

To insure that expenditures, planned or started while the economy was suffering from unemployment, are important enough that the public is willing to pay for them when they must, it is sometimes proposed that tax rates be set to cover the spending at full employment. In terms of Figure 22-1, the fiscal program line would rotate to become steeper but would still intersect the balanced budget line at the same point.

We have been speaking here as if the question of balanced versus unbalanced budgets were purely an economic question. In fact, as our news media often remind us, the political implications of taxing and spending are often the controlling influences.

Long-Run Growth Policy

Until recently the role of the government in promoting short-run stability has received more attention than its role in promoting long-run growth. The analysis of growth in Chapter 21 indicated that growth depended on some factors in the public sector, as well as some in the private sector, of the economy. If optimum growth is to be achieved, services provided by the government must also grow to meet the needs of the economy. This includes all the services regularly provided by state and local governments. If some areas cannot afford adequate services, such as education, growth would be aided by having the overall economy provide them. Although this raises questions about states' rights and governmental interference in education, there is little question about it as a means for promoting growth. Services provided by the federal government must also keep pace with the economy. These include building federal highways, waterways, and other major projects called "social capital" and such programs as the United States Employment Service, the activities of the Department of Labor to promote labor peace and help settle strikes, and the work of the Federal Trade Commission.

The need for a growing governmental program in these areas, growing as the economy grows, by and large, is not subject to much disagreement, except who will do it—local units, the states, or the federal government—and who will pay for it. Some people believe that the government's contribution to growth should end with providing the needed services for an expanding economy. Beyond this, they believe that the greatest contribution that government can make is to provide an environment in which private investment can grow. Governmental programs to stimulate private investment, including aid to research, are currently in place. Some people have advocated governmental investment programs, which are greatly increased in scope and in the volume of funds involved. Such programs have long been advocated by those who feel they are needed by society. Recently, however, some have advocated programs of increased governmental investment, as a means of speeding up economic growth, in such fields as public housing, schools, hospitals, public buildings, and power projects.

Increased governmental investment programs can, of course, only speed up the rate of growth when it is not at optimum levels. Those advocates of an expanded governmental investment program on a regular basis believe that this is generally true, or true so much of the time that the loss of goods to the private sector would not be material.

The Dual Budget

Certain countries, notably Denmark and Sweden, have adopted a dual budget in which the ordinary operating expenses of government and capital expenditures are separated. Under such a budget system, tax rates are set high enough so that, on the average, in both good and bad years, the operating budget is in balance. With fixed tax rates, there is a surplus in prosperity and a deficit in depressions. Capital expenditures for all types of public construction are planned on a long-term basis and budgeted separately. The funds are raised initially by borrowing, but interest payments and depreciation are added to the operating budget. Only such public construction is carried on as the public is willing to pay for over its life in the operating budget. In short, the same accounting and cost determination practices used in private businesses are used in governmental accounting and financial planning. Insofar as possible, capital expenditures are made in years of recession and depression.

A dual budget is not necessarily related to the use of fiscal policy for growth and stability. It is primarily a device to put governmental operations on a basis of sound planning. Public construction is carried out only if the electorate is willing to assume its full cost over the life of the project. The dual budget prevents deficits for which no repayment procedure exists, yet facilitates compensatory fiscal planning. It also helps remove many fears of the consequences of growing deficits, since plans are made to meet the costs of all expenditures over their period of usefulness.

Governmental Programs to Influence Sector Behavior

To now, we have dealt with the overall impact of the federal budget on economic activity. Here, we shall consider what can be done to influence the spending behavior of the other economic sectors—consumption by households, investment by business, and foreign trade with the rest of the world. The focus is not upon the amount of spending or taxing that may be involved, but upon the particular method or direction the spending or taxing may take. Furthermore, some of the programs require little or no taxing or spending.

The Propensity to Consume Out of a Given Level of Disposable Income. The government can use its powers to influence the propensity to consume out of a given level of income. To some extent, the government has done so in peacetime, but primarily in wartime when programs in this area were designed to reduce inflationary pressures.

The propensity to consume can be affected by changing the relative relationship between the level of wages and profits, which has been done on a limited basis by laws favorable to union bargaining positions. Since the marginal propensity to consume (MPC) out of wages appears to be greater than the MPC out of profit or other property earnings, such actions are defended when it is assumed that the long-run problem is too low a level of consumer demand. Excess profits taxes also alter the division of the national income, but they have usually been instituted during wartime on emotional, rather than on economic, grounds. Direct price, wage, and production controls, along with rationing, also have an important effect on the propensity to consume and have been used in wartime, as well. In the early 1970s, the Nixon administration imposed price controls and freeze phases somewhat half-heartedly in an attempt to break what was considered to be an inflation expectations psychology.

Another possibility that has not been used to date is taxing consumption and saving at different rates. In periods of inflation, a tax on consumption has been advocated in the form of a federal sales tax or a value added tax (VAT).

Excise taxes on particular commodities have been imposed during inflations and reduced or eliminated during slack periods as countercyclical acts. In depressions, a tax on savings to encourage spending was advocated. The proposal to tax spending in an inflationary period was given serious consideration in the World War II and postwar period, but it has not yet been used.

Another possibility is to stimulate saving so as to reduce the propensity to consume, which was done through campaigns to buy bonds, especially through payroll savings plans. This worked reasonably well during World War II, but it has had little effect in the postwar period of inflation. Proposals have been made for compulsory savings programs in inflationary periods, but they have received little support, except during wartime. Pronouncements by the President and other primary government officials to encourage or discourage consumption spending are made at different times. It is not likely that this kind of "jawbone fiscal policy" is very effective.

The Social Security program probably has had a long-run effect on the propensity to consume. If some of the economic uncertainties of life due to unemployment, sickness, and old age are lessened, there is less need for current saving. To the extent that a single, large-scale insurance-type program is more efficient than many individual programs, the propensity to consume is increased. Guaranteed annual incomes and guaranteed financing of education presumably would have the same effect. These programs could not be used countercyclically, but could be used as secular stimulants to consumption. The important issue here is the realization of the proper balance between consumption and investment uses of our resources.

Investment in Plant and Equipment. Governmental programs have an influence on private-sector investment expenditures, primarily on expenditures for plant and equipment and for housing, but also, to a limited degree, on expenditures for inventories. Tax incentives have been used to stimulate investment in plant and equipment. Rapid amortization of facilities that were necessary to meet defense needs stimulated such construction. There have been proposals to use rapid amortization in a period of recession to stimulate capital goods demand. A conscious effort to encourage investment in durable capital goods was the 7-percent tax credit granted to firms making such expenditures. The tax was instituted in 1962 when it was thought that such stimulation was needed, and it was revoked in 1966 when the fear of an overheated economy prevailed.

In the 1981 Tax Act, Congress instituted the Accelerated Cost Recovery System (ACRS), which permits greater depreciation in the early years of the life of the capital equipment. The system also allows relatively short periods of time for the depreciation schedule: three years and up for various categories of capital goods. In addition, a 10-percent investment tax credit in the year of purchase has been used to encourage investment. Some investments can be written off in the year in which they are purchased, and a number of economists have advocated a system wherein all investment expenditures could be 100 percent written-off at the time of purchase. The tax codes of Canada and England basically employ this system, and, indeed, most other countries allow faster write-offs than does the United States. Such a tax plan could not be used to stimulate or retard capital spending over the cycle but would be designed to promote more rapid secular economic growth.

The effect of corporate income taxes and changes in the corporation tax on investment is different from the effect of the personal income tax and changes therein on consumption. Actually, the important effect of an increase in the corporation tax is likely to be on consumption, since it lowers the disposable income of stockholders and/or of the other suppliers of resources.[5] Although any tax change that influences expectations of future consumption will certainly affect investment spending, we will now demonstrate that any direct effect on investment by corporate income taxes is likely to be very small.

This conclusion, which is initially surprising, can be demonstrated with a simple example. Suppose a firm has an investment opportunity under consideration that is expected to yield a net return of 10 percent. If we can show that the decision to invest or not invest is the same if the corporate tax is 50 percent or if the tax is zero, we should agree that the tax has no effect on investment. For this example, we will assume that the firm borrows the $10,000 needed to buy a machine at 5-percent

---

5. The incidence of the corporate profits tax is not entirely resolved in the theoretical literature of the subject. For our purposes, identification of the final bearer of the tax is unimportant.

interest, although the same principles are involved if the financing is through internal funds or by issuance of additional equity capital.

The pertinent figures are the following:

$10,000 cost of machine
$ 2,500 gross annual return
$ 1,000 annual depreciation
$ 500 annual interest cost
$ 1,000 net annual return if taxes are zero ($2,500 – $1,000 – $500)
$ 500 net annual return if taxes are 50 percent
[($2,500 – $1,000 – $500) × 0.50]

This example shows that the firm is better off with no taxes than with taxes, but this is completely irrelevant to the question asked. Will the firm invest in both cases? The answer is yes. This may be objected to on the grounds that the firm is not likely to risk $10,000 to earn just $500 annually under these conditions. But that is exactly the point. If the tax rate is 50 percent, the firm risks only 50 percent of the initial capital. This can be seen in two ways. First, if the gross return were zero instead of $2,500 in our first case, the loss to the firm when no taxes exist is $1,500; but if taxes are 50 percent, the loss to the firm is just $750. Thus, while a firm gains more profit when profits are positive if there are no taxes, it also bears the full loss when there are losses. When the corporate tax rate is 50 percent, the government absorbs 50 percent of all losses.

The second way to see the issue involved is to assume that the machine becomes obsolete or is physically destroyed before operations can start. If there are no taxes, the firm has lost the full $10,000. If the taxes are 50 percent, the firm can deduct $5,000 of the loss from its other income, so that its actual loss is just $5,000. In other words, the government is a full partner in both gains and losses, and the private firm's decision is unaffected by the proportion of the investment the two partners undertake. Returning to our original example, the return on risked capital is 10 percent in both the tax and the no-tax case,

50 percent tax: $500/$5,000 = 10 percent return
       no tax: $1,000/$10,000 = 10 percent return

Relating the simple example to the real world, some qualifications are necessary. For the example to work as presented, it is necessary to

assume (1) that the tax is not progressive, which with only minor qualifications is true of the corporate income tax in the United States, and
(2) either that the firm has other income that can be offset by any losses,
or that unlimited carry forward and back of profit and loss is permitted,
which is also quite close to the case in the United States.

Accelerated depreciation allowances for tax purposes are a stimulant to investment, but not to the extent that is frequently assumed.
If, as is typically the case, exactly 100 percent depreciation is permitted, then the only difference between fast and slow "write-offs" is that
the taxpayer is permitted to use the tax funds for a longer or shorter
period of time. The amount of the tax over the lifetime of the capital
is the same in both cases. To calculate the advantage of accelerated depreciation to the firm, it is necessary to multiply the difference in after-
tax profit by the interest rate for the period of time involved. The most
effective way to use this instrument is to create the impression that
depreciation schedules will be shortened if increased investment is
desired. The best way to create that impression is to shorten them
"temporarily." Similarly, if excessive demand pressure seems to be the
problem, a lengthening of depreciation schedules may induce some
investors to wait until more favorable rules apply.

Capital investment is also encouraged by governmental programs
that make financing more easily available to business firms than would
otherwise be the case. This is done on a long-run basis by such agencies
as the Small Business Administration (SBA) as well as on a cyclical
basis by making larger amounts of funds available to the SBA in recessionary periods. Investment is also encouraged at certain times
through general financing programs as was done when the Reconstruction Finance Corporation was established during the depression of the
1930s. Capital investment could be, and to a limited degree, has been,
stimulated by governmental research programs. These programs have
been restricted to the fields of health and scientific developments related to defense and space-age needs. However, they could be used
more generally not only to develop new products and industries and
thus create more demand for capital goods, but also to do the basic
research that is needed to make applied research possible.

Construction Investment. During inflationary periods, it is generally desirable to depress capital-goods construction, primarily
through monetary policy. This was done during wartime through direct controls by requiring special permits to get scarce materials for
building. (To date, this has not been used in highly inflationary periods
in peacetime.) Demand for housing in our economy is also affected by

governmental programs. During the depression of the 1930s, steps were taken to stabilize mortgage markets by taking low quality mortgages out of the hands of private investors and by setting up government guarantees of new mortgages that met preestablished standards. In more recent years, the terms of financing on government-guaranteed mortgages have been varied to either stimulate or depress housing demand by changing downpayments and repayment periods as well as interest rates.

Direct governmental construction of public housing has also been used to stabilize total housing demand, although some public housing has been built even in years of a housing boom. Governmental programs of urban redevelopment to replace slums with planned housing projects could also be used to foster stability. The pressure for such programs on a long-run basis, however, has kept their use as a stabilization device minor.

Inventory Investment. Inventory investment is largely unaffected by fiscal policies. However, monetary policy has an important effect on inventory investment. When credit becomes tight in recovery, funds are not available for investment in additional inventory without cutting other uses, and this is difficult because all demand is high. Since inventories are financed significantly by short-term bank credit, monetary policy is especially restrictive. Monetary policy is only partially successful, however, in stabilizing inventory investment. Easy credit in recession encourages inventory build-ups, and stocks usually are being built up at a rate that cannot be sustained by increases in demand before credit becomes tight. This situation has led to a search for other programs to supplement monetary programs. The government has done little in this area, but it has helped management control stocks more adequately by making current data available on the levels of inventories by basic fields and by stages of manufacture. These data help show when inventories are out of line with past relationships to sales. Although this has been helpful, fluctuations in the rate of inventory holding have continued to be one of the major factors leading to changes in economic activity in minor cycles.

Foreign Trade and Investment. Governments have been engaged in efforts to influence foreign trade and foreign investments since early modern times and even before. They have had only a very limited measure of success with such programs, however, in promoting growth and stability in foreign trade. In the worldwide depression of the late 1920s and early 1930s, foreign trade and investment collapsed almost completely.

In the absence of governmental restrictions, a boom or severe depression in a major industrial country has a tendency to spread to other industrialized countries. For example, if a boom exists in the United States, imports are likely to rise. Since imports from Great Britain are substantial, the demand for British goods is increased, which creates increased demand and increased price pressure in Great Britain. If these are great enough, they can initiate an upward movement in business after a recession. If a boom already exists, they can add to inflationary pressures. The situation is just the reverse in a depression.

For example, assume that Great Britain and the United States are both experiencing a period of prosperity and that a severe depression develops in the United States. Imports from Britain will be cut, which will cut demand for British goods. It will also cut the means of payment for goods from the United States. To pay for these imports from the United States, gold and other reserves will need to be transferred to the United States, which will reduce the money supply and lead to deflation. The Bank of England will take steps to stop the outflow of gold, which will tend to reduce business further. Thus, depression will spread to Britain, from Britain to countries with which it trades, and so on.

Additional problems arise in a severe depression. Traders in a country experiencing low demand will try to sell goods in foreign markets at a price low enough to move them. This action helps demoralize business in the foreign countries.

This spread of business cycles from one country to another led most nations to take steps during the 1930s to insulate their economy from the rest of the world by means of high tariffs, trade quotas, bilateral trade agreements, barter arrangements, and the like. It was also done by changing the value of domestic currency in relation to gold to make exports cheaper in world markets and imports more expensive and, therefore, less desirable. The result was an almost complete breakdown of world trade and investment.

Trade stability is furthered by the International Monetary Fund. The Fund provides for short-term credits to take care of temporary imbalances in foreign trade. It also provides an orderly procedure for changing the value of currencies, when necessary, to promote long-run trade equilibrium. Various steps have been taken to make funds available for foreign investment. The U.S. government has made loans through the Export-Import Bank. The World Bank has financed capital development projects in many countries and obtains funds by selling bonds that are guaranteed by the member countries. Increasingly frequent proposals are made for guarantees of foreign investments made by the U.S. government. Some of these proposals call for a general guarantee; others would only guarantee losses due to confiscation of property by foreign governments, confiscatory taxes, and changes in exchange rates.

The last series of proposals we will discuss provide for some form of international stockpiling of goods. This could be done by coordinating domestic stockpiling programs, as well as by a world agency buying stocks in periods of surpluses and disposing of them in periods of excess supplies. More extreme proposals call for international quotas for production of basic materials. Except for international agreements to stabilize wheat production and prices, such proposals have had a poor reception in the United States. Some people propose using international stockpiles as collateral for currency issued by a world bank to be used for settling international balances. But again, such proposals have received little serious consideration in the United States.

INTERRELATIONSHIP OF FISCAL AND MONETARY POLICY

The discussions in this and the preceding chapters show clearly that monetary policy and fiscal policy are operating to meet similar objectives. Therefore, these policies should be coordinated. If the government is adding to purchasing power by means of a deficit, it makes little sense to have a monetary policy of restraint. Both usually should be working in the same direction. This is just as true in a period of inflation as in recession. The only reason a question might be asked is that in the U.S. economy, these two groups of policies are administered by two separate agencies.

Monetary policies are largely the responsibility of the Board of Governors of the Federal Reserve System, a nonpolitical board to which members are appointed for fourteen-year terms and cannot succeed themselves. Since only one member is appointed every two years, there never is a wholesale shift in board membership. Fiscal policy is determined by Congress and the Treasury Department, who usually work in harmony, except, perhaps, when Congress is controlled by one political party and the President is of another.

Conflicts have periodically arisen between fiscal and monetary policy. For example, in the early 1980s, Federal Reserve monetary policy had raised interest rates materially, which also raised the cost of financing the public debt. In the hope that interest rates would decline significantly in late 1982 or early 1983, the Treasury resorted to short-term borrowing. Ceilings on the national debt also regularly force the Treasury to act in ways that are inconsistent with its stabilization goals. In such circumstances, the Federal Reserve is forced into being the active agent.

Such conflicts of interest and the possibility of more serious conflicts have led to repeated proposals for a central agency to coordinate monetary and fiscal policy. One proposal calls for a national monetary authority. This agency would be composed of representatives of both the Federal Reserve and Treasury and would develop policies that both groups would enact. Other proposals would put the Federal Reserve Board under the Treasury's jurisdiction or would make it a board appointed by the President on a political basis. To date, the desire to keep monetary policies out of politics and to prevent inflation from becoming a political tool has kept the Federal Reserve Board of Governors an independent, nonpolitical agency.

In the original proposal for the Federal Reserve Reform Act of 1989, the legislation would have made the Secretary of the Treasury a member of the Federal Open Market Committee (FOMC). This provision was later changed to require periodic meetings between the FOMC and representatives of the Administration. Alan Greenspan, Chairman of the Board of Governors, opposed both provisions on the grounds of the need to maintain the independence of the Federal Reserve System.[6] During the 1980s, there was a great deal of writing in the economic literature concerning the mix of monetary and fiscal policy. It is often argued that there are times when fiscal policy should be expansive and monetary policy tight and times when monetary policy should be easy and fiscal policy tight. In general, economists feel that fiscal policy acts more directly on the real economy and employment and that monetary policy is effective in stabilizing price levels and influencing interest rates.

The management of the national debt is another tool that can be used to promote economic stability. There is some question about whether debt management should be considered monetary policy or fiscal policy, since it is the responsibility of the Treasury, but its impact is on the liquidity of the economy.

By debt management we mean the changing of the composition of the debt, mainly in its term structure, but also other terms, including

---

6. Alan Greenspan, "Statements to Congress," *Federal Reserve Bulletin* (December 1989), pp. 795–803.

marketability, callability, interest rates, ownership restrictions, denominations, and redeemability characteristics. The absolute size of the debt is not viewed as a part of debt management, although when the debt is expanded or a portion is retired, important questions of debt management do arise.

There are many considerations the Treasury must bear in mind, such as cost and legality, but we shall restrict our attention to the role that debt management can play in a stabilization program. The general proposition is that long-term and less liquid government securities should be increased when inflation is the devil; and when depressed conditions exist, the debt should be shifted to a larger proportion of short-term and more liquid forms of securities. Issues must be tailored to fit the needs of particular classes of potential holders, such as insurance companies, commercial banks, wage earners, and industrial concerns.

With a national debt in excess of $3 trillion, its maturity structure is likely to have some impact on the term structure of interest rates of private borrowers. There are times when it seems desirable to try to increase rates at the short end and decrease long-term rates. Debt management can play a part in such an attempt.

Management of the public debt is so closely related to the activities of the Federal Reserve System, particularly in its open-market operations, that coordination is absolutely essential. Significant gains could undoubtedly be achieved by making the Federal Reserve System completely responsible for debt management.[7]

QUESTIONS

1. Distinguish between Roosa's defensive and dynamic policies of the Federal Reserve.
2. Outline the connection between:
   (a) the monetary authority, the monetary base, the money supply, and
   (b) real income, price levels, interest rates, and employment.
3. Contrast the flexibility of prices and wages, both upward and downward.
4. What kind of time lags exist between the time the need for monetary policy occurs and the time its effect on the economy takes place?
5. Evaluate the several tools of monetary policy.

---

7. A. G. Hart and P. B. Kenen, *Money, Debt, and Economic Activity*, 3d ed. (Englewood Cliffs, NJ: Prentice-Hall, Inc., 1961), pp. 454–457.

6. Describe the factors that affect bank reserves. Which of these does the Federal Reserve control?
7. Evaluate arguments for and against the use of selective credit controls to combat inflation and influence growth.
8. Which factors support the case for a long-run inflationary bias?
9. Explain the concept of "automatic stabilizers."
10. Explain the full employment surplus concept.
11. Explain the concept of "social capital."
12. Evaluate the principle of annually balanced budgets for the federal government.
13. Do you think that the individual states should engage in countercyclical fiscal policy to the same extent and with the same techniques as the federal government?
14. Evaluate the statement that countercyclical fiscal policy is necessary only because of the imperfections of the free enterprise system and such rigidities in wages, prices, and immobility of resources as are characteristic of our economy.
15. What considerations are involved in determining whether a particular amount of increased government spending should be handled by additional taxes, by increasing the national debt, or by increasing the money supply? State in each case what major effects would be expected and the relative merits or evils of these effects.

READINGS

American Economic Association. *Readings in Business Cycle Theory*. Homewood, IL: Richard D. Irwin, Inc., 1951. Chapters 13 and 14.

American Economic Association. *Readings in Fiscal Policy*. Homewood, IL: Richard D. Irwin, Inc., 1955.

Aronson, J. Richard. *Public Finance*. New York: McGraw-Hill Book Company, Inc., 1989.

Brunner, Karl, and Allan H. Meltzer, eds. *Stabilization of the Domestic and International Economy*. New York: Elsevier North-Holland Publishing Co., Inc., 1977.

Clark, John J., and Morris Cohen, eds. *Business Fluctuations, Growth and Economic Stabilization*. New York: Random House, Inc., 1963.

Courant, Paul N., and Edward M. Gramlich, *Federal Budget Deficits: America's Great Consumption Binge*. Englewood Cliffs, N.J.: Prentice-Hall, 1986.

The Economic Report of the President. Washington, D.C.: United States Government Printing Office, annually.

Goldfeld, Stephen M., and Lester V. Chandler. *The Economics of Money and Banking*, 10th ed. New York: Harper & Row Publishers, Inc., 1990.

Hafer, R. W., ed. *The Monetary Versus Fiscal Policy Debate*. Totowa, NJ: Rowman and Littlefield, 1986.

Horrigan, Brian. "Sizing Up the Deficit: An Efficient Tax Perspective." *Business Review*, Federal Reserve Bank of Philadelphia (May/June 1984).

Issues in Monetary Policy. Kansas City: Federal Reserve Bank of Kansas City, 1982.

Pechman, Joseph A., ed. *Setting National Priorities: The —— Budget*. New York: Brookings Institution, Inc., annually.

U.S. Congress, Joint Economic Committee. *The Business Cycle and Public Policy*. Washington, D.C.: United States Government Printing Office, 1980.

Walsh, Carl E. "The Federal Reserve's Operating Procedures and Interest Rate Fluctuations." *Economic Review*, Federal Reserve Bank of Kansas City (May 1982): pp. 8–18.

Willett, Thomas D., ed. *Political Business Cycles: The Economics and Politics of Stagflation*. San Francisco: Pacific Institute for Public Policy Research, 1986.

INDEX